Total Truth is marked by Nancy Pearcey's signature clarity, readability, and intellectual depth. It presents a passionate case for an integral and culturally relevant biblical worldview. It is rare to find a book of such religious and intellectual integrity which is at the same time so accessible and enjoyable.
—AL WOLTERS, author, *Creation Regained*

Anybody who has read Nancy Pearcey knows to expect a careful review of the literature, a keen discussion of the issues, and a creative analysis of the way ahead—all expressed in a clear and lively way. *Total Truth* does not disappoint: it addresses the most important issue facing the Christian church today.
—PAUL MARSHALL, Senior Fellow at Freedom House's Center for Religious Freedom, author, *Heaven Is Not My Home*

Nancy Pearcey has written a book that spans intersections of secular thought and Christian orientation over a wide cultural horizon. While Francis Schaeffer gave a whole generation a credible framework in Christianity for the flow of ideas and their consequences, Pearcey goes more into the text and demonstrates how correct Schaeffer was in his analysis.
—UDO MIDDELMANN, Director, Francis A. Schaeffer Foundation

In an easy-to-read, well-documented, sometimes provocative text, Nancy Pearcey has provided a superb worldview lens through which we can see things more clearly. All who read it will live their lives differently.
—BECKY NORTON DUNLOP, VP for External Relations, the Heritage Foundation

Nancy Pearcey is a gifted writer and thinker. She offers clarity and insight in the midst of a cacophony of cultural trends and competing political and philosophical points of view.
—FRANCIS J. BECKWITH, Associate Director, J. M. Dawson Institute of Church-State Studies, and Associate Professor of Church-State Studies, Baylor University

It doesn't matter how many Christians gain positions of influence in the cultural gatekeeping institutions if we don't permit our worldview to shape what we do. *Total Truth* recovers the biblical admonition to live all of life to God's glory.
—WILLIAM WICHTERMAN, congressional aide

Nancy Pearcey takes the analysis of worldviews to another level, in the most insightful applications since Francis Schaeffer.
—GENE EDWARD VEITH, Culture Editor, *World* magazine

Total Truth is well written, clear, and insightful. The prose is extremely easy to read, even though Pearcey is often dealing with heady philosophical subjects. . . . a great book.
—JAY RICHARDS, VP, the Discovery Institute

The important point Nancy Pearcey makes in her excellent and well-documented book is that Christians must not check their worldviews on the way out the church door. Christians need to do more than slap a veneer of Christianity over their work, hobbies, and studies. They need to fully integrate their faith with all of life.
—CURT LOVELACE, Executive Director, Lifework Forum

A fascinating study! The perspective is fresh, helpful, moving, and challenging. *Total Truth* is simple yet profound, passion-filled without being "preachy," broad in scope and centered on fundamental issues.
—JOHN VANDER STELT, Professor Emeritus of Philosophy,
  Dordt College

I like the way Nancy Pearcey tells personal stories that help to incarnate the issues and make them come alive. I appreciate her clear, concrete, lively writing style. This message should get a wide hearing.
—MICHAEL GOHEEN, Professor of Worldview Studies,
  Redeemer University College

With the passion of an advocate and the skill of a surgeon, Nancy Pearcey sets forth the elements of a Christian worldview and then makes a persuasive case for Christian involvement in society.
—KERBY ANDERSON, National Director, Probe Ministries,
  Cohost, "Point of View"

Total Truth

TOTAL TRUTH

*Liberating Christianity
from Its Cultural Captivity*

NANCY R. PEARCEY

FOREWORD BY
Phillip E. Johnson

CROSSWAY BOOKS

A DIVISION OF
GOOD NEWS PUBLISHERS
WHEATON, ILLINOIS

Total Truth: Liberating Christianity from Its Cultural Captivity

Published by Crossway Books,
        a division of Good News Publishers
        1300 Crescent Street
        Wheaton, Illinois 60187

Published in association with Yates & Yates, LLP, Attorneys and Counselors, Orange, California.

Cover design: Chris Gilbert, UDG / Designworks, www.udgdesignworks.com

Cover photo: "Le Semeur 1" http://www.kmm.nl/index_flash.html#voorpagina

First printing 2004

Printed in the United States of America

Unless otherwise indicated, all Scripture quotations are from The Holy Bible, English Standard Version, copyright © 2001 by Crossway Bibles, a division of Good News Publishers. Used by permission. All rights reserved.

The Scripture quotation marked KJV is from the King James Version of the Bible.

All emphases in Scripture quotations have been added by the author.

Library of Congress Cataloging-in-Publication Data
Pearcey, Nancy.
  Total truth: liberating Christianity from its cultural captivity / Nancy R.
Pearcey ; foreword by Phillip E. Johnson.
    p. cm.
  Includes bibliographical references and index.
  ISBN 1-58134-458-9 (HC : alk. paper)
  1. Christianity—Philosophy. 2. Apologetics. 3. Christian life.
4. History—Religious aspects—Christianity. 5. History—Philosophy.
I. Title.
BR100.P37   2004
261—dc22   2003019514

Q		14	13	12	11	10	09	08	07	06	05	04
15	14	13	12	11	10	9	8	7	6	5	4	3	2	1

CONTENTS

FOREWORD BY PHILLIP E. JOHNSON   11

INTRODUCTION   17

Politics Is Not Enough • Losing Our Children • Heart Versus Brain
Just a Power Grab? • Mental Maps • Not Just Academic
Worldview Training • Acknowledgments

1: WHAT'S IN A WORLDVIEW?

CHAPTER 1: BREAKING OUT OF THE GRID   31

Divided Minds • Bible School Drop-Outs • Subtle Temptation
Enlightenment Idol • Two Cities • Absolutely Divine • Aristotle's Screwdriver
Biblical Toolbox • Read the Directions • Born to Grow Up
A Personal Odyssey • Manifesto of Unbelief • Like a Swiss Farmer • God Wins
Scolds and Scalawags • In Love With Creativity
Christian Philosophers Out of the Closet • Religion: Good for Your Health
Benevolent Empire

CHAPTER 2: REDISCOVERING JOY   63

Sealy's Secret • Capitol Hill Guilt • Becoming Bilingual • The Faith Gap
Disconnected Devotion • Christian Schizophrenia • Why Plato Matters
That Rascal Augustine • Aristotle and Aquinas • Fluffs of Grace
The Reformers Rebel • Escape from Dualism
Creation: God's Fingerprints All Over • Fall: Where to Draw the Line
Redemption: After the Great Divorce • Christianity Out of Balance
More Than Sinners • God's Offspring • Jars of Clay • A Higher Consciousness?
The Great Drama • Serving Two Masters • All Together Now

CHAPTER 3: KEEPING RELIGION IN ITS PLACE   97

Reason Unbound • Collateral Damage • Cartesian Divide • Kantian Contradiction
Intellectually Fulfilled Atheists • Secular Leap of Faith • War of Worldviews
Your Worldview Is Too Small • Imperialistic "Facts" • Conflicted on Campus
Leftovers from Liberalism • Evangelism Today • Spirit of the Age
C. S. Lewis's True Myth • The Whole Truth

CHAPTER 4: SURVIVING THE SPIRITUAL WASTELAND   123

Mystique of the Forbidden • Not a Smokescreen • Hands-On Worldview
Repairing the Ruins • Retooling the Family • For the Love of Children
Mobilizing the Trinity • The Worldview Next Door • Marx's Heresy
Rousseau and Revolution • Sanger's Religion of Sex • Buddhist in the Sky
Worldview Missionaries

2: *STARTING AT THE BEGINNING*

CHAPTER 5: DARWIN MEETS THE BERENSTAIN BEARS   153

A Universal Acid • Kindergarten Naturalism • Spinmeisters in Science
Darwin's Beaks • Dysfunctional Fruit Flies • Doctored Moths
Most Famous Fake • Baloney Detectors • Punk Scientists • Birds, Bats, and Bees
Divine Foot in the Door • Evolution Gets Religion • Berkeley to the Rescue
Closed System, Closed Minds • Winning a Place at the Table
What Every Schoolchild Knows

CHAPTER 6: THE SCIENCE OF COMMON SENSE   179

Little Green Men • Blind Watchmaker? • Marks of Design
Roller Coaster in the Cell • Behe and the Black Box • A Universe Built for You
Cosmic Coincidences • Who Wrote the Genetic Code? • Explanatory Filter
Up from Chance • Against the Law • No Rules for *Hamlet*
The Medium Is Not the Message • Testing Positive • Three to Get Ready
Christian Relativists • Fairy Dust • Out of the Naturalist's Chair

CHAPTER 7: TODAY BIOLOGY,
TOMORROW THE WORLD   207

Universal Darwinism • Evolution for Everyman
Darwinian Fundamentalism on Rape • Mothers Red in Tooth and Claw
Peter Singer's Pet Theme • Darwinizing Culture • The Acid Bites Back
Telling Genes to Jump in the Lake • Mental Maps
Beware Scientists Bearing Values • Dilemma of Leo Strauss
Born-Again Darwinists • The Kitchen As Classroom

CHAPTER 8: DARWINS OF THE MIND   227

Holmes Loses His Faith • Darwin's New Logic • Cash Value of an Idea
What's Religion Worth to You? • Tough Versus Tender • Disciples of Darwin
Transforming America • Let God Evolve • Why Judges Make Law
Dewey's Dilemmas • Hamstrung Teachers • Inventing Your Own Reality
"Keeping Faith" with Darwin • Tom Wolfe and Darwin's Doubt
Truth from the Barrel of a Gun • He Is There and He Is Not Silent
The Cognitive War

3: HOW WE LOST OUR MINDS

CHAPTER 9: WHAT'S SO GOOD ABOUT
EVANGELICALISM?   251

Denzel Asked the Deacon • Forward to the Past • Identity Check
And the Winner Is • When Government Help Hurts • Wild West Religion
Riders in the Storm • Frontier Fallout • Whitefield Across America
Heart Versus Head • Defiant Individualism

CHAPTER 10: WHEN AMERICA MET CHRISTIANITY —
GUESS WHO WON?   273

Democracy Comes to Church • A Politician for a Priest • Fetters for Our Children?
Half American • Salvation on the Spot • America the Natural
Leapfrogging 1,800 Years • Christians for Jefferson • No Traffic Cop
Self-Made People • Preacher, Performer, Storyteller • Celebrity Style
In PR We Trust • Pulling Strings • Not a Rogues' Gallery
Rise of the Sovereign Self

CHAPTER 11: EVANGELICALS' TWO-STORY TRUTH   295

Scotch Tip • The Science of Scripture • Campbell's Rationalist Soup
Old Books for Modern Man • Sola Scriptura? • The View from Nowhere
Becoming Double-Minded • A Science of Duty • Celestial Mathematician
Blinded by Bacon • Religion on the Side • Making Sense of Common Sense
Reid Romans 1 • Colors and Shapes • Just a Habit? • Are You Nobody?
Mere Chemistry? • Disinformation Minister • Philosophical "Cheating"
Signs of Intelligent Life • Boxed-In Believers

CHAPTER 12: HOW WOMEN STARTED THE CULTURE WAR   325

Women and the Awakening • Households At Work • Communal Manhood
Home as Haven • Why Men Left Home • The Passionate Male • Taming Men
Feminizing the Church • Morals and Mercy • Female Standards, Male Resentment
Manly Men • Romper Room Dads • Feminist Fury • What Hath Woman Lost?
Remoralizing America • No Double Standard • Reconstituting the Home
Private and Personal • Blueprint for Living

4: WHAT NEXT? LIVING IT OUT

CHAPTER 13: TRUE SPIRITUALITY AND CHRISTIAN WORLDVIEW   351

Wurmbrand's Freedom • Schaeffer's Crisis • Idols of the Heart
Theology of the Cross • Rejected, Slain, Raised • Life-Producing Machines
His Work, His Way • Gold, Silver, Precious Stones • Results Guaranteed
Marketing the Message • More Money, More Ministry • Operating Instructions
From Good to Great • Loving Enough to Confront • No Little People
Real Leaders Serve • Getting It Right by Doing It "Wrong" • True Spirituality

APPENDICES

APPENDIX 1   381

How American Politics Became Secularized

APPENDIX 2   385

Modern Islam and the New Age Movement

APPENDIX 3   389

The Long War Between Materialism and Christianity

APPENDIX 4   393

Isms on the Run: Practical Apologetics at L'Abri

NOTES   397

RECOMMENDED READING   451

INDEX   467

FOREWORD

When Nancy Pearcey invited me to write a foreword for her "worldview" book, I hastened to accept the honor. I was honored by the invitation because this is a book of unusual importance by an author of unusual ability.

It has been a treat for me to read and study the manuscript, and I feel that I am doing a great favor to every potential reader whom I can persuade to enjoy these pages as I have done. Nancy Pearcey is an author who is greatly respected by all who know her work. I hope that, with this book, she will receive the acclaim that her thought and writing has so long deserved, and that readers will find in its message of liberation the key to intellectual and spiritual renewal.

It would be an understatement to say that worldview is an important topic. I would rather say that understanding how worldviews are formed, and how they guide or confine thought, is the essential step toward understanding everything else. Understanding worldview is a bit like trying to see the lens of one's own eye. We do not ordinarily see our own worldview, but we see everything else by looking through it. Put simply, our worldview is the window by which we view the world, and decide, often subconsciously, what is real and important, or unreal and unimportant.

It may be that a worldview is commonly a collection of prejudices. If so, the prejudices are necessary, because we can't start from a blank slate and investigate everything from scratch by ourselves. When somebody tells me that he receives guidance from God in prayer, or that science is our only way of knowing anything for sure, or that there is no objective difference between good and evil, I need to have some verifiable frame of reference to tell me at once whether he is merely deluded or is saying something that is sufficiently sensible to merit serious consideration.

Similarly, when I tell my fellow Berkeley professors that I don't believe the theory of evolution, I need to know why they find it so difficult to take me seriously or to believe that my objection to the theory is based on scientific evidence rather than on the book of Genesis. The reason is that evolution with its accompanying philosophy is identified with their worldview at such a deep level that they cannot imagine how the theory could possibly be contrary to the evidence.

Every one of us has a worldview, and our worldview governs our thinking even when—or especially when—we are unaware of it. Thus, it is not uncommon to find well-meaning evildoers, as it were, who are quite sincerely convinced that they are Christians, and attend church faithfully, and may even hold a position of leadership, but who have absorbed a worldview that makes it easy for them to ignore their Christian principles when it comes time to do the practical business of daily living. Their sincerely held Christian principles are in one mental category for them, and practical decision making is in another. Such persons can believe that Jesus is coming again to judge the world and yet live as if the standards of this world are the only thing that needs to be taken into account.

Likewise, Christian education is likely to be an exercise in futility if it does not prepare our young people to confront and survive the worldview challenges that they will surely meet as soon as they leave the security of the Christian home, and probably even while they are still living at home and being educated in a Christian environment, due to the pervasive influence of the media and the Internet. For example, a youngster may be taught very fine Christian principles, but he or she may also grow up understanding that these principles fit into a specialized category called "religious belief."

Sooner or later, that youngster will find out that secular college professors, and sometimes even Christian professors, proceed from an implicit assumption that religious beliefs are the kind of thing one is supposed to set aside when learning how the world really works, and that it is usually praiseworthy to "grow" gradually away from those beliefs as a part of the normal process of maturing.

Why do those professors think that? Of course they are being influenced by the dominant belief system in their academic culture, which is also the culture of the newsroom at most daily newspapers or television stations. But just to say that people are influenced by their cultural environment does not explain how our culture has come to be the way it is, when it used to be very different. To survive in modern or postmodern American culture without being overwhelmed by its concealed prejudices, everyone needs to know how to recognize those prejudices, to understand what kind of thinking brought them into existence, and to be able to explain to ourselves and others what is wrong with the pervasive assumptions that often come labeled only as "the way all rational people think," and that will swamp our faith if we are not alert to them.

A fine education in worldview analysis is as basic an element of a modern Christian's defense system as a shield was in the days when a prudent traveler needed to be prepared to repel an attack by sword-wielding robbers. Today the intellectual brigands rob unwary youths of their faith, and they do it with arguments based on the shifting sand of "what everybody knows" and "the way we think today." Those youths need to find the solid rock, and they need to know both why the rock is solid, and why the world prefers the shifting sand.

Only a very gifted author is capable of writing a book about worldview analysis that will make exciting reading for the ordinary person, but which is also sufficiently informed by scholarship to convey a deep understanding of the subject rather than merely a superficial acquaintance. Everyone is aware that American culture changed enormously during the twentieth century, but very few people understand how the change was brought about by ideas and habits that seemed at first to be eccentric or of only minor importance, but that eventually crept into the popular culture and proved to be almost irresistible. The situation we find ourselves in today has deep roots in the thinking of earlier times. Conduct that not very long ago was regarded as perverse or criminal has become not only tolerated but the new norm. Those who dare to disapprove of that conduct, or just fail to applaud the new norm with sufficient enthusiasm, are themselves likely to feel the full weight of society's disapproval. The change in conduct was brought about by changes in worldview, which caused those who followed the new fashions to think differently.

With that much of an introduction, I invite you to read Nancy Pearcey. You will find not only pleasant reading but all the elements and basic information necessary to produce a Christian mind with a map of reality that really works. When Christian parents, pastors, educators, and other leaders learn to give this subject the importance it deserves, and to practice it even as they teach it thoroughly in the home, from the pulpit, and in every classroom, then Christians will find that they are no longer fearful and timid when they have to address claims of worldly wisdom. So let's get started.

—Phillip E. Johnson
Berkeley, California
January 2004

Christianity is not a series of truths in the plural,
but rather truth spelled with a capital "T."
Truth about total reality, not just about religious things.

Biblical Christianity is Truth concerning total reality —
and the intellectual holding of that total Truth
and then living in the light of that Truth.

FRANCIS SCHAEFFER
Address at the University of Notre Dame.
April 1981

INTRODUCTION

"Your earlier book says Christians are called to redeem entire cultures, not just individuals," a schoolteacher commented, joining me for lunch at a conference where I had just spoken. Then he added thoughtfully, "I'd never heard that before."

The teacher was talking about *How Now Shall We Live?*[1] and at his words I looked up from my plate in surprise. Was he really saying he'd never even *heard* the idea of being a redemptive force in every area of culture? He shook his head: "No, I've always thought of salvation strictly in terms of individual souls."

That conversation helped confirm my decision to write a follow-up book dealing with the worldview themes in *How Now Shall We Live?* Just a few years ago, when I began my work on that earlier volume, using the term *worldview* was not on anyone's list of good conversation openers. To tell people that you were writing a book on *worldview* was to risk glazed stares and a quick change in subject. But today as I travel around the country, I sense an eagerness among evangelicals to move beyond a purely privatized faith, applying biblical principles to areas like work, business, and politics. Flip open any number of Christian publications and you're likely to find half a dozen advertisements for *worldview* conferences, *worldview* institutes, and *worldview* programs. Clearly the term itself has strong marketing cachet these days, which signals a deep hunger among Christians for an overarching framework to bring unity to their lives.

This book addresses that hunger and offers new direction for advancing the worldview movement. It will help you identify the secular/sacred divide that keeps your faith locked into the private sphere of "religious truth." It will walk you through practical, workable steps for crafting a Christian worldview in your own life and work. And it will teach you how to apply a worldview grid to cut through the bewildering maze of ideas and ideologies we encounter in a postmodern world. The purpose of worldview studies is nothing less than to liberate Christianity from its cultural captivity, unleashing its power to transform the world.

"The gospel is like a caged lion," said the great Baptist preacher Charles Spurgeon. "It does not need to be defended, it just needs to be let out of its cage." Today the cage is our accommodation to the secular/sacred split that reduces Christianity to a matter of private personal belief. To unlock the cage, we need to become utterly convinced that, as Francis Schaeffer said, Christianity is not merely religious truth, it is total truth—truth about the whole of reality.

POLITICS IS NOT ENOUGH

The reason a worldview message is so compelling today is that we are still emerging from the fundamentalist era of the early twentieth century. Up until that time, evangelicals had enjoyed a position of cultural dominance in America. But after the Scopes trial and the rise of theological modernism, religious conservatives turned in on themselves: They circled the wagons, developed a fortress mentality, and championed "separatism" as a positive strategy. Then, in the 1940s and 50s, a movement began that aimed at breaking out of the fortress. Calling themselves *neo-evangelicals,* this group argued that we are called not to escape the surrounding culture but to engage it. They sought to construct a redemptive vision that would embrace not only individuals but also social structures and institutions.

Yet many evangelicals lacked the conceptual tools needed for the task, which has seriously limited their success. For example, in recent decades many Christians have responded to the moral and social decline in American society by embracing political activism. Believers are running for office in growing numbers; churches are organizing voter registration; public policy groups are proliferating; scores of Christian publications and radio programs offer commentary on public affairs. This heightened activism has yielded good results in many areas of public life, yet the impact remains far less than most had hoped. Why? Because evangelicals often put all their eggs in one basket: They leaped into political activism as the quickest, surest way to make a difference in the public arena—failing to realize that politics tends to reflect culture, not the other way around.

Nothing illustrates evangelicals' infatuation with politics more clearly than a story related by a Christian lawyer. Considering whether to take a job in the nation's capital, he consulted with the leader of a Washington-area ministry, who told him, "You can either stay where you are and keep practicing law, or you can come to Washington and *change the culture.*" The implication was that the only way to effect cultural change was through national politics. Today, battle-weary political warriors have grown more realistic about the limits of that strategy. We have learned that "politics is downstream from culture, not the other way around," says Bill Wichterman, policy advisor to Senate Majority Leader Bill Frist. "Real change has to start with the culture. All we can do on Capitol Hill is try to find ways government can nurture healthy cultural trends."[2]

On a similar note, a member of Congress once told me, "I got involved in politics after the 1973 abortion decision because I thought that was the fastest route to moral reform. Well, we've won some legislative victories, but *we've lost the culture.*" The most effective work, he had come to realize, is done by ordinary Christians fulfilling God's calling to reform culture within their local spheres of influence—their families, churches, schools, neighborhoods, workplaces, professional organizations, and civic institutions. In order to effect lasting change, the congressman concluded, "we need to develop a Christian worldview."

LOSING OUR CHILDREN

Not only have we "lost the culture," but we continue losing even our own children. It's a familiar but tragic story that devout young people, raised in Christian homes, head off to college and abandon their faith. Why is this pattern so common? Largely because young believers have not been taught how to develop a biblical worldview. Instead, Christianity has been restricted to a specialized area of religious belief and personal devotion.

I recently read a striking example. At a Christian high school, a theology teacher strode to the front of the classroom, where he drew a heart on one side of the blackboard and a brain on the other. The two are as divided as the two sides of the blackboard, he told the class: The heart is what we use for religion, while the brain is what we use for science.

An apocryphal story? A caricature of Christian anti-intellectualism? No, the story was told by a young woman who was in the class that day. Worse, out of some two hundred students, she was the only one who objected. The rest apparently found nothing unusual about restricting religion to the domain of the "heart."[3]

As Christian parents, pastors, teachers, and youth group leaders, we constantly see young people pulled down by the undertow of powerful cultural trends. If all we give them is a "heart" religion, it will not be strong enough to counter the lure of attractive but dangerous ideas. Young believers also need a "brain" religion—training in worldview and apologetics—to equip them to analyze and critique the competing worldviews they will encounter when they leave home. If forewarned and forearmed, young people at least have a fighting chance when they find themselves a minority of one among their classmates or work colleagues. Training young people to develop a Christian mind is no longer an option; it is part of their necessary survival equipment.

HEART VERSUS BRAIN

The first step in forming a Christian worldview is to overcome this sharp divide between "heart" and "brain." We have to reject the division of life into a sacred realm, limited to things like worship and personal morality, over against a secular realm that includes science, politics, economics, and the rest of the public arena. This dichotomy in our own minds is the greatest barrier to liberating the power of the gospel across the whole of culture today.

Moreover, it is reinforced by a much broader division rending the entire fabric of modern society—what sociologists call the public/private split. "Modernization brings about a novel dichotomization of social life," writes Peter Berger. "The dichotomy is between the huge and immensely powerful institutions of the public sphere [by this he means the state, academia, large corporations] . . . and the private sphere"—the realm of family, church, and personal relationships.

The large public institutions claim to be "scientific" and "value-free," which means that values are relegated to the private sphere of personal choice. As Berger explains: "The individual is left to his own devices in a wide range of activities that are crucial to the formation of a meaningful identity, from expressing his religious preference to settling on a sexual life style."[4] We might diagram the dichotomy like this:

Modern societies are sharply divided:

PRIVATE SPHERE
Personal Preferences

PUBLIC SPHERE
Scientific Knowledge

In short, the private sphere is awash in moral relativism. Notice Berger's telling phrase "religious preference." Religion is not considered an objective truth to which we *submit*, but only a matter of personal taste which we *choose*. Because of this, the dichotomy is sometimes called the fact/value split.

Values have been reduced to arbitrary, existential decisions:

VALUES
Individual Choice

FACTS
Binding on Everyone

As Schaeffer explains, the concept of truth itself has been divided—a process he illustrates with the imagery of a two-story building: In the lower story are science and reason, which are considered public truth, binding on everyone. Over against it is an upper story of noncognitive experience, which is the locus of personal meaning. This is the realm of private truth, where we hear people say, "That may be true for you but it's not true for me."⁵

The two-realm theory of truth:

UPPER STORY
Nonrational, Noncognitive

LOWER STORY
Rational, Verifiable

When Schaeffer was writing, the term *postmodernism* had not yet been coined, but clearly that is what he was talking about. Today we might say that in the lower story is modernism, which still claims to have universal, objective truth—while in the upper story is postmodernism.

Today's two-story truth:

POSTMODERNISM
Subjective, Relative to Particular Groups

MODERNISM
Objective, Universally Valid

The reason it's so important for us to learn how to recognize this division is that it is the single most potent weapon for delegitimizing the biblical perspective in the public square today. Here's how it works: Most secularists are too politically savvy to attack religion directly or to debunk it as false. So what do they do? They consign religion to the *value* sphere—which takes it out of the realm of true and false altogether. Secularists can then assure us that of course they "respect" religion, while at the same time denying that it has any relevance to the public realm.

As Phillip Johnson puts it, the fact/value split "allows the metaphysical naturalists to mollify the potentially troublesome religious people by assuring them that science does not rule out 'religious *belief*' (so long as it does not pretend to be *knowledge*).⁶" In other words, so long as everyone understands that it is merely a matter of private feelings. The two-story grid functions as a gate-keeper that defines what is to be taken seriously as genuine knowledge, and what can be dismissed as mere wish-fulfillment.

JUST A POWER GRAB?

This same division also explains why Christians have such difficulty communicating in the public arena. It's crucial for us to realize that nonbelievers are constantly filtering what we say through a mental fact/value grid. For example, when we state a position on an issue like abortion or bioethics or homosexuality, *we* intend to assert an objective moral truth important to the health of society—but *they* think we're merely expressing our subjective bias. When we say there's scientific evidence for design in the universe, *we* intend to stake out a testable truth claim—but *they* say, "Uh oh, the Religious Right is making a political power grab." The fact/value grid instantly dissolves away the objective content of anything we say, and we will not be successful in introducing the *content* of our belief into the public discussion unless we first find ways to get past this gatekeeper.

That's why Lesslie Newbigin warned that the divided concept of truth is the primary factor in "the cultural captivity of the gospel." It traps Christianity in the upper story of privatized values, and prevents it from having any effect on public culture.[7] Having worked as a missionary in India for forty years, Newbigin was able to discern what is distinctive about Western thought more clearly than most of us, who have been immersed in it all our lives. On his return to the West, Newbigin was struck by the way Christian truth has been marginalized. He saw that any position labeled *religion* is placed in the upper story of values, where it is no longer regarded as objective knowledge.

To give just one recent example, in the debate over embryonic stem cell research, actor Christopher Reeve told a student group at Yale University, "When matters of public policy are debated, *no religions should have a seat at the table.*"[8]

To recover a place at the table of public debate, then, Christians must find a way to overcome the dichotomy between public and private, fact and value, secular and sacred. We need to liberate the gospel from its cultural captivity, restoring it to the status of public truth. "The barred cage that forms the prison for the gospel in contemporary western culture is [the church's] accommodation . . . to the fact-value dichotomy," says Michael Goheen, a professor of worldview studies.[9] Only by recovering a holistic view of total truth can we set the gospel free to become a redemptive force across all of life.

MENTAL MAPS

To say that Christianity is the truth about total reality means that it is a full-orbed worldview. The term means literally a *view* of the *world*, a biblically informed perspective on all reality. A worldview is like a mental map that tells us how to navigate the world effectively. It is the imprint of God's objective truth on our inner life.

We might say that each of us carries a model of the universe inside our heads that tells us what the world is like and how we should live in it. A classic book on worldviews is titled *The Universe Next Door*, suggesting that we all have a mental or conceptual universe in which we "live"—a network of principles that answer the fundamental questions of life: Who are we? Where did we come from? What is the purpose of life? The author of the book, James Sire, invites readers to examine a variety of worldviews in order to understand the mental universe held by other people—those living "next door."

A worldview is not the same thing as a formal philosophy; otherwise, it would be only for professional philosophers. Even ordinary people have a set of convictions about how reality functions and how they should live. Because we are made in God's image, we all seek to make sense of life. Some convictions are conscious, while others are unconscious, but together they form a more or less consistent picture of reality. Human beings "are incapable of holding purely arbitrary opinions or making entirely unprincipled decisions," writes Al Wolters in a book on worldview. Because we are by nature rational and responsible beings, we sense that "we need some creed to live by, some map by which to chart our course."[10]

The notion that we need such a "map" in the first place grows out of the biblical view of human nature. The Marxist may claim that human behavior is ultimately shaped by economic circumstances; the Freudian attributes everything to repressed sexual instincts; and the behavioral psychologist regards humans as stimulus-response mechanisms. But the Bible teaches that the overriding factor in the choices we make is our ultimate belief or religious commitment. Our lives are shaped by the "god" we worship—whether the God of the Bible or some substitute deity.

The term *worldview* is a translation of the German word *Weltanschauung*, which means a way of looking at the world (*Welt* = world; *schauen* = to look). German Romanticism developed the idea that cultures are complex wholes, where a certain outlook on life, or spirit of the age, is expressed across the board—in art, literature, and social institutions as well as in formal philosophy. The best way to understand the products of any culture, then, is to grasp the underlying worldview being expressed. But, of course, cultures change over the course of history, and thus the original use of the term *worldview* conveyed relativism.

The word was later introduced into Christian circles through Dutch neo-Calvinist thinkers such as Abraham Kuyper and Herman Dooyeweerd. They argued that Christians cannot counter the spirit of the age in which they live unless they develop an equally comprehensive biblical worldview—an outlook on life that gives rise to distinctively Christian forms of culture—with the important qualification that it is not merely the relativistic belief of a particular culture but is based on the very Word of God, true for all times and places.[11]

NOT JUST ACADEMIC

As the concept of *worldview* becomes common currency, it can all too easily be misunderstood. Some treat it as merely another academic subject to master—a mental exercise or "how to" strategy. Others handle worldview as if it were a weapon in the culture war, a tool for more effective activism. Still others, alas, treat it as little more than a new buzzword or marketing gimmick to dazzle the public and attract donors.

Genuine worldview thinking is far more than a mental strategy or a new spin on current events. At the core, it is a deepening of our spiritual character and the character of our lives. It begins with the submission of our minds to the Lord of the universe—a willingness to be taught by Him. The driving force in worldview studies should be a commitment to "love the Lord your God with all your heart, soul, strength, and mind" (see Luke 10:27).

That's why the crucial condition for intellectual growth is *spiritual* growth, asking God for the grace to "take every thought captive to obey Christ" (2 Cor. 10:5). God is not just the Savior of souls, He is also the Lord of creation. One way we acknowledge His Lordship is by interpreting every aspect of creation in the light of His truth. God's Word becomes a set of glasses offering a new perspective on all our thoughts and actions.

As with every aspect of sanctification, the renewal of the mind may be painful and difficult. It requires hard work and discipline, inspired by a sacrificial love for Christ and a burning desire to build up His Body, the Church. In order to have the mind of Christ, we must be willing to be crucified with Christ, following wherever He might lead—whatever the cost. "Through many tribulations we must enter the kingdom of God" (Acts 14:22). As we undergo refining in the fires of suffering, our desires are purified and we find ourselves wanting nothing more than to bend every fiber of our being, including our mental powers, to fulfill the Lord's Prayer: "Thy Kingdom come." We yearn to lay all our talents and gifts at His feet in order to advance His purposes in the world. Developing a Christian worldview means submitting our entire self to God, in an act of devotion and service to Him.

WORLDVIEW TRAINING

This book approaches the topic of worldview by weaving together insights from three strands.[12] Part 1 sheds light on the secular/sacred dichotomy that restricts Christianity to the realm of religious truth, creating double minds and fragmented lives. To find personal wholeness, we must be willing to lay bare all aspects of our work and life to God's direction and power. Worldview thinking proves to be a rich avenue to joy and fulfillment—a means of letting the spark of God's truth light up every nook and cranny of our lives.

This section also provides practical, hands-on worldview training. It will walk you through concrete steps for crafting a biblically based worldview in any field using the structural elements of Creation, Fall, and Redemption. It will also give you an opportunity to practice apologetics by analyzing non-Christian worldviews. After all, every philosophy or ideology has to answer the same fundamental questions:

1. CREATION: How did it all begin? Where did we come from?

2. FALL: What went wrong? What is the source of evil and suffering?

3. REDEMPTION: What can we do about it? How can the world be set right again?

By applying this simple grid, we can identify nonbiblical worldviews, and then analyze where they go wrong.

Part 2 zeroes in on Creation, the foundational starting point for any worldview. In the West, the reigning creation myth is Darwinian evolution; thus, no matter what our field of work is, we must begin by critiquing Darwinism—both its scientific claims and its worldview implications. In this section, you will discover how the latest findings of science discredit naturalistic theories of evolution, while supporting the concept of Intelligent Design. You may also be surprised to learn how aggressively Darwinism has been extended far beyond the bounds of science, even reconfiguring America's social and legal institutions—with devastating effects.

Part 3 peers into the looking glass of history to ask *why* evangelicals do not have a strong worldview tradition. Why is the secular/sacred dichotomy so pervasive? Here we step back from the present to take a tour of the history and heritage of evangelicalism in America. By rummaging about in the attic of our past, we can diagnose the way inherited patterns of thought continue to shape our own thinking today. We can learn how to identify self-defeating barriers to worldview thinking and how to overcome them.

Part 4 reminds us that the heart of worldview thinking lies in its practical and personal application. The renewal of our minds comes about only through the submission of our whole selves to the Lordship of Christ. We must be willing to sit at the feet of Jesus and be taught by Him, as Mary of Bethany did, realizing that only "one thing is necessary" (Luke 10:42). Given our fallen human nature, we typically do not really *sit* before the Lord until our legs are knocked out from under us by crises—sorrow, loss, or injustice. It is only when stripped of our personal dreams and ambitions that we truly die to our own agendas. Union with Christ in His death and resurrection is the only path to sanctification of both heart and mind—to being conformed to the likeness of Christ.

ACKNOWLEDGMENTS

It is a joyful task to express gratitude to those whose ideas and lives have helped shape this book's message. Foremost is Francis Schaeffer, through whose ministry I returned to the Christian faith I had rejected as a teenager. After my first visit to L'Abri (described in chapter 1), I returned a year later for another round of study, when I also met the young man who became my husband. Later we both earned degrees at Covenant Seminary in St. Louis, where Schaeffer once taught. For further graduate studies we attended the Institute for Christian Studies in Toronto, where we were steeped in the philosophy of Dutch Reformed thinkers like Kuyper and Dooyeweerd, whose ideas were seminal for *How Now Shall We Live?* especially its overall framework of Creation, Fall, Redemption, and Restoration. The same background will be evident to readers of this present book as well, and by making frequent references to the original writings, I hope to inspire readers to discover these rich resources for themselves.

Second, I owe much to Dr. Phillip Johnson, professor emeritus of law at the University of California at Berkeley, who provides strategic leadership for the Intelligent Design movement. I have known Phil since 1990, when I interviewed him for the *Bible-Science Newsletter*,[13] and his original way of framing the argument for design has revolutionized the origins debate. His name likewise appears frequently throughout the text, in order to direct readers to his original works.

In my early years as a young Christian, Denis and Margie Haack (founders of Ransom Fellowship) provided crucial support and stability. At Covenant Seminary, I benefited especially from the fine teaching of Dr. David Jones. At the Institute for Christian Studies, a year-long course on neo-Platonism demonstrated that Dr. Al Wolters has a rare gift for bringing ancient Greek philosophy to life. I also had the privilege of taking the last class on neo-Calvinist philosophy taught by Dr. Bernard Zylstra before his untimely death from cancer.

I am grateful to my uncle Bill Overn, a brilliant physicist, whose recommendation helped open a position for me at the *Bible-Science Newsletter* in 1977, where I worked for thirteen years, writing in-depth monthly articles for a section titled "Worldview" on the relation between science and Christian worldview. These lengthy articles traced the impact of evolutionary concepts on education, psychology, law, Marxism, sexuality, New Age religion, and much more—material that later formed the basis for much of my contribution to *How Now Shall We Live?*[14] as well as the present book.

The material for this book was honed through interaction with various audiences, and I would like to thank the following groups: World Journalism Institute and its director Bob Case; Faith and Law (a fellowship of congressional staffers); the *How Now Shall We Live?* reading groups on Capitol Hill; Regent University School of Law; L'Abri in Rochester, Minnesota; the Association of Christian Schools International; the Renaissance Group (Christian artists and entertainers); Christian Schools International; Trinity Forum Academy; and several Christian colleges and universities. I have also benefited from the opportunity to address events organized by Christian campus groups at Princeton, Dartmouth, Ohio State University, UC Santa Barbara, the University of Minnesota, and USC. Special thanks to John Mark Reynolds, director of the Torrey Honors Institute at Biola University, who invited me to give seminars on the book when it was still in manuscript form, and to the students who contributed by their feedback and comments.

I wish to thank the Discovery Institute's Center for Science and Culture and its director Steve Meyer for a grant that underwrote the initial research stage of the book. The center's staff and fellows form a highly professional group of scientists and scholars who inspire and inform one another's work in countless ways.

I am grateful to those who read or discussed sections of the manuscript: Ila Anderson, Lael Arrington, Michael Behe, Katie Braden, David Calhoun, Bob and Kathy Case, Nancy Chan, Roy Clouser, Jim DeKorne, Michael Goheen, Os Guinness, Darryl Hart, Dana Hill, David Jones, Ranald Macaulay, George Marsden, Tim McGrew, Steven Meyer, Udo Middelmann, Kathleen Nielson, J. I. Packer, Dieter Pearcey, Dorothy Randolph, Karl Randolph, Jay

Richards, Jim Skillen, John Vander Stelt, Tyrone Walters, Linda McGinn Waterman, Richard Weikart, and Al Wolters.

It is an honor to have as my agent Sealy Yates, a man of enormous integrity and a servant's heart. The publisher of Crossway Books, Lane Dennis, along with his wife, Ebeth, welcomed the book project with prayerful enthusiasm from the beginning. Many thanks to the Crossway staff, especially vice president Marvin Padgett and editor Bill Deckard.

The deepest gratitude is due, as always, to family. Thanks to my parents, who sacrificed greatly to send their children to Lutheran schools. I owe an unspeakable debt to my husband, Rick, whose unflagging support, professional editorial expertise, and background in worldview studies contribute to a fruitful writing partnership. The perspective he developed through years of editorial experience on Capitol Hill keeps me grounded in the real world. Finally, I dedicate the book to my two sons, Dieter and Michael, in the hope that they will craft a Christian worldview in their own fields of work, liberating the gospel's power to transform their lives and their world.

—Nancy Randolph Pearcey
Lake Ridge, Virginia
March 2004

PART ONE

WHAT'S
IN A
WORLDVIEW?

1

Breaking Out of the Grid

Sundays were Sundays,
with the rest of the week largely detached,
operating by a different set of rules.
Can these two worlds that seem so separate ever merge?
JOHN BECKETT[1]

A fashionably dressed college student stepped into the counselor's office, tossing her head in an attempt at bravado. Sarah recognized the type. The Planned Parenthood clinic where she worked often attracted students from the elite university nearby, and most were wealthy, privileged, and self-confident.

"Please sit down. I have your test result . . . and you are pregnant."

The young woman nodded and grimaced. "I kind of thought so."

"Have you thought about what you want to do?" Sarah asked.

The answer was quick and sure. "I want an abortion."

"Let's go over your options first," Sarah said. "It's important for you to think through all the possibilities before you leave today."

Sometimes the young women sitting in her office would grow impatient, even hostile. They had already convinced themselves that there *were* no other viable options. After years of experience in her profession, however, Sarah knew that women who have abortions are often haunted afterward. She hoped to help the students consider the impact an abortion might have in years to come, so they would make an informed decision. If they balked, she fell back on protocol: "This is my job, I have to do it."

Why did Sarah care? Because she was a practicing Christian, as she explained to me many years later,[2] she thought that's what being a believer meant—showing compassion to women who were considering abortion. Nor was she alone: The Planned Parenthood clinic where she worked was located in the Bible belt, and virtually all the women on staff were regular church-goers. During breaks they would discuss things like their Bible study groups or their children's Sunday school programs.

Sarah's story illustrates how even sincere believers may find themselves drawn into a secular worldview—while remaining orthodox in their theological beliefs. Sarah had grown up in a solidly evangelical denomination. As a teenager, she had undergone a crisis of faith and had emerged from it with a fresh confidence. "I still have the white Bible my grandmother gave me back then," she told me. "I underlined all the passages on how to be sure you were saved." From then on, she never doubted the basic biblical doctrines.

So how did she end up working at Planned Parenthood and referring women for abortion? Something happened to Sarah when she went off to college. There she was immersed in the liberal relativism taught on most campuses today. In courses on sociology, anthropology, and philosophy, it was simply assumed that truth is culturally relative—that ideas and beliefs emerge historically by cultural forces, and are not true or false in any final sense.

And Christianity? It was treated as irrelevant to the world of scholarship. "In a class on moral philosophy, the professor presented every possible theory, from existentialism to utilitarianism, but never said a word about Christian moral theory—even though it's been the dominant religion all through Western history," Sarah recalled. "It was as though Christianity were so irrational, it didn't even merit being listed alongside the other moral theories."

Yet Sarah had no idea how to respond to these assaults on her faith. Her church had helped her find assurance of salvation, but it had *not* provided her with any intellectual resources to challenge the ideologies taught in her classes. The church's teaching had assumed a sharp divide between the sacred and secular realms, addressing itself solely to Sarah's religious life. As a result, over time she found herself absorbing the secular outlook taught in her classes. Her mental world was split, with religion strictly contained within the boundaries of worship and personal morality, while her views on everything else were run through a grid of naturalism and relativism.

"I may have started out picking up bits and pieces of a secular worldview to sprinkle on top of my Christian beliefs," Sarah explained. "But after I graduated and worked for Planned Parenthood, the pattern was reversed: My Christianity was reduced to a thin veneer over the core of a secular worldview. *It was almost like having a split personality.*" To use the categories described in the Introduction, her mind had absorbed the divided concepts of truth characteristic of Western culture: secular/sacred, fact/value, public/private. Though her faith was sincere, it was reduced to purely private experience, while public knowledge was defined in terms of secular naturalism.

Sarah's story is particularly dramatic, yet it illustrates a pattern that is more common than we might like to think. The fatal weakness in her faith was that she had accepted Christian doctrines strictly as individual items of belief: the deity of Christ, His virgin birth, His miracles, His resurrection from the dead—she could tick them off one by one. But she lacked any sense of how Christianity functions as a unified, overarching system of truth that applies to social issues, history, politics, anthropology, and all the other subject areas. In short, she lacked a Christian worldview. She held to Christianity as a collection of truths, but not as Truth.[3]

Only many years later, after a personal crisis, were Sarah's relativistic views finally challenged. "When Congress held hearings on partial-birth abortion, I was appalled. And I realized that if abortion was wrong at nine months, then it was wrong at eight months, and wrong at seven months, and six months— right back to the beginning." It was a shattering experience, and Sarah found she had to take apart her secular worldview plank by plank, and then begin painstakingly constructing a Christian worldview in its place. It was tough work, yet today she is discovering the joy of breaking out of the trap of the secular/sacred split, and seeing her faith come alive in areas where before she had not even known it applied. She is learning that Christianity is not just religious truth, it is total truth—covering all of reality.

DIVIDED MINDS

Like Sarah, many believers have absorbed the fact/value, public/private dichotomy, restricting their faith to the religious sphere while adopting whatever views are current in their professional or social circles. We probably all know of Christian teachers who uncritically accept the latest secular theories of education; Christian businessmen who run their operations by accepted secular management theories; Christian ministries that mirror the commercial world's marketing techniques; Christian families where the teenagers watch the same movies and listen to the same music as their nonbelieving friends. While sincere in their faith, they have absorbed their views on just about everything else by osmosis from the surrounding culture.

The problem was phrased succinctly by Harry Blamires in his classic book *The Christian Mind*. When I was a new Christian many years ago, Blamires's book was almost a fad item, and everyone walked around intoning its dramatic opening sentence: "There *is* no longer a Christian mind."[4]

What did Blamires mean? He was not saying that Christians are uneducated, backwoods hayseeds, though that remains a common stereotype in the secular world. A few years ago an infamous article in the *Washington Post* described conservative Christians as "poor, uneducated, and easily led."[5] Immediately the *Post* was overwhelmed with calls and faxes from Christians across the country, listing their advanced degrees and bank account balances!

But if that's not what Blamires meant, what *did* he mean? To say there is no Christian mind means that believers may be highly educated in terms of technical proficiency, and yet have no biblical worldview for interpreting the subject matter of their field. "We speak of 'the modern mind' and of 'the scientific mind,' using that word *mind* of a collectively accepted set of notions and attitudes," Blamires explains. But there is no "Christian mind"—no shared, biblically based set of assumptions on subjects like law, education, economics, politics, science, or the arts. As a moral being, the Christian follows the biblical ethic. As a spiritual being, he or she prays and attends worship services. "But as a *thinking* being, the modern Christian has succumbed to secularism," accepting "a frame of reference constructed by the secular mind and a set of criteria reflecting secular evaluations."[6] That is, when we enter the stream of discourse in our field or profession, we participate mentally as non-Christians, using the current concepts and categories, no matter what our private beliefs may be.

Living in the Washington, D.C., area, I have witnessed firsthand the growing numbers of believers working in politics today, which is an encouraging trend. But I can also say from experience that few hold an explicitly Christian political philosophy. As a congressional chief of staff once admitted, "I realize that I hold certain views because I'm politically conservative, *not* because I see how they're rooted in the Bible." He knew he should formulate a biblically based philosophy of government, but he simply didn't know how to proceed.

Similarly, through decades of writing on science and worldview, I have interacted with scientists who are deeply committed believers; yet few have crafted a biblically informed philosophy of science. In Christian ministries, I've met many who take great pains to make sure their *message* is biblical, but who never think to ask whether their *methods* are biblical. A journalism professor recently told me that even the best Christian journalists—sincere believers with outstanding professional skills—typically have no Christian theory of journalism. In popular culture, believers have constructed an entire parallel culture of artists and entertainers; yet even so, as Charlie Peacock laments, few "think Christianly" about art and aesthetics.[7] The phrase is borrowed from Blamires, and when I addressed a group of artists and musicians in Charlie's home, he showed me a shelf with half a dozen copies of Blamires's book—enough to lend out to several friends at once.

"Thinking Christianly" means understanding that Christianity gives the truth about the whole of reality, a perspective for interpreting every subject matter. Genesis tells us that God spoke the entire universe into being with His Word—what John 1:1 calls the *Logos*. The Greek word means not only Word but also reason or rationality, and the ancient Stoics used it to mean the rational structure of the universe. Thus the underlying structure of the entire universe reflects the mind of the Creator. There is no fact/value dichotomy in the scriptural account. Nothing has an autonomous or independent identity, separate from the will of the Creator. As a result, all creation must be interpreted in light of its relationship to God. In any subject area we study, we are discovering the laws or creation ordinances by which God structured the world.

As Scripture puts it, the universe speaks of God—"the heavens declare the glory of God" (Ps. 19:1)—because His character is reflected in the things He has made. This is sometimes referred to as "general" revelation because it speaks to everyone at all times, in contrast to the "special" revelation given in the Bible. As Jonathan Edwards explained, God communicates not only "by his voice to us in the Scriptures" but also in creation and in historical events. Indeed, "the whole creation of God preaches."[8] Yet it is possible for Christians to be deaf and blind to the message of general revelation, and part of learning to have the mind of Christ involves praying for the spiritual sensitivity to "hear" the preaching of creation.

The great historian of religion Martin Marty once said every religion serves two functions: First, it is a message of personal salvation, telling us how to get right with God; and second, it is a lens for interpreting the world. Historically, evangelicals have been good at the first function—at "saving souls." But they have not been nearly as good at helping people to interpret the world around them—at providing a set of interrelated concepts that function as a lens to give a biblical view of areas like science, politics, economics, or bioethics. As Marty puts it, evangelicals have typically "accented personal piety and individual salvation, leaving men to their own devices to interpret the world around them."

In fact, many no longer think it's even the *function* of Christianity to provide an interpretation of the world. Marty calls this the Modern Schism (in a book by that title), and he says we are living in the first time in history where Christianity has been boxed into the private sphere and has largely stopped speaking to the public sphere.[9]

"This internalization or privatization of religion is one of the most momentous changes that has ever taken place in Christendom," writes another historian, Sidney Mead.[10] As a result, our lives are often fractured and fragmented, with our faith firmly locked into the private realm of church and family, where it rarely has a chance to inform our life and work in the public realm. The aura of worship dissipates after Sunday, and we unconsciously absorb secular attitudes the rest of the week. We inhabit two separate "worlds," navigating a sharp divide between our religious life and ordinary life.

BIBLE SCHOOL DROP-OUTS

At the same time, most believers find this highly frustrating. We really *want* to integrate our faith into every aspect of life, including our profession. We want to be whole people—people of integrity (the word comes from the Latin word for "whole"). Not long ago, I met a recent convert who was agonizing over how to apply his newfound faith to his work as an art teacher. "I want my whole life to reflect my relationship with God," he told me. "I don't want my faith to be in one compartment and my art in another."

We would all agree with Dorothy Sayers, who said that if religion does not speak to our work lives, then it has nothing to say about what we do with the vast majority of our time—and no wonder people say religion is irrelevant! "How can anyone remain interested in a religion which seems to have no concern with nine-tenths of his life?"[11]

In the secular/sacred dualism, ordinary work is actually denigrated, while church work is elevated as more valuable. In his book *Roaring Lambs*, Bob Briner describes his student days at a Christian college, where the unspoken assumption was that the only way to *really* serve God was in full-time Christian work. Already knowing that he wanted a career in sports management, Briner writes, "I felt I was a sort of second-class campus citizen. My classmates who were preparing for the pulpit ministry or missionary service were the ones who were treated as if they would be doing the *real* work of the church. The rest of us were the supporting cast."

The underlying message was that people in ordinary professions might contribute their prayers and financial support, but that was about it. "Almost nothing in my church or collegiate experiences presented possibilities for a dynamic, involved Christian life outside the professional ministry," Briner concludes. "You heard about being salt and light, but no one told you how to do it."[12] Lip service was paid to the idea of dedicating your work to God, but all it seemed to mean was, *Do your best, and don't commit any obvious sins.*

The same secular/sacred dualism nearly snuffed out the creative talents of the founders of the whimsically funny Veggie Tales videos. Phil Vischer says he always knew he wanted to make movies, but "the implicit message I received growing up was that full-time ministry was the only valid Christian service. Young Christians were to aspire to be either ministers or missionaries." So he dutifully packed his bags and went off to Bible college to study for the ministry.

Yet the more he saw the powerful influence movies have on kids, the more he thought it was important to produce high-quality films. Finally he made up his mind: "I figured God could use a filmmaker or two, regardless of what anyone else said." Dropping out of Bible college, he and his friend Mike Nawrocki started a video company. As their former classmates turned into pastors and youth ministers, they turned into the voices of Bob the Tomato and Larry the Cucumber.[13] The videos have become immensely popular, with their biblical messages and quirky humor. Yet if these two Bible school drop-outs had not broken free from the secular/sacred mentality and decided that Christians have a valid calling in the field of filmmaking, their talents may well have been lost to the church. Every member of the Body of Christ has been gifted for the benefit of the whole, and when those gifts are suppressed, we all lose out.

The pervasiveness of the secular/sacred split is less surprising when we realize that many pastors and teachers have absorbed it themselves. A school superintendent once told me that most educators define "a Christian teacher" strictly in terms of personal behavior: things like setting a good example and showing concern for students. Almost none define it in terms of conveying a biblical worldview on the subjects they teach, whether literature, science, social studies, or the arts. In other words, they are concerned about being a Christian *in* their work, but they don't think in terms of having a biblical framework *on* the work itself.

In many Christian schools, the typical strategy is to inject a few narrowly defined "religious" elements into the classroom, like prayer and Bible memorization—and then teach exactly the same things as the secular schools. The curriculum merely spreads a layer of spiritual devotion over the subject matter like icing on a cake, while the content itself stays the same.

SUBTLE TEMPTATION

The same pattern holds all the way up to the highest academic levels. "Christians in higher education are strongly, though subtly, tempted to compartmentalize our faith," says a sociology professor after teaching for many years at a Christian college. Religion is considered relevant to special areas like church and campus religious activities, he says. "But when we are teaching and doing our research, we usually center our attention upon the theories, concepts, and other subject matter that are conventional in our respective disciplines."

Here we see the danger of the secular/sacred split: It concedes the "theories, concepts, and other subject matter" in our field to nonbelievers. Christians have essentially accepted a trade-off: So long as we're allowed to hold our Bible studies and prayer meetings, we've turned over the *content* of the academic fields to the secularists.

I encountered a particularly egregious example many years ago when I interviewed a physics professor for an article I was writing. He was a sponsor for a well-known campus ministry at a large secular university, so I asked him to explain a Christian perspective on his field, and especially on the "new physics"—relativity theory and quantum mechanics. Now, claims and counterclaims have been tossed back and forth about the supposedly revolutionary impact of the new physics—that it demolished the Newtonian worldview which had held sway for three hundred years, that it destroyed determinism and made room for free will, that it undercut materialism, and much more. In fact, many popular books on the subject even claim that quantum mechanics confirms Eastern metaphysics (the classic example is *The Tao of Physics*[14]). As a young writer, I was intrigued to learn how a Christian professor would evaluate the wide-ranging philosophical implications being drawn from the new physics.

To my dismay, the professor had nothing to offer. Physics and faith are completely separate domains, he told me. The exact words he used are branded into my memory: "Quantum mechanics is like auto mechanics. It has nothing to do with my faith."

This man was deeply involved in campus ministry, but obviously he kept his faith and his science in separate, parallel tracks—running along side by side like train rails that never touch or intersect. He was a Christian and he was a physicist—but he did not have a Christian worldview that brought the two together.[15]

Clearly, developing a Christian mind involves much more than merely earning an advanced degree. Many Christians with Ph.D.'s have simply absorbed a two-track approach to their subject, treating science or sociology or history as though it consisted of religiously neutral knowledge, where biblical truth has nothing important to say. In these areas, the attitude seems to be that God's Word is not a light to our paths after all, and that we must simply accommodate to whatever the secular experts decree.[16] God's Word is robbed of its power to transform our minds, and we become inwardly divided, deprived of the joy of living whole and integrated lives.

ENLIGHTENMENT IDOL

Secularists reinforce this split mentality by claiming that *their* theory does not reflect any particular philosophy—that it is just "the way all reasonable people think." They thus promote their own views as unbiased and rational, suitable for the public square, while denouncing religious views as biased or prejudiced. This tactic has often cowed Christians into being defensive about our faith, which in turn has taken a steep toll on our effectiveness in the broader culture.

The mistake lies in thinking there *is* such a thing as theories that are unbiased or neutral, unaffected by any religious and philosophical assumptions. We know, of course, that in the *sacred* realm, each group has its own religious views—Christian, Jewish, Muslim, New Age, and so on. But in the *secular* realm, it is often thought that we all have access to neutral knowledge where religious and philosophical values are not supposed to interfere.

The irony is that this ideal is itself a product of a particular philosophical tradition. The notion that it is possible to strip the mind of all prior assumptions and religious commitments in order to get down to the bare, unvarnished truths of "reason" comes from the Enlightenment. It was expressed most forcefully in the seventeenth century by René Descartes, often considered the first modern philosopher. The way to find truth, Descartes said, was to strip the mind of everything that can possibly be doubted until we finally reach a bedrock of truths that cannot possibly be doubted. He believed that he himself had dug deep enough to hit that infallible bedrock in his famous *cogito:* "I think, therefore I am." After all, even when we are doubting everything, we are still thinking, and therefore the surest thing we can know is the existence of the thinking subject.

The idea emerged that by a method of systematic doubt, the human mind—or Reason (often capitalized)—could attain to godlike objectivity and certainty. In one of my college philosophy courses, the professor liked to define objectivity as "the way God sees things." Though not a believer, his point was that true objectivity could be attained only by a Being who transcends this world and knows everything as it truly is. The hubris of the Enlightenment lay in thinking that Reason was just such a transcendent power, providing infallible knowledge. Reason became nothing less than an idol, taking the place of God as the source of absolute Truth.

Ironically, Descartes himself was a devout Catholic; he was so certain that God had revealed to him the irrefutable logic of the *cogito* that he vowed to make a pilgrimage to the shrine of Our Lady of Loreto in Italy—which he did a few years later. Thus he is a tragic example of how one may be a sincere Christian and yet promote a philosophy that is certainly *not* Christian. Descartes helped to establish a form of rationalism that treated Reason not merely as the human ability to think rationally but as an infallible and autonomous source of truth. Reason came to be seen as a storehouse of truths independent of any religion or philosophy.

TWO CITIES

The Enlightenment project was in sharp contrast to the classic Christian tradition, which suggested a far humbler and more realistic view of knowledge (or epistemology). It recognized that what we count as knowledge is profoundly shaped by our spiritual condition. This insight was best expressed by St. Augustine in his image of two cities: the City of God and the City of Man. Augustine wasn't speaking about the divide between church and state, as some have thought; he was talking about two systems of thought and allegiance. We help to build the City of God when our actions are animated and directed by the love of God, offered up to His service. We build the City of Man whenever our actions are motivated by self-love, serving sinful purposes.

Applied to the life of the mind, the image of two cities means we all come to the table with a spiritual motivation already in place, which affects what we will accept as true. Far from being blank slates, our minds are colored by our spiritual stance—either for God or against Him. As Romans 1 puts it, we either worship and serve the true God or we worship and serve created things (idols). Humans are inherently religious beings, created to be in relationship with God—and if they reject God, they don't stop being religious; they simply find some other ultimate principle upon which to base their lives.

Often that idol is something concrete, like financial security or professional success; in other cases, it may be an ideology or set of beliefs that substitutes for religion. Whatever form the idolatry takes, according to Romans 1:18 those who worship idols *actively suppress* their knowledge of God, while seeking out substitute gods. They are far from religiously neutral.

Of course, Christianity is not deterministic: It teaches that, by God's grace, people may be enlightened by His truth to bow before Him, so that they are moved from one side to the other—transferred from the kingdom of darkness to the kingdom of Christ (see Col. 1:13). That's called conversion. Yet at any particular point in time, we are either on one side or the other. We are interpreting our experience in the light either of divine revelation or of some competing system of thought. Our calling as Christians is to progressively clean out all the "idols" remaining in our thought life, so that we may pursue every aspect of our lives as citizens of the City of God.[17]

In recent decades, this classic Christian view has received support from what may seem a surprising source. Contemporary philosophy of science has rejected the older, positivistic definition of knowledge, which treated scientists in white coats as though they were magically freed from preconceptions and prior beliefs the moment they entered the laboratory. Instead philosophers are much quicker today to acknowledge the human factor in deciding what counts as knowledge—to admit that it is impossible to approach the facts from a purely neutral philosophical stance. We all come to the scientific enterprise as whole persons, bringing into the laboratory a panoply of prior experiences, theoretical assumptions, personal beliefs, ambitions, and socioeconomic interests. These preconceptions color virtually every aspect of the scientific endeavor: what we consider worth studying, what we expect to find, where we look, and how we interpret the results.[18]

"All facts are theory-laden," is a popular slogan in philosophy of science today. A bit of an exaggeration, perhaps, but it makes the point that even what we choose to consider a "fact" is influenced by the theories we bring to the table. We always process data in light of some theoretical framework that we have adopted for understanding the world.

ABSOLUTELY DIVINE

The upshot is that no system of thought is a product purely of Reason— because Reason is not a repository of infallible, religiously autonomous truths, as Descartes and the other rationalists thought. Instead, it is simply a human capacity, the ability to reason from premises. The important question, then, is what a person accepts as ultimate premises, for they shape everything that follows.

If you press any set of ideas back far enough, eventually you reach some starting point. Something has to be taken as self-existent—the ultimate reality and source of everything else. There's no reason for it to exist; it just "is." For the materialist, the ultimate reality is matter, and everything is reduced to material constituents. For the pantheist, the ultimate reality is a spiritual force or substratum, and the goal of meditation is to reconnect with that spiritual oneness. For the doctrinaire Darwinist, biology is ultimate, and everything, even religion and morality, is reduced to a product of Darwinian processes. For the empiricist, all knowledge is traceable ultimately to sense data, and anything not known by sensation is unreal.

And so on. Every system of thought begins with some ultimate principle. If it does not begin with God, it will begin with some dimension of creation— the material, the spiritual, the biological, the empirical, or whatever. Some aspect of created reality will be "absolutized" or put forth as the ground and source of everything else—the uncaused cause, the self-existent. To use religious language, this ultimate principle functions as the divine, if we define that term to mean the one thing upon which all else depends for existence. This starting assumption has to be accepted by faith, not by prior reasoning. (Otherwise it is not really the ultimate starting point for all reasoning—something else is, and we have to dig deeper and start there instead.)

In this sense, we could say that every alternative to Christianity is a religion. It may not involve ritual or worship services, yet it identifies some principle or force in creation as the self-existent cause of everything else. Even nonbelievers hold to some ultimate ground of existence, which functions as an idol or false god. This is why the "Bible writers always address their reader as though they already believe in God or some God surrogate," explains philosopher Roy Clouser.[19] Faith is a universal human function, and if it is not directed toward God it will be directed toward something else.

"The need for religion appears to be hard-wired in the human animal," writes philosopher John Gray (though as an atheist he bemoans the fact). "Certainly the behaviour of secular humanists supports this hypothesis. Atheists are usually just as emotionally engaged as believers. Quite commonly, they are more intellectually rigid."[20] In short, it is not as though Christians have faith, while secularists base their convictions purely on facts and reason. Secularism itself is based on ultimate beliefs, just as much as Christianity is. Some part of creation—usually matter or nature—functions in the role of the divine. So the question is not which view is religious and which is purely rational; the question is which is true and which is false.

This is what Augustine meant by his image of two cities. Ever since the Fall, the human race has been divided into two distinct groups—those who follow God and submit their minds to His truth, and those who set up an idol of some kind and then organize their thinking to rationalize their worship of that idol. Over time, as people's ultimate commitments shape the choices they make, their perspective is inevitably molded to support those choices. A false god leads to the formation of a false worldview.

This is why Christians cannot complacently abandon so-called *secular* subject areas to nonbelievers—just so long as they grant us some restricted *sacred* area where we are free to sing hymns and read the Bible. Instead we must identify and critique the dominant intellectual idols, and then construct biblically based alternatives.

ARISTOTLE'S SCREWDRIVER

This is not to deny that Christians and non-Christians often agree across a wide range of subject matter. Nonbelievers may even be *more* capable at constructing buildings, running banks, performing surgery, or writing computer software. The reason is grounded in the doctrine of creation: We are all made in God's image, in order to live in God's world, and our faculties were designed to give us real knowledge of that world. Thus in many fields there can be a significant range of agreement between believers and nonbelievers.

In addition, the Bible teaches the doctrine of common grace. Whereas *special grace* refers to salvation, *common grace* means God's providential care—the way He actively upholds all of creation. God "sends rain on the just and on the unjust," Scripture says (Matt. 5:45). That is, His gifts are given even to nonbelievers, including the intellectual gifts of knowledge and insight. That's why Jesus could say that even sinners "know how to give good gifts to [their] children" (Matt. 7:11) and can be good parents. He could also chide His opponents for failing to interpret the signs of the times: Since they were able to interpret the signs of impending weather, He expected them to be able to discern the meanings of history as well (Matt. 16:1-4). Thus, the Bible itself teaches that nonbelievers are capable of effective functioning in the world, including cognitive functioning.

Yet as soon as we try to *explain* what we know, then our spiritual and philosophical assumptions come into play. Take, for example, mathematics. You might not think there is a Christian view of mathematics, but there is. Certainly everyone, believer or not, will agree that 5+7=12. But when you ask how to *justify* mathematical knowledge, people split into several competing camps.

The ancient Greeks, standing at the dawn of Western history, are famous for having discovered Euclidean geometry. But they did not believe the material world itself exhibited a precise mathematical order, because they regarded matter as independently existing, recalcitrant stuff that would never completely "obey" mathematical rules. So they kept mathematics locked up in an abstract Platonic "heaven."

By contrast, most of the early modern scientists were Christians; they believed that matter was *not* preexisting but had come from the hand of God. Thus it had no power to resist His will but would "obey" the rules He had laid down—with mathematical precision. Historian R. G. Collingwood writes, "The possibility of an applied mathematics is an expression, in terms of natural science, of the Christian belief that nature is the creation of an omnipotent God."[21]

Since my father is a mathematics professor, I like to remind him of Collingwood's words. "The very *existence* of your field," I tell him, "is a product of the Christian worldview."

Today, however, most philosophers no longer even regard mathematics as a body of truths. The dominant philosophy of mathematics treats it as a social construction, like the game of baseball. "Three strikes and you're out" is an arbitrary rule. It's not true or false; it's just the way we choose to play the game. By the same token, mathematical rules are regarded as just the way we play the game.[22]

Even American schoolchildren are now taught this postmodern view of math. A popular middle school curriculum says students should learn that "mathematics is man-made, that it is arbitrary, and good solutions are arrived at by consensus among those who are considered expert."[23] Man-made?

Arbitrary? Clearly, our public schools have waded deeply into the murky waters of postmodernism.

Moreover, if math is arbitrary, then there are no wrong answers, just different perspectives. In Minnesota, teachers are instructed to be tolerant of "multiple mathematical worldviews."[24] In New Mexico, I met a young man who had recently graduated from high school, where a mathematics teacher had labeled him a "bigot" for thinking it was important to get the right answer. As long as students worked together in a group and achieved consensus, the teacher insisted, the outcome was acceptable.

This means that even the simplest, most universal form of knowledge— mathematics—is subject to sometimes radically differing worldview interpretations. Clearly, the impact of worldview will grow even larger as we move up the scale into more complex fields, like biology, economics, law, or ethics.[25]

The danger is that if Christians do not *consciously* develop a biblical approach to the subject, then we will *un*consciously absorb some other philosophical approach. A set of ideas for interpreting the world is like a philosophical toolbox, stuffed with terms and concepts. If Christians do not develop their own tools of analysis, then when some issue comes up that they want to understand, they'll reach over and borrow *someone else's* tools—whatever concepts are generally accepted in their professional field or in the culture at large. But when Christians do that, Os Guinness writes, they don't realize that "they are borrowing not an isolated tool but a whole philosophical toolbox laden with tools which have their own particular bias to every problem." They may even end up absorbing an entire set of alien principles without even realizing it—like Sarah did in our opening story. Using tools of analysis that have non-Christian assumptions embedded in them is "like wearing someone else's glasses or walking in someone else's shoes. *The tools shape the user.*"[26]

In other words, not only do we fail to be salt and light to a lost culture, but we ourselves may end up being shaped by that culture.

BIBLICAL TOOLBOX

What is the antidote to the secular/sacred divide? How do we make sure our toolbox contains biblically based conceptual tools for every issue we encounter? We must begin by being utterly convinced that there *is* a biblical perspective on everything—not just on spiritual matters. The Old Testament tells us repeatedly that "The fear of the LORD is the beginning of wisdom" (Ps. 111:10; Prov. 1:7; 9:10; 15:33). Similarly, the New Testament teaches that in Christ are "all the treasures of wisdom and knowledge" (Col. 2:3). We often interpret these verses to mean spiritual wisdom only, but the text places no limitation on the term. "Most people have a tendency to read these passages as though they say that the fear of the Lord is the foundation of *religious* knowledge," writes Clouser. "But the fact is that they make a very radical claim—the claim that somehow *all* knowledge depends upon religious truth."[27]

This claim is easier to grasp when we realize that Christianity is not unique in this regard. All belief systems work the same way. As we saw earlier, *whatever* a system puts forth as self-existing is essentially what it regards as divine. And that religious commitment functions as the controlling principle for everything that follows. The fear of some "god" is the beginning of every proposed system of knowledge.

Once we understand how first principles work, then it becomes clear that all truth must begin with God. The only self-existent reality is God, and everything else depends on Him for its origin and continued existence. Nothing exists apart from His will; nothing falls outside the scope of the central turning points in biblical history: Creation, Fall, and Redemption.

Creation

The Christian message does not begin with "accept Christ as your Savior"; it begins with "in the beginning God created the heavens and the earth." The Bible teaches that God is the sole source of the entire created order. No other gods compete with Him; no natural forces exist on their own; nothing receives its nature or existence from another source. Thus His word, or laws, or creation ordinances give the world its order and structure. God's creative word is the source of the laws of *physical* nature, which we study in the natural sciences. It is also the source of the laws of *human* nature—the principles of morality (ethics), of justice (politics), of creative enterprise (economics), of aesthetics (the arts), and even of clear thinking (logic). That's why Psalm 119:91 says, "all things are your servants." There is no philosophically or spiritually neutral subject matter.

Fall

The universality of Creation is matched by the universality of the Fall. The Bible teaches that all parts of creation—including our minds—are caught up in a great rebellion against the Creator. Theologians call this the "noetic" effect of the Fall (the effect on the mind), and it subverts our ability to understand the world apart from God's regenerating grace. Scripture is replete with warnings that idolatry or willful disobedience toward God makes humans "blind" or "deaf." Paul writes, "The god of this world has blinded the minds of the unbelievers, to keep them from seeing the light of the gospel" (2 Cor. 4:4). Sin literally "darkens" the understanding (Eph. 4:18).[28]

Of course, nonbelievers still function in God's world, bear God's image, and are upheld by God's common grace, which means they are capable of uncovering isolated segments of genuine knowledge. And Christians should welcome those insights. All truth is God's truth, as the church fathers used to say; and they urged Christians to "plunder the Egyptians" by appropriating the best of secular scholarship, showing how it actually fits best within a biblical worldview. There may even be occasions when Christians are mistaken on some point while nonbelievers get it right. Nevertheless, the overall *systems* of thought constructed by nonbelievers will be false—for if the system is not built on biblical truth, then it will be built on some other ultimate principle. Even individual truths will be seen through the distorting lens of a false worldview. As a result, a Christian approach to any field needs to be both critical and constructive. We cannot simply borrow from the results of secular scholarship as though that were spiritually neutral territory discovered by people whose minds are completely open and objective—that is, as though the Fall had never happened.

Redemption

Finally, Redemption is as comprehensive as Creation and Fall. God does not save only our souls, while leaving our minds to function on their own. He redeems the whole person. Conversion is meant to give new direction to our thoughts, emotions, will, and habits. Paul urges us to offer up our entire selves to God as "living sacrifices," so that we will not be "conformed to this world" but be "transformed by the renewal of [our] minds" (Rom. 12:1-2). When we are redeemed, *all things* are made new (2 Cor. 5:17). God promises to give us "a new heart, and a new spirit" (Ezek. 36:26), animating our entire character with new life.

This explains why the Bible treats sin primarily as a matter of turning away from God and serving other gods, and only secondarily in terms of lists of specific immoral behaviors. The first commandment is, after all, the *first* commandment—the rest follows only *after* we are straight about whom or what it is that we are worshiping. By the same token, redemption consists primarily in casting out our mental idols and turning back to the true God. And when we do that, we will experience His transforming power renewing every aspect of our lives. To talk about a Christian worldview is simply another way of saying that when we are redeemed, our entire outlook on life is re-centered on God and re-built on His revealed truth.

READ THE DIRECTIONS

How do we go about constructing a Christian worldview? The key passage is the creation account in Genesis, because that's where we are taken back to the beginning to learn what God's original purpose was in creating the human race. With the entrance of sin, humans went off course, lost their way, wandered off the path. But when we accept Christ's salvation, we are put back on the right path and are restored to our original purpose. Redemption is not just about being saved *from* sin, it is also about being saved *to* something—to resume the task for which we were originally created.

And what was that task? In Genesis, God gives what we might call the first job description: "Be fruitful and multiply and fill the earth and subdue it." The first phrase, "be fruitful and multiply," means to develop the *social* world: build families, churches, schools, cities, governments, laws. The second phrase, "subdue the earth," means to harness the *natural* world: plant crops, build bridges, design computers, compose music. This passage is sometimes called the Cultural Mandate because it tells us that our original purpose was to create cultures, build civilizations—nothing less.[29]

This means that our vocation or professional work is not a second-class activity, something we do just to put food on the table. It is the high calling for which we were originally created. The way we serve a Creator God is by being creative with the talents and gifts He has given us. We could even say that we are called to continue God's own creative work. Of course, we do not create from nothing, ex nihilo, as God did; our job is to develop the powers and potentials that God originally built into the creation—using wood to build houses, cotton to make clothes, or silicon to make computer chips. Though modern social and economic institutions are not explicitly referred to in the Garden of Eden, their biblical justification is rooted in the Cultural Mandate.

In the first six days of the Genesis narrative, God forms then fills the physical universe—the sky with the sun and moon, the sea with its swimming creatures, the earth with its land animals. Then the narrative pauses, as though to emphasize that the next step will be the culmination of all that has gone before. This is the only stage in the creative process when God announces His plan ahead of time, when the members of the Trinity consult with one another: Let Us make a creature in Our image, who will represent Us and carry on Our work on earth (see Gen. 1:26). Then God creates the first human couple, to have dominion over the earth and govern it in His name.

It is obvious from the text that humans are not supreme rulers, autonomously free to do whatever they wish. Their dominion is a delegated authority: They are representatives of the Supreme Ruler, called to reflect His holy and loving care for creation. They are to "cultivate" the earth—a word that has the same root as "culture." The way we express the image of God is by being creative and building cultures.

This was God's purpose when He originally created human beings, and it remains His purpose for us today. God's original plan was not abrogated by the Fall. Sin has corrupted every aspect of human nature, but it has not made us less than human. We are not animals. We still reflect, "through a glass, darkly" (1 Cor. 13:12, KJV), our original nature as God's image-bearers. Even nonbelievers carry out the Cultural Mandate: They "multiply and fill the earth"—which is to say, they get married, raise families, start schools, run businesses. And they "cultivate the earth"—they fix cars, write books, study nature, invent new gadgets.

After I spoke at a conference, a young woman said to me, "When you talk about the Cultural Mandate, you're not talking about anything distinctively Christian; these are things everybody does." But that's precisely the point: Genesis is telling us our true nature, the things we can't help doing, the way God created everyone to function. Our purpose is precisely to fulfill our God-given nature.

The Fall did not destroy our original calling, but only made it more difficult. Our work is now marked by sorrow and hard labor. In Genesis 3:16 and 17, the Hebrew uses the same word for the "labor" of childbearing and the "labor" of growing food. The text suggests that the two central tasks of adulthood—raising the next generation and making a living—will be fraught with the pain of living in a fallen and fractured world. All our efforts will be twisted and misdirected by sin and selfishness.

Yet when God redeems us, He releases us from the guilt and power of sin and restores us to our full humanity, so that we can once again carry out the tasks for which we were created. Because of Christ's redemption on the cross, our work takes on a new aspect as well—it becomes a means of sharing in His redemptive purposes. In cultivating creation, we not only recover our original purpose but also bring a redemptive force to reverse the evil and corruption introduced by the Fall. We offer our gifts to God to participate in making His Kingdom come, His will be done. With hearts and minds renewed, our work can now be inspired by love for God and delight in His service.

The lesson of the Cultural Mandate is that our sense of fulfillment depends on engaging in creative, constructive work. The ideal human existence is not eternal leisure or an endless vacation—or even a monastic retreat into prayer and meditation—but creative effort expended for the glory of God and the benefit of others. Our calling is not just to "get to heaven" but also to cultivate the earth, not just to "save souls" but also to serve God through our work. For

God Himself is engaged not only in the work of salvation (special grace) but also in the work of preserving and developing His creation (common grace). When we obey the Cultural Mandate, we participate in the work of God Himself, as agents of His common grace.

This is the rich content that should come to mind when we hear the word *Redemption*. The term does not refer only to a one-time conversion event. It means entering upon a lifelong quest to devote our skills and talents to building things that are beautiful and useful, while fighting the forces of evil and sin that oppress and distort the creation. *How Now Shall We Live?* added a fourth category—Creation, Fall, Redemption, *and Restoration*—to emphasize the theme of ongoing vocation. Some theologians suggest the fourth category should be *Glorification,* to call to mind our final goal of living in the new heavens and new earth, for which our work here is a preparation. Whatever term we use, being a Christian means embarking on a lifelong process of growth in grace, both in our personal lives (sanctification) and in our vocations (cultural renewal). The new heavens and new earth will be a continuation of the creation we know now—purified by fire, but recognizably the same, just as Jesus was recognizable in His resurrection body. As C. S. Lewis puts it at the end of his Narnia tales, we have started a great adventure story that will never end. It is the "Great Story which no one on earth has read: which goes on for ever: in which every chapter is better than the one before."[30]

BORN TO GROW UP

In many churches, the message of justification—how to get right with God—is preached over and over again. But much less is said about sanctification—how to live *after* you're converted. In the Lutheran churches where I grew up, it seemed we were always fighting the Reformation over again: Every sermon came back to justification by faith. Shortly after my conversion, I remarked in frustration to my great-aunt Alice, a devout and intelligent woman, that we really didn't need to hear the basic message of salvation by faith *every* Sunday.

Her eyes sparkled at me behind wire-rimmed glasses, and she replied patiently, "But we always need to be reminded, dear, because grace is so contrary to our human tendencies."

She was right, of course, but it remains true that most churches are strong on teaching about conversion but weak on teaching about how to live after conversion. Think of an analogy: In one sense, our physical birth is the most important event in our lives, because it is the beginning of everything else. Yet in another sense, our birth is the *least* important event, because it is merely the starting point. If someone were to mention every day how great it was to be born, we would find that rather strange. Once we have come into the world, the important task is to grow and mature. By the same token, being born again is the necessary first step in our spiritual lives, yet we should not focus our message constantly on how to be saved.[31] It is crucial for churches to lead people forward into spiritual maturity, equipping the saints to carry out the mission God has given us in the Cultural Mandate.

Each of us has a role to play in cultivating the creation and working out God's norms for a just and humane society. By sheer necessity, of course, a large percentage of our time is devoted to running businesses, teaching schools, publishing newspapers, playing in orchestras, and everything else needed to keep a civilization thriving. Even those who work in "full-time Christian service" still need to clean the house, take care of the kids, and mow the lawn. It is imperative for us to understand that in carrying out these tasks, we are not doing inferior or second-tier work for the Kingdom. Instead we are agents of God's common grace, doing His work in the world.

Martin Luther liked to say that our occupations are God's "masks"—His way of caring for creation in a hidden manner through human means. In our work, we are God's hands, God's eyes, God's feet. There are times, says the Lutheran writer Gene Edward Veith, when God works directly and miraculously, as when He fed the Israelites manna from heaven. But ordinarily He feeds people through the myriad workers in agriculture, transportation, food processing, and retailing. Sometimes God may heal the sick miraculously, as Jesus did in the New Testament. But He works just as surely through the work of doctors, nurses, and health care specialists. At times God may rout an enemy army miraculously, as He did in the book of Judges. But in everyday life, He protects us from evil by the means of police officers, attorneys, and judges—and from outside enemies by the military. He raises children through parents, teachers, pastors, and soccer coaches. Even nonbelievers can be "masks" of God, avenues of His providential love and care.[32]

The metaphor of God's "mask" presses home the fact that our vocation is not something *we* do for God—which would put the burden on us to perform and achieve. Instead, it is a way we participate in *God's* work. For God Himself is engaged not only in the work of salvation but also in the work of preserving and maintaining His creation.

Understanding this profound truth also helps prevent a triumphalistic attitude. I have encountered people who are averse to the concept of Christian worldview because they think it means trying to take over the world and impose our beliefs, top down, on everyone else. This is when we must remind them (and ourselves) that God's means of salvation was, after all, the cross. He came in humility and human weakness, even submitting to death at the hands of sinners. In a fallen world, we too may pay a price for being faithful to God's calling. If we stand up for what is right against injustice, we may not be as successful in our careers, or win public and professional recognition, or earn as much money as we might have. Those who follow Christ may end up sharing in His suffering. Luther emphasized these themes in his "theology of the cross,"[33] which can help us to guard against triumphalism, pride, and self-righteousness.

By God's grace, we *can* make a significant difference within our sphere of influence—but only as we "crucify" our craving for success, power, and public acclaim. "If anyone would come after me," Jesus said, "let him deny himself and take up his cross daily and follow me" (Luke 9:23). If we long to be given the mind of Christ, we must first be willing to submit to the pattern of suffering He modeled for us. We should expect the process of developing a Christian worldview to be a difficult and painful struggle—first inwardly, as we uproot the idols in our own thought life, and then outwardly, as we face the hostility of a fallen and unbelieving world. Our strength for the task must come from spiritual union with Christ, recognizing that suffering is the route to being conformed to Him and remade into His image.

A PERSONAL ODYSSEY

To flesh out the theme of Christian worldview on a personal level, I'd like to tell my own conversion story, and then the stories of others who have applied a Christian perspective—often with revolutionary impact. To some people, *worldview* may be a stuffy academic-sounding term that conjures up images of tweedy professors and dusty lecture halls. When *How Now Shall We Live?* was published, Prison Fellowship kicked off the publicity campaign with a conference where one of the invited speakers was a television producer, who seemed a bit discomfited about speaking at a *worldview* conference. I had suggested that she speak along the lines of "A Christian Framework for Popular Culture"—and throughout her presentation she made dismissive, almost mocking comments about "frameworks" and "worldviews" and "perspectives," with audible scare quotes around the words, as though that were something for nerds with plastic pencil guards in their pockets. Certainly not the thing for an *artiste!*

I was scheduled to give my testimony the next morning, so I stayed up half the night completely recasting my personal story in order to emphasize that *worldview* is not something abstract and academic, but intensely personal. Our worldview is the way we answer the core questions of life that everyone has to struggle with: What are we here for? What is ultimate truth? Is there anything worth living for?

I began asking these questions in a serious way myself as a teenager. Since I had grown up in a Scandinavian Lutheran home and attended Lutheran elementary school, I had a good background in knowing *what* Christianity teaches. But I came to realize I didn't know *why* it was true.

Like many teenagers, I was influenced in part by non-Christian friends, particularly one girl who was Jewish. We both played violin in the school orchestra; we attended music camps together; and over time, I came to realize that *she* was Jewish because of her ethnic background and because she respected her parents . . . and in the same way, *I* was Christian because of *my* family background and because I wanted to please my parents. It struck me that if the same motivation led to contrary results, then obviously it was not an adequate epistemological principle.

I didn't quite think of it in those terms, of course. But I did realize that I had no reason for believing Christianity was true over against the other belief systems I was encountering.

When I began asking questions of my parents and pastors, the typical response, unfortunately, was a patronizing pat on the head. One pastor told me, "Don't worry, we all have doubts sometimes." No one seemed to grasp that I was not merely troubled by psychological "doubts" but had stepped outside the circle of faith and was questioning the truth of the whole system.

Manifesto of Unbelief

Failing to find answers, I eventually took a very significant step: I decided that the most intellectually honest course would be to reject my faith—and then to analyze it objectively alongside all the other major religions and philosophies, in order to decide which one was really true. A pretty ambitious project for a sixteen-year-old! Yet I began visiting the high school library and pulling out books from the philosophy shelf and struggling through them. I didn't have the background to understand much of the material, but I thought this must be the place where people discussed the Big Questions—questions about Truth and the Meaning of Life.

I want to emphasize that this was not merely an academic study, but a very dark and difficult period of my life. People who grow up outside the church may not know what they are missing. But I'd had a genuine faith, even though it was only a child's faith: I knew that God created me, that He loved me, that He had a wonderful purpose for my life. These principles seem very simple—until you reject them. Then suddenly I became acutely aware that I had no answers to the most basic questions: Where did I come from? Was life just a chance accident of blind forces? Did it have any purpose? Were there any principles so true and so real that I could build my life on them?

Eventually I embraced relativism and subjectivism and several of the other popular "isms" of modern culture. For I was determined to be ruthlessly honest about the logical consequences of unbelief. If there is no God, then what can be the basis for objective or universal Truth? I realized that it is impossible to step outside our limited experience—our insignificantly small slot in the vast scope of the history of the universe—in order to gain access to universal knowledge, valid for all times and places.

And if there is no God, then what can be the basis for universally valid moral standards? Once, when a classmate described someone's action as "wrong," I shook my head and began arguing that we cannot know right or wrong in any ultimate sense.

Eventually I began to wonder whether I could even be sure about any reality outside my own head. I began doodling little cartoons of the entire world as nothing more than a thought bubble in my mind. When I graduated from high school, I wrote a senior paper on the topic of "Why I Am Not a Christian." Later I would discover that Bertrand Russell had written a famous essay by that title (which I had not read yet)—but this was my own manifesto of unbelief.

Like a Swiss Farmer

It was a few years later, when I was attending school in Germany and studying violin at the Heidelberg Conservatory, that I stumbled across L'Abri in Switzerland, the residential ministry of Francis Schaeffer. I was stunned by this place. It was the first time I had ever encountered Christians who actually answered my questions—who gave reasons and arguments for the truth of Christianity instead of simply urging me to have faith. When I arrived, the most obvious thing that struck me was that most of the guests were not even Christian. The place was crowded with hippies sporting long hair, beards, and bell-bottom jeans. At the time, it was extremely rare to discover Christian ministries capable of crossing the countercultural divide to reach alienated young people, and my curiosity was sparked. Who *were* these Christians?

Schaeffer himself used to strike people as somewhat odd, with his goatee and knickers. (Though when you were actually at L'Abri, it didn't seem odd at all: After all, this was the Alps—and he dressed like a Swiss farmer.) But when he opened his mouth and began to speak, people were transfixed: Here was a *Christian* talking about modern philosophy, quoting the existentialists, analyzing worldview themes in the lyrics of Led Zeppelin, explaining the music of

John Cage and the paintings of Jackson Pollock. You must remember that this was in an era when Christian college students were not even allowed to go to Disney movies—yet here he was, discussing films by Bergman and Fellini.[34]

Seeing Christians who engaged with the intellectual and cultural world was a complete novelty. In fact, it was such a novelty that I was afraid that I might make a decision for Christianity based on emotion instead of genuine conviction, and so, after only one month, I returned to the States. (To be honest, I *fled* back home.) And I thought, "I'm going to test these ideas in my college philosophy classes, and see how well they stand up in a secular university setting."

The most dramatic response came almost immediately. Signing up for my first philosophy course, I discovered it was a huge introductory class, with some three hundred students. Pretty intimidating. For the first major assignment, I took out my copy of Schaeffer's *Escape from Reason* and wove some of its themes into my paper. A week or so later, the professor said, "I have your papers to hand back . . . but first I would like to read one of them to the entire class."

It was my paper.

Needless to say, I was astonished. And even more so when the professor went on to say, "I have never seen such mature thought in an undergraduate." Of course, it wasn't really *my* thought—it was the Christian worldview analysis I had been learning through L'Abri.[35] Again and again, I tested these ideas in my university classes, and I saw that Christianity really does have the intellectual resources to stand up in a secular academic setting.

God Wins

While still at L'Abri, I had once accosted another student, demanding that he explain why he had converted to Christianity. A pale, thin young man with a strong South African accent, he responded simply, "They shot down all my arguments."

I continued gazing at him somewhat quizzically, expecting something more, well, dramatic. "It's not always a big emotional experience, you know," he said with an apologetic smile. "I just came to see that a better case could be made for Christianity than for any of the other ideas I came here with." It was the first time I had encountered someone whose conversion had been strictly intellectual, and little did I know at the time that my own conversion would be similar.

Back in the States, as I tested out Schaeffer's ideas in the classroom, I was also reading works by C. S. Lewis, G. K. Chesterton, Os Guinness, James Sire, and other apologists. But inwardly, I also had a young person's hunger for reality, and one day I picked up David Wilkerson's *The Cross and the Switchblade*. Now, *here* was a story exciting enough to suit anyone's taste for the dramatic—stories of Christians braving the slums and witnessing supernatural healings from drug addiction. Fired up with the hope that maybe God would do something equally spectacular in my own life, that night I begged Him, if He was real, to perform some supernatural sign for me—promising that if He did, I would believe in Him. Thinking that maybe this sort of thing worked better with an aggressive approach, I vowed to stay up all night until He gave me a sign.

Midnight passed, then one o'clock, two o'clock, four o'clock . . . my eyes were closing in spite of myself, and still no spectacular sign had appeared. Finally, rather chagrined about engaging in such theatrics, I abandoned the vigil. And as I did, suddenly I found myself speaking to God simply and directly from the depths of my spirit, with a profound sense of His presence. I acknowledged that I did not really need external signs and wonders because, in my heart of hearts, I had to admit (rather ruefully) that I was already convinced that Christianity was true. Through the discussions at L'Abri and my readings in apologetics, I had come to realize there were good and sufficient arguments against moral relativism, physical determinism, epistemological subjectivism, and a host of other isms I had been carrying around in my head. As my South African friend had put it, all my own ideas had been shot down.[36] The only step that remained was to acknowledge that I had been persuaded—and then give my life to the Lord of Truth.

So, at about four-thirty that morning, I quietly admitted that God had won the argument.

What I hope you take from my experience is that *worldview* is not an abstract, academic concept. Instead, the term describes our search for answers to those intensely personal questions everyone must wrestle with—the cry of the human heart for purpose, meaning, and a truth big enough to live by. No one can live without a sense of purpose and direction, a sense that his or her life has significance as part of a cosmic story. We may limp along for a while, extracting small installments of meaning from short-term goals like earning a degree, landing a job, getting married, establishing a family. But at some point, these temporal things fail to fulfill the deep hunger for eternity in the human spirit. For we were made for God, and every part of our personality is oriented toward relationship with Him. Our hearts are restless, Augustine said, until we find our rest in Him.[37]

Once we discover that the Christian worldview is really true, then living it out means offering up to God all our powers—practical, intellectual, emotional, artistic—to live for Him in every area of life. The only expression such faith can take is one that captures our entire being and redirects our every thought. The notion of a secular/sacred split becomes unthinkable. Biblical truth takes hold of our inner being, and we recognize that it is not only a message of salvation but also the truth about all reality. God's Word becomes a light to *all* our paths, providing the foundational principles for bringing every part of our lives under the Lordship of Christ, to glorify Him and to cultivate His creation.

SCOLDS AND SCALAWAGS

Looking back after three decades, I've come to appreciate L'Abri more than ever, because it gave me a worldview conception of Christianity right from the beginning of my spiritual life. Schaeffer didn't just *teach* about the Cultural Mandate, he *demonstrated* it. From the moment I arrived at L'Abri, hitchhiking up the mountain and knocking on the door of a quaint Swiss chalet, I was struck by the respect for art and culture evident in even the little things—the simple beauty of a small vase of wildflowers on the dinner table, the natural elegance of the Swiss mountain decor, the depth and range of the conversation, the after-dinner readings in classical literature.[38] Listening to Schaeffer's lectures was an education in itself, as they ranged over politics, philosophy, education, art, and popular culture—showing by example that there can be a Christian perspective in all these areas.

After becoming a Christian, I returned to L'Abri for a longer period of study, and discovered how liberating a worldview approach can be. There is no need to *avoid* the secular world and hide out behind the walls of an evangelical subculture; instead, Christians can *appreciate* works of art and culture as products of human creativity expressing the image of God. On the other hand, there is no danger of being naive or uncritical about false and dangerous messages embedded in secular culture, because a worldview gives the conceptual tools needed to analyze and critique them. Believers can apply a distinctively biblical perspective every time they pick up the newspaper, watch a movie, or read a book.

Schaeffer modeled this balanced approach in his lectures and writings. He would draw attention to the artistic quality of, say, a Renaissance painting, even while critiquing the Renaissance *worldview* of autonomous humanism expressed in it. He would appreciate the color and composition of an Expressionist painting, or the technical quality of a Bergman film, or the musicianship of a piece of rock music—even while identifying the relativistic or nihilistic worldview it expressed.[39]

Artists are often the barometers of society, and by analyzing the world-views embedded in their works we can learn a great deal about how to address the modern mind more effectively. Yet many Christians critique culture one-dimensionally, from a moral perspective alone, and as a result they come across as negative and condemning. At a Christian college, I once took an English course from a professor whose idea of critiquing classic works of literature was to tabulate how many times the characters used bad language or engaged in illicit sexual relations. He seemed blind to the books' literary quality—whether or not they were good *as literature*. Nor did he teach us how to detect the worldviews expressed there. Similarly, a Christian radio personality recently wagged a stern finger at Elvis Presley for the immoral content of his songs, without ever asking whether his songs were good *as music* (which they certainly were), or raising other worldview questions, such as why popular culture has such a powerful impact. When the only form of cultural commentary Christians offer is moral condemnation, no wonder we come across to non-believers as angry and scolding.

Our first response to the great works of human culture—whether in art or technology or economic productivity—should be to celebrate them as reflections of God's own creativity. And even when we analyze where they go wrong, it should be in a spirit of love. Today on religious radio or in ministry fund-raising letters, it is common for Christian activists to attack Hollywood or television or rap music in tones of aggrieved anger, berating their immoral content or mocking the pretensions of postmodern political correctness. But Schaeffer would have none of that. Even when raising serious criticisms, he expressed a burning compassion for people caught in the trap of false and harmful world-views. When describing the pessimism and nihilism expressed in so many movies, paintings, and popular songs, he demonstrated profound empathy for those actually living in such despair. These works of art "are the expression of men who are struggling with their appalling lostness," he wrote. "Dare we laugh at such things? Dare we feel superior when we view their tortured expressions in their art?" The men and women who produce these things "are dying while they live; yet where is our compassion for them?"[40]

Today, Christian activists are quick to organize a boycott or pressure a politician to de-fund some artistic group, and these strategies have their place. But how many reach out to the artists with compassion? How many do the hard work of crafting real answers to the questions they are raising? How many cry out to God on behalf of people struggling in the coils of false worldviews?

IN LOVE WITH CREATIVITY

The best way to drive out a bad worldview is by offering a good one, and Christians need to move beyond *criticizing* culture to *creating* culture. That is the task God originally created humans to do, and in the process of sanctification we are meant to recover that task. Whether we work with our brains or with our hands, whether we are analytical or artistic, whether we work with people or with things, in every calling we are culture-creators, offering up our work as service to God.

A church in Los Angeles that ministers to Hollywood artists includes among its core principles this wonderful statement: "Creativity is the natural result of spirituality."[41] Exactly. Those in relationship with the Creator should be the most creative of all. By creatively developing a biblical approach to their subject area, believers may even transform an entire discipline. Consider a few inspiring examples.

Christian Philosophers Out of the Closet

The philosophical journal *Philo* recently carried an article deploring the way Christians are taking over philosophy departments in universities across the country.[42] At least, that's what the author claims is happening. Quentin Smith is an aggressive proponent of philosophical naturalism (he publicly debates Christian apologists[43]), and in this article he warns his colleagues that the field of philosophy is being "de-secularized." In informal surveys, Smith reports, professors around the country consistently say that one-quarter to one-third of their departments now consist of theists, generally Christians.

Why is this happening? Largely because of the work of one Christian philosopher: Alvin Plantinga. In the past, Christians working in philosophy kept their theism restricted to their "private lives," never mentioning it in "their publications and teaching," Smith says. Then came Plantinga's influential *God and Other Minds*,[44] which demonstrated that theists could match their naturalistic colleagues in "conceptual precision, rigor in argumentation, technical erudition, and an in-depth defense of an original worldview." Other books by Plantinga followed quickly, Smith notes, all showing that Christians are capable of "writing at the highest qualitative level of analytic philosophy."

Soon other forms of theistic realism, most of them influenced by Plantinga, began sweeping through the philosophical community. While in other fields Christian academics still tend to compartmentalize their beliefs from their scholarly work for fear of committing academic suicide, Smith writes, "in philosophy, it became, almost overnight, 'academically respectable' to argue for theism."

He concludes morosely: "God is not 'dead' in academia. He returned to life in the later 1960s and is now alive and well in his last academic stronghold, philosophy departments."

Plantinga's far-ranging influence shows that it is possible for believers to do better work than their opponents, and even begin to reverse the direction of an entire academic discipline. It is an astonishing example of what Christians can do when they obey the command to take every thought captive to Christ. Smith castigates his fellow naturalistic philosophers for "the embarrassment" of belonging to the only academic field being de-secularized, and spends the rest of the article urging them to reverse this pernicious trend.[45] We can pray that, by God's grace, they will not succeed.

Religion: Good for Your Health

Another inspiring example is the work of the late David Larson, who practically single-handedly turned around the medical community on the subject of religion and health. As a graduate student in psychiatry, Larson was actually advised to leave the field. The settled stereotype was that religious belief is associated with mental illness. Ever since Freud had declared belief in God a "universal obsessional neurosis,"[46] it had become dogma that religion is harmful to mental health, and even pathological.

Nevertheless, Larson persisted in his studies, and over time he began to notice that the negative stereotype of religion was not supported by actual research results. In fact, the facts pointed to the *opposite* conclusion: Subjects who were more religious tended to show up in the healthy groups, not the sick groups. Eventually Larson began doing his own research and founded the National Institute for Healthcare Research (NIHR), which has published scores of studies confirming that religious belief (which in America generally means Christianity) actually correlates with better mental health. It is now widely accepted that religious people have lower rates of depression, suicide, family instability, drug and alcohol abuse, and other social pathologies.

How did scientists overlook for so long the fact that religion is a powerful source of mental well-being? How did they even mistake it for a form of mental *disorder*? If the study of mental health is a science, as its practitioners like to claim, this was no "minor oversight," writes Patrick Glynn, in *God: The Evidence.* "It shows to what degree the term 'science' has been abused by the thinkers of modernity to mask what amounts to little more than a prior prejudice against the idea of God."[47]

Even more surprising, religious belief also correlates with better *physical* health—with lower rates of virtually everything from cancer to hypertension to cardiovascular disease. When religious people do get sick, they recover faster. They even have lower mortality rates—that is, they live longer—which is the bottom line for medical professionals. (Modern demographers regard life expectancy as the best indicator of quality of life.) All told, people who attend church regularly are happier, healthier, and even live longer.

What a stunning irony, writes Glynn. The heralds of modernity had "assumed that spirituality would be shown to have a physical basis"—but "instead something like the reverse has occurred: Health has been shown to have a spiritual underpinning."[48]

Only fifteen years ago, research on the topic of religion and health could not even get published. "Research of this type could almost be described as 'anti-tenure' activity," Larson once observed. "Research on religion was almost unheard of and my colleagues considered it hazardous to one's academic health."[49] Yet today it is rapidly gaining acceptance. Even non-Christian researchers are beginning to acknowledge the correlations. Herbert Benson of Harvard, who claims no religious faith, is famous for his catchy saying that we are all "wired for God."[50] Our bodies simply function better, he says, when we believe in God.

Another non-Christian persuaded by the sheer weight of the evidence was Guenter Lewy, author of *Why America Needs Religion*. Interestingly, Lewy started out to write a book on the opposite theme—why America does *not* need religion. Many political conservatives have argued that religion is foundational to morality and social stability, and Lewy intended to prove them wrong. His book would be, in his own words, "a defense of secular humanism and ethical relativism."[51]

But as he examined the evidence, Lewy turned around 180 degrees. He ended up writing a book arguing that religion, particularly Christianity, correlates with lower rates of social pathologies such as crime, drug abuse, teen pregnancy, and family breakdown. Or, to put it positively, Christianity motivates attitudes that signal social health, such as responsibility, moral integrity, compassion, and altruism. "Contrary to the expectations of the Enlightenment," Lewy concludes, "freeing individuals from the shackles of traditional religion does not result in their moral uplift." To the contrary, the evidence now shows clearly that "no society has yet been successful in teaching morality without religion."[52]

Today the facts are in: Science itself confirms that biblical principles work in the real world—which is strong evidence that they are true. The Bible describes the way we were created to function, and when we follow its prescriptions, we are happier and healthier. The best explanation of the positive data is that our lives are lining up with the objective structure of reality.

Benevolent Empire

A final example is Marvin Olasky, who unexpectedly and decisively transformed the welfare debate. A slim, bespectacled former Marxist from a Russian Jewish background, Olasky is a journalism professor and editor of *World* magazine. But in the early 1990s he received a grant to write a book, so he holed up in a small office at the Heritage Foundation in Washington, D.C., just two blocks from where I was living at the time. When I walked over for a visit, he told me about the project that would catapult him to fame a few years later.

American welfare policy had come to an impasse: Though welfare had done some good for those who needed only a temporary boost to get back on their feet, it had also created a permanent underclass—the chronically poor, whose poverty was related to social pathologies such as alcohol addiction, drug abuse, fatherless homes, and crime. Everyone on both sides of the political aisle agreed that welfare needed to be reformed, but no one knew how to do it.

It was Olasky who discovered the answer, and he did it by analyzing the traditional Christian approach to charity. In researching the vast proliferation of Christian charities in the nineteenth century, often dubbed the Benevolent Empire,[53] Olasky found that the churches specialized in personal assistance that fulfilled the literal meaning of *compassion*—"suffering with" others. They didn't just hand out money; they helped people change their lives, focusing on job training and education. They required that the poor do some useful work, giving them a chance to rebuild their dignity by making a worthwhile contribution to society. They helped outcasts to build a social network—to reconnect with family and church for ongoing support and accountability. Most of all, they addressed the moral and spiritual needs that lie at the heart of dysfunctional behavior.

Clearly, this goes beyond what any government can do. In fact, government aid can actually make things worse. By handing out welfare checks impersonally to all who qualify, without addressing the underlying behavioral problems, the government in essence "rewards" antisocial and dysfunctional patterns. And any behavior the government rewards will generally tend to increase. As one perceptive nineteenth-century critic noted, government assistance is a "mighty solvent to sunder the ties of kinship, to quench the affections of family, to suppress in the poor themselves the instinct of self-reliance and self-respect—to convert them into paupers."[54]

The churches' successful approach is described in Olasky's book *The*

Tragedy of American Compassion, where he coined the term *compassionate conservatism.* The book was picked up by former Speaker of the House Newt Gingrich, who liked it so much that he distributed it to all incoming freshmen in Congress. Overnight, Olasky began to be feted as the guru who had discovered a way out of the welfare impasse. He became an advisor to George W. Bush, who campaigned for the presidency on the slogan of "compassionate conservatism," promising to create a special office to support faith-based initiatives. Though policy analysts continue to debate the details, Olasky has brought about a decisive paradigm shift in America's approach to welfare.

The successes of people like Plantinga, Larson, and Olasky can inspire all of us to take our theistic beliefs out of hiding and into the public sphere. If Christianity really is true, then it will yield a better approach in every discipline.

Why do many Christians still compartmentalize their faith in the private sphere? Why do they accept the secular/sacred split that limits the revolutionary impact of God's Word? The only way to break free from this confining grid is to trace it back to its roots—to diagnose where it came from, how it grew over time, and how it came to shape the way most Christians think today. In the next chapter, we will sleuth our own history for clues to why we think the way we do. How can we recover the conviction that Christianity is not only religious truth but total truth?

2

REDISCOVERING JOY

The problem is not only to win souls but to save minds.
If you win the whole world and lose the mind of the world,
you will soon discover you have not won the world.
CHARLES MALIK[1]

By the time Sealy Yates was just twenty-five years old, he had already ful-filled his life's dreams. He had gone to law school, passed the bar exam, landed a great job. He had married a wonderful woman, and they were busy raising their first child. Life was good.

That's when Sealy slumped into a profound depression. He was too young for a midlife crisis, yet he found himself asking all the same questions: Is this all there is? Is this what I want to do for the rest of my life? What's the mean-ing of it all?

Sealy was not naturally depressive, so he probed for some reason behind it. And the answer he discovered was one that no psychologist would have guessed: The key to recovering joy and purpose turned out to be a new under-standing of Christianity as total truth—an insight that broke open the dam and poured the restoring waters of the gospel into the parched areas of his life.

Years ago, at the age of fifteen, Sealy had responded to an altar call at a Baptist church. From that moment on, he knew deep in his bones that what he wanted most was to serve God. At first, he figured that meant doing church work of some kind—becoming a pastor, missionary, or music leader. "I wanted to live for God," Sealy told me,[2] "and the only frame of reference I had said that meant full-time Christian work."

There was only one problem: He didn't have the skills for any church-based profession. In reviewing his aptitude tests, however, a high school guid-ance counselor suggested that he consider becoming an attorney. The idea was electrifying. No one in Sealy's family had even gone to college, let alone law school. The very thought seemed to soar beyond the bounds of possibility. Nevertheless, he prayed, he worked hard, and now . . . he had made it.

So why wasn't he happy? Sealy's impossible dream had come true, yet he was miserable. He maintained a heavy schedule of church activities, but a spiritual hunger still gnawed at his heart. Maybe he had made a mistake? Maybe he really *had* been called to full-time church work but had ignored God's call? Maybe he should drop his job and go to the mission field?

Christians who are seriously committed to their faith often experience this inner tug-of-war. Like Sealy, most of us absorb the idea that serving God means primarily doing church work. If we end up in other fields of work, then we think serving the Lord means piling religious activities on top of our existing responsibilities—things like church services, Bible study, and evangelism. But where does that leave the job itself? Is our work only a material necessity, something that puts food on the table but has no intrinsic spiritual significance? Is it merely utilitarian, a way of making a living?

Sealy discovered that it was just such questions that were driving his depression: He had no idea how to integrate his Christian faith with his professional life. In his law classes at UCLA there had never been any mention of Christianity; none of his professors or classmates had shared his faith commitment; nor did any colleagues at the law firm where he now worked. And since his professional work took up most of his waking hours, that meant a large segment of his life was sealed off from what mattered most to him.

"Where is God in my life?" Sealy found himself asking. What he thought was depression turned out to be an agonized longing for spiritual meaning in his work. Adding church activities to a completely secularized job was like putting a religious frame on a secular picture. The tension between his spiritual hunger and the time demands of a purely "secular" job was tearing him apart inside.

Sealy's search for a solution was finally rewarded when he discovered a Christian study program that taught him how to address clients' spiritual lives. Instantly, a whole new world opened to him, as he came to realize that the law addresses issues connected to the whole person. After all, "people typically come to lawyers when they're in a crisis," he explained. "It's a phenomenal opportunity to help them do what's right." Lawyers can minister to troubled spouses seeking a divorce, counsel misguided teens in trouble with the law, advise ethically conflicted businessmen to do what's right, confront Christian ministries that are compromising biblical principles. The law is not merely a set of procedures or an argumentative technique. It is God's means of confronting wrong, establishing justice, defending the weak, and promoting the public good.

In every profession, the prevailing views stem from some underlying philosophy—basic assumptions about what is ultimately true and right. That means Christians need not feel out of place bringing their *own* assumptions into the field. Sealy began to claim the freedom to bring biblical understandings of justice, rights, and reconciliation into the legal arena.

SEALY'S SECRET

The dilemma Sealy faced is not uncommon for Christians in any profession. As we saw in the previous chapter, modern society is characterized by a sharp split between the sacred and secular spheres—with work and business defined as strictly secular. As a consequence, Christians often live in two separate worlds, commuting between the private world of family and church (where we can express our faith freely) and the public world (where religious expression is firmly suppressed). Many of us don't even know what it means to have a Christian perspective on our work. Oh, we know that being a Christian means being ethical on the job—as Sealy put it, "no lying or cheating." But the work itself is typically defined in secular terms as bringing home a paycheck, climbing the career ladder, building a professional reputation.

For lawyers like Sealy, success is defined primarily as winning cases. The attitude in today's legal profession is that law has nothing to do with morality. Lawyers are little more than "hired guns" who are expected to defend their clients, right or wrong, with no regard for moral principles of truth or justice. They are admonished to keep their own moral perspective tucked tightly away in the private sphere; in the public sphere, their job is to give strictly legal advice.[3]

But no Christian, in any profession, can be happy when torn in two contrary directions. We all long for our work to count for something more than paying the bills or impressing our colleagues. How can we experience the full power of our Christian faith when it is locked away from the rest of life? How can we lead whole and integrated lives when we're required to shed our deepest beliefs along the way as we commute to work, functioning there from a purely "secular" mindset?

The dichotomies we've been talking about—secular/sacred and public/private—are not merely abstractions. They have a profoundly personal impact. When the public sphere is cordoned off as a religion-free zone, our lives become splintered and fragmented. Work and public life are stripped of spiritual significance, while the spiritual truths that give our lives the deepest meaning are demoted to leisure activities, suitable only for our time off. The gospel is hedged in, robbed of its power to "leaven" the whole of life.

How do we break free from the dichotomies that limit God's power in our lives? How can love and service to God become living sparks that light up our whole lives? By discovering a worldview perspective that unifies *both* secular and sacred, public and private, within a single framework. By understanding that all honest work and creative enterprise can be a valid calling from the Lord. And by realizing there are biblical principles that apply to every field of work. These insights will fill us with new purpose, and we will begin to experience the joy that comes from relating to God in and through every dimension of our lives.

For Sealy, that meant discovering that practicing law is much more than a way to make money and win cases. It is fundamentally a way to execute God's own purposes in the world—to advance justice and contribute to the good of society. "God showed me how to live for him *in* my professional life," Sealy told me. "It's not just about running a business or making a living. In our work, we do the work of God. That's when I rediscovered joy."

CAPITOL HILL GUILT

Probably most of us had not linked together the idea of Christian worldview with finding joy in life. Yet Sealy is right. It is only when we offer up everything we do in worship to God that we finally experience His power coursing through every fiber of our being. The God of the Bible is not only the God of the human spirit but also the God of nature and history. We serve Him not only in worship but also in obedience to the Cultural Mandate. If Christian churches are serious about discipleship, they must teach believers how to keep living for God after they walk out the church doors on Sunday.

Not long ago, after speaking on Capitol Hill, I was approached by a congressional chief of staff who confided, with some frustration, that many of the Christian young people who come to Washington feel "guilty" about their interest in politics.

"Guilty?" The notion was incomprehensible to me. "But why?"

"Well," he explained, "they feel that if they were *really* committed to God, they wouldn't be here. They'd be in the ministry." Though many of these young people were graduates of Christian colleges, they had not been taught a Christian worldview. They still placed their professional work on the *secular* side of the secular/sacred split, regarding it as less valuable than religious activity.

A high-ranking Washington official once lamented how difficult it was to find people for government positions who were committed Christians and at the same time outstanding professionals. The problem, he told me, is that most Christians don't have a biblical sense of calling in their jobs—and thus they fail to treat it as frontline work for the Kingdom. As an example, he related the story of a doctor who had stopped practicing medicine in order to join the staff of a Christian organization.

"I left my medical practice to work in ministry," the doctor told him.

"Hold it," the official broke in. "That's exactly the problem: Your medical practice *was* a ministry, just as much as what you're doing now." Taken aback, the doctor confessed he had never thought of it that way before.

Ordinary Christians working in business, industry, politics, factory work, and so on, are "the Church's front-line troops in her engagement with the world," wrote Lesslie Newbigin. Imagine how our churches would be transformed if we truly regarded laypeople as frontline troops in the spiritual battle. "Are we taking seriously our duty to support them in their warfare?" Newbigin asked. "Have we ever done anything seriously to strengthen their Christian witness, to help them in facing the very difficult ethical problems which they have to meet every day, to give them the assurance that the whole fellowship is behind them in their daily spiritual warfare?"[4] The church is nothing less than a training ground for sending out laypeople who are equipped to speak the gospel to the world.

BECOMING BILINGUAL

In a sense, Christians need to learn how to be bilingual, translating the perspective of the gospel into language understood by our culture. On one hand, we all learn to use the language of the world: If we've gone through the public education system, "we have been trained to use a language which claims to make sense of the world without the hypothesis of God," as Newbigin puts it. But then, "for an hour or two a week, we use the other language, the language of the Bible."[5] We are like immigrants—like my own grandparents, who came to America from Sweden. During the Lutheran church service on Sunday, they spoke their familiar mother tongue; but for the rest of their lives they had to employ the strange-sounding English of the land where they had settled.

Yet Christians are not called to be *only* like immigrants, simply preserving a few customs and phrases from the old country. Instead, we are to be like missionaries, actively translating the language of faith into the language of the culture around us.

The uncomfortable truth is that we don't seem to be doing very well as linguists. Columnist Andy Crouch tells the story of a Christian professor at Cornell University who was concerned about the Christian students in his classes. They "hardly say a thing," the professor complained. The only way I even know that they're fellow believers is when "they come up after class and furtively thank me." Here was a professor actively seeking to create a friendly environment where Christian students would feel free to participate—"but they won't say anything!"[6]

Why not? The answer is that most Christian students simply don't know how to express their faith perspective in language suitable for the public square. Like immigrants who have not yet mastered the grammar of their new country, they are self-conscious. In private, they speak to one another in the mother tongue of their religion, but in class they are uncertain how to express their religious perspective in the accents of the academic world.

THE FAITH GAP

Polls consistently show that a large percentage of Americans claim to believe in God or to be born again—yet the effect of Christian principles is decreasing in public life. Why? Because most evangelicals have little training in how to frame Christian worldview principles in a language applicable in the public square. Though Christianity is thriving in modern culture, it is *at the expense* of being ever more firmly relegated to the private sphere.

Another way to phrase it is that the private sphere has become increasingly religious, while at the same time the public sphere has become increasingly secular. In a 1994 poll, 65 percent of Americans said religion is losing its influence in public life—yet almost the same number, 62 percent, said the influence of religion was actually *increasing* in their personal lives.[7] This means the divide between public and private realms has widened to a yawning chasm, making it harder than ever for Christians to cross over in order to bring biblically based principles into the public arena.

Privatization has also changed the *nature* of religion. In the private realm religion may enjoy considerable freedom—but only because the private sphere has been safely cordoned off from the "real" world where the "important" activities of society take place. Religion is no longer considered the source of serious truth claims that could potentially conflict with public agendas. The private realm has been reduced to an "innocuous 'play area'," says Peter Berger, where religion is acceptable for people who need that kind of crutch—but where it won't upset any important applecarts in the larger world of politics and economics.[8]

By allowing religion to be restricted to a segregated area of life, however, we have undercut one of its primary purposes, which is precisely to provide a sense of life's overarching meaning. As Berger writes, privatization "represents a severe rupture of the traditional task of religion, which was precisely the establishment of an integrated set of definitions of reality that could serve as a common universe of meaning for the members of a society."[9] In fact, many evangelicals no longer even think it *is* the task of religion to provide a "common universe of meaning." Today religion appeals almost solely to the needs of the private sphere—needs for personal meaning, social bonding, family support, emotional nurturing, practical living, and so on. In this climate, almost inevitably, churches come to speak the language of psychological needs, focusing primarily on the therapeutic functions of religion. Whereas religion used to be connected to group identity and a sense of belonging, it is now almost solely a search for an authentic inner life.

People often become very attached to a religion that addresses their emotional and practical needs in this manner. In an increasingly impersonal public world, people are hungry for resources to sustain their personal and private world. Nonetheless, it represents a truncated view of Christianity's claims to be the truth about all of reality. "Secularization did not cause the death of religion," says theologian Walter Kasper, but it did cause it to "become but one sector of modern life along with many others. Religion lost its claim to universality and its power of interpretation."[10] That is, Christianity no longer functions as a lens to interpret the whole of reality; it is no longer held as total truth.

In essence, Christians have accepted a trade-off: By acquiescing in the privatization process, Newbigin says, Christianity "has secured for itself a continuing place, at the cost of surrendering the crucial field."[11] In other words, Christianity has survived in the private sphere, but at the cost of losing the ability to make a credible claim in the public sphere or to challenge the reigning ideologies.

The reason Newbigin was so sensitive to the problem is that he lived for forty years as a missionary in India, which is not plagued by the same secular/sacred, public/private split. The mentality of Indian Christians is that *of course* religion permeates all of life. The same is true of African Christians. "In most human cultures, religion is not a separate activity set apart from the rest of life," Newbigin explains. In these cultures, "what we call religion is a whole worldview, a way of understanding the whole of human experience."

On a global scale, then, the secular/sacred dichotomy is an anomaly—a distinctive of Western culture alone. "The sharp line which modern Western culture has drawn between religious affairs and secular affairs is itself one of the most significant peculiarities of our culture, and would be incomprehensible to the vast majority of people."[12] In order to communicate the gospel in the West, we face a unique challenge: We need to learn how to liberate it from the private sphere and present it in its glorious fullness as the truth about all reality.

DISCONNECTED DEVOTION

The first step in the process is simply identifying the split mentality in our own minds, and diagnosing the way it functions. The dichotomy is so familiar that

Christians often find it difficult *even to recognize* it in their own thinking. This struck me personally when I read about a survey conducted a few years ago by Christian Smith, a sociologist at the University of North Carolina (and himself an evangelical believer).[13] The results of the survey highlight both the good news and the bad news about American evangelicalism.

The good news was that, on several measures of religious vitality, evangelicals came out consistently on top. It's clear that evangelicals are highly committed to their faith; they speak the language of the gospel fluently. On the other hand, when asked to articulate a Christian worldview perspective on *other* subjects—areas such as work, business, and politics—they had little to say. They seemed unable to translate a faith perspective into language suitable for the public square.

The survey compared evangelicals to four other groups: fundamentalists, mainline Protestants, liberal Protestants, and Roman Catholics.[14] Let's look at a few examples of the findings. First, the good news. When asked about their view of the Bible, some 97 percent of evangelicals said it is inspired by God and without errors. Compare that to the other groups surveyed:

    97% of evangelicals
    92% of fundamentalists
    89% of mainline Protestants
    78% of liberal Protestants
    74% of Catholics

Evangelicals were also the most likely to say they have committed their life to Jesus Christ as personal Lord and Savior:

    97% of evangelicals
    91% of fundamentalists
    82% of mainline Protestants
    72% of liberal Protestants
    67% of Catholics

Here's the percentage who say their religious faith is very important to them:

    78% of evangelicals
    72% of fundamentalists
    61% of mainline Protestants
    58% of liberal Protestants
    44% of Catholics

Do absolute moral standards exist? "Yes":

75% of evangelicals
65% of fundamentalists
55% of mainline Protestants
34% of liberal Protestants
38% of Catholics

Do you have doubts about your faith? "Never":

71% of evangelicals
63% of fundamentalists
62% of mainline Protestants
44% of liberal Protestants
58% of Catholics

A question particularly relevant to this book: How important is it to defend a biblical worldview in intellectual circles? "Very important":

63% of evangelicals
65% of fundamentalists
46% of mainline Protestants
49% of liberal Protestants
(Catholics not polled)

The numbers make it clear that on many measures of religious vitality, evangelicalism is doing very well.[15] Historians and sociologists are notorious for predicting the demise of Christianity in the modern world: Most accept the "secularization thesis," which states that as societies modernize, they inevitably secularize. But the secularization of America has been vastly overstated. The evidence shows that evangelicalism is thriving even in today's highly modernized society.

If that's the good news, then what's the bad news? The bad news is that when asked to articulate a biblical worldview perspective on issues in the public square, no one could do it. *Not one person* in the entire survey. Respondents spoke strictly in the language of individual morality and religious devotion; they seemed unable to express a Christian philosophy of business, politics, or culture.[16]

This comes alive if we read a few examples in their own words. When asked how to have a transforming effect on the broader culture, a Baptist woman replied, "I just feel that if each individual lived the Christian life, . . . it influences society. We just need to live the life that Christ wants us to live, the best we can, to influence society in general." A Christian charismatic told the survey takers, "For me, the solution to the world's problems is becoming a Christian, okay?" A Church of Christ man said, "Just believe in Christ and live the best you can the way he wants you to, and that would change the whole world."[17]

These answers contain a great deal of truth, of course; but that truth is limited to individual conversion and personal influence. None of the respondents talked about critiquing the worldviews that shape modern public life, or about developing a Christian theory of social order.

When asked how Christianity should affect the world of work and business, most thought only of injecting religious activities into the workplace. A woman from a seeker church said, "There are opportunities . . . to have Bible study on company time, a prayer breakfast, outreach of some kind." A Pentecostal man (with apparently a tough job), said, "I don't let them cuss excessively on the job. . . . No drinking, no alcohol, no coming to work drunk. Also, we pray most of the time before we start work in the morning."[18]

Other respondents stressed their own moral witness on the job. Christians "should be the most honest employees they have," a Presbyterian man replied. "If you are working for someone, you shouldn't steal or take an extra ten minutes for lunch break." In fact, honesty was the single factor most often mentioned—listed by more than one out of three evangelicals. When survey-takers pressed the issue, asking whether Christians could do anything else for the economy, a Church of Christ man answered, "No, because if everybody would be honest, that's all it would take." A Baptist woman said, "If you [are honest], most everything will take care of itself."[19]

Of course, we have to commend those who start Bible studies in the work place or try to exert a moral influence. But what about a biblical perspective on the work itself? There's something missing when we don't hear any respondents talking about their work itself as service to God or as fulfillment of the Cultural Mandate—the biblical command to subdue the earth (see chapter 1). Even when pressed, none of the respondents offered any biblical principles of economics or seemed aware of the impact of systemic economic forces or institutions.

Finally, what about politics? A woman attending an evangelical Moravian church told the survey, "What can a Christian accomplish in politics? Be a moral presence." A Church of Christ man said, "Why should Christians be active [in politics]? Because I think souls should be saved. . . . If I can help somebody [go to heaven] by being in the government, . . . that would make me feel good."[20]

No one would deny that Christians are called to be evangelists *wherever* they are—including politics. But political office is not just a platform for sharing the gospel. We are also called to work out a biblical perspective on the state and politics. God created the state for a purpose, and we need to ask what that purpose is. How do Christians work to advance justice and the public good?

On occasions when respondents did address specific political issues, they typically mentioned abortion and homosexuality. Why these particular issues? Because they are easy to conceptualize in terms of individual morality. By the same token, solutions to social problems were phrased almost solely in terms of individual voluntary activities—missions of mercy to the poor, the homeless, the addicted. "Worthy as these projects may be," Smith comments, "none of them attempt to transform social or cultural systems, but merely to alleviate some of the harm caused by the existing system."[21]

The study provides a fascinating snapshot of contemporary evangelical Christians, pinpointing with deadly accuracy both their strengths and their weaknesses. On one hand, their hearts are in the right place: They are sincere, serious, committed. On the other hand, their faith is almost completely privatized: It is usually restricted to the area of personal behavior, values, and relationships. Even when evangelicals do try to influence the public sphere, their main strategy is to import activities from the private sphere, like prayer meetings and evangelism. Friends who work on Capitol Hill tell me there are several Christian groups that minister to politicians and staffers, yet virtually all of them limit their ministry to one's personal devotional life—"How's your walk with Jesus?" Few challenge those in politics to think about the issues themselves from a biblical perspective—"What is a Christian political philosophy? How does your faith perspective influence the way you're going to vote today on the bills before Congress?"

Before we can even begin to craft a Christian worldview, we first need to identify the barriers that prevent us from applying our faith to areas like work, business, and politics. We need to try to understand why Western Christians lost sight of the comprehensive call God makes on our lives. How did we succumb to a secular/sacred grid that cripples our effectiveness in the public sphere? To break free of this destructive thought pattern, we need to understand where it came from, identify the forms it has taken, and trace the way it became woven into the pervasive patterns of our thinking. We will discover that, from the beginning, Christianity has been plagued by dualisms and dichotomies of various kinds. And the only way to free ourselves from dualistic thinking is to make a clear diagnosis of the problem.

CHRISTIAN SCHIZOPHRENIA

To make that diagnosis, we must go back to the early church and its encounter with Greek thought. Imagine the earliest believers: Small, embattled groups surrounded by an alien culture with its own established language, literature, culture, civic institutions—and, most powerful of all, the rich intellectual tradition of Greek philosophy. How would the early church defend its faith in the resurrection of Jesus over against the highly developed philosophies of the day?

The classical thinkers taught much that was good. You know the names: Homer, Socrates, Plato, Aristotle. They emphasized the rational order of the universe, which was later to become an important inspiration for the development of modern science. They stood against the materialists and hedonists of their day, asserting the eternal ideals of Truth, Goodness, and Beauty. They argued that knowledge was objective, not merely a social convention. Plato even offered an argument from design based on the goal-directed order in nature.[22] All this and more, Christian thinkers found very congenial, and eventually they began adopting many elements of classical philosophy as intellectual tools to give philosophical expression to their own biblical faith.

Yet the Greek thinkers were pagans, and many of their doctrines were incompatible with biblical truth. Instead of giving a comprehensive description of classical thought, we will zero in on some of these problematic elements. To be fair, the church fathers almost couldn't help absorbing a good bit of Greek thought. It was, after all, the only conceptual language available to them as they sought to address the educated world of their day. But it came with some serious negative baggage—especially what Schaeffer calls a "two-story" view of reality.[23] Classical thought drew a stark dichotomy between matter and spirit, treating the material realm as though it were less valuable than the spiritual realm—and sometimes outright evil. Thus salvation was defined in terms of ascetic exercises aimed at liberating the spirit from the material world so that it could ascend to God.

This may sound abstract, so let's make it concrete by examining the two key figures who had the greatest impact on Christian thought.

Why Plato Matters

The dualism just described was especially strong in Plato, the philosopher who had by far the greatest impact on Christian thinkers through the Middle Ages (especially through a later adaptation known as neo-Platonism).[24] Plato taught that everything is composed of Matter and Form—raw material ordered by rational ideas. Think of a statue: It consists of marble crafted into a beautiful shape according to a design or blueprint in the artist's mind. Matter on its own was regarded as disordered and chaotic. The Forms were rational and good, bringing about order and harmony.

In fact, the realm of pure Form was actually considered *more real* than the material world, strange as that sounds to us today. Plato painted a powerful word picture to suggest that the world of ordinary experience—the world we know by sight and sound and touch—is merely a play of shadows cast on the wall of a cave. Most people are captivated by the shadow show and mistake it for reality, he said. But the philosopher is the enlightened one who manages to escape the cave and discover the genuinely real world of immaterial Forms, the highest being Goodness, Truth, and Beauty. The point of Plato's word picture is that the material world is the realm of error and illusion: The path to true knowledge is to free ourselves from the bodily senses, so that reason can gain insight into the realm of Forms.

Why did Plato view the material world as inferior? As we saw in our discussion of mathematics in chapter 1, Plato regarded Matter as preexisting from all eternity. The role of the creator was merely to impose rational Form upon it. But the preexistence of Matter meant it had independent properties over which the creator had no control; as a result, the deity was never fully successful in forcing it into the mold of the Forms. This explains why there is always some chaos, disorder, and irrationality in the world.

In essence, Plato was offering a twofold origin for the world. Both Form and Matter are eternal: Form represents reason and rationality, while the eternal flow of formless Matter is inherently evil and chaotic. This twofold view of origins led to a two-story view of reality, with *Form* in the upper story and *Matter* in the lower story.

Platonic dualism can be represented like this:

FORM
Eternal Reason

MATTER
Eternal Formless Flux

From a biblical perspective, the problem with Platonic dualism was that it identified the source of chaos and evil with some *part* of God's creation—namely, Matter. Creation was divided into two parts: the spiritual (superior, good) and the material (inferior, bad). This stands in clear opposition to the biblical worldview, which teaches that *nothing* exists from eternity over against

God. Matter is not some preexisting stuff with its own independent properties, capable of resisting God's power. God created it and thus has absolute control over it. This was the operative meaning of the doctrine of creation ex nihilo—that nothing is independent of God, but everything came from Him and is subject to Him.

In contrast to the Greeks, then, the Bible presents the material world as originally good: Since it was created by God, it reflects His good character.[25] The Bible does not identify evil with Matter or with any other part of creation, but with sin, which twists and distorts God's originally good creation. For example, Scripture does not treat the body as inherently sinful or less valuable.[26] When Paul urges us in Galatians 5 to avoid "the lusts of the flesh," he is not referring to the body but is using "flesh" as a technical term for the sinful nature.[27] Indeed, if the body were inherently sinful, the Incarnation would have been impossible, for Jesus took on a human body yet had no sin. The sheer, monumental fact that God Himself took on human form speaks decisively of the dignity of the body. For Greek thinkers, the most shocking claim Christians made was that God had become a historical person, who could be seen, heard, and touched. Rational inquiry could no longer simply reject the world of the senses but had to take account of history—events in time and space like Christ's incarnation, death, and resurrection.[28]

That Rascal Augustine

Another way to put it is that Scripture defines the human dilemma as *moral*—the problem is that we have violated God's commands. But the Greeks defined the human dilemma as *metaphysical*—the problem is that we are physical, material beings. And if the material world is bad, then the goal of the religious life is to avoid, suppress, and ultimately escape from the material aspects of life. Manual labor was regarded as less valuable than prayer and meditation. Marriage and sexuality were rejected in favor of celibacy. Ordinary social life was on a lower plane than life in hermitages and monasteries. The goal of spiritual life was to free the mind from the evil world of the body and the senses, so it could ascend to God.

Does this sound familiar? It describes much of the spirituality of the church fathers and the Middle Ages. The *really* committed Christian was the one who rejected ordinary work and family life, withdrawing to a monastery to live a life of prayer and contemplation. A Christian vocation was conceived of as separate from ordinary human life and community.

These ideas were derived not from the Bible but from Greek philosophy. Many of the church fathers were deeply influenced by Platonism, including

Clement of Alexandria, Origen, Jerome, and Augustine. On one hand, in their writings they took a strong stand for the goodness of creation, rejecting the twofold origin of the world. Every aspect of creation comes from the hand of God and bears the stamp of His handiwork. Yet, on the other hand, in practice most of them absorbed at least some of the Greeks' negative attitude toward the material world.[29]

The most influential was Augustine, a bright but rascally youngster (as he himself tells us) who rebelled against his mother's Christian faith and embarked on an intellectual quest for truth. He was first attracted to Manicheism (there are two gods, one good and the other evil). Later he became a Platonist, then finally converted to Christianity—without, however, ever quite giving up all the elements of Platonism. Most important, he retained an adapted notion of the double creation, teaching that God first made the Platonic intelligible Forms, and afterward made the material world in imitation of the Forms.

The effect of this modified dualism proved devastating. Even though Augustine explicitly affirmed the goodness of creation, his concept of a dual creation had the effect of undercutting what he said and leading to a two-story hierarchy: The immaterial world (the Forms) functioned as his upper story, which he regarded as superior to the material creation in the lower story. "Despite his averrals of the goodness and reality of the created order," says theologian Colin Gunton, "the sensible world is for him manifestly inferior to the intellectual—that Platonic dualism is never long absent from his writing."[30]

This dualistic view of creation led naturally to a dualistic view of the Christian life. Thus Augustine embraced an ethic of asceticism, based on the assumption that the physical world and bodily functions were inherently inferior, a cause of sin. The way to reach the higher levels of spiritual life was by renunciation and deprivation of physical wants. He regarded ordinary work in the world—what he called the "active" life—as inferior to the "contemplative" life of prayer and meditation shut away in monasteries. He also treated marriage as inferior to celibacy, and even recommended that married clergy not live with their wives.[31]

Partly because Augustine was such a towering figure in church history, a kind of Christianized Platonism remained the *lingua franca* among theologians all the way through the Middle Ages. It is a prominent thread woven through the writings of Boethius, John Scotus Erigena, Anselm, and Bonaventure, and was not challenged until the thirteenth century, when the works of Aristotle were reintroduced into Europe.

Aristotle and Aquinas

In fact, the rediscovery of Aristotle's work represented a serious challenge to Christianity itself, for it presented a comprehensive pagan system that included not only philosophy but also ethics, aesthetics, science, and politics. Some Christians were so impressed that they resorted to an extreme two-story dichotomy—the so-called double-truth theory, where the upper and lower stories were regarded as actually contradictory to one another.

For example, Aristotle taught that the world was eternal, while of course Scripture teaches that it was created—and somehow, it was said, *both* are true. The most notorious proponent of the double-truth theory was a French theologian named Siger de Brabant, whose views are described in acid tones by G. K. Chesterton: "There are two truths; the truth of the supernatural world, and the truth of the natural world, which contradicts the supernatural world. While we are being naturalists, we can suppose that Christianity is all nonsense; but then, when we remember that we are Christians, we must admit that Christianity is true even if it is nonsense."[32]

Of course, this itself was nonsense, and the man who rallied to oppose it was a Dominican named Thomas Aquinas. A gentle giant of a man, Aquinas was so taciturn that his friends nicknamed him the Dumb Ox. But his words flowed fluently when he rose to attack the double-truth theory. Aquinas labored mightily to "Christianize" Aristotle's philosophy, rejecting what was clearly unscriptural and seeking to reinterpret the rest in a form compatible with Christianity (just as earlier thinkers had done with Plato).[33]

The end result was that Aquinas retained the dualistic framework of Greek philosophy while changing the terminology. In the upper story he put *grace,* and in the lower story he put *nature*—not nature in the modern scientific sense but in the Aristotelian sense of the "nature of a thing," meaning its ideal or perfect form, its full potential, the goal toward which it strives, its *telos.* In Aristotle's philosophy, all natural processes are *teleological,* tending toward a purpose or goal.[34]

This adaptation of Aristotle had several beneficial effects on Christian thought. For example, Aristotle had taught that natural processes are *good* because they are the means by which things fulfill their "nature" and arrive at their ideal or perfected form—as an acorn grows to become a full-grown oak or an egg matures into a rooster. This argument was picked up by Aquinas and aimed as a weapon against the Platonic idea that the material world (Matter) is inherently inferior. Against that view, Aquinas argued that the creation (nature) is good because it is the handiwork of a good Creator. As one historical account put it, the message of Christian Aristotelianism "was that God is good, His creation is good, [and] the goodness and the causality of the Creation are evidence of the goodness of God."[35]

Thus Aquinas struck a blow at the world-denying asceticism so common during the Middle Ages, and recovered a more biblical view of creation. This had an immediate effect in the arts, where it inspired a more natural and realistic style of painting in the works of artists like Cimabue and Giotto. It also encouraged the study of nature, preparing the ground for the scientific revolution.[36]

Fluffs of Grace

Yet the fact that Aquinas retained a bi-level schema was eventually to undercut much of the good that he achieved. The Aristotelian definition of nature that Aquinas borrowed contained a hidden dynamite that was to blow the system apart. Why? Because it defined the "nature" of things—their goal or purpose or teleology—as immanent within the world. That meant the world did not need God, but was perfectly capable of reaching its purpose or full potential strictly on its own, by its own resources. This was particularly troublesome in the case of human beings: Is the purpose of our lives really circumscribed by the horizons of this world? Don't we have a higher purpose? Can we really live the way we were meant to by our natural faculties alone? Don't we need to be in relationship to God to be truly fulfilled?

The biblical answer, of course, is that all creation is ordered toward relationship with God, as Aquinas knew. But how could he make room for this biblical truth? His solution was to keep the Aristotelian concept of *nature* but restrict it to the lower story. Then, in the upper story, he added God's supernatural *grace*. That is, over and above our natural faculties, God had endowed humans with a supernatural gift or faculty that enables them to be in relationship with God: "In the state of pure nature man needs a power *added to* his natural power by grace . . . in order to do and to will supernatural good."[37] The state of "pure nature" had to be supplemented by an added-on state of grace. In his words, grace was a *donum superadditum*—meaning a gift (donum) that is added on (superadditum).

Aquinas's reworking of the two stories can be diagrammed like this:

GRACE
A Supernatural Add-On

NATURE
A Built-In Ideal or Goal

But this two-tiered schema of nature and grace proved unstable, and after Aquinas the two orders of existence had a tendency to separate and grow increasingly independent. Why? Because there was no real interaction or interdependence between them. Aristotelian "nature" remained complete and sufficient in itself, with grace merely an external add-on. No matter how much icing you spread on a cake, it's still a separate substance. The things of the world and the things of God coexisted on parallel tracks, without relating in any intrinsic way. Those who came after Aquinas (the later scholastics) even tended to speak as though human life had two distinct goals or ends: an earthly one and a heavenly one—a view still held by some Roman Catholic theologians today. Here's a recent expression: "There are in us, then, since there are two ends, one natural, one supernatural, two sets of virtues, two sets of habits, two sets of gifts, the one set natural the other supernatural."[38]

The problem with this radical dichotomy was that it divided human nature itself in half. "Man, such as mediaeval Christendom conceived him, has been split in two," writes Catholic philosopher Jacques Maritain.

On the one hand, one has a man of pure nature, who has need only of reason to be perfect, wise, and good, and to gain the earth; and on the other, one has a celestial envelope, a believing double, assiduous at worship and praying to the God of the Christians, who surrounds and pads with fluffs of grace this man of pure nature and renders him capable of gaining heaven.

Thus, Maritain comments with heavy irony, "by a sagacious division of labor that the Gospel had not foreseen, the Christian will be able to serve two masters at once, God for heaven and Mammon for the earth, and will be able to divide his soul between two obediences each alike absolute and ultimate—that of the Church, for heaven, and that of the State, for the earth."[39]

The practical impact of this nature/grace dualism was to reinforce the medieval two-tiered spirituality: Laypeople were thought to be capable of attaining only natural, earthly ends, which were clearly inferior, while the religious elites alone were thought capable of spiritual perfection, defined primarily in terms of performing rituals and ceremonies. Thus the religious professionals took over the spiritual duties of those deemed unable to fulfill them for themselves—saying prayers, attending mass, doing penance, going on pilgrimages, and performing acts of charity on behalf of the common folk.

The Reformers Rebel

One of the driving motives of the Reformers was to overcome this medieval dualism and to recover the unity of life and knowledge under the authority of

God's Word. They argued that the medieval scholastics had accommodated far too much to pagan philosophers such as Aristotle, and they urged a more critical attitude toward the alleged truths of reason arrived at apart from divine revelation. (This is how we must understand Luther's overstated charge that "reason is the devil's whore"—he was not against reason per se but against reason applied outside the bounds of God's Word.) The Reformers sought a return to a unified field of knowledge, where divine revelation is the light illuminating all areas of study.

Above all, they soundly rejected the spiritual elitism implied by the nature/grace dualism. They threw out the two-tiered system of religious professionals versus lay believers, replacing it with a robust teaching of the priesthood of all believers (1 Pet. 2:9). Rejecting monasticism, they preached that the Christian life is not a summons to a state of life *separate from* our participation in the creation order of family and work, but is *embedded within* the creation order. Whereas in the Middle Ages the word *vocation* was used strictly of religious callings (priest, monk, or nun), Martin Luther deliberately chose the same term for the vocation of being a merchant, farmer, weaver, or homemaker. Running a business or a household was not the least bit inferior to being a priest or a nun, he argued, because all were ways of obeying the Cultural Mandate—of participating in God's work in maintaining and caring for His creation.

This was backed up theologically by rejecting the definition of grace as something added to nature (*donum superadditum*). That definition assumed that human nature on its own, as God created it, was not fit for relationship with Him but required the infusion of an additional power—which seemed to suggest that human nature was defective in some way. The Reformers were eager to banish any form of dualism that denigrated God's creation, and so they argued that God created human nature as good *in itself*. Grace was not a substance added onto human nature, but was God's merciful acceptance of sinners, whereby He redeems and restores them to their original perfect state.

We get a clearer picture of why this was so revolutionary from the Augsburg Confession, which gives us a window into the attitudes of that time. Prior to the Reformation, it says, "Christianity was thought to consist wholly in the observance of certain holy-days, rites, fasts, and vestures. These observances had won for themselves the exalted title of being the spiritual life and the perfect life." As a result, obedience to God in ordinary life was devalued. As the text explains:

> The commandments of God, according to each one's calling, were without honor: namely, that the father brought up his offspring, that the mother bore

children, that the prince governed the commonwealth—these were accounted works that were worldly and imperfect, and far below those glittering observances.

This dual ranking system created genuine distress among spiritually committed lay believers: "This error greatly tormented devout consciences, which grieved that they were held in an imperfect state of life, as in marriage [or] in the office of magistrate. . . . They admired the monks and such like, and falsely imagined that the observances of such men were more acceptable to God."[40] The Reformers' hearts went out to these devout but devalued laypeople, and they strove to restore spiritual significance to the activities of ordinary life, performed in obedience to the Cultural Mandate.

Thus the Reformers contrasted the monastic call *from* the world with the biblical call *into* the world. As Jesus says to the Father in John 17:15, "I do not ask that you take them out of the world, but that you keep them from the evil one" while still in the world. Calvin articulated a view of ordinary work so distinctive that it later came to be called the Protestant work ethic. "He taught that the individual believer has a vocation to serve God in the world—in *every* sphere of human existence—lending a new dignity and meaning to ordinary work," explains theologian Alister McGrath.[41] Calvin taught that Christ was the Redeemer of every part of creation, including culture, and that we serve him in our everyday work.

Despite all this, the Reformers' emphatic rejection of the nature/grace dualism was not enough to overcome an age-old pattern of thought. The problem was that they failed to craft a *philosophical* vocabulary to express their new theological insights. Thus they did not give their followers any tools to defend those insights against philosophical attack—or to create an alternative to the dualistic philosophy of scholasticism.[42] As a result, the successors of Luther and Calvin went right back to teaching scholasticism in the Protestant universities, using Aristotle's logic and metaphysics as the basis of their systems—and thus dualistic thinking continued to affect all the Christian traditions.

ESCAPE FROM DUALISM

Over the centuries, of course, the definition of what is sacred and what is secular, or worldly, has been redefined. Among the Puritans, some defined worldliness in terms of wearing colorful clothing and ruffled collars; to be holy meant wearing dark, plain clothing. Today many older Christians can remember growing up in churches where it was still forbidden to dance, smoke, play cards, chew tobacco, wear makeup, or go to movies. When a friend of mine attended a Christian college several years ago, "mixed bathing" was still forbidden in the college swimming pool. Even now, walk into some fundamentalist churches and you feel like you've been transported back to the 1950s: All the men are in dark suits while all the women wear skirts below the knees with pumps and hose. The congregation might not exactly call it a sin for a woman to wear pants, but they certainly regard it as a "bad witness."

The problem with this secular/sacred dualism is that it does exactly what Plato did so many years ago: It identifies sin with some *part* of creation (dancing, movies, tobacco, makeup). Spirituality is defined as avoiding that part of creation, while spending as much time as possible in another part (church, Christian school, Bible study groups). This explains why work in the spiritual realm as a pastor or missionary is regarded as more important or valuable than being a banker or businessman. No wonder someone like Sealy Yates absorbed the attitude that the only way to really serve God was in full-time Christian ministry.

In *Loving Monday*, a businessman named John Beckett tells how he struggled to overcome this same dualistic thinking. Having come to God as an adult, Beckett soon discovered "a wide gulf" between his new faith and his work life. He realized, of course, that clear moral principles apply across the board. "But by and large," he says, "I found myself living in two separate worlds."[43]

Longing for "a much fuller integration of my two worlds," he began reading books by Francis Schaeffer and discovered, much as we have in this chapter, that ever since the Greeks the world of work and occupations has been demoted to the lower story. The obvious implication of this dualistic outlook was that it was "'impossible' to serve God by being a man or woman in business," Beckett writes. "For years, I thought my involvement in business was a second-class endeavor—necessary to put bread on the table, but somehow less noble than more sacred pursuits like being a minister or a missionary."[44]

Beckett's story reminds us that the Greek perspective is still alive and well, continuing to rob believers of the integrated life God promises. How did he free himself from this pervasive dualism? Through a new understanding of the cosmic scope of Creation, Fall, and Redemption. And you and I can overcome dualistic thinking in the same way, to bring healing and wholeness to our lives.

Creation: God's Fingerprints All Over

Dualism was born, you will recall, because the Greeks thought Matter was preexisting and eternal, capable of resisting the rational order imposed by the Forms. The obvious answer to that dualism, then, is the biblical doctrine that *nothing* is preexisting or eternal except God. He is the sole source of all creation; every part bears His fingerprints and reflects His good character in its original, created form. "The earth is the LORD's and the fullness thereof," writes the psalmist (Ps. 24:1). Everything bears the stamp of its Maker. Genesis presses the point home by repeating over and over again, of the newly created world, "And God saw that it was good" (Gen. 1:4, 10, 12, etc.).

The implication is that no *part* of creation is inherently evil or bad. "Everything created by God is good, and nothing is to be rejected if it is received with thanksgiving," Paul says (1 Tim. 4:4). Being spiritual cannot be defined simply in terms of roping off and avoiding certain parts of creation—whether movies, cards, dancing, or makeup. Once we understand this, Christians will never come across as negative kill-joys. While hating sin, we should exhibit a deep love for this world as God's handiwork, seeing through its brokenness and sin to its original created goodness. We should be known as people in love with the beauties of nature and the wonders of human creativity.

Among the Reformers, it was Calvin who sounded this theme most consistently. Whereas Plato explained the order of the universe in terms of abstract ideals (Matter is ordered by rational Forms), Calvin explained its order as a product of God's word or law or creative decree. The divine word gives things their "nature" or identity, governing both human life (moral law) and the physical universe (laws of nature). Modern people tend to place morality and science in completely different categories, but for Calvin both were examples of God's law. The difference is only that humans must *choose* to obey the moral law, whereas natural objects have no choice but to obey the laws of physics or electromagnetism. If we look at the world through Calvinist eyes, we see God's law governing every element in the universe, God's word constituting its orderly structure, God's truth discoverable in every field.

Fall: Where to Draw the Line

Just as we must insist on the cosmic scope of Creation—that all creation came from God's hand—so too we must insist on the cosmic scope of the Fall. Even the natural world has been affected by human sin, as we are told in Genesis 3 and Romans 8. Because humans were created to be God's deputies exercising dominion over creation, their sin had a ripple effect that has extended into the natural world. This is simply one of the consequences of authority: If a father is harsh, the whole family is unhappy; if a CEO is unethical, the whole company is likely to be corrupt.

Against the Greek conception, we must insist that evil and disorder are not intrinsic in the material world but are caused by human sin, which takes God's good creation and distorts it to evil purposes. "When Adam fell, it was the result of a rebellious will, and not because he had a body," writes philosopher Gordon Clark.[45] That's why Paul can write, "Nothing is unclean in itself"

(Rom. 14:14). It *becomes* unclean only when sinners use it to express their rebellion against God. The line between good and evil is not drawn between one part of creation and another part, but runs through the human heart itself—in our own disposition to use the creation for good or for evil.

For example, music is good, but popular songs can be used to glorify moral perversion. Art is a good gift from God, but books and movies can be used to convey nonbiblical worldviews and encourage moral decadence. Science is a vocation from God, but it can be used to undermine belief in a Creator. Sexuality was God's idea in the first place, but it can be distorted and twisted to serve selfish, hedonistic purposes. The state is ordained by God to establish justice, but it can be perverted into tyranny and injustice. Work is a calling from God, but in American corporate culture it is often an addiction—a frenzied scramble for a higher rung on the corporate ladder, a bigger salary, a more impressive résumé. In every area of life, we need to distinguish between the way God originally created the world, and the way it has been deformed and defaced by sin.

Reformed thinkers label this *structure* versus *direction*. Structure refers to the created character of the world, which is still good even after the Fall— music, art, science, sexuality, work, the state (to use the examples above). Direction refers to the way we "direct" those structures to serve either God or idols. In every enterprise in which we are engaged, we need to ask: (1) What is the original structure that God created, and (2) how is it being distorted and directed to sinful purposes?[46]

Even religious activity can be directed toward sin. We've probably all had the tragic experience of knowing pastors and ministry leaders who, despite impressive God-talk and skillful PR, are actually driven by spiritual pride, using their position as a means for power and influence instead of for service. Spiritual sin can be difficult to spot precisely because we are blinded by the secular/sacred split, which inclines us to classify the spiritual realm as the "good" part of creation. This makes it easy for religious leaders to gloss over wrongdoing by claiming it is necessary "to advance the ministry" or "to reach more people." We need to bear in mind the powerful words of Alexander Solzhenitsyn, when he wrote, "The line separating good and evil passes not through states, nor between classes, nor between political parties either, but right through every human heart."[47]

Redemption: After the Great Divorce

Finally, just as all of creation was originally good, and all was affected by the Fall, so too all will be redeemed. God's ultimate promise is a new heavens and a new earth, which means earthly life is not simply going to end; instead it's going to be fully sanctified. Heaven will not be a place of insubstantial spirits or disembodied minds floating around. Our physical bodies will be resurrected and restored, and we will dwell in a new earth. In the Apostles' Creed we affirm both Jesus' bodily resurrection and our own as well. His resurrection is the guarantee that we too will rise (1 Corinthians 15). As part of God's good creation, the material world will participate in the final redemption. In eternity, we will continue to fulfill the Cultural Mandate, though without sin—creating things that are beautiful and beneficial out of the raw materials of God's renewed creation.

This means that every valid vocation has its counterpart in the new heavens and new earth, which gives our work eternal significance. We cannot know exactly what life will be like in eternity, but the fact that Scripture calls it a new "earth," and tells us we will live there with glorified physical bodies, means that it will not be a negation of the life we have known here on the old earth. Instead it will be an enhancement, an intensification, a glorification of this life. In *The Great Divorce,* C. S. Lewis pictures the afterlife as recognizably similar to this world, yet a place where every blade of grass seems somehow more real, more solid, more substantial than anything experienced here on earth.[48]

A young woman working as a technical writer once told me that her job was merely a way of establishing a financial base to do the things she *really* wanted—which consisted mostly of church activities. "I considered going back to school to learn how to write better," she explained. "But then I realized this won't exist in heaven, so it isn't worth studying." The young woman's commitment to spiritual matters is commendable, but she was mistaken in regarding her earthly vocation as merely a temporary expedient. In our work we not only participate in God's providential activity today, we also foreshadow the tasks we will take up in cultivating a new earth at the end of time. God's command to Adam and Eve to partner with Him in developing the beauty and goodness of creation revealed His purpose for *all* of human life. And after He has dealt with sin once for all, we will joyfully take up that task once again, as redeemed people in a renewed world.

This comprehensive vision of Creation, Fall, and Redemption allows no room for a secular/sacred split. All of creation was originally good; it cannot be divided into a good part (spiritual) and a bad part (material). Likewise, all of creation was affected by the Fall, and when time ends, all creation will be redeemed. Evil does not reside in some part of God's good creation, but in our abuse of creation for sinful purposes (structure versus direction). Paul defined sin as "anything not of faith"—that is, *anything* not directed to God's glory and service. The other side of the coin is that, in redemption, *"all things* are ours" (see 1 Cor. 3:21).

This holistic vision can be wonderfully liberating. When John Beckett finally overcame the secular/sacred split, for the first time he was able to regard his work "as having great worth to God." As "a business person, I was no longer a second-class citizen," he exulted. "Nor did I need to leave my Christian convictions and biblical values outside the office entrance when I headed into work on Monday morning."[49] This same liberating experience can be available to all of us, as we shed dualistic thinking and embrace a holistic Christian worldview.

CHRISTIANITY OUT OF BALANCE

The task of identifying dualistic thinking can be somewhat tricky, because several different forms exist. However, the three-part grid of Creation-Fall-Redemption gives us a powerful tool of analysis. Throughout the history of the church, various groups have tended to seize upon one of these three elements, overemphasizing it to the detriment of the other two—producing a lopsided, unbalanced theology. For example, stressing the Fall too heavily tends toward pessimism and negativism, while overemphasizing Redemption can lead to triumphalism and complacency.

Let's practice using the three-part grid by applying it to some common tendencies among Christian groups. Perhaps the most common imbalance in American evangelicalism is to overemphasize the Fall. Consider the typical evangelistic message: "You're a sinner; you need to be saved." What could be wrong with that? Of course, it's true that we are sinners, but notice that the message starts with the Fall instead of Creation. By beginning with the theme of sin, it implies that our essential identity consists in being guilty sinners, deserving of divine punishment. Some Christian literature goes so far as to say we are nothing, completely worthless, before a holy God.

This excessively negative view is not biblical, however, and it lays Christianity open to the charge that it has a low view of human dignity. The Bible does not begin with the Fall but with Creation: Our value and dignity are rooted in the fact that we are created in the image of God, with the high calling of being His representatives on earth. In fact, it is only *because* humans have such high value that sin is so tragic. If we were worthless to begin with, then the Fall would be a trivial event. When a cheap trinket is broken, we toss it aside with a shrug. But when a priceless masterpiece is defaced, we are horrified. It is because humans are the masterpiece of God's creation that the destructiveness of sin produces such horror and sorrow. Far from expressing a low view of human nature, the Bible actually gives a far *higher* view than the dominant secular view today, which regards humans as simply complex computers made of meat—products of blind, naturalistic forces, without transcendent purpose or meaning.

If we start with a message of sin, without giving the context of Creation, then we will come across to nonbelievers as merely negative and judgmental. After an extended trip through Africa (described in *Dark Star Safari*), the writer Paul Theroux said one of the saddest moments in his journey was "hearing a young woman [missionary] tell me that she was heading for Mozambique and adding, 'They're all sinners, you know.'" Theroux concluded that missionaries only make people "despise themselves."[50] We need to begin our message where the Bible begins—with the dignity and high calling of all human beings because they are created in the image of God.

More Than Sinners

Moreover, in our secularized culture, starting with the Fall renders the rest of our message incoherent. In an earlier age, when most Americans were brought up in the church, they were familiar with basic theological concepts—which meant that the revivalist's simple message of sin and salvation was often adequate. When people heard, "You're a sinner," they had the context to understand what it meant, and many were moved to repentance. But contemporary Americans often have no background in biblical teaching—which means that the concept of sin makes no sense to them. Their response is likely to be, What is *sin*? What right does God have to judge me? How do you know He even exists? Beginning with sin instead of creation is like trying to read a book by opening it in the middle: You don't know the characters and can't make sense of the plot.

As a result, even a pulpit-pounding, fire-and-brimstone sermon is likely to have only a limited effect at best. In my own pilgrimage back to faith as a teenager, I encountered a message of sin and judgment in the unlikeliest of places—in James Joyce's semi-autobiographical book *A Portrait of the Artist as a Young Man,* which was required reading in a high school English class. When I read its description of Father Arnall's hellfire sermons, dwelling in exquisite detail on the suffering of the damned, I had to admit that it was a bit frightening. I was impressed with a sense that *if* Christianity were true, then the decision to believe would be a genuinely life-and-death matter. I began to tell friends that maybe we should reconsider our relaxed relativism: *What if* there really is one single, universal Truth? A small step in the right direction, perhaps, but it certainly did not bring me to faith or repentance. The hellfire images in Joyce's book served as nothing more than a metaphor for the seriousness of the search for truth. Isolated doctrines taken out of their biblical context do not even make sense to modern people, because they no longer have the background to supply the context on their own.

Finally, if we begin with the Fall instead of Creation, we will not be able to explain Redemption—because its goal is precisely to *restore* us to our original, created status. If it were true that we are worthless, and that being sinners is our core identity, then in order to have something of value God would have to destroy the human race and start over again. But He doesn't do that; instead He restores us to the high dignity originally endowed at Creation—recovering our true identity and renewing the image of God in us.

God's Offspring

We can take a lesson from the way the apostles addressed various audiences in New Testament times. Their initial audiences consisted of the Jews of their day—people steeped in the Old Testament, with a firm grasp of key concepts like covenant, law, sin, and sacrifice. When addressing these audiences, the apostles could simply start with Jesus as the supreme sacrifice, the Lamb of God. With people already looking for the coming Messiah, the apostles could simply announce that Jesus was the One they were waiting for.

By contrast, when Paul addressed secular Greek philosophers in Acts 17, the Stoics and Epicureans on Mars Hill, where did he begin? With Creation. Notice how carefully he builds his argument, step by step. First he identifies God as the ultimate origin of the world: "The God who made the world and everything in it" is the "Lord and heaven and earth" (v. 24). Then he identifies this God as the source of our own humanity: "He made from one man every nation of mankind" (v. 26). Finally, he draws the logical conclusion: "Being then God's offspring, we ought not to think that the divine being is like gold or silver or stone" (v. 29). That is, God cannot be akin to material things like idols. Since He made us, He must have at least the qualities we have as personal, moral, rational, creative beings. As water cannot rise above its source, so a nonpersonal object or force could not have produced personal beings like ourselves. It is logical to conclude that God too is a personal Being.

In that case, however, we stand in a personal relationship with God—we owe Him our allegiance, just as children owe honor and allegiance to the parents who brought them into the world. In fact, failure to acknowledge God is a moral fault and calls for repentance: "Now He commands all people everywhere to repent" (v. 30). Notice that it is only *after* having built a case based on Creation that Paul introduces the concepts of sin and repentance. In addressing the pagan Greek culture, he first lays a foundation in the doctrine of creation. As Robert Bellah comments, "In order to preach Jesus Christ and him crucified to the biblically illiterate Athenians, Paul must convince them of the fundamentally Jewish notion of a creator. . . . Only in that context does the incarnation, crucifixion, and resurrection of Jesus Christ make sense."[51]

Today, as we address the biblically illiterate Americans of the twenty-first century, we need to follow Paul's model, building a case from Creation before expecting people to understand the message of sin and salvation. We need to practice "pre-evangelism," using apologetics to defend basic concepts of who God is, who we are, and what we owe Him, before presenting the gospel message.

Jars of Clay

If beginning with sin and judgment has historically been the most typical imbalance among Protestants, it is also possible to tilt in the opposite direction. Some groups weight Redemption more heavily than the Fall, leading to the doctrine of Christian Perfection or Holiness—the idea that we can become completely holy even in this life. For example, a central doctrine in the Wesleyan and Nazarene tradition is "entire sanctification," the teaching that we can be made completely holy or freed from sin in the present life, instead of waiting for eternal life. These churches hold that believers are "made free from original sin, or depravity, and brought into a state of entire devotement to God, and the holy obedience of love made perfect" (in the words of the articles of faith of the Church of the Nazarene).[52]

The error here consists in holding that Redemption overcomes the Fall completely in this life. The Bible teaches that sin will not be completely conquered until Christ returns. On the cross, Christ defeated sin and Satan and won the decisive victory; yet much of the world remains under the power of the enemy until Christ returns as conquering King. We need to hold both of these truths together in proper balance. When the Pharisees asked Jesus when the kingdom would come, He answered, "the kingdom of God is in the midst of you" (Luke 17:21). Yet he also instructed His disciples to pray, "Thy kingdom come," and taught that its coming has not yet been fully accomplished. Between Christ's first and second coming, we must balance both the "already" and the "not yet" aspects of this interim phase.[53]

Picture the world as God's territory by right of Creation. Because of the Fall, it has been invaded and occupied by Satan and his minions, who constantly wage war against God's people. At the central turning point in history, God Himself, the second person of the Trinity, enters the world in the person of Jesus

Christ and deals Satan a deathblow through His resurrection. The Enemy has been fatally wounded; the outcome of the war is certain; yet the occupied territory has not actually been liberated. There is now a period where God's people are called to participate in the follow-up battle, pushing the Enemy back and reclaiming territory for God. This is the period in which we now live—between Christ's resurrection and the final victory over sin and Satan. Our calling is to apply the finished work of Christ on the cross to our lives and the world around us, without expecting perfect results until Christ returns.

This is not an excuse for complacency. We should still strive to develop a character of such quality that people can see a difference between the redeemed and the unredeemed. Our lives should exhibit a supernatural dimension that nonbelievers cannot explain away in terms of merely natural talent or energy.

Paul expressed the proper balance by saying we have a powerful spiritual treasure but it is held in fragile, breakable jars of clay (2 Cor. 4:7). This side of heaven, we should strive to live with all three elements held in balance: recognizing the created goodness of God's world (Creation), fighting the corruption of ongoing sin and brokenness (Fall), and working toward the healing of creation and the restoration of God's purposes (Redemption).

A Higher Consciousness?

Some groups hold an even more extreme imbalance—that Redemption overcomes not only the Fall but even Creation itself. This is the conviction embraced by all sorts of utopian movements, including monasticism: the idea that the highest calling is not to recover God's purpose in Creation but to presage the final Redemption. Monasticism recognized that marriage is part of the creation order; nevertheless it rejected marriage as inferior and aspired instead to prefigure the glorified state, where there will be neither marrying nor giving in marriage, but we will be "like angels in heaven" (Mark 12:25). Thus in the monastic interpretation of this verse, celibacy was exalted as a way to foreshadow the final Redemption.[54]

Similarly, monasticism recognized that owning property is a natural right, rooted in creation and protected by the eighth commandment; nevertheless, by abandoning all property, monks and nuns sought to rise above the natural order to a higher state. Monasticism recognized a natural right to protect oneself, and for a nation to protect itself; yet it claimed for itself the higher calling of pacifism. And so on. Nor are these ideas restricted to monks and nuns: Throughout history, Christianity has seen the rise of various radical, utopian movements that rejected ordinary life, rooted in the creation order, for the sake of some supposed higher spirituality that would be an anticipation of eternity.

The error here is to assume that the order of Redemption destroys the order of Creation. And the antidote is to realize that Redemption is intended not to demolish God's good creation but to fulfill it. As we have seen, this was a theme in the writings of the Reformers, and of Thomas Aquinas before them. The way Aquinas put it was that grace does not *destroy* nature in order to replace it with something higher—instead grace *perfects* nature. He was using the verb "perfect" in the biblical sense of reaching a goal, achieving a purpose, fulfilling an ideal—as when James calls on believers to become "perfect and complete, lacking in nothing" (James 1:4).[55] In Redemption, God does not call us to become something *other* than human but rather to *recover* our true humanity. He empowers us to achieve the purpose for which we were originally created—to fulfill our created nature, which He declared in Genesis to be "very good."

Notice how Jesus Himself replied when the Jewish leaders challenged His teaching on marriage. What was His response? "He who created them from the beginning made them male and female" (Matt. 19:4). In other words, the creation order that God established "from the beginning" remains normative throughout human history. It is not an inferior order to be overcome or destroyed by Redemption. Genesis reveals what God intended for humanity from the start, and what it still means to live a fully human life today.

The Great Drama

The tragedy is that in applying this corrective to medieval thought, Aquinas overcompensated and ended up with a new imbalance. We've talked about what happens when groups overemphasize the Fall or Redemption. But what happens when someone overemphasizes Creation? That's what Aquinas did, and it led to a truncated or incomplete view of the Fall.

Think back to our earlier discussion of Aquinas's nature/grace dualism, which treated grace as an addendum to nature—a suprahuman faculty given to Adam at Creation to supplement his natural faculties. What did this imply for Aquinas's view of the Fall? The answer is that when humans fell into sin, they lost *only* the added-on gift of supernatural grace (the upper story). They fell from the state of grace to the state of pure nature, losing the extra, suprahuman faculties but retaining their human faculties (the lower story) essentially intact and unchanged.[56]

But notice what this implies: If only the upper story fell, then only the upper story needs to be redeemed. The lower story does not. Spiritually, we need a re-infusion of supernatural grace, but our ordinary human nature does not participate in either the Fall or Redemption.[57]

As a result, the gospel was restricted to the upper-story realm of religion and theology. In those areas, humans needed divine revelation and the enlightening of God's Spirit. But in the lower-story realm of science, philosophy, law, and politics, human reason was thought to function quite adequately on its own. Reason was regarded as spiritually neutral or autonomous, not affected by the Fall nor in need of direction from God's Word. In other words, in these subject areas, there was *no distinctively biblical perspective*. Everyone could simply accept whatever "reason" decrees.

This differs sharply from classic Protestant teaching, which defines sin as turning away from God at the core of our being—thus coloring *everything* we think or do. Our entire being is involved in the great drama of sin and redemption. There is no aspect of human nature unaffected by the Fall, no independent realm known by a spiritually neutral reason. Indeed, it's a mistake even to think of reason as neutral, in the sense of being independent of any philosophical or religious commitments. As we saw in chapter 1, all systems of thought begin with some basic premise—some ultimate principle that is regarded as self-existing or divine. Reason is merely the human capacity to reason from those starting premises.

In short, reason is always exercised in service to some ultimate religious vision. People interpret the facts in the light of either biblical revelation or some competing system of thought. When Calvinists use the phrase *total depravity,* this is what they mean: not that humans are hopelessly evil but rather that *every aspect* of human nature has been affected by the Fall, including our intellectual life—and thus *every aspect* needs to be redeemed. Nothing was left pristine and innocent. Even our minds are tempted to worship idols instead of the true God.

Serving Two Masters

This analysis explains why Protestant thinkers have long argued that the medieval nature/grace dualism led to an incomplete view of the Fall. If only the upstairs fell, then the range of God's revelation and redemption is limited to the religious sphere. "By restricting the scope of fall and redemption to the supranatural," writes Herman Dooyeweerd, the nature/grace dualism robbed the Christian message of its integral, all-encompassing character, so that it "could no longer grip man with all its power and absoluteness." In practical terms, the nature/grace dualism implied that we need *spiritual* regeneration in the upper story of theology and religion, but we don't need *intellectual* regeneration in order to get the right view of politics, science, social life, morality, or work. In these areas, human reason is treated as religiously neutral, and we can all go ahead and accept whatever the secular experts decree. It should come as no surprise, then, that this dichotomy led believers to accommodate with the world in these areas. (It also functioned as a stepping-stone to secularism, as we will see in the next chapter.)

Today many Catholic scholars have come to agree with this critique of the nature/grace dualism. For example, Louis Dupré notes that the dualistic scheme allowed *pure nature* (downstairs) to be conceived of as "independent of the historical stages of the fall and redemption." And he praises Reformed theology for expressing "man's *total* involvement in the drama of sin and redemption far more profound than the late medieval theologies with their dual vision of a supernatural order 'added' to nature."[58]

We must never forget, however, that the same dualism permeated the Protestant denominations nearly as thoroughly as it did Catholicism. Because the Protestant Reformers did not craft an alternative philosophy to scholasticism (as we saw earlier), many of their followers slipped back into the same medieval nature/grace dualism. We see the effects today when Christians assume they can attend church and Bible study on the weekends and then, during the week, simply accept whatever concepts and theories are current in their professional field.

In practice, the notion that reason is religiously neutral means that secularism and naturalism are often promoted under the guise of "neutrality." They are presented as objective, rational, and binding on everyone, while biblical views are dismissed as biased private opinions. This equivocation has created enormous pressure on Christians to abandon any distinctively biblical perspective in their professional work. One Christian philosopher goes so far as to insist that it would be "wrong" to apply biblical principles to his work: "I have, myself, definite religious convictions: but I would consider it entirely wrong to make them intrude as tacit presuppositions in the actual process of analysis I undertake."[59] This scholar has clearly acquiesced to the idea that intellectual work can be autonomous of religious or philosophical commitments.

The effect of such a stance, however, is that Christians will abandon the world of ideas to the secularists. They will fail to see that secularism is itself a philosophical commitment—and that if they don't bring *biblical* principles to bear on various issues, then they will end up promoting *nonbiblical* principles. It is impossible to think without some set of presuppositions about the world. This illustrates why it is crucial for Christians to understand the ongoing pitfalls of the nature/grace dualism—so that we can break free from faulty thought patterns and open our whole lives to the transforming power of God's Word.

ALL TOGETHER NOW

What we learn from this brief survey of theological traditions is that Creation, Fall, and Redemption are not only the fundamental turning points of biblical history—they also function as marvelously useful diagnostic tools. A genuinely biblical theology must keep all three principles in careful balance: that all created reality comes from the hand of God and was originally and intrinsically good; that all is marred and corrupted by sin; yet that all is capable of being redeemed, restored, and transformed by God's grace.

These three principles also provide a way to overcome the secular/sacred dichotomy in our lives. The biblical message is not just about some isolated part of life labeled "religion" or "church life." Creation, Fall, and Redemption are cosmic in scope, describing the great events that shape the nature of all created reality. We don't need to accept an inner fragmentation between our faith and the rest of life. Instead we can be integrally related to God on all levels of our being, offering up everything we do in love and service to Him. "Whether you eat or drink or whatever you do, do all to the glory of God," Paul says (1 Cor. 10:31). The promise of Christianity is the joy and power of an integrated life, transformed on every level by the Holy Spirit, so that our whole being participates in the great drama of God's plan of redemption.

Yet when we work to overcome the long-standing secular/sacred dualism in the Christian world, our efforts will run up against powerful dualisms in the *secular* world as well, aimed at privatizing and marginalizing the biblical message. After all, in the West, secular thought grew out of the same stream of intellectual history that we have been surveying. The nature/grace dualism was simply secularized, producing the fact/value dichotomy that remains potent right up to our own times. To liberate Christianity from its cultural captivity, we need to diagnose the modern secular dualism as well. And that is what we will do in the next chapter.

3

KEEPING RELIGION
IN ITS PLACE

When all is said and done, science is about *things*
and theology is about *words*.
FREEMAN DYSON[1]

Alan Sears of the Alliance Defense Fund patted his right jacket pocket. "Most Christian lawyers keep their faith in one pocket," he told me. Then he patted his left pocket. "And they keep the law in the other. Their ability to integrate the two is very poor."[2]

Sears was explaining why the ADF had set up a program to train practicing attorneys in a Christian approach to the law. Educated in mainstream law schools, many Christian attorneys simply absorb a secularized view of the law as nothing more than a utilitarian set of procedures that can be manipulated at will to further their client's interests. Their professional lives remain completely separate from their personal walk with the Lord. As Christians, of course, they realize that they should behave morally on the job—not lie or steal. But few have any background in Christian apologetics or worldview that would provide an alternative approach to legal philosophy itself.

"Our first step in the educational programs," Sears explained, "is to deconstruct the legal philosophy these lawyers have absorbed from their secular training." This is done in small groups, he added, "because it is far too painful to be done publicly."

"Painful?" I asked. "Why is that?"

"Because it can be devastating to discover how much they have compromised with the secular mindset," Sears replied. In spite of their personal religious beliefs, in their professional work many Christian lawyers have slipped into a mindset of relativism and pragmatism.

A particularly striking example was a Christian lawyer who worked for a Fortune 500 company. A deacon in his church, he tithed generously, taught

Sunday school, and was in every way a model church member. But on the job, his sole responsibility was . . . to break contracts. Whenever the company decided it was no longer in its interest to work with someone, this man's job was to find a legal loophole that allowed the company to break the contract. He seemed to have no sense that his work involved violating moral principles every day—ideals of truth, integrity, and keeping one's word. He was just "doing his job."

How can even committed Christian believers be so blind? Because they often undergo many years of professional training in a secular setting where they have no opportunity to develop a biblical worldview. In fact, they know that if they *did* express a biblical perspective, it would be a barrier to getting into most graduate schools. And so, most believers learn to compartmentalize their lives, absorbing the reigning secular assumptions in their field of study, while maintaining a devotional life on the side in their private time.

Sears recounted a story about the chief justice of a state supreme court who once told a group of lawyers, "If you think the law has anything to do with morality, you won't last long in this profession." So how *do* most Christians last in the legal profession? By locking away their religious beliefs while on the job and adopting the prevailing concepts and procedures in their field.

In fact, the very concept of being "professional" has come to have connotations of being secular. In the late nineteenth and early twentieth centuries, explains Christian Smith, there was a drive to professionalize all fields—which meant in practice throwing off a Christian worldview and cultivating a secular approach that was touted as *scientific* and *value-free*. The process was nothing less than a "secular revolution," Smith says. In higher education, colleges that used to promote "a general Protestant worldview and morality" were transformed into universities "where religious concerns were marginalized in favor of the 'objective,' a-religious and irreligious pursuit and transmission of knowledge."[3]

This "secular revolution" affected every part of American culture—not only higher education but also the public schools, politics, psychology, and the media. In each of these areas, Christianity was privatized as "sectarian," while secular philosophies like materialism and naturalism were put forth as "objective" and "neutral," and therefore the only perspectives suitable for the public sphere.

Of course, they were nothing of the sort. There is nothing neutral about the claim that the only way to get at truth is to deny God's existence. That is a substantive religious claim, just as it is to affirm God's existence. Yet because of the secular revolution, even many believers came to believe that speaking from a distinctively Christian perspective was biased—that to be truly objective they must bracket their faith and think like nonbelievers in their professional work. To adapt to modernity's professional ethos, Christians found themselves pressured to adopt a naturalistic, secularized approach to the subject matter of their field.

Across the board Christians have been taught (in Alan Sears's image) to keep their faith in one pocket and their work in the other pocket. Many have accepted the idea that the secularized concepts in their field really *do* constitute neutral knowledge, requiring no biblical critique. Faith is often reduced to a separate add-on for personal and private life—on the order of a private indulgence, like a weakness for chocolates—and not an appropriate topic in the public arena.

Today believers are sometimes so intimidated "that they bend over backwards not to sound too 'Christian'," says English professor Kathleen Nielson. Speaking from her experiences in teaching literature in Christian colleges, she says evangelicals are so eager to fit into the standard ideal of neutral scholarship that "we're sometimes afraid to notice a worldview within a novel [even when it] is profoundly un-Christian, or anti-Christian, because we don't want to appear condemnatory or unappreciative of the art."[4] In other words, we don't want to come across as unsophisticated. The rules of professional scholarship rigidly enforce the public/private dichotomy, so that Christians are often made to feel they have no choice but to play by the rules.

Why does this bifurcation between public and private have such force? In the last chapter, we examined the nature/grace dualism that arose within Christianity from the early church through the Middle Ages. In this chapter, we will pick up the story from there and trace the way the dualism became secularized, producing the modern dichotomies between public and private, fact and value. When we think of medieval society, what strikes us most often are the vast differences between that period and our own. For example, despite its dualistic worldview, medieval society remained much more unified and holistic than modern society, which is split institutionally between public and private spheres. In the Middle Ages, moreover, it was the upper story that was valued more highly, whereas in the modern age we have witnessed a stunning reversal. Nevertheless, important continuities link the historical process together, as we will see. In order to craft an effective strategy for bringing Christian truth back into the public sphere, we must understand how secular dualisms arose—so we can strike them right at the root. By tracing their development, we will be equipped to diagnose the way they function today. In the process, we will also develop an effective strategy for evangelism in the postmodern age.

Reason Unbound

If we begin with an overview of the process of secularization—the big picture—then it will be easier to break it down and examine key steps along the way. We pick up the story with the nature/grace dualism as it developed after Thomas Aquinas. Recall that *grace* meant theology and the mysteries of faith (the upper story), while *nature* meant knowledge of this-worldly things, supposedly known by unaided reason apart from divine revelation (the lower story). But serious problems were raised by the very notion of unaided or autonomous reason, for if the ordinary affairs of life could be understood and managed by reason alone, then the realm of grace seemed increasingly irrelevant. Oh, people knew they'd better perform the correct church rituals to make sure they got into the *next* life on good terms. But in *this* life, Christian truth began to seem superfluous. Human reason was regarded as perfectly competent on its own for understanding the state, society, science, economics, philosophy—in fact, everything outside of theology. Thus the Christian mind itself began to be split. God's Word was limited to the upper story, but was deemed irrelevant and unnecessary in directing the lower story.

Aquinas managed to maintain a balanced synthesis of both stories; but his synthesis was not to last. Increasingly, religion was seen as nothing more than a negative check on what reason was allowed to say. Revelation provided a set of truths that reason was not allowed to contradict, which made it a useful yardstick for detecting error. But it did not provide any positive guidance in the lower story.[5] By the time of the later scholastics, faith and reason began to be split into separate, unrelated categories. Religion was reduced to a matter of arbitrary faith, while reason was made increasingly autonomous from revelation, as though it were an independent source of truth. We could picture it by saying that late medieval thinkers thickened the line of demarcation between the upper and lower stories until it became a dense, impenetrable wall.

Just prior to the Reformation, the separation between faith and reason was stretched to the breaking point. The key person was William of Ockham, who denied that God could be understood in rational categories at all. Prior to this, many Christian thinkers had labored to show that God's plan of salvation was fitting, suitable, and perfectly reasonable. For example, in the twelfth century Anselm had offered a case for salvation that was concise and logical: *Because* human beings sinned, therefore a human being had to render payment. *However,* the debt we owe God is so great that only God Himself is able to pay it. *Therefore* God became a human being in order to pay the price exacted by divine justice. Anselm's point was that God's plan of salvation makes perfect sense.[6] By contrast, Ockham argued that if we apply rational principles to

God in any way, we deny His absolute freedom. From the perspective of reason, God's plan of salvation is completely arbitrary; God could have chosen a completely different way to save us. Instead of becoming a human being, Ockham said, He could have become a stone or a donkey. In matters of religion, we cannot consider what seems rational; religion derives solely from revelation, accepted by faith.

In short, faith and reason had split into two independent categories. And from this radical dichotomy, it was only a small step to complete secularism. For if virtually everything needed for ordinary life could be known by reason alone, eventually people began to ask why we need revelation at all. A type of rationalism arose that regarded "Reason" as a storehouse of truths known autonomously, apart from divine revelation.[7] In fact, it seemed as though these autonomous truths could even be used to *judge* the claims of religion. Thus the balance of power shifted: Instead of religion functioning as a yardstick of error, reason was now held up as the yardstick of truth. And in applying that yardstick, many concluded that religion failed to measure up.

As the medieval period merged into the Renaissance (beginning roughly in the 1300s), a drumbeat began to sound for the complete emancipation of reason from revelation—a crescendo that burst into full force in the Enlightenment (beginning in the 1700s). The credo of the Enlightenment was autonomy. Overthrow all external authority, and discover truth by reason alone! Impressed by the stunning successes of the scientific revolution, the Enlightenment enthroned science as the sole source of genuine knowledge. Claiming to "liberate" the lower story from the upper story, it insisted that nature was the sole reality, and scientific reason the sole path to truth. Whatever was not susceptible to scientific study was pronounced an illusion. Though reason was touted as philosophically neutral, in reality it began to be identified with scientific materialism.

COLLATERAL DAMAGE

Yet scientific materialism, with its vision of a mechanistic universe, was unattractive to many people, and it galvanized a reaction known as the Romantic movement. For religion was not the only casualty of scientific materialism masquerading as neutral reason. Morality and the arts came under attack as well—after all, things like moral ideals and beauty and creativity are not subject to scientific investigation either. The Romantics responded by trying to preserve some cognitive territory for things that are not reducible to scientific materialism, including religion and morality and the arts and humanities. Romanticism rejected the philosophy of materialism in favor of the philosophy of idealism, which says that ultimate reality is not material but mental or spiritual—usually capitalized as Mind or Spirit or the Absolute.

Yet Romanticism made a fatal concession: It largely conceded the study of nature to mechanistic science, and sought only to carve out a parallel arena for the arts and humanities. Thus scientific materialism continued to reign unchallenged in the lower story, while Romantic idealism was limited to the upper story, leaving the dualistic schema intact.

In a thumbnail sketch, then, the Enlightenment and its intellectual heirs were given jurisdiction over the lower story, where we deal with knowledge that is rational, objective, and scientific—the public sphere. Romanticism and its heirs were given jurisdiction over the upper story, where we deal with religion, morality, and the humanities—the private sphere. We can diagram the division like this:

Modern forms of dualism began with the Enlightenment:

ROMANTICISM
Religion and the Humanities

ENLIGHTENMENT
Science and Reason

This is the overall picture of the secularization process; but to understand it more effectively, we need to trace key steps along the way.

CARTESIAN DIVIDE

The beginning of secular dualism is generally traced to the seventeenth-century French philosopher René Descartes, who proposed a sharp dichotomy between matter and mind. The material world he pictured as a vast machine moving in fixed patterns set by natural laws, subject to mathematical necessity. For Descartes, even animals were machines, and so was the human body. By contrast, the human mind or spirit was the realm of thought, perception, emotions, and will.

Few people realize that in drawing such a sharp opposition between matter and mind, Descartes' purpose was actually to *defend* the realm of mind. As noted in chapter 1, Descartes was a pious Catholic, and by drawing a sharp distinction between the mechanical universe and the human spirit, he hoped to defend belief in the latter. His famous phrase "I think, therefore I am" was intended as a religious affirmation: Since thought is a spiritual activity, he had proved the existence of the human spirit.

But in one of the ironies of history, the enduring impact of Descartes' philosophy was precisely the opposite of what he had intended. What survived was not his defense of the human spirit but his mechanistic conception of the universe. Mind was cast into the upper story, where it was reduced to a shadowy substance totally irrelevant to the material world known by science—a kind of ghost only tenuously connected to the physical body. The novelist Walker Percy speaks of the "dread chasm that has rent the soul of Western man ever since the famous philosopher Descartes ripped body loose from mind and turned the very soul into a ghost that haunts its own house."[8]

The legacy of Descartes' secular dualism can be diagrammed like this:

MIND
Spirit, Thought, Emotion, Will

MATTER
A Mechanical, Deterministic Machine

This "dread chasm" between upper and lower stories grew even wider after the stunning success of Newtonian physics. Newton's law of gravity subsumed a vast number of natural processes under a single mathematical formula—from the fall of an apple to the orbit of the planets. Nature began to be pictured as a huge machine, governed by natural laws as strictly as the gears of a clock. How could there be any room in such a mechanism for the human soul or spirit? Though these concepts were crucial for religion and morality, in the conceptual world of science there seemed to be no room for them in the inn.[9]

If one had to choose between the two, science seemed to promise far greater certainty than religion or metaphysics. During the religious wars of the sixteenth century, Christians actually fought and killed one another over religious differences—and the fierce conflicts led many to conclude that universal truths were simply not knowable in religion. The route to unity lay not in religion but in science. This conviction gave rise to philosophies like positivism and scientific materialism, which grant science a monopoly on knowledge (downstairs) while consigning everything else to merely private belief and cultural tradition (upstairs).

KANTIAN CONTRADICTION

A pivotal figure in the demotion of the upper story was the great German philosopher Immanuel Kant. A thin, spare man, Kant ordered his personal life like clockwork (it was said that his neighbors could set their watches by his daily walks). He also eagerly embraced the Enlightenment's clockwork image of the universe. Deeply absorbed in the new scientific findings of his day, Kant actually spent most of his life writing on science rather than philosophy, developing the first completely naturalistic account of the origin of the solar system (the nebular hypothesis). His interest in philosophy arose only after he encountered the writings of a skeptical Scot named David Hume, who seemed to undermine the credibility of Newtonian science itself.[10] This was an outrage, and Kant turned to philosophy as a tool for defending Newtonian physics from such scandalous skepticism. In the process, he recast the upper and lower stories in terms of *nature* versus *freedom*.[11]

Kant's version of the two-realm theory of truth:

FREEDOM
The Autonomous Self

NATURE
The Newtonian World Machine

What did these terms mean for Kant? *Nature* was no longer the Aristotelian nature of Thomas Aquinas; it now meant the deterministic machine of Newtonian physics. As Kant wrote, it is "necessary that everything which takes place should be infallibly determined in accordance with the laws of nature."[12]

Yet Kant also sensed the beginnings of the Romantic reaction against Newtonian determinism, which explains why he put *freedom* in the upper story. He was intensely aware that the machine image of the universe was becoming distasteful to creative and sensitive people, like artists, writers, and religious thinkers. The machine model implied that the vivid colors and sounds and smells that make the world so beautiful were not real; they were merely the secondary effects of atoms impinging on our senses. Worse, if the machine included everything, even humans, then there could be no such thing as creativity, morality, freedom, or spirit. Enlightenment science, with its clockwork universe, had begun to loom as an enemy of the humane values.

The first person to reject Enlightenment notions of progress and civilization had been Jean-Jacques Rousseau, the flamboyant Swiss rebel who gave birth to Romanticism. Humans are *not* part of the machine, he declared; they are inherently free and autonomous. Rousseau himself fled the courts of Paris for the countryside, where he could throw off cultivated manners and live freely, in harmony with nature.[13] Kant was captivated by Rousseau's idea of autonomy (though he was far too straight-laced to live it out personally). Having been raised in a devout pietistic family, Kant also believed firmly in the need for morality, and morality presupposes the freedom to make moral choices. Thus in the upper story he put freedom or autonomy—defining *autonomy* literally as being subject only to laws imposed on oneself by oneself. (In Greek, *autos* = self, *nomos* = law.) His ideal was to be influenced by nothing but one's own moral will.

This was a radical concept of autonomy. As one theologian comments, "The creation of universal [moral] law was traditionally the function of God alone, and this function is now arrogated to the individual human rational will." Thus one might even say, "Kant has made reason into God."[14]

It is crucial to realize that the two sides in Kant's dichotomy were not just independent but outright contradictory. For if nature really is the deterministic machine of Newtonian physics, then how is freedom possible? Even Kant admitted that this was a paradox (an "antinomy") that he never succeeded in resolving. The trick, he said, is somehow to think of ourselves in both ways at once: On one hand, we operate within a physical world completely determined by natural laws (downstairs); and at the same time, we participate in a conceptual world where we conceive of ourselves as free moral agents (upstairs). In that purely conceptual world, Kant also placed God, the soul, and immortality.

Yet try as he might, Kant could not maintain both sides of the paradox as equally true. For in the lower story he was talking about things that actually exist, the constituents of the real world—while in the upper story he was talking about a realm of concepts or principles that we assume only because they are necessary for morality. Since morality requires freedom of the will, we must *suppose* ourselves to be free, no matter what science says to the contrary. Since the correspondence of happiness with virtue cannot be left to mere coincidence, we must *suppose* there is a God who guarantees it. And since moral perfection cannot be attained in this life, we must *suppose* ourselves to live forever. Kant himself admits that he did "not demonstrate freedom as something actual in ourselves and in human nature," but only something that "we must presuppose." It is "only an idea of reason whose objective reality is in itself questionable."[15]

In short, the lower story is what we *know;* the upper story is what we *can't help believing.*

In the end, Kant threw up his hands and simply insisted that regardless of what science says, we must act "as if" we were free. But that little phrase gives away the store: It implies that we know better, that we're tricking ourselves, and that moral freedom is little more than a useful fiction. In Kant's formulation, says philosopher Colin Brown, freedom, God, and immortality "look suspiciously like pieces of wishful thinking."[16]

INTELLECTUALLY FULFILLED ATHEISTS

Another way to describe Kant's dichotomy is to say that the lower story became the realm of publicly verifiable *facts* while the upper story became the realm of socially constructed *values*. This is the terminology that has become widespread in our own day through the work of social scientists.

The most common terminology today is fact versus value:

VALUE
Socially Constructed Meanings

FACT
Publicly Verifiable Truth

The divide between *fact* and *value* was clinched in the late nineteenth century by the rise of Darwinism. Though Kant and others had speculated on a naturalistic origin of the universe, the picture was not complete until Darwin offered a plausible naturalistic mechanism for the origin of life. He provided the missing puzzle piece that rendered naturalism a complete and comprehensive philosophy. That's why contemporary biologist Richard Dawkins says "Darwin made it possible to be an intellectually fulfilled atheist."[17] As he explains, before Darwin it was certainly possible to be an atheist, but not an intellectually satisfied one—because you could not have a complete, comprehensive worldview. Darwin filled in the final gap in a naturalistic picture of the universe. The lower story was now seamless and self-contained.

As a result, the upper story was now completely cut off from any connection to the realm of history, science, and reason. After all, if evolutionary forces produced the human mind, then things like religion and morality are no longer transcendent truths. They are merely ideas that appear in the human mind when it has evolved to a certain level of complexity—products of human subjectivity. We create our own morality and meaning through our choices.

Of course that means we can also *re*create them whenever we choose. Nothing justifies the normative definition of, say, marriage as a lifetime union between a husband and a wife. That social pattern is not inherent and original in human nature—because *nothing* is inherent and original in human nature. Cultural patterns emerge gradually over the course of human evolution, arising by naturalistic causes and lasting only as long as they are expedient for survival.[18]

SECULAR LEAP OF FAITH

Today the fact/value dichotomy has become part of the familiar landscape of the American mind. Children pick it up every day in the typical school classroom. Fields like the humanities and social studies have been taken over by postmodernism. In English classes, teachers have tossed out their red pencils, and act as though things like correct spelling or grammar were forms of oppression imposed by those in power.

But paradoxically, if you go down the hallway to the science classroom, you'll find that there the ideal of objective truth still reigns supreme. Theories like Darwinian evolution are *not* open to question, and students are not invited to judge for themselves whether or not it is true. It is treated as public knowledge that everyone is expected to accept, regardless of their private beliefs.

By the time these students go to college, they've learned the lesson very well. Describing the students who troop into his classroom year after year, philosopher Peter Kreeft says, "They are perfectly willing to believe in objective truth in science, or even in history sometimes, *but certainly not in ethics or morality.*"[19] Do you recognize the dichotomy? The vast majority of students arrive in the classroom already convinced that science constitutes *facts* while morality is about *values*.

And what they learn in the college classroom typically reinforces this split. Let's do a close analysis of a few contemporary thinkers to show how widespread the two-realm theory of truth remains today.[20] Take, for example, Steven Pinker of MIT, a leader in the field of cognitive science, and his bestselling book *How the Mind Works*. The message of science, Pinker writes, is that the human mind is nothing more than a data-processing machine, a complex computational device. At the same time, he goes on to say, the very possibility of morality depends on the idea that we are *more* than machines—that we are capable of making free, uncoerced, undetermined choices. Here's how he states the dilemma: "Ethical theory requires idealizations like free, sentient, rational, equivalent agents *whose behavior is uncaused,*" and yet "the world, as seen by science, does not really have uncaused events."[21]

What is Pinker saying here? Let me restate it to make it even clearer: The postmodern dilemma can be summed up by saying that ethics depends on the *reality* of something that materialistic science has declared to be *unreal*.

You might think Pinker is arguing that science has disproved the foundational premise of ethics. At least, you might think that if you had not just read about Kant. For like Kant, Pinker wants to maintain *both* sides of the contradiction—by putting concepts like moral freedom in the upper story. As a scientist, Pinker accepts a materialistic, mechanistic model of human nature: "The mechanistic stance allows us to understand what makes us tick and how we fit into the physical universe." (That's his lower story.) But when he takes off his lab coat and goes home, he reverts to the traditional language of moral responsibility: "When those discussions wind down for the day, we go back to talking about each other as free and dignified human beings." (That's his upper story.)

This is not just a *divided* field of truth, it's an out-and-out contradiction—one that Pinker finds no way to resolve. He simply holds both sides of the contradiction at the same time: "A human being is *simultaneously* a machine *and* a sentient free agent, depending on the purposes of the discussion." Or, as he also puts it, depending on whether we are playing the "science game" or the "ethics game."[22]

We could represent Pinker's two-realm theory like this:

THE ETHICS GAME
Humans Have Moral Freedom and Dignity

THE SCIENCE GAME
Humans Are Data-Processing Machines

We must never forget that this is a real person, not just Exhibit A in a taxonomy of ideas—a person living in sharp existential tension between two contradictory modes of thought. It is impossible for Pinker to conduct his *personal* life on the basis of the philosophy that guides his *professional* life. Real people stubbornly refuse to act according to the mechanistic paradigm. So he is virtually forced to affirm the reality of things like freedom and dignity—*even though there is no basis for them within his own philosophy.*

Schaeffer uses a vivid image to describe this dilemma: He says modern thinkers often make a "leap of faith" from the lower story to the upper story. Intellectually they embrace scientific naturalism; that's their professional ideology. But this philosophy does not fit their real-life experience, so they take a leap of faith to the upper story where they affirm a set of contradictory ideas like moral freedom and human dignity—*even though these things have no basis within their own intellectual system.*

Pinker comes close to calling it a leap as well—he labels it *mysticism.*

"Consciousness and free will seem to suffuse the neurobiological phenomena at every level," he writes. "Thinkers seem condemned either to denying their existence or to wallowing in mysticism."[23] That is, *either* you can try to be consistent with evolutionary naturalism in the lower story—in which case you have to deny the existence of consciousness and free will. Or *else* you can affirm their existence even though they have no basis within your intellectual system—which is sheer mysticism. An irrational leap.

The secular "leap of faith":

POSTMODERN "MYSTICISM"
Moral and humane ideals have no basis in truth,
as defined by scientific naturalism.
BUT WE AFFIRM THEM ANYWAY

SCIENTIFIC NATURALISM
Humans are machines

You can understand why Schaeffer titled one of this books *Escape from Reason.* This is the great intellectual lostness of our age: that many are forced to hang their entire hopes for dignity and meaning on an upper-story realm that they themselves regard as noncognitive and unverifiable.

WAR OF WORLDVIEWS

To show how common this pattern is, let's consider a few more examples. Pinker's colleague at MIT, Marvin Minsky, is famous for his catchy phrase that the human mind is nothing but "a three-pound computer made of meat." But in his book *The Society of Mind,* he too takes a leap of faith. "The physical world provides no room for freedom of will," he writes. And yet, "that concept is essential to our models of the mental realm. Too much of our psychology is based on it for us to ever give it up. [And so] We're virtually forced to maintain that belief, *even though we know it's false.*"[24]

This is an astounding statement. Because people are made in the image of God, they unavoidably and inescapably believe in things like human freedom—yet they "know" these ideas are false, based on materialistic philosophy. The upper story has been reduced to a realm of false but necessary illusions.

Philosopher John Searle says there are two pictures of the universe that "are really at war" with one another. Science gives a picture of the universe as a vast machine, regular and law-like in its behavior. But everyday experience gives a picture of humans as agents capable of conscious, rational decision making. This universal experience is so compelling, Searle says, that "we can't give up our conviction of our own freedom, *even though there's no ground for it.*"[25] No ground, that is, within scientific materialism.

What he's saying is that he has to take a leap into the upper story—where he believes things even though there's no rational ground for them.

This is the tragedy of the postmodern age: The things that matter most in life—freedom and dignity, meaning and significance—have been reduced to nothing but useful fictions. Wishful thinking. Irrational mysticism.

YOUR WORLDVIEW IS TOO SMALL

The key to understanding the dynamics of the two stories is to recognize the symbiotic relationship between them. It is *because* the lower story has been defined in terms of scientific naturalism that there is "no ground" for upper-story beliefs. Naturalism leads to a mechanistic, deterministic model of human nature that reduces ideas like freedom and dignity to useful fictions. We might say that it's *because* modernism is in the lower story that postmodern skepticism has taken over the upper story.

Whenever we hear the language of "separate realms," we can be sure that one of them will be accorded the status of objective truth, while the other is demoted to private illusion. Since the Enlightenment, the *fact* realm has steadily expanded its territory into the *value* realm until there is little or no content left there. It has been reduced to empty words that merely express our irrational wishes and fantasies, with no basis in reality as defined by scientific naturalism. Using graphic terms, Schaeffer warns that the lower story "eats up" the upper story, dissolving away all traditional concepts of morality and meaning.[26]

Again, this is not merely an intellectual analysis. We are talking about a split that divides a person's inner life, creating enormous tension. When we evangelize among people who have accepted a divided field of knowledge, we must press them to face squarely the terrifying reality of this jagged split running through their own thought world. The very fact that they have to make a leap of faith shows that the scientific naturalism they have accepted in the lower story is not an adequate worldview. It does not explain human nature as everyone experiences it—as even they themselves experience it.

When a person's worldview is too "small," there will always be some element in human nature that fails to fit the paradigm. It's like trying to stuff a person into a garbage can, to borrow an analogy from Schaeffer—an arm or a leg will always stick out.[27] Adherents of scientific naturalism freely acknowledge that in ordinary life they have to switch to a different paradigm. That ought to tell them something. After all, the purpose of a worldview is to explain the *world*—and if it fails to explain some part of the world, then there's something wrong with that worldview. "Although man may *say* that he is no more than a machine," Schaeffer writes, *"his whole life denies it."*[28]

In evangelism, our task is to bring people face to face with this contradiction—between what a person *says* he believes and what his *whole life* is telling him. The gospel then becomes good news indeed: The doctrine that we are created in the image of God gives a solid foundation for human freedom and moral significance. We do not have to resort to an irrational upper-story leap. Given the starting point of a personal God, our own personhood is completely explicable. It no longer "sticks out of the garbage can." The Christian worldview provides a firm basis for the highest human ideals.

Now we can see why it's so important that we do not put Christianity in the upper story—because then *we will have nothing to offer to people trapped in the two-story dichotomy.* We will be offering just one more irrational upper-story experience—"true for me" but not universally, objectively true. We have to insist on presenting Christianity as a comprehensive, unified worldview that addresses all of life and reality. It is not just religious truth but total truth.

IMPERIALISTIC "FACTS"

The fact/value dichotomy gives us the tools to explain a host of cultural and intellectual trends. Take, for example, the process of reductionism, or what Schaeffer referred to as the lower story "eating up" the upper story. In our own day, this process has advanced very far indeed. If the upper story has traditionally been the realm for the spirit or soul—or, as moderns say, the self—today these concepts are under heavy shelling from cognitive science (philosophy of mind). At best, our sense of self is regarded as an accidental by-product of the interaction of particles. "The physical world is a perfectly natural place," writes Searle. "It consists of particles organized into systems, some of which have evolved consciousness and intentionality."[29] That is, you and I are merely particles that have somehow evolved consciousness and a sense of personal identity.

Many scientific materialists have even begun to say there is no "self" at all—no central "I" that resides in the body and makes decisions, holds opinions, loves and hates. The popular computational theory of the mind breaks it up into an array of independently evolved modules—a collection of computers, each of which performs a highly specialized function. In a recent public forum, Pinker argued that the concept of a unified self is sheer fiction: "It's only an illusion that there's a president in the Oval Office of the brain who oversees the activity of everything."[30] Appropriately, the forum was titled, "Is Science Killing the Soul?"

One school of thought, called eliminative materialism, goes so far as to dismiss consciousness itself as an illusion. Proponents insist that mental states do not exist; and they urge us to replace language about beliefs and desires with statements about the nervous system's physical mechanisms—the activation of neurons and so on.[31] Searle suggests that we describe the product of brain processes as "mentation," just as the product of stomach processes is digestion. We may *think* that we act deliberately and consciously, but in fact the brain acts on its own, and then deceives us into thinking we acted intentionally. A Harvard psychologist named Daniel Wegner has even written a book called *The Illusion of Conscious Will*, arguing that unconscious forces control all our actions.[32]

Yet in true Kantian form, even eliminative materialists concede that the concept of a self remains a convenient fiction—one that, in practice, we cannot do without. Even though our actions are produced by unconscious forces, Wegner writes, the *feeling* of a conscious will is a useful illusion because it helps us to sort out who did what, so that we can accept moral responsibility for our actions (even though we didn't actually choose to do them).

Do you recognize the leap of faith again? Scientific naturalism rules out the objective existence of conscious will; but in ordinary experience we can't get along without it. And so it is tossed into the upper story with other useful fictions.

In a similar vein, philosopher Daniel Dennett argues that language about purposes, intentions, feelings, and so on, does not belong to science but only to what he calls "folk psychology"—the idiom of ordinary discourse. Yet *there* it is all but indispensable. Predicting people's behavior is much more reliable if we think of them *as if* they had beliefs, desires, and purposes than if we assume they are simply physical mechanisms. (It's easier to predict that Sally will go to the refrigerator if we know that she *wants* milk and that she *believes* it is in the fridge.) But that Kantian phrase *as if* is a dead giveaway that Dennett is describing an upper-story concept—one that is useful but technically false. Folk psychology is useful, says one philosopher, if we keep in mind that it is "a way of looking at things which is strictly speaking, or in some sense, false."[33]

Clearly, the *fact* realm has grown aggressively imperialistic and is rapidly colonizing the *values* realm, reducing traditional concepts of the self and moral responsibility to convenient fictions.

CONFLICTED ON CAMPUS

The dynamic between the upper and lower stories often leads to outright hostility between people representing the two sides. On today's university campus, the antagonism between them is almost palpable. On the *fact* side of the campus, in the hard sciences, an ideal of objective knowledge still holds sway. Many Christians attending secular universities can tell horror stories about Darwinist professors who ridicule students for their religious faith. By contrast, on the *value* side of campus, in the humanities and social sciences, the idea of objective truth is long since passé, and subjectivism rules in the form of postmodernism, multiculturalism, deconstructionism, and political correctness. Here we are told that truth is relative to particular interpretive communities, and that knowledge claims are at best social constructions, at worst nothing but power plays. As a university student, I found that by far the toughest challenge to my newfound faith came from a sociology class: The assumption of relativism was so pervasive that it was tough to maintain hope in the sheer *possibility* of objective truth, let alone the conviction that Christianity was true. In a recent Zogby poll, 75 percent of American college seniors said their professors teach that there is no such thing as right and wrong in a universal or objective sense—that "what is right and wrong depends on differences in individual values and cultural diversity."[34]

We might explain the campus wars by saying that as the *fact* realm grows ever more imperialistic, the *values* realm is fighting back. Postmodernists are taking aim at Enlightenment concepts of rationality and science, debunking them as expressions of Western, white, male power. In feminist algebra, the common idiom of "attacking" mathematical problems is denounced as oppressive and violent. In feminist biology, the concept of DNA as the "master molecule" directing the cell's activities is denounced as a product of masculine bias. The scientific method itself is criticized for incorporating sexist overtones of male dominance and control, which justify the "rape of the earth." Feminist Sandra Harding is notorious for suggesting that Newton's principles of mechanics should be called Newton's "rape manual."[35] Women have often introduced helpful new perspectives into scholarship, but here I'm talking about a radical, ideological feminism that works hand-in-glove with postmodernism and multiculturalism in debunking the very idea of rationality and objectivity.

Why are these movements driven by such hostility to Western rationalism? It's important to recall that the rise of Enlightenment scientism put not only religion on the defensive, but also the arts and humanities. Traditionally, the arts had been regarded as an expression of Truth. Even though they make use of myth and metaphor, the arts conveyed deep truths about the human condition. In the Enlightenment, however, rationalist critics began to denounce the arts. They argued that poetry and fairy tales—with their unicorns and dragons, monsters and fairies—were nothing but harmful illusions. The "true world" revealed by science was contrasted to the "false world" invented by poets and painters.

"Science had persuaded the intelligent that the universe was nothing but the mechanical interaction of purposeless bits of matter," writes historian Jacques Barzun. As a result, "Thoughtful people in the nineties [1890s] told themselves in all seriousness that they should no longer admire a sunset. It was nothing but the refraction of white light through dust particles in layers of air of variable density."[36] By the same token, why *paint* a sunset? It would only be painting an illusion. At best, art was nothing more than a pleasing falsehood, a Noble Lie.

As the arts lost status and prestige, artists and writers found themselves adrift, without their historical function in society. Many responded by going on the offensive, attacking the mechanistic science and industrial society that they regarded as dehumanizing—and that had made their own status so precarious.[37] Today they continue to seek redress by demonstrating the superiority of their own new analytical tools of literary analysis and deconstruction. And why not apply these tools even to the sacrosanct area of science? If all texts can be deconstructed, what makes scientific texts immune to that process?

I witnessed a fascinating altercation at a conference at Boston University on science and postmodernism several years ago. Postmodernist philosophers led off by arguing that "there are no metanarratives," meaning no overarching, universal Truths. Responding on behalf of the scientists was Nobel Prize–winning physicist Steven Weinberg, who replied: But of course there are metanarratives. After all, there's evolution—a vast metanarrative from the Big Bang to the origin of the solar system to the origin of human life. And since evolution is true, that proves there is at least *one* metanarrative.

To which the postmodernist philosophers responded, ever so politely: That's just *your* metanarrative. Evolution is merely a social construct, they said, like every other intellectual schema—a creation of the human mind.

Thus postmodernism reduces even the most cherished scientific theories to relativistic, culture-bound social constructs. Moreover, it does so in the name of "liberation" from the dead hand of rationalism—and from the impersonal, industrialized society that rationalism has produced. Even sheer irrationality is sometimes portrayed as an escape from the naturalistic "machine" of the lower story. This explains the celebration of irrationality that we witnessed in the drug culture of the 1960s, then again in the New Age movement of the 70s, and yet again in today's postmodernism. In 1978, a *New York Times* article commented that California was the first state to shift "from steel to plastic, from hardware to software, from materialism to mysticism, from reality to fantasy."[38] Mysticism? Fantasy? A stunning example of romantic postmodernism offered as a redemptive alternative to the deadening impact of materialism.

As the lower story becomes ever more naturalistic and mechanistic, it seems that the upper story compensates by becoming ever more irrational and fanciful. Flight from logic and rationality has been embraced as an escape to a larger experience of meaning.

LEFTOVERS FROM LIBERALISM

The shift to a two-story view of truth also helps to explain the rise of liberal theology. Liberalism can be tough to pin down, because individual theologians may retain different bits and pieces of historic Christian doctrine. One accepts that Jesus was divine, while another denies it. One accepts the reality of the Resurrection, or the Virgin Birth, or Jesus' miracles, while another denies it. And so on. For a long time, conservative theologians tried to oppose liberalism by scurrying about arguing individual points of doctrine, one after another. But a much more effective way to critique liberalism is to expose its epistemology (theory of truth): The crucial flaw in liberalism is that it adopts the two-layer concept of truth. It accepts a naturalistic account of science and history in the lower story, while relegating theology to the upper story where it is reduced to personal, noncognitive experience.[39]

This explains why liberal theologians insist that Scripture is full of mistakes. After all, naturalistic science and history have decreed that miracles and other supernatural events are impossible.[40] Convinced that they must accommodate to naturalism, liberals either deny the supernatural elements in Scripture or else translate them into naturalistic terms. For example, an Irish clergyman recently wrote an article claiming that "there are possible natural explanations" for all the biblical miracles: "One natural explanation of the loaves-and-fishes miracle is that the people in the crowd, moved by the words of Jesus, so effectively and generously shared the little they had that there was enough for all." Astonishingly, the clergyman intended this as a *defense* of Christianity against scientific detractors. He concludes, hopefully: "If you think about it, this could work."[41] I doubt that his scientific opponents were impressed.

After accepting naturalism in the lower story, liberal theology then tries to rebuild a new form of Christianity strictly in the upper story, cut off from any roots in nature or history. "Creation" is not something God actually did; it is merely a symbolic term for our dependence on God. "The Fall" was not an event in history; it is merely a symbol of pervasive moral corruption. "Redemption" refers to a sense of meaning and purpose that has nothing to do with whether Jesus' tomb was empty as a historical fact. The theology left over after this process is typically so thin that liberalism ends up borrowing an interpretative framework from some other source—from existentialism (neo-orthodoxy) or Marxism (liberation theology) or feminism (feminist theology) or process thought (process theology) or postmodernism. Christian categories are then reinterpreted in terms of this external conceptual framework.

The defining feature of liberalism, then, does not lie in the details of its scriptural interpretation but in its two-realm view of truth. Liberalism rips Christianity from its roots in historical fact and casts it into the upper story, where it is demoted to subjective, contentless symbols and metaphors. It then becomes, in practice, little more than spiritualized window dressing for some other, more substantial system of thought.

This segmentation of the concept of truth is completely alien to historic Christianity, which teaches that spiritual truths are firmly rooted in historical events. Paul went so far as to say that if Christ's resurrection had not happened in real history—if there were no empty tomb—then our faith would be worthless (see 1 Corinthians 15). He even claimed to know of some five hundred people who were eyewitnesses to the fact that Christ was alive after His crucifixion—which meant he was treating religious truth as susceptible to the ordinary means of verification for historical events. Of course, the Resurrection is not *only* a historical event; it also has profound and far-reaching spiritual implications. But the point is that the two are not partitioned off from one another: An event that did not occur can have no spiritual implications. The orthodox Christian holds a unified field of truth, because the God who acts in our hearts is also the God who acts in history.

EVANGELISM TODAY

The holistic unity of Christian truth has to be at the heart of our message when we engage in evangelism in a postmodern age. For many people, the traditional forms of apologetics have become ineffective. For example, arguments based on the historical reliability of the Bible work well when nonbelievers still function within an older framework where religious claims are still considered to be either true or false.[42] But today if you talk about Christianity being true or historically verifiable, many people would be puzzled. Religion is assumed to be a product of human subjectivity, so that the test of a "good" religious belief is not whether it is objectively true but only whether it has beneficial effects in the lives of those who believe it.

During my own agnostic stage, I had absorbed this attitude wholesale. My older brother Karl once quizzed a friend and me about our religious beliefs. Hesitant to admit her doubts openly, the friend was being evasive until finally my brother said, "Look, do you believe in the Resurrection—that Jesus rose historically from the dead?"

My friend paused. "Well, that's the crux of the matter, isn't it?" she replied thoughtfully.

"No, it's not," I jumped in. "The Resurrection could be a kind of parable—not historically true but expressing some spiritual truth for those who believe it." In this exchange, my friend represented the older, rationalist skeptic, who still thought in categories of true and false and empirical verifiability. I was already swept up into postmodern subjectivism, where religion is not even susceptible to such categories anymore. President Eisenhower presaged the same attitude when he said, "Our government makes no sense unless it is founded in a deeply felt religious faith—and I don't care what it is."[43] In a postmodern world, it doesn't matter whether a religion is objectively true but only whether it performs a beneficial function.

Indeed, today people are less likely to talk about *religion* at all, preferring the term *spirituality*. The magazine *American Demographics* noted that five words are rapidly becoming the mantra of the new millennium: "I'm into spirituality, not religion."[44]

What's the difference between the two? *Religion* has come to refer to the public realm of institutions, denominations, official doctrines, and formal rituals—while *spirituality* is associated with the private realm of personal experience. "Spirit is the inner, experiential aspect of religion," explains Wade Clark Roof, "institution is the outer, established form of religion."[45] Isn't it interesting that even the realm of faith itself has now been divided between public and private? And since spirituality is firmly located in the private realm of personal experience, many people find something suspect about the *very notion* of public religious institutions and official religious doctrines. This pervasive sense that faith is by definition individual and subjective may be the prime reason for the loss of credibility on the part of religious institutions in our day.

This cleavage came to light in polls tracking Americans' spiritual response to the terrorist attacks. When surveys asked people how September 11 affected their religious *feelings*, the poll numbers soared. But when surveys were asked about their actual religious *beliefs and practices* (e.g., how often do you go to church or read the Bible?), the numbers dropped down to the same level as before the attacks. "The emerging consensus seems to be that vague, comforting spirituality is healthy," concludes columnist Terry Mattingly, "but that doctrinal, authoritative religion may even be dangerous."[46] The concept of *spirituality* has come to mean an experience devoid of doctrinal content and detached from any testable historical claims—something that belongs strictly in the upper story.

SPIRIT OF THE AGE

In this climate, the crucial challenge is to present Christianity as a unified, comprehensive truth that is not restricted to the upper story. We must have the confidence that it is true on *all* levels—that it can stand up to rigorous rational and historical testing, while also fulfilling our highest spiritual ideals.

Christians are called to resist the spirit of the world, yet that spirit changes constantly. The challenges facing our generation are not the same that faced an earlier generation. In order to resist the spirit of the world, we must recognize the form it takes in our own day. Otherwise, we will fail to resist it, and indeed may even unconsciously absorb it ourselves.[47]

And haven't many of us done just that? Haven't many evangelicals shifted their beliefs to the upper story, holding them as subjective, personalized truths—"true for me" but not universally, objectively true? "A significant percentage of Americans have inherited a theistic world from previous generations which they have 'syncretized' with the cultural elite's relativism," writes Bill Wichterman. As a result, they end up "holding fundamentally incompatible ideas and affirming both simultaneously."[48]

For example, a survey done in the 1970s of the three largest Lutheran synods found that 75 percent of Lutherans agreed that belief in Jesus Christ is absolutely necessary for salvation. But 75 percent also agreed that all roads lead to God and it does not matter which way one takes. Based on these numbers, at least half the Lutherans polled held two mutually exclusive theological positions at the same time. How is that possible? Christians often have "bifurcated minds," explains historian Sidney Mead. "When an American asserts that belief in Jesus Christ is essential for salvation, he speaks as one programmed by exposure to Christendom's orthodox tradition. . . . But when he asserts that all roads lead to God and are equally valid, he speaks as the creature of an eighteenth-century 'Enlightenment' perspective."[49]

Have you and I made faith a matter of the heart, while letting our minds be shaped by an Enlightenment perspective? Far too often the answer is yes, writes Phillip Johnson: "Even conservative Christians have so privatized their faith that they do not regard it as a source of knowledge but as merely theological 'reflection' on topics given by secular academia."[50] As he explains, "The typical strategy is to cede to science the authority to determine the 'facts,' then try to salvage some area of Christian faith in the realm of 'value.'"[51]

But such a strategy is ultimately self-defeating. Since values are not granted the status of genuine knowledge, they end up being dismissed as subjective and arbitrary. The appeal of the term *values,* writes historian Douglas Sloan, is that it seems to refer to "the most important dimensions of human experience," such as right and wrong, good and evil, the beautiful and the ugly. "But this is an illusion," Sloan warns; "in reality it means a capitulation to the modern dualism between . . . value and fact, in which the most important domains of human experience can only be dealt with in arbitrary, irrational, and ultimately dogmatic ways."[52] Christians must find ways to make it clear that we are making claims about reality, not merely our subjective experience.

After I had given a presentation explaining the fact/value dichotomy at an education conference, a teacher stood up and said cheerfully, "In Christian education, we have both: Christianity is about *values* while education is about *facts.* So I think we're doing pretty well." Without realizing it, the teacher had completely absorbed the modern split mindset. If we really understood what those terms mean today, we would utterly reject both. Christians do not promote *values,* because we hold that Christianity is objectively true, not merely our private preference. Nor do we teach *facts* in the modern sense, because that term means "value-free" science—free from any religious framework. What Christianity offers is a unified, integrated truth that stands in complete contrast to the two-level concept of truth in the secular world.

C. S. LEWIS'S TRUE MYTH

Traditional evangelism addressed a person's *moral* "lostness," which can be an effective method when that person is aware of standing guilty before a holy God. But today many people do not believe in a transcendent moral standard; if you speak about guilt, they think you're talking about a psychological problem that requires therapy, not about true moral guilt that requires forgiveness.

Yet there is also a *metaphysical* "lostness" that we can address. The tragedy of the two-story split is that the things that matter most in life—like dignity, freedom, personal identity, and ultimate purpose—have been cast into the upper story, with no grounding in accepted definitions of knowledge. We must never treat the divided concept of truth as not merely academic; it produces an inner division between what people *think they know* (that we are merely machines in a deterministic universe) and what they desperately *want to believe* (that our lives have purpose and meaning).

This can be a soul-wrenching dilemma, and it is illustrated dramatically in the life of the well-loved writer C. S. Lewis. As a young man, Lewis abandoned his childhood faith in favor of atheism and materialism. Yet the bracing new philosophies that tantalized his intellect left his imagination hungry. As he wrote later, "Nearly all that I loved [poetry, beauty, mythology] I believed to be imaginary; nearly all that I believed to be real I thought grim and meaningless."[53]

Do you recognize the two-story division? What Lewis *thought* was real was the lower-story world of scientific materialism—but it was "grim and meaningless." What he *wished* were real was the upper-story world of myth and meaning—but he believed it to be only "imaginary."

This inner conflict created such agony that it drove Lewis's religious quest. He became desperate to find a truth that satisfied the whole person, including his longing for meaning and beauty. Eventually he abandoned materialism and adopted philosophical idealism, followed by pantheism, in an earnest effort to bring together the two conflicting realms he called "reason" and "romanticism."

C. S. Lewis spoke of reason versus romanticism:

ROMANTICISM
Beautiful but Imaginary

REASON
Repulsive but Real

What a joy it was when Lewis eventually discovered that Christianity resolved his lifelong struggle. He saw that Christ's incarnation was the fulfillment of the ancient myths that he had always loved—while at the same time a confirmable fact of history. Christianity was "the true myth to which all the others were pointing," explains one biographer. "It was a faith grounded in history and one that satisfied even his formidable intellect."[54]

To use Lewis's own punchy phrase, Christ's resurrection was a myth that became fact. It had all the wonder and beauty of a myth, answering to humanity's deepest needs for contact with the transcendent realm. And yet—wonder of wonders!—it had actually happened in time and space and history:

> The heart of Christianity is a myth which is also a fact. The old myth of the Dying God, without ceasing to be myth, comes down from the heaven of legend and imagination to the earth of history. It happens—at a particular date,

in a particular place, followed by definable historical consequences. We pass from a Balder or an Osiris, dying nobody knows when or where, to a historical Person crucified (it is all in order) under Pontius Pilate.[55]

Ironically, the turning point for Lewis came through a conversation with "the hardest boiled" atheist he'd ever known, who startled him by observing that the evidence for the historicity of the Gospels was surprisingly good: "All that stuff of [mythology] about the Dying God. Rum thing. It almost looks as if it had really happened once."[56]

Those few words brought Lewis's thoughts into sharply concentrated focus: He realized that Christianity rests on historical events that are confirmable by empirical evidence, and that at the same time express the most exalted spiritual meanings. There is no division into contradictory, opposing levels of truth—and therefore no division in a person's inner life either. Christianity fulfills both our reason and our spiritual yearnings. This is truly good news. We can offer the world a unified truth that is intellectually satisfying, while at the same time it meets our deepest hunger for beauty and meaning.

THE WHOLE TRUTH

Are we prepared to make that case to our postmodern neighbors? When we read James's injunction to "keep oneself unstained from the world" (James 1:27), we tend to interpret that in strictly moral terms—as an injunction not to sin. But it also means to keep ourselves "unstained" from the world's wrong ways of thinking, its faulty worldviews. We must learn how to identify and resist the false worldviews dominant at our moment in history. And the most pervasive thought pattern of our times is the two-realm view of truth. If we aspire to engage the battle where it is really being fought, we must find ways to overcome the dichotomy between sacred and secular, public and private, fact and value—demonstrating to the world that a Christian worldview alone offers a whole and integral truth. It is true not about only a limited aspect of reality but about total reality. It is total truth.

How do we go about crafting such a comprehensive Christian worldview? Where do we begin? In the next chapter, you will have a chance to practice hands-on worldview analysis, learning to handle the basic tools for building a Christian worldview. At the same time, you will be equipped with a simple but effective strategy for critiquing nonbiblical worldviews—so you will be ready to be used by God to liberate others from the power of false ideas as well.

4

SURVIVING THE
SPIRITUAL WASTELAND

[A Christian worldview] involves three fundamental dimensions:
the original good creation,
the perversion of that creation through sin,
and the restoration of that creation in Christ.
ALBERT WOLTERS[1]

As a teenager, I once went searching for books on Christianity at the local university library, wandering the aisles like a babe in the woods. I had just finished my senior year in high school, where I had taken an experimental class in intellectual history taught by a teacher who was a militant atheist. That was fine with me, since I had already rejected the Christian faith in which I had been reared, and was searching for my own truth. I had even written a senior paper for the class on why I no longer found Christianity credible.

But to my great surprise, when he read my paper, the same aggressively atheistic teacher urged me to slow down. "Make sure you know what you're rejecting before you try something new," he said. "Why don't you research some books on Christian philosophy before you decide to give it up." He reassured me that it was perfectly possible to be a "liberal-minded Christian"(or conversely a "closed-minded atheist"), so I didn't need to slam the door on my family background in order to pursue an honest, open-minded search for truth.

Having never heard before that there was such a thing as Christian philosophy (as opposed to theology), I promptly made my way to the local university library and looked in the card catalog under "Philosophy—Christian." Going to the shelves, I pulled out a book titled *Behold the Spirit,* by Alan Watts. Those familiar with the counterculture of the 1960s will instantly recognize that I had stumbled into a trap: Watts was a key figure in introducing Eastern religions to the West, and despite the Christian-sounding title, the book's theme was that if you delve under the surface details, Christianity really teaches the same things as Eastern mysticism. In fact, Watts taught that *all* religions are merely cultural window dressing over a common core of beliefs—a "perennial philosophy"—which regards everything as an emanation from the divine Being.

Now, I had gone to church all my life (my parents made sure of that) and also attended Lutheran elementary school. Over the years, I had memorized hymns, Bible verses, the creeds, and the Lutheran catechism, and I remain immensely grateful for that background. Yet I had never been trained in apologetics, or given tools for analyzing ideas, or taught to defend Christianity against competing "isms"—and when I read Watts's book, I was entranced. Through trips to the local bookstore, I brought home more of his books, along with works by Aldous Huxley (who promoted the same "perennial philosophy" in a book by that title) and Teilhard de Chardin (who offered a mystical spiritual evolutionism).[2]

The only person who looked over my shoulder and offered a critical perspective was my troublesome older brother Karl, who was annoying enough to point out that the content of these books deviated far from orthodox Christianity. But of course that was precisely their appeal. If I could explore exotic religious ideas while at the same time holding on to the genuine mystical core of Christianity, as these books promised, so much the better.

The story illustrates one of the most important reasons for developing a Christian worldview: to protect against absorbing alien philosophies unaware. Like so many young people, I had learned my Bible but had no clue how to relate biblical doctrine to the realm of ideas and ideologies. When I first encountered the broader intellectual world beyond the circle of family and church, I was an easy target. I had no conceptual tools to ward off challenges to the faith.

"Always [be] prepared to make a defense to anyone who asks you for a reason for the hope that is in you," Peter says (1 Pet. 3:15). The Greek word for "defense" is *apologia* (the root word in *apologetics*) and it was originally a legal term, meaning the defendant's reply to the prosecutor in a court of law. Later the same term was used of the early Christian apologists—philosophically trained theologians who defended the new faith against the rampant paganism of the Roman Empire.

But defending the faith is not only for professionally trained apologists. Just as all Christians are called to practice evangelism, so all have a responsibility to learn how to give reasons supporting the credibility of the gospel message. By "translating" Christian theology into contemporary language, we can set it side by side with other systems of thought, demonstrating that it offers a more consistent and comprehensive account of reality.

A few months ago I saw a clever advertisement that featured a rumpled, tweedy college professor glaring out at the reader, while the copy said: "Meet your son's first college professor. He is a Marxist, Atheist English professor who eats Christian freshmen for lunch."[3] That's exactly the image that ought to pop up in the minds of Christian parents when they are preparing their teens to go off to secular universities. Today basic apologetics has become a crucial skill for sheer survival. Without the tools of apologetics, young people can be solidly trained in Bible study and doctrine, yet still flounder helplessly when they leave home and face the secular world on their own. The tragedy is replayed over and over again, as Christian teenagers pack their bags, kiss their parents goodbye, and head off to secular universities, only to lose their faith before they graduate, falling prey to the latest intellectual fads.

MYSTIQUE OF THE FORBIDDEN

Like many others caught up in the counterculture of the 1960s and 70s, I plunged into Eastern thought, explored existentialism, read the early feminists, experimented with drugs, and "discovered" that truth was relative and subjective. For some teenagers, of course, the counterculture was merely fun and high jinks, but for me it was a serious search for truth and meaning. I tried mind-altering drugs only after reading books on the subject by philosophers like Aldous Huxley, who recommended drugs as a means of tapping into the cosmic consciousness. In *The Doors of Perception*, he promised that using hallucinogens would open the "reducing valve" of ordinary rationality that restricts our perceptions to the dull, mundane everyday world. Inspired by Huxley, I dipped into psychedelic drugs as part of a philosophic search for wider horizons of truth.[4]

Strange as it seems in retrospect, I first read Francis Schaeffer's *Escape from Reason* because I thought it sounded like yet another book on drugs. Before ever hearing about L'Abri, I happened on the first British edition of the book, which had a slightly eerie-looking cover illustration. And the title seemed to promise exactly what I was looking for—liberation from the dull grid of ordinary rationality. Yes, *I* want to "escape from reason," I thought as I picked up the book. Of course, I soon saw that Schaeffer's theme is precisely the opposite—that postmodern irrationality is a dead end, and that Christianity alone offers a logically consistent answer to the basic philosophical questions of life.

We need to make sure our own children leave home with that same conviction burned deeply into their minds—that Christianity is capable of holding its own when challenged in the marketplace of ideas. It is not enough to teach young believers how to have a personal quiet time, follow a Scripture memory program, and link up with a Christian campus group. We also need to equip them to respond to the intellectual challenges they will face in the classroom. Before they leave home, they should be well acquainted with all the "isms" they will encounter, from Marxism to Darwinism to postmodernism. It is best for young believers to hear about these ideas first from trusted parents, pastors, and youth leaders, who can train them in strategies for analyzing competing ideologies.

At the very least, these ideologies should be stripped of the mystique of forbidden ideas. When I was a teenager, my older sister initiated me into some of the mysteries of the wider culture—like evolution and ethical relativism—and I remember how much added allure these ideas had simply because they were something "Mother never told me." The dominant methodology in many Christian schools and churches has been to protect children from nonbiblical ideologies, and in part that is educationally sound. It makes sense to protect children until they are developmentally ready to handle complex ideas. But in many cases students are *never* exposed to competing ideas within their families, churches, or Christian schools, and as a result they go out into the world unprepared for the intellectual battles they are about to encounter, especially on secular college campuses.

NOT A SMOKESCREEN

When these young people start their classes and are confronted by new, plausible-sounding ideas, they may begin to wonder whether the adults in their lives were covering something up. They may suspect that their parents and teachers did not criticize competing ideas because there *are* no good criticisms—that they did not demonstrate how to defend Christianity because it is indefensible.

Nor do students get much help from the typical Christian campus group. The group I associated with after my conversion was spiritually committed but hopelessly anti-intellectual. As a new believer, I was still wrestling with the "isms" that had been so seductive in my pre-Christian days, but the fellowship group was unable to provide any support. One day, almost overwhelmed by the pervasive relativism taught in a sociology class, I sought the advice of one of the group leaders, asking desperately for some intellectual tools for defending the notion that there is genuine, objective truth—otherwise, how can we be sure that *Christianity* is true? His response was to steer the conversation out of intellectual territory and into familiar spiritual territory: "Nancy, it sounds like you're having a problem with assurance of salvation."

Now, I knew that I had done what was necessary for salvation: At my conversion I had carried out the requisite transaction, asking Jesus to pay the penalty for my sin, which is all that God requires. So my concerns were not theological. Instead I was struggling with doubts and second thoughts about whether God even existed, brought on by the almost smothering atmosphere of relativism in the classroom.

Despite the common stereotype, intellectual questions are not always merely a smokescreen for spiritual or moral problems. To be effective in equipping young people and professionals to face the challenges of a highly educated secular society, the church needs to redefine the mission of pastors and youth leaders to include training in apologetics and worldview. We must refuse to dismiss objections to the faith as mere spiritual subterfuge, but instead prepare ourselves to give what Schaeffer called "honest answers to honest questions."

When America was a young nation, the clergy were often the most highly educated members of the community. The congregation looked up to them and respected their intellectual expertise. But today those sitting in the pews are often as highly educated as the pastor; among the general population the clergy may even be looked down upon as narrowly trained functionaries. In this climate, it is imperative for seminaries to broaden the education of pastors to include courses on intellectual history, training future pastors to critique the dominant ideologies of our day. Pastors must once again provide intellectual leadership for their congregations, teaching apologetics from the pulpit. Every time a minister introduces a biblical teaching, he should also instruct the congregation in ways to defend it against the major objections they are likely to encounter. A religion that avoids the intellectual task and retreats to the therapeutic realm of personal relationships and feelings will not survive in today's spiritual battlefield.

HANDS-ON WORLDVIEW

Let's move now to the heart of this section of the book, giving you a chance to practice hands-on worldview construction. The grid of Creation, Fall, Redemption is not only helpful in diagnosing theological traditions, as we saw in earlier chapters. It also provides the scaffolding for constructing a Christian perspective on any topic, along with a grid for analyzing competing worldviews.

In any field, the way to construct a Christian worldview perspective is to ask three sets of questions:

1. CREATION: How was this aspect of the world originally created? What was its original nature and purpose?

2. FALL: How has it been twisted and distorted by the Fall? How has it been corrupted by sin and false worldviews? Cut off from God, creation tends to be either divinized or demonized—made into either an idol or an evil.

3. REDEMPTION: How can we bring this aspect of the world under the Lordship of Christ, restoring it to its original, created purpose?

Let's apply these categories to a few key areas—to education, the family, and then to a broad Christian social theory.

Repairing the Ruins

In Scripture, parents are repeatedly urged to pass on biblical truths to the next generation. As the Israelites were poised to enter the Promised Land, Moses emphasized the need to pass on their religious heritage to their children: "You shall teach [these words of mine] to your children, talking of them when you are sitting in your house, and when you are walking by the way, and when you lie down, and when you rise" (Deut. 11:19). The language paints an image of families passing on the faith not only through formal instruction but also through everyday conversation.

In every period of history, Christians have taken the charge of education seriously—founding schools, promoting literacy, and preserving the literary heritage of the surrounding culture. After the fall of Rome, it was the monks who carefully preserved the great literary and philosophical masterpieces of the classical world, painstakingly copying ancient manuscripts, along with commentaries and glosses to explain the meaning of the text.[5] The Reformers preached the priesthood of all believers—the responsibility of each person to know and understand the Scriptures—and they founded catechism schools to teach children the principles of the faith from an early age. When the Puritans landed on American shores and began to clear the wilderness, within a mere six years they had founded the first university (Harvard) to train young men for the ministry and for political leadership.

How, then, do we apply the categories of Creation, Fall, and Redemption to education? Creation tells us that children are created in the image of God, which means they have the great dignity of being creatures with a capacity for love, morality, rationality, artistic creation, and all the other uniquely human capabilities. Education should seek to address *all* aspects of the human person. We cannot be content with a behaviorist methodology that treats students as complex stimulus-response machines. Nor can we adopt a constructivist methodology that treats students as organisms adapting to their environment, using concepts merely as tools to organize subjective experience. Christianity gives the basis for a higher view of human nature than any alternative worldview that begins with nonpersonal forces operating by chance.[6]

Yet the biblical view of human nature is also solidly realistic. The doctrine of the Fall teaches us that children are, like all of us, prone to sin and in need of moral and intellectual direction. In the aftermath of the Fall, God gave verbal revelation to enable us to order our lives by timeless and universal truths that would otherwise be unavailable to fallen, finite creatures. Thus Christian educators will not accept the Enlightenment optimism that unaided reason, apart from divine revelation, is capable of achieving a "God's-eye" view of the world. Nor will we accept the Romantic notion that children come to earth naturally innocent, "trailing clouds of glory." Both of these philosophies deny the reality of the Fall and give birth to progressive methods of education that refrain from teaching students true from false, or right from wrong, but instead expect them to discover their own "truths."[7]

Finally, Redemption means that education should aim at equipping students to take up their vocation in obedience to the Cultural Mandate. Each child should understand that God has given him or her special gifts to make a unique contribution to humanity's task of reversing the effects of the Fall and extending the Lordship of Christ in the world. As the poet John Milton once wrote, the goal of learning "is to repair the ruins of our first parents."[8] To do that, every subject area should be taught from a solidly biblical perspective so that students grasp the interconnections among the disciplines, discovering for themselves that all truth is God's truth.

At the same time, we must be alert to the false visions of redemption that shape various theories of education today. Proponents of virtually every ideology seek to gain a foothold in the classroom, because they know that the key to shaping the future is shaping the minds of children. We may have to fend off New Age methods of meditation and guided imagery applied to the classroom (redemption through cultivating a higher consciousness); or the misuse of therapeutic techniques to change students' attitudes to fit some progressive agenda (redemption through psychological adjustment); or programs of political correctness and multiculturalism (redemption through leftist politics).[9] Many educators no longer even define education as helping students learn skills and gain knowledge, but as empowering students to enlist in approved social causes. As American culture moves away from its Christian heritage, the public classroom is becoming a battleground for competing ideologies, so that one of our most important tasks is to teach students how to identify and critique worldviews.

Retooling the Family

How does the grid of Creation, Fall, and Redemption give us tools for crafting a biblical concept of the family? As the foundational social institution, the family has functioned as the laboratory for countless social experiments. Every political visionary dreams up some scheme for retooling the family—often abolishing it altogether in favor of either radical statism or radical individualism.

Statism has been a recurring theme since the dawn of Western culture. To an astonishing degree, Western political and social thought has been hostile to the role of the family in proposed visions of the ideal society. Secular intellectuals from Plato to Rousseau to B. F. Skinner to Hilary Clinton have been enamored with the idea of putting the child directly under the care of the state rather than the family.

To counter such utopian schemes, we must begin with Creation. The biblical doctrine of creation tells us the family is a social pattern that is original and inherent in human nature itself. It is therefore normative for all times and all historical situations. Although there can be variety in the details, its essential nature cannot be remodeled at will. Any utopian scheme that seeks to cast the family into the dustbin of history will find itself working against human nature itself.

Utopians who deny Creation also deny the Fall, totally rejecting the idea that human nature is corrupt and prone to evil. Instead they redefine all social problems as temporary disorders that can be resolved through education and social engineering. "Utopians are motivated by a desire to overcome the effects of the Fall without relying on divine redemption," writes Bryce Christensen in *Utopia Against the Family.* "Most utopians wish to 'be as gods' (Gen. 3:5) through self-will and human engineering, not through the blessings of heaven."[10]

Thus is born a seductive image of Redemption through the creation of a new Eden—a return to the original state of innocence. In B. F. Skinner's famous novel *Walden Two,* the founder describes his utopian community as "an improvement on Genesis."[11]

Yet, ironically, virtually every actual historical attempt to improve on Genesis has ended in a coercive, totalitarian state. Why? Because, contrary to the utopian vision, sin is real and cannot be simply engineered out of existence. Thus the state always finds itself having to *force* people to fulfill its utopian schemes. The destruction of the family is often simply one tool for increasing government power over individuals by eliminating competing loyalties, in an attempt to create total allegiance to the state. To defend the family against statist agendas, we need to make the case that only the biblical drama of Creation, Fall, and Redemption gives a realistic yet humane account of human nature and of the structure and purpose of the family in society.

For the Love of Children

Alongside the tendency toward statism runs what seems a paradoxical tendency to reduce all social relationships to individual choice. A dramatic example can be found in Ted Peters's *For the Love of Children,* which urges a complete overhaul of the American family. Peters recommends that each parent be required to make a legal contract with each of his or her children—preferably with a public ceremony similar to a wedding ceremony. The purpose of this odd-sounding proposal? To shift the foundation of the family from biology to choice.[12]

"Whether we like it or not, the end of the road for a disintegrating liberal society is individual choice," Peters argues, implying that there is no alternative but to go along. As a liberal Lutheran, he urges Christians to discard "any premodern formalism based on divine dicta or traditional authority or natural law that would try to make an end run around choice"[13]—which is to say, not even God's commands ("divine dicta") have any force to stop us from reconfiguring the family on the basis of choice. Peters's proposal would turn the family into a collection of disconnected, atomistic individuals, bound by no attachments or obligations they do not choose for themselves. This is called ontological individualism, which means that individuals are the only ultimate reality. Relationships are not ultimate in the same sense but are derivative, created by individual choice.

It is significant that Peters begins by rejecting the biblical doctrine of creation in favor of the evolutionary approach of Process Theology—which frees him to jettison traditional Christian social philosophy.[14] For Creation implies that we are not merely disembodied wills, forming families by sheer choice; instead we are holistic beings who procreate "after our kind." We exercise our wills by choosing to submit to an objective moral order that God has ordained, not by inventing alternatives to it. The family provides a rich metaphor for the Kingdom of God precisely because it is the primary experience we have of an obligation that transcends mere rational choice, and is constitutive of our very nature.

Mobilizing the Trinity

The tug-of-war between statism and individualism in regard to the family is easier to understand if we jump to a higher level and consider social theory in general. The Rosetta Stone of Christian social thought is the Trinity: The human race was created in the image of God, who is three Persons so intimately related as to constitute one Godhead—in the classic theological formulation, *one in being* and *three in person*. God is not "really" one deity, who only appears in three modes: nor is God "really" three deities, which would be polytheism. Instead, both oneness and threeness are equally real, equally ultimate, equally basic and integral to God's nature.

The balance of unity and diversity in the Trinity gives a model for human social life, because it implies that both individuality and relationship exist within the Godhead itself. God is being-in-communion. Humans are made in the image of a God who is a tri-unity—whose very nature consists in reciprocal love and communication among the Persons of the Trinity.[15] This model provides a solution to the age-old opposition between collectivism and individualism. Over against collectivism, the Trinity implies the dignity and uniqueness of individual persons. Over against radical individualism, the Trinity implies that relationships are not created by sheer choice but are built into the very essence of human nature. We are not atomistic individuals but are created for relationships.

As a result, there is harmony between being an individual and participating in the social relationships that God intended for our lives together. This may sound abstract, but think of it this way: Every married couple knows that a marriage is more than the sum of its parts—that the relationship itself is a reality that goes beyond the two individuals involved. The social institution of marriage is a moral entity in itself, with its own normative definition. This was traditionally spoken about in terms of the common good: There was a "good" for each of the individuals in the relationship (God's moral purpose for each person), and then there was a "common good" for their lives together (God's moral purpose for the marriage itself).

In a perfect marriage unaffected by sin, there would be no conflict between these two purposes: The common good would express and fulfill the individual natures of both wife and husband. In fact, certain virtues necessary for spiritual maturity—such as faithfulness and self-sacrificing love—can be practiced *only* within relationships. That means individuals cannot fully develop their true nature unless they participate in social relationships, such as marriage, family, and the church.[16]

Ever since the Fall, however, societies have tended to tilt toward either the individual or the group. In modern cultures, family bonds are rapidly dissolving in the acids of personal autonomy. By contrast, in some traditionalist cultures, the clan or tribe still takes precedence over the individual. When I attended a Lutheran Bible school in the mid-1970s, a fellow student, a young Japanese woman, was under enormous pressure from her Buddhist family back home to renounce her Christian faith. The main barrier to Christianity in her homeland, she told me, was that most young people refused to adopt a religion different from that of their parents and extended family. This was a novel idea to me since, as a young American, being different from one's parents seemed a good reason in *favor* of adopting a religion, or anything else.

The doctrine of the Trinity has repercussions not only for our concept of the family but also for virtually every other discipline. In philosophy, the triune nature of God provides a solution to the question of the One and the Many (sometimes called the problem of unity and diversity): Ever since the ancient Greeks, philosophers have asked, Does ultimate reality consist of a single being or substance (as in pantheism) or of disconnected particulars (as in atomism)?[17] In politics, the opposing poles play out in the two extremes of totalitarianism versus anarchy. In economics, the extremes are socialism or communism versus laissez-faire individualism.

In practice, of course, most societies shuffle toward some middle ground between the two opposing poles—like America's "mixed" economy today. Yet merely hovering between two extremes is not a theoretically coherent position. A consistent worldview must offer a way to reconcile them within a consistent system. By offering the Trinity as the foundation of human sociality, Christianity gives the only coherent basis for social theory.

Nor is the answer merely theoretical. In Redemption, believers are called to form an actual society—the church—that demonstrates to the world a balanced interplay of the One and the Many, of unity and individuality. In John 17:11, Jesus prays for the disciples He is about to leave behind, asking the Father "that they may be one, *even as we are one.*" Jesus is saying that the communion of Persons within the Trinity is the model for the communion of believers within the church. It teaches us how to foster richly diverse individuality within ontologically real relationships. "The Church as a whole is an icon of God the Trinity, reproducing on earth the mystery of unity in diversity," writes

Orthodox bishop Timothy Ware. "Human beings are called to reproduce on earth the mystery of mutual love that the Trinity lives in heaven."[18] And as we learn to practice unity-in-diversity within the church, we can bring that same balance to all our social relationships—our families, schools, workshops, and neighborhoods.

THE WORLDVIEW NEXT DOOR

Apologetics involves not only defending the Christian faith but also critiquing other faiths or worldviews. Part of the task of evangelism is to free people from the power of false worldviews by diagnosing the points where they fail to stack up against reality. Just as Isaiah had to argue against the wooden idols of Old Testament times, showing how silly it was to bow down to the work of one's own hands (Isa. 44:6ff.), so today we have to deconstruct the conceptual idols that hold so many people captive.

A wonderfully simple and effective means of comparing worldviews is to apply the same grid of Creation, Fall, and Redemption. After all, every worldview or ideology has to answer the same three sets of questions:

1. CREATION: Translated into worldview terms, Creation refers to ultimate origins. Every worldview or philosophy has to start with a theory of origins: Where did it all come from? Who are we, and how did we get here?

2. FALL: Every worldview also offers a counterpart to the Fall, an explanation of the source of evil and suffering. What has gone wrong with the world? Why is there warfare and conflict?

3. REDEMPTION: Finally, to engage people's hearts, every worldview has to instill hope by offering a vision of Redemption—an agenda for reversing the "Fall" and setting the world right again.

Let's practice applying the three-part grid to some of the worldviews we all encounter. In the passages that follow, I will offer brief descriptions and excerpts from representative worldviews, and as you read along, stop and think how *you* would break down these ideas into Creation, Fall, and Redemption.

Marx's Heresy

Marxism fits the three categories of Creation, Fall, and Redemption so neatly that many have called it a religious heresy, which makes it a good sample to

start with. It also remains an important philosophy for Christians to understand: Though the Iron Curtain has fallen, Marxism retains a powerful influence in many places of the world—especially on the American university
campus. A French political philosopher recently said that nowadays when he
wants to debate a Marxist, he has to import one from an American
university.

Even more important, all of us encounter various leftist movements such
as multiculturalism, feminism, and political correctness. These liberation
movements are sometimes called *neo*-Marxist because they apply Marxist
forms of analysis to groups identified by race or gender, urging them to raise
their consciousness and throw off their oppressors. The characters have
changed, but it's still the same play.

How, then, can we use the categories of Creation, Fall, and Redemption
to analyze these various forms of Marxism?[19] For Karl Marx, the ultimate creative power was matter itself. This was a new form of philosophical materialism, for earlier versions had been static, picturing the world as a vast machine.
The problem with that conception, for Marx, was that it seemed to open the
door to the idea of God: Since a machine is designed to fulfill a particular function, it virtually requires a designer, just as a watch implies the existence of a
watchmaker.[20] To avoid that conclusion, Marx proposed that the material universe is not static but dynamic, containing within itself the power of motion,
change, and development. That's what he meant by *dialectical* materialism. He
embedded the Prime Mover within matter as the dialectical law.

In short, Marx made matter into God. His disciple, Vladimir Ilyich Lenin,
did not shy away from using explicitly religious language: "We may regard the
material and cosmic world as the supreme being, the cause of all causes, the
creator of heaven and earth."[21] The universe became a self-originating, self-
operating machine, moving inexorably toward its final goal of the classless
society.

Marx's counterpart to the Garden of Eden was the state of primitive communism. And how did humanity fall from this state of innocence into slavery
and oppression? Through the creation of private property. From this economic "Fall" arose all the evils of exploitation and of class struggle.

Redemption comes about by reversing the original sin—in this case,
destroying the private ownership of property. And the "redeemer" is the proletariat, the urban factory workers, who will rise up in revolution against
their capitalist oppressors. One historian, though not a professing Christian,
brings out the religious overtones nicely: "The savior proletariat [will], by
its suffering, redeem mankind, and bring the Kingdom of Heaven on
earth."[22]

Let's break this down now by applying the three-part grid. Without looking ahead at the answers, how would you analyze Marx's thought into
Creation, Fall, and Redemption?

CREATION

Q: What is Marxism's counterpart to Creation,
the ultimate origin of everything?

A: Self-creating, self-generating matter

A crucial subpoint under the category of Creation is one's view of human
nature. You see, humanity is always defined by its relationship to God—to
whatever is regarded as ultimate reality. In Marxism, then, we are defined by
the way we relate to matter—the way we manipulate it and make things out
of it to meet our needs. In short, by the means of production. Thus Marx's
materialism explains why he embraced economic determinism—why he
regarded everything from politics to science to religion as mere superstructure
built upon economic relations.

FALL

Q: What is Marxism's version of the Fall,
the origin of suffering and oppression?

A: The rise of private property

Notice that Marx does not identify the ultimate source of evil as a moral failing, for that would imply that humans are morally culpable—which means the
solution must be forgiveness and salvation. Instead he locates evil in social and
economic relations; thus the solution is to change those relations through revolution. Marxism assumes that human nature can be transformed simply by
changing external social structures.

REDEMPTION

Q: How does Marxism propose to set the world right again?

A: *Revolution! Overthrow the oppressors*
and recreate the original paradise of primitive communism

The day of judgment in Marxism is the day of revolution, when the evil bourgeoisie will be condemned. Marx and Engels even used the liturgical term *Dies
Irae* (the Day of Wrath), looking forward to the day when the mighty would be
cast down.[23] Marxism "is nothing less than a program for creating a new humanity and a new world in which all present conflicts will be solved," says theologian Klaus Bockmuehl. It "is a secularized vision of the kingdom of God."[24]

This analysis explains why Marxism continues to have such widespread
influence despite its dramatic failure ever to produce a classless society anywhere on earth—and why it keeps spawning neo-Marxist movements. By
incorporating all the elements of a comprehensive worldview, it taps into a
deep religious hunger for redemption. Marx's idea of the end of history, when
communism will triumph and conflict will vanish from the world "is trans-
parently a secular mutation of Christian apocalyptic beliefs," writes philosopher John Gray. It is "myth masquerading as science."

Of course, that's why it is far more powerful than science. It takes other-
worldly religious hope and secularizes it into this-worldly revolutionary zeal.[25]
"Like Christianity, Marx's thought is more than a theory," writes philosopher
Leslie Stevenson. "It has for many been a secular faith, a vision of social
salvation."[26]

Rousseau and Revolution

Let's go back before Marx to one of the sources of his ideas—Jean-Jacques
Rousseau. Most of the ideologies that bloodied the twentieth century were
influenced by Rousseau. His writings inspired Robespierre in the French
Revolution, as well as Marx, Lenin, Mussolini, Hitler, and Mao. Even Pol Pot,
who massacred a quarter of the population in Cambodia, was educated in Paris
and read his Rousseau. So if you get a grip on Rousseau's thinking, you have
a key to understanding much of the modern world.

What exactly was it that made his worldview so revolutionary? Rousseau said the way to grasp the essence of human nature was to hypothesize what we would be like if we were stripped of all social relationships, morals, laws, customs, traditions—of civilization itself. This original, pre-social condition he called the "state of nature." In it, all that exists are lone, disconnected, autonomous individuals, whose sole motivating force is the desire for self-preservation—what Rousseau called self-love (*amour de soi*). Social relationships are not ultimately real; instead they are secondary or derivative, created by individual choice.

What did that mean for Rousseau's view of society? If our true nature is to be autonomous individuals, then society is *contrary* to our nature: It is artificial, confining, oppressive. That's why Rousseau's most influential work, *The Social Contract,* opens with the famous line, "Man is born free, and everywhere he is in chains." He did not mean chains of *political* oppression, as we Americans might think: For Rousseau, the really oppressive relationships were *personal* ones like marriage, family, church, and workplace.

This line of thought represented a stark break from traditional Christian social theory, which takes the Trinity as the model of social life (as we saw above). The picture of ultimate origins given in the Bible is not one of disconnected solitary individuals wandering under the trees in a state of nature. Instead, the picture is one of a couple—male and female—related from the beginning in the social institution of marriage, forming the foundation of social life.

The implication of the doctrine of the Trinity is that relationships are just as ultimate or real as individuals; they are not the creation of autonomous individuals, who can make or break them at will. Relationships are part of the created order and thus are ontologically real and good. The moral requirements they make on us are not impositions on our freedom but rather expressions of our true nature. By participating in the civilizing institutions of family, church, state, and society, each with its own "common good," we fulfill our social nature and develop the moral virtues that prepare us for our ultimate purpose, which is to become citizens of the Heavenly City.

This explains why it was so revolutionary when Rousseau proposed that individuals are the sole ultimate reality. He denounced civilization, with its social conventions, as artificial and oppressive. And what would liberate us from this oppression?

The state. The state would destroy all social ties, releasing the individual from loyalty to anything except itself. Rousseau spelled out his vision with startling clarity: "Each citizen would then be completely *independent* of all his fellow men, and absolutely *dependent* on the state."[27] No wonder his philosophy inspired so many totalitarian systems.

Let's run these ideas through the three-part grid.

CREATION

Q: What is the starting point for Rousseau's philosophy,
his substitute for the Garden of Eden?

A: *The state of nature*

Rousseau was not alone in starting with the concept of a state of nature. Other early modern political thinkers like Thomas Hobbes and John Locke had proposed the concept as well, picturing the original human condition in terms of disconnected, atomistic individuals. They were taking their cue from Newtonian physics, which pictured the physical world in terms of atoms combining and recombining under the force of attraction or repulsion. Reflecting the same model in the social world, these early political thinkers recast society in terms of human "atoms" who are logically prior to the social arrangements in which they "bond."

The notion of a state of nature was clearly an alternative to the Garden of Eden, a new account of human origins. It "is a new myth of origins at variance with the account in Genesis," says philosopher Nancey Murphy.[28] Standing at the dawn of modernity, these thinkers sensed that in order to propose a new view of civil society, they needed to begin by offering a new creation myth. Because they were writing prior to Darwin, they were ambiguous about whether they were offering an actual historical account or merely a thought experiment. But in any case they realized that to propose a new political philosophy, they had to ground it in a new creation story.

Rousseau went further than either Hobbes or Locke, however: In his state-of-nature scenario the individual is stripped not only of social ties but of human nature itself. The earliest human is unformed, indeterminate, nothing more than a beast—a gentle, peaceful, and happy beast (in contrast to Hobbes), but a beast nonetheless. Thus Rousseau's definition of human nature is, paradoxically, not to have a nature at all—to be free to create oneself.[29] Humans have the distinctive ability to develop and transform themselves. The reason social relationships are oppressive is that they interfere with the individual's freedom to create himself.

With this concept of human nature, revolution in the modern sense became possible—not just revolt against a political regime but the attempt to destroy the entire social order and rebuild an ideal one from scratch, one that would transform human nature itself and create "the New Man." As Rousseau put it, the ideal legislator "should feel within himself the capacity to change human nature."[30] For if human nature is indeterminate and can no longer be defined positively, then there is an unlimited space for the state to impose its own definition of human nature.

FALL

Q: For Rousseau, what is the Fall, the source of oppression and suffering?

A: *Society or civilization*

In the state of nature, human beings are autonomous selves, with no ties to others except those they choose for themselves. Virtually by definition, then, any relationships *not* a product of choice are oppressive—such as the biological bonds of family, the moral bonds of marriage, the spiritual bonds of the church, or the genetic bonds of clan and race.

The only social bond where individuals retain their pristine autonomy is the contract—because there the parties are free to choose for themselves how they wish to define the terms and the extent of their agreement. The terms are not preset by God, church, community, or moral tradition but are strictly voluntary.[31] That's why Rousseau, Hobbes, and Locke all called for a state based on a "social contract." In it, all social ties would be dissolved and then reconstituted as contracts, based on choice. This was always presented in terms of liberating the individual from the oppression of convention, tradition, class, and the dead hand of the past.[32]

REDEMPTION

Q: What is the source of Redemption for Rousseau?

A: *The state*

The idea that the state could be a liberator was completely novel. In actual experience, of course, the state is a locus of power, authority, and coercion. No one had ever suggested before that it might be a liberator. Thus one Christian political theorist says Rousseau gave birth to "the politics of redemption."[33]

Historians tell us the twentieth century was the bloodiest ever, but the problem is not that large numbers of people suddenly underwent some mysterious moral degeneration. The problem is that they adopted worldviews based on faulty definitions of Creation, Fall, and Redemption.[34]

It may seem paradoxical that a philosophy of radical individualism would lead to radical statism. But as Hannah Arendt points out in *The Origins of Totalitarianism*, disconnected, isolated individuals are actually the most vulnerable to totalitarian control because they have no competing identity or loyalties.[35] That's why one of the best ways to protect *individual* rights is by protecting the rights of *groups* such as families, churches, schools, businesses, and voluntary associations. Strong, independent social groupings actually help to limit the state because each claims its own sphere of responsibility and jurisdiction, thus preventing the state from controlling every aspect of life. Neo-Calvinist political philosophy describes the independence of the social spheres using the term *sphere sovereignty,* meaning the right of each to its own limited jurisdiction over against the other spheres.[36] Catholic social thought uses the term *subsidiarity* for basically the same idea. Contrary to Rousseau, protecting moral, social, and kinship bonds actually protects individual freedom.

Unfortunately, most American political thought—both liberal and conservative—continues to rest on the atomistic view that society is made up of autonomous individuals. It is the unconscious assumption that students bring into the classroom today says one Christian professor: "Without ever having read a word of Locke, they could reproduce his notion of the social contract without a doubt in the world."[37]

In fact, I suggest that the assumption of autonomous individualism is a central factor in the breakdown of American society today. Take public policy: In *Democracy's Discontent,* Michael Sandel says the background belief of modern liberalism is the concept of the "unencumbered" self—by which he means "unencumbered by moral or civic ties they have not chosen."[38] In liberalism, the individual exists prior to its membership in moral communities such as marriage, family, church, and polity. The self is even prior to any definition of its own nature. Thus for liberalism the core of our personhood is our ability to choose our own identity—to create ourselves. This is why relationships and responsibilities are often considered separate from, and even contradictory to, our essential identity—why individuals often feel they need to break free from their social roles (as husband, wife, or parent) in order to find their "true self."[39] It is Rousseau redux.

Or take legal philosophy: In *Rights Talk,* Mary Ann Glendon says modern American law typically depicts the "natural" human person as a solitary creature. Our law is "based on an image of the rights-bearer as a self-determining, unencumbered individual, a being connected to others only by choice."[40] In other words, relationships are not constituent of our identity but are creations of individual choice—a direct echo of Rousseau's "state-of-nature" theory.

Finally, political philosophy: In *Modern Liberty and Its Discontents,* Pierre Manent says the basic tenet of liberalism is that no individual can have an obligation to which he has not consented. All human attachments are to be dissolved, and then reconstituted on the basis of choice—that is, contracts. "Through the contracts that he makes with his fellows, each individual is the author of his every obligation."[41] We now understand why Ted Peters wanted to dissolve the biological base of the family to reconstitute it on the basis of sheer choice.

Ideas like these do not remain purely abstract and academic. They filter down from professors to their students, who may well put them into practice. For example, with marriage reduced to sheer choice, many students are deciding that saying "I do" has become too risky—that it's not worth the trade-off involved in giving up their autonomy. A study from the National Marriage Project at Rutgers University found that today's young people view marriage "as a form of economic exposure and risk, largely due to the prevalence of divorce." This is the deadly fruit of the atomistic view of society. Instead of being reverenced as a social good, marriage is now feared as an economic risk. "Today's singles mating culture is not oriented to marriage," the study says. "Instead it is best described as a low-commitment culture of 'sex without strings, relationship without rings'."[42] Clearly, the ontological individualism of Hobbes, Locke, and Rousseau remains at the heart of America's social and political crisis. (For more on this subject, see appendix 1, "How American Politics Became Secularized.")

Sanger's Religion of Sex

Having raised the subject of "sex without strings," let's apply a worldview analysis to some of the cutting-edge social issues of our day. The left-right split in American politics used to be over economic issues, such as the distribution of wealth. But today the split tends to be over issues of sex and reproduction:

abortion, homosexual rights, no-fault divorce, the definition of the family, fetal experimentation, stem cell research, cloning, sex education, pornography.

In fact, a few years ago, *The Boston Globe* reported that college students have a new way to make the grade—by watching pornographic movies. Many colleges now offer courses where students analyze hard-core pornography. They're even required to shoot their own explicit films as homework to show in class. It's a new trend called "porn studies."[43]

How did students go from studying Homer to studying "Debbie Does Dallas"? The answer is that sexual liberation itself has become nothing less than a full-blown ideology, with all the elements of a worldview.

Just listen to some of the architects of the sexual revolution, like Margaret Sanger, the founder of Planned Parenthood. Most of us know Sanger as an early champion of birth control, but not everyone knows that she also wrote several books expounding a complete worldview. Sanger was a committed Darwinist, a champion of Social Darwinism and eugenics, which was very much in vogue in the early part of the twentieth century. Her goal was to construct a "scientific" approach to sexuality based squarely on Darwinism.

Sanger portrayed the drama of history as a struggle to free our bodies and minds from the constraints of morality—what she called the "cruel morality of self-denial and sin." She touted sexual liberation as "the only method" to find "inner peace and security and beauty." She even offered it as the way to overcome social ills: "Remove the constraints and prohibitions which now hinder the release of inner energies [her euphemism for sexual energies], [and] most of the larger evils of society will perish."[44]

Finally, Sanger offered this sweeping messianic promise: "Through sex, mankind will attain the great spiritual illumination which will transform the world, and light up the only path to an earthly paradise."[45]

Clearly this is a religious vision if there ever was one. Let's run it through the three-part grid:

CREATION

Q: What functions as Sanger's creation myth?
Where did humans come from?

A: *Evolution: She was an avid proponent of both
biological and Social Darwinism*

What did this mean for Sanger's view of human nature? If we are products of evolution, then our ultimate human identity is located in the biological, the natural, the instinctual—especially the sexual instincts. A few years ago, the *New Yorker* ran an article on "porn studies," and even interviewed some of the professors who teach these courses. As one of them explained: "Sex is now seen as the motive force of our beings"—our "ultimate" identity.[46]

In Sanger's day, scientists were just discovering the glands, and she concluded that healthy human development depended on the free functioning of the reproductive glands. This suggested to her that sexual restraint was actually physiologically harmful. Today those older notions have been debunked—no one knowledgeable in the field believes that sexual restraint is physically harmful. Yet sexologists do continue to believe that sexual liberation is the foundation of healthy personality development.

FALL

Q: For Sanger, what is the source of our social and personal dysfunctions?

A: The rise of Christian morality

It is Christianity, with its repressive morality, that prevents people from finding their true sexual identity, which is the core of their being—and this in turn causes all sorts of other dysfunctions. Sanger condemned "the 'moralists' who preach abstinence, self-denial, and suppression."[47]

Of course, not all sexual liberals come right out and condemn Christian morality so openly. A more common strategy is to claim that they simply want to be scientific, and that science requires a morally neutral stance. For example, Alfred Kinsey opened his major study *Sexual Behavior in the Human Male* by complaining about scientists who divide human behavior into categories of normal and abnormal. "Nothing has done more to block the free investigation of sexual behavior" than the acceptance of this moral distinction, he fumed; and he urged scientists to describe all forms of human behavior "objectively," without ethical comment. Repeatedly he emphasized that sex is "a normal biologic function, *acceptable in whatever form it is manifested.*"[48]

But of course, that statement itself expresses a moral stance. Kinsey was completely committed to a form of ethical relativism based on Darwinian naturalism—and he was smuggling in his *own* values masked as objective and neutral science. Kinsey often insisted that science is only descriptive—that it cannot prescribe what people should do. But in reality, writes historian Paul Robinson, he "had very strong opinions about what people should and should not do, and his efforts to disguise those opinions were only too transparent." The very categories of analysis he chose to use "clearly worked to undermine the traditional sexual order." Indeed, Kinsey sometimes spoke as if the introduction of a Bible-based sexual morality were *the* watershed in human history[49]—a sort of "fall" from which we must be redeemed.

REDEMPTION

Q: What do people like Sanger and Kinsey offer as means of healing and wholeness?

A: *Sexual liberation*

In the *New Yorker* article on porn studies, one professor explained that "the cultural left" has turned from changing society to "inner change"—defined primarily as discovering the true nature of one's sexuality.[50] In short, sexual liberation has itself become a moral crusade, in which Christian morality is the enemy and opposition to it is a heroic moral stance.

This is a difficult concept for Christians to get their minds around, because when we hear the word *morality* we think of biblical morality. But for many secularists, biblical morality is nothing less than the source of evil and dysfunction—while their own position has all the fervor and self-righteousness of a moral call to arms.

The conservative Jewish film critic Michael Medved learned this the hard way. He once publicly praised the work of a couple who were both Hollywood film producers. They had been together for fifteen years, had two children, and he spoke of them as a married couple. Immediately he heard from friends of the couple, who said they were certainly *not* married—and that they would be "offended" to hear themselves described that way.[51]

Offended? Why would anyone consider it an insult to be regarded as married? By rejecting marriage, you see, this couple meant to take a high-minded stand for freedom against an oppressive moral convention. The philosopher John Stuart Mill once wrote, "The mere example of nonconformity, the mere refusal to bend the knee to custom, is itself a service."[52] By giving an example of liberation, folks like this Hollywood couple feel they are performing a service to humanity. When Madonna was asked in a recent interview why she had published her raunchy book *Sex* back in 1992, she responded, "I thought I was doing a service to mankind, being revolutionary, liberating women."[53]

This attitude explains why it is so difficult to stop the sexualizing of our culture. Sexual liberation is not just a matter of sensual gratification or titillation: It is a complete ideology, with all the elements of a worldview. To stand against it, we cannot simply express moral disapproval or say, *That's wrong.* We have to remember that morality is always derivative—it stems from one's worldview. In order to be effective, we have to engage the underlying worldview.

Buddhist in the Sky

On an airplane I once found myself sitting beside a sweet-faced, black-haired woman from Thailand who was a devout Buddhist. Determined not to miss this opportunity to learn more about an Eastern religion firsthand, I peppered her with questions—and discovered that the real article is vastly different from the version that is trendy among Hollywood celebrities. Take reincarnation. In the Westernized version, cycling through ever-higher levels has the optimistic ring of evolutionary progress.[54] But for a real Buddhist, reincarnation is the wheel of *suffering*. The whole purpose of life is to escape from it.

How? Through self-denial and detachment from the things of the world. This earnest Thai woman traveled to a Buddhist monastery for a week out of each month to live in a hut with a dirt floor and no electricity in order to practice meditation. Through long hours of practice, she explained, your "muddy mind" (full of worldly concerns) can be transformed into a "clear mind" (free from all earthly attachments). And if you finally attain that level of consciousness, you will break free from the cycle of suffering. Few succeed within a single lifetime, the woman told me—mostly monks, because they have rejected the attachments of marriage and family. Yet out of hundreds of thousands of monks, maybe only one will make it.

"What about you?" I asked, knowing that she was married and had children. "Haven't you already blown it, then?"

"I don't worry about that; I just keep practicing meditation," the woman replied. She went on to explain the law of karma: "Bad thoughts attract bad things, good thoughts attract good things."

"What if you are good, and bad things still happen?" I asked.

"Then you are paying for what you did in a previous life." It struck me that Buddhism is a pretty bleak religion. Everything bad that happens is your own fault—caused by what you did either in this life or in an earlier one. There is no grace, no real hope of redemption in this lifetime. And meditation is not contact with a God who responds by listening and loving; it's merely a set of mental exercises to train the mind to detach from the material world.

In fact, there *is* no personal God in Eastern religions like Buddhism and Hinduism. The divine is a nonpersonal, noncognitive spiritual force field. The ultimate goal in these religions is not so much happiness as relief from the burden of the self: Nirvana is the merging of the individual spirit with the universal spiritual substratum to all things—losing your individuality in the pantheistic One.

When Eastern thought came to America in the 1960s, it combined with Western elements to form the New Age movement. But the core pantheistic concepts remain essentially the same. So let's apply our three-part grid to New Age thought.

CREATION

Q: What is the ultimate reality, the origin of all things, in New Age pantheism?

A: *The Absolute, the One, a Universal Spiritual Essence*

In pantheism, ultimate reality is a unified mind or spiritual essence pervading all things. It is an undifferentiated Unity beyond all human categories of thought—beyond the divisions of good and evil, subject and object. This is not a personal Being with consciousness and desires, but a nonpersonal spiritual essence of which we are all part. In fact, a personal God like the Christian deity is regarded as inferior because personality implies differentiation, which to the Eastern mind suggests limitation. The biblical idea of a God who is *both* personal *and* infinite is regarded as incomprehensible.

FALL

Q: In pantheism, what is the source of evil and suffering?

A: *Our sense of individuality*

In pantheism, the great dilemma of human existence is not sin—after all, an unconscious spiritual essence cannot care about what humans do to each other. The human dilemma is that we *don't know* we are part of god. We think we're individuals, with separate existences and identities. This is what gives birth to greed and selfishness, conflict and warfare. In Hinduism, our sense of individuality is even called "maya," which means illusion. The goal of spiritual exercises is to free our minds from the illusion of individuality.

REDEMPTION

Q: How does pantheism tell us to solve the problem of evil and suffering?

A: *By being reunited with the Universal Spiritual Essence from which we all came*

The goal of Eastern religious exercises is to reunite with the god within—to recover a sense that we are all god. This analysis helps make sense of the bewildering proliferation of techniques in the New Age movement—yoga, transcendental meditation, crystals, centering, tarot cards, diets, guided imagery, and all the rest. In spite of their vast variety, the purpose of all these techniques is to dissolve the boundaries of the self and recover a sense of universal oneness.

One reason it is important to learn how to do worldview analysis is to protect ourselves and our children from being taken in by false worldviews. A few years ago a friend of mine, a very committed Christian woman, recommended a book to me. "It's a classic," she said. "You must read it." But when I bought it, I was stunned to find that it featured a clear statement of Eastern pantheism in story form. It is a book sure to be familiar to most of you: *The Secret Garden,* by Frances Hodgson Burnett.

The main character is a ten-year-old boy named Colin, and Burnett uses him as the main mouthpiece for her pantheistic philosophy. Colin tells the other characters in the story that everything in the world is made of a single spiritual substance, which he calls "Magic." The word is always capitalized in the book—a dead giveaway that it is a code word for the divine. Colin says, "Everything is made out of Magic, leaves and trees, flowers and birds. . . . The Magic is in me. . . . It's in every one of us."[55] This Magic has marvelous, even miraculous, powers—it makes things grow, heals the sick, and makes people good. It is the ultimate power in the universe, for as one character in the book says, there could not be any "bigger Magic." Significantly, Colin even borrows explicitly Christian language: "Magic is always . . . making things out of nothing."[56]

It turns out that this is not a personal God who loves us but an impersonal force to be tapped, like electricity. As Colin puts it, "We need to get hold of Magic and make it do things for us, like electricity and horses and steam."[57] (Burnett was writing back in 1911.) And the way to "get hold" of this power is through spells and incantations. The children in the story cross their legs, "like sitting in a sort of temple," and Colin begins to chant "in a High Priest tone": *"the Magic is in me—the Magic is in me. . . . Magic, Magic, come and help."*[58]

If this isn't outright religion, I don't know what is. Yet I have known countless Christian parents and teachers who have read the book with their children—*without detecting the Eastern pantheistic worldview.* After reading the book, I wrote an article analyzing its not-so-hidden religious themes,[59] and not long afterward, my own son was assigned to read it . . . in a Christian school.

Several years later I researched Burnett's life, and learned that she was involved in Spiritualism and Theosophy (a Buddhist-inspired philosophy involving concepts such as karma, reincarnation, and pantheism).[60] But even if readers do not know her personal history, the Eastern worldview is recognizable throughout the book. It is a prime illustration of the principle that if we do not learn how to do worldview analysis—and teach our children as well—we will have no defense against the alien worldviews we encounter in the surrounding culture. And then we are likely to absorb them without even being aware of it. (For more detail on the New Age movement, see appendix 2.)

WORLDVIEW MISSIONARIES

In thinking about why we need a Christian worldview, I suggest that it is nothing less than obedience to the Great Commission. As Christians we are called to be missionaries to our world, and that means learning the language and thought-forms of the people we want to reach. In America we don't have to master a new language, but we *do* have to learn the thought-forms of our culture.[61] We need to speak to philosophers in the language of philosophy, to politicians in the language of public policy, and to scientists in the language of science.

A student in international relations once told me that the courses she was taking, designed to prepare professionals to work in other cultures, focused almost entirely on worldviews. Learning another language was considered only a preliminary step, she explained; to communicate effectively, the most important requirement was to know the habits of thought in a culture. It is no accident that Paul says Christians are called to be "ambassadors" for the heavenly King to an alien culture (2 Cor. 5:20). To be effective ambassadors, we need to prepare ourselves as thoroughly as any professional in international relations.

If the grid of Creation, Fall, and Redemption provides a simple and effective tool for comparing and contrasting worldviews, it also explains why the biblical teaching of Creation is under such relentless attack today. In any worldview, the concept of Creation is foundational: As the first principle, it shapes everything that follows. Critics of Christianity know that it stands or falls with its teaching on ultimate origins.

To become more effective ambassadors for Christ, then, we must learn how to defend the biblical view of Creation, both scientifically and philosophically. That is the theme of the next four chapters (Part 2).[62] As you work through these chapters, you will learn how to defend your faith against the challenges of Darwinian naturalism while also crafting a positive case for Intelligent Design. You will learn how a Darwinian worldview helped propel a host of damaging cultural trends, from the legalization of abortion to the decline in public education. To communicate a Christian worldview, the first step is learning how to make a winsome case for creation.

PART TWO

Starting at the Beginning

5

DARWIN MEETS
THE BERENSTAIN BEARS

[Darwinism] is supported
more by atheistic philosophical assumptions
than by scientific evidence.

HUSTON SMITH[1]

It was Darwinism that first raised doubts about my faith," recalls Patrick Glynn, author of *God, the Evidence*.[2] Raised in a Catholic home, Glynn describes himself as a serious child who was "very devout." He became an altar boy at a younger age than was officially permitted, and recalls that at the Catholic school he attended, a good half of the books in the library consisted of lives of the saints.

In seventh grade, however, the teacher presented the theory of evolution, and like the clear-sighted child in *The Emperor's New Clothes*, young Patrick immediately recognized that it contradicted all his prior religious teaching. "I stood up in class and asked the nun, If Darwin's theory is true, then how can the creation story in the Bible be true?" The poor nun was flummoxed . . . and thus the seeds of doubt were planted.

Patrick's mother urged him to talk to a local priest, who took the boy to a baseball game, bought him a hot dog, and took the opportunity to have *the talk*. Between innings, the priest explained how to reconcile Genesis with an evolutionary origin of the human race: "You don't have to believe that Adam and Eve were the *only* beings around at the time," he said. "You only have to believe that God took them and gave them souls." This seemed such an obviously ad hoc strategy that it only reinforced the boy's growing doubts.

"By the time I became a student at Harvard, I was ripe for its atmosphere of naturalism and secularism," Glynn says. In his classes, it was simply assumed that religious belief had become impossible for any rational human being. After all, "Darwin had demonstrated that it was not necessary to posit a God to explain the origin of life." If natural causes working on their own are capable of producing everything that exists, then the obvious implication is that there's nothing left for a Creator to do. He's out of a job. And if the existence of God no longer serves any explanatory or cognitive function, then the only function left is an emotional one: Belief in God is reduced to an escape hatch for people afraid to face modernity. At Harvard, Glynn says, religion was regarded as a human construct invented by primitive cultures as a defense mechanism to help them cope with the rigors of surviving. By the end of his graduate studies, he had reached the conclusion that there was no God, no soul, no afterlife, no inherent justice in the universe. "I prided myself on being realistic, even Machiavellian, in my view of the world."

It was some twenty years later, after a personal crisis, that Glynn began to question his settled certitudes of rationalism and naturalism. In *God, The Evidence* he recounts the various lines of argument that finally persuaded him that God exists after all, including the stunning evidence for design in the physical universe (which we will cover in chapter 6).

Glynn's personal story illustrates the foundational role played by a theory of origins in the formation of a worldview. As we have seen, every worldview starts with an account of Creation, which shapes its concepts of the Fall and Redemption.[3] As a result, whoever has the authority to shape a culture's Creation myth is its de facto "priesthood," with the power to determine what the dominant worldview will be. To break the power of today's secular "priesthood," Christians need to have a basic grasp of the origins controversy, with its wide-ranging impact on American thought.

As we will discover over the next four chapters, the major impact of Darwinian evolution does not lie in the details of mutation and natural selection, but in something far more significant—a new criterion of what qualifies as objective truth. As one historian explains, Darwinism led to a naturalistic view of knowledge in which "theological dogmas and philosophical absolutes were at worst totally fraudulent and at best merely symbolic of deep human aspirations."[4] Let's unpack that phrase: If Darwinism is true, then both religion and philosophical absolutes (like Goodness, Truth, and Beauty) are strictly speaking false or "fraudulent." We can still hold on to them if we really want to, but only if we're willing to place them in a separate category of concepts that are not genuinely true but "merely symbolic" of human hopes and ideals.

Do you recognize the two-story division of truth? A naturalistic view of knowledge places Darwinism in the lower story of public *facts*, while relegating religion and morality to the upper story where they are merely symbols of private *values*. As one philosophy textbook tells the story, prior to Darwin, most thinkers in America assumed "the fundamental unity of knowledge" based on the conviction of a single universal order established by

God—encompassing both the natural and the moral order. The impact of Darwinian evolution "was to shatter this unity of knowledge," reducing religion and morality to "noncognitive subjects."[5] In short, Darwinism completed the cleavage between the upper and lower stories. Today the two stories run along on parallel tracks, never meeting or merging. As you read through Part 2, you will see how this bifurcation was solidified and cemented in place, until in our own day it has become a potent instrument for debunking the objectivity of religious truth claims.

To start off, we will examine the key scientific claims and counterclaims. The current chapter will bring you up to date on the scientific case against Darwinism, while the next chapter will equip you to make a positive case in favor of Intelligent Design. After that, we will trace the broad implications of the origins controversy across all of Western culture—from ethics to education, from movies to music. Virtually every part of society has been affected by the Darwinian worldview, and in order to be effective worldview missionaries, you and I need to be prepared to show why it is mistaken, while offering a credible alternative.

A UNIVERSAL ACID

For some three hundred years after the scientific revolution, Christianity and science were thought to be completely compatible and mutually supporting. Most scientists were Christian believers, and a parson collecting biological specimens was a common sight in the countryside. The stunning complexities of nature unveiled by science were not feared as a challenge to belief in God but hailed as confirmation of His wisdom and design. Scholars as diverse as Copernicus, Kepler, Newton, Boyle, Galileo, Harvey, and Ray felt called to use their scientific gifts in praise to God and service to humanity. The application of science in medicine and technology was justified as a means of reversing the effects of the Fall by alleviating suffering and tedium.[6]

Secularizing trends eventually began to threaten the harmony between science and religion, but its final collapse came abruptly in the late nineteenth century when Charles Darwin published his theory of evolution. Darwinism was implacably naturalistic, explaining life's origin and development by strictly natural causes. It was (as we saw in chapter 3) the missing puzzle piece that completed a naturalistic picture of reality. This is when historians began concocting images of "warfare" between science and religion—especially historians who hoped the victor in the conflict would be science.

Many people are surprised to learn how recently the warfare stereotype was constructed, because today it is part of folk culture. I was once preparing a lecture while sitting outside my son's karate class. (This is how mothers of

young children get much of their work done—by the playground or the soccer field.) Another mother came over to chat, and when she heard that my topic
was Christianity and science, her eyebrows shot up in surprise: "Why? Aren't
religion and science always in conflict? Don't they disagree on just about everything?" More recently, a graduate student in aerospace engineering told me
that when her unchurched roommate learned she was a believer, her first
response was, "How can you be a Christian and study science?" Stories like
these remind us that many people still unthinkingly assume that science and
religion are in deadly opposition to one another.

To be fair, it's a stereotype deliberately cultivated in some quarters. A few
years ago, a friend of mine decided to educate himself on the origins issue, and
browsing in a bookstore he came across a book titled *Darwin's Dangerous
Idea*. "Just the thing," he thought, "for a good critique of Darwinism."

To his chagrin, my friend discovered that far from offering a critique, the
book actually gives an enthusiastic *endorsement* of Darwinism. The theory is
"dangerous" only to irrational superstitions, like traditional religion and
ethics, says the author Daniel Dennett. He calls Darwinism a "universal acid,"
an allusion to the children's riddle about an acid so corrosive that it eats
through everything—including the flask in which you are trying to contain it.
The point is that Darwinism is likewise too corrosive to be contained. It spreads
through every field of study, corroding away all traces of transcendent purpose
or morality. As Dennett puts it, Darwinism "eats through just about every traditional concept and leaves in its wake a revolutionized world-view."[7]

Public schools are urged to revolutionize their students' worldviews by
applying Darwin's "universal acid" to the beliefs they bring in from home. And
what if meddlesome parents persist in teaching their children that Darwinism
is *not* the whole story of human origins? In that case, Dennett growls, "we will
describe your teachings as the spreading of falsehoods, and will attempt to
demonstrate this to your children at our earliest opportunity." As a final insult,
he suggests putting traditional churches and rituals in "cultural zoos," along
with other artifacts from defunct cultures.[8]

Obviously, what Dennett is promoting here is not objective science but his
own personal philosophy of evolutionary materialism or naturalism. Making
an appearance in the eight-part PBS series "Evolution," Dennett informed the
audience that Darwin's great accomplishment was to reduce the design of the
universe to a product of "purposeless, meaningless matter in motion."[9] But
think about it: Is there any possible way such a statement could be tested scientifically? Any laboratory test that could confirm that the universe arose from
"meaningless matter in motion"? Clearly not. It is not a scientific theory at all,
but merely Dennett's personal philosophy.

Yet it is the philosophy that has become official orthodoxy in the public square. Half a century ago G. K. Chesterton was already warning that scientific materialism had become the dominant "creed" in Western culture—one that "began with Evolution and has ended in Eugenics." Far from being merely a scientific theory, he noted, materialism "is really our established Church."[10]

To defend a Christian worldview in our generation, we must learn how to challenge this "established Church." And a crucial first step is to demonstrate precisely that it *is* a church—a belief system or personal philosophy. Much of what is packaged and sold under the label of *science* is not really science at all but philosophical materialism. Which is to say, it is not objective truth but merely the expression of someone's personal "values." We can use the fact/value dichotomy to turn the tables, arguing that evolution itself belongs in the sphere of private, subjective "values"—which means the rest of us have no reason to regard it as authoritative. Scientists may have authority to tell us how to hybridize corn or manufacture medicines, but they have no special expertise to tell us what worldview to believe. They have no valid claim on us when they leave the bounds of science and issue metaphysical proclamations that the universe is a product of "purposeless, meaningless matter in motion." We need to develop sales resistance to such aggressive philosophical proselytizing.

KINDERGARTEN NATURALISM

These days, even young children need to be primed to think critically. Several years ago I picked up a science book for my little boy Michael, and was shocked to discover that along with the science it gave a whopping dose of philosophical naturalism. Titled *The Bears' Nature Guide*,[11] the book featured the Berenstain Bears from the extremely popular children's picture book series. As the book opens, the Bear family invites us to go on a nature walk; and after turning a few pages, we come to a two-page spread with a dazzling sunrise and the words spelled out in capital letters: "Nature . . . is all that IS, or WAS, or EVER WILL BE!"

Where have we heard those words before? You might remember them from Carl Sagan's PBS program "Cosmos." Its trademark slogan was: "The Cosmos is all that is or ever was or ever will be."[12] Those who attend a liturgical church will recognize that Sagan was offering a substitute for the *Gloria Patri* ("As it was in the beginning, is now, and ever will be").[13] The authors of the Berenstain Bear books have now repackaged Sagan's naturalistic religion for young children.

And just in case a child misses the naturalistic message, at the bottom of the page the authors have drawn a bear pointing out at the reader, saying, "Nature is you! Nature is me!"

The point is that if philosophical naturalism is appearing in books even for young children, then you *know* it has permeated the entire culture. Under the guise of teaching science, a philosophical battle is being waged. And if Christians do not frame the philosophical issues, someone else will do it—and they will not balk at preaching their message even to small children.

SPINMEISTERS IN SCIENCE

To grasp the defining role played by naturalistic philosophy, all we have to consider is how limited the evidence for Darwinian evolution really is. When pressed for observable, empirical support for the theory, Darwinists invariably reach into the same grab bag and pull out their favorite stock examples, which you can easily master. Let's look at a few of them, following loosely the lead of Jonathan Wells in *Icons of Evolution*,[14] which analyzes the illustrations used most frequently in high school and college textbooks. These are images familiar to all of us—and probably to our children as well—which means it is crucial that we learn how to evaluate them.

Darwin's Beaks

One of the most widely cited pieces of evidence for evolution is the variation among finches on the Galapagos Islands off the coast of South America. The finches are small, rather dull-looking birds, whose main claim on our interest is that their beak size differs according to the habitats where they live—suggesting that they have adapted to differing conditions. Virtually every biology textbook repeats the story of Darwin's voyage to the Galapagos as a young naturalist,[15] and contemporary biologists have gone back there to confirm his theory.

Sure enough, one study found that during a period of drought, the average beak size among the finches actually increased slightly. Apparently the only food available in the dry period were larger, tougher seeds, so that the birds with slightly larger beaks survived better. Now, we're talking about a change measured in tenths of a millimeter—about the thickness of a thumbnail. Yet it was hailed enthusiastically as confirmation of Darwin's theory. As one science writer exulted, this is evolution happening "before [our] very eyes."[16]

But that was not the end of the story. Eventually the rains returned, restoring the original range of seeds. And what happened then? The average beak size returned to normal. In other words, the change that Darwinists were so excited about turned out to be nothing more than a cyclical fluctuation. It did not put the finches on the road to evolving into a new kind of bird; it was simply a minor adaptation that allowed the species to survive in dry weather.

Which is to say, the change was a minor adjustment that allowed the finches *to stay finches* under adverse conditions. It did not demonstrate that they originally evolved from another kind of organism, nor that they are evolving into anything new (see fig. 5.1).[17]

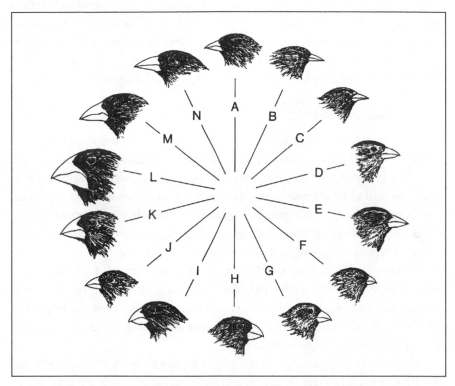

Fig. 5.1 DARWIN'S FINCHES: The change in beak size was a cyclical variation that allowed the birds to *stay finches* under adverse conditions. *(Copyright Jody Sjogren. Used with permission.)*

When the National Academy of Sciences (NAS) put out a booklet on evolution for teachers, it decided this story really needed a more positive spin. And so the booklet *did not mention* that the average beak size returned to normal. Instead it speculated what might happen if the change were to continue indefinitely for some two hundred years—whether the process would even produce a "new species of finch."[18]

This was clearly a misleading treatment of the facts, suggesting that the change was directional instead of reversible. The *Wall Street Journal* responded with an apt rejoinder by Phillip Johnson: "When our leading scientists have to resort to the sort of distortion that would land a stock promoter in jail," he said, "you know they are in trouble."[19]

Nor is the problem limited to finch beaks. Examples of minor, reversible diversification are the stock-in-trade of textbooks on biological evolution.

Another frequent example is the development of resistance to antibiotics. A highlight of the PBS "Evolution" series was a section explaining how the HIV virus becomes resistant to the drug used in treatment, due apparently to a mutation. Once again, this was hailed as evolution in action. But once again, as soon as the drug was removed, the change was reversed, and the virus returned to normal. (It became drug sensitive again.)[20] Such limited, reversible change is hardly evidence for a theory that requires *un*limited, directional change.[21]

Dysfunctional Fruit Flies

To come up with better evidence than nature offers, scientists have tried producing mutations in the laboratory, typically using fruit flies. These tiny insects reproduce in a matter of only days, which means researchers can expose them to radiation or toxic chemicals and then observe the resulting mutations over several generations. What kinds of mutations have they produced? Larger wings. Smaller wings. Shriveled wings. No wings. They even get oddities like a fly with legs growing out of its head instead of antennae.

So what does it all add up to? To be frank, dysfunctional fruit flies. After half a century of bombarding fruit flies with radiation, scientists have not coaxed them into becoming a new kind of insect—or even a new and improved fruit fly. None of the mutated forms fly as well as the original form, and probably would not survive in the wild.

There's only one mutation that could even appear to be an improvement: The PBS "Evolution" series featured a mutation that produces four wings instead of two (see fig. 5.2). Now, *that* might seem to be an evolutionary advance. But if you were watching the program, and looked closely at the television screen, you would have seen that the extra wings don't actually move. That's because they don't have any muscles; they just hang motionless, weighing down the fly like a suit of armor. If mutations are the engine that drives evolution, as Darwinism claims,[22] they certainly don't seem to be *taking* evolution anywhere.

The key to Darwin's theory is an extrapolation: It assumes that the same kind of small-scale changes we see in nature today can be extrapolated backward in time, allowing us to explain the major differences between taxonomic groups by the slow accumulation of minor changes. The problem is that minor changes simply do not add up the way the theory requires. After experimenting with fruit flies for nearly half a century, geneticist Richard Goldschmidt finally threw up his hands and said that even if you could accumulate a thousand mutations in a single fruit fly, it would still be nothing but an extremely odd fruit fly.[23] To produce a new species, you cannot simply accumulate changes in the details. Instead you need a new overall design.

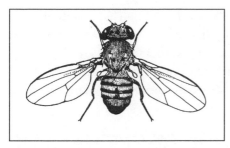

Fig. 5.2 **NORMAL and FOUR-WINGED FRUIT FLIES:** Because the mutated forms are weaker, they are *less* likely to survive in the wild. *(Copyright Jody Sjogren. Used with permission.)*

The limited nature of organic change has been common knowledge among farmers and breeders for centuries. You can breed for faster horses or larger apples, but eventually you reach a boundary that cannot be crossed, no matter how intensively you continue the breeding program. A horse will never be as fast as a cheetah, or an apple as large as a pumpkin. What's more, as you approach the boundary, organisms become progressively weaker and more prone to disease, until eventually they become sterile and die out. This has been the bane of breeding efforts since the dawn of time. Luther Burbank, possibly the most famous breeder of all times, suggested that there might even be a natural law that "keeps all living things within some more or less fixed limitations."[24]

An enormous amount of research has been carried on within the Darwinian paradigm over the past century and a half, yet success has been limited to changes *within* those "fixed limitations," like mutations in fruit flies. Research has cast virtually no light on the really important questions, like how there came to be fruit flies in the first place.[25] As one wag put it, Darwinism might explain the *survival* of the fittest, but it fails to explain the *arrival* of the fittest.

Doctored Moths

The case for naturalistic evolution has been seriously damaged in recent years by reversals in key evidence. Take the peppered moths in England, which most of us remember from photos in our high school science textbooks. The moths appear in two variants—a light gray and a darker gray—and the standard textbook story goes like this: During the Industrial Revolution, the new factories poured out smoke and soot, which darkened the tree trunks where the moths perched and made it easier for birds to see the lighter variety and eat them. Over time this process led to a larger proportion of the darker moths. This has long been touted as *the* showcase example of natural selection.

In recent years, however, a small problem has come to light: Peppered moths don't actually perch on tree trunks in the wild. (They are thought to perch in the upper canopy of trees.) How, then, do we explain the photographs we see in the textbooks? It turns out that they were staged: To create the photos, scientists glued dead moths onto the tree trunks. One scientist who helped make a television documentary acknowledged that he glued dead moths on the trees in producing the film (see fig. 5.3).[26]

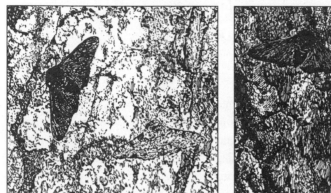

Fig. 5.3 **PEPPERED MOTHS ON TREE TRUNKS:** It turns out that the photographs were staged. *(Copyright Jody Sjogren. Used with permission.)*

Why was such a shoddy piece of scientific research accepted in the first place? And how did it attain to iconic status in evolutionary biology? Because scientists desperately wanted to believe it, says journalist Judith Hooper in a recent exposé. The problem with Darwin's theory is that evolutionary change requires thousands or millions of years, so we never actually see it happening. In the case of the peppered moth, however, for the first time evolutionary change seemed fast enough to be actually observed. It was just what Darwinists had been waiting for, and before long it had become "an irrefutable article of faith."[27]

The scandal has now been thoroughly aired in the scientific literature, to the great embarrassment of evolutionists. The peppered moth was a "prize horse in our stable of examples," lamented one well-known evolutionary biologist. Learning the truth, he said, was like learning "that it was my father and not Santa Claus who brought the presents on Christmas Eve."[28]

Yet amazingly, the moths continue to appear in science textbooks. One enterprising reporter interviewed a textbook writer who admitted he *knew* the photos were faked—but used them anyway. "The advantage of this example," the writer said, "is that it is extremely visual." "Later on," he added, students "can look at the work critically."[29] Apparently even falsified evidence is acceptable, if it reinforces Darwinian orthodoxy.

Most Famous Fake

As a junior high student, I was immensely impressed when my parents took me to a museum featuring an exhibit sure to be familiar to everyone: It showed vertebrate embryos lined up side by side—fish, amphibian, reptile, bird, and human. The point of the exhibit was to show how similar the embryos are, in order to suggest common ancestry. Darwin himself said the similarity among vertebrate embryos was "by far the strongest single class of facts in favor of" his theory.[30]

But it turns out that Darwin was misled. The embryo series was created by one of his most ardent supporters, a German scientist named Ernst Haeckel. His goal was to support a polysyllabic slogan he had coined—*ontogeny recapitulates phylogeny*—which means each individual embryo replays all the prior stages of evolution (see fig. 5.4).

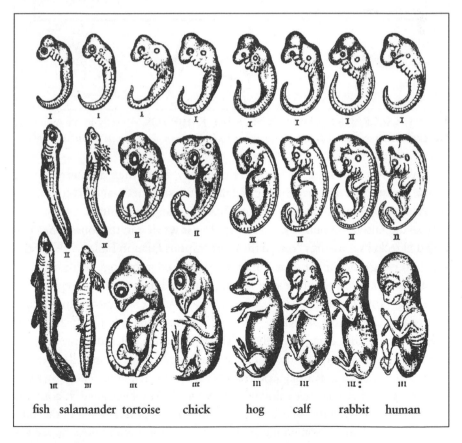

fish   salamander   tortoise   chick   hog   calf   rabbit   human

Fig. 5.4 **HAECKEL'S EMBRYOS:** Darwin was fooled by a supporter who was overly eager to "confirm" evolutionary theory. *(Copyright Jody Sjogren. Used with permission.)*

Shocking as it may seem, however, Haeckel fudged his sketches, making them look far more similar than they really are. Compare his illustrations with the more accurate ones in fig. 5.5.

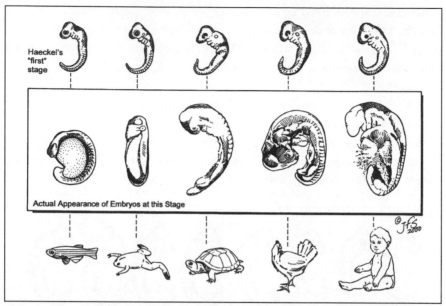

Fig. 5.5 HAECKEL'S DRAWINGS VS. REAL EMBRYOS. Already in his own day, Haeckel was accused of fraud. *(Copyright Jody Sjogren. Used with permission.)*

Even more shocking, in Haeckel's own day, more than a hundred years ago, scientists *already knew* that he had faked the sketches—and his colleagues accused him of fraud. Yet only recently has the scientific community begun to expose the falsehood publicly. An embryologist writing in the journal *Science* called Haeckel's drawings "one of the most famous fakes in biology."[31] Yet the same drawings, or similar ones, continue to be used in biology textbooks.

Haeckel's principle of recapitulation (that the human embryo replays the steps of evolution) has likewise been debunked, yet it continues to live a kind of postmortem zombie existence—often in arguments used to justify abortion. ("After all, at that stage it's only a fish or a reptile.") Columnist Michael Kinsley even used it in an attempt to support embryonic stem cell research. Technically speaking, Kinsley acknowledged, the principle of *ontogeny recapitulates phylogeny* has been discredited. Nevertheless, he argued, it contains a kernel of truth: Restated in ordinary language, in the development of the individual human being, "something similar" to evolution really does happen— namely, "that we each start out as something less than human, that the transformation takes place gradually."[32]

But if a principle is false, then restating it in the vernacular does not make it true. Biologically speaking, it is simply incorrect to say that we all start out as something less than human. The embryo is human from day one—a self-integrating organism whose unity, distinctness, and identity remain intact as it develops.

It is no coincidence that Haeckel, with his low view of life in the womb, supported race-based eugenics, and is often considered a progenitor of National Socialism. But it is odd that a contemporary liberal like Kinsley would resurrect the long-defunct argument of a racist German scientist.

BALONEY DETECTORS

How have Darwinists responded to the debunking of their icons?[33] Astonishingly, most have closed ranks to defend the use of falsified stories. For example, Bassett Maguire, a biology professor at the University of Texas, admits that the moths were staged, the embryos exaggerated. But, he told a reporter, the examples don't really matter so much as the concepts they teach. The icons represent flawed but nevertheless historic moments in science, he said, and the concepts they illustrate remain valid.[34]

This certainly shatters the idealized image of scientists as noble seekers after truth. Instead they are coming across as propagandists ready to employ useful lies.

My children have the advantage (if you can call it that) of having a mother who was a science writer for many years, and even as youngsters their antennae were super-alert to evolutionary messages. When my older son Dieter was only about six years old, he picked up an endearing habit of singing out, every time he encountered Darwinian concepts in library books or television nature programs, "Hey, Mom—evo-LOO-shun!" Together we would then examine the claims being made, contrasting them to what the evidence really shows. My goal was to help my children develop finely tuned "baloney detectors" (to borrow a phrase from Phillip Johnson[35]) to equip their young minds to evaluate the claims made on behalf of evolution.

Let's get out our own "baloney detectors" and identify the flaws in the standard Darwinian argument. The essence of Darwin's theory is that minor adaptations (sometimes called *micro*evolution) can be extrapolated over vast periods of time to explain the major differences dividing taxonomic groups (*macro*evolution). But as we have seen, small changes simply don't add up the way the theory requires. What's more, this has been public knowledge since at least 1980.

I recall the shock of opening a copy of *Newsweek* that year and reading about a landmark conference titled "Macroevolution," held at Chicago's Field Museum of Natural History.[36] What made the conference such a watershed was that the paleontologists bravely told the biologists what they least wanted to hear: that the fossil record does not, and never will, support the Darwinian scenario of a smooth, continuous progress of life forms, nicely graded from simple to complex. Instead the rocks show a pervasive pattern of gaps: New life forms appear suddenly, with no transitional forms leading to them, followed by long periods of stability during which they show little or no change at all. The late Stephen Jay Gould of Harvard dubbed this "the trade secret of paleontology"—revealing, perhaps inadvertently, how powerful the peer pressure can be among scientists. (Why did they feel the need to keep it secret?)

Darwin himself acknowledged that the most damaging evidence against his theory was the discontinuous nature of the fossil record—the lack of intermediate forms. However, he held out the hope that someday all the missing links would be discovered. And when that happened, the fossil record would finally reveal the continuous stream of transitional forms that his theory predicted.

What made the Macroevolution conference so significant was that many paleontologists finally seemed to be throwing in the towel. Since Darwin, fossil hunting has been carried on intensively for more than a century, but instead of filling in the gaps, new findings have actually made the gaps more pronounced than ever. Why? Because the fossil forms tend to fall *within* existing groups, leaving clear gaps *between* groups—just as there are clear gaps between modern animals like horses and cows, dogs and cats. Put another way, variation tends to be limited to change *within* groups, instead of leading gradually from one group to another.

Given this consistent pattern in the rocks, the paleontologists at the Macroevolution conference announced that it is irrational to keep hoping that the gaps will one day be filled in. It's time to recognize that they are here to stay. The standard picture of evolution will simply have to be revised: Instead of a smooth, continuous chain of life forms, evolution must be reconfigured as an erratic, leap-frog process. The new view was dubbed *punctuated equilibrium* (irreverently shortened to "punk eek") to denote an overall pattern of stability broken by occasional eruptions in which new forms appear suddenly out of nowhere. "Most species exhibit no directional change during their tenure on earth," Gould explained. "They appear in the fossil record looking much the same as when they disappear."[37]

This is a far cry from classic Darwinian gradualism, and it sent biologists scurrying to identify some new mechanism capable of generating sudden, large-scale, systemic changes—a search that continues to this day.[38] To use an image from Aesop's fables, evolutionary change was once modeled on the tortoise (slow and steady), but is now modeled on the hare (sudden spurts, followed by a long nap). Yet there seems to be no genetic mechanism capable of producing such a herky-jerky pattern. Large-scale mutations are usually deleterious, and often fatal. (Think: birth defects.) Thus evolution is, as the title of one influential book puts it, *A Theory In Crisis*.[39] Darwinian gradualism has been discredited, but there is as yet no broadly accepted alternative mechanism to replace it.

PUNK SCIENTISTS

With all this ferment going on, it's astonishing to see how leading scientists respond when challenged publicly—like during the public school controversies in Kansas and Ohio a few years ago. Immediately they trot out all the old examples of limited variation, like finch beaks and fruit flies and antibiotic resistance, as though they had never heard about the macroevolution controversy. The point of the controversy, after all, was that minor variations like these are *not* the engine driving macroevolution. "The central question of the Chicago [Macroevolution] conference was whether the mechanisms underlying microevolution can be extrapolated to explain the phenomena of macroevolution," wrote Roger Lewin in *Science*. With some qualifications, "the answer can be given as a clear No."[40]

Yet rather than admit that all the classic evidence is now irrelevant, the scientific establishment papers over the controversy by using the word *evolution* to cover two very different processes. On one hand, the term is applied to *limited* variation within *existing* groups, like finches and fruit flies, which is readily observed and which no one denies. On the other hand, the term is also applied to *un*limited change leading to the creation of *new* groups, which has no observational support and is completely speculative. This seems to be a deliberate equivocation of terms, a verbal trick designed to enhance the credibility of speculative evolutionary scenarios by linking them with minor variations familiar to everyone. Our baloney detectors should start ticking loudly whenever we encounter this ruse.

Nor does the newer paradigm of "punk eek" solve the problem. If you point out the problems with classic Darwinism in a typical science classroom, you will quickly be reassured that punctuated equilibrium has solved them all. But since there is no known mechanism capable of producing sudden, large-scale evolutionary change, most biologists sneak classic Darwinism in the back door. The typical tactic is to say that Darwinist evolution occurs very rapidly, and in very small populations, so that it leaves no record in the fossils. In short, the mechanism is still Darwinian variation plus natural selection, with the process merely speeded up until it is invisible. In that case, however, punk eek is nothing but a variation on the same old theme, and is subject to the same problems as classic Darwinism.[41]

BIRDS, BATS, AND BEES

Where, then, is the evidence that natural selection has the power to create the vast diversity of living things on earth? Where do we see that creative power at work? Certainly not in the standard examples cited in the typical biology textbook.

And that is a clue that something else is at work—that it is not really the evidence that persuades. The reason people can find such minor, reversible change persuasive is that they are already persuaded on other grounds—on philosophical grounds—that nature alone *must* be capable of creating all life forms. In other words, they are already persuaded of philosophical naturalism: that nature is all that exists, or at least that natural forces are all that may be invoked in science. And once people have made that philosophical commitment, they can be persuaded by relatively minor evidence.[42]

The place to focus our attention, then, is not on the scientific details but on the philosophy of naturalism. Should the definition of science restrict inquiry to natural causes alone? Or should inquiry be free to follow the evidence wherever it leads—whether it points to a natural or an intelligent cause?

Most ordinary people hold an idealized image of science as impartial, unbiased empirical investigation that attends strictly to evidence. That's the official definition found in the standard science textbook, bristling with objective-sounding words like *observation* and *testing*. The problem is that, in practice, science has been co-opted into the camp of the philosophical naturalists, so that it typically functions as little more than applied naturalism.

How do we know that? Because the only theories regarded as acceptable are naturalistic ones. Consider these words by the well-known science popularizer Richard Dawkins: *"Even if there were no actual evidence* in favor of the Darwinian theory . . . we should still be justified in preferring it over all rival theories."*[43] Why? Because it is naturalistic.

Here's the same argument, flipped over. A Kansas State University professor published a letter in the prestigious journal *Nature*, stating: *"Even if all the data point to an intelligent designer,* such an hypothesis is excluded from science because it is not naturalistic."[44] Pause for a moment and let that sink in: Even if there is *no* evidence in favor of Darwinism, and if *all* the evidence favors Intelligent Design, still we are not allowed to consider it in science. Clearly, the issue is not fundamentally a matter of evidence at all, but of a prior philosophical commitment.

A few more examples drive the point home. During the Ohio controversy, one of the drafters of the controversial state guidelines wrote a letter to *Physics Today,* insisting that, in order to be considered at all, *"the first criterion* is that any scientific theory must be naturalistic."[45] In other words, unless a theory is naturalistic, it will be ruled out before any consideration of its merits. The editor in chief of *Scientific American* then entered the fray, stating that "a central tenet of modern science is methodological naturalism—it seeks to explain the universe purely in terms of observed or testable natural mechanisms."[46] But who says we have to accept naturalism as a "central tenet" of science? As one professor I know retorted, "Who made up that rule? I don't remember voting on it."

In other words, why should we acquiesce in letting philosophical naturalists prescribe the definition of science itself? The only reason for restricting science to *methodological* naturalism is if we assume from the outset that *philosophical* naturalism is true—that nature is a closed system of cause and effect. But if it is not true, then restricting science to naturalistic theories is not a good strategy for getting at the truth.[47]

Today a naturalistic definition of science is taught as unquestioned dogma throughout the public education system, even to young students who lack the background to challenge it. Read this quotation from a typical high school textbook: "Many people believe that a supernatural force or deity created life. That explanation is not within the scope of science."[48] Notice that the book does not say creation has been proven false or discredited by facts, but only that it falls outside a certain definition of science. It has been ruled out by definition.

Another high school textbook says, "By attributing the diversity of life to natural causes rather than to supernatural creation, Darwin gave biology a sound scientific basis."[49] Note how the text equates "sound" science with philosophical naturalism.

One more example, this time from the college level: "Biological phenomena, including those seemingly designed, can be explained by purely material causes, rather than by divine creation."[50] An aggressive assertion of materialism like this is deemed acceptable in a college textbook. But a parallel passage asserting design would be deemed unacceptable.

Clearly, philosophy has gained primacy over the facts. The first question many scientists ask is not whether a theory is true, but whether it is naturalistic. They no longer consider it appropriate to ask *whether* life evolved by natural forces, but only *which* natural processes were at work. And once science has been defined in terms of naturalism, then something very close to Darwinism has to be true.[51]

Anyone who believes in naturalism or materialism "must, as a matter of logical necessity, also believe in evolution," writes Tom Bethell. "No digging for fossils, no test tubes or microscopes, no further experiments are needed." He goes on to explain:

> For birds, bats, and bees do exist. They came into existence somehow. Your consistent materialist has no choice but to allow that, yes, molecules in motion succeeded, over the eons, in whirling themselves into ever more complex conglomerations, some of them called bats, some birds, some bees. *He 'knows' that is true, not because he sees it in the genes, or in the lab, or in the fossils, but because it is embedded in his philosophy.*[52]

Precisely. Evolution wins the debate by default. Getting an exact theory of how the process happened is secondary.

Surprisingly, Darwin himself was willing to countenance alternative theories of evolution—so long as they were naturalistic. He was not wedded to his own theory of natural selection as the only mechanism of evolution, but regarded any mechanism as acceptable as long as it got rid of the concept of divine creation. "If I have erred" by exaggerating the power of natural selection, he wrote, "I have at least, as I hope, done good service in aiding to overthrow the dogma of separate creations." After listing some of the other theories offered in his day, he added: "Whether the naturalist believes in the views given by [these other writers] or by myself, signifies extremely little in comparison with the admission that species have descended from other species, and have not been created immutable."[53] It's clear that, for Darwin, evolution was not so much a specific theory as a philosophical stance—a stance that could be described as, *any mechanism is acceptable, as long as it is naturalistic.* Darwinian evolution is not so much an empirical finding as a deduction from a naturalistic worldview.

DIVINE FOOT IN THE DOOR

Harvard biologist Richard Lewontin gave the game away in a highly revealing article in the *New York Review of Books* a few years ago. Lewontin starts out by admitting the darker side of science (it makes extravagant claims, causes environmental problems, and so on). And yet, he quickly adds, we must still prefer science to any form of supernaturalism. Why? Because, "we have a prior commitment, a commitment to materialism."

This is a stunning admission that what drives the show is not the facts but the philosophy. (And who is this *we* Lewontin keeps addressing? Clearly he is assuming that his audience consists of the elites who have made that "prior commitment to materialism.")

"It's not that the methods and institutions of science somehow compel us to accept a material explanation" of the world, Lewontin explains. "On the contrary," he says, "we are forced by our *a priori* adherence to material causes to create an apparatus of investigation and a set of concepts that produce material explanations." Translation: We first accepted materialism as a philosophy, and then refashioned science into a machine for cranking out strictly materialist theories.

Finally, he warns that this materialism must be "absolute, for we cannot allow a divine foot in the door."[54] That final phrase points to what's really at stake in the evolution controversy. Why does Lewontin urge us to define science as applied materialism? Because otherwise we might let a "divine foot in the door." And we all know what happens then: When a salesman gets his foot in the door, pretty soon his brooms and brushes are all over your living room. If a "divine foot" ever got in the door of science, that would provide the groundwork for the entire Christian worldview, with its theology and biblical morality. That's what sends a shiver of fear up the spine of many secularists.

The famous duo who discovered the double-helix structure of DNA, Francis Crick and James Watson, freely admit that anti-religious motivations drove their scientific work. "I went into science because of these religious reasons, there's no doubt about that," Crick said in a recent interview. "I asked myself what were the two things that appear inexplicable and are used to support religious beliefs." He decided the two things that support religion were "the difference between living and nonliving things, and the phenomenon of consciousness."[55] He then aimed his own research specifically at demonstrating a naturalistic view of both.

Religion is just so many "myths from the past," Watson chimed in during the same interview. The discovery of the double helix, he said, gives "grounds for thinking that the powers held traditionally to be the exclusive property of the gods might one day be ours."[56]

Steven Weinberg was even more aggressively anti-religious when addressing the aptly named Freedom From Religion Foundation. "I personally feel that the teaching of modern science is corrosive to religious belief, and I'm all for that!" he said. The hope that science would liberate people from religion, he went on, is "one of the things that in fact has driven me in my life." If science helps bring about the end of religion, he concluded, "it would be the most important contribution science could make."[57] Clearly, the motives driving many evolutionists have as much to do with religion as with science.

EVOLUTION GETS RELIGION

We could even say that Darwinism itself often functions as an alternative religion. In fact, that's exactly what philosopher of science Michael Ruse does say. Ruse is a pugnacious and aggressive evolutionist, who testified in court against an Arkansas creationist statute back in 1982. While there, however, he had a conversation with the well-known creationist Duane Gish that brought him up short. "The trouble with you evolutionists is that you just don't play fair," Gish told him. You accuse us of teaching a religious view, he said, but "you evolutionists are just as religious in your way. Christianity tells us where we came from, where we're going, and what we should do on the way. I defy you to show any difference with evolution. It tells you where you came from, where you are going, and what you should do on the way."[58] In short, evolution itself functions as a religion.

The comment rankled Ruse, and he couldn't get it out of his mind. Eventually, he decided that Gish was right—that evolution really *is* "more than mere science," as he put it in a recent article. "Evolution came into being as a kind of secular ideology, an explicit substitute for Christianity." Even today, it "is promulgated as an ideology, a secular religion—a full-fledged alternative to Christianity, with meaning and morality."

Ruse hastens to reassure his readers that he himself remains "an ardent evolutionist and an ex-Christian." And yet, "I must admit that in this one complaint . . . the [biblical] literalists are absolutely right. Evolution is a religion. This was true of evolution in the beginning, and it is true of evolution still today."[59]

Ruse announced his new insight at the 1993 annual meeting of the American Association for the Advancement of Science (AAAS), where his presentation was met by stunned silence. A conference report published by an evolution advocacy group wondered, "Did Michael Ruse Give Away the Store?"[60]

But Ruse wasn't making wild allegations. He backed them up with solid examples, citing people like Stephen Jay Gould, who once claimed that evolution "liberates the human spirit." For sheer excitement, Gould added, evolution "beats any myth of human origins by light years." Since evolutionary history is entirely contingent, "in an entirely literal sense, we owe our existence, as large and reasoning mammals, to our lucky stars."[61]

"If this is not a rival to traditional Judaeo-Christian teaching," Ruse comments wryly, "I do not know what is."[62]

Ruse's analysis certainly throws new light on the controversy over teaching evolution in the classroom. Critics typically accuse Intelligent Design supporters of trying to inject religion into the classroom. For example, during the

Ohio controversy an editorial in a Columbus newspaper said, "The problem is that intelligent-design proponents want to bring religion into science classes, where it doesn't belong."[63]

The correct response is that religion is *already* in the classroom—because naturalistic evolution is itself a religion or worldview. "The so-called warfare between science and religion," wrote historian Jacques Barzun, should really "be seen as the warfare between two philosophies and perhaps two faiths." The battle over evolution is merely one incident "in the dispute between the believers in consciousness and the believers in mechanical action; the believers in purpose and the believers in pure chance."[64] To promote one faith in the public school system at public expense, while banning the other, is an example of viewpoint discrimination, which the Supreme Court has declared unconstitutional in a wide variety of cases.[65]

BERKELEY TO THE RESCUE

If the evolution controversy really is a "warfare between two philosophies," the next question is whether Christians are prepared to fight it. As we saw in Part 1, American evangelicals have not historically had a robust intellectual tradition. When I first started writing on science and worldview back in 1977, the Christian world had splintered over the issue. Most people involved had been trained as scientists, and while they were doing (and continue to do) excellent work in developing critiques of evolutionary theory, they were still losing the battle. Why? Because they did not think in terms of underlying worldviews.

As a result, instead of joining together to oppose the hegemony of the naturalistic worldview, Christians often got caught up in fighting each other. The bitterest debates were often not with atheistic evolutionists but among believers with conflicting scientific views: young-earth creationists, old-earth creationists, flood geologists, progressive creationists, "gap" theorists, and theistic evolutionists. There were endless arguments over theological questions like the length of the creation "days" and the extent of the Genesis flood.

Meanwhile, secularists were happy to fan the flames. As Phillip Johnson once put it, "They all but said, 'Let us hold your coats while you fight.'"[66] For if Christians were going to endlessly divide, then it was clear that secularists would conquer.

It was Johnson himself, more than anyone else, who refocused the debate and brought about a rapprochement of the warring camps under the umbrella of the Intelligent Design movement.[67] Johnson converted to Christianity in his late thirties, at the peak of a highly successful career as a law professor at the

University of California at Berkeley. Perhaps he was suffering the malaise of those to whom success has come too easily and too early, for he was already asking the classic midlife questions: Is this all there is to life? Then his wife got caught up in the trendy feminism of the seventies and walked out, leaving him with the house and kids. Disillusioned with both his professional and his personal life, Johnson began to look for something more than the pragmatic success ethic that had governed his thinking so far, and he began considering the case for Christianity.

That meant taking on Darwinism. If you want to know whether the Christian worldview is "fact or fantasy," Johnson said in a recent interview, then "Darwinism is a logical place to begin because, if Darwinism is true, Christian metaphysics is fantasy." More than any other factor, Darwinism is the reason Christianity is marginalized and dismissed in mainstream academia.[68]

Johnson's critiques of evolution (in books like *Darwin on Trial* and *Reason in the Balance*)[69] have had an enormous impact. Having spent much of his life as a cynical secularist, Johnson was well versed in the latest intellectual fads and knew how to speak the language of secular academia. Equally important, Johnson crafted a new battle strategy that has proven remarkably effective in winning a respectful hearing for the concept of Intelligent Design. What made his strategy so effective is that Johnson did not come into the fray with yet another position to defend. Instead he introduced a paradigm shift: He urged Christians to stop fighting *each other* and to rally together behind the crucial point of confrontation with the *secular* world—namely, its embrace of naturalistic philosophy.

Luther once said that if we fight on all fronts except the one actually under attack at the moment, then we are not really fighting the battle. And what is the point under attack today? Mainstream evolutionists may disagree with one another over the precise mechanism and timing of evolution (whether natural selection needs to be supplemented by other mechanisms); but they all agree that it happened by blind, undirected natural causes. On the other side of the divide, Christians may argue with one another over secondary questions like *when* God created the universe (whether it is young or old); but they all agree that the universe is the handiwork of a personal God. Thus the heart of the battle is whether the universe is the result of Intelligent Agency or of blind, noncognitive forces—and that's where we must direct our energies. Christians need to bracket peripheral issues and focus on the crucial point of whether there is evidence for Intelligent Design in the universe.[70]

CLOSED SYSTEM, CLOSED MINDS

Johnson's way of framing the debate parallels in many ways the approach Francis Schaeffer crafted for cultural apologetics. When long-haired, bearded young people began flocking to his chalet in the Alps in the 1960s and 70s seeking answers to life, Schaeffer sketched in stark outline what the basic choices are. When it comes to first principles, he noted, there are not really many viable options—in fact, only two: Either the universe is a closed system of cause and effect, or it is an open system, the product of a Personal Agent. Everything that follows stems from that fundamental choice.

During the course of my own studies at L'Abri, I listened to a tape of one of Schaeffer's best-known lectures, "Possible Answers to the Basic Philosophical Questions"[71]—replaying the tape several times because it simplified so neatly the quest for truth. Every worldview has to start somewhere, Schaeffer said, and either we can start with "time plus chance plus the impersonal" or we can begin with a Personal Being who thinks, wills, and acts. Once we grasp these two basic categories and all their implications, then worldview analysis is greatly streamlined. By showing that a nonpersonal starting point fails to account for the world, we can eliminate a vast variety of philosophical systems that fall within that category—materialism, determinism, behaviorism, Marxism, utilitarianism—without needing to investigate the myriad details that distinguish them.

In a similar way, the Intelligent Design argument wonderfully streamlines the debate over origins. It cuts through the conflicting claims of a vast variety of positions by grouping them within two basic categories: Either nature is a closed system, and science is permitted to consider only blind, material forces; or else nature is an open system, and intelligence is an irreducible reality alongside natural forces. Darwinism functions as the scientific underpinning for the first view: that the universe is a closed system. That is why the cultural ruling class will not allow it to be seriously questioned.

The website for Internet Infidels greets visitors with an unusually candid statement of their beliefs: "Our goal is to promote a nontheistic worldview, which holds that the natural world is all that there is, a closed system in no need of a supernatural explanation and sufficient unto itself."[72] That certainly puts the matter bluntly. The fundamental question is whether the universe is a closed system or an open system, and focusing on this basic antithesis will help us follow Luther's dictum to direct our forces to the actual point of attack.

WINNING A PLACE AT THE TABLE

If the key issue is naturalistic philosophy, then the main *consequence* of naturalism, as we saw at the beginning of the chapter, is a new view of knowledge. Historically speaking, it was Darwinism more than anything else that barred the door on any consideration of Christianity as objective truth. It cemented in place the two-story division of truth that pushed religion into the upper story of *values,* defined as the irrational beliefs of certain reactionary subcultures.

As one historian explains, Darwinism caused a shift "from religion as *knowledge* to religion as *faith.*" Since there was no longer any function for God to carry out in the world, "He was, at best, a gratuitous philosophical concept derived from a personal need." If you still wanted to believe in God, that was fine, so long as you realized that your belief was "private, subjective, and artificial."[73]

Unless we understand this shift, we will not be able to decipher the debates going on all around us. For example, see if you can detect the two-story divide in these words from a position paper put out by the Arkansas Science Teachers Association (ASTA) in 2001: "Science strives to explain the nature of the cosmos while religion seeks to give the cosmos and the life within it a purpose."[74] Notice that, in this definition, religion doesn't give any actual *knowledge* about the cosmos; it addresses only questions of "purpose." Even then, it doesn't *reveal* the purpose of the cosmos but instead "gives" it one—language implying that purpose is not objectively real but only a human construction that we impose upon the material world.

Logically enough, the ASTA paper concludes that religion-based views are relativistic, and should be restricted to the private realm within "the home or within the context of religious institutions." By contrast, naturalistic evolution is universally true and should be taught to everyone in the public schools: "The goal of science is to discover and investigate universally accepted natural explanations. This process of discovery and description of natural phenomena should be taught in public schools."[75]

Thus the first hurdle for Christians is simply reintroducing the very concept that religion can be genuine knowledge. Julian Huxley once said, "Darwinism removed the whole idea of God as the Creator . . . from the sphere of rational discussion."[76] We must learn how to bring God back into the sphere of rational discussion—to win a place at the table of public discourse. We must find a way to talk about Christianity as objective knowledge, not our personal values. We must stake out a cognitive territory and be prepared to defend it.

WHAT EVERY SCHOOLCHILD KNOWS

It is unwise for Christians even to use the terminology of *values* in referring to our beliefs. Many evangelicals have become active in the public arena today, proclaiming the need to defend "Christian values." Some groups have even adopted the term in their name, like the Values Action Team in the U.S. Congress. These groups often do excellent work, yet by adopting the label *values* they unwittingly pick up baggage that could ultimately discredit their efforts. As one historian explains, "Values are for the modern mind subjective preferences, personal and social, over against the objective realities provided by scientific knowledge."[77] Allan Bloom (author of the best-seller *The Closing of the American Mind*) puts it more tersely: "Every school child knows that values are relative," and not objectively true.[78] If this meaning of the word is so obvious to "every school child" in the secular world, why haven't Christians picked up on it?

When we use the term *values,* we are broadcasting to the secular world a message that says *we are talking only about our own group's idiosyncrasies, which the rest of society should tolerate as long as it doesn't upset any important public agendas.* After all, everyone knows that ethnic subcultures often hold irrational beliefs and quaint customs, and these can be accommodated as long as we all understand that no one really believes that stuff anymore—rather like humoring an eccentric old aunt.

Some Christians don't just use the lingo but have actually capitulated wholesale to the fact/value dichotomy. Delaware was recently in the news for instituting a particularly aggressive program for teaching evolution in high schools. The reporter asked a fifteen-year-old Christian student what effect the course had on her religious beliefs. It didn't really have *any* effect, the student replied. Why not? "Religion is what you believe because of *faith*," she explained. "With science, you need *evidence* and need to back it up."[79] Notice the assumption that religion has nothing to do with evidence or reason.

In another recent example, the website for the PBS "Evolution" series includes a statement from two young people identified as science students attending a conservative Christian college. The statement says, "Science deals with the material world of genes and cells, religion with the spiritual world of value and meaning."[80] Do you see how the students have absorbed the fact/value dichotomy? Science is about facts; religion is about values. This is not even accurate: Christianity does make claims about the material world—about the origin of the cosmos, the character of human nature, and events in history, preeminently the Resurrection. Yet these students were willing to deny that their faith has any cognitive content, reducing it to subjective questions of "value and meaning."

When Christians are willing to reduce religion to noncognitive categories, unconnected to questions of truth or evidence, then we have already lost the battle. We have thrown away our chance of evangelizing people who long for a unified truth that escapes the pervasive fact/value dichotomy.

If the broader impact of Darwinism was to remove Christianity from the sphere of objective truth, then the broader significance of the Intelligent Design movement will be to bring it back. By providing evidence of God's work in nature, it restores Christianity to the status of a genuine knowledge claim, giving us the means to reclaim a place at the table of public debate. Christians will then be in a position to challenge the fact/value dichotomy that has marginalized religion and morality by reducing them to irrational, subjective experience.

To accomplish that goal, however, we must go beyond negative critiques of naturalistic evolution and lay out the positive evidence for design, putting forward a viable research program. Let's turn now to the exciting new ways Christians are crafting a positive case for Intelligent Design in the public square.

6

The Science
of Common Sense

When I first started studying,
I saw the world as composed of particles.
Looking more deeply I discovered waves.
Now after a lifetime of study,
it appears that all existence is the expression of information.

John Wheeler[1]

In a public library in Toronto, I was once chatting with a recent émigré from Ukraine named Bogdan about an article I was writing on evolution. Suddenly he looked around furtively, as if afraid of being overheard, dropped his voice, and asked, "Do you believe in Darwinism?"

Startled, and assuming that he was probably a Marxist materialist, I launched into a rambling discussion about the lack of a plausible mechanism . . . when he cut me short, leaned closer, and asked in more urgent tones, "But do you *believe* in Darwinism?"

I paused, then shook my head. "Uh. No."

Bogdan smiled ever so slightly, looked around again, and then said conspiratorially, "Neither do I."

This was 1986, before the fall of the Berlin Wall, and prior to emigrating to Canada this man had been an officer in the KGB, the Soviet secret police. Handpicked at an early age, Bogdan had been educated at the Marxism-Leninism University in Moscow, from which he had emerged as a true believer in atheistic communism. That is, until he traveled to Canada, ostensibly to visit family members but in fact on a KGB mission. Having been steeped in Marxist propaganda all his life, the experience of seeing the West firsthand destroyed all his prior mental categories, and soon after returning to Moscow he put in an application to emigrate. His wife promptly divorced him and he was shunted off to a dead-end job. But this was after the Stalin era (when he would have been summarily executed), and after many years he was finally permitted to emigrate.

As I got to know Bogdan, I learned that he was in the process of painfully dismantling the atheistic ideology that had formed the bones and sinews of his thinking for his entire life. And the crucial foundation for it all was evolution. For decades, communist authorities had held up Darwinian evolution as the trump card supporting an atheistic, materialist worldview.

"No," Bogdan repeated thoughtfully. "I don't *believe* it." And he began to talk about the obvious design and complexity of the world. His sense of design was intuitive, and he had not yet worked out all the implications. He was just beginning to open his mind to the possibility that there were more things in heaven and earth than Marx had dreamed of. But of one thing he was certain: Darwinism, along with the entire edifice of atheistic materialism that it supported, was simply false.

A sense that the universe was designed is an intuitive awareness found in virtually all cultures from the beginning of time. Even the Soviets' official state policy of atheism could not completely stamp it out. Here in America, a 1998 survey by the Skeptics' Society found that among highly educated Americans the number one reason for believing in God was seeing "good design" and "complexity" in the world. Design was cited by almost a third of respondents—29 percent—while only 10 percent said they believed in God because religion was comforting or consoling. The results were quite surprising, especially for the skeptics who had conducted the study, because it shot down the common stereotype that religion is nothing but an emotional or psychological crutch. On the contrary, for most believers the ground for faith is an essentially rational intuition: They are convinced that there is a God because the universe seems so highly ordered that it suggests the hand of a conscious Mind or Creator.[2]

That conviction would certainly have resonated with the founders of the scientific revolution—figures like Copernicus, Kepler, Newton, and Galileo—all of whom were inspired in their scientific discoveries by the conviction that they were revealing the intricate plan of a Divine Artisan.[3] If the intuition of design is so common and compelling, can we restate it in rigorous scientific terms? Can we formalize it as a scientific research program? That, in a nutshell, is the aim of the Intelligent Design movement.

LITTLE GREEN MEN

The heart of design theory is the claim that design can be empirically detected. When you think about it, this is something we do all the time in ordinary life. We distinguish readily between the products of nature and the products of intelligence. Walking on the beach, we may admire the lovely pattern of ripples running across the sand, but we know it is merely a product of the wind and the waves. If, however, we come across a sand castle with walls and turrets and a moat, do we assume it too was created by the wind and waves? Of course not. The material constituents of the castle are nothing but sand and mud and water, just like the ripples all around it. But we intuitively recognize that those starting materials have a different kind of order imposed upon them. Design theory merely formalizes this ordinary intuition—just as all of science is largely formalized common sense.[4]

An illustration that design theorists often use is Mount Rushmore. If you were driving through the mountains in South Dakota, and suddenly came upon the faces of four famous presidents carved into the rock, you would not think for a moment that they were the product of wind and rain erosion. You would instantly recognize the handiwork of an artist.

A friend of mine once took a ship up the West Coast to Canada, where he was greeted by a colorful display of flowers spelling out "Welcome to Victoria." It was a sure guarantee that the seeds were not blown there randomly by the wind.[5]

Critics say the concept of design does not belong in science. They argue that it is a "science-stopper" that puts an end to scientific investigation. The head of an evolution advocacy group recently told CNN that design theory is "not a very good science, because it's basically giving up and saying: We can't explain this; therefore, God did it."[6]

But that accusation is based on a misunderstanding. The process of detecting design is thoroughly empirical. In fact, it is already an important element in several areas of science. Back in 1967, I was startled to read a newspaper headline announcing that astronomers may have discovered radio messages coming from outer space. They dubbed the signals "LGM" to signify "Little Green Men." Later, however, they realized that the radio pulses were coming in a regular, recurring pattern like the flashing of a lighthouse, not an irregular pattern like the sequence of letters in a message. What they had discovered were not aliens but pulsars—rotating stars.

Today astronomers involved in the search for extraterrestrial intelligence (SETI) have worked out extensive criteria for recognizing when a radio signal is an encoded message and when it is just a natural phenomenon, like a pulsar. In other words, they have developed criteria for distinguishing between products of design and products of natural causes.

The same distinction is made in several other fields:

- Detectives are trained to distinguish murder (design) from death by natural causes.
- Archeologists have criteria for distinguishing when a stone has the distinctive chip marks of a primitive tool (design), and when its shape is simply the result of weathering and erosion.
- Insurance companies have steps for deciding whether a fire was a case of arson (design) or just an accident.
- Cryptologists have worked out procedures to determine whether a set of symbols is a secret message (design) or merely a random sequence.

Across all the scientific disciplines, researchers also need to know how to identify the telltale signs that an experiment has been rigged, that someone has tampered with the results. There is even a U.S. Office of Research Integrity, dubbed the Fraud Squad, which has the job of scrutinizing scientific research for signs that the data has been fudged—graphs that are a bit too neat, random numbers that are not completely random, protein blots that look too similar, and so on.[7]

A bizarre case of detecting design involved a standardized test used in the Washington state school system in 2001. Students were asked to identify a bus route based on the distances among four cities, with the correct answer being a sequence of city names: Mayri, Clay, Lee, and Turno. A perceptive tenth-grader thought the sequence sounded suspiciously like the name of Mary Kay Letourneau, a teacher who had been convicted of child molestation. When authorities investigated the company that had produced the test, sure enough, they confirmed that it was an intentional act and tracked down the culprit.[8] The student who had spotted the pattern was making a design inference—correctly, as it turned out.

It should be possible to formalize the thinking process used in all these examples, which is exactly what design theory does. Its central tenet is that the characteristic marks of design can be empirically detected. As the title of one book puts it, in nature we can uncover *Signs of Intelligence*.[9]

BLIND WATCHMAKER?

In one sense, the concept of design in nature is completely uncontroversial. Evidence for design shows up in laboratories all the time. Biologists have found that the best way to tease out the functions of various molecules in the cell is to practice "reverse engineering"—the same backward reasoning we would use if we wanted to figure out how some gadget was manufactured. Working in their laboratories, biologists take apart the complicated "molecular machines" within the cell, and then try to reconstruct the "blueprints" by which they were designed.[10]

If you listen carefully to nature programs on television, you'll often hear language that is sprinkled with references to design or biological engineering. "Every couple of minutes the narrator was talking about 'the designs of nature' and 'the blueprint of life,'" a friend of mine commented after watching a PBS nature program. "It seems scientists can't get away from the language of design."

Surprisingly, Darwin himself never denied the evidence for design. His goal, however, was to show that the same evidence could be accounted for by purely natural forces. In other words, he hoped to demonstrate that living things only *appear* to be designed, while actually being products of noncognitive forces. Natural selection was proposed as an automatic, mechanistic process that could *mimic* the effects of intelligence. As one historian puts it, Darwin hoped to show "how blind and gradual adaptation could *counterfeit* the apparently purposeful design" that seemed so obviously "a function of mind."[11]

In fact, design is such a defining feature of living things that biologist Richard Dawkins begins one of his books with this startling sentence: "Biology is the study of complicated things that give *the appearance of having been designed for a purpose.*"[12] Being an evolutionist, he then spends the rest of the book seeking to demonstrate that this prima facie "appearance" of design is false and misleading.

Titled *The Blind Watchmaker,* Dawkins's book plays off a famous metaphor formulated two hundred years ago by a clergyman named William Paley. If you find a gadget like a watch lying on the ground, Paley said, you don't have any trouble deciding that it is a product of human manufacture—made by a watchmaker. For a watch has all the diagnostic signs of design: It is a set of interconnecting, coordinated parts all directed toward a purpose (to tell time). In living things we find the same type of integrated, purposeful structures: The purpose of the eye is to see, the ear to hear, the fin to swim. Thus, Paley argued, they must likewise be products of an intelligent agent. Dawkins's claim is that Paley's intelligent agent can be replaced by a blind, unconscious process—one that produces purposeful structures without itself having any purpose or intention. Natural selection is a "blind watchmaker."

The same claim was put in remarkably clear language by George Gaylord Simpson, sounding rather like Paley except for a tendency to speak of "apparent" purpose instead of the real thing. It does seem obvious, Simpson conceded, that organisms are designed for a purpose—that "fishes have gills in order to breathe water, that birds have wings in order to fly, and that men have brains in order to think." Echoing Paley, Simpson admits that living things remind us forcefully of machines:

> A telescope, a telephone, or a typewriter is a complex mechanism serving a particular function. Obviously, its manufacturer had a purpose in mind, and the machine was designed and built in order to serve that purpose. An eye, an ear, or a hand is also a complex mechanism serving a particular function. It, too, looks as if it had been made for a purpose. This *appearance of purposefulness* is pervading in nature.

Accounting for this "apparent purposefulness," Simpson says, is a central problem for biology. But not to worry, he hastens to conclude, because Darwin has already solved it. Natural selection "achieves the aspect of purpose *without* the intervention of a purposer, and it has produced a vast plan *without* the concurrent action of a planner."[13]

In other words, both sides of the evolution debate agree that, taken at face value, living things look for all the world as though they are designed. To salvage the notion of evolution, its proponents have to show that this obvious design is not real but is instead a deceptive illusion produced by natural selection. Design theorists, on the other hand, have the advantage that design is prima facie plausible, and all they have to do is identify reliable empirical markers of intelligent agency.

Marks of Design

There are three main areas where exciting new evidence for design is being uncovered: (1) the world of the cell (biochemistry), (2) the origin of the universe (cosmology), and (3) the structure of DNA (biological information). Let's get acquainted with the major lines of argument being developed in each of these areas.

Roller Coaster in the Cell

As a young man, Darwin was greatly impressed by Paley's argument for a watchmaker; in fact, he even formulated his own theory explicitly to counter it. So let's examine Paley's reasoning more closely. When we inspect a watch, he wrote, we perceive "that its several parts are framed and put together for a purpose," namely, to tell time. The intricate interplay of parts makes no sense apart from the purpose it serves. Hence, Paley concluded, "the inference we think is inevitable, that the watch must have had a maker . . . who comprehended its construction and designed its use."

Now, living systems likewise are made of interconnected parts that are ordered toward a purpose, Paley noted; thus it is reasonable to conclude that they too were designed by a Maker. As he put it, "The marks of design are too strong to be got over."[14]

Paley adduced many examples, some of which did not support his argument well, with the result that his work was eventually discredited. Yet the core of his reasoning continues to have a great deal of validity. Paley's central argument "has actually never been refuted," says Michael Behe in his influential book *Darwin's Black Box*.[15] Behe himself has gone on to refine and update the design argument with new findings from the field of biochemistry.

Behe is a short, personable fellow with a disarming, aw-shucks manner, who is rarely seen wearing anything but his trademark jeans and plaid shirt. As a Roman Catholic, he was taught evolution as a youngster in parochial schools, and thus had no religious motivation for rejecting it. Instead it was his work in biochemistry that caused him to question Darwinian orthodoxy, by revealing the almost unthinkable complexity contracted into the tiny space of the living cell.

More than a hundred years ago, Darwin thought the living cell was extremely simple—nothing but a bubble of jelly (protoplasm). Over the past few decades, however, new technologies like the electron microscope have produced a revolution in molecular biology. We now know that the cell bristles with high-tech molecular machinery far more complex than anything devised by mere humans. Each cell is akin to a miniature factory town, humming with power plants, automated factories, and recycling centers. In the nucleus is a cellular library, housing blueprints and plans that are copied and transported to factories, each of which is filled with molecular machines that function like computerized motors. These manufacture the immense array of products needed within the cell, with the processes all regulated by enzymes that function as stopwatches to ensure that everything is perfectly timed.[16]

"The cell is thus a minute factory, bustling with rapid, organized chemical activity," writes Francis Crick of DNA fame. "Nature invented the assembly line some billions of years before Henry Ford."[17] The outside surface of the cell is studded with sensors, gates, pumps, and identification markers to regulate traffic coming in and out. Today biologists cannot even describe the cell without resorting to the language of machines and engineering.

Behe piles example upon example, but consider just one. Each cell has an automated "rapid transit system" in which certain molecules function as tiny monorail trains running along tracks to whisk cargo around from one part of the cell to another. Other molecules act as loading machines, filling up the train cars and attaching address labels. When the train reaches the right "address" in another part of the cell, it is met by other molecules that act as docking machines, opening them up and removing the supplies. To frame a mental image of the cell, picture it as a large and complex model train layout, with tracks crisscrossing everywhere, its switches and signals perfectly timed so that no trains collide and the cargo reaches its destination precisely when needed.[18]

For kids raised on computer games, a good image might be the highest level on Roller Coaster Tycoon. This is a level of complexity Darwin never dreamed of, and his theory utterly fails to account for it. Why? Because a system of coordinated, interlocking parts like this can only operate *after* all the pieces are in place—which means they must appear simultaneously, not by any gradual, piece-by-piece process. Behe coined the term *irreducible complexity* to refer to the minimum level of complexity that must be present before such a tightly integrated system can function at all.

Behe's favorite illustration is the humble mouse trap. You cannot start with the wooden base and catch a few mice . . . then add the spring and catch a few more mice . . . then add a hammer and catch even more mice. No, all the parts have to be assembled at once, or you don't catch *any* mice at all. You cannot get gradual improvement in function by adding the pieces incrementally, one at a time. Instead, the entire system has to be in place from the beginning in order to perform at all.

You see, natural selection is said to work on tiny, random improvements in function—which means it does not kick in until there is at least *some* function to select from. But irreducibly complex systems don't have *any* function until a minimum number of parts are in place—which means those parts themselves cannot be products of natural selection. We're talking about a minimum number of interacting pieces that must be present before natural selection even begins to operate.

As an example, consider the tiny string-like flagellum attached like a tail to some bacteria. As the bacterium swims around in its environment, the flagellum whips around exactly like a propeller, and from a diagram, you would think you were looking at some kind of tiny motorized machine (see fig. 6.1). It is a microscopic outboard rotary motor that comes equipped with a hook joint, a drive shaft, O-rings, a stator, and a bi-directional acid-powered motor that can hum along at up to 100,000 revolutions per minute. Structures like these require dozens of precisely tailored, intricately interacting parts, which could not emerge by any gradual process. Instead the coordinated parts must somehow appear on the scene all at the same time, combined and coordinated in the right patterns, for the molecular machine to function at all.

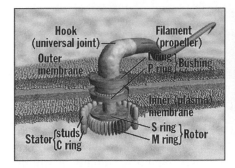
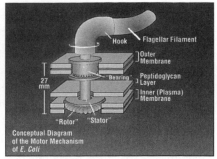

Fig. 6.1 MOLECULAR MACHINES: Many structures within the cell bear an uncanny resemblance to manufactured gadgets. *(Reprinted with permission from Access Research Network, www.arn.org.)*

"More so than other motors, the flagellum resembles a machine designed by a human," writes biologist David DeRosier.[19] That resemblance suggests that the tiny molecular machines within the cell were designed by an intelligent agent.

Behe and the Black Box

In Darwin's day, scientists knew next to nothing about biochemistry. Living things were "black boxes," their inside workings a mystery—hence the title of Behe's book. It was easy to speculate about large-scale scenarios where fins gradually turned into legs, or legs into wings, since no one had a clue as to how limbs and organs actually worked from the inside. It's as though we were to ask how a stereo system is made and the answer was: by plugging a set of speakers into an amplifier and adding a CD player, radio receiver, and tape deck.[20] What we really want to know is how things like speakers and CD players themselves were assembled. What is *inside* those plastic boxes?

Today, through the use of the electron microscope, the "black box" of the cell has been opened, and biologists are intimately familiar with its inside workings. The older broad-stroke speculations about fins becoming legs won't cut it anymore. Today any theory of life's origin must explain molecular systems.

Darwin himself once admitted that the existence of irreducible complexity (though he didn't use that term) would stand as a refutation of his theory. He even offered it as a test: "If it could be demonstrated that any complex organ existed which could not possibly have been formed by numerous, successive, slight modifications, my theory would absolutely break down."[21] With the explosion of knowledge from molecular biology, it appears that Darwin's theory has indeed broken down.

Critics charge that irreducible complexity is nothing more than an argument from "personal incredulity." As they see it, people like Behe are simply saying, *We can't imagine any naturalistic way to explain this high level of complexity, so there isn't one.* If that were really all Behe meant, then his argument would only reveal the poverty of his own imagination. After all, there was a time when no one thought it would be possible to fly, either.

But the critics are missing the point. The argument from irreducible complexity is not a statement about what is psychologically possible to imagine. Instead, it is a *logical* argument about how wholes are constructed from parts. An *aggregate* structure, like a pile of sand, can be built up gradually by simply adding a piece at a time—one grain of sand after another. By contrast, an *organized* structure, like the inside of a computer, is built up according to a preexisting blueprint, plan, or design. Each interlocking piece is structured to contribute to the functioning of the whole—which in turn becomes possible only after a minimal number of pieces are in place.

The logical question, then, is whether living structures are aggregates or organized wholes. And the answer is clear: Not only on the level of body systems, but also within each tiny cell, living structures are incredibly complex organized wholes. The most plausible theory, then, is that the pieces were put together according to a preexisting blueprint.[22]

A Universe Built for You

Until recently, the controversy over evolution has centered on design in biology. But today evidence of design is being uncovered in physics and cosmology as well. The cosmos itself is exquisitely fine-tuned to support life.

Cosmologists have discovered that the universe's fundamental forces are intricately balanced, as though on a knife's edge. Take, for example, the force of gravity: If it were only slightly stronger, all stars would be red dwarfs, too cold to support life. But if it were only slightly weaker, all stars would be blue giants, burning too briefly for life to develop. (The margin of error in the universe's expansion rate is only 1 part in 10^{60}.) Cosmologists speak of "cosmic coincidences"—meaning that the fundamental forces of the universe just *happen* to have the exact numerical value required to make life possible. The slightest change would yield a universe inhospitable to life.[23]

This is sometimes dubbed the Goldilocks dilemma: How did these numerical values turn out not too high, not too low, but just right?

What makes the question so puzzling is that there is no physical cause explaining why these values are so finely tuned to support life. "Nothing in all of physics explains why its fundamental principles should conform themselves so precisely to life's requirement," says astronomer George

Greenstein.[24] And since there is no known *physical* cause, it looks suspiciously as though they are the product of *intention*—as though someone designed them that way. "Why is nature so ingeniously, one might even say suspiciously, friendly to life?" asks astrophysicist Paul Davies. "It's almost as if a Grand Designer had it all figured out."[25]

To make the logic clearer, imagine that you found a huge universe-creating machine, with thousands of dials representing the gravitational constant, the strong nuclear force, the weak nuclear force, the electromagnetic force, the ratio of the mass of the proton and the electron, and many more. Each dial has hundreds of possible settings, and you can twirl them around at will—there is nothing that pre-sets them to any particular value. What you discover is that each of the thousands of dials *just happens* to be set to exactly the right value for life to exist. Even the slightest tweak of one of the cosmic knobs would produce a universe where life was impossible. As a science reporter puts it, "They are like the knobs on God's control console, and they seem almost miraculously tuned to allow life."[26]

Since the "knobs" are not constrained by any natural law, they have all the earmarks of being a product of design or intention. "I am not a religious person, but I could say this universe is *designed very well* for the existence of life," says astronomer Heinz Oberhummer. "The basic forces in the universe are tailor-made for the production of . . . carbon-based life."[27]

Nobel Prize–winner Arno Penzias, who has a Jewish background, is quick to see the religious implications: "Astronomy leads us to a unique event, a universe which was created out of nothing, one with the very delicate balance needed to provide exactly the conditions required to permit life, and one which has an underlying (one might say 'supernatural') plan."[28] In fact, he says, "The best data we have are exactly what I would have predicted, had I had nothing to go on but the five books of Moses, the Psalms, the Bible as a whole."[29]

Cosmic Coincidences

Critics admit that the fine-tuning of the universe suggests design, but they grope around for an alternative explanation. Astronomer Fred Hoyle is often quoted as saying, "A common sense interpretation of the facts suggests that a superintellect has monkeyed with the physics."[30] But who is that "superintellect"? Adamantly opposed to the Christian teaching of creation, Hoyle proposed that it was an alien mind from another universe.[31]

Others have proposed the quasi-pantheistic notion that the universe itself is intelligent, with a mind of its own. For example, Greenstein starts out *appearing* to agree with Christianity: "As we survey all the evidence, the thought insistently arises that some supernatural agency—or, rather Agency—must be involved. Is it possible that suddenly, without intending to, we have stumbled upon scientific proof of the existence of a Supreme Being? Was it God who stepped in and so providentially crafted the cosmos for our benefit?"

Yet, no matter how "insistently" this thought arises, Greenstein firmly suppresses it. He wants no part of a personal God. Instead, making a wild extrapolation from quantum mechanics, Greenstein says the universe could not fully exist until human beings emerged to observe it—and thus, in order to become fully real, the universe decided to evolve human consciousness. The "cosmos does not exist unless observed," he writes, and thus "the universe brought forth life in order to exist."[32]

This implausible notion has proven surprisingly popular. Sounding like an Eastern mystic, the Nobel Prize–winning biologist George Wald said the reason intelligent life evolved is that "the universe wants to be known."[33] And physicist Freeman Dyson, noting "the many accidents of physics and astronomy that have worked together to our benefit," wrote these eerie-sounding words: "It almost seems as if the Universe must in some sense have known that we were coming."[34] How ironic that scientists who dismiss the idea of design as unscientific will turn around and embrace the bizarre, almost mystical notion of a conscious universe that "knew" we were coming.

Less mystical astronomers take a different tack to explain away the "cosmic coincidences," proposing to beat the low probabilities by inflating the number of possibilities. They stack the deck by suggesting that there are multiple universes besides our own (the "Many Worlds" hypothesis). Most of these universes would be dark, lifeless places, but a few might possibly have the right conditions for life—and ours just happens to be one of them. This is sheer, unbridled speculation, of course, since it is impossible to know if any other universes actually exist. "The multiverse theory requires as much suspension of disbelief as any religion," comments Gregg Easterbrook. "Join the church that believes in the existence of invisible objects 50 billion galaxies wide!"[35] The only reason for proposing such a far-fetched idea is that it makes our own universe seem a little less like a freak improbability.

Surveying all these bizarre speculations, physicist Heinz Pagels remarks that scientists seem reluctant to draw the most straightforward inference from the evidence—that "the reason the universe seems tailor-made for our existence is that it *was* tailor-made."[36] The design inference is the simplest, most direct reading of the evidence. It's amazing what exotic theories some scientists will propose in order to avoid that inference. David Gross, director of the Kavli Institute for Theoretical Physics, recently admitted that his objection to the concept of fine-tuning is "totally emotional": It's a dangerous idea because "it smells of religion and intelligent design."[37] Convoluted theories of a conscious cosmos, or of countless unknowable universes, are little more than desperate attempts to avoid the obvious evidence for design.

Who Wrote the Genetic Code?

The most powerful evidence for design in my own view is the DNA code. You may remember the burst of publicity a few years ago, when scientists announced that they had decoded the human genome. At a White House press conference, all the ceremonial language crafted for the occasion stressed the analogy between DNA and a written language. The director of the National Human Genome Research Institute, Dr. Francis Collins, an evangelical Christian, said: "We have caught the first glimpses of our instruction book, previously known only to God." Not to be outdone, then-President Clinton resorted to God talk as well: "Today we are learning the language in which God created life."[38]

These are actually very apt analogies. The DNA molecule is built up of four bases that function as chemical "letters"—adenine (A), thymine (T), cytosine (C), and guanine (G)—which combine in various sequences to spell out a message. The discovery of this chemical code means we can now apply the categories of information theory to DNA. "What has happened is that genetics has become a branch of information technology," writes Dawkins. "The genetic code is truly digital, in exactly the same sense as computer codes. This is not some vague analogy, it is the literal truth."[39]

The result is that the origin of life has now been recast as the origin of biological information: How do we get highly specified, complex biological information?

In ordinary life, when we find a message, we don't have any doubt where it came from. We *know* that natural causes do not produce messages. I once took my little boy to a park, where we sat under a large old beech tree with hearts and slogans carved into the bark—"George loves Wendy" and "Class of '95." It was a sure sign that the squiggles were not the product of natural forces. When Egyptian hieroglyphics were discovered, no one knew how to decipher them for 1,400 years (until the Rosetta Stone was discovered in 1799). Yet everyone knew without a doubt that the hieroglyphs were made by an intelligent agent, and were not patterns etched into the rock by some naturally occurring acid.

An amusing episode took place shortly after September 11 in Palm Beach, Florida. A minor panic broke out when residents spied a crop duster flying overhead, using skywriting to spell out, "God is great." Afraid that the pilot might be a terrorist praising Allah, several people called the cops. But the pilot turned out to be a Christian, who periodically uses his skywriting skills to send inspirational messages—and who was rather amused by all the furor.[40]

The point is that when you see a message, a language, you immediately conclude that it is not a product of natural causes. When the citizens of Palm Beach saw fluffy white shapes that looked like letters in the sky, they did not for a moment start discussing interesting patterns of water condensation. They correctly inferred that the pattern was the product of an intelligent agent—though they were a little worried about *who* the agent was!

This kind of reasoning is intuitive—it seems to be natural to the human mind. But how do we make it logically and scientifically rigorous? What are the empirical markers of design? Under what conditions do we draw the design inference? And can we apply the same reasoning to nature?

Explanatory Filter

We begin by distinguishing among three types of events: those that occur by chance, by law, and by design. Back in 1970, the French geneticist Jacques Monod wrote a book titled *Chance and Necessity*,[41] which achieved cult-like status among college students at the time. (I still have my dog-eared copy from those days.) Monod was presenting standard Darwinian theory, but he did so in a manner that was strikingly streamlined—conceiving it as the interplay between chance (randomness) and necessity (law). Intelligent Design theory adopts the same simplified schema but adds a third category: design.

Thus, (1) some things are the result of random processes, occurring by chance; (2) others are the result of regular, predictable processes which can be formulated as laws of nature; (3) still others are the result of design—like houses, cars, computers, and books.

Which category best explains the origin of life? William Dembski has formulated a rigorous mathematical analysis of the reasoning we use to assign things to each category, which he calls the Explanatory Filter, described in his book *The Design Inference*.[42] His explanation is highly complex, as befits a book published by Cambridge University Press. But I'm going to offer a much simpler treatment, using the analogy of Scrabble letters. After all, if DNA is made up of chemical "letters," like a language, then it is the *sequence* of those "letters" that makes biological function possible, just as the sequence of letters on this page makes its message intelligible. How can we best account for the origin of complex specified sequences in DNA—by chance, by law, or by design?

UP FROM CHANCE

If we have an infinite number of monkeys sitting at typewriters, and an infinite amount of time, eventually they will type out the works of Shakespeare. So goes the theory, at least. But researchers in England recently put the theory to the test. They placed a computer in a cage with six monkeys to see what would happen. The monkeys' main response was to bang the computer with stones; for some reason many of them also found it appealing as an outhouse. When a few actually got around to pressing the keys, the result was a lot of *s*'s, along with about four other letters. After a month the monkeys had not written anything even close to a word of human language. Shakespeare? Not a chance.[43]

The experiment was done partly as a gag, but it does suggest that a bit of skepticism is in order about the standard assumption that life arose by sheer chance. Darwin himself did not write much about the origin of life (his main interest was the origin of species), but in a private letter he once dropped a casual comment about life arising by random chemical interactions in a "warm little pond." When spelled out in greater scientific detail by others, this became the dominant view until recent decades. Ask ordinary people what the theory of evolution is, and typically they will say it's the theory that life arose by pure chance. Yet, among professional scientists, chance-based theories have been all but completely rejected.

The heyday of chance theories was in the early 1950s, when scientists first discovered that they could produce a few simple organic compounds (like amino acids—the building blocks of proteins) in laboratory experiments. But those heady days are over. The early successes have petered out; the excitement has died down. Having created a few simple building blocks, researchers found it much more difficult to create the larger molecules (macromolecules like proteins and DNA) that are crucial for life.[44] It has become clear that simply mixing chemicals in a flask and sparking them with an electrical charge does not produce any biologically significant results.[45]

But if the core of life is biological information, this is exactly what we should expect. Why? Because chance processes do not produce complex information. Take our Scrabble analogy: Imagine that you put a blindfold over your eyes, then pull out a random string of Scrabble letters. Are they going to spell out an intelligible sentence? Of course not. You might get a few short words like "it" or "can," but a random process will not produce Shakespeare's *Hamlet*. Chance simply does not give rise to complex, specified information. Theologian Norman Geisler once offered a spunky illustration: "If you came into the kitchen and saw the Alphabet cereal spilled on the table, and it spelled out your name and address, would you think the cat knocked the cereal box over?"[46]

194 TOTAL TRUTH

In fact, instead of *creating* information, chance events tend to *scramble* information. Think of random typos sprinkled throughout a page of text: They are much more likely to make nonsense than better sense. Applied to origin-of-life theories, this means that if any short chains of molecules *did* arise by chance processes in that warm little pond, they would quickly break down again—because the same chance processes would go on to insert "typos" into the chemical "text." It's as though every time your string of Scrabble letters spelled out "it" or "can," a mischievous child grabbed some of the letters and replaced them with new random letters. The upshot is that chance interactions of chemicals will never accumulate any significant concentrations of biologically important compounds. The primeval pond would be as dilute as the Atlantic Ocean is today.[47]

This is not an argument from probability, because the point is not merely that the odds are against the chance formation of life. The point is that, *in principle,* chance events do not create complex information. As a result, virtually all origin-of-life researchers today have abandoned theories based on chance.

AGAINST THE LAW

The second possibility is that the origin of life can be accounted for by some law of nature. This is the most popular view among scientists today—that life arose by natural forces within the constituents of matter itself. The idea is that every time the right preconditions exist, life will arise automatically and inevitably. It is no coincidence that one of the most widely used graduate textbooks expounding this view is titled *Biochemical Predestination.*[48] But instead of God, it was some force within matter itself that "predestined" the chemical compounds to line up in just the right sequences to create the building blocks of life.

The theory is based on the fact that chemical compounds react more easily with certain substances than with others, and it proposes that these chemical preferences are responsible for the highly specified sequences in protein and DNA. Yet the predestinarians turned out to be better biologists than theologians. When the textbook's authors, Dean Kenyon and Gary Steinman, conducted experiments to confirm their theory of biochemical predestination, the chemicals appeared to be Arminians with wills of their own: They stubbornly refused to line up in the proper sequences to form biologically significant results. When I interviewed Kenyon in 1989, he told me, "If you survey the experiments to date, designed to simulate conditions on the early earth, one thing that stands out is that you do not get ordered sequences of amino acids. These simply do not appear among the products of any experiments." And he added wryly: "If we thought we were going to see a lot of spontaneous order-ing, something must have been wrong with our theory."[49]

When the experiments failed, Kenyon faced the implications squarely: Eventually he repudiated his own theory and became a proponent of Intelligent Design.[50]

Once again, however, if life consists in information, then Kenyon's failed experiments are exactly what we should expect—because, *in principle,* laws of nature do not give rise to information. Why not? Because laws describe events that are regular, repeatable, and predictable. If you drop a pencil, it will fall. If you put paper into a flame, it will burn. If you mix salt in water, it will dis-solve. That's why the scientific method insists that experiments must be repeat-able: Whenever you reproduce the same conditions, you should get the same results, or something is wrong with your experiment. The goal of science is to reduce those regular patterns to mathematical formulas. By contrast, the sequence of letters in a message is *ir*regular and *non*repeating, which means it cannot be the result of any law-like process.

NO RULES FOR *HAMLET*

To illustrate the point, let's invoke our imaginary Scrabble game again, but this time when you organize the letters, you decide to follow a certain formula or rule (an analogy to laws of nature). For example, the formula might require that every time you have a D, it is followed by an E. And every time you have an E, it's followed by a S, then an I, then a G, and an N. The result would be that every time you started with D, you would get DESIGN, DESIGN, DESIGN, over and over again. Obviously, if the letters in a real alphabet fol-lowed rules like that, you would be limited to spelling only a few words—and you could not convey very much information. The reason a real alphabet works so well is precisely that the letters do *not* follow rules or formulas or laws. If you know that a word begins with a T, you cannot predict what the next letter will be. With some minor exceptions (in English, *q* is always fol-lowed by *u*), the letters can be combined and recombined in a vast number of different arrangements to form words and sentences.

When I was a youngster and computers were still new, my father used the huge, whiz-bang computer at work to create wrapping paper with "Happy Birthday" printed all over. It was a novelty at the time, though today you can easily do the same thing on your PC using a macro. It's a matter of program-ming the computer to write "Happy Birthday," and then cycle back and do the same thing—over and over again. The result is an ordered pattern, but one that conveys very little information. The entire page contains only as much information as the first two words. On the other hand, if you want your computer to write out Shakespeare's *Hamlet,* there is no rule or formula you can program it to follow. Instead, you have to specify each individual letter one by one.

The same is true of the DNA code. If the chemical "letters" in DNA followed some law or formula, they would line up automatically into only a few repeated patterns, storing very little biological information. But in fact, every cell in your body contains more information than the entire thirty volumes of the *Encyclopedia Britannica.* Why is that possible? Because with some minor exceptions, there are no laws of chemical attraction and repulsion that cause the "letters" in DNA to link up in any particular pattern. If you were to decode one section of DNA, there is no rule or formula determining what comes next. Instead the chemical "letters" are free to combine and recombine in a vast variety of sequences.[51]

What holds the DNA molecule together is a sugar-phosphate chain that functions like a backbone, and of course there is a chemical bond that makes the "letters" (bases) stick to that backbone. But there are no chemical bonds connecting one letter to the next in order to form a particular sequence. "DNA is like the magnetic letters your kid sticks on the refrigerator," says Steve Meyer. "The magnetic force explains how the letters stick to the fridge, but it doesn't explain how the letters are sequenced to spell 'I love Daddy.'"[52]

Thus it is futile for scientists to keep looking for some natural law or force within matter to explain the origin of life. It's not just that experiments to create life in a test tube have failed so far; it's that, *in principle,* law-like processes do not generate high information content.

Nor is the problem solved by the newer theories of complexity that are so fashionable these days. At the Santa Fe Institute, Stuart Kauffman holds out the hope that complexity theory will finally uncover the laws that make life inevitable. Kauffman and his colleagues have found that they can construct intricate structures on their computer screens that resemble frost and ferns and snowflakes. This has been touted as evidence that the complexity of life might be the result of self-organizing forces in matter.[53]

The problem, however, is that these structures represent the same kind of order as the birthday wrapping paper—they are products of a simple instruction that cycles back on itself again and again. In Kauffman's own words, they are constructed by the application of a few "astonishingly simple rules," repeated over and over again.[54] While the patterns on the computer screens may look impressive, they lack high information content.

THE MEDIUM IS NOT THE MESSAGE

If neither chance nor law accounts for complex biological information, the final option is design. The distinctive feature of design is an irregular sequence that fits a prescribed pattern—the kind of order found in Scrabble games, books, magazines, and radio scripts. The sequence of letters and words you are reading right now convey information because it fits the prescribed pattern of the English language.

The most popular analogy, however, is a computer program. DNA is the "software" that makes the cell operate, and the sequence of its bases carries information in the same way that sequences of 0 and 1 carry information in a computer code. "The machine code of the genes is uncannily computer-like," writes Dawkins. "Apart from differences in jargon, the pages of a molecular biology journal might be interchanged with those of a computer engineering journal."[55]

The upshot is that we can now apply information theory to biology, which opens whole new vistas on the origin of life.[56] For example, information theory tells us that a message is independent of the material medium used to convey it. The words you are reading right now were printed with ink on paper, but they could also be written with crayon or paint or chalk, or even scratched into sand with a stick. The message remains the same, no matter what kind of material you use to store and transmit it.

But if information is independent of the material medium, *then it was not created by the forces within that medium.* The words on this page were not created by chemical forces within the ink and paper. If you see "Math Test Today" written on a chalkboard, you do not think the message is a product of the chemical properties of calcium carbonate. Applied to the origin of life, this principle means the message encoded in DNA was not created by chemical forces within the molecule itself.

We can now explain why all the experiments to create life in a test tube have failed—because they tried to build life from the bottom up, by assembling the right materials to form a DNA molecule. But life is not about matter, it's about information. "Evolutionary biologists have failed to realize that they work with two more or less incommensurable domains: that of information and that of matter," writes George Williams (himself an evolutionary biologist). "The DNA molecule is the medium, it's not the message."[57] And information theory tells us that the medium does not write the message.

This becomes even clearer if we press the analogy a step further. DNA is a "genetic databank" that transmits information using the genetic code, writes Paul Davies. As a result, he concludes:

Trying to make life by mixing chemicals in a test tube is like soldering switches and wires in an attempt to produce Windows 98. *It won't work because it addresses the problem at the wrong conceptual level.*[58]

This is a devastating critique of the dominant origin-of-life scenarios. Proposing that matter gave rise to life is not just mistaken; it is addressing the question "at the wrong conceptual level."

The argument from information theory was developed by the late A. E. Wilder-Smith, a brilliant British-Swiss scientist with multiple earned doctorates.[59] I had the good fortune to meet Wilder-Smith when he was teaching in Ankara, Turkey, and I had just graduated from high school. (My father was teaching at the Middle East Technical University in Ankara.) I was still in a rebellious stage where I wanted nothing to do with Christians—and to my great surprise, that made Wilder-Smith very interested in talking to me. He had a broad, genial face, with eyes that twinkled intently through wire-rimmed spectacles. And unlike most of the Christians I knew, he did not condemn me for my lack of faith but showed genuine interest in my questions and objections. I was impressed that he would take the time to talk to a somewhat hostile teenager about things like DNA and information theory.

As a consequence, after becoming a Christian, I immediately sought out his books and studied them intensively. That's when I realized that he was pioneering what would become the heart of the design argument: that information does not arise from natural forces within matter but has to be imposed *upon* matter from outside by an intelligent agent.

Testing Positive

Negative evidence that matter does not write messages will not clinch the case, however. We also need to identify positive evidence for an intelligent agent. And once again, information theory provides the key: The tell-tale sign of design is what information theorists call *specified complexity.*[60]

To translate that phrase into simple English, we can once again use the three-part Explanatory Filter to compare chance, law, and design. (1) Chance alone may account for simple order (in our Scrabble example, short words like "it" and "can")—but products of design are *complex*. (2) Laws describe regular patterns ("DESIGN, DESIGN, DESIGN")—but products of design exhibit an irregular pattern. (3) That pattern is pre-selected, or *specified* in advance. Hence the distinctive mark of design in *specified complexity*.

Take the example of a language. There is no law of nature that determines the meaning of a sequence of sounds like G-I-F-T. In English the sequence means *present;* in German it means *poison;* in Norwegian it means *married.* A language takes what is an otherwise arbitrary sequence of sounds like G-I-F-T and confers meaning on it through a linguistic convention—formalized in dictionaries, rules of grammar, and so on. Out of all the possible combinations of sounds, a language selects only a few and confers meaning on them.

The DNA code is precisely parallel. The sequences of chemical "letters" are chemically arbitrary. There is no natural force that determines the meaning of certain combinations. Out of all the possible combinations of chemical "letters," somehow only a few carry meaning. But where did the cell's linguistic convention come from?

Clearly, linguistic conventions and rules of grammar do not arise out of chemical reactions. They come from the mental realm of information and intelligence.

The concept of specified complexity was first applied to the origins debate by Charles Thaxton and his coauthors, Walter Bradley and Roger Olsen, in their groundbreaking book *The Mystery of Life's Origin.*[61] Many years before the book came out, I had heard Charlie make the case when he was on staff at L'Abri and I was still an agnostic. Lecturing in the wood-paneled chapel, with the snow-covered Alps blazing through the windows, Charlie covered an easel with symbols for amino acids and proteins and DNA molecules, while I madly scribbled notes. I came away knowing that whatever other objections I might still harbor against Christianity, I could no longer cavalierly argue that it was disproved by science.

What made Thaxton an innovator in the design movement was that he was unwilling to stop short with building a negative case against evolution. Since Darwin's day, a wide variety of people (not only creationists) had rejected evolution, but no one had built a *positive* case for Intelligent Design. Thaxton argued that it is not enough to show the inadequacies of *natural* causes; we must go on to demonstrate the plausibility of *intelligent* causes. And the hallmark of intelligence is that elusive quality we just discussed: specified complexity. The structure of DNA is precisely parallel to the structure of languages and computer programs. Can we infer that specified complexity in DNA is likewise the product of an intelligent agent? Unless we define science from the outset in terms of naturalistic philosophy, the answer should be yes.

Three to Get Ready

Notice that the design inference is not an argument from ignorance: It does not say, *We don't know* the cause of a certain phenomenon, so we just throw up our hands and invoke a miracle. Instead, the argument is based on what we *do* know

about the kinds of structures produced by chance, law, and design.[62] Faced with
any phenomenon, a scientist can run it through the Explanatory Filter: Is it a random event? Then all we need to invoke is chance. Does it occur in a regular,
repeated pattern? Then it is an instance of some natural law. Is it a complex, specified pattern? Then it exhibits design, and was produced by intelligence.

The Explanatory Filter is also useful for cutting through the surface detail
in order to see what competing theories are really proposing. Take, for example, Darwin's theory. Stripped of the details, its core claim is that science should
be limited to the first two categories of explanation—chance and law. In fact,
its goal is precisely to eliminate design as a permissible category within science.
How? By showing that chance and law, working together, can substitute for
design. Darwinism proposes that when random mutations (chance) are run
through the sieve of natural selection (law), then over time organisms become
better and better adapted until they *appear* to be designed. In this way, the theory claims, a wholly naturalistic process can mimic the effects of Intelligent
Design—which means design is no longer required as a separate category. As
one philosopher puts it, Darwin was offering "a scheme for creating Design
out of Chaos without the aid of Mind."[63]

This explains why Darwin himself had no patience with theistic, or God-
guided, evolution. In his theory, natural selection functions to sift out any
harmful variations, while letting only beneficial variations through. If God
were guiding the process, however, then He would create only good variations
in the first place—in which case the sifting action of natural selection would
be unnecessary. In Darwin's words, "The view that each variation has been
providentially arranged seems to me to make Natural Selection entirely superfluous, and indeed takes the whole case of the appearance of new species out
of the range of science."[64]

Notice that Darwin was offering two objections to design. First, that it
makes natural selection "entirely superfluous." In other words, if you invoke
natural selection *plus* design then one of the two is redundant and unnecessary.
And Darwin intended to make sure it was design that would be rejected as
redundant. Thus a widely used college textbook says, "By coupling undirected,
purposeless variation [chance] to the blind, uncaring process of natural selection [law], Darwin made theological or spiritual explanations of the life processes superfluous."[65]

Second, and more importantly, Darwin's remarks show that he wanted to
transform the definition of science itself. That's why he objected that attributing the origin of species to providential purpose would take it "out of the range
of science." The implication is that science cannot countenance intelligent causation in any form. In Darwin's mind, theistic or divinely ordained evolution

was no different in principle from direct creation—and neither was admissible in science. To use our three categories, chance and law were permitted in science, but design was not. As one philosopher of science explains, "Darwin insisted on telling a totally consistent naturalistic story or none at all."[66]

Today, however, it is clear that the naturalistic story did not succeed. Chance and law do not mimic design. Applying the Explanatory Filter to life's origin, we find that the sequence in DNA is neither random (chance) nor regular (law). Instead, it exhibits specified complexity, the hallmark of design. Chance and law may explain many other events in the history of the cosmos. But to explain the origin of life, we need to include an additional tool in the scientist's tool chest.[67]

It's beginning to look like the key to interpreting the organic world is not natural selection but information. In science we are hearing echoes of John 1:1, "In the beginning was the Word." The Greek word *Logos* means intelligence, wisdom, rationality, or information. Modern genetics seems to be telling us that life is a grand narrative told by the divine Word—that there is an Author for the text of life.

CHRISTIAN RELATIVISTS

If Darwin's goal was to get rid of design, then clearly his motivation was not strictly scientific but also religious. We should avoid the misleading dichotomy that says evolution is scientific, while design is religious. Darwinism and design theory are not about different subjects—science versus religion. Instead they are competing answers to the *same* question: How did life arise in the universe? Both theories appeal to scientific data, while at the same time both have broader philosophical and religious implications.

Christians will only be able to make this case effectively, however, when we challenge the science/religion dichotomy in our own thinking. We must be confident that the biblical teaching on creation is objectively *true* and not just a matter of religion—in the modern sense of merely personal, subjective values. Consider the Bible's opening claim: "In the beginning God created the heavens and the earth." Is this true or false? For many people, even asking such a question amounts to making a category mistake.[68] Genesis is religion, they might say, which is not a matter of true or false. Religion is a personal commitment, a way of life, a source of ultimate meaning. And of course, Christianity *is* all these things. But are we also prepared to say it is *true?*

Many Christians have come to think of religion as a matter of experience rather than truth. I discovered this shortly after my conversion, after I had returned to the States from L'Abri. Living in New Mexico, I heard about a

Christian "crash pad" in Albuquerque. (Do you even *remember* that term? It meant a household that took people in for the night as a ministry.) Immediately I hitched a ride to Albuquerque, and ended up living in the household all summer. Those who lived or gathered regularly at His House, as it was called, were all ex-hippies, "Jesus freaks." But because of my studies at L'Abri, I talked about my recent conversion in terms of becoming convinced that Christianity is *true*—that it answers the basic philosophical questions better than any other system of thought.

My new friends, with their long hair and granny dresses, looked puzzled. They would often go to the park to evangelize among teens tripping on drugs, and they said, "We tell the people, 'Jesus works for me. Why don't you try Him.' Isn't that good enough?"[69]

It's *not* enough, of course, and the weakness of reducing Christianity to "what works" came home to me when I joined my friends in their witnessing expeditions. One evening I had a long, engaging discussion with a young teenager who expressed interest in converting. When I asked if he was convinced that Christianity was true, however, he frowned and burst out, "Well, of course it's true. If you believe it, it's true for you!"

Clearly, the evangelistic message was being sieved through a relativistic grid that reduced all truth claims to whatever is "true for you." The reason Christians often fail to break through that relativistic framework is partly that we ourselves have absorbed a form of religious relativism—in practice, even if not in belief. By accepting the fact/value dichotomy, many of us have come to think of religion and morality in terms of a privatized, upper-story experience.

FAIRY DUST

If we privatize our faith, however, we will play right into the hands of the philosophical naturalists, who likewise relegate religion to the upper story. Rather than attacking religion directly as *false*, which would risk arousing public protest, philosophical naturalists deftly relegate it to the "values" realm—which keeps the question of true and false off the table altogether. As Johnson writes, religion is consigned "to the private sphere, where illusory beliefs are acceptable 'if they work for you.'"[70]

Unless Christians tackle this attitude head on, our message will continue to pass through a grid that reduces it to an expression of merely psychological need. I witnessed a breathtaking example a few years ago at a scientific conference at Baylor University. One of the speakers was the Nobel Prize–winning physicist Steven Weinberg, and he opened his presentation by announcing that he intended to lump together all spiritual beings—whether Buddha or Jesus or whoever—under a single rubric, which he would call "fairies." And then he would explain why as a scientist he did not believe in "fairies." A murmur of awkward laughter rippled through the audience, many of whom were Christians. And no wonder: It's pretty tough to defend your beliefs with any dignity when they've just been labeled nothing more than fairy tales.

Yet Weinberg was only bluntly stating the logical consequence of redefining religion in terms of noncognitive experience—exactly what many Christians themselves do, at least implicitly, when they accept the fact/value dichotomy.

OUT OF THE NATURALIST'S CHAIR

Some even do it explicitly. Consider Christians who are theistic evolutionists: Though they would never agree with atheists that nature is all that exists (*metaphysical* naturalism), they do agree that science must be limited to natural causes (*methodological* naturalism). As philosopher Nancey Murphy of Fuller Theological Seminary writes: "Christians and atheists alike must pursue scientific questions in our era without invoking a Creator." Why? Well, because that's what atheists have decided: "For better or worse, we have inherited a view of science as *methodologically* atheistic."[71]

But who says that we have to play by the rules set down by atheists? If Christianity is true, then it's not at all obvious that valid science can be done only by making the counterfactual assumption that atheism is true. Theistic evolutionists generally accept exactly the same scientific theories as atheists or naturalists; the only thing they ask is that they be allowed to propose a theological meaning behind it all—known only by faith, and not detectable by scientific means. In essence, they allow atheists to define scientific knowledge, so long as theology is allowed to put a religious spin on whatever science comes up with.

In that case, however, what does this theological meaning amount to? It is reduced to a subjective gloss on the story told by naturalistic science. God's existence doesn't make any difference scientifically because He does not act in ways that can be detected. As a result, theology is no longer regarded as an independent source of knowledge; it is merely an overlay of *value* on otherwise value-free facts.

"As the scientific concept of truth came to dominate modernity," explains theologian Ellen Charry, "theologians came to assign religious claims to the realm of myth and meaning." Theology lost its status "as genuine truth and knowledge," while "a small space was carved out for theological claims as symbolic terms that render life meaningful."[72] A merely symbolic religion does not threaten the ruling regime of materialistic science, and hence the scientific establishment is generally willing to tolerate it. It is seen as a harmless delusion for those who need that kind of crutch—provided they keep it contained within Sunday worship and don't bring it into the science classroom, where we talk about what *really* happened. The attitude is summed up in H. L. Mencken's aphorism: "We must respect the other fellow's religion, but only in the sense and to the extent that we respect his theory that his wife is beautiful and his children smart."

Theistic evolutionists tend to be content with this arrangement, but secularists understand very well that it is an untenable halfway house. John Maddox, former editor of *Nature* and a self-identified atheist, put the matter bluntly when he reviewed a book by a liberal churchman: "The religious explanation of the world is not free standing, but an optional add-on," he wrote. In other words, religion is not an independent source of knowledge, but merely an optional emotional overlay to what we already know from science—like adding a color overlay to a photograph.[73]

The attempt to accommodate to philosophical naturalism was illustrated nicely by Francis Schaeffer in an image of two chairs. Those who sit in the naturalist's "chair," he said, view the world filtered through a lens that limits their sight to the natural world. But those who sit in the supernaturalist's "chair" view the world through a much larger lens that makes them aware of an unseen realm that exists in addition to the seen realm. Christians are called to live out their entire lives, including their scientific work, from the perspective of the supernaturalist's chair, recognizing the full range of reality.[74] This is what it means to "walk by faith, not by sight" (2 Cor. 5:7), with a day-by-day awareness of the unseen dimension of reality.

Sadly, however, even sincere believers keep wandering over to the naturalist's chair. They may embrace biblical doctrine with their minds, and follow biblical ethics in their practical behavior—and yet still conduct their day-to-day professional lives on the basis of a naturalistic worldview. You might say that in confessing their beliefs they sit in the supernaturalist's "chair," but in pursuing their professional work, they walk over and sit in the naturalist's "chair." This is what happens when Christians accept methodical naturalism in science.

By contrast, design theory demonstrates that Christians can sit in the supernaturalist's "chair" even in their professional lives, seeing the cosmos through the lens of a comprehensive biblical worldview. Intelligent Design steps boldly into the scientific arena to build a case based on empirical data. It takes Christianity out of the ineffectual realm of *value* and stakes out a cognitive claim in the realm of objective truth. It restores Christianity to its status as genuine knowledge, equipping us to defend it in the public arena.

Finally, by challenging naturalism in science, it provides the basis for challenging naturalism in theology, morality, politics, and every other field. And none too soon, because naturalism is spilling over the banks of science and making deep inroads into the rest of culture. In the next chapter we will see how naturalistic evolution is being transformed into a universal worldview that is aggressively taking over every aspect of human life and society.

7

TODAY BIOLOGY,
TOMORROW THE WORLD

What is in our genes' interests
is what seems "right"—morally right.
ROBERT WRIGHT[1]

A first-grader came home from school one day and asked: "Who's lying, Mom—you or my teacher?" That day, it turned out, the teacher had informed the class that humans and apes are descended from a common ancestor. Little Ricky was bright enough to figure out that this didn't square with what his mother had taught him from the Bible, so he figured one of them must be making things up. Surely, it couldn't be the teacher; after all, in his young eyes she was the expert, the professional. No, the person he decided to doubt was his mother. With sorrow, she realized that she had better start on a long process of counter-education.

It is because of incidents like this, repeated over and over in the classroom, that the controversy over teaching evolution refuses to die. When Ohio debated the topic in 2002, the Department of Education received more public response than to any previous issue. The public senses intuitively that there's much more at stake than just science—that when naturalistic evolution is taught in the science classroom, that will lead to a naturalistic view of ethics and religion being taught down the hallway in the history classroom, the social studies classroom, the family life classroom, and all the rest of the curriculum. A leader in the Ohio controversy put it well: "A naturalistic definition of *science* has the effect of indoctrinating students into a naturalistic *worldview*."[2]

The public is right to be concerned, and the purpose of the next two chapters is to show why.[3] Darwinism functions as the scientific support for an overarching naturalistic worldview, which is being promoted aggressively far beyond the bounds of science. Some even say we are entering an age of "universal Darwinism," when it will no longer be just a scientific theory but a comprehensive worldview. In order to have a redemptive impact on our culture, Christians need to engage Darwinian evolution not only as science but also as a worldview.

UNIVERSAL DARWINISM

I'd like to begin with a sentence from one of Francis Schaeffer's books. The central reason Christians have not been more effective in the public square, he says, is that we tend to see things in "bits and pieces." We worry about things like family breakdown, violence in schools, immoral entertainment, abortion and bioethics—a wide array of *individual* issues. But we don't see the big picture that connects all the dots.

And what *is* that big picture? All these forms of cultural dissolution, Schaeffer writes, have "come about due to a shift in worldview . . . to a worldview based on the idea that the final reality is impersonal matter or energy shaped into its current form by impersonal chance."[4] In other words, long before there was an Intelligent Design movement, Schaeffer saw that everything hangs on your view of origins. If you start with impersonal forces operating by chance—in other words, naturalistic evolution—then over time (even if it takes several generations) you will end up with naturalism in moral, social, and political philosophy.

Many evolutionists today would agree with that. In fact, one of the fastest-growing disciplines today is the application of Darwinism to social and cultural issues. It goes by the name of evolutionary psychology (an updated version of sociobiology), and its premise is that if natural selection produced the human body, then it must also account for all aspects of human belief and behavior. Evolutionary psychology is spreading rapidly to virtually every subject area, with new books appearing on the shelves almost faster than you can keep up with them. Let's run through a smattering of recent titles, just to get a flavor of what's coming out on the subject.

One of the topics tackled most frequently is morality. After all, if human behavior is ultimately programmed by "selfish genes" (as Dawkins argues in *The Selfish Gene*), then it becomes enormously difficult to explain unselfish or altruistic behavior. Thus new books keep being churned out with titles like *The Moral Animal* and *Evolutionary Origins of Morality,* seeking to explain morality as a product of natural selection. The theme is that we learn to be kind and helpful only because that helps us survive and produce more offspring.[5]

"The basis of ethics does not lie in God's will," write E. O. Wilson and Michael Ruse. Ethics is "an illusion fobbed off on us by our genes to get us to cooperate." For some unexplained reason, humans simply "function better if they are deceived by their genes into thinking that there is a disinterested objective morality binding upon them, which all should obey."[6] In other words, evolution practices a kind of benign deception to get us to be nice to one another.

If natural selection is the reason we're good, it's also the reason we're bad. So says a new book called *Demonic Males: Apes and the Origins of Human Violence*. The authors take aim at the biblical teaching of "original sin," insisting that even the September 11 attacks had nothing to do with moral "evil"— they merely show that a predisposition to violence "is written in the molecular chemistry of DNA." Their genes made them do it.[7]

Religion is another favorite target, and recent books include *In Gods We Trust* and *Religion Explained: The Evolutionary Origins of Religious Thought*. The basic theme is that religion is a malfunction to which brains are susceptible when the nervous system has evolved to a certain level of complexity.[8]

EVOLUTION FOR EVERYMAN

If you are interested in politics, there are books like *Darwinian Politics: The Evolutionary Origin of Freedom*. For economists, there's *Economics as an Evolutionary Science*. Lawyers may want to consult *Evolutionary Jurisprudence* or *Law, Biology and Culture: The Evolution of Law*.[9]

For educators, there's *Origins of Genius: Darwinian Perspectives on Creativity*. The book defines intelligence as a Darwinian process of generating a variety of ideas, then selecting those that are "fittest." There are even books targeted specifically to English teachers, like *Evolution and Literary Theory*.[10]

If you work in medicine, a slew of new books have come out, such as *Evolutionary Medicine* and *Why We Get Sick: The New Science of Darwinian Medicine*. Mental health workers can choose either *Darwinian Psychiatry* or *Genes on the Couch: Explorations in Evolutionary Psychology*.[11]

If you're a woman, there's *Divided Labours: An Evolutionary View of Women at Work*. For parents, there's *The Truth About Cinderella: A Darwinian View of Parental Love*. If you're a businessman, there's even something for you: *Executive Instinct: Managing the Human Animal in the Information Age*. The author asks, How do we manage people whose brains were hardwired in the Stone Age?[12]

Of course, to really sell books you have to talk about the racier topics, and scientists have not been shy about doing so. A sampling of recent titles includes *The Evolution of Desire: Strategies of Human Mating* and *Ever Since Adam and Eve: The Evolution of Human Sexuality*.[13] Science seems to be descending to the level of soap opera.

The PBS "Evolution" series featured an evolutionary psychologist named

Geoffrey Miller, author of *The Mating Mind: How Sexual Choice Shaped the Evolution of Human Nature.*[14] On the program Miller told the audience that the origin of the human brain "wasn't God, it was our ancestors . . . choosing their sexual partners." As he was talking, you could hear the strains of Handel's "Messiah" playing in the background, while a voice-over explained that even artistic expression began as a form of sexual display.

After September 11, evolutionary psychologists suddenly had a real-world opportunity to apply their theory. Pundits of every stripe rushed to offer some explanation for the terrible tragedy, and even the science desk at the *New York Times* got into the act. It claimed that the heroism of the rescue workers was a product of evolution—akin to the cooperative instincts of ants and bees.

Selfless behavior is a product of "kin selection," the article said—the idea that your genes are passed on not only to your own children but also to close relatives. As a result, you can enhance your own reproductive success by caring for a wider group of genetic relatives.[15] A leading evolutionist, J. B. S. Haldane, once explained the calculus of kin selection by saying he was prepared to sacrifice his life for two brothers, or possibly eight cousins.[16]

Other theories of altruistic behavior are based on game theory, which shows that cooperative strategies—"tit for tat"—work best in getting what we want. Of course, neither of these explanations accounts for altruism in the ordinary sense; they are merely extended forms of self-interest. They tell us that what *appears* to be sacrificial behavior—for example, on the part of a mother for her child—is *really* just a strategy for passing on her own genes.

We could go further and argue that genuine altruism actually provides a powerful apologetic argument for Christianity. Heroic self-sacrifice of the type we witnessed on September 11 can *only* be explained by the Christian understanding of human nature as genuinely moral beings, made in the image of God.[17]

DARWINIAN FUNDAMENTALISM ON RAPE

If Christians remain skeptical of the claims of evolutionary psychology, they are in good company. Many mainstream scientists are likewise critical. After all, it's easy to come up with imaginary scenarios of how some behavior *might* be adaptive under certain circumstances, and then jump to saying it *was* adaptive—even when there is no actual evidence. The literature of evolutionary psychology is full of "cocktail party" speculation devoid of any real data from genetics or neurology. Some critics have dismissed the theory as "Darwinian fundamentalism"—a provocative phrase implying that Darwinism itself has become a rigid orthodoxy.[18]

"The ugly fact is that we haven't a shred of evidence that morality in humans did or did not evolve by natural selection," says geneticist H. Allen Orr. Evolutionary psychologists have constructed a host of hypothetical scenarios on questions like *What would happen if we had a gene that said be nice to strangers?* "But, in the end, a thought experiment is not an experiment," Orr states acerbically. The reality is, "We have no data."[19]

We have to realize, however, that once someone has accepted the evolutionary premise, the question of evidence becomes all but irrelevant. Applying Darwinian explanations to human behavior is a matter of simple logic. After all, if evolution is true, then how else did the mind emerge, if *not* by evolution? How else did human behavior arise, if *not* through adaptation to the environment?

This became clear a few years ago when a book appeared offering an evolutionary account of sexual assault. It was titled *The Natural History of Rape: Biological Bases of Sexual Coercion,* and the authors were two university professors who made the rather inflammatory claim that rape is not a pathology, biologically speaking. Instead it is an evolutionary adaptation for maximizing reproductive success. In other words, if candy and flowers don't do the trick, some men may resort to coercion to fulfill the reproductive imperative. The book calls rape "a natural, biological phenomenon that is a product of the human evolutionary heritage," akin to "the leopard's spots and the giraffe's elongated neck."[20]

Demonstrating how insulated many scientists are, the authors said they were genuinely surprised by all the controversy the book caused. After all, to a Darwinist it is simple logic that any behavior that survives today *must* have conferred some evolutionary advantage—otherwise it would have been weeded out by natural selection. So the authors were virtually forced to identify some benefit even in the crime of rape.[21]

When one of the authors, Randy Thornhill, appeared on National Public Radio, he found himself deluged by angry calls, until finally he insisted that the logic is inescapable: If evolution is true, then "every feature of every living thing, including human beings, has an underlying evolutionary background. *That's not a debatable matter.*"[22] Three times during the program, he hammered home the same phrase: It's "not a debatable matter."

This explains why opponents of evolutionary psychology have failed to halt its rapid growth: Many accept the same evolutionary premise, which means ultimately they have no defense against its application to human behavior. For example, critics of the rape thesis tended to focus their arguments at the level

of details: Many victims of rape are either too young or too old to bear children—and in some cases, are even males (e.g., prison rape)—which clearly
undercuts the idea that rape is driven by a biological imperative to reproduce.
The entire theory, said *Nature,* rests on "statistical sleight of hand."[23]

Yet the critics were hamstrung by the fact that most of them accept the
same evolutionary assumptions as the book—which left them no principled
means of opposing its conclusion. To borrow an elegant phrase from Tom
Bethell, "The critics were disarmed by their shared worldview."[24]

There was an amusing episode in the NPR program when Thornhill faced
off against a leading feminist, Susan Brownmiller, who authored an influential
book on rape many years ago called *Against Our Wills.* Not surprisingly, she
objected strenuously to the rape thesis, and Thornhill fired back with the worst
insult he could dream up: He said she was starting to sound just like "the
extreme religious right."

No doubt she *was* insulted, but the underlying point was actually serious.
Thornhill was saying that *evolution* and *evolutionary ethics* are a package deal.
If you accept the premise, then you must accept the conclusion. And if you
don't like it, you may as well join the "religious right" and challenge evolution
itself. It's just as Schaeffer said: All the dots connect back to your view of
origins.

MOTHERS RED IN TOOTH AND CLAW

A few years ago, Steven Pinker wrote an article in the *New York Times* applying evolutionary psychology to another troubling moral issue—infanticide.
This was shortly after the news media had picked up the story about a teenage
girl, dubbed the "Prom Mom," who delivered her baby at a school dance, then
dumped it in the trash. At around the same time, an unmarried teen couple
killed their newborn as well. The public was shocked, and so Pinker arose to
reassure them with the wisdom of science.

We must "understand" teenagers who kill their newborns, Pinker began,
because infanticide "has been practiced and accepted in most cultures throughout history." Its sheer ubiquity implies that it *must* have been preserved by natural selection—which in turn means it *must* have an adaptive function.
Speaking of human mothers in terms more suitable to cats, Pinker said, "If a
newborn is sickly, or if its survival is not promising, they may cut their losses
and favor the healthiest in the litter or try again later on." Thus, "the emotional
circuitry of mothers has evolved" to commit infanticide in certain situations.
Because of natural selection, "a capacity for neonaticide is built into the biological design of our parental emotions."[25]

Pinker's interpretation should have come as no surprise to anyone who remembered an earlier article that appeared in *Newsweek* back in 1982 under the startling title "Nature's Baby Killers." It was a report on the first major symposium studying infanticide among animals, convened with the hope that it might explain similar behavior in humans. Many of the participating scientists agreed that "infanticide can no longer be called 'abnormal.' Instead it is as 'normal' as parenting instincts, sex drives and self-defense," and may even be a beneficial evolutionary adaptation.[26]

But all this is little more than smoke and mirrors. There is no evidence that neonaticide is a genetic trait to begin with, let alone one selected by evolution. "Where are the twin studies, chromosome locations, and DNA sequences supporting such a claim?" demands Orr. "The answer is we don't have any. What we do have is a story—there's an undeniable Darwinian logic underlying the murder of newborns in certain circumstances." And it's this logic, more than any factual evidence, that drives the theory: The evolutionary story sounds persuasive; evolution requires genes; therefore, the behavior is genetic. "The move is so easy and so seductive," Orr says, "that evolutionary psychologists sometimes forget a hard truth: a Darwinian story is not Mendelian evidence. A Darwinian story is a story."[27]

The "Darwinian logic" is so compelling that even Darwin himself was taken in by it. In *The Descent of Man* he argued that the "murder of infants has prevailed on the largest scale throughout the world, and has met with no reproach." Indeed, "infanticide, especially of females, has been thought to be good for the tribe."[28] More than a century ago, Darwin already understood where the logic of his theory led.

Ultimately, the fatal weakness of evolutionary psychology is that it is so elastic that it can explain anything. Evolution is said to account for mothers who kill their newborn babies—but if you were to ask why most mothers do *not* kill their babies, why, evolution accounts for that too. A theory that explains any phenomenon and its opposite, too, in reality explains nothing. It is so flexible that it can be twisted to say whatever proponents want it to say.

PETER SINGER'S PET THEME

In the past, it was Christians who warned that Darwinian evolution would ultimately destroy morality, by reducing it to behavioral patterns selected only for their survival value. Back then, evolutionists would often respond with soothing reassurances that getting rid of God would not jeopardize morality—that "we can be good without God." But in recent years, evolutionists themselves have begun bluntly declaring that the theory undercuts the basis of morality.

For example, biologist William Provine of Cornell travels the lecture circuit telling university students that the Darwinian revolution is still incomplete, because we have not yet embraced all its moral and religious implications. What are those implications? Provine lists them: "There is no ultimate foundation for ethics, no ultimate meaning in life, and no free will."[29] Thus evolutionary psychologists are simply completing the Darwinian revolution by drawing out its full implications. They are connecting the dots, by showing what consistent Darwinism means for morality.

The results can be quite abhorrent. A few years ago, conservative commentators around the country gave a collective gasp when an article appeared by a Princeton University professor supporting—of all things—sexual relations between humans and animals. The professor was Peter Singer, already notorious for his support of animal rights. (Apparently we didn't realize what kind of rights he meant . . .)

The article was titled "Heavy Petting," and in it Singer makes it clear that his real target is biblical morality. In the West, he writes, we have a "Judeo-Christian tradition" that teaches that "humans alone are made in the image of God." "In Genesis, God gives humans dominion over the animals." But evolution has thoroughly refuted the biblical account, Singer maintains: Evolution teaches us that "We are animals"—and the result is that "sex across the species barrier [isn't that a scientific-sounding euphemism?] ceases to be an offence to our status and dignity as human beings."[30]

These sentiments do not remain carefully contained within academia, but trickle down into popular culture—where they have a much greater impact on the public. In 2002 a play opened on Broadway to rave reviews called *The Goat, or, Who Is Sylvia?* featuring a successful architect who confesses to his wife that he has fallen in love with someone else. The object of his affection turns out to be a goat named Sylvia.[31] Apparently, playwrights no longer feel that they can get enough dramatic tension out of an ordinary affair; to really create drama, they must probe the theme of bestiality.

A culture is driven by a kind of logic: It will eventually begin to express the logical consequences of the dominant worldview. If evolution is true—if there really is an unbroken continuity between humans and animals—then Singer is absolutely right about what he calls "sex across the species barrier."

Once again, all the dots connect back to your view of origins.

In another example, few years ago a song by a group called the Bloodhound Gang soared to number 17 on Billboard's top 200 chart. It featured a catchy refrain punched out over and over again: "You and me baby ain't nothin' but mammals; so let's do it like they do on the Discovery Channel." The video featured band members dressed up as monkeys in antic sexual poses.[32]

Back in the 1940s, Alfred Kinsey, himself a committed Darwinist, said the only source of sexual norms for humans is what the other mammals do—whatever fits within "the normal mammalian picture."[33] What Kinsey stated in academic jargon half a century ago is now showing up in punchy rhymes for teenagers.

And not just teenagers. A friend tells me he heard two young boys belting out a song while playing in the park, and as he came closer he could make out the words—"You and me baby ain't nothing but mammals." The boys were only about eight years old.

DARWINIZING CULTURE

In the past, most social scientists tried to limit the implications of evolution by erecting a wall between biology and culture. Evolution created the human body, they said, but then humans created culture, which is independent of biology.[34] This conviction was a key plank in defending against biological determinism. Today, with the rise of evolutionary psychology, that wall is crumbling. Scientists realize they can no longer put any arbitrary limit on the logic of evolution. Consistency requires that they apply it across the board—to religion, morality, politics, everything.

For a fascinating example of the change in outlook, consider the dramatic turnabout that brought Singer into the sociobiology camp. When the theory first appeared, Singer went into fierce opposition mode. As he later explained, sociobiology raised hackles because it was regarded as a revival of Social Darwinism with its "nasty, right-wing biological determinism." Social Darwinism had long harnessed the idea of the survival of the fittest to the ruthless pursuit of self-interest; and sociobiology, it seemed, merely replaced the selfish individual with the selfish gene.[35]

In his recent book *A Darwinian Left,* however, Singer makes an astounding reversal, pressing liberals and leftists to accept sociobiology's offshoot, evolutionary psychology. The left must "face the fact that we are evolved animals," he intones, "and that we bear the evidence of our inheritance, not only in our anatomy and our DNA, but in our behavior too."[36]

Singer seems to have realized that it is impossible to limit the implications of Darwinian evolution. There is no way to cordon off politics or morality or whatever you happen to care most about, and say, *This* is immune to the implications of evolution. Once you accept the Darwinian premise, there is logical pressure to be consistent, applying it to every aspect of culture. Today evolutionary psychologists are putting out books with all-encompassing titles like *The Evolution of Culture* and *Darwinizing Culture,* which contend that culture can no longer be separated from biology, but is itself merely a product of evolutionary forces.[37]

In other words, Darwinists are connecting all the dots, tracing everything back to origins. And that's why Christians had better connect the dots as well. If *they* offer "universal Darwinism," then *we* had better offer "universal Design," showing that design theory gives scientific support for an all-encompassing Christian worldview.

THE ACID BITES BACK

Given that evolutionary psychology often leads to morally outrageous conclusions, as we have seen, why is it gaining such rapid acceptance? The reason is that, for many people, it promises to provide a morality based on the solid ground of science instead of the myths of religion. Some twenty years ago, sociologist Howard Kaye wrote what is now a classic critique of sociobiology, in which he calls it nothing less than a secularized natural theology—an attempt to use nature to justify a secular worldview. Evolutionary psychology engages in a two-part process: First it debunks traditional morality by reducing it to genetic self-interest ("an illusion fobbed off on us by our genes"); then it offers to construct a new morality with all the authority of science. Extending Darwinian principles from bodies to behavior, it claims that adaptive forms of behavior survive, while maladaptive ones are weeded out by natural selection.[38]

But it is painfully clear from the examples we have surveyed that literally *any* behavior that is practiced today can be said to have survival value—after all, it has *survived* to our own times. Evolution fails as a moral guide because it provides no standard for judging any existing practices.

The logical flaw in the theory, however, is that it undercuts itself. For if all our ideas are products of evolution, then so is the idea of evolutionary psychology itself. Like all other constructs of the human mind, it is not true but only useful for survival. Daniel Dennett may call Darwinism a "universal acid" that dissolves away traditional religion and ethics (as we saw in an earlier chapter)—but it is the height of wishful thinking for him to presume that the acid will dissolve only *other* people's views, while leaving his own views untouched.[39] Once the very possibility of objective truth has been undermined, then Darwinian evolution itself cannot be objectively true.

Once when I was presenting these ideas at a Christian college, a man in the audience raised his hand and said, "I have only one question: These guys who think all our ideas and beliefs evolved . . . , do they think *their own* ideas evolved?" The audience burst into laughter, because of course the man had nailed the crux of the matter in a single, punchy question. If all ideas are products of evolution, and not really true but only useful, then evolution *itself* is not true either. And why should the rest of us pay it any attention?

To use philosophical labels, a statement that undercuts itself is self-defeating or self-referentially absurd. Other examples would include using logical arguments to refute the validity of logic; or stating (in English) that you cannot speak English; or arguing that there are absolutely no moral absolutes; or saying "My brother is an only child." Discovering that a philosophy is self-referentially absurd is a sure sign that it is fatally flawed.

TELLING GENES TO JUMP IN THE LAKE

Another way to evaluate a theory is by submitting it to the practical test: Can we live by it? Does it fit our experience of human nature? Many proponents of evolutionary psychology admit that it is a dark doctrine, with repugnant implications. After all, if humans are nothing more than "gene machines" or "robots" programmed to behave in certain ways by natural selection, then what becomes of moral freedom and human dignity? Ironically, when evolutionary psychologists reach that point, they will suddenly turn around and contradict everything they have just said—urging us to act *against* our genetic programming by embracing traditional moral ideals of love and altruism.

Our earlier discussion of the two-story view of truth helps us recognize the dynamic taking place here. As ever-greater areas of life are absorbed into the lower story of Darwinian determinism, the only way to defend any concept of moral freedom is to leap to the upper story—no matter how self-contradictory and irrational it renders the resulting theory.

A prime example is *The Moral Animal*, where Robert Wright starts with the premise that "our genes control us"—that "we are all machines, pushed and pulled by [physical] forces." Even our noblest beliefs are products of natural selection: "We believe the things—about morality, personal worth, even objective truth—that lead to behaviors that get our genes into the next generation." The implications of all this are as clear as they are troubling: "Free will is an illusion," a "useful fiction," part of an "outmoded worldview." Darwinism even calls into question "the very meaning of the word *truth*." All truth claims "are, by Darwinian lights, raw power struggles." Wright doesn't flinch from concluding that Darwinism leads to utter "cynicism."[40]

But then, ignoring all he has just said, he takes a grand leap of faith by urging us to work on "correcting the moral biases built into us by natural selection" and practicing the ideal of "brotherly love."[41] But if we really are "machines" created by natural selection, how can we "correct" the force that created us?

Dawkins gives a similar display of stunning inconsistency in *The Selfish Gene*. Again and again he insists that the genes "created us, body and mind"; that we are their "survival machines"—merely sophisticated "robots" built by the genes to perpetuate themselves. Yet astonishingly, he then turns around and issues a stirring declaration of independence from our genetic masters: "We have the power to defy the selfish genes of our birth," he says with rhetorical flourish. Although "we are built as gene machines, . . . we have the power to turn against our creators. We, alone on earth, can rebel against the tyranny of the selfish replicators."[42]

But where does this power to rebel come from? How does a machine rise up against its creator? Like all of us, Dawkins knows from actual experience that we do make genuine choices. Yet there is nothing in evolutionary psychology to account for this power of choice—and so he simply makes a leap of faith to a conclusion totally unwarranted by his own philosophy.

What these examples tell us is that evolutionary psychology fails the practical test: No one can live by it. Since universal human experience confirms the reality of moral choice, evolutionary psychologists cannot actually live on the basis of their own deterministic theory. They may try to, but when the contradiction between theory and life grows too pressing, they suddenly abandon the theory and proclaim their autonomy from the power of the genes. As Steven Pinker once wrote, noting that his choices contradicted the genetic imperative, "If my genes don't like it, they can go jump in the lake."[43]

A rather humorous example came to light back when former president Bill Clinton was in trouble for various escapades, and it became fashionable to offer evolutionary explanations for his behavior couched in terms of "alpha males." Dawkins jumped on the bandwagon, explaining that our evolutionary ancestors were not monogamous (like Canada geese), but instead were harem builders (like seals and walruses), where any male who monopolized power and wealth could also monopolize females, thus ensuring the survival of his genes. Ergo, Clinton's behavior was simply a fossilized remnant from our genetic past.

At this point, Dawkins seemed to grow uncomfortable about offering a genetic excuse for immorality. So he confided to readers that he himself had made the "un-Darwinian personal decision" to be "deliberately monogamous."[44] But think about this for a moment—if we really are programmed by our genes through Darwinian selection, how *could* anyone make an "un-Darwinian" decision? In fact, how could anyone make free moral decisions at all? The notion that we are free to act in un-Darwinian ways is completely irrational within the Darwinian worldview.

The reason people are compelled to take an irrational leap is that no matter what they believe, they are still made in the image of God. Even when they reject the witness of Scripture, they still face the constant witness of their own human nature. At some point, even the most adamant scientific materialists find that their own humanity resists the deterministic implications of the Darwinian worldview—that human nature stubbornly refuses to remain within the cramped confines of any mechanistic philosophy (the lower story). When that happens, they simply issue a declaration of independence from the power of the selfish genes, and take a leap of faith to a traditional concept of moral freedom and responsibility (the upper story), even though it is completely unwarranted within their own worldview.[45]

Ironically, critics often dismiss Christianity as irrational—yet it does not require any irrational, self-contradictory leap of faith. Because it begins with a personal God, Christianity provides a consistent, unified worldview that holds true *both* in the natural realm *and* in the moral, spiritual realm. The biblical doctrine of the image of God gives a solid basis for human dignity and moral freedom that is compatible with the compelling witness of human experience. Unlike the evolutionary psychologist, Christians can live consistently on the basis of their worldview because it fits the real world.

MENTAL MAPS

Since the leap of faith is endemic in the way people think today, let's analyze one final example in greater detail. The theme of Singer's book *A Darwinian Left* is that people along the entire political spectrum must now accept a Darwinian account of human nature. Yet at the end of the book Singer contradicts everything he has just said, by pronouncing that morality must be based on a power that *transcends* Darwinian forces. What power is that? Human reason. In a way not explained, natural selection has made us "reasoning beings"—which, paradoxically, enables us to transcend the impulses instilled by natural selection. Through reason, he promises, we will develop genuine altruism, not merely the pseudo-altruism of evolutionary psychology (the enlightened self-interest of kin selection or tit for tat). "We do not know," he writes wistfully, "to what extent our capacity to reason can . . . take us beyond the conventional Darwinian constraints on the degree of altruism that a society may be able to foster."[46]

Singer does not account for this novel capacity that frees us from "Darwinian constraints"—he simply pulls it out of a hat. Reason may eventually even "overcome the pull of other elements in our evolved nature," he hopes, until we embrace "the idea of an impartial concern for all of our fellow humans." To that end, we are urged to consider "deliberately cultivating and nurturing pure, disinterested altruism—something that has no place in nature, something that has never existed before in the whole history of the world."[47]

If *this* isn't a leap of faith, I don't know what is. Reason is presented as a mysterious capacity capable of creating something de novo, something that has never existed before—one might even say ex nihilo. This godlike power will enable us to rise above our evolutionary origins. Here reason is treated as far more than a utilitarian instrument: It is nothing less than the means of achieving freedom—metaphysical and moral freedom. "In a more distant future that we can still barely glimpse," Singer writes, scientific knowledge "may turn out to be the prerequisite for a new kind of freedom."[48]

Translation: Singer finds no basis for morality and altruism within the Darwinian worldview in the lower story—so he takes a leap to a hypothetical upper-story realm far beyond the constraints of "our evolved nature." Somehow the evolutionary process has produced a power that liberates us from the evolutionary process. Singer has cut humanity completely loose from its Darwinian anchor in biology, and set it free to soar to dizzying heights. But his philosophy is left behind in a hopeless crumple of contradictions.

Taking a leap of faith is a sure sign that a person's philosophy fails to explain human nature *as he himself experiences it.* When his worldview points in one direction while his lived experience points in another direction, then he cannot consistently live on the basis of his professed worldview.

This in turn is a reliable indicator that the worldview itself is faulty. After all, a worldview is a mental map of the *world*—and if it is accurate, it will enable us to navigate reality effectively. Most of us have a mental map of our bedroom, for example, so that if we get up at night, we can walk around in the dark and not bump into things. But if we're spending the night in an unfamiliar place, then we're liable to hit our shin on the furniture or knock our nose on the door frame. Our mental map of the new place isn't accurate yet—it doesn't fit reality. And so we find ourselves bumping up against reality in painful ways.

By the same token, if our worldview doesn't fit the larger reality we are trying to explain, then at some point we will find that we cannot follow it—that it is not a workable guide for navigating the world. C. S. Lewis once wrote, "The Christian and the Materialist hold different beliefs about the universe. They can't both be right. The one who is wrong will act in a way which simply doesn't fit the real universe."[49] That's why it is a potent criticism of evolutionary psychology to point out that proponents cannot live consistently on the basis of their own theory. Because they act in ways that don't "fit the real universe," at some point, they bump up against reality. And when they find the consequences too painful, they tell their genes to go jump in the lake—then take a leap to the upper story where, in some subjective way, human values can still be affirmed.

BEWARE SCIENTISTS BEARING VALUES

The rise of evolutionary psychology makes it clear that the debate over Darwinism is not just over scientific facts but over conflicting worldviews—the mental maps we use to navigate the world. "The Darwinian revolution was not merely the replacement of one scientific theory by another," wrote zoologist Ernst Mayr, "but rather the replacement of a worldview, in which the supernatural was accepted as a normal and relevant explanatory principle, by a *new worldview* in which there was no room for supernatural forces."[50] Worldview clashes are far too important to leave to scientists to adjudicate. All of us need to understand the debate over Darwinian evolution and be prepared to discuss it with our family and neighbors, and in the public square. It is nothing less than a debate over how we should order our personal lives and our corporate lives—and the stakes are very high indeed.

For if Darwinism is true, then religion and morality are nothing more than irrational, upper-story beliefs inhabiting the realm of *value* rather than *fact*. We are sometimes reassured that this is not a bad thing, because after all the subjectivity of the *value* realm renders it immune to rational scrutiny. The marketing pitch can be quite seductive: Scientific naturalists say they will acknowledge that there are certain moral and religious feelings that science cannot account for—if, in return, theology will agree not to intrude into realms investigated by science. In other words, if Christians would just relinquish all claims to objective truth, then they would be granted an arena where their beliefs are secure from criticism.

But it has become evident that such a bargain offers a false security. So great is the intellectual imperialism of naturalistic evolution that it will not leave the *value* realm in peace. Evolutionary psychology is recklessly invading the *value* territory and claiming ground once off-limits to science—seeking to explain moral behavior, human relationships, cultural customs, and yes, even religion, as products of natural selection. A recent book by Dawkins denounces religion as a virus of the mind—a "malignant infection" that invades the mind like a computer virus.[51] Clearly, the *fact* realm is mounting a continued siege on the *value* realm.

That's why it is dangerous to engage in any cognitive bargaining that relegates Christianity to the *value* realm. The human mind has a natural drive toward unity and consistency, and for the Darwinist, that means dragging everything down into the lower story so that evolution itself may become a unified, holistic system. The only way to counter that system is to show that Christianity is equally holistic. It is not an irrational, upper-story leap, but a comprehensive truth that meets the human hunger for an overarching, consistent worldview. As Christians we must make it clear that we are not offering a subjective, private faith that is immune to rational scrutiny. We are making cognitive claims about objective knowledge that can be defended in the public arena.

DILEMMA OF LEO STRAUSS

The historic Christian conception of morality rests on a cognitive claim about human nature. It says humans were designed for a purpose—to be conformed to spiritual ideals of holiness and perfection, so that we may live in love with God and our fellow creatures. Moral rules are simply the instructions telling us how to fulfill those ideals, how to reach that goal, how to live according to that divine purpose. In the Fall we went off the track, but in salvation God puts us back on course and empowers us to resume the journey to developing our full humanity, to become the people He originally intended us to be. To use a technical term, Christian morality is *teleological,* based on the concept of human progress toward the purpose or ideal (*telos*) for which we were designed.

Under the Darwinian regime, however, the very concept of purpose or teleology has come under attack. For if the world itself was not designed, then there can be no design or purpose for human life either. Morality is reduced to a product of biology—an expression of our subjective desires and impulses, programmed into us by natural selection. That's why the political philosopher Leo Strauss once said "the fundamental dilemma" in locating a moral basis for public life today "is caused by the victory of modern natural science." For "the teleological view of the universe, of which the teleological view of man forms a part, would seem to have been destroyed by modern natural science."

Just so. If evolution is correct in portraying a world without purpose, then the traditional teleological conception of morality cannot be sustained. (For more on this subject, see appendix 3.) Now, Strauss took Darwinian evolution to be an irrefutable fact, and he tried to work around it by grounding morality in the realm of Platonic ideals. Yet that was not "an adequate solution to the problem," as he himself recognized, because it implied a two-story view of knowledge—the "fundamental, typically modern, dualism of a nonteleological natural science" (in the lower story), along with "a teleological science of man" (in the upper story).[52]

The liberating message of Design theory is that we don't have to take Darwinian evolution as an irrefutable fact, nor resign ourselves to the "typically modern dualism." As we saw in the previous chapter, design and purpose have once again become core concepts in explaining nature itself—both in the organic world (the cell and DNA) and in the physical world (the fine-tuning of the universe). Design theory thus provides the scientific basis for the recovery of a holistic, teleological worldview. It releases us from the modern dualism, making it reasonable once again to speak of morality as a form of objective knowledge.

BORN-AGAIN DARWINISTS

The destructive impact of the Darwinian worldview on religion and morality has become so commonplace that it hardly even registers as news anymore. For example, when yet another article came across my desk about someone challenging the Boy Scouts' exclusion of atheists and homosexuals, I nearly set it aside without reading it. But then a small item caught my eye. It turned out that an Eagle Scout was being threatened with ejection because he was an atheist, counter to the Scout pledge, and the significant phrase read like this: The young man, who was nineteen, "has been an atheist since studying evolution in the ninth grade."[53] The fact was reported as though it were perfectly normal, even routine, for kids to lose their religious faith when they encounter the theory of evolution in science classes.

Admittedly the pattern is distressingly common. "In my senior year of high school I accepted Jesus as my Savior and became a born-again Christian," says one writer. "I had found the One True Religion, and it was my duty—indeed it was my pleasure—to tell others about it, including my parents, brothers and sisters, friends, and even total strangers."[54] But this young man's religious conviction did not survive a serious encounter with evolutionary theory: He underwent a "deconversion in graduate school six years later when I studied evolutionary biology."[55] Who is the writer? Michael Shermer, the director of the Skeptics Society and publisher of *Skeptic* magazine. Shermer now makes a cottage industry of debunking Christianity, while defending Darwinism against design theorists.

Another prominent atheist tells a similar story. "I was a born-again Christian. When I was fifteen, I entered the Southern Baptist Church with great fervor and interest in the fundamentalist religion." But once again, the religious fervor did not survive its confrontation with evolution. "I left [the church] at seventeen when I got to the University of Alabama and heard about evolutionary theory."[56] The encounter was nothing less than an "epiphany." "I was enthralled, couldn't stop thinking about the implications evolution has . . . for just about everything."[57] Who is this? Harvard professor E. O. Wilson, the founder of sociobiology. After losing his Christian faith, he says, science itself became the object of his religious longings, and he sought to channel the power of religion into the service of materialism. Religion itself "had to be explained as a material process, from the bottom up, atoms to genes to the human spirit. It had to be embraced by a single grand naturalistic image of man."[58]

THE KITCHEN AS CLASSROOM

This is the metaphysical motivation that drove sociobiology, and that now drives its offspring, evolutionary psychology—the desire to craft "a single grand naturalistic image of man." The only way to stand against such a comprehensive naturalistic worldview, as Abraham Kuyper said, is by articulating a Christian worldview "of equally comprehensive and far-reaching power."[59] We must prepare young people *before* they leave for college by teaching them that Christianity is not just religious truth but the truth about all reality. It is total truth.

One of the most inspiring models I've encountered was my own grandfather, Oswald Overn. With five rambunctious children close in age, he was determined to prepare them all to defend their faith by the time they left home. And so he turned the evening dinner table into a classroom—a place for serious teaching and discussion. "My father would bring books and articles to the dinner table, to read and discuss with us," recalls my uncle Bill Overn. "He taught us Latin, physics, math. He also had us memorize the creeds, the Lutheran catechism, and passages from the Bible." In fact, that's how all five children learned how to read: "We would read a passage by going around the table, and everyone from the oldest to the youngest had their verses to read."

He also created opportunities for one-on-one discussions. "My father would take one of the children with him when he went into town, and always he would expound on some topic," Bill says. "It was a three-mile walk into town, and he made use of every minute." As a physicist, my grandfather was especially attuned to the sciences, and he would often bring clippings of recent science news to the dinner table to discuss. He taught the children how to counter the standard evidences for evolution, so that by the time Bill went off to college to study physics, following in his father's footsteps, he was solidly grounded in apologetics and knew in his bones that the Christian faith was intellectually defensible.[60]

Unless we give our children that same level of confidence, they will not survive the cognitive warfare they face in the secular world today. Evolutionary psychologists, with their blatant, in-your-face applications of Darwinism, are the shock troops of evolution. Yet there is also a more hidden impact of Darwinism on American thought—and precisely because it is hidden, it is more pervasive and thus more dangerous. In the next chapter I will take you behind the scenes, so to speak, to reveal how Darwinism has permeated the American mind at a deeper level—even reshaping America's social, educational, and legal institutions. If Christians hope to speak effectively to modern culture, we need to diagnose the way these ideas have rippled out far beyond the sciences.

8

DARWINS OF THE MIND

They mean to tell us all was rolling blind
Till accidentally it hit on mind . . .
ROBERT FROST[1]

The impact of Darwin on worldview came home to me starkly one day while I was homeschooling my son. One of the joys of teaching your own children is that you get a chance to read all the wonderful books you missed when you were growing up. Thus it was that when Dieter was in junior high, we were reading together several young adult biographies of famous people—including Joseph Stalin. Suddenly I came across a startling dialogue from the days when the young Stalin was a seminary student, studying to become a priest in the Russian Orthodox Church. As one of his friends relates, they were discussing religion:

> "Joseph heard me out, and after a moment's silence, said: "'You know, they are fooling us, there is no God. . . .'
> "I was astonished at these words. I had never heard anything like it before.
> "'How can you say such things, Soso?' I exclaimed.
> "'I'll lend you a book to read; it will show you that the world and all living things are quite different from what you imagine, and all this talk about God is sheer nonsense,' Joseph said.
> "'What book is that?' I enquired.
> "'Darwin. You must read it,' Joseph impressed on me."[2]

We all know what happened after that: Having become an atheist, Stalin went on to murder literally millions of his own people in his attempt to construct an officially atheistic state.

Here in the West, the impact of Darwinism has been more subtle, yet it runs far deeper than most of us imagine. In the 1950s a group of scholars produced a thick volume titled *Evolutionary Thought in America* surveying its impact across the curriculum. The book included chapters on the influence of evolution on sociology, psychology, economics, political thought, moral theory, theology, and even literature.[3] Simply reading the table of contents hammers home the wide-ranging impact Darwinism has exerted on virtually every field of study. It is impossible to understand twentieth-century America unless we grasp the implications of evolutionary thinking.

In fact, in the late nineteenth century when Darwinism crossed the Atlantic, it was welcomed to American shores by a group of scholars who founded an entire school of philosophy upon it. The school was called philosophical pragmatism, and its core assumption was that if *life* has evolved, then the human *mind* has evolved as well—and all the human sciences must be rebuilt on that basis: psychology, education, law, and theology.[4] Pragmatism is America's only "home-grown" philosophy (most of the others were imported from Europe), and for that reason alone it has been enormously influential. By taking a closer look at philosophical pragmatism, we will get a good handle on the way Darwinism has altered not only the way Americans think but also the very structure of American social institutions.

HOLMES LOSES HIS FAITH

The central figures in developing philosophical pragmatism were John Dewey, William James, Charles Sanders Peirce, and Oliver Wendell Holmes, Jr. Their goal was to expand Darwinian naturalism into a complete worldview to rival traditional religion. As one historian explains, the pragmatists "sought ways of preserving some of the heart values of the older religion"—not by retaining any of the actual *content* of religion, but by finding "rich and inspiring versions of naturalism to replace it." Which is to say, by turning Darwinian naturalism itself into a comprehensive philosophy that would satisfy the need to make sense of life.[5]

The pragmatist's core beliefs can be illustrated in a dramatic way in the personal odyssey of Oliver Wendell Holmes, Jr. As a Harvard student prior to the Civil War, Holmes held conventional religious views. He joined a student group called the Christian Union, and wrote school essays on themes such as "the relations of man to God" and the need to base morality on ideas "in the mind of the Creator" instead of on arbitrary human concepts.[6] Later he became deeply involved in the abolitionist cause, and when war broke out he risked his college degree by dropping out right before graduation to enlist in the Massachusetts Militia.

But the horrors of war proved almost too much for Holmes—the blood, the chaos, and everywhere the dead and wounded bodies. He watched many of his friends die, and was wounded himself three times. The third time, he was shot in the foot and hoped desperately that it would have to be amputated, so he could be discharged. That's how much he had come to hate the war.

Somewhere along the way he began losing his Christian faith, a process that reached a crisis the first time he was wounded. Bleeding profusely, he was told by hospital personnel that he might die. And so, lying in a makeshift field hospital, with soldiers dying all around him, Holmes commenced a reexamination of his personal beliefs—or rather, by this time, his lack of beliefs. It struck him forcefully, as he later wrote, that "the majority vote of the civilized world declared that with my opinions I was *en route* to Hell"—and he was terrified. Should he undergo a deathbed conversion? Upon reviewing the options, he decided against it, feeling that conversion would be "nothing but a cowardly giving way to fear." Instead he determined to adopt the rather simplistic credo, "whatever shall happen is best." And with a whispered prayer, "God forgive me if I'm wrong," he went to sleep.[7]

Holmes had gone off to fight because of his moral beliefs (abolitionism), but he came home a moral skeptic. "The war did more than make him lose those beliefs," writes one historian. "It made him lose his belief in beliefs."[8] That is, he emerged from his wartime experience with the firm conviction that firm convictions lead only to conflict and violence. While recovering from his third war wound, he began reading books by Herbert Spencer, the enormously influential popularizer of Social Darwinism, and became a convinced Darwinist. From then on he began to argue that evolution applies not only to physical organisms but also to the sphere of beliefs and convictions. The great, towering principles that have shaped civilizations are not transcendent truths, he wrote, but simply those that won out in the "struggle for life among competing ideas."[9] These were to become the core teachings of philosophical pragmatism.

DARWIN'S NEW LOGIC

At its heart, pragmatism is a Darwinian view of knowledge (epistemology). The pragmatists asked, What does Darwinian naturalism mean for the way we understand the human mind? And they answered, It means the mind is nothing more than a part of nature. They rejected the older view that the human mind is *transcendent to* matter, in favor of the Darwinian view that mind is *produced by* matter.

In a single stroke, this assumption subverted both traditional and liberal forms of theism. Why? Because both forms make mind prior to matter. In traditional theology, a transcendent God creates the world according to His own design and purpose; in liberal theology, an immanent deity externalizes its purposes through the historical development of the world. Either way, mind precedes matter, shaping and directing the development of the material world.

Darwin reversed that order: In his theory, mind emerges very late in evolutionary history, as a product of purely natural forces. Mind is not a fundamental, creative force in the universe but merely an evolutionary by-product. In short, Darwin "naturalized" the mind.[10]

For the pragmatists, this naturalizing of the mind was the most revolutionary impact of Darwinian theory. It seemed to imply that mental functions are merely adaptations for solving problems in the environment. Ideas originate as chance mutations in the brain, parallel to Darwin's chance variations in nature. And the ideas that stick around and become firm beliefs are those that help us adapt to the environment—a sort of mental natural selection. Concepts and convictions develop as tools for survival, no different from the lion's teeth or the eagle's claws.

John Dewey even wrote a famous essay called "The Influence of Darwin on Philosophy," in which he said Darwinism gives us a "new logic to apply to mind and morals and life."[11] In this new evolutionary logic, ideas are nothing more than mental tools for getting things done. We don't decide if a tool is any good by judging it against a transcendent, eternal ideal; instead we test it by how successfully it does the job, how well it works in coping with the environment. If a fork works, Dewey said, you go ahead and use it. If you're trying to eat soup and it doesn't work, you don't engage in philosophical disquisitions on the essential "nature" of forks; instead you go get a spoon.[12]

CASH VALUE OF AN IDEA

The pragmatists were highly influenced by the experimental psychologists of their day, who were engaged in a similar project of applying Darwinism to the mind. Through most of the nineteenth century, psychology had been understood as the science of the soul, and its method was introspection—the examination of consciousness. But the new experimental approach was behavioristic, claiming that the mind could be known only through external actions of the body that can be observed and measured. These ideas reinforced the pragmatists' view that mind is not a distinct spiritual substance but merely part of nature.

William James, for example, was quite impressed by the laboratory work of one of his students, Edward Thorndike, who put chickens and other tame animals in boxes, then measured how long it took them to learn to press a lever to open a door and get food pellets. You may remember this from a Psychology

101 course. Sure enough, over time the chickens learned to press the lever as soon as they were in the box. The pattern had been imprinted. James decided that ideas were imprinted in the human mind the same way. If believing something produces results—if it gets us "pellets" that we want—then over time that belief is imprinted in our minds. In his famous phrase, truth is the "cash value" of an idea: If it pays off, then we call it true.[13]

In short, beliefs are not reflections of reality but rules for action.[14] Peirce liked to say that beliefs are a kind of prediction—a bet. When we say something is true, we are merely predicting that if we perform a certain action we will get a certain response. The model for this definition was scientific knowledge: If we say quartz is hard, we mean it will not be scratched if we rub it with wood or cork or plastic. Given the meaning of the word *hard,* we may predict the outcome of various operations on a lump of quartz. For Peirce, a successful belief is simply a winning bet.[15]

To understand how revolutionary all this was, we must realize that until this time the dominant theory of knowledge was based on the biblical doctrine of the image of God. It is because human reason reflects the divine reason that we can trust human knowledge to be generally reliable. God created our minds to "fit" the universe that He made for us to inhabit; and when our cognitive faculties are functioning properly, they are designed to give us genuine knowledge. Even thinkers who moved outside the sphere of traditional Christian theology still retained the philosophical assumption that the human mind is akin to a higher Mind, an absolute Mind, as the guarantee of human knowledge.[16]

But the pragmatists faced squarely the implications of evolution: If blind, undirected natural forces produced the mind, they said, then it is meaningless to ask whether our ideas reflect reality. Ideas are simply mental survival strategies—continuations of the struggle for existence by other means. "'The true' is only the expedient in the way of our thinking," James wrote, "just as 'the right' is only the expedient in the way of our behaving."[17]

WHAT'S RELIGION WORTH TO YOU?

James was even tolerant toward religious beliefs, at least more so than some of the other pragmatists. His father had converted to Christianity during the Second Great Awakening, then converted just as enthusiastically to Swedenborgianism, with the result that James never quite shook off an awareness of the spiritual realm. His view was that if a religion gives some sense of happiness and meaning, then it is "true." In his words, "If the hypothesis of God works satisfactorily in the widest sense of the word, it is true."[18]

True, at least, for the individual who believes it. James was perhaps the most personable of the pragmatists—charming, creative, emotionally effusive, and totally maddening to his colleagues because of his extreme individualism. The other pragmatists all held that knowledge is a social construction; individuals don't create knowledge, groups do. By contrast, James was willing to let each individual decide what "works satisfactorily" for him, and then believe accordingly.

In some passages, James even seemed to say that any system of thought, scientific or religious, is "true" insofar as it meets a person's needs. Presented with a complex world, he wrote, humans naturally wonder what its ultimate nature is: "Science says molecules. Religion says God." How do we decide which is true? Well, on one hand, James answered, "science can do certain things for us." (By that he meant that scientific reasoning enables us to "deduce and explain" events.) Yet on the other hand, "God can do other things" for us. (Religion can "inspire and console" us.) So the question each individual must ask is: "*Which things* are worth the most?"[19] Whatever you decide, that's your truth.

James was toying with ideas we now call postmodern, and it evoked a stinging rebuke from the British philosopher Bertrand Russell. James's pragmatic defense of religion "simply omits as unimportant the question whether God really is in His heaven," Russell objected; "if He is a useful hypothesis, that is enough." What a ridiculously narrow frame of reference, he fumed: The pragmatists act as though all that matters is the effect ideas have "upon the creatures inhabiting our petty planet."[20] Plainly, beliefs can be useful and yet be false, Russell pointed out; thus it really does matter whether a religion is true, not just how it makes us feel.

There is a kernel of truth in pragmatism, of course. If a belief system is true, then it ought to work in the real world, as we argued in the previous chapter. One of the ways we can check out a truth claim is to submit it to the practical test. But pragmatic success does not *make* a claim true. As with all "isms," pragmatism fastens upon one aspect of reality and elevates it into a system that reduces everything else to a single dimension.

TOUGH VERSUS TENDER

To understand any philosophy, it is crucial to ask what question people were trying to answer. The problem the pragmatists wanted to solve was the division of knowledge that has plagued Western thought for centuries. They wanted to bridge the gap between fact and value—to merge the lower and upper stories—and bring about a reunification of knowledge.

Recall the thumbnail sketch given in chapter 3: When the two-story dichotomy was secularized, the downstairs was occupied by the Enlightenment and the upstairs by Romanticism. What did these categories mean in the late nineteenth century? In the lower story, the Enlightenment had given rise to British empiricism and utilitarianism. Society was reduced to a collection of individuals held together by sheer choice (atomism). And individuals in turn were reduced to complex mechanisms.

Meanwhile, the upper story was taken over by Romantic idealism. Here we're talking about people like Hegel, who taught that the material world is the outworking of an Absolute Spirit or Mind or God. Romanticism was fiercely opposed to the Enlightenment: In contrast to utilitarianism, it upheld moral idealism. Instead of atomism, it offered holism. Instead of physical reductionism, it affirmed the reality of Spirit.

This dualism was even reflected in the university curriculum, in a division between the sciences and the humanities. As the sciences were taken over by philosophical naturalism, the humanities adopted philosophical idealism and historicism (the Absolute externalizes itself over time through the historical process).[21]

The two-tiered truth led to a division within the university curriculum:

THE ARTS AND HUMANITIES
Philosophical Idealism

THE SCIENCES
Philosophical Naturalism

By the late nineteenth century, these two contradictory streams stood in tense opposition to one another. Nor was it merely an academic problem. The two contradictory pictures of reality were experienced by thoughtful people as an agonizing internal division, a painful tension that cried out to be resolved.[22] This was the existential dilemma that drove the pragmatists, especially Dewey and James.

"Dewey's condemnation of dualism was the central feature of his philosophy," says one philosopher; "he vigorously attacked this in virtually everything he wrote."[23] Dewey traced the dichotomy back to the Form/Matter dualism of the ancient Greeks (just as we did in chapter 2). Then he offered pragmatism as a "via media," a middle way that would overcome the dichotomy that pitted naturalism in the lower story against idealism in the upper story.[24]

William James experienced the inner conflict even more intensely.[25] He was particularly sensitive to the imperialism of science in the lower story. While respecting legitimate science, James despised what he saw as an aggressive naturalistic philosophy masquerading as science, which led to "determinism, atheism, and cynicism." It undercut the objective status of values, driving students to agnostic despair (here James spoke from painful personal experience).[26] Caught in the conflict, he spiraled into a profound depression, which finally precipitated what he described as a "collapse."

James would later describe his spiritual crisis as a tension between the Tough-Minded (who care only about science and facts) and the Tender-Minded (who long for meaning and values).[27] The pragmatists hoped their own philosophy would bridge the gulf: "You want a system that will combine both things," James wrote: "the scientific loyalty to facts . . . but also the old confidence in human values." The two have become "hopelessly separated," he went on, but "I offer the oddly-named thing pragmatism as a philosophy that can satisfy both kinds of demand."[28]

DISCIPLES OF DARWIN

How did the pragmatists hope to accomplish this reunification of knowledge? By taking a little from each of the two conflicting streams of thought and melding them together. From Romantic idealism (the upper story), the pragmatists took its historicism—the definition of ideas as products of evolving custom. For if reality was the unfolding of an Absolute Mind, then everything was in a process of constant change and evolution—not only living things but also cultures, customs, and concepts.

From British empiricism (the lower story), the pragmatists took its instrumentalism—the definition of ideas as tools for achieving social goals. By combining these two approaches, the pragmatists transformed Hegel's historicism from a *spiritual* process into a thoroughly *naturalistic* process.

As a result, however, they never actually succeeded in combining *fact* and *value,* but only offered a new flavor of naturalism. The model for their strategy was Darwin, who had effected virtually the same merging of the two philosophical traditions within biology. Darwin's theory of evolution was in part a product of Romantic historicism applied to biology (there are no stable essences; everything is in constant flux). But being a good British empiricist, he gave the evolutionary process a completely materialistic mechanism. In other words, he melded historicism with naturalism. As one historian puts it, "Darwin gave Hegel the respectability of science."[29] That's exactly what the pragmatists aspired to do in areas *beyond* biology—take over Hegel's cultural evolutionism, but give it the respectability of science by rendering it completely naturalistic.

The pragmatists were not the only ones who wanted to naturalize Hegelian historicism. Many of the early anthropologists and other social scientists of the nineteenth century had tried to do the same thing, the most notable being Karl Marx. (That's why it is often said that Marx turned Hegel on his head.) The difference was that these earlier thinkers tended to be determinists: They decreed that all societies everywhere must pass through the same inevitable stages of cultural evolution, governed by unchanging "laws" of social evolution. (For Marx, the stages were based on economic relationships.) What made the pragmatists unique is that they rejected determinism outright, and instead conceived of history as completely contingent—spontaneous, unpredictable, open to genuine novelty.

Why did the pragmatists break the mold of deterministic thinking? The answer, again, was the influence of Darwin. As we saw in chapter 6, Darwin's theory consists of two elements: chance and law. The pragmatists seized on the role of chance and turned it into the basis for a philosophy of indeterminacy, freedom, and innovation. In their interpretation, the "openness" of the world takes the form of *chance* at lower levels of complexity, and takes the form of *choice* at the human level.[30] An incomplete and indeterminate world left room for humans to play a role in creating reality by their free choices.

TRANSFORMING AMERICA

How do these ideas affect the world we live in today? The answer is that they have radically reshaped American social institutions. Let's focus on four crucial areas: theology, law, education, and philosophy.

Let God Evolve

In theology, the pragmatists asked: What kind of God is compatible with evolution? And they answered that *if* you keep any notion of God at all, it has to be an immanent God—a finite deity evolving in and with the world. "With the advent of evolution," writes one philosopher, "the tendency of those who took science seriously was to conceive of God increasingly as immanent in the world process."[31]

Among the pragmatists, the most influential in this area was Charles Sanders Peirce. The quirkiest of the group, Peirce had a prickly, arrogant character that made it difficult for him to keep a job. He violated prevailing moral sensibilities by getting divorced and then living with his second wife before marrying her. Back then, this kind of scandal was enough to shut the door on teaching positions at the universities, and often Peirce had to rely on the generosity of his friends just to keep body and soul together. But he was a brilliant abstract thinker and made significant contributions to logic and probability theory.

Peirce felt strongly about religion, but despised traditional and orthodox forms of it. Instead, he proposed a form of panpsychism (everything in the universe has a mind or consciousness). He envisioned the entire cosmos evolving toward Mind or the Absolute or God, in a teleological process he called "evolutionary love."[32]

Where do we hear these ideas in our own day? In Process Theology, which some say is the fastest-growing movement in mainline seminaries today. Its founder, Charles Hartshorne, said Peirce was one of the few thinkers who had the greatest influence on him.[33]

Process Theology teaches that God and the world are both in a process of constant change and evolution. God is a divine spirit evolving in and with the world, the soul of the world, the evolving cosmic life of which our lives are a part. This is not strictly speaking *pantheism* (all is God), but rather *panentheism* (all is *in* God), where the physical world is a concrete emanation of God's own essence.[34] Process Theology teaches that as we make the choices that shape our lives and experiences, we also shape God and His experiences, since our lives give concrete form to the divine life. In short, we are not only co-creators *with* God, we are also co-creators *of* God. When we die, then, the life we have lived merely becomes a past stage in God's own ongoing life, while we as individuals cease to exist. There is no afterlife.

By placing God Himself within the evolutionary nexus, Process Theology breaks sharply with traditional theism. It holds that God is limited—He does not know in advance what is going to happen (He is not omniscient), nor does He have the power to prevent evil from happening (He is not omnipotent). Instead, He simply evolves along with the world over the course of history.

Surprisingly, some of these same themes have spilled over into evangelical circles as well, in what is known as Open Theism, promoted by Clark Pinnock and others. The term itself echoes the pragmatists' language when they described an evolving universe as an "open" universe—a world of novelty, innovation, emergence, and unpredictable possibilities, which cannot be known in advance, even by God.[35]

Clearly, one reason for challenging evolutionary *science* is that otherwise we may find our churches and seminaries teaching evolutionary *theology*.[36]

Why Judges Make Law

Oliver Wendell Holmes, Jr., influenced legal thought more than anyone else in the twentieth century. Applying philosophical pragmatism to the law, he founded a movement called—not surprisingly—legal pragmatism. As we saw at the beginning of the chapter, Holmes was greatly influenced by Herbert Spencer, and he often sprinkled Social Darwinist concepts throughout his writings, speaking of the law as merely a product of the "survival of the fittest" among competing interest groups.[37] But Holmes did more than just use Darwinian metaphors. Earlier we saw how pragmatism followed the Darwinian model by weaving together German idealism with British empiricism—and Holmes followed exactly the same strategy in the field of jurisprudence. He took the historical school of jurisprudence (from German idealism) and wove it together with the analytical school of jurisprudence (from British empiricism).[38]

From the historical school, Holmes took the idea that the source of law is nothing but evolving custom. Whereas traditional Western legal philosophy had based law on an unchanging source (on natural law, derived ultimately from divine law), Holmes treated law as a product of evolving cultures and traditions, completely relative to particular times and cultures. In fact, the whole reason for doing historical research, he said, was not to defend traditional concepts of law against would-be reformers, but precisely the opposite: By tracing legal ideas over the course of history, we can see for ourselves that they are *not* based on any unchanging, universal moral order, but are always the product of a particular local culture and its unique history. Once we grasp this, Holmes said, then judges will be liberated from the past and free to change the law to reflect whatever social policy they think works best. As Holmes put it, "History sets us free and enables us to make up our minds dispassionately" as to whether the old legal rules still serve any purpose.[39]

And how do we determine whether the old rules still serve any purpose? By their practical consequences. From the analytical school of jurisprudence Holmes took the idea that the criterion for law is social utility, as measured by the social sciences. In his words, the law should be established "upon accurately measured social desires."[40] This is the source of one of Holmes's famous aphorisms: "The man of the future is the man of statistics and the master of economics."[41] In other words, the law should be judged by what works—and what works is determined by empirical studies done by social scientists. Law is reduced to a tool for social engineering. The justification for any given law, Holmes wrote, is "not that it represents an eternal principle" such as Justice, but "that it helps bring out a social end which we desire."[42]

In practice, of course, this means a social end that the *judge* desires. Holmes unabashedly agreed that judges do not merely interpret the law but make law.

Where have we seen these ideas at work in our own day? The idea that law is about enacting social policies? That judges don't just interpret the law but make law?[43] The most significant example is the 1973 *Roe v. Wade* abortion decision. Even supporters of the decision agree that the court essentially legislated from the bench. In the majority opinion, Justice Harry Blackmun wrote that abortion must be considered in relation to "population growth, pollution, poverty, and racial" issues. In other words, the Court made its decision not by what the *law* said but by the social outcomes it favored.[44]

This is the heritage of legal pragmatism. And it will shape the way the courts deal with a host of new bioethical issues on the horizon, unless we challenge the underlying Darwinian worldview.

Dewey's Dilemmas

John Dewey did more to shape educational methodology than anyone else in the twentieth century. Born in 1859, the same year Darwin published his *Origin of Species,* Dewey grew up in an evangelical home (Congregational) and was profoundly influenced by his devout mother. In his early twenties, he underwent a conversion—a "mystic experience," he called it—and afterward he attended church regularly and even taught Bible classes.[45]

Eventually, however, Dewey embarked on a slow and gradual process of losing his faith—so gradual that it never seemed to cause him any mental trauma. That may have been due partly to his inherent temperament, for Dewey had a phlegmatic, unflappable, almost colorless personality. In any case, his spiritual decline began in college, where he encountered a liberal form of theology shaped by German idealism. Later he was to say that Hegel "left a permanent deposit in my thinking." His early writings are attempts to meld Hegel and Darwin by proposing an immanent God embodied in matter, like the soul in the body—similar to Process Theology. Later Dewey accepted the Social Gospel, which redefined salvation as social progress. God did not impart grace to individuals, he argued, but was immanent in culture; if the culture embraced Christian values, the individual would be redeemed.[46]

In his thirties, Dewey shed even this attenuated form of Christianity and adopted a consistently naturalistic philosophy. He stopped being active in church and student religious associations, and his children stopped attending Sunday school.[47] Naturalism itself would now be his religion. He offered himself "as a quiet-spoken evangelist of a redeeming form of humanism and naturalism," says one historian.[48] Dewey even presented his "redeeming" naturalism in a book titled *A Common Faith*, urging his followers to cultivate a "religious" devotion to social ideals. This was a form of religion consistent with his belief that humans were merely biological organisms seeking to control the environment through scientific inquiry.

These ideas then became the basis of Dewey's educational philosophy. He recast intellectual inquiry as a form of mental evolution, and said it should proceed on the same pattern as biological evolution: by posing problems and then letting students construct their own answers based on what works best—a kind of mental adaptation to the environment. Teachers are not instructors but "facilitators," guiding students as they try out various pragmatic strategies to discover what works for them.[49] Of course, this is inherently relativistic: After all, what works for me may not work for you. (In fact, it might not even work for *me* all the time.) Thus pragmatism inevitably leads to a pluralism of beliefs, all of them transient and none of them eternally or universally true.

Does this sound familiar? Dewey is the source of much of today's moral education, where all values are treated as equally valid and students simply clarify what they personally value most. Teachers are rigorously instructed not to be directive in any way, but only to coach students in a process of weighing alternatives and making up their own minds. Any value that students choose is deemed acceptable, whether or not it comports with accepted moral standards, as long as they have gone through the prescribed series of steps. Why? Because, as one textbook puts it, "None of us can be certain that our values are right for other people."[50] Each individual has to become an autonomous decision maker, determining his values strictly on his own.

The underlying assumption of this approach is philosophical naturalism. A naturalistic approach to ethics does not acknowledge any transcendent standard, so that the only standard available is whatever the individual in fact values. As Dewey argued, we all experience things as good or bad, pleasurable or painful, rewarding or disturbing. And since science is supposed to be based on experience, moral inquiry must begin by analyzing our experience. We first clarify what we in fact value, and then weigh various courses of action to decide which will lead most reliably to consequences that match our values.

The first step—clarifying what we value—sounds easy, but in reality it may not be so simple, Dewey said. For our experience is often distorted by religious and moral dogmas telling us what we *ought* to want or do. Thus it becomes crucial to disentangle our thoughts and feelings from preexisting moral dogmas in order to clarify what we *really* want. This explains why most programs of moral education start by presenting students with difficult moral dilemmas: These are designed to jolt students out of their preexisting moral framework, absorbed from family and church and other sources, so they can probe their true feelings about right and wrong.

For example, one mother tells of a dilemma used in her daughter's class, where students were required to imagine they were planning to murder their best friend. What alternatives could they come up with for accomplishing that goal? Some students were appalled, objecting that they would not choose *any* methods because murder is wrong. Period. But that answer was not acceptable. The teacher required students to leave behind their preexisting moral convictions, by mentally rehearsing behavior they held to be wrong. The goal of such activities is to detach students from the moral teachings absorbed from outside, so that they will get in touch with their own personal, authentic values.

HAMSTRUNG TEACHERS

By "liberating" students from the moral standards they bring in from home and church, however, the inquiry approach leaves them with nothing higher than their own subjective likes and dislikes—or worse, the pressures of the peer group. Thomas Lickona, an education professor, relates the story of a teacher who used the values clarification strategy with a class of low-achieving eighth-graders. Having worked through the requisite steps, the students concluded that their most valued activities were "sex, drugs, drinking, and skipping school." The teacher was hamstrung: Her students had clarified their values, and the method gave her no leverage for persuading them that these values were morally wrong.[51] Moral education no longer means teaching students about the great moral ideals that have inspired virtually all civilizations, but training them to probe their own subjective feelings and values.

In spite of such criticisms, the inquiry approach remains immensely popular among educators. Another professor of education, William Kilpatrick, speaks frequently to parent and teacher groups around the country, and he often poses the following question: Which approach would you prefer at your own school—Model A, where students are encouraged to develop their own values, with no right or wrong answers; or Model B, where students are encouraged to develop specific virtues like courage, justice, and honesty, with inspiring illustrations from literature and history? The vast majority of *parents* choose Model B, Kilpatrick reports. By contrast, *teachers* almost invariably prefer Model A, and many "say they would not use the second approach under any circumstances"![52] Clearly, a wide chasm separates the educational establishment from the public on the sensitive issue of moral education.

Kilpatrick tells the story in a book aptly titled *Why Johnny Can't Tell Right from Wrong*. American educators have imbibed deeply at the well of Dewey, and many toe the professional line even when their own experience shows that the method does not work.

INVENTING YOUR OWN REALITY

The same teaching method is being applied to other subject areas as well. One of the trendiest fads today is called constructivist education. If knowledge is a social construction, as Dewey said, then the goal of education should be to teach students how to *construct* their own *knowledge*. Read this description by a proponent of the method:

> Constructivism does not assume the presence of an outside objective reality that is revealed to the learner, but rather that learners actively *construct their own reality*.[53]

That's a pretty tall order: Before kids are big enough to cross the street, they're supposed to learn how to "construct their own reality." Teachers are not to tell students that their ideas are right or wrong, either, but merely to encourage them "to clarify and articulate their own understandings." Just as in values clarification, the teacher is left with no mechanism to adjudicate between the answers students come up with. Thirty different students may well offer thirty different answers, but each must be considered viable. After all, there are many different possible ways to construct the world, and constructivism cannot rule out any viable theory that encapsulates personal experience.[54]

This explains why schools now have classes where children construct their own spelling systems ("invented spelling"), their own punctuation and grammar rules, their own math procedures, and so on. In one state, the history standards say that by high school, students "should have a strong sense of how to reconstruct history."[55] Isn't *that* an Orwellian phrase?

When I began writing on educational issues back in 1982 for a statewide citizens group, I would send my articles to my mother, who has a doctoral degree in education. "But, Nancy," she would say, "these things are taught to teachers as merely the latest teaching techniques"—as instructional methodologies based on practical experience in the classroom. But actually most educational theories are *not* inspired by teaching experience. Instead they are applications of a philosophy, and constructivism is no exception: It is a direct application of Dewey's evolutionary epistemology.[56] As one prominent constructivist writes, "To the biologist, a living organism is viable as long as it manages to survive in its environment. To the constructivist, concepts, models, theories, and so on are viable if they prove adequate in the contexts in which they were created."[57] Notice that the passage speaks of ideas being *viable,* not *true.* Constructivism is based on the assumption that we are merely organisms adapting to the environment, so that the only test of an idea is whether it works.

Astonishingly, even some Christian teachers have accepted constructivism, apparently without discerning its philosophical roots. After I spoke on the subject at an education conference, a Christian school superintendent came up to me and said, "All my teachers are constructivists—all of them."

"But don't they realize what that means for their faith?" I asked in surprise. "If knowledge is a social construction, then that applies to Christianity as well—it's just a product of social forces."

"I know, I know," the superintendent replied. "But constructivism is what they learned at the university under the auspices of the 'experts,' and they don't question it. They just keep their religious beliefs in a separate mental category from their professional studies." As a result of this compartmentalization, the teachers had unwittingly embraced a radical postmodernism that reduces all truth claims to merely social constructions.[58]

"Keeping Faith" with Darwin

If this is starting to sound like postmodernism in the classroom, that's exactly what it is. One of the most influential philosophers in America today is the postmodernist Richard Rorty—and the interesting thing is that he calls himself a *neo*-pragmatist. If you spell out the logical consequences of Dewey's pragmatism, he says, you end up with a postmodernism very much like the thought of Jacques Derrida, Martin Heidegger, and Michel Foucault.[59]

For Rorty, the key slogan of postmodernism is, "Truth is made, not found." In other words, it is not "out there," objective, waiting to be discovered. Beliefs are merely human constructions, like the gadgets of modern technology. And they function the same way as commodities in the marketplace: Echoing James's economic metaphor of the "cash value" of an idea, Rorty says we accept ideas when they "pay off"—when we find them "profitable."[60]

Like Dewey, Rorty bases his philosophy ultimately on Darwinian evolution. He once wrote that "keeping faith with Darwin" (a telling phrase in itself) means understanding that all our beliefs and convictions "are as much products of chance as are tectonic plates and mutated viruses."[61] Ideas arise by random variations in the brain, just like Darwin's random variations in nature.

Thus Rorty reduces all the great formative ideas of Western culture to evolutionary accidents: Just as "a cosmic ray scrambles the atoms in a DNA molecule" to produce a mutation, so too the great work of Aristotle or St. Paul or Newton could be "the results of cosmic rays scrambling the fine structure of some crucial neurons in their respective brains."[62] The reason these ideas have exhibited great staying power is not that they reflect reality, but that they help people organize their experience and get ahead in the struggle for existence. Thus the human species is not oriented "toward Truth" (note the capital T) but only "toward its own increased prosperity." The very notion of Truth, he says, frankly is "un-Darwinian."[63]

TOM WOLFE AND DARWIN'S DOUBT

What this means is that, despite postmodernism's rejection of the notion of objectivity, paradoxically there is *one* idea that it treats as unquestioned truth—namely, Darwinism itself. Evolution is treated as an objective fact and not merely a human construction—because unless it is true, there's no reason for accepting postmodernism. If the mind is a product of Darwinian evolution, then ideas and words are merely tools for controlling the environment, including other people. As Rorty says, language evolved because it is a "useful tactic in predicting and controlling [people's] future behavior."[64]

I once attended a luncheon with the well-known writer Tom Wolfe, who understood very well what Rorty was saying. According to postmodernism, Wolfe said, "language is merely one beast using words as tools to get power over another beast."

Precisely.

The most devastating argument we can use against this radical reductionism is that it undercuts itself. If ideas and beliefs are not true but only useful for controlling the environment, then that applies to the idea of postmodernism itself. And if postmodernism is not *true*, then why should the rest of us give it any credence?

Interestingly, Darwin himself wrestled with the same question—not just once, but several times—calling it his "horrid doubt." In one typical example he wrote, "With me, the horrid doubt always arises whether the convictions of man's mind, which has been developed from the mind of the lower animals, are of any value or at all trustworthy."[65] But of course, Darwin's own theory was likewise one of "the convictions of man's mind," and so he was cutting off the branch he himself was sitting on.

In short, Darwinian evolution is self-refuting. "What evolution guarantees is (at most) that we *behave* in certain ways—in such ways as to promote survival," explains Alvin Plantinga. But "it does not guarantee mostly true or verisimilitudinous beliefs."[66] British philosopher Roger Trigg agrees: For evolution, "it does not matter if a belief is true or false, as long as it is useful, from a genetic point of view."[67]

Thus postmodernists like Rorty are merely showing us where a consistent naturalistic view of knowledge ends up.[68] Once again we see the symbiotic nature of the two stories: It's *because* Darwinian naturalism was put in the lower story that we now have postmodernism (or neo-pragmatism) in the upper story:

The symbiotic relationship between the two stories:

NEO-PRAGMATISM
Truth Is What Works

NATURALISM
The Mind Evolved by Natural Selection

Some find it hard to take postmodernism and its radical implications seriously, shrugging them off as the antics of campus radicals. But ways of thinking that strike us as strange and out of the ordinary may have their roots in very ordinary worldview assumptions. People often do not understand the full implications of the ideas they have picked up from their education and the culture around them.

That's why an effective method of apologetics can be to compel people to face the logical conclusions of their own premises. Francis Schaeffer called this strategy "taking the roof off"—removing the shield of denial that people erect to protect themselves from the dangerous and unsettling implications of their own views, which might otherwise storm in on them.[69] In talking with nonbelievers, we need to press them to recognize the logical conclusions of naturalism. If they were utterly consistent, those who hold naturalistic premises would end up holding postmodern skepticism in science, morality, and every other field of knowledge. The fact that most people are *not* postmodern skeptics means they disagree with the consequences of their own premises—which is a good reason to go back and reconsider those premises. (To read more about Darwinism and pragmatism, see appendix 3.)

TRUTH FROM THE BARREL OF A GUN

"There is an old joke among philosophers that the problem with pragmatism is that it doesn't work," writes Phillip Johnson. After all, "Who wants to rely upon people who think that the only truth is that we should employ the most effective means to get whatever it is we happen to want?"[70] The only measure that pragmatism offers for evaluating an idea is whether it works—whether it achieves social desires and goals. But how do we know whether those goals *themselves* are good or bad, right or wrong?

As a result, in practice, pragmatism easily leads to an endorsement of whatever values a particular society happens to hold.[71] Or, more ominously, whatever the powerful happen to want.

Holmes, the most cynical of the pragmatists, saw these implications clearly—and endorsed them. He was willing to support the powerful even when the consequences were socially destructive: "I quite agree that a law should be called good if it reflects the will of the dominant forces of the community, even if it will take us to hell." And: "Wise or not, the proximate test of a good government is that the dominant power has its way."[72] Applying the same principle to international relations, he famously defined truth as "the majority vote of the nation that can lick all the others."[73]

In short, a rule based on what the pragmatists called "social desires" turns out to be the rule that the most powerful come out on top. If pragmatism has its way, Bertrand Russell warned darkly, then "ironclads and Maxim guns must be the ultimate arbiters of metaphysical truth."[74]

HE IS THERE AND HE IS NOT SILENT

In a remarkable passage, Rorty admits that the very notion of capital-T Truth is coherent only within the context of a Christian worldview. "The suggestion that truth . . . is out there" (that is, objective and universal), he says, "is a legacy of an age in which the world was seen as the creation of a being who had a language of his own," a "nonhuman language" written into the cosmos.[75] Here Rorty is harkening back to an image that Christians have used since the church fathers—the idea of two books: the book of God's word (the Bible) and the book of God's world (nature). His point is that objective truth is possible only if the world itself is a kind of book, created by God's word—language, Logos—so that there is an objective message and meaning in the universe itself.

Of course, that's precisely what science is proving to be the case, as we saw in chapter 6. The discovery of DNA, the coded instructions in every cell of every living thing, means that at the heart of life is a language, a message, information. In other words, the organic world really *is* a book, packed with complex biological information. And not only the organic world—information has become the key for interpreting the physical universe as well. The fine-tuning of the fundamental forces bespeaks a designing intelligence.

"Ask anybody what the physical world is made of, and you are likely to be told 'matter and energy,'" said a recent article in *Scientific American*. "Yet if we have learned anything from engineering, biology, and physics, information is just as crucial an ingredient." Indeed, some physicists now "regard the physical world as made of information, with energy and matter as incidentals."[76]

And where does information come from? In all of human experience, information is generated not by blind material forces but only by an intelligent agent. The reality of the Logos in the material realm underscores the reality of the Logos *beyond* the material—an Intelligent Agent who is the source of its order and rationality.

Rorty agrees that the very idea of objective truth and morality is possible only on the basis of the Logos doctrine. As he puts it, the idea of a truth beyond human subjectivity "is a remnant of the idea that the world is a divine creation, the work of someone who had something in mind, *who Himself spoke some language in which He described His own project.*"[77] In other words, objective truth is possible only if there is a Creator who has spoken to us—giving us divine revelation. As Schaeffer put it in the title of one of his books, only if *He Is There and He Is Not Silent.*[78] The only way of escape from postmodern skepticism is if God has revealed something of His own perspective to us—not about spiritual matters only, and not just a noncognitive emotional experience, but revelation of objective truth about the cosmos we live in.

In short, the biblical doctrine of revelation is the only way to close the gap between fact and value, between the upper and lower stories. The pragmatists sought to bring the two together, but their noble enterprise failed. Once they had put Darwinian evolution in the lower story, then ideas were reduced to mental mutations selected only for their survival value. Instead of uniting the two stories, pragmatism cast the net of naturalism over the upper story and drew it down into the lower story, leaving only postmodern irrationalism and skepticism on top.

Rorty states the choice with utter clarity: Either we "keep faith with Darwin" and embrace postmodernism, or we keep faith with a personal God who is not silent—whose Logos is the source of unified, universal, capital-T Truth.

THE COGNITIVE WAR

It has become commonplace to say that Americans are embroiled in a culture war over conflicting moral standards. But we must remember that morality is always derivative—it stems from an underlying worldview. If Christians hope to engage effectively in the *culture* war, we must be willing to engage the underlying *cognitive* war over origins. Darwinism was the turning point that sealed a naturalistic worldview in the lower story, while reducing religion and morality to noncognitive, upper-story categories.

Thus the key to restoring a unified concept of truth is to recover a robust concept of creation. Christianity has always taught that there is "a single reality" because it was created by a single omnipotent and all-wise God, explains one historical account. *"Given this creation story,* it followed that knowledge, too, comprised a single whole."[79] It was the doctrine of creation that undergirded confidence in the unity of truth.

To be loyal to the great claims of our faith, we can no longer acquiesce in letting Christianity be shunted aside to the *value* sphere. We must throw off metaphysical timidity, be convinced that we have a winning case, and take the offensive. Armed with prayer and spiritual power, we need to ask God to show us where the battle is being fought today, and enlist under the Lordship and leadership of Christ.

Why are evangelicals so prone to metaphysical timidity? Why don't we have a strong and robust intellectual tradition? To advance, we sometimes first need to go backward, retracing our steps to discover where we went wrong, so we can identify negative patterns and replace them with more positive ones. In the next section, we will dig into the history of American evangelicalism to uncover what went wrong on the intellectual front. We will ask why Christians have not had a strong worldview tradition, and what we can do about it. A better understanding of where we have come from can help us adjust the compass, set a better direction, and then go forward confidently to make a difference in our world today.

PART 3

HOW WE
LOST OUR MINDS

9

WHAT'S SO GOOD
ABOUT EVANGELICALISM?

Is Christianity a felt thing?
If I were converted would I feel and know it?
JAMES MCGREADY[1]

When Denzel was a teenager, he prayed fervently that he would lose his virginity. A basketball star in an inner-city high school, Denzel was tired of telling lies about his nonexistent sex life to impress his teammates. "All my friends had a lot more sexual experience than I did, and I didn't want them to think I was unpopular with the girls," he told me. "I had this idea that God just wanted me to be happy. So I kept praying that I would lose my virginity."[2]

Growing up, Denzel had attended church only sporadically with his mother and brother. (His father was a drug dealer, who had been sent to prison for robbing a credit union when Denzel was very young.) "I thought of church as a wonderful, holy place—the Sunday clothes, the choir, the rituals, the baptisms. But I didn't really know anything about God." Clearly not, if he thought God would answer a prayer in favor of fornication.

Eventually Denzel would learn to know this God better, but only after undergoing a personal conversion experience. He did not harbor any intellectual objections against Christianity. He respected the church and accepted the foundational principles taught there: that the Bible is God's Word, that Christ rose from the dead, that we need to be saved. What brought about his conversion was a simple message of sin and repentance, which won over his heart. In many ways, Denzel's story illustrates both the strengths and weaknesses of the old-fashioned evangelical message, and provides a helpful entrée into understanding its history and heritage.

We can begin Denzel's story of sin and salvation in his senior year of high school, when he finally found that girlfriend he'd been praying for. By that time, he was also drinking heavily. ("My friends considered me an alcoholic.") After high school, he tried college but after the first semester he dropped out. He tried working but after six months he was fired. Then his girlfriend announced that she was pregnant.

The news hit Denzel hard. So hard that it drove him, for the first time in his life, to take stock of his actions. "I was seventeen, and I thought, *I can't raise a child*. But most important, I knew it would hurt my mother, and I didn't want to do that."

His mother had gone through several bad relationships with men, who always ended up being drug addicts or alcoholics. Denzel longed to protect her somehow. And she in turn was fiercely protective of her two sons. For years, she had been cutting ethical corners just to put food on the table and a roof over their heads—writing bad checks, falsifying her financial status, opening new accounts under a relative's name. Every few years, things would catch up with her, and she and her sons would be evicted again. Eventually she tried starting her own business, but it was not going well. At just the time Denzel was facing the greatest personal crisis of his young life, she was facing an accusation of financial mismanagement. It looked likely that she would be convicted and end up behind bars.

The thought of his mother being gone, leaving him totally on his own, made Denzel panic. And as one crisis after another pressed in on him, he began praying again—this time in agonizing earnestness. "Many nights I would hide out in the bathroom and cry for hours. I didn't know how to pray, so I would read the Psalms as prayers."

As the court date loomed, his mother decided they needed to resort to drastic measures: She announced that they would go to church. Denzel quickly agreed. "As I got dressed, it somehow became very real to me that this is where I would meet God—the same God I'd been trying to pray to every night. My heart was almost shivering with excitement and fear." As he and his mother slipped into a pew, he could not hold back tears. "I cried through the whole service. I don't remember a thing that was said."

His mother ended up with a six-month prison sentence, and since his older brother was working, Denzel was alone in the house all day with his grief and desperation. Reaching out to God, he sat and read the Bible for hours every day. "One day I read the book of Revelation, and I was struck forcefully by the beauty of the new heavens and the new earth. But I was also struck by the fact that I knew I wasn't going there. Though no one had told me, somehow I knew that fornication was wrong, that I was drinking too much, that I was not living for God. I felt so guilty. I dropped to my knees and cried out, '*God, forgive me! God, forgive me!*'"

Suddenly Denzel recalled an old box of books left behind by his father many years ago, shoved into the corner of a dark closet. He pulled the box out, rummaging around until he uncovered a few dusty Christian books and tracts. One tract caught his eye: It presented a simple, old-fashioned message of guilt and forgiveness, along with a prayer. "I read the tract, prayed the prayer, and immediately I sensed God's forgiveness. I was overwhelmed with joy—I knew now that I could go to heaven." From that moment on, Denzel was utterly and totally committed to his newfound faith.

Denzel's conversion is a classic evangelical story of sin and repentance. He wasn't struggling with questions about positivism or postmodernism; he just knew he was a sinner. He didn't need a complicated apologetic to persuade him that God exists; he just wanted assurance of forgiveness. He couldn't unravel the theological subtleties that divide the denominations; he just longed to know he was going to heaven. His conversion was spiritual and emotional—a profound experience that Christ's atonement applied to *him* personally. In that sense, it was not unlike the conversion of the great evangelist John Wesley, who wrote, "I felt my heart strangely warmed. . . . And an assurance was given me, that [Christ] had taken away *my* sins, even *mine*, and saved *me* from the law of sin and death."[3] In the same way, Denzel's conversion involved personally appropriating God's forgiveness for his own sins. (Later that day he told his girlfriend, with more enthusiasm than theological precision, "God *did* something to me!")

Historically, evangelicalism began as a renewal movement within the churches, not as a separate denomination—and that explains why at first it did not develop an independent intellectual tradition. It didn't need to. It could take for granted the inherited theological and ecclesiastical structures within the denominations where it arose. Like the pietists before them, evangelicals focused on the personal appropriation of theological teachings like sin and atonement. Their goal was to cultivate a *subjective* experience of *objective* biblical truths.[4] As a result, when evangelicalism became dominant within various groups—or when evangelical groups broke away from existing denominations altogether and became independent—they suffered from a certain theological weakness. Evangelical groups tended to downplay the role of theology in favor of practical application such as personal devotion, moral living, and social reform.

DENZEL ASKED THE DEACON

Soon after Denzel's conversion, he began to sense the missing cognitive element in the churches he sought out. Having felt God move in his soul, he was now eager to learn more about *who* this God was. By the time I met Denzel two years later, he had developed an insatiable hunger for spiritual knowledge and was attending three services every Sunday—at three different churches!—in his eagerness to discover what the various denominations teach. (His girlfriend, a preacher's daughter, wanted nothing to do with his newfound faith; as they broke up, she revealed that she had not been pregnant after all.)

Unfortunately, Denzel's hunger for theological knowledge went largely unmet. "At my baptism, I asked the deacon about the Trinity. She told me, just believe Jesus is God, and don't worry about the details." He tried to engage pastors, Sunday school teachers, anyone he could buttonhole in the church hallway, but few had answers to the flurry of questions that came tumbling out.

The pressure to find answers grew even stronger after Denzel got a job. Many of his coworkers were Muslims or Jehovah's Witnesses who were quite vocal about their beliefs. "Everyone at work was able to defend their spiritual convictions—except the Christians. They were the only ones who seemed to have no answers." It became clear to Denzel that in a pluralistic society, Christians need to master apologetics in order to defend their faith in the public arena.

Finally he came up with the idea of applying for a job at a Christian bookstore, to gain access to serious spiritual reading. There he became friends with my son Dieter, who had undergone his own spiritual awakening a few months earlier and had come on staff for the same purpose! Through the world of books, both young men finally tracked down writers on theology and apologetics who helped slake their deep intellectual thirst—Francis Schaeffer, C. S. Lewis, R. C. Sproul, James Montgomery Boice, and J. I. Packer. Browsing the web, Denzel also dug up classic works by Augustine, Aquinas, Luther, Calvin, and Spurgeon.

Denzel's story of sin and salvation illustrates both the fortes and the flaws of American evangelicalism. When he unearthed that dusty, dog-eared tract and read the simple gospel message, he immediately felt freedom from his burden of guilt. Assurance of salvation swept over his soul like a life-giving stream. His church welcomed him, baptized him, and gave him a place to worship. But when he began looking for more solid intellectual food—theological teaching and apologetics—he had to search long and hard to find resources to satisfy his hunger. Today he is still trying to track down a church that ministers to the whole person, including the mind.

Why are evangelical churches typically weak in apologetics and worldview? To answer that question, we need to open up the archives on the history of the evangelical movement. In Part 1, we traced the crucial importance of having a Christian worldview—of not letting ourselves be "conformed to this world" (Rom. 12:1) with its two-story division of truth. In Part 2 we identified the crucial role that Darwinian naturalism plays in maintaining the two-tiered fact/value split—by reducing religion and morality to meaningless products of a mindless process. Now, in Part 3, we will dig into the history of American evangelicalism in order to discover why it has largely acquiesced in the two-story division of truth. Why did evangelicalism largely accept the secular/sacred split that locks Christianity into the upper story of merely personal experience? How did we lose a full-bodied conception of Christianity as truth about all reality—as total truth? Only by backtracking over the path that brought us here will we be equipped to chart a better course for the future.

FORWARD TO THE PAST

Questions about the history of evangelicalism became pressing for me personally after I had finished my work on *How Now Shall We Live?* Having immersed myself in the theme of Christian worldview through the writing process, the burning question that arose at the end was *why* this is such a difficult message to communicate. What are the mental barriers people have against worldview thinking? Why have evangelicals accepted a largely privatized faith? This was not merely an academic question but also a personal one, because I was trying to understand how to communicate the book's themes to the real people I encountered.

I began digging into books on evangelicalism, and as I identified various paradigms from the past, all the pieces fell into place. Many of the trends we confront today were characteristic of the evangelical movement right from the beginning, and if we trace them down from colonial times, they come alive as never before. Often we do not recognize patterns even in our own thinking unless we gain some outside vantage point, just as a fish can't tell you what water is, because it is all the fish has ever known. Getting a historical perspective is like going up high for an aerial shot, and as we look down through the scope of time we can detect various trends unfolding gradually, which makes them much easier to recognize—and gives us insight into our own time as well. After all, we are heirs to more than two hundred years of American history, and these inherited habits of thought shape our ideas and practices still today.

I will not be giving anything like a comprehensive historical account, but only looking for clues to diagnose the intellectual weakness of the church today. Our goal is to pinpoint patterns that throw light on the contemporary situation of the church. A book by Alister McGrath includes a chapter titled, "The Dark Side of Evangelicalism,"[5] and in a sense that is our theme here as well. Though there is much that is good and praiseworthy within evangelicalism, our focus will be on elements in our history and heritage that continue to pose barriers to Christian worldview thinking.

Historically, the evangelical movement divided roughly into two wings. The first we might call populist: It had a strong revivalist style that downplayed doctrine and appealed to ordinary folk. Strongest in the Southern states, this stream included mostly Baptists, Methodists, and the Restoration movement (the Churches of Christ, the Disciples of Christ, and the "Christian" Churches). The second wing was rationalist and scholarly. Centered in the North, it included evangelicals within the Congregationalist, Presbyterian, and Episcopalian churches, who united evangelical fervor with these denominations' traditional emphasis on theology and scholarship.[6]

In this chapter and the next, we'll examine the populist stream, which has become dominant today in terms of sheer numbers and influence within the churches. We will bring this tradition to life with colorful anecdotes of lively camp meetings and impassioned revivalists. Then in chapter 11 we will turn to the scholarly stream, getting acquainted with some of the most interesting and inspiring figures in the history of American thought. Finally, in chapter 12, we will take a fascinating side trip to see how religion in America was reshaped by changes in social and economic life. After all, religion is not just about abstract ideas. It is part of the fabric of concrete reality, and new ideas about religion were woven in with new ideas about the family, the church, work, and even the relationship between men and women.

IDENTITY CHECK

What does it mean to be evangelical? Most of us probably apply the term to all Christians who are Bible-believing and personally committed. I certainly used the word in this broad sense for many years. Thus when I began researching the subject, I was puzzled to turn up literature by conservative Lutheran clergy (the church I grew up in) insisting that they were certainly *not* evangelical—and warning darkly that evangelicalism was seeping into the Lutheran churches!

So what *does* the term mean? American historians typically use it in a more technical sense to refer to a movement that grew out of the First and Second Great Awakenings, embracing a revivalist style of preaching and an emphasis on personal conversion (the "New Birth").[7] Because it was a renewal movement within the church, its goal was not so much to convert nonbelievers as to enliven the faith of nominal believers—to bring individuals to a subjective experience of the saving truths of the gospel.

Classic Protestantism stemming from the Reformation defined the

Christian life largely in terms of participation in the church's corporate worship and liturgy. A church expressed its identity through creeds and confessions, maintained by the authority of clerical office. But the revival movement cast much of that aside. It stressed the individual's direct access to God apart from any church, defining the Christian life primarily in terms of individual devotion and holiness. Thus the rhetoric of revival tended to have an anti-authoritarian and anti-traditionalist flavor, denouncing liturgy and ceremonies as empty, external ritualism. Even today, says one historian, we must not "lose sight of this central point, namely, that any Protestant who emphasizes the subjective and ethical aspects of Christianity, rather than its official and churchly characteristics, is an evangelical."[8]

Some religious groups stood aloof from the revivalist movement, notably Catholics, Lutherans, German Reformed, Dutch Reformed, and Old Side Presbyterians. These are sometimes called the confessional churches. Yet the boundaries are not watertight: Even within the confessional churches, some groups were more sympathetic to revivalism.[9] Moreover, the very fact that today groups like Lutherans need to patrol their borders so diligently is evidence of how pervasive the evangelical style of spirituality has become. For good or ill, over a period of more than two hundred years of American history, populist evangelicalism has triumphed over the confessional churches.

"Evangelicals now constitute the largest and most active component of religious life in North America," says historian Mark Noll.[10] And not only here but also across the globe. In *The Next Christendom,* Philip Jenkins shows that the fastest-growing Christian groups in Africa, Asia, and Latin America tend to exhibit the characteristics of populist evangelicalism as well (experiential, theologically conservative, with an emphasis on personal conversion and supernatural signs and wonders).[11] That's why the populist branch of evangelicalism is something we all need to grapple with, no matter what our own denominational background, if we hope to communicate a worldview message to those around us.

And the Winner Is

In evaluating the impact of evangelicalism, we might say there is good news and bad news. The good news is that the evangelical movement has been remarkably effective in "Christianizing" American society. Look at fig. 9.1, which shows church membership in America from the colonial era. The graph is from *The Churching of America,* by Roger Finke and Rodney Stark,[12] and surprisingly it shows that religious adherence in America has actually *increased* significantly since the colonial period. The common stereotype that in colonial times virtually everyone belonged to a church turns out to be false.[13] And the correlative stereotype that in the modern world religion is withering away is likewise false. In terms of adherents, churches are doing very well today.

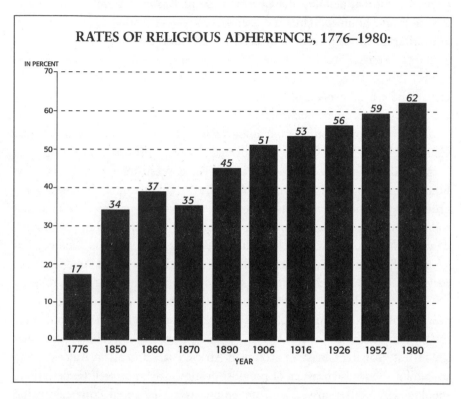

RATES OF RELIGIOUS ADHERENCE, 1776–1980:

Fig. 9.1 The numbers contradict the common assumption held by sociologists that as societies modernize, they inevitably secularize. *(Finke and Stark, 16, adapted with permission.)*

The sheer rise in numbers doesn't tell the whole story, however. Turn to fig. 9.2, which shows the sizes of various denominations between 1776 and 1850 (from the American Revolution to the climax of the Second Great Awakening).[14] Notice the stunning reversals in fortune. At the time of the Revolution, more than half of Americans who belonged to a religious group (55 percent) were Congregationalist, Episcopalian, or Presbyterian. At the time it seemed almost certain that these groups would remain dominant. Yet by 1850, Congregationalism had virtually collapsed. The Episcopalians had suffered greatly (partly because they supported England during the War; many returned to the homeland). The Presbyterians enjoyed some growth, but the increase shown in the graph only kept pace with the growing population; they actually lost ground in terms of "market share"—percentage of religious adherents. The Catholics grew, but through immigration, not conversion.

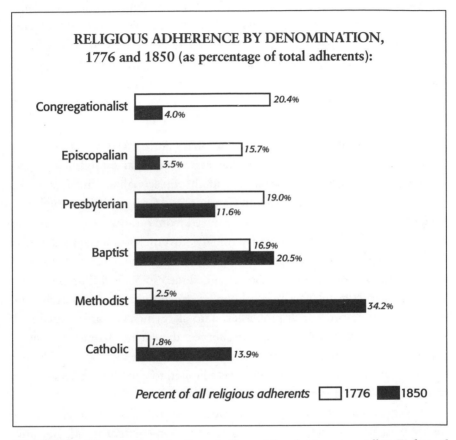

RELIGIOUS ADHERENCE BY DENOMINATION,
1776 and 1850 (as percentage of total adherents):

Congregationalist — 20.4% / 4.0%
Episcopalian — 15.7% / 3.5%
Presbyterian — 19.0% / 11.6%
Baptist — 16.9% / 20.5%
Methodist — 2.5% / 34.2%
Catholic — 1.8% / 13.9%

Percent of all religious adherents ☐ 1776 ■ 1850

Fig. 9.2 Why did some denominations decline, while others grew rapidly? *(Finke and Stark, 55, adapted with permission.)*

The most striking growth took place among the Baptists and the Methodists. During the Revolutionary War, most Methodist preachers returned to England at John Wesley's command, so they were starting over again—yet even so, they enjoyed phenomenal success. By 1850, they had become the largest Protestant denomination, accounting for 34 percent of all church members in the country. Some historians even call the nineteenth century "the Methodist Age." In 1906 they were overtaken by the Baptists, which tells us that *their* growth rate continued steadily as well.

When we talk about the "growth" of religion in America, then, we need to understand that it was not uniform: After the nation gained its independence, some groups went into decline, while others grew like wildfire, especially the Baptists and Methodists, and also (though not on the chart) the Churches of Christ.

How do we explain this pattern? Why did some churches flourish, while others declined? The answer, in a nutshell, is that the winners were the evangelical groups that participated in the First and Second Great Awakenings, while the losers were the established churches that largely failed to compete in the free marketplace of religion that arose in the new nation.

WHEN GOVERNMENT HELP HURTS

We sometimes forget that, in pre-Revolutionary America, the religious landscape was dominated by churches that rested on legal establishment: the Congregationalists in New England, and the Episcopalians in New York, Virginia, Maryland, North and South Carolina, and Georgia. What exactly did legal establishment mean? It is so far removed from our own experience that we may not realize what an intensive role the government played in administering the churches. Typically, the state collected tithes (which all citizens were legally required to pay, whether they attended the established church or not). The state also laid out new parish boundaries, subsidized new church construction, maintained parish properties, paid clergymen's salaries, hired and fired them, and even took measures to suppress dissenters. (Baptist preachers, for example, were sometimes jailed and beaten. Yes, here in America!) Finally, in many states, government positions were limited to church members—there were religious tests for office.[15]

It might seem that having the government on their side would have given the established churches quite an edge, and to some extent it did. But ultimately, it weakened them. Monopolies tend to be lazy, whether we're talking about businesses or schools or churches. The established clergy often lived like members of the gentry (the class that did not work but lived off of investments and rents), enjoying ample time for leisure activities. For example, in Scotland's state church, which was Presbyterian, Thomas Chalmers observed that after holding worship services, "a minister may enjoy five days in the week of uninterrupted leisure."[16]

By contrast, the evangelical ministers were enthusiastic activists, throwing themselves into ceaseless efforts to spread the gospel. They set up additional worship services, started Sunday schools, taught Bible classes, made personal visits, established charities, and founded missionary societies. Chalmers himself later became an evangelical, after which he is reputed to have visited

11,000 homes in his Glasgow parish during a single year! Becoming an evangelical made a significant difference in one's style of ministry.

People at the time were keenly aware of the difference in ethos. A document from 1837 (after all American churches had been disestablished), describes the vivid contrast between America's free churches and England's established church. Having seen both firsthand, the writer observed that legal establishment made the clergy "indolent and lazy," since a person with a guaranteed income would never "work as hard as one who has to exert himself for a living." As a result, the writer concluded, the Americans had a threefold advantage: "they have *more* preachers; they have more *active* preachers, and they have *cheaper* preachers than can be found in any part of Europe."[17]

A monopoly faith breeds religious indifference not only among the clergy but among members as well. This is one reason rates of religious adherence were lower in colonial days than we typically suppose. A modern analogy might be societies like Sweden where everyone is putatively Lutheran, or Italy where everyone is Roman Catholic. The level of religious participation in these countries is astonishingly low compared to that in America.[18]

Finally, the established churches tended to be the first to drift into theological liberalism. The wealthier the church, the more likely its clergy were to enjoy social status and formal academic training—and thus also the more likely to welcome the liberalism emerging from European universities at the time. Well before the American Revolution, leading scholars at Harvard and Yale had become Unitarian. Instead of exhorting their congregations to repent and be saved, they delivered elegantly styled lectures on "reasonable religion," with the supernatural elements increasingly stripped away. When the First and Second Great Awakenings broke out, the liberal clergy firmly opposed them, declaring themselves on the side of "Reason" against the revivalists' "religion of the heart."

That was a sure recipe for failure. It is a common assumption that, in order to survive, churches must accommodate to the age. But in fact, the opposite is true: In every historical period, the religious groups that grow most rapidly are those that set believers at odds with the surrounding culture. As a general principle, the higher a group's tension with mainstream society, the higher its growth rate.

"Religious organizations are stronger to the degree that they impose significant costs in terms of sacrifice and even stigma upon their members," write Finke and Stark. Why? Because religions that demand a lot also give a lot. A frankly supernatural religion may demand more from adherents than a watered-down gospel of "reasonable religion" or social activism. But in turn it gives much greater rewards in terms of doctrinal substance, intense spiritual experience, and a sense of direct access to God. As Finke and Stark comment dryly, people go to church "in search of salvation, not social service."[19]

WILD WEST RELIGION

While these principles hold true in any society, they apply especially to American history—because throughout most of our nation's history, there has been a large frontier. The map in fig. 9.3 shows the percentage of religious adherents in America in 1850, at the height of the Second Great Awakening (the same year the previous chart ended). Notice that the country is only half settled! To make these dates concrete, I remind myself that I was born in the 1950s, which means this map shows conditions a mere hundred years before my birth. And notice which states are on the frontier: Michigan, Missouri, Texas! This means that *most* of American history can be mapped as the gradual westward movement of the frontier—a process that lasted nearly three hundred years. The dynamics of frontier life continued to shape much of American culture right up to the dawn of the twentieth century.

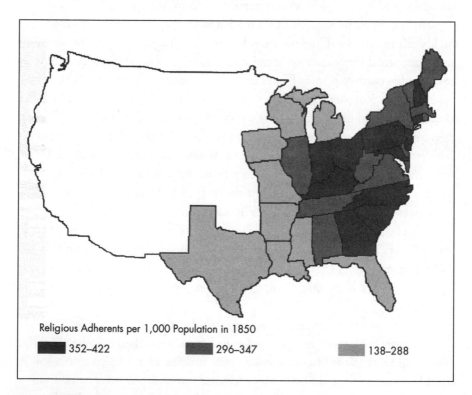

Religious Adherents per 1,000 Population in 1850

352–422   296–347   138–288

Fig. 9.3 Throughout most of America's history, there has been a frontier to evangelize. *(Finke and Stark, 68, adapted with permission.)*

What were conditions like on the frontier? First, it was rough and dangerous. Think of it this way: People were moving west faster than social institutions could keep up with them. Often there were no schools, no churches, no local governments, not even families (large numbers of single men went west).[20] Many who went west were drifters and people in trouble with the law, fleeing their past. Listen to this firsthand account from 1840 by the French nobleman Alexis de Tocqueville, a perceptive observer of American culture. Those going west, he noted, were "adventurers impatient of any sort of yoke, greedy for wealth, and often outcasts from the States in which they were born. They arrive in the depths of the wilderness without knowing one another. *There is nothing of tradition, family feeling, or example to restrain them.*"[21]

So when you think of the frontier, think Dodge City. As Finke and Stark write, you should picture "towns filled with male drifters, gamblers, confidence tricksters, whores, and saloon keepers, and *without* churches, schools, or respectable women."[22]

The question facing the Christian churches, then, was how do you make an effective religious appeal to such uncivilized, rough-hewn people? How do you bring religion to Dodge City? And the answer is that you do exactly what the Methodists and Baptists did in the revival movements: You grab people by the throat with an intense emotional experience to persuade them of the power of the supernatural—then you tell them to stop drinking, stop shooting each other, and live straight.

This kind of intense emotional conversion experience is exactly what the camp meetings of the First and Second Great Awakenings aimed to produce. No profound teaching, no high church ceremonies, no theological subtleties, no solemn hymns. Instead the revivalists used simple, vernacular language and catchy folk tunes, delivered with lively theatrics to catch people's attention and move their emotions. Evangelical preachers broke with the older pattern of using sermons to instruct, and began to use their sermons to press hearers to a point of crisis, in order to produce a conversion experience. Instead of talking about a gradual growth in faith through participation in a church, evangelicals began to treat a one-time conversion event as the only sufficient basis for claiming to be a Christian.[23]

RIDERS IN THE STORM

Another key to success on the frontier is that you have to *be* there. You have to be willing to sacrifice the comforts of the settled cities in order to minister among rough people living rough lives. As a rule, the established clergy were not willing to do that. In the state-supported churches (and in wealthier churches generally), the training for pastors was a long, expensive process that led to a chronic shortage of clergy, thus giving them considerable bargaining power over salary and location. Many simply refused to go to the unsettled frontier areas.

Fig. 9.4 **METHODIST CAMP MEETING, March 1, 1819:** People flocked from miles around to hear the revivalists' message of sin and grace. *(Engraving. Library of Congress, Prints and Photographs Division [LC-USZC4-772].)*

By contrast, the Methodist circuit preachers became a legend on the frontier. They traveled constantly, virtually living in the saddle. They were willing to preach to tiny frontier outposts, even to individual households. Most were single (they were on the road too often to maintain a family), worked for almost no money, and literally died young from the sheer hardship of their lives. One minister dubbed them God's "light artillery," perfectly adapted to the frontier. They had a reputation for braving terrible conditions and bad weather, so that during particularly bad storms it used to be said, "There's nobody out tonight but crows and Methodist preachers."[24]

Similarly, most Baptists preachers were simple farmers, ministering to their own neighbors. Many had only minimal theological education, speaking the same language as the people they were trying to reach. It was not unusual for someone to be converted at one revival meeting, then turn around and immediately start helping to run others, picking up a little theological education along the way only if he had the time and money.[25]

This was a complete novelty. We often forget that ever since Christianity was made the state religion of the Roman Empire in the fourth century, the church had been associated with the ruling class. As America was becoming a nation, most European countries still had state churches, in which church authorities wielded considerable political power—often even holding government office. In England, for example, Anglican bishops sat in the House of Lords (and still do). Even in colonial America, clerical and government authority were intertwined, since things like tithing and Sunday attendance were matters of legal coercion. Typically ministers were also the most highly educated in a community, which meant they were given deference as leaders.

This elitism was utterly abhorrent to the revivalists, and they set out to "popularize" religion. Fired by a profound concern for ordinary people, they pronounced the right of the unlearned to investigate religion for themselves. They made the gospel accessible by using simple language and spontaneous preaching. They delivered sermons that were emotive and extemporaneous— a refreshing novelty at a time when it was customary for clergy to simply *read* sermons written out ahead of time. In John Wesley's words, the revivalists wanted to preach nothing but "plain truth for plain people."[26] Ordinary believers were no longer regarded as passive recipients, as they were under the old hierarchical model, but as active participants.

The revivalists' concern for the poor and outcast reached even to slaves. At the time of the Revolutionary War, few blacks, whether slave or free, were Christians. "Well into the nineteenth century Episcopalians and Presbyterians were still wringing their hands about their failure to Christianize their own slaves," says historian Nathan Hatch.[27] Over the next three decades, however, thousands of African-Americans turned to the gospel. What attracted them? The simple, colloquial preaching style of the revivalists. "Other denominations preached so high-flown that we were not able to comprehend their doctrine," said Richard Allen, founder of the African Methodist Episcopal Church.[28] But the preaching style of the Methodists and Baptists was simple, direct, and dramatic. Instead of imposing a solemn, restrained style of worship, they encouraged spontaneous singing, chanting, and shouting, affirming the rich heritage of folk expression among African-Americans.

When we consider the growth of religious affiliation in America, then, the most striking thing is that it did *not* take place among the respectable or established churches, but among the evangelical groups—the "upstart" groups, as they were called at the time. This is the good news about evangelicalism. Later, the revivalist techniques that had been honed on the frontier were adapted to the cities by men like Charles Finney. He took the camp meeting style, dressed it in a suit, upgraded to a more urbane language, and pitched his appeal to the professional classes (lawyers and businessmen).[29]

Meanwhile, what happened to the established churches? They went into a slow but steady process of decline that has continued to our own day. For a long time they were able to mask their decline: The overall population in America was growing so fast that their numbers continued to increase in absolute terms, even though they were not actually keeping pace with the population increase. To leap ahead for a moment, by the 1960s the mainline churches could no longer hide the fact that even absolute numbers were falling. In 1972 Dean Kelley, an executive of the theologically liberal National Council of Churches, wrote a book called *Why Conservative Churches Are Growing*,[30] which stated frankly for the first time that mainline and liberal churches were dying. Kelley's colleagues excoriated him for airing unpleasant truths in public, but today even liberals admit that evangelical denominations have confounded all predictions by refusing to die out in the modern world, but instead continuing to grow and thrive.[31]

Overall, the Great Awakenings are largely responsible for the fact that America remains the most religious of the industrialized nations. By popularizing Christianity, evangelicalism permeated all the social classes. "In 1790 something like only 10 percent of Americans professed membership in a Christian church," writes Noll, "but by the time of the Civil War [1861], the proportion had multiplied several times." And the main cause of this dramatic increase was "the active labors of the revivalists."[32]

FRONTIER FALLOUT

If that is the good news about the populist wing of evangelicalism, what's the bad news? What happened along the way to the evangelical mind? Why did the evangelical movement become largely anti-intellectual, with little sense of how to relate to the mainstream culture? Ironically, the answer lies in some of the same factors that made it so successful. Let's outline some of the major factors, and then watch them unfold more dramatically in a series of short narratives through the rest of this chapter and into the next.

First, the focus on an intense conversion experience was highly effective in bringing people to faith. But it also tended to redefine religion in terms of emotion, while contributing to a neglect of theology and doctrine and the whole cognitive element of belief. This tendency did enormous damage by reinforcing a conception of Christianity as a noncognitive upper-story experience.

Second, the use of vernacular language and simple folk songs was highly effective in reaching ordinary people. But the revivalists often went much further, practically wearing their ignorance on their sleeves, as though being theologically educated equated with being spiritually dead. One of their favorite themes was poking fun at the educated clergy "back east."

Third, addressing individuals apart from their family or church was very effective in forcing a crisis of faith. But it could also lead to a radically individualistic view of the church that rejected the intellectual riches developed over the centuries by the great minds throughout church history—including the distillations of doctrine in corporate statements of faith, such as creeds and confessions. Many evangelicals uncritically absorbed the individualism that was coming into vogue in American *political* life, and simply transferred it to the church. An atomistic, voluntaristic ecclesiology was born that did not reflect biblical teaching so much as the political philosophy of the day.

Finally, revivalism led to a new model of leadership. The pastor was no longer a teacher who instructs a covenanted congregation, but a celebrity who is able to inspire mass audiences.

Of course, these trends were not embodied by all evangelical groups, nor did they appear full-blown right from the beginning. We will find seeds of the new attitudes being planted in the first Awakening (the rest of this chapter), coming to full fruition only in the second Awakening (the topic of the next chapter). See if you can spot the characteristic themes as I flesh them out with a few historical sketches.

Whitefield Across America

The First Great Awakening began when a young English evangelist named George Whitefield made a sensational appearance in the American colonies. He preached in the open air, in the fields, in the streets—anywhere he could gather an audience. Having been an actor as a youngster, Whitefield always retained a love for dramatic flair, which he now employed in his passion to build God's kingdom. One biographer even titles his book *The Divine Dramatist*, and says Whitefield pioneered a new preaching style: "an actor-preacher, as opposed to a scholar-preacher."[33] He raised his arms, stamped his feet, acted out Bible stories, and wept aloud.

To recapture the novelty of all this, we have to realize how contrary it was to the somber, reserved preaching fashion of the day. Living in Europe, I once got a taste of the old-world preaching style when we visited a seven-hundred-year-old Lutheran church in rural Sweden. The pastor literally read an hour-long sermon in a monotonous tone of voice, rarely even looking up at the congregation. It was the revivalists who pioneered extemporaneous preaching, aimed at evoking an emotional response and changing hearts. Whitefield's delivery was so effective, people joked he could bring an audience to tears just by the way he pronounced the word *Mesopotamia*.

To promote his tours, Whitefield pioneered the use of mass marketing, borrowing heavily from marketing techniques in the commercial world of his day. I had always assumed that the huge crowds attracted to Whitefield's evangelistic crusades were spontaneous gatherings, but most were carefully orchestrated: When he planned to visit a city, he would send out assistants—up to two years in advance—to distribute flyers and line up the facilities. He also issued a constant stream of advance publicity, from press releases to newspaper ads to printed copies of his sermons. He "followed a strategy of self-promotion and publicity that was unheard of in religious circles" of his day, says one historian. He would sometimes even "inflate the numbers to generate greater attention in the press," or "stage events again to draw crowds and publicity in newspapers."[34] All told, these were some of the best publicized events in colonial America.

Historian Harry Stout sums up Whitefield's novelty by calling him America's "first modern celebrity." In what sense? In the sense that his claim to influence did not rest on institutional validation—things like degrees and ordination, by which a church or denomination qualifies a person to represent it. Instead his claim to credibility rested on personality and popularity—the sheer ability to move a crowd. Unlike local pastors, revivalists like Whitefield did not address regular congregations who knew them personally. Instead they drew mass audiences made up of strangers who had no way of knowing them personally, and who therefore could only be attracted by publicity and advertising.[35]

Do you recognize some of our themes emerging here? The focus on an emotional response; the celebrity-style leader; the engineered publicity; the individual detached from his local congregation. Again, my purpose is not to give a complete historical account but only to highlight key patterns that help explain the loss of a Christian mind in our own day. There is no question that in both Awakenings, God performed a mighty work in the land. Great numbers of people became aware of their sin, then discovered the joys of forgiveness and grace. One cannot read firsthand accounts by Whitefield and other revivalists without being impressed by their fervent love for God and their hunger to see people brought into the Kingdom. But if we hope to make an unflinching diagnosis of the anti-intellectualism in our midst, we must recognize that crucial seeds were being sown.

Heart Versus Head

Contemporary Christians tend to have such a positive picture of the great Awakenings that it is difficult to grasp why they provoked such bitter contention at the time. In the First Great Awakening, some churches, like the Presbyterians, actually split between revivalist and confessional groups, while other groups broke away entirely to become independent (often Baptist). What drove the two sides was a disagreement over the role of emotion or experience in conversion.

Opponents of the Awakening treated the Christian life as a gradual growth in faith and holiness by what they called "Christian nurture," through participation in the rituals and teaching of the church. It was, they insisted, a thoroughly rational growth in knowledge. As one critic put it, "The Acts of the Soul in Conversion" are "the most rational Acts."[36] This reflected the Enlightenment view (revived from classical Greek culture) that humans are preeminently rational creatures. The "passions" were distrusted as forces that interfere with reason. The critics often charged that the revivalists were subverting the social order by rousing the passions of the ignorant rabble.

By contrast, supporters of the Awakening insisted that a merely intellectual assent to theological propositions was not enough. What was needed was "a Change of Heart" or a "New Birth." This theme came from European pietism, which had rejected the Enlightenment focus on reason to embrace the emerging Romantic focus on feelings. "Our people do not so much need to have their heads stored, as to have their hearts touched," wrote Jonathan Edwards, the preeminent theorist of the First Great Awakening, in 1743.[37] One of his protégés described the best preacher as one "whose heart is ravished with the glory of divine things."[38]

The emphasis on emotion was perhaps inevitable, given that most people in the colonial era were at least nominally Christian, which meant that the primary goal of the Awakenings was to counter spiritual coldness and indifference. With few outright atheists to address, the revivalists did not seek to convert people to Christianity so much as to what they called "experimental religion"—the idea that religious truth should not merely be believed but also experienced.

Consider a typical conversion account from very early in the second Awakening. James McGready was studying for the Presbyterian ministry when it struck him that, even though his theological beliefs were orthodox and his moral behavior impeccable, these things were not enough. "When he came to examine *his feelings,* to try them by such passages as, being 'filled with the Spirit; filled with joy; filled with the Holy Ghost; joy of the Holy Ghost . . . ,' it seemed to him that he did not understand these things experimentally," wrote an early historian.[39] After being ordained, McGready said the goal of his own preaching was to get people to ask themselves, "Is Christianity a *felt* thing? If I were converted would I *feel* and know it?" [40]

The emphasis on making Christianity "a felt thing" did not mean evangelicals were outright anti-intellectual—not in the early stages, at least. What they opposed was a *merely* intellectual knowledge of God. Many succeeded in maintaining a balance between piety and rationalism, Edwards being the outstanding example. Highly educated, Edwards maintained an admirable blend of theological learning and spiritual fervor. Even secular historians count him as one of the greatest minds in American history. Supporters of the revival also founded several universities, including Princeton, Rutgers, Brown, and Dartmouth.

And yet, the New Birth was consistently described in emotional terms, as producing "sudden rapturous joys" and "boundless felicity." A convert at the time called it the surest "Way to Happiness." One historian comments, somewhat sarcastically, that the incessant search for emotional rapture through the New Birth "represented the evangelical version of the pursuit of happiness."[41] We could say that Protestantism was being split into two stories, with the revivalists pushing for emotional conversions (upper story) while their opponents defended reasonable religion (lower story).[42]

Defiant Individualism

Moreover, the revivalists of the first Awakening engaged in an attack on church authority that tended to undercut, in the long run, even the natural authority of learning and scholarship. Although many were themselves well-born and well-educated, ironically they tended to identify themselves as outsiders. At every opportunity they pictured their opponents as "the Noble and Mighty" elders of the church, while identifying themselves with the poor and the "common People."[43]

Unlike the local pastor ministering to his own covenanted congregation, the revivalist often preached to crowds of people drawn together from across several congregations and denominations. This was a significant change, for it meant the individual was addressed *as an individual,* apart from his membership in a church. In fact, the revivalists often went further, explicitly urging people to leave their local churches to find ministers who were truly converted—an idea that was shocking in light of Puritan covenant theology.

To understand why this message was so unsettling, we have to realize that the seventeenth-century view of social order was highly communal and organic. A person simply did not conceive of himself apart from the family, church, local community, and so on. When a pastor was called to a local parish, it was almost like a marriage proposal: He was expected to bond permanently with the congregation and stay there for life.[44] By the same token, members were bound by a covenant to the local parish.

Thus it was a radical departure when the revivalists directed their message to individuals, exhorting them to make independent decisions in regard to religion—and to act on those decisions regardless of their effect on the larger society. "Piety was no longer something inextricably bound up with local community and corporate spirituality," explains Stout. "The emphasis shifted to a more individualistic and subjective sense of piety that found its quintessential expression in the internal, highly personal experience of the 'New Birth.'"[45]

To wrench individuals free from tenacious traditional bonds, the revivalists often adopted a contentious, even defiant tone. For example, Samuel Finley, who later became president of the College of New Jersey (Princeton), urged his listeners to take sides immediately for or against their parish ministers: "Away with your carnal Prudence! And either follow *God* or *Baal. He that is not actually with us, is against us.*" He then urged parishioners to act on their decisions even if it "rends the Church; divides Congregations and Families; [and] sets People at Variance"—even if "your Neighbours growl against you, and reproach you."[46] His words illustrate what one historian calls "the new spirit of defiant individualism that was one of the most radical manifestations of the Awakening."[47]

Partisans of the revival also gave vent to harsh denunciations of the local clergy, pronouncing them spiritually dead and carnal. One of the most famous sermons in the first Awakening was a flaming address by a leader of the New Side Presbyterians named Gilbert Tennent, titled "The Danger of an Unconverted Ministry," urging people to exercise their Christian liberty by deserting their parish minister for ministers who had been genuinely converted by undergoing a "New Birth." Not surprisingly, such declarations of religious independence were especially popular among young people. Taunting religious authorities became so widespread on college campuses that in 1741 the trustees at Yale University had to pass a college law forbidding students to call college officers "carnal" or "unconverted."[48]

The shock and outrage these actions produced at the time can be sensed in these anguished words from an opponent of the Awakening: "You have no liberty, no right, to forsake the communion of these churches . . . you cannot do it without breaking the covenant . . . and incurring the awful guilt of schism."[49] What was emerging was a new theology of conversion: The older view that believers are nurtured *within* the corporate church as whole persons, including the mind (through study and catechesis), was giving way to a new view that individuals undergo a one-time emotional decision that takes place *outside* the church.

The focus on individual choice and experience would eventually contribute to the idea that Christian belief is a noncognitive, upper-story phenomenon. Despite the overall positive legacy of the First Great Awakening, we cannot avoid the conclusion that seeds of anti-intellectualism were being planted. They did not come into full bloom, however, until the Second Great Awakening.[50] The two Awakenings were divided historically by the Revolutionary War, and so we will divide our narrative at this point as well, to resume our account with the dawning of the Second Great Awakening.

WHEN AMERICA MET CHRISTIANITY— GUESS WHO WON?

We have it in our power to begin the world over again.
THOMAS PAINE[1]

After moving to a new suburb a few years ago, my family began the search for a church home, visiting a Bible church not far down the road. In the middle of the sermon, the pastor launched into the most blatant expression of anti-intellectualism I had ever encountered. "In college I once took a philosophy course," he said, "and when I tried to read the textbook, I discovered it was pure nonsense. Gobbledygook."

He smiled expansively at the congregation, as though proud of his discovery. "From that time on, I knew Christians didn't have to worry about reading books on philosophy or any of that intellectual stuff. Those philosophers don't know what they're talking about."

My husband and I exchanged looks of utter amazement. Yet the attitude we were witnessing—a disdain for the things of the mind—had already begun to take root in the First Great Awakening, as we saw in the previous chapter. And it was to grow even more pronounced in the Second Great Awakening. In this chapter, we pick up the story again and trace its enduring legacy. The purpose is not to give a complete or comprehensive history, but only to zero in on patterns that help us understand why so much of the Christian world finds itself trapped in a two-story view of truth today.

As the Second Great Awakening got underway, open-air camp meetings became huge affairs. People would come from miles around to live in tents for days, even weeks, at a time. Paintings from the time show row upon row of peaked white tents filling a forest clearing, with a speaker's stand in the middle, surrounded by wooden benches. Several speakers' stands might even be scattered throughout the camp, so that at virtually any time *someone* could be heard preaching.[2]

Fig. 10.1 **THE SECOND GREAT AWAKENING:** In the Second Great Awakening, camp meetings became huge social gatherings. *(The Camp Ground, courtesy of the Billy Graham Center Museum, Wheaton, Ill.)*

In many ways, the second Awakening carried forward the themes of the first Awakening, so as we tell some of its stories, bear in mind the major characteristics listed in the previous chapter: the focus on an intense emotional conversion experience; the celebrity model of leadership; a deep suspicion of theological learning, especially as embodied in creeds and confessions; and an increasingly individualistic view of the church, which borrowed heavily from the political philosophy of the day. In fact, if there is one factor especially distinctive of the second Awakening, it is a surprising lack of critical distance from the political ideology of the American Revolution. This provides a handy way to remember what distinguishes the two Awakenings: the first came *before* the American Revolution, while the second came *after* it—at a time when the Revolution was becoming the template for the way people thought about virtually every area of life. It became common for leaders in the second Awakening to transfer the rhetoric of independence uncritically from the political sphere to the religious sphere.

For example, in the first Awakening, revivalists had not attacked church structure or learning per se, but only the abuses that had turned the clergy into a privileged class. By contrast, in the second Awakening, church authority itself was denounced as "tyranny." Creeds and liturgies were nothing but "popery" and "priestcraft." (Charles Finney denounced the Westminster Confession as a "paper pope.") Many began to argue that the American Revolution was not yet complete: We have cast off *civil* tyranny, they said, but now we need to cast off *ecclesiastical* tyranny. The priesthood of all believers was taken to mean religion of the people, by the people, and for the people.

This assault on authority and learning was part of a general "democratization of truth," says historian Gordon Wood. The concept of "unalienable rights" was transferred from the political realm to the realm of ideas, where it meant the right of ordinary people to think as they pleased without deferring to the judgments of the well-bred and well-educated. As a result, "Americans of the early Republic experienced *an epistemological crisis* as severe as any in their history," Wood writes. Truth itself seemed to be shattered, and everything was left to the individual—the voter, the buyer, the religious believer—to make decisions strictly on his own.[3]

Unfortunately, many evangelicals were caught up in the same "epistemological crisis." They absorbed the American ethos, and in some respects even led the way to an anti-authoritarian, anti-historical, individualistic outlook—which, as we will see, had devastating consequences for the Christian mind.

DEMOCRACY COMES TO CHURCH

One way to bring these themes to life is by telling stories, which Nathan Hatch does remarkably well in *The Democratization of American Christianity*. His book will be our major source as we draw vignettes of some of the key figures in the Second Great Awakening.

A Politician for a Priest

Lorenzo Dow played a significant role in the growth of Methodism. He traveled more miles, preached to more people, and attracted larger crowds to camp meetings than any other preacher of his day. Cultivating a John-the-Baptist image, he sported long, loose hair, unkempt clothes, and a weather-beaten face. Theatrical in the extreme, he could hold an audience spellbound, bringing them to tears or laughter with his vivid stories. He was a master of the vernacular style in preaching and had a rollicking sense of humor—which he used especially to make fun of the genteel educated clergy.

The most striking thing about Dow, however, was that his religious views were thoroughly intertwined with his political views. He was a radical

Jeffersonian who would begin a sermon by quoting Tom Paine. He railed against "the galling yoke of Tyranny and priest-craft"—putting political oppression side by side with church authority. In one of his many pamphlets Dow wrote, "if all men are 'BORN EQUAL,' and endowed with unalienable RIGHTS by their CREATOR . . . then there can be no just reason . . . why he may or should not think, and judge, and act for himself in matters of religion."[4] Notice how he applies the words of the Declaration of Independence to the church. The title of the pamphlet was the *Rights of Man,* an Enlightenment phrase if there ever was one. Instead of offering a distinctively biblical perspective on the current political culture, many evangelicals virtually equated spiritual liberty with political liberty.[5]

Do you detect our themes emerging? The appeal to the emotions; the distrust of learning; the lack of critical distance from the secular philosophies of the day. In fact, the borrowing of political slogans was so common among the revivalists that when Tocqueville visited America, he wrote that you would "meet a politician where you expected to find a priest."[6]

Fetters for Our Children?

Another key person in the Second Great Awakening was John Leland, one of the most popular and controversial Baptists in the early nineteenth century. Leland, too, was a fervent Jeffersonian, taking the concept of self-government in *politics* to imply personal autonomy in *religion.* "We will be free, we will rule ourselves," he wrote. It is fitting that the inscription on Leland's tombstone praises him for protecting both civil and religious rights. (It reads, "Elder John Leland, who labored . . . to protect piety and to vindicate the civil and religious rights of men.")

Leland took the concept of religious autonomy so far that he was even opposed to parents teaching their own children. He warned that "it is very iniquitous [for a man] to bind the consciences of his children." And to show that he did not mean only adult children, he went on: "to make fetters for them before they are born, is very cruel."[7] This was a radically individualistic conception of the divine economy: He urged people to make a deliberate effort to free themselves from all natural authorities, whether church, state, teachers, or even the family.

Leland's rejection of religious authority led him to insist that the simple and the ignorant are actually *more* competent than the learned clergy to read and understand the Bible: "Is not the simple man, who makes nature and reason his study, a competent judge of things?"[8] Here we see an early expression of the Baptist concept of *soul competency.*

The troubling thing about all this is that Christianity was not shaping the culture so much as the culture was shaping Christianity. In the classic Protestant churches—Lutheran, Reformed, Anglican—corporate statements of faith such as creeds, confessions, and formal liturgies were considered necessary means of expressing communal identity and structuring communal worship. But now all theological formulations were denounced as nothing but man-made devices to keep the people "under the thumb of clerical tyrants."[9] As liberal individualism was taking root in politics, it was being uncritically applied to the churches, producing a highly individualistic and democratic ecclesiology. Modern values like autonomy and popular sovereignty became simply taken for granted in evangelical churches.

Half American

The Disciples of Christ, Churches of Christ, and "Christian" Churches merged to form the first indigenous American denomination, and one of its most fascinating figures was Elias Smith. Starting out as a Baptist minister, Smith fell under the spell of a radical Jeffersonian political writer—and then began translating the idea of popular sovereignty from the political sphere to the religious sphere. He resigned from his church as a manifesto of his liberty, and began denouncing formal religion of every kind.

In one pamphlet Smith wrote, "Many are *republicans* as to *government,* and yet are but half republicans, being in matters of religion still bound to a catechism, creed, covenant, or a superstitious priest." In other words, the American Revolution was only a halfway measure: We've thrown off political tyranny, now we must throw off ecclesiastical tyranny. (Smith is using the word *republican* to mean essentially what we would call *democratic*.) And he ended with this heady challenge: "Venture to be as independent in things of religion, as those which respect the government in which you live."[10]

Notice again how the paradigm is borrowed from politics. Similarly with Barton Stone (who founded the Disciples of Christ): When he broke away from the Presbyterian Church where he had been a pastor, he couldn't resist calling it the "declaration of our independence."[11] Thus the American Revolution was taken as a precedent for toppling authority and elitism of all kinds. A letter published in a "Christian" newspaper drew an explicit parallel: The conflict to free the Bible from "creeds and confessions," it said, was "perfectly analogous to the revolutionary war between Britain and America."[12] So deeply intertwined were democratic themes with biblical themes that any real political analysis was short-circuited.

Salvation on the Spot

To be fair, the borrowing did not go one way only. Key phrases like "inalienable rights" were actually first developed by religious dissenters. The difference in usage was this: Prior to the Revolution, slogans about rights and autonomy were used primarily by dissenting *groups* against coercive state churches. After the Revolution, the same slogans were used by dissenting *individuals* against their own churches.[13] Many began to declare the right of each person to reject historic churches, ancient creeds, and theological scholarship in order to decide strictly on his own what the Bible really teaches. For example, Elias Smith argued that each individual Christian had an "unalienable right" to follow "scripture wherever it leads him"—even if he ended by embracing positions "contrary to what the Reverend D.D.'s call Orthodoxy."[14]

What was emerging in the populist branch of evangelicalism was a new individualistic, even atomistic, view of the church. The shift can be illustrated by a new theology of conversion. In early New England, to become a member of a church, a candidate went through a long process of learning the Bible, the creeds, the Lord's Prayer, the Ten Commandments, the catechism. Then he or she was required to submit to an initial examination by the church elders and minister. After that, he had to present a credible narrative of his conversion experience before the entire congregation. Next came an investigation of the candidate's life and moral conduct: The townspeople would be questioned about his character and reputation. And so on. Only if the candidate passed these various tests was he or she received into the covenant. The whole process was "a kind of community rite."[15]

The conversion experience alone was expected to take years of struggle before a person sensed the inner testimony of the Holy Spirit, giving assurance of being forgiven and counted among the elect. Memoirs of the time show that some people suffered through years of haunting doubt and anxiety before gaining assurance of salvation.[16]

By contrast, the revivalists offered assurance of salvation on the spot. Instead of going through a lengthy process, the individual made a decision—and he was saved instantly.[17] Instead of being taught and tested by the church, the convert announced to others what he had experienced.

Eventually, of course, some procedures for membership had to be re-created, but the American mind had been altered. What need was there for things like catechism, liturgy, or sacraments if what counted for salvation was the crisis of conversion? The church was no longer an organic community into which one was received, and certainly not a spiritual authority to which one submitted. Rather, it was a collection of equal, autonomous individuals coming together by choice.

AMERICA THE NATURAL

If you have read chapter 4, that last sentence should set off loud bells in your mind: Populist evangelicals were sounding the same note as the early social contract theorists—Hobbes, Locke, and Rousseau—who regarded social structures as the creation of sheer choice, formed by the consent of autonomous individuals living in a "state of nature." (For more detail, see appendix 1.) After the Revolution, social contract theory gained enormous plausibility among Americans, because it seemed to describe what they were actually experiencing. Even Christians echoed similar themes in their views of the church.

Back when social contract theories were first proposed, the state of nature had been offered as a merely hypothetical scenario, a myth of how society might have originated in the misty past. After all, no one has actual experience of a state of nature; we are all born into a preexisting family, church, clan, village, nation. And yet, the settlement of the New World broke the norm, and actually seemed to fit the hypothetical paradigm. Here in America, some began to say, a genuine state of nature had existed; then a society of independent farmers and entrepreneurs had come together and formed a state through deliberation and choice—just as social contract theory prescribes. The people themselves had created the structures of government, distributing power as they wished.[18]

In short, in America it seemed that the state of nature had been real and historical. Here at last was a genuine natural equality among independent individuals. Here at last humanity had the chance to start over and build civil society from the ground up. For many Americans, the meaning of the Revolution was not just that they had eliminated a king but that they had started a new world from scratch. "We have it in our power to begin the world over again," Thomas Paine exulted. "A situation similar to the present has not happened since the days of Noah until now."[19] This was an astonishing comparison—as though in the New World, the earth itself had been swept clean so that human civilization could begin again.

For the first time, in other words, social contract theory seemed to fit people's actual experience instead of being merely hypothetical—and as a result, liberalism became the dominant political philosophy. As Wood explains, many Americans adopted an atomistic image of civil society based on "isolated and hostile individuals" who exist intrinsically "outside all governments" (that is, in a state of nature), and who then come together and create power by their own choices.

This was a new and exhilarating view of society. In the colonial period, the dominant political philosophy had been classical and Christian republicanism, which was highly communal. It called on individuals to submit to a set of preexisting, normative social structures—family, church, state—instituted and sanctioned by the Creator. Virtue consisted in accepting the responsibilities attached to one's prescribed role within the social organism, practicing self-sacrifice for the common good. But in the new liberalism, social structures were not instituted by God; they came into being only when individuals created them in order to protect their interests. The ethos of self-sacrifice was replaced by one of self-assertion and self-interest.[20]

LEAPFROGGING 1,800 YEARS

This was a momentous intellectual revolution, and soon the ideas were echoing throughout every sphere of society, including the churches. Instead of analyzing the new ideas from a biblical perspective, many evangelicals embraced them uncritically. If the people could form their own state, why not their own church as well? There was a widespread conviction that the rise of democracy was the most significant historical event in two millennia—a *novus ordo seclorum* ("new order of the ages," the phrase on the back of our dollar bills). And just as Americans felt they were establishing a "new order" politically, so many also hoped that they could start a new church. They would sweep away the rubble of the ages and start over from scratch, recreating the church of New Testament times.

There arose a conviction that Christianity had become hopelessly corrupted sometime after the apostolic age, and that the great task at hand was to leapfrog back over 1,800 years of history to restore the original purity of the primitive church. This is sometimes called the assumption of the "fallen" church—that the visible church has suffered a great falling away. Various groups located the fall at different points in history: Some placed it at the age of Constantine, with its merging of state and church; others placed it at the time the papacy was established; and so on. The common theme, however, was that the forms and practices that had developed over the ages within the church were not normative, nor even valuable. Instead they represented a process of corruption and degeneration in which the purity of primitive Christianity had been lost.[21] Things like creeds and ceremonies were merely human inventions that had crusted over the gospel like barnacles on a ship, which must be scraped away so that authentic New Testament worship could be restored.

This attitude is sometimes called primitivism, and it stands in striking contrast to the stance of Catholics, Orthodox, and Anglicans, who vie with one another even today in claiming an unbroken historical continuity back to the apostolic age, which is regarded as a mark of authenticity. It was the Reformation that first introduced the new theme—the idea that the past was a morass of corruption and that the true church could be found only by throwing out centuries of historical development to recover an earlier, purer pattern. For populist evangelicals, however, even the Reformers' work was inadequate; after all, they had still retained a host of churchly trappings like creeds and liturgies. Evangelicals wanted to go much further: They vigorously denounced creeds, confessions, ceremonies, and ecclesiastical structures as violations of Christian liberty that must be stripped away.

"The fresh start in the New World was seen as a providential chance to begin over again at a selected point in history where it was thought the Christian Church had gone astray," writes historian Sidney Mead.[22] Admittedly, this was more rhetoric than reality, for most evangelicals in fact retained the basic teachings of Christian orthodoxy spelled out in such statements as the Apostles' and the Nicene Creeds. Yet there was a heady sense that just as the American Revolution had started the world over again, so evangelicals would start the church over again—rebuilding it, plank by plank, on the New Testament alone.

On one hand, this kind of primitivism could be liberating: It put the individual on notice that he could no longer passively accept whatever his church taught, but had to conduct his own independent study of the Bible. The focus on the early church also inspired a wealth of empirical study of the New Testament's original linguistic and cultural context. On the other hand, however, the cavalier rejection of the past stripped the church of the rich resources of centuries' worth of theological reflection, Scriptural meditation, and spiritual experience. It inculcated an attitude that there was nothing to be gained from grappling with the thought of the great minds of the past—Augustine and Tertullian, Bernard of Clairvaux and Thomas Aquinas, Martin Luther and John Calvin. It was an approach doomed, almost by definition, to anti-intellectualism and theological shallowness.

I am not making a theological point about whether tradition should be accorded religious authority, but only a historical point about the effects that an anti-historical attitude had on the life of the mind. "The greatest danger besetting American Evangelical Christianity is the danger of anti-intellectualism," warned Charles Malik at the dedication of the Billy Graham Center at Wheaton College. Evangelicals are in a hurry to preach the gospel, Malik said, but "they have no idea of the infinite value of spending years of leisure in con-

versing with the greatest minds and souls of the past, and thereby ripening and
sharpening and enlarging their powers of thinking."[23] This cavalier rejection
of the past had roots in the great Awakenings. Evangelicals were eagerly "liberating" themselves from their own Christian heritage, without recognizing
how impoverished this left them.

CHRISTIANS FOR JEFFERSON

Why did these ideas become so popular? Why did this atomistic, anti-historical conception of the church spread like wildfire? In many ways, evangelicals
were caught up in the great transformations taking place in the culture around
them. Ideas take hold when they seem to match people's experience, and the
most common experience in America was that of an expanding democracy—
in both the political and the economic spheres.

First, the political sphere. Prior to the Revolution, as we have mentioned,
most colonials held the classical republican view of society: Social institutions
like family, church, and state were thought of as organic wholes, each with a
common good transcending the interests of its individual members. In this context, certain words had a completely different meaning from the way we understand them today. For example, virtue was primarily public, not private: It
meant fulfilling the responsibilities laid on the individual through his or her role
within a social group—husband and wife, parent and child, pastor and laity,
magistrate and citizen. (Think of the way Paul ends many of his New
Testament letters with instructions to each of these groups.) Liberty was
defined in public terms as well, as the right of each social institution to govern
itself. Leadership was an "office" with divine sanction; and the person in office
was called upon to be "disinterested," sacrificing his personal interests and selfish ambitions in order to protect and promote the common good of the group.

As we know all too well, such sacrifice and selflessness are not typical of
human nature, and so classical republicanism was typically hierarchical and
elitist: Only certain classes of persons were qualified by birth, breeding, and gender to practice the high ideal of disinterested leadership.[24] The great masses were
considered hopelessly self-interested, fractious, and incapable of self-government.
This seemed to accord with the biblical teaching that people are prone to sin,
making civil order difficult to maintain. As a result, a kind of Christian republicanism was widespread among the Calvinists who predominated in colonial
America. Wood even calls it a "secularized version" of Puritanism.[25]

After the Revolution, however, many Americans began to reject classical
republicanism (represented politically by the Federalists) and to replace it with
modern liberalism (represented by the Jeffersonians). Based on social contract

theory, liberalism regarded civil society as a voluntary gathering of individuals. There was no organic "whole" beyond the individuals involved. As a result, there was no common good either—no purposes or values for the group beyond the discrete aims of individual members—and thus no need for a leadership class responsible for *protecting* the common good. With this logic, liberals rejected the elitism of classical republicanism.

They also began to attack the biblical doctrine of sin because it was now associated in their minds with the idea that people were incapable of governing themselves, which had provided a rationale for elitism and paternalistic government.[26] In place of the old elitism, liberals promoted a new confidence that ordinary people are perfectly capable of making rational, constructive choices for themselves, if only they are given their freedom. Liberalism denied that government was a locus of public virtue, called upon to execute Justice; instead, the state was a product of individual choices—which meant its worth was merely functional, measured in terms of how effectively it facilitated the individual pursuit of happiness and prosperity.[27]

Of course, these new ideas took hold only gradually, so that republican and liberal ideas were often combined in various blends. Yet, against this backdrop, it is easier to understand why the populist branch of evangelicalism spread so quickly. Most *opponents* of the revival movement, whether orthodox Calvinists or Unitarians, tended to be Federalist in political philosophy, holding to the older view of classical republicanism. By contrast, *supporters* of the revival movement, especially Methodists, Baptists, and Disciples, tended to be Jeffersonian, sharing its deep aversion to elitism and its trust of the common folk. They knew that Jefferson himself was a deist, who took a scissors to the New Testament and snipped out all the supernatural elements, leaving only Jesus' moral teaching intact; yet they supported Jefferson's presidential bid in 1800. Their attitude was summed up by Samuel Miller, an evangelical Presbyterian, who announced that he would "much rather have Mr. Jefferson President of the United States than an aristocratic Christian." Isaac Backus, a leader of the New England Baptists, even regarded Jefferson's election as a harbinger of the millennium.[28]

In this context, it is understandable why popular evangelicalism rejected the older conception of the church as organic and hierarchical (reflecting classical republicanism), in favor the church as atomistic and egalitarian (reflecting liberalism). This is sometimes called a believers-church or free-church ecclesiology, and it shares the liberal conception of social institutions as merely collections of their members, with no overarching organic "whole." Noll speaks of "the triumph of the believers' church, defined as the sum of its members, whose own choices brought it into existence."[29] Church authority was no longer thought of as a spiritual gift conferred by God through the office itself, but merely as a functional difference among equals.

NO TRAFFIC COP

This egalitarian revolution in *political* philosophy was supported by an *economic* revolution occurring at the same time. Throughout the vast scope of human history, most societies have lived at the subsistence level, with some 90 percent of the people's labor being required just to produce food for the community. This gave rise to an organic view of society, focusing on the survival of the whole rather than the liberty of the individual. With little defense against bad weather and poor harvests, "the survival of the whole was clearly linked to the diligence of each member," says one historian. And "with so many lives always at risk, concern for the public good predominated." The precariousness of life justified authoritarian control of economic relations.[30]

With the rise of capitalism and the Industrial Revolution, however, for the first time many people were freed from the fear of want and hunger—a truly historic benchmark. What's more, the new economic network crisscrossing the country was being created by ordinary men and women: farmers, craftsmen, traders, merchants, shopkeepers, cattle drovers. It began to seem that, contrary to the old Calvinist pessimism concerning human nature, ordinary people were quite capable of making rational choices to advance their own interests. And when they did, lo, they created wealth all around. Adam Smith's *The Wealth of Nations* was only the clearest expression of what by that time had become a common "discovery"—that ordinary people, operating freely and autonomously, were quite competent and capable after all.

Astonishingly, by the middle of the eighteenth century in the larger American colonies, per capita wealth was far higher than anywhere else in the world.[31] There was no longer any need for an authoritarian government to stand as traffic cop over limited resources. In fact, opportunities for enterprise were growing at a much more rapid rate than the government's capacity to oversee them. "It was increasingly clear that no one was really in charge of this gigantic, enterprising, restless nation," writes Wood. And yet, order seemed to emerge spontaneously as individuals pursued their own self-interest. "The harmony emerging out of such chaos was awesome to behold, and speaker after speaker and writer after writer commented on it."[32] In this economic climate, radical theories about individual liberty suddenly acquired plausibility. They seemed to make sense of the real conditions of life that people were experiencing.

Against this backdrop, we can better understand why Christianity became a matter of "making a decision for Christ." The focus was on individual choice, not on fitting into an inherited tradition. It is no coincidence that the populist branch of evangelicalism flowered in the age of Thomas Jefferson in politics and Adam Smith in economics.[33] People's experience in these other realms made them open to a religious message that rejected elitism and authority, while championing the right of ordinary people to assert themselves and make their own decisions. Instead of critically challenging the emerging culture of modernity, populist evangelicals were reshaping Christianity to fit the categories of the modern experience.

SELF-MADE PEOPLE

We can make this more concrete with a word picture suggested by sociologist Gary Thomas. In post-Revolutionary America, Thomas says, a Calvinist minister might stand in the pulpit on a Sunday morning and preach to his congregation that they were morally corrupt by nature and slaves to sin, that they did not have the capability to choose salvation, that God had chosen some and rejected others, and that there was nothing they could do about it. The trouble is, this Calvinist message would not fit the congregation's actual experience. They were no longer born into a static society, where people had no choice about their status, and where virtue was defined in terms of the duties attached to one's unchanging station in life. Instead, they were active participants in a mobile society, which they were creating by their own choices. They were self-made men and women in an expanding economy where success rested largely on their own choices, drive, and ambition. A Calvinist message, says Thomas, "would run counter to the individual's self-determinism in the everyday life of market and polity," and as a result, the sermon simply would not seem plausible. It would not make sense.

On the other hand, a traveling Methodist revivalist might ride into town and address the same people that night in an open-air revival meeting. He might preach that they had the power to choose God, that their salvation hung upon their own decision, and that salvation was open to any who chose to call upon the Lord. Given their everyday experience, this message would make sense. An Arminian message and a free-church ecclesiology fit with their experience as independent, autonomous actors in a democratic polity and an expanding capitalist economy.[34]

This explains why historians often characterize evangelicalism as a quintessentially modern religion. At first blush, that claim might seem implausible, running contrary to the typical stereotype that Christianity is a conservative, even reactionary, force in Western society. But consider: Though populist evangelicalism preached the age-old message of sin and salvation, at the same time its spirituality and ecclesiology were thoroughly modern—anti-historical, anti-authoritarian, individualistic, and voluntaristic (hinging on the individual's decision). Thus Wood writes that "by challenging clerical unity, shattering the communal churches, and cutting people loose from ancient religious bonds," the religious revivals became "a massive defiance of traditional authority."[35] On a similar note, Michael Gauvreau says evangelicalism actually helped to assert "the independence of the individual from the social constraints of the old order" while promoting "a rival vision of community based upon the free association of equal, autonomous individuals."[36] In short, evangelicalism did not provide a critical stance from which to evaluate the new developments in politics and economics, but was itself in many ways a powerful force for modernization.[37]

PREACHER, PERFORMER, STORYTELLER

The new model of human community called forth a new model of leadership as well. When Richard Hofstadter wrote his Pulitzer Prize–winning book *Anti-Intellectualism in American Life,* whom do you suppose he highlighted as Exhibit A? Right: evangelicals. Tracing the history of revivalism, much as we have done, he concluded that one of its most significant results was a new style of leadership. The populist branch of the evangelical movement cast aside an older model of leaders as holy men and instead gave rise to leaders who were entrepreneurs—pragmatic marketers who were willing to use whatever worked to get conversions. Hofstadter quoted the evangelist Dwight L. Moody, who once said, "It makes no difference how you get a man to God, provided you get him there." And the Congregationalist divine Washington Gladden said his theology was "hammered out on the anvil for daily use in the pulpit. The pragmatic test was the only one that could be applied to it: 'Will it work?'"[38] Long before pragmatism was developed into a full-blown American philosophy (see chapter 8), it had already been formulated and practiced by evangelical leaders.

Revivalism altered the seminaries as well: "The Puritan ideal of the minister as an intellectual and educational leader was steadily weakened in the face of the evangelical ideal of the minister as a popular crusader and exhorter," Hofstadter writes.[39] Theological education began to focus more on practical techniques and less on intellectual training.

Even the style of preaching was transformed: Expository preaching on biblical texts gave way to topical sermons on the felt needs of the congregation. "Earlier, a minister had been expected to provide his congregation with a comprehensive intellectual [theological] system," explains historian Donald Scott. The traditional sermon was essentially a formal argument—moving point by point through a logical progression in order to show that a particular doctrine was grounded in Scripture, then concluding with an application. But now congregations no longer expected to be taught theology; they wanted a minister who would move them emotionally and give them practical guidance for daily living. The pastor was no longer "expected to articulate a general intellectual structure by which life in all its facets could be comprehended." Instead, "the pastoral role had become almost exclusively a devotional and confessional one."[40]

Scott offers a striking example in a well-known sermon by the famous Congregationalist preacher Henry Ward Beecher, titled "How to Become a Christian." Beecher portrayed conversion as a simple step that required absolutely no doctrinal knowledge or assent. The sermon consisted almost entirely of an extended word picture of Jesus inviting the hungry to eat at a banquet. Don't "wait for somebody to explain it," Beecher urged his listeners. "Try it yourself today." The sermon was virtually free of theological content, focusing on the pragmatic appeal to simply "try it."[41]

Increasingly, the populist preacher became a performer, stringing together stories and anecdotes, often from his own life. This method engaged the audience's emotions, while subtly enhancing the speaker's own image by highlighting his own ministry and spiritual experiences.

CELEBRITY STYLE

The outcome of all this was the rise of personality cults, the celebrity system that has become so entrenched in evangelicalism. The traditional clergy had earned authority by going through a long process of training and certification; they were ordained by a recognized religious body and spoke on its behalf. But the leaders of the populist evangelical movement made an end run around denominational structures and built movements based on sheer personality— on their ability to move people and win their confidence. Starting with Whitefield, as we saw earlier, they became Christian celebrities: Their authority came not from having met accepted standards of education or training but from their magnetism and ability to gather a large following. As one account puts it, the revivalists went forth "armed only with a sense of divine calling and the sheer talent of being able to move people," relying on little besides "presence and charisma."[42] No wonder Hofstadter could say that "the 'star' system prevailed in religion before it reached the theater."[43]

These self-appointed leaders tended to be shrewd entrepreneurs and talented entertainers, adept at arousing (or manipulating) people's emotions. They honed the sermon into an effective "recruiting device,"[44] using language peppered with provincial expressions and colloquialisms. They were also quick to make use of the growing technology of print journalism to publish vast quantities of newspapers, books, and pamphlets, which resulted in many becoming well-known far beyond any local congregation.

The local rootedness of the traditional clergy had provided at least some measure of genuine accountability: Their character was known and tested in ongoing, long-term contact with a regular congregation. By contrast, the evangelist addressed mass audiences made up of strangers, who could not possibly judge his character by personal knowledge. He could dazzle them with sheer image-making and marketing hype. Many evangelical leaders became "successful, polished politicians," says Hofstadter, "well versed in the secular arts of manipulation."[45]

In PR We Trust

Some evangelicals even began to speak as though revivals could be produced simply by applying the right techniques in a near-mechanical fashion. During the first Awakening and earlier stages of the second, most regarded revivals as movements of the Spirit that could not be predicted or controlled; as a result, no one even considered using special techniques to spark them. Many of the preachers had been laboring in the pulpit for years when revival suddenly erupted, surprising them as much as anyone else. Jonathan Edwards spoke for many when he called the Awakening a "Surprizing Work of God."[46]

As the Second Great Awakening proceeded, however, preachers began to employ methods calculated to pressure people into making a decision. The most aggressive was Charles Finney, a lawyer-turned-evangelist who toned down the revivalist style and added a note of rational persuasion to make it palatable to educated, middle-class audiences. His innovations also included several high-pressure tactics, however, that were to become quite controversial. Finney "had a flair for pulpit drama," Hofstadter comments. "But his greatest physical asset was his intense, fixating, electrifying, madly prophetic eyes,"[47] which he used to great effect in confronting sinners by name in his revival meetings. That was one of his special tricks. Another was the use of the "anxious seat" at the front of the crowd: Those who felt convicted of sin were urged to come forward and sit on a bench, a technique that focused everyone's attention on them, creating pressure to reach a resolution (an early form of the altar call, an innovation that also began around this time).

By coming down to the front, converts became visible—which meant for the first time they could be counted. Not surprisingly, the practice of counting converts only fed the results-oriented mentality. Already in 1817 a critic of the revivalists could write, "They measure the progress of religion by the numbers, who flock to their standard; not by the prevalence of faith, and piety, justice and charity."[48]

Finney insisted that revivals had to be carefully staged. "A revival is not a miracle," he stated flatly; it is merely "the result of the right use of the appropriate means." Using the right methods, he said, a revival can be produced just as certainly as farmers using scientific methods can "raise grain and a crop of wheat." His recommendations included techniques such as holding "protracted" meetings (nightly gatherings for several weeks), ensuring good ventilation, making effective use of music, and so on, in order to engineer mass conversions. One of Finney's famous sayings was, "Religion is a work of man"—and clearly he regarded *revivals* of religion as a work of man as well.[49]

Supporters said Finney was merely pointing out that a revival must use the means God had ordained. And God apparently blessed his efforts: Finney was instrumental in the conversion of thousands of people, in addition to inspiring a surge of social reform movements. But his "new measures," as they were called, aroused considerable opposition and were ultimately rejected by many of the other revivalists, especially among his fellow Presbyterians. In the face of criticism, his defense was largely pragmatic: "The results justify my methods."[50] That same pragmatic attitude lives on today, as Christian organizations build large internal PR machines relying heavily on the latest secular marketing and publicity techniques. The natural outcome of this mechanical mentality, both then and now, is a tendency to measure success by numbers and impact, instead of by the minister's personal virtue and faithfulness to the gospel.

PULLING STRINGS

One of the dangers in personality cults is that they lead easily to demagoguery. The revivalists were often strong-willed leaders who, ironically, ended up exercising an even higher degree of dogmatism and control than pastors in traditional denominations, whom they denounced. A critic of the Awakening at the time, a Reformed theologian named John Nevin, argued that the revivalists' "high-sounding phrases" of liberty and free inquiry were merely masks for a new form of domination. Though they called loudly for "liberty," he said, most evangelical groups pressed every member into "thinking its particular notions, shouting its shibboleths and passwords, dancing its religious hornpipes, and reading the Bible only through its theological goggles." Nevin compared these

restrictions to "so many wires, that lead back at last into the hands of a few
leading spirits, enabling them to wield a true hierarchical despotism over all
who are thus brought within their power."[51] Thus, ironically, the magnetic
leaders who encouraged people to break away from traditional theological
structures often ended up becoming authoritarian leaders within their own
groups, sometimes verging on demagoguery.

Yet this was an almost inevitable result of having revamped the role of the
Christian leader. The traditional minister relied upon the institutional authority of his office to influence his flock. But since the revivalists rejected the notion
of institutional authority, all they had to rely on was personal charisma and
power. Thus Henry Ward Beecher once insisted that sermons should aim not
to impart knowledge so much as to gain "direct power on men's minds and
heart." As one historian writes, the minister became not so much a spiritual
teacher as "a personality exercising power."[52]

NOT A ROGUES' GALLERY

How do the patterns we have traced throw light on evangelicalism today? Not
long ago, I met a young man who had moved to Washington, D.C., as part of
the advance team for an event to be hosted by a major evangelist, scheduled
to take place two years from then. Two years? I thought I must have heard
wrong. Yes, he assured me, the speaker's organization sent out full-time, paid
staffers a full two years in advance to set up the event. I could not help thinking how the earliest revivalists first began orchestrating events a year or two in
advance. The pattern was set right from the beginning. Contemporary practices become easier to understand when we trace their emergence through
history.

How should we evaluate the enduring impact of the populist branch of
evangelicalism? On one hand, with their simple language and emotional
appeals, the revivalists were wildly successful in Christianizing broad segments
of the population. They imparted a sense of dignity and independence to the
laity. "A compelling theme in popular preaching throughout this era was the
Jeffersonian notion that people should shake off all servile prejudice and learn
to prove things for themselves," writes Hatch.[53] The revivalists' deep concern
for the poor and the downtrodden continues to inspire respect in all who know
of their work.

Even critics have been turned around. Catholic writer Ronald Knox was
highly critical when he began research on his book *Enthusiasm* (an older
derogatory term applied to the revivalist movement). At the outset, he intended
the book to be a "broadside, a trumpet-blast," a "rogues' gallery" of

disheveled, eccentric, wild-eyed preachers sowing confusion. But to his great surprise, as he came to know his subjects—great men like Wesley and Whitefield—he could not help respecting their sincerity and single-mindedness, their commitment to truth, their concern for simple folk. By the time Knox finally finished writing *Enthusiasm,* he had painted a highly positive portrayal of the early evangelicals.[54] Afterward he even translated the Catholic Bible into more accessible English, in the hope of inspiring a little more "enthusiasm" among Catholics!

On the other hand, as America moved beyond being a nation of settlers and farmers and small towns, a "religion of the heart" was not enough to respond to the intellectual challenges emerging in the nineteenth century, especially Darwinism and higher criticism. Later evangelists like Dwight L. Moody and Billy Sunday tried to counter the new ideas with sheer revivalist fervor. The fervor, however, began to take on a brittle, defensive edge. And the more Christians sought to prop up their faith with mere emotional intensity, the more it appeared to be an irrational belief that belonged in the upper story of private experience.

Unable to answer the great intellectual questions of the day, many conservative Christians turned their back on mainstream culture and developed a fortress mentality. This led to the fundamentalist era of the early twentieth century, when separatism was adopted as a positive strategy, and Christianity was reduced to the jargon of a distinct subculture. "The result was a near-abdication of any voice in academe at a time when the intellectual foundations of Judeo-Christian theism were being questioned as never before," writes historian Joel Carpenter. "Fundamentalist leaders were caught unprepared to respond to the critiques of scientific naturalism, whether applied to natural history [Darwinism] or the study of the Bible [higher criticism]."[55]

This is not to overlook the fundamentalist movement's enormous vitality and worthy accomplishments. In its zeal to protect the basic teachings of historic Christian orthodoxy, it founded large numbers of schools, seminaries, radio programs, youth organizations, Bible study groups, missions, and so on. Yet fundamentalism tended to be marked by an attitude of defiant defensiveness against mainstream culture.

Today evangelicalism is still emerging from the fundamentalist era—still working to regain a more holistic understanding of the Lordship of Christ over all of life and culture.[56] In recent decades, evangelicals have moved up the social and economic ladder. We are more likely to be educated and have high incomes. Yet I would suggest that in our churches and parachurch ministries, we still encounter many of the basic patterns from an earlier age—the tendency to define religion primarily in emotional terms; the anti-creedal, anti-historical attitude that ignores the theological riches of the past; the assertion of individual choice as the final determinant of belief; the atomistic view of the church as merely a collection of individuals who happen to believe the same things; the preference for social activism over intellectual reflection. Most of all, perhaps, evangelicalism still produces a celebrity model of leadership—men who are entrepreneurial and pragmatic, who deliberately manipulate their listeners' emotions, who subtly enhance their own image through self-serving personal anecdotes, whose leadership style within their own congregation or parachurch ministry tends to be imperious and domineering, who calculate success in terms of results, and who are willing to employ the latest secular techniques to boost numbers.[57]

Through the lens of history we can see these patterns more clearly, which helps us to identify the way they persist in our own churches and parachurch groups. "Today we rail against the celebrity system within Christianity, thinking it was imported from Hollywood culture," a university student recently said to me. "But when we look back historically, we find that the star system began in Christian circles." Exactly. Only by recognizing the source of various trends can we craft the tools to correct them. We need to diagnose the way historical patterns continue to shape the way we operate our churches and ministries. History holds up a mirror to the way we think and act today.

RISE OF THE SOVEREIGN SELF

The populist branch represents the dominant form of evangelicalism in North America in our day. "We are now entering a new chapter of evangelical history," Carpenter wrote in 1997, "in which the pentecostal-charismatic movement is quickly supplanting the fundamentalist-conservative one as the most influential evangelical impulse today." By *pentecostal-charismatic,* he meant populist, experiential, anti-creedal.[58] Especially in some megachurches and seeker churches, the evangelical worship style is becoming less doctrinal, more experiential, more geared to contemporary tastes.

This same worship style is even crossing religious boundaries. "We are all evangelicals now," says a provocative new book by sociologist Alan Wolfe. What he means is that the evangelical pattern is becoming dominant in all religions in America—a pattern he describes as "more personalized and individualistic, less doctrinal and devotional." Evangelicalism is growing "theologically broad to the point of incoherence," he adds; we may even be witnessing "the gradual disappearance of doctrine."[59]

This style may not be so much distinctively Christian as it is distinctly American, Wolfe says—in the sense that its individualism and experientialism align closely with the modern American ethos.[60] In many churches, the individual alone with his Bible is regarded as the core of the Christian life. A poll taken in the mid-1990s by sociologist Wade Clark Roof found that 54 percent of evangelical Christians said "to be alone and meditate" was more important than "to worship with others." And more than half agreed that "churches and synagogues have lost the real spiritual part of religion." Roof concluded that "the real story of American religious life in this half-century is the *rise of a new sovereign self* that defines and sets limits on the very meaning of the divine."[61] In other words, instead of challenging modern liberalism's notion of the autonomous self, evangelicalism tends to reflect the same theme in religious language.

As Wolfe puts it, "In every aspect of the religious life, American faith has met American culture—and American culture has triumphed."[62] Evangelicalism has largely given in to the two-story division that renders religion a matter of individual experience, with little or no cognitive content.

If we hope to retain what is best in the evangelical heritage, we must also soberly assess its weaknesses, praying for wisdom and strength to bring about reformation. And one of the best places to seek help is from other resources within evangelicalism itself—from its more scholarly branch. In the next chapter, we will meet some of the intellectual leaders in the history of evangelicalism—teachers and professors who sought to shape the thought of the entire nation from their positions at universities and seminaries. To diagnose what happened to the evangelical mind, let's take a closer look at those who did the most to cultivate it. Did they succeed in breaking out of the two-story division of truth? What resources did they develop that could help us today in developing a Christian worldview?

11

EVANGELICALS'
TWO-STORY TRUTH

*Religious forces accepted a division of labour;
they were boxed in.*
MARTIN MARTY[1]

everal years ago, a lively controversy flared up in the pages of the *Christian
Scholar's Review* over the correct way to define evangelicalism. Which
groups are included? Who should be allowed to lay claim to the label?

Two historians faced off against each other, while others cheered along the
sidelines. On one side was Donald Dayton, who traced a "Methodist" lineage
for evangelicalism. Starting with the Reformation, this line moves through
European pietism, John Wesley in England, the Great Awakenings in America,
through Dwight L. Moody to Billy Graham—with a focus on individual conversion and the subjective experience of faith. By now, you recognize this pattern: Dayton was identifying evangelicalism with the populist branch described
in the previous two chapters.

Taking the other side in the journal debate was George Marsden, who
traced a "Presbyterian" lineage for evangelicalism. Starting with the
Reformation, this line moves through Protestant Orthodoxy, to the Old School
Presbyterians, especially Charles Hodge and B. B. Warfield at Princeton, to
J. Gresham Machen at Westminster Seminary. The focus of this line has been
on theological orthodoxy and biblical authority.[2]

Which definition of evangelicalism is correct? Answer: Both are. As we
mentioned at the outset, historically the evangelical movement has consisted
of two wings, one populist and the other scholarly—and we need to be familiar with both in order to craft an effective strategy for reviving the evangelical
mind in our own day. Surveying the populist wing revealed the roots of long-
standing patterns of anti-intellectualism. Surveying the scholarly wing will
reveal why even a rational approach was not fully successful in confronting the

challenges from secular academia. Yet we will also discover important resources within our heritage for reviving a Christian worldview in our day.

The scholarly wing of evangelicalism actually included more than the "Presbyterian" line that Marsden traced. As the decades passed, the populist wing of evangelicalism outgrew its adolescent stage of rebuffing all religious authority and began giving rise to its own scholars. Alongside fiery preachers there appeared distinguished professors, teaching at seminaries and universities. Together with stalwarts among the Old School Presbyterians, they labored to develop moral and political philosophies; honed apologetics arguments against Deists, Unitarians, and infidels; responded to the latest scientific theories; and in general sought to relate the evangelical faith to the intellectual currents of the day.

And to a large degree, they were successful. The scholarly wing of evangelicalism, says one historian, became "the most powerful shaping influence" in nineteenth-century American culture.[3] The Presbyterians alone established forty-nine universities prior to the Civil War—more than any other denomination—thereby dominating American education. Though in terms of sheer numbers they were quickly overtaken by the populist wing, in terms of influencing American public life they were far more effective. "Conservative Presbyterians were zealous campaigners against the anti-intellectualism" pervasive during this period, says one historian. They "considered themselves missionaries to the American intellect."[4]

What can we learn today by getting to know these "missionaries to the intellect"? In every age, Christians have sought to address the issues of their day by "translating" timeless biblical truths into contemporary language. They have commended the ancient faith by using up-to-date terms understood by the people around them. The trick is to find a language that communicates effectively *without* compromising the gospel in the process. How well did nineteenth-century evangelicals succeed at this task? What philosophical language did they adopt, and did it compromise their spiritual message? What enduring legacy did they leave for us today?

SCOTCH TIP

To give philosophical expression to their faith, most evangelicals of the eighteenth and nineteenth centuries called on the services of a philosophy imported from Scotland called Common Sense realism, which was immensely popular across the entire intellectual landscape in America at the time. It was embraced by both supporters and critics of the Awakenings. It was held by Unitarians and other theological liberals. It was even adopted by deists (who denied all supernatural elements in the Bible) like Thomas Jefferson. "The Scottish Enlightenment was probably the most potent single tradition in the American Enlightenment," concludes one account.[5] Common Sense realism has even been called "the official philosophy of nineteenth-century America."[6]

How many of you know about this aspect of our history? When I was studying philosophy at the university, we read about the great European thinkers—Descartes, Kant, Hegel, and so on. But we never read about the philosophy that was dominant for more than a century in our own country.[7] This is an astonishing oversight, and crucial gap to fill in, if we want to understand our own history.

Common Sense realism was imported to America by John Witherspoon, who left Scotland in 1768 to become president of Princeton University (then called the College of New Jersey). From Princeton, Common Sense philosophy spread throughout the academic world of the day. "It became an *evangelical worldview* that permeated every classroom and which eventually influenced hundreds of ministers, countless schoolmasters, and dozens of practicing scientists and physicians," says one historian. It "became practically identified with the evangelical point of view."[8]

If this was nothing less than the "evangelical worldview" for such a long time, then certainly we should know more about it. What was this philosophy and why was it so popular?

Common Sense realism was crafted by the Scottish philosopher Thomas Reid in response to the radical skepticism of a fellow Scot, David Hume (discussed briefly in chapter 3). In fact, Hume's skepticism was so radical that Immanuel Kant famously said it roused him from his "dogmatic slumbers." It seems to have roused Reid as well, because he aimed his own philosophical efforts at refuting Hume and formulating a new foundation for knowledge. The way to avoid skepticism, Reid proposed, is to realize that some knowledge is "self-evident"—that is, it is forced upon us simply by the way human nature is constituted. As a result, no one really doubts or denies it. It is part of immediate, undeniable experience.

For example, no one really doubts that he or she exists (not in practice, at least). No one doubts that the material world is real (we all look both ways before crossing the street). Nor do we doubt our inner experiences like memories or pain. (If I say I have a headache, you don't ask, *How do you know?*) If anyone does deny these basic facts, we call him insane—or a philosopher. And even philosophers deny them only theoretically: Hume himself said that, after reasoning his way to radical skepticism in the solitude of his study, he would clear his mind by playing a good game of backgammon with his friends.[9]

In practical life, everyone has to simply take a good many propositions for granted. As Reid put it, "The statesman continues to plod, the soldier to fight, and the merchant to export and import, without being in the least moved by the demonstrations that have been offered of the non-existence of those things about which they are so seriously employed."[10]

The core claim of Common Sense realism was that these undeniable or self-evident truths of experience provide a firm foundation upon which to build the entire edifice of knowledge—like the foundation of a house. (By "common sense," Reid did not mean practicality or horse sense, as we use the term today, but rather those truths known by universal human experience—*common* to all humanity.) Most nineteenth-century thinkers included among the self-evident truths many of the basic teachings of Christianity, such as God's existence, His goodness, and His creation of the world. These were taken to be self-evident to reasonable people.

Having laid a foundation in self-evident truths, how did Common Sense realism build the house on top? For this task, Reid recommended the work of Francis Bacon, a seventeenth-century thinker often credited with establishing the inductive method of science.[11] The reason earlier ages got their science all wrong, Bacon had said, was that they deduced their ideas about nature from metaphysical speculations. Genuine science must start not with philosophy but with facts, then reason strictly by induction. "Taught by Lord Bacon," Reid wrote, people had at last been freed from the treadmill of medieval "deductivism," and set on "the road to the knowledge of nature's works."[12]

To a wide range of Americans, this linkage of Common Sense realism with Baconian induction seemed an unbeatable combination for countering the skepticism of Hume and other radical Enlightenment philosophers. Soon it was being applied to virtually every field of thought: science, political philosophy, moral theory, and even biblical interpretation (hermeneutics). Its central concept was even enshrined in the Declaration of Independence: "We hold these truths to be self-evident." Where did the idea of self-evident truths come from? From Common Sense realism.[13]

To evaluate these ideas, let's first zero in on how the Baconian method was applied to biblical studies and various other disciplines. Then we will back up for a wider perspective on Common Sense realism as a whole, focusing on how it has continued to be developed by Christians right up to our own day. I will not be attempting in any way to give a comprehensive description of these ideas or the figures who propounded them. Our goal here is to draw out key patterns that contributed to the decline of the evangelical mind, in order to get a better handle on how to bring about intellectual revival in our own day.

THE SCIENCE OF SCRIPTURE

What did Baconianism mean when applied to biblical interpretation? For Bacon, standing at the dawn of the scientific revolution, the main enemy had been Aristotelian philosophy. Thus he taught that science must start by clearing the decks—by liberating the mind from all metaphysical speculation, all received notions of truth, all the accumulated superstition of the ages. "With minds washed clean from opinions" (in his words), we sit down before the facts "as little children" and let the facts speak for themselves—then compile them inductively into a system.[14]

The very notion that facts can "speak for themselves" would send contemporary philosophers into babbling fits about *paradigm shifts* and *conceptual frameworks*. Yet this positivistic approach to knowledge became a powerful ideal among virtually all Enlightenment thinkers. Applied to biblical interpretation, the Baconian method stipulated that the first step is to free our minds from all historical theological formulations (Calvinist, Lutheran, Anglican, or whatever). With minds washed clean from merely human speculations, we confront the biblical text as a collection of "facts" that speak for themselves—and then compile individual verses inductively into a theological system. Statements in Scripture were treated as analogous to facts in nature, knowable in exactly the same way.

Among the most influential to embrace the Baconian method were the Old School Presbyterians at Princeton. For example, James Alexander said, "The theologian should proceed in his investigation precisely as the chemist or the botanist proceeds"—which "is the method which bears the name of Bacon."[15] Charles Hodge even compared the propositions in the Bible with the "oceans, continents, islands, mountains and rivers" studied by geography. That's why he could say: "The Bible is to the theologian what nature is to the man of science. It is his store-house of facts."[16]

It is important to realize that the term *science* had not yet acquired the narrow, specialized meaning it has today. Instead, it meant any form of systematized knowledge (Latin for *knowledge* is *scientia*), so that the term was applied even to subjects like politics, morality, and theology ("the queen of the sciences"). This explains why so many clergymen at the time assumed that a scientific method like Bacon's could be applied to theology. It did not necessarily mean they were selling out to scientism, as some critics have suggested.

It did mean, however, that they were seeking to meet the challenge of modern science in part by arguing that theology followed the same inductive method. In other words, they were trying to co-opt the Enlightenment. After the American Revolution, all traditional and inherited authorities were discredited as "tyranny" and "oppression." The only public authority to which one could credibly appeal was science because, ideally at least, science was democratic. By following the scientific method, one was not supposed to bow to any established authority; each individual could examine the evidence and decide for himself. Applied to theology, the Baconian method claimed that the Bible was accessible to everyone who cared to look at its "facts"—an idea that appealed to a newly born democratic culture.[17]

CAMPBELL'S RATIONALIST SOUP

Let's flesh out some of these themes through a personal vignette. Few embraced Baconian hermeneutics more enthusiastically than members of the Restoration movement (Disciples of Christ, Churches of Christ, and the "Christian" Church). In fact, theologians within this tradition continue to debate the merits of the method even today. When I ran an Internet search on "Baconian" and "hermeneutics" a few years ago, half a dozen articles from the *Restoration Quarterly* popped up. So we're talking about a question that is still a live issue.

One of the founders of the Restoration movement was Alexander Campbell. Born in Ireland, Campbell underwent an intense conversion experience as a young man. After weeks of wandering the fields alone in prayer, he writes, "finally, after many strugglings, I was enabled to put my trust in the Saviour, and to *feel* my reliance on him as the only Saviour of sinners."[18] Several years later, he set off for America and began to preach.

In many respects, then, Campbell was as evangelical as any of the revivalists we have discussed. Like them, he treated the American Revolution as a paradigm for inaugurating a new age within the church, insisting that America's "political regeneration" gave her the responsibility to lead an "ecclesiastical renovation" as well. Thoroughly anti-clerical and populist, he called for "the inalienable right of all laymen to examine the sacred writings for themselves." He even favored abolishing the traditional distinction between clergy and laity: "Liberty is no where safe in any hands excepting those of the people themselves."[19]

Yet Campbell was critical of the emotionalism of the revivalist movement, and he became known for a highly rationalist approach to theology—based on an application of Baconian hermeneutics. "We are in science and philosophy Baconians," he asserted proudly. "We build on Bible facts and documents and not on theories and speculations."[20] Like so many others in his day, Campbell described the Bible as a book of "plain facts," defining "its science or doctrine [as] merely the meaning of its facts, . . . inductively gathered and arranged by every student for himself."[21]

The main attraction of the Baconian method for Campbell was its promise of creating Christian unity. The overriding goal of the Restoration movement was to reverse the splintering of the denominations, reuniting them within a single church. And his model of unity was science: "Great unanimity has obtained in most of the sciences, in consequence of the adoption of certain rules of analysis and synthesis," he wrote; "for all who work by the same *rules,* come to the same *conclusions.*"[22] Campbell was convinced that the main cause of disunity in the church was that everyone read Scripture from the perspective of a particular theological system. That was like reading through "colored glasses," he said—it distorts our perception. If we would clean the glasses (clear our minds), then we would all observe the facts of the Bible correctly and arrive at the same interpretation. Using himself as a happy example, Campbell wrote: "I have endeavored to read the scriptures as though no one had read them before me."[23] The Baconian doctrine of the perspicuity of nature for science seemed to underscore the Protestant doctrine of the perspicuity of Scripture for theology.[24]

OLD BOOKS FOR MODERN MAN

What are some of the enduring effects of evangelicals' embrace of a Baconian hermeneutic? The method suffered from several serious weaknesses, which we need to grasp in order to understand how it continues to shape the way we read the Bible today.[25] First, the very notion that Christians needed a "scientific" exegesis of Scripture represented a degree of cultural accommodation to the age. By embracing the most widely held scientific theory of their day—and even applying it to theology—evangelicals came close to losing the critical distance that Christians are called to have in every age.

Moreover, the empiricist insistence that theology was a collection of "facts" led easily to a one-dimensional, flat-footed interpretation of Scripture. Metaphorical, mystical, and symbolic meanings were downplayed in favor of the "plain" meaning of the text. And by treating Bible verses as isolated, discrete "facts," the method often produced little more than proof-texting— pulling out individual verses and aligning them under a topical label, with little regard for literary or historical context, or for the larger organizing themes in Scripture.[26]

Perhaps most serious, however, was the Baconian hostility to history—its rejection of the creeds and confessions that had been hammered out by the church over the course of centuries. When Campbell admonished believers to remove the "colored glasses" and read the Scriptures "as though no one had read them before," he was suggesting that each individual had to start over from scratch to figure out what the Bible teaches. But notice what this means: It means the church loses the wisdom of the luminous intellects that have appeared throughout church history—Augustine, Aquinas, Luther, Calvin. By adopting the Baconian method, many American evangelicals lost the intellectual riches of two millennia of theological reflection. As we noted in the previous chapter, the idea that a single generation can reject wholesale all of Christian history and start over again is doomed to theological shallowness. The very language and concepts in currency today—like *Trinity* or *justification*—were defined and developed over centuries of controversy and heresy-fighting, and unless we know something of that history we don't really know the meaning of the terms we are using.

Moreover, in our own age, with its keener sense of the historical context of knowledge, we recognize that it is unrealistic to think people are capable of approaching Scripture with minds swept clean, like blank slates. Those who attempt to jettison the past are likely to simply sanction their own current prejudices and preconceptions as unquestioned truth. They lose the critical distance afforded by checking their ideas against those of Christian scholars across a wide range of different cultures and historical periods. Instead of seeing farther by standing on the shoulders of giants, they are limited to what they are able to see from their own narrow perspective within a tiny slice of history.

That's why C. S. Lewis urged Christians to read "old books," not just contemporary ones. It is difficult *not* to be taken in by the prejudices of our own age, he wrote, unless we have access to another perspective—which is what old books provide.[27] The great figures in church history are our brothers and sisters in the Lord, members of the Body of Christ extended across the ages, and we can learn much by honing our minds on the problems they wrestled with and the solutions they offered.[28]

SOLA SCRIPTURA?

At first blush, it may seem that nineteenth-century evangelicals were simply following the Reformation principle of *sola Scriptura*. Not so: Their anti-historical individualism was a far cry from the Reformation meaning of the phrase. In spite of their insistence that the Bible was plain to anyone, the Reformers retained an allegiance to the ecumenical creeds and councils of the church's first five centuries (including the Apostles' Creed, the Nicene Creed, the Athanasian Creed, and the councils of Chalcedon, Orange, and Constantinople), where fundamental doctrines like the Trinity and the deity of Christ were deliberated and defined. Moreover, after their break with Rome, the Reformers and their followers promptly set to work writing their own confessions and catechisms (including the Augsburg Confession, the Westminster Confession, the Belgic Confession, the Lutheran Catechism, and the Heidelberg Catechism).[29] For the Reformers, *sola Scriptura* meant that Scripture was the final authority, but clearly it did not mean a radical rejection of history or of corporate statements of faith.

Nor did the Reformers deny the importance of theological study or the natural authority of scholarship and learning. To the radical egalitarians of his day, Luther responded sarcastically that from Scripture alone one might prove anything: "Now I learn that it suffices to throw many passages together helter-skelter whether they fit or not," he said. "If this is the way to do it, I certainly shall prove with Scripture that Rastrum beer is better than Malmsey wine." John Calvin likewise stood against the idea that anyone's private reading of Scripture is as valid as another's: "I acknowledge that Scripture is a most rich and inexhaustible fountain of all wisdom; but I deny that its fertility consists in the various meanings which any man, at his pleasure, may assign."[30]

In short, among the Reformers, the principle that the Bible is the final authority was not intended to deny other forms of religious authority. Thus when nineteenth-century evangelicals urged common people to cast aside the rich heritage of creeds, confessions, and theological systems, they were embarking on a radical departure from the Reformation heritage. The most distinctive principle among evangelicals was "No creed but the Bible,"[31] which clearly goes far beyond the Reformers' position.

THE VIEW FROM NOWHERE

Ironically, after nineteenth-century evangelicals had thoroughly embraced the Baconian method, to their great consternation scientists themselves began to discard it. At the dawn of the scientific revolution, when Francis Bacon had first proposed his empiricist approach to knowledge, it probably did good service in drawing people's attention away from theoretical speculations to focus on the facts of nature. As a full-blown philosophy of science, however, it had serious shortcomings. For one thing, science does not proceed by sheer induction—by collecting and organizing facts. It proceeds by proposing hypotheses and then testing them (the hypothetico-deductive method), and theories are accepted based on a wide range of factors, from simplicity to how well they cohere with existing knowledge.[32]

More fundamentally, the very idea that our minds can be "washed clean from opinions," as Bacon put it, was eventually rejected as an illusory Enlightenment ideal. The Baconian method assumes that it is possible to shed all metaphysical commitments and stand outside our limited slot in history and culture in order to observe the unadorned "facts," stripped of any philosophical framework. This imaginary stance is sometimes called the "God's-eye view" or "the view from nowhere," as though individuals were capable of transcending their particular location in time and space to gain a universal perspective on reality. Such godlike objectivity is clearly impossible for unaided human reason. To think at all, we have to make at least some initial assumptions. Even scientific investigation always proceeds under the guidance of control beliefs—a set of premises that indicates which ideas are worth pursuing, and then provides a framework for interpreting the results.

Moreover, by stressing the need to shed all presuppositions, the Baconian ideal of objectivity blinded people to the presuppositions they actually continued to hold. Thus, in the nineteenth century, religious groups would often charge that *everyone else* imposed a preexisting, humanly constructed framework of interpretation on the Bible, but *they* did not; *they* merely accepted the self-evident meaning of the text. As one historical account explains, their "reliance on Baconianism had convinced them that they had escaped the constraints of history, culture, and tradition and simply stood with the apostles in the first Christian age," understanding the text precisely as the apostles originally intended.[33]

The paradox is that the very notion that we are capable of freeing ourselves from human systems of thought was itself the product of . . . a human system—one inherited from Francis Bacon. Historians have pointed out "the irony of claiming to overturn all human traditions and interpretive schemes while at the same time being wedded to an empirical theological method drawn from early Enlightenment thought." For example, Campbell and his colleagues "never quite saw that in addition to being Disciples of Christ they also had become disciples of Baconian empiricism."[34]

The enduring legacy of Baconianism, then, was an anti-historical and somewhat positivist view of biblical interpretation—the idea that we may safely ignore the wisdom of the church's heritage over the centuries; that the best way to read the biblical text is to approach it as an isolated individual. The beauty and wonder of God's personal approach is that He often *does* speak to individuals as they come to Him in humility and openness, simply reading the Scripture as they understand it. The Holy Spirit graciously enlightens our hearts to apply biblical truth to our personal lives. As a formal method of determining what biblical truth is in the first place, however, Baconianism was unrealistic and self-deceptive—while also tending to reinforce the same primitivism and disdain for history we found so prominent in populist evangelicalism.

The defining theme in nineteenth-century American Christianity, says one historian, was a profound sense of "historylessness."[35] Artistic people picked up on this attitude and portrayed it in the literature of the time: In Anthony Trollope's novel *Barchester Towers,* an evangelical minister repeatedly announces that the time has come for "casting away the useless rubbish of past centuries."[36] We might say that evangelicalism became characterized by a rejection of C. S. Lewis's advice about reading old books.

BECOMING DOUBLE-MINDED

Applied to other fields, Baconianism led to even more pernicious results. Its primary effect was to reinforce the two-story division of truth, by promoting a kind of methodological naturalism in the lower story. By promising that knowledge could be based on empirical facts unfiltered through any religious or philosophical grid, Baconianism persuaded Christians to set aside their *own* religious framework. At the same time, it allowed *alien* philosophical frameworks, like naturalism and empiricism, to be introduced under the banner of "objectivity" and "free inquiry." By insisting that science operated without any philosophical framework, Baconianism disarmed evangelicals by blinding them to these new anti-Christian frameworks . . . until it was too late.

Another way to picture the process is that Baconianism drove Christian perspectives out of the lower story, where we deal with subjects like science and history, and into the upper story. The Baconian ideal of knowledge as religiously neutral made believers feel that it was illegitimate to bring their faith into the classroom or the science lab—for that would mean they were biased. To be objective and unbiased, one must treat the world as though it were a naturalistic system known by strictly empirical methods. The upshot was that religion was limited to the upper story, while methodological naturalism was given free rein in the lower story.

A Science of Duty

Let's flesh out the way this worked by looking at a few examples, starting with moral philosophy. The heyday of evangelicals' influence was in the mid-nineteenth century, when they controlled many of the nation's universities. At that time, the capstone of a student's university career was a course in moral philosophy—or, as it was called, "moral science." Generally taught by the college president, it was a senior course intended to draw together everything the student had learned, integrating it into an uplifting moral vision for life.

But that label *science* is a dead giveaway that the very definition of morality had shifted. A new approach to moral philosophy had arisen that rejected the Aristotelian ethic (which had been taught by Christian scholasticism up to that time) in favor of what was heralded as a scientific approach. And that meant a Baconian approach. An effort was made, says Mark Noll, "to construct ethics as Francis Bacon had defined the doing of science."[37] The starting data would be our sense of right and wrong; by examining the moral sense, one could gather the data into general laws to create a science. Thus, in 1859 a Methodist college president wrote that moral philosophy was a "science of duty" for investigating the "laws of morality" through rational methods.[38]

To turn morality into a science, it was assumed that cause and effect operate there exactly as in Newtonian physics—that virtue leads to health and happiness, while vice causes misery. Thus Witherspoon urged that progress could be made by "treating moral philosophy as Newton and his successors have done natural [philosophy]."[39] And Francis Wayland, a Baptist minister who became president of Brown University, taught that the laws of morality consist of "sequences connected by our Creator" (behaviors followed by reward or punishment) that are "just as invariable as an order of sequence in physics."[40]

Labeling ethics a *science* was a good public relations move, because it gave Christian clergy a credibility boost in an age when traditional and historical authorities were being cast aside. Claiming to be scientific put them "in a position to prescribe a Christian moral order without looking *too* Christian," as one historian comments wryly.[41] They did not appeal to the Bible or revelation, but tried to base ethics on induction from experience. For example, Witherspoon described his own moral philosophy as one that proceeded "by reason, as distinct from revelation."[42]

As a result, however, what evangelical scholars offered to the public was *an ethic not explicitly grounded in a Christian worldview.* "Wayland's text and others like it also written by clergymen did not expound a specifically Christian ethics," explains one account. "They found the basis of ethics . . . in the natural order and in the experience of rational creatures rather than in the revealed will of God."[43]

In one sense, of course, there was nothing new in this approach. It was just putting "scientific" window dressing on the age-old concept of natural law. From ancient times, Christians have acknowledged that all humans, because they are created in the image of God, have a basic sense of right and wrong. C. S. Lewis referred to it as the Tao—the conviction found in virtually every culture that there is an objective moral order, and that wisdom consists in aligning our personal lives with that order.[44]

Yet the moral sense itself is not enough to ground a full-blown moral philosophy. Our sense of right and wrong is merely a datum of experience—which must be explained and accounted for by an overarching worldview. And if the

Christian worldview is ruled out as an explanatory framework, then anti-Christian worldviews will rush in to fill the vacuum.

Historically, that is exactly what happened. Because of their Baconian view of knowledge, nineteenth-century evangelicals tried to build a moral science that was religiously autonomous—a lower-story science based on empirical and rational grounds alone. It was, as one philosophy textbook puts it, an approach based "on *an entirely naturalistic view of human nature.*"[45] Of course, evangelical scholars assumed that the findings of moral science would turn out to be parallel to the teachings of the Bible—and thus would provide confirmation of Christianity. But within the discipline itself, they adopted a form of methodological naturalism.

In doing so, however, they opened the door to full-fledged *philosophical* naturalism (nature is all that exists). And it was not long before scholars who embraced that philosophy walked right through the door that had been opened for them. They abolished the courses on moral philosophy, replacing them with empirically oriented courses on experimental psychology and sociology that spelled out the full implications of a naturalistic view of human nature. The American university was being secularized.

Celestial Mathematician

The same secularization process was proceeding apace in the natural sciences. Ever since Isaac Newton established classical physics, science seemed to be creating an image of the universe as a huge clockwork, wound up at the beginning but ever since running by mechanistic forces. Inevitably, tension emerged between this machine model of the universe, which portrayed God as a kind of celestial mathematician, and the belief in a personal God who lovingly supervises every event by His direct providence. If all physical phenomena could be explained by natural law, what room was there for divine causality? It began to seem that the natural world operated autonomously by inbuilt natural laws known by science (the lower story), while the supernatural world was limited to the invisible realm of the spirit, known only by religion (the upper story).

The outcome was what one historian calls "a schizophrenic conception of God." On one hand, "intellectual assurance came from the Divine Engineer," while on the other hand, "personal religious experience assumed the Heavenly Father." Yet the relationship between them was far from equal, for science had been defined as the sole source of genuine knowledge, which meant religion was demoted to subjective feelings. Thus as science progressed, eventually "the personal God retreated into an impalpable spiritual world."[46]

In short, a chasm was opening in the minds of believers. Many struggled to keep the upper and lower stories connected, insisting that in the end the two realms would prove complementary—that scientific knowledge would harmonize with biblical teachings. The design argument was immensely popular during this period, especially William Paley's analogy that the universe is like a finely-made watch, and thus requires a watchmaker. Yet this did not prevent Christianity from being reduced eventually to little more than a ceremonial benediction pronounced over the results of science. At the end of his research, the typical scientist would round off with a flourish by praising God for His wise and benevolent design; but he denied that biblical assumptions were foundational in making science possible in the first place, or that they played any role as control beliefs in directing his scientific work.

"By the end of the eighteenth century, American Protestants of almost all sorts had adopted this two-tiered worldview, founded on an empiricist epistemology, with the laws of nature below, supporting supernatural belief above," writes George Marsden.[47] Christians were treating fields outside theology as essentially autonomous disciplines, operating by the methodology of "value-free" science. This was reflected in the increasing specialization within the university curriculum, so that when the Duke of Argyll gave his inaugural address as chancellor of the University of St. Andrews in 1852, he warned that theology no longer provided an overarching unity of knowledge: "An absolute separation has been declared between science and religion; and the theologian and the [scientist] have entered into a sort of tacit agreement that each is to be left free and unimpeded by the other within his own walk and province." This was a dangerous development, he warned, for if the true meaning of nature and history is not recognized, then "a false one will be invented."[48]

Just so. If a Christian philosophy does not provide the control beliefs for science, then false philosophies will fill the vacuum—naturalism and materialism. The Enlightenment claim that science can operate without any philosophical premises proved, in the end, to be a cover for discarding Christian premises while smuggling in naturalistic ones. As Marsden writes, the ideal of "free inquiry" became merely a tactic for debunking traditional religion, while science itself was elevated to "the new orthodoxy."[49]

Blinded by Bacon

Unfortunately, once again the Baconian view of science prevented many Christians from recognizing what was happening. An example is the way some responded to the appearance of Darwinism in 1859. The reason Darwinian evolution was so revolutionary was not its concept of natural selection but its definition of knowledge, or epistemology. The older epistemology assumed an open universe, where concepts like design and purpose (teleology) made sense and were considered perfectly rational. But as we saw in chapter 6, Darwin wanted to establish a naturalistic epistemology that assumed a closed system of cause and effect—one that ruled design and purpose out of bounds. Thus the heart of the conflict revolved around two rival epistemologies: Which definition of knowledge should govern in science?[50]

The tragedy is not just that evangelicals failed to meet the challenge: For the most part they did not even recognize it. As good Baconians, evangelicals denied the role of philosophical assumptions in science—and thus they were powerless to critique and counter the new assumptions when they appeared on the intellectual horizon. A great many of them simply took the *facts* that Darwin presented and inserted them into the older *philosophy* of nature as an open system—not realizing, apparently, that *the older philosophy was precisely what was under attack*. In the late nineteenth century, explains historian Edward Purcell, the majority of thinkers failed to realize that Darwinism implied "a fully naturalistic worldview." They inserted Darwinism into a religious and providential framework, trying to somehow fit it into a "belief in nature as part of a comprehensive divine order, and in science as part of a larger and morally oriented natural philosophy."[51]

An example was the Princeton theologian B. B. Warfield. As a young man, he had bred shorthorn cattle on his father's ranch, where he noticed that wild cattle developed distinctive traits through interaction with their environment. In short, he had witnessed natural selection. Thus when he encountered the concept of evolution, he accepted it easily, describing himself as "a Darwinian of the purest water." Yet when Warfield explained what he *meant* by evolution, he spoke of the constant supervision of divine providence, punctuated by "occasional supernatural interference."[52] Anyone expressing those views today would be branded a flaming creationist.

Princeton president James McCosh likewise called himself a Darwinian. Yet he held that several pivotal events could not be explained by natural causes alone—that God worked by "immediate fiat" at the origin of life, intelligence, and morality.[53] Finally, one of the most influential theistic evolutionists of the nineteenth century, Asa Gray, also inserted Darwin's concept of natural selection into the older theistic cosmology open to divine supervision and design. He apparently failed to understand that Darwin's intention was to replace that cosmology with a naturalistic one.[54]

One of the few to recognize what was at stake philosophically was Charles Hodge. "The distinctive element" in Darwinism, he wrote, is not natural selection but the denial of design or purpose. And "the denial of design in nature is virtually the denial of God."[55]

Despite Hodge's protest, the debate was not really engaged on the level of philosophy until the rise of the Intelligent Design movement in our own day. When I began writing on science and worldview back in the 1970s, the debate was still being carried on almost solely at the level of scientific details (fossils, mutations, geological strata). One reason the Intelligent Design movement has had such a powerful impact is that Phillip Johnson finally succeeded in shifting the argument to Darwin's naturalistic definition of science. "Christians often think the controversy is primarily a dispute about scientific facts, and so they become trapped into arguing scientific details rather than concentrating on the fundamental assumptions that generate the evolutionary story," Johnson writes in his latest book.[56] The rise of the Intelligent Design movement signals that Christians are finally moving beyond a Baconian view of science, recognizing the formative role that philosophical assumptions play in what counts as genuine knowledge. As we saw in Part 2, factual evidence is important, but it will not persuade unless at the same time we challenge the reigning naturalistic epistemology in science.

Religion on the Side

As the nineteenth century progressed, the Baconian two-story schema filtered down from the realm of abstract ideas and began to be expressed in the institutional structure of the university itself. Universities that had been founded as Christian schools, like Harvard, Princeton, and Yale, began pushing theology off into a separate department instead of allowing it to permeate the curriculum as a whole. Religion became an extracurricular activity that students pursued in their private time on the side—like going to chapel or participating in Christian student groups. The public/private split was becoming part of the institutional structure: Religion was being removed from the curriculum, where we teach public knowledge, and relegated to the private sphere of subjective experience.

In the curriculum, religion was replaced by the humanities, which were supposed to fill the vacuum by dealing with higher questions of meaning, morality, and the spiritual life. But the humanities remained strictly in the upper story, leaving the lower story to science. In 1906 Daniel Coit Gilman, the first president of Johns Hopkins University, wrote, "While the old line between the sciences and the humanities may be invisible as the equator, it has an existence just as real." The difference between them, he said, is that science is "true everywhere and all the time" whereas the humanities depend on "our aesthetic preferences, our intellectual traditions, our religious faith."[57] Notice that by this time Gilman can simply assume the fact/value split: Science is universally true, but the humanities are a matter of preferences, traditions, and faith.

The bi-level division of truth began to be internalized by individuals as well. As the world of the intellect became secularized and divorced from spiritual experience, Christians began talking about a schism between the *head* and the *heart*. A German man spoke for many educated people in 1817 when he said, I "am a heathen in my reason and a Christian with my whole heart."[58]

It is nothing less than tragic that Christians themselves were partly responsible for the privatizing of religion, by accepting the Baconian definition of science as religiously neutral. Evangelicalism fostered a split, says historian Douglas Sloan, between "an emotional conversion experience as the heart of religion" (upper story) and "a narrow, technical utilitarian reason for dealing with this world" (lower story).[59] In other words, for the things of this world, they adopted a form of *methodological* naturalism, which eventually opened the door to *metaphysical* naturalism. After all, if you can interpret the world perfectly well without reference to God, then His existence becomes a superfluous hypothesis, and those who are intellectually honest and courageous will dump it altogether. Historically, that is exactly what happened: "The naturalistic definition of science," Marsden writes, was "transformed from a *methodology* into a dominant academic *worldview.*"[60]

To bring about a restoration of the Christian mind, we would do well to follow the Intelligent Design movement in challenging the Baconian model of autonomous or neutral knowledge in every field. We must reject the presumption that holding Christian beliefs disqualifies us as "biased," while the philosophical naturalists get a free pass by presenting their position as "unbiased" and "rational." Most of all, we need to liberate Christianity from the two-story division that has reduced it to an upper-story private experience, and learn how to restore it to the status of objective truth.

MAKING SENSE OF COMMON SENSE

We can draw resources for the task from some of the other strands within nineteenth-century thought. The Baconian method was just one element of Common Sense realism, and as we raise our sights to a higher level, we will discover new intellectual terrain yielding valuable insights and strategies for today.

In nineteenth-century America, as we saw earlier, Scottish realism became immensely popular. It was applied to virtually every discipline in the college curriculum, becoming the *lingua franca* of the day. What exactly did it teach? Thomas Reid said all knowledge begins with those things we cannot help believing because of the very way the human mind is constituted (self-evident truths). Our inner awareness of pain and pleasure, our moral sense of right and wrong, our instinctive belief in the reality of the physical world—things like these do not need any philosophical justification. They are virtually forced upon us by the constitution of our own nature in order to function in the world God created.[61]

You might say that Common Sense realism is not so much a philosophy as an anti-philosophy[62]—because it actually describes the experiential knowledge that forms the raw material for formal philosophy. Using the image of a plant, Reid said philosophy "has no other root but the principles of Common Sense; it grows out of them, and draws its nourishment from them."[63] Common Sense is the *pre-theoretical experience* that provides the starting material for our *theories* in philosophy, science, morality, and so on. The role of philosophy is to explain *why* it is possible to know the things we already know by experience.

This experiential knowledge also serves as a touchstone for error. When philosophers concoct abstract systems that contradict the self-evident truths of Common Sense, we can be sure that something has gone wrong. After all, the purpose of philosophy is to *explain* what we know by direct experience, not to contradict or deny it. "When a man suffers himself to be reasoned out of the principles of common sense, by metaphysical arguments," Reid said, "we may call this metaphysical lunacy."[64] That is, embracing a philosophy that denies the truths known by experience is sheer craziness.

Scottish realism was particularly attractive to Christians because it was a theistic philosophy, resting on the assumption of divine creation. Reid was a moderate Presbyterian clergyman, and he argued that the reason our minds and senses are trustworthy is that God designed them to work reliably in the world He created. James Henley Thornwell, an Old School Presbyterian, explained that God created the mind to know truth, just as He made "the eye to see, the ear to hear, or the heart to feel."[65]

REID ROMANS 1

What is the legacy of Scottish realism for our own day? Critics charge that it fostered a type of intellectual laziness among nineteenth-century evangelicals, by short-circuiting careful theoretical reflection. It seemed to imply that they did not need to invest in the hard work of defending their core beliefs—because, after all, those beliefs were undeniable and self-evident. "For much of the history of the United States," writes Noll, "evangelicals denied that they *had* a philosophy. They were merely pursuing common sense."[66] What's worse, they included in that category a good number of theological propositions that, to a later generation, did not seem at all self-evident—beliefs that very much required defending in a new, more hostile intellectual climate.

Yet Common Sense philosophy has continued to have remarkable vitality, and has even enjoyed somewhat of a resurgence in our own day, especially among Reformed thinkers. Since the late nineteenth century, there have been essentially two major strands within Reformed thought. Common Sense realism was the *Scottish* Reformed tradition. It fostered an evidentialist form of apologetics, emphasizing truths knowable by believer and unbeliever alike, which function as testing grounds to evaluate competing worldviews. A later strand is the *Dutch* Reformed tradition, consisting of the neo-Calvinism of Abraham Kuyper and Herman Dooyeweerd. It fostered a presuppositionalist form of apologetics, emphasizing the formative impact of worldviews themselves and the need to evaluate them as unified wholes—starting with first principles and tracing out their logical conclusions. "In almost every field today," Marsden notes, "evangelical scholars are divided basically into [these] two camps, with some hybrids in between."[67]

One hybrid was proposed by Francis Schaeffer, who showed how evidentialist and presuppositionalist elements can actually work in tandem in practical evangelism.[68] His method proved remarkably effective for an entire generation of young people. I personally found it persuasive many years ago after arriving on the doorstep at L'Abri as a nonbeliever. And today whenever I give my testimony in public, invariably half a dozen people come up afterward with their own stories of how Schaeffer's ministry and writings brought them to conversion, or helped them through a crisis of faith. Let's do a closer analysis of his hybrid method, then, to see how he crafted a method of apologetics that is still relevant and workable today.

On one hand, Schaeffer agreed with the basic tenet of Common Sense realism that everyone has immediate, pre-theoretical knowledge derived from direct experience. We are all made in the image of God, live in God's universe, and are upheld by God's common grace—and thus we share certain universal experiences, insights, and ways of thinking. Most basic would be the truths of common sense—our fundamental sense of personal identity, right and wrong, the rules of logic, and so on.

Yet these truths do not interpret themselves. They are merely *data* that need to be explained and accounted for by an overall metaphysical system. And so, on the other hand, Schaeffer agreed with neo-Calvinism that even our basic beliefs must be interpreted within a Christian framework. When speaking with nonbelievers, our goal is to show them that Christianity is the only *theoretical* system that accounts for the truths we know by *pre-theoretical* experience. All truth is God's truth, wherever we may find it, as the church fathers said so long ago; but those truths make sense only within a Christian worldview.

This approach is based on Romans 1:19-20. The passage starts by asserting that everyone has genuine knowledge of God through the world He has made: "what can be known about God is plain to them, because God has shown it to them. For his invisible attributes, namely, his eternal power and divine nature, have been clearly perceived, ever since the creation of the world, in the things that have been made. So they are without excuse." In other words, the most pervasive, inescapable experiences—of our own human nature and of an orderly and beautiful universe—give ample reasons for believing in God. Why? Because only His revelation accounts for those experiences.

Nonbelievers try to "suppress" their knowledge of God, Romans goes on to say, by inventing all sorts of alternative explanations for the world. Yet none of these explanations is adequate—and as a result, at some point the nonbeliever's account of the world will be contradicted by his lived experience. That ought to tell him something. The term rendered "without excuse" (v. 20) literally means "without an apologetic." The task of evangelism starts with helping the nonbeliever face squarely the inconsistencies between his professed beliefs and his actual experience. As philosopher Roy Clouser explains, one test of a worldview involves "seeing whether certain data can have *any plausible account at all* on its standpoint."[69] After showing that the nonbeliever's worldview cannot give "any plausible account" of the data of experience, we can then present Christianity as the only worldview that gives a consistent and logical answer.

Or, to turn the argument around, we want to help people see that if their worldview contradicts commonsense experience, then it cannot be true. As Dooyeweerd put it, experience is "a pre-theoretical datum" and "any philosophical theory of human experience which cannot account for this datum in a satisfactory way must be erroneous."[70] To borrow Reid's colorful phrase, it is metaphysical lunacy.

Colors and Shapes

What are some practical examples of how we might use this line of argument in apologetics? Common Sense realism points out that no one can really deny the testimony of the senses. To function at all in the world, we must have a basic trust in the things we see and hear. The entire scientific enterprise is based on the trustworthiness of sense data, and would collapse without the assurance that our sensations provide a reliable picture of reality. Yet how do we know that the images or impressions from our senses match up with the real world? The fatal flaw in any empiricist philosophy is that we cannot step *outside* our sensations and gain some independent vantage point, from which we can test sense data against the external world. How, then, can we explain the trustworthiness of our senses?

The only adequate basis for our confidence is the biblical teaching that there is a Creator who designed our mental capacities to function reliably in the world He created. The doctrine of creation is the epistemological guarantee that the constitution of our human faculties conforms to the structure of the physical world. As Alvin Plantinga writes, it is part of the "human design plan" to trust our own sense perceptions. When our perceptual faculties are in good working order, and functioning in the environment for which they were designed, we naturally trust that the colors and shapes we perceive represent real objects in a real world.[71]

Udo Middelmann (Schaeffer's son-in-law) uses a wonderful phrase to explain why the Christian can have epistemological confidence: Because God created us in His image, to function in His world, there is a "continuity of categories" between God's mind, our minds, and the structure of the world.[72]

The concept of creation or design is the crucial assumption that believers of the nineteenth century overlooked when they thought the sciences could proceed without any distinctively Christian presuppositions. Apart from the doctrine of creation or design, there is no basis for trusting that the ideas in my mind have any correlation to the world outside. If the human mind is a product of chance events, preserved by natural selection, then there is no basis for trusting any of our ideas. Recall Darwin's "horrid doubt" that the human mind could be trusted at all, if it is a product of evolution (chapter 8). The non-Christian pursuing his research has no choice but to rely on his senses, just as everyone else does; but he has no philosophical *basis* for doing so. He is being inconsistent with his own worldview.

Just a Habit?

Take another example. No one can function in daily life without assuming regular patterns of cause and effect. All our actions are based on the conviction that if we perform action A, we will produce effect B. If we put food on the stove, we expect it to cook. If we put fuel in our car, we expect it to run. Science likewise depends on the reality of a consistent order in nature. "Belief in the absoluteness of nature's laws is a deeply-rooted part of the scientific culture," writes an astrophysicist. "To do science, you have to have faith that something is sacrosanct and utterly dependable."[73]

Yet skeptics have argued that our belief in causation is merely a habit, resulting from the flow of sense impressions in our head. When we perceive event A followed by event B, then over time we come to expect the pattern to continue. There is no real basis for that expectation, however, for we cannot know that nature has any plan or order that justifies our thinking. If the universe is a product of chance, then there is no guarantee that the sun will rise tomorrow, or that *any* of the regularities we observe today will hold in the future.

Hume states the problem in a famous passage: "The bread which I formerly ate, nourished me . . . but does it follow that other bread must also nourish me at another time?"[74] In other words, the sheer fact that in the past we have always experienced that bread nourishes us, or that the sun rises, or that fires burns, gives no ground for projecting the same pattern into the future. The tendency to think inductively, Hume says, is grounded in nothing but "custom" and "habit." It has no rational justification.

Science offers mathematical formulas to express the cause-and-effect relationships in nature, but that only intensifies the dilemma. For if the universe evolved by blind, material forces acting randomly, why should it fit so neatly into the mathematical formulas we invent in our minds? In short, why does math work? In a famous essay titled "The Unreasonable Effectiveness of Mathematics in the Natural Sciences," Eugene Wigner says the fact that math works so well in describing the world "is something bordering on the mysterious." Indeed, "there is no rational explanation for it."[75]

No explanation *within scientific materialism,* that is. But within the Christian worldview there is a perfectly rational explanation—namely, that a reasonable God created the world to operate as an orderly progression of events. This was the conviction that inspired the early modern scientists, says historian Morris Kline: "The early mathematicians were sure of the existence of mathematical laws underlying natural phenomena and persisted in the search for them because they were convinced *a priori* that God had incorporated them in the construction of the universe."[76]

By the same token, it was God who outfitted humans with the ability to discover that order in nature. Our instinctive tendency to draw predictions for the future based on the past is part of the human "design plan."[77] In order to function in the world, the nonbeliever has no choice but to reason inductively, but his worldview gives no *basis* for believing in cause-and-effect regularities. To live in the real world, he has to be inconsistent with his own worldview.

Are You Nobody?

The same argument can be applied to our sense of personal identity or self-hood. "I take it for granted that all the thoughts I am conscious of, or remember, are the thoughts of one and the same thinking principle, which I call *myself* or my *mind,*" Reid wrote. "Every man has an immediate and irresistible conviction, not only of his present existence, but of his continued existence and identity as far back as he can remember."[78]

That seems to be an obvious point, but the reason Reid made an issue of it was that skeptics were contesting it. His nemesis, Hume, had pointed out that, on strictly empirical premises, we cannot justify believing even in something as basic as the existence of a unified self. Scanning the contents of our consciousness, all we can detect is an ever-flowing series of perceptions and impressions. "When I enter most intimately into what I call *myself,* I always stumble on some particular perception or other, of heat or cold, light or shade, love or hate, pain or pleasure," Hume wrote. "I never can catch *myself* at any time without a perception, never can observe any thing but the perception."[79] As we saw in chapter 3, some cognitive scientists today side with Hume, denying the reality of a single unified self.

But the purpose of a worldview is to *explain* the data of experience—not to *deny* it. Any philosophical system that fails to offer a plausible account of our sense of personal selfhood should be rejected as inadequate. And that includes both scientific materialism (which defines reality in terms of nonpersonal *natural* forces) as well as Eastern and New Age thought (which defines reality as nonpersonal *spiritual* forces).[80] Any system that begins with nonpersonal forces must, in the end, reduce persons to components of an unconscious matrix of being.

Only Christianity, with its teaching of a personal Creator, provides an adequate metaphysical explanation of our irreducible experience of personhood. It alone accounts for the raw material of experience within a comprehensive worldview. In the modern world, with its large, impersonal institutions where people are treated as ciphers in the machine, the Christian message is good news indeed. Ultimate reality is not the machine; it is a personal Being who loves and relates to each individual in a personal manner.

Mere Chemistry?

Indeed one of the central characteristics of human nature is the capacity for relationships of love and self-giving. Young children deprived of love do not thrive. Yet reductionists tell us that feelings of "love" are merely the effects of chemical reactions in the brain—or, as cognitive science puts it, an illusion caused by patterns of neural activity.

Evolutionary psychologists (as we saw in chapter 7) tell us that altruistic behavior is merely a calculated strategy of helping others so they will help us in return. Tit for tat. It is a strategy of "reciprocal altruism," programmed into our genes by natural selection so that we will get along and survive better. It would be more candid, however, to call this "pseudo-altruism" (as Daniel Dennett does)[81] because the assumption is that individuals practice cooperation and self-control only when it secures their larger interests. Every good deed is ultimately selfish.

What do these same scientists do when they take off their lab coats and go home to their families? Do they treat their love for their spouses and children with the same skepticism? If they have ordinary human emotions, they are all but forced to live inconsistently with the philosophy they have embraced professionally.

The only worldview that supports the highest aspirations of the human heart is Christianity. It gives a basis for believing that love is real and genuine because we were created by a God whose very character is love. The Bible teaches that there has been love and communication between the members of the Trinity from all eternity. Love is not an illusion created by the genes to promote our evolutionary survival, but an aspect of human nature that reflects the fundamental fabric of ultimate reality. Moreover, by submitting to God's plan of salvation and becoming His children, we have the astonishing possibility of participating in that eternal love.

DISINFORMATION MINISTER

The principle running through these examples is that, on one hand, Common Sense realism was right to argue for universal, undeniable human experiences. Human nature is constituted in such a way that we can't help functioning as though our senses are reliable, that cause-and-effect relationships are real, that we have a personal self, and so on. Believer and nonbeliever alike, we were all created in God's image, to live in God's universe, supported by God's common grace, and thus we all share certain fundamental experiences. It rains on the just and the unjust alike.

But the truths of experience are not self-explanatory. Instead they merely constitute the data that cries out to be explained within an overarching worldview. *Why* is it that the bits of matter we call our bodies have consciousness and are able to navigate the world so effectively? *Why* are we capable of building societies with some measure of justice and compassion? As I write, NASA has just released stunning new photographs of the surface of Mars—but why is it possible for humans to calculate a trajectory and land a spacecraft on another planet? What kind of world permits these fascinating achievements? Our claim as Christians is that only a biblically based worldview offers a complete and consistent explanation of why we are capable of knowing scientific, moral, and mathematical truths. Christianity is the key that fits the lock of the universe.

Moreover, since all other worldviews are false keys, we can be absolutely confident, when talking with nonbelievers, that they themselves know things that are *not accounted for* by their own worldview—whatever it may be. Or, to turn it around, they will not be able to live consistently on the basis of their own worldview. Since their metaphysical beliefs do not fit the world God created, their lives will be more or less inconsistent with those beliefs. Living in the real world requires them to function in ways that are not supported by their worldview.

This creates a state of cognitive dissonance, and at that point of tension, the gospel may find an opening. In evangelism we can draw people's attention to the conflict between what they *know* on the basis of experience and what they *profess* in their stated beliefs—because that is a sure sign that something is wrong with their beliefs.[82]

The level of tension will depend on how logically consistent the person is. During the invasion of Iraq, the Iraqi Minister of Information appeared daily before a bank of microphones to repeat over and over again: "There are no American infidels in Baghdad! Never!" This, as American soldiers were taking over government buildings a few blocks away. Presuming that the minister was not simply lying, he was being utterly, unshakably consistent in the face of contrary evidence.

Most people, however, are less consistent. They may hold a philosophy of materialism or Darwinian naturalism, yet in practice they live in ways that contradict those worldviews. After all, who really treats their convictions as the products of natural selection, and not really true but only useful for survival? Who could survive emotionally if they really believed that self-sacrificing love is nothing but "pseudo-altruism"? Because nonbelievers are created in the image of God, the force of their own human nature compels them to live in ways that are inconsistent with their professed worldview. In evangelism, our goal is to highlight that cognitive dissonance—to identify the points at which the nonbeliever's worldview is contradicted by reality. Then we can show that only Christianity is fully consistent with the things we all know by experience to be true. (For more on how this works, see appendix 4.)

PHILOSOPHICAL "CHEATING"

Often people are not fully aware of the logical conclusions of their own beliefs—in which case we may have to press them to follow them out to the end. We cannot let them "cheat" by sneaking in conclusions that are not rationally supported by their starting premises. I recall the regular Saturday night discussions in the L'Abri chapel, where Schaeffer would sit before the large stone fireplace interacting with students and guests, many of them seekers or nonbelievers. Often they would try to defend some purely secular basis for morality or freedom or whatever—and relentlessly he would press them back to their starting premises. "If you want to maintain that something is real, then you have to say what it is and where it came from," as he put it during one discussion. A closed system of naturalistic cause and effect simply gives no basis for things like moral freedom or human dignity—as B. F. Skinner stated so forcefully in the title of his book *Beyond Freedom and Dignity.* In fact, if non-believers were utterly consistent, they would all be amoral skeptics.

Yet in reality very few people in the West are either completely amoral or completely skeptical. Why not? Because they "cheat" by borrowing ideas from the Christian heritage.

A recent example is Dennett's latest book, *Freedom Evolves,* in which he seeks to reconcile Darwinism with a belief in moral freedom. British philosopher John Gray penned a scathing review accusing Dennett of being inconsistent with his self-professed philosophy of naturalism. After all, Gray explained, "the notion that humans are free in a way that other animals are not does not come from science. Its origins are in religion—above all, in Christianity." He charged Dennett with "seeking to salvage a view of humankind derived from Western religion."[83]

To use our terminology, Dennett is "cheating" by borrowing concepts from the Christian heritage that have no basis within his own naturalistic system.

This is far more common than we might think. Gray argues that the whole of Western liberalism is actually parasitic on Christianity. The high view of the human person in liberalism, he says, is derived directly from Christianity: "Liberal humanism inherits several key Christian beliefs—above all, the belief that humans are categorically different from all other animals." No other religion has given rise to the conviction that humans have a unique dignity.

Think of it this way: If Darwin had announced his theory of evolution in India, China, or Japan, it would hardly have made a stir. "If—along with hundreds of millions of Hindus and Buddhists—you have never believed that humans differ from everything else in the natural world in having an immortal soul, you will find it hard to get worked up by a theory that shows how much we have in common with other animals." The West's high view of human dignity and human rights is borrowed directly from Christianity. "The secular world-view is simply the Christian take on the world with God left out," Gray concludes. "Humanism is not an alternative to religious belief, but rather a degenerate and unwitting version of it."[84]

Do we believe this ourselves? Are we convinced that concepts like moral freedom and human dignity have no basis outside of Christianity? We need to press people to stop "cheating" and face squarely the bankruptcy of their own belief systems. For postmodern people, this may be what the Holy Spirit uses to create an awareness of their need—and an openness to the biblical answer. A realization of their "metaphysical lostness" may be the means by which God brings them to salvation.

Signs of Intelligent Life

Francis Schaeffer's method of evangelism, which we have just described, was highly effective with the stream of seekers who stopped in at his chalet in Switzerland. Yet his was not the only possible adaptation of Common Sense realism. In chapter 1 we told the story of Alvin Plantinga's stunning success in restoring theistic philosophy to academic respect in recent years—but what we did *not* mention was that the philosophy he has expounded so brilliantly is an updated version of Thomas Reid's realism. "Human beings are constructed according to a certain design plan," Plantinga argues—including our cognitive faculties. We don't need to construct a complex philosophical defense of the basic beliefs of common sense. Those beliefs are warranted if our cognitive faculties are functioning properly in the environment for which they were designed.[85] This revival of Common Sense philosophy is shared by other Reformed thinkers (such as William Alston and Nicholas Wolterstorff), and their approach has been labeled Reformed Epistemology.

The work of Schaeffer, Plantinga, and many others testifies to the fact that both Scottish Common Sense realism and Dutch neo-Calvinism remain viable philosophical traditions among evangelical thinkers today, capable of sustaining substantial philosophical work. Even outsiders have begun to sit up and take notice. A few years ago, *Commonweal* ran an article titled "The Evangelical Mind Awakens,"[86] remarking that the majority of evangelical scholars who have achieved academic recognition in mainstream academia have ties to neo-Calvinism. Three historians mentioned in the article—George Marsden, Mark Noll, and Nathan Hatch—are so prolific in their scholarship that a Yale professor has even warned that an "evangelical thesis" may be taking over the study of American history![87]

Ordinary believers are expressing a hunger to recover a richer heritage as well, by acquainting themselves with the spiritual classics. When I visited a small Christian bookstore near my home, the owner told me that the shelf he can't restock fast enough is the one devoted to the older classics, from Augustine to St. John of the Cross—an encouraging sign of a new interest in worshiping God with our minds as well as our hearts.

BOXED-IN BELIEVERS

Let's summarize what we've learned from the history of American evangelicalism over the past three chapters. To begin with, we cannot help recognizing its overall positive impact. By inspiring an intensely personal commitment to Christianity, it is the main reason America remains the most religious nation in the industrialized world today. Yet we also need to realize that evangelicalism did not overcome the age-old two-story division of knowledge—on the contrary, it intensified the split. The populist branch of evangelicalism contributed to the idea that religion is a private emotional experience (upper story), while the scholarly branch reinforced the idea that public knowledge must be religiously neutral and autonomous (lower story). As a result, religion was removed from the public realm and shunted off into the private realm. There it might flourish, as in fact it has. But it would be carefully kept in its cage. Meanwhile, secular ideologies took advantage of the vacuum and quickly filled the public arena.

What happened in the nineteenth century, explains historian Martin Marty, was that religion in America "accepted a division of labour." On one hand, "religion acquiesced in the assignment to address itself to the personal, familial, and leisured sectors of life" (the private dimension). On the other hand, "the public dimensions—political, social, economic, cultural—were to become autonomous," and were eventually taken over by non-Christian ideologies.[88]

This division of labor was "a momentous concession," Marty says, and yet today Americans have grown so used to it that we no longer realize what a novel development it was. He calls it the Modern Schism and says it was a complete "novelty in Western culture." Of course, Christian thought had been marked by the two-story dichotomy for centuries, as we have seen. But in the nineteenth century that dichotomy began to be expressed externally in social institutions. Society was divided into "an outer, encompassing culture," on one hand, and on the other hand "an inner, sequestered largely ecclesiastical religious culture within."[89] Individual believers began to inhabit two worlds, commuting from one to the other across the Modern Schism.

No longer were religious leaders the public spokesmen of society, as they had once been. Instead, they were permitted to appear in public only to perform the limited role of inspiring and legitimating the larger culture. They could perform invocations and benedictions—like opening prayers in Congress—but they were not welcome to comment on the substance of legislation; that would be "meddling" in politics. Visitors from other countries were amazed at the way the clergy in America were boxed in. The ever-observant

Tocqueville commented, "In America, religion is a distinct sphere, in which the priest is sovereign but out of which he takes care never to go."[90]

The overall pattern of evangelicalism's history is summarized brilliantly by Richard Hofstadter in a single sentence. To a large extent, he writes, "the churches *withdrew* from intellectual encounters with the secular world, *gave up* the idea that religion is a part of the whole life of intellectual experience, and often *abandoned* the field of rational studies on the assumption that they were the natural province of science alone."[91] Let's break that sentence down, for it sums up the entire story of what happened to the evangelical mind. Notice that Hofstadter mentions three factors: One, churches and seminaries themselves largely *withdrew* from intellectual confrontation with the secular world, limiting their attention to the realm of practical Christian living. Two, they *gave up* the idea that Christianity gives a comprehensive framework to interpret all of life and scholarship, allowing it to become boxed into the upper story. Three, in the process, they *abandoned* an entire range of intellectual inquiry to the lower story. They gave in to the demand that the academic disciplines must be religiously and philosophically autonomous, without realizing that it was just a cover to introduce *new* philosophies like positivism and naturalism.

Yet that is not the whole story. Ideas do not remain in the realm of the abstract; they also influence the concrete ways people construct their society and its institutions. The Modern Schism was not just a set of ideas about religion, it was also a profound change in the way real people lived and organized their lives. It was part of a larger reordering of society that affected the structure of the workplace, the family, and even the relations between the sexes. Turn to the next chapter for a fascinating excursion into the personal and social consequences of the public/private split in American life—consequences that include religion but also go far beyond it.

12

HOW WOMEN STARTED
THE CULTURE WAR

Modernization brings about
a novel dichotomization of social life.
The dichotomy is between
the huge and immensely powerful institutions
of the public sphere . . . and the private sphere.
PETER BERGER[1]

I had just spoken on a panel at a large secular university when a woman in the audience stood up and said, "I'm not a feminist, but . . ." That was a pretty good tip-off that she was about to say something from a feminist perspective.

"Why didn't this program mention any women? None of the speakers cited works by women. Why are you ignoring half the human race?" The woman glared around the room, then added: "Don't bother to answer." She began to stalk out of the auditorium, staging a dramatic exit.

I grabbed the microphone. "Don't leave," I said. That night I had talked about the divided concept of truth that runs like a chasm through all of Western thought. "The fact/value split is not merely academic," I said. "It has been incarnated in modern social institutions as a split between public and private life—which affects even the relationships between men and women."

That got her attention, and the room grew hushed. I explained that the two-story conception of knowledge has restructured not only the university curriculum but also the home, the church, and the workplace. This is an important aspect of the two-tiered division of truth, because it reminds us that it is not just a matter of ideas but also a powerful force reshaping the way we live.

WOMEN AND THE AWAKENING

Come with me back to the middle of the Second Great Awakening. In 1838, a controversial article appeared urging laypeople to "think for themselves" in matters of religion.[2] Ordinarily, a message like that would hardly have caused a ripple. As we have seen, the call to ordinary people to read and interpret the Bible for themselves was a central theme in the evangelical movement of the time. What made this article so controversial, however, was that it was written by a woman—and she was calling on *women* to read the Bible for themselves: "I believe it to be the solemn duty of every individual to search the Scriptures for themselves, with the aid of the Holy Spirit, and not be governed by the views of any man, or set of men."[3]

Once the evangelical movement had embraced spiritual populism, it was difficult to contain the logic of equality to white males. In terms of sheer numbers, the Awakenings reached more women than men, especially younger women. The revivalists also permitted women to pray and speak publicly, and even to become "exhorters" (teaching assistants), which scandalized critics. Moreover, because the revivalists stressed the emotional side of religion, their message seemed to be pitched especially to women. They began to speak of women as being more naturally religious than men, and urged wives to be the means of converting their more worldly husbands.

Like the other trends we have traced, this one has continued into our own day. American churches still typically attract more women than men, giving rise to the stereotype that religion is for women and children. This pattern is so widespread that some have spoken of the "feminization" of the church. "Men still *run* most churches," one study concludes, but "in the *pews* women outnumber men in all countries of Western civilization."[4]

Interestingly, this is not true of other faiths: In Eastern Orthodoxy, the membership is roughly balanced, and in Judaism and Islam men actually predominate.[5] So the pattern cannot be explained by saying that men are just naturally less religious than women. Instead, Western Christianity is unusual in this regard. Why is that?

The answer is found in the split between the public and the private, fact and value, which cast Christianity into the upper story. This was not merely a change in ideas about religion; it involved changes in the material world as well—in the institutional structures of society. Once we grasp this process, it will shed new light not only on the state of evangelicalism today but also on issues like the role of the church in society and the roles of men and women in the home.[6]

HOUSEHOLDS AT WORK

Historically speaking, the key turning point was the Industrial Revolution, which eventually divided the private realm of family and faith from the public realm of business and industry. To grasp these changes more clearly, let's start by painting a picture of life *before* the Industrial Revolution.

In the colonial period, families lived much the way they have lived for millennia in traditional societies. The vast majority of people lived on farms or in peasant villages. Productive work was done in the home or its outbuildings.[7] Work was done not by lone individuals but by families or households. A household was a relatively autonomous economic unit, often including members of the extended family, apprentices, servants, and hired hands. Stores, offices, and workshops were located in a front room, with living quarters either upstairs or in the rear.[8] This meant that the boundary between home and world was highly permeable: The "world" entered continually in the form of clients, business colleagues, customers, and apprentices.

This integration of life and work actually survives in pockets of modern society. When I was twelve years old, my family lived for a year in a small village outside Heidelberg, Germany. To go shopping we would take a large basket and walk down the street to the baker, then the butcher, then the grocer, and so on. Each storefront was located in the front room of a house, with the family living upstairs or in the back rooms. Husband and wife worked together all day, and school let out at noon (all the way through high school), so the kids could come home and help out too, stocking shelves and running the cash register. Each business was a genuine family enterprise.

One evening when I visited a small gift shop down the street, a woman came out of a back room with a baby on her hip. She waited on me holding her baby in one arm, then waved goodbye and went back to making dinner. As late as the 1960s, in German villages, one could still experience the preindustrial form of the family enterprise.

What did the colonial integration of work and life mean for family relationships? It meant that husband and wife worked side by side on a daily basis, sharing in the same economic enterprise. For a colonial woman, one historian writes, marriage "meant to become a co-worker beside a husband . . . learning new skills in butchering, silversmith work, printing, or upholstering— whatever special skills the husband's work required."[9] A useful measure of a society's treatment of women is the status of widows, and historical records show that in colonial days it was not uncommon for widows to carry on the family enterprise after their husbands died—which means they had learned the requisite skills to keep the business going on their own.[10]

Of course, women were also responsible for a host of household tasks requiring a wide range of skills: spinning wool and cotton; weaving it into cloth; sewing the family's clothes; gardening and preserving food; preparing meals without preprocessed ingredients; making soap, buttons, candles, medicines. Many of the goods used in colonial society were manufactured by women, and, as Dorothy Sayers writes, they "worked with head as well as hands."[11]

Now, the fact that all this took place in the home meant that mothers were able to combine economically productive work with raising children. It also meant that *fathers* were much more involved in raising children than they are today. In fact, we cannot understand changes in women's roles unless we consider changes in men's roles at the same time.

COMMUNAL MANHOOD

In the colonial period, the husband and father was regarded as the head of the household—and headship had a highly specific definition: It was defined as a divinely sanctioned office that conferred a duty to represent *not* his own individual interests but those of the entire household. This was an extension of the classical republican political theory discussed in chapter 10, in which a social institution (family, church, or state) was regarded as an organic unity where all shared in a common good. There was a "good" for individuals, but there was also a "good" of the whole, which was more than the sum of its parts— and this latter was the responsibility of the one in authority. He was called to sacrifice his own interests—to be *dis*interested—in order to represent the interests of the whole.[12] Husbands and fathers were not to be driven by personal ambition or self-interest but to take responsibility for the common good of the entire household.

We might say that the culturally dominant definition of masculinity was "communal manhood," a term coined by Anthony Rotundo in *American Manhood*. It meant that a man was expected to rank duty above personal ambition. To use a common phrase of the time, he was to fulfill himself through "publick usefulness" more than through economic success.[13]

In their day-to-day life, fathers enjoyed the same integration of work and childrearing responsibilities that mothers did. With production centered on the family hearth, fathers were "a visible presence, year after year, day after day" as they trained their children to work alongside them. Being a father was not a separate activity to come home to after a day at work; rather, it was an integral part of a man's daily routine.[14] Historical records reveal that colonial literature on parenting—like sermons and child-rearing manuals—were not addressed to mothers, as the majority are today. Instead, they were typically addressed to *fathers*. Fathers were considered the primary parent, and were held to be particularly important in their children's religious and intellectual training.[15]

Each household was a small commonwealth, headed by a Hausvater (literally: "house father"). In the mid-nineteenth century, writes historian John Gillis, "Not only artisans and farmers but business and professional men conducted much of their work in the house, assisted by their wives and children." As a result, "There was no difference between [the Hausvater's] time and that of his wife, children, and servants. They all ate and prayed together; they got up and went to bed on the same schedule." Indeed, surprising as it may seem, "Males . . . were as comfortable in the kitchen as women, for they had responsibility for provisioning and managing the house. Until the nineteenth century, cookbooks and domestic conduct books were directed primarily to them, and they were as devoted to décor as they were to hospitality."[16]

In terms of the father's constant presence in the home, nineteenth-century America was actually closer to the world of Martin Luther than to our own. "When a father washes diapers and performs some other mean task for his child, and someone ridicules him as an effeminate fool," Luther wrote, he should remember that "God with all his angels and creatures is smiling."[17]

This is not to idealize colonial life, which was often a rugged life of back-breaking labor. Yet in terms of family relations, there is no doubt that families benefited from an integration of life and labor that is extremely rare in our fragmented age.

HOME AS HAVEN

All of that changed with the Industrial Revolution. The main impact of the Industrial Revolution was to take work out of the home. This apparently simple change—in the physical location of work—set off a process that led to a sharp decline in the social significance accorded the home, drastically altering the roles of both men and women.

Industrialization took place in America at breakneck speed, roughly between 1780 and 1830. In the early stages, whole families went to work in the factories or did piecework at home—after all, they were used to working together as a unit. But it soon became evident that industrial work was shockingly different from the older family-centered work culture.

Since we've grown used to an industrialized workplace, we have to use a bit of historical imagination to grasp the differences. The old pattern was based on *personal* relations between a farmer and his sons and hired hands, or between craftsman and apprentices. In the Industrial Revolution, that gave way to *impersonal* relations based on wages. Or again, in the old handcraft tradition, a single craftsman would plan, design, and then carry out a project. But under capitalism there arose an ever-increasing class of managers and contractors, who took over all the creative planning and decision making, while leaving workers with mechanical tasks divided into simple, repetitive steps— the assembly line. In the traditional agrarian society, farming and handcrafts were "task-oriented," structured by human need and seasonable requirements. But in an industrial society, factory work was "time-oriented," structured by the clock and the regularity of the machine.

The new workplace fostered an economic philosophy of atomistic individualism, as workers were treated as so many interchangeable units to be plugged into the production process—each struggling to advance himself at the expense of others. To many, the world of industry seemed to be a Social Darwinist war of each against all. (Some have even suggested that Darwin's concept of the struggle for existence was merely an extrapolation into biology of the competitive ethos of early industrialism.[18])

It was not long before a great social outcry was raised against this new and alien work style, while large-scale efforts were mobilized to restrict its dehumanizing effects. The primary strategy was to delineate one outpost where the "old" personal and ethical values could be protected and maintained— namely, the home. It came to stand for enduring values and ideals that people desperately wanted to maintain in the face of modernity: things like love, morality, religion, altruism, and self-sacrifice.

To protect these endangered values, laws were passed limiting the participation of women and children in the factories. This was followed, beginning in the 1820s, by an outpouring of books, pamphlets, advice manuals, and sermons that delineated what historians call a doctrine of separate spheres: The public sphere of business and finance was to be cordoned off from the private sphere of home and family—so that the home would become a refuge, a haven, from the harsh and competitive world outside, a place of solace and spiritual renewal.[19]

WHY MEN LEFT HOME

How did these changes affect men and women? The most obvious change is that men had little choice but to follow their work out of households and fields, and into factories and offices. As a result, their physical presence around the household dropped sharply. It became difficult for them to continue acting as the primary parent. Fathers simply no longer spent enough time with their children to educate them, enforce regular discipline, or train them in adult skills and trades.

As a result, the most striking feature of child-rearing manuals of the mid-nineteenth century is the disappearance of references to fathers. For the first time we find sermons and pamphlets on the topic of child-rearing addressed exclusively to mothers rather than to fathers or both parents.[20] Men began to feel connected to their children primarily through their wives. The story is told of one Victorian father with sixteen children, who failed to recognize his own daughter at a parish Christmas party: "And whose little girl are you?" he asked. To which the miserable child replied, "I am yours, Daddy." The incident was probably exceptional, yet there is no doubt that middle-class fathers were becoming secondary parents.[21]

The impact on women was, if anything, even more dramatic. After the Industrial Revolution, the home eventually ceased being the locus of production and became a locus of consumption—which meant that women at home were gradually reduced from producers to consumers. Household industries with their range of mutual services were replaced by factories and waged labor. Instead of developing a host of varied skills—spinning, weaving, sewing, knitting, preserving, brewing, baking, and candle-making—women's tasks were progressively reduced to basic housekeeping and early childcare. Instead of enjoying a sense of economic indispensability, women were reduced to dependents, living off the wages of their husbands. Instead of working in a common economic enterprise with their husbands, women were shut off in a world of private "retirement." Instead of working with other adults throughout the day—servants, apprentices, clients, customers, and extended family—women became socially isolated with young children all day.[22]

Indeed, the role of mothers in childrearing actually became *more* salient than it had been in the past, when they had shared the task with other adults in the household—grandparents, single relatives, older siblings, servants, and especially fathers. As these others left home for the workplace, raising children became almost solely the mother's responsibility.

In a nutshell, women experienced a drastic *decrease* in the range of work available to them in the home—while, at the same time, experiencing a dramatic *increase* in responsibility for the narrow range of tasks that remained. Historical records give evidence of the dramatic change: Women "vanished more or less entirely from a number of occupations; they appeared less frequently in public records as printers, blacksmiths, arms-makers, or proprietors of small business concerns."[23] As I mentioned earlier, colonial widows often took over the business when their husbands died—but no longer. "By the early nineteenth century," writes one historian, "widows were conventionally viewed as pitiful charity cases,"[24] lacking the work skills to support themselves.

THE PASSIONATE MALE

Even the portrayals of masculine and feminine character came in for social redefinition. In the older ideal of "communal manhood," the key word was *duty:* duty to one's superiors and to God. Manly virtue was defined as keeping one's "passions" in submission to reason (with *passion* defined primarily as self-interest and personal ambition). The good man was one who exercised self-restraint and self-sacrifice for the sake of the common good.

But the emerging world of industrial capitalism fostered a new definition of virtue. The capitalist world seemed to require each man to function as an individual in competition with other individuals. In this new context, it was appropriate, even necessary, to act under the impulse of self-interest and personal ambition. Economic theories appeared—like Adam Smith's *The Wealth of Nations*—that treated self-interest as a universal natural force, analogous to the force of gravity in physics.

At the same time, political theory was shifting from the household to the individual as the basic unit of society. Classical republican political philosophy—with its organic view of an overarching, unifying common good—gave way to an atomistic view of society as an aggregate of warring, self-interested individuals. There emerged a new vision of the individual as free from settled social bonds, free from generational ties to the past, free to find his own place in society through open competition.[25]

We discussed these trends earlier in relationship to the evangelical movement, but they also had an enormous impact on the family. Eventually the values of the colonial period were actually turned upside down: The Puritans had viewed the "passions" as a threat to social order, requiring control and self-restraint for the public good. But by the end of the nineteenth century, male "passions" and self-interest had come to be viewed in a positive light—as the source of equality and economic prosperity.

In fact, the word *competitive* now entered the English language for the first time. Until then, the English did not even have a word for a person who relished the challenge of a contest. But by the end of the nineteenth century, competition had become an obsession among American men. It was firmly believed that free competition was the engine of prosperity and political life.[26] "By a remarkable inversion," writes Lesslie Newbigin, people began to find "in covetousness not only a law of nature but the engine of progress by which the purpose of nature and nature's God was to be carried out."[27] And as men went forth to do battle in the tough, competitive world of commerce and politics, the masculine character itself was redefined as morally hardened, competitive, aggressive, and self-interested.

TAMING MEN

For women, however, the doctrine of separate spheres meant an entirely different story. They were called on to maintain the home as an arena cordoned off from the competitive, dog-eat-dog ethos of economics and politics. Women were to cultivate the softer virtues—of community, morality, religion, self-sacrifice, and affection. They were urged to act as moral guardians of the home, making it a place where men could be renewed, reformed, and refined—a place of "retirement" from the competitive, amoral world outside. As Frances Parkes wrote in 1829, "The world corrupts; home should refine."[28]

Thus the public/private split was reflected in a sharp contrast between the sexes as well. As Kenneth Keniston of MIT writes: "The family became a special protected place, the repository of tender, pure, and generous feelings (embodied in the mother) and a bulwark and bastion against the raw, competitive, aggressive, and selfish world of commerce (embodied by the father)."[29]

This was a startling reversal. In colonial days, husbands and fathers had been admonished to function as the moral and spiritual leaders of the household. But now men were being told that they were naturally crude and brutish—and that they needed to learn virtue from their wives. And many men acquiesced to the new ethos. For example, during the Civil War, General William Pender wrote to his wife, "Whenever I find my mind wandering upon bad and sinful thoughts I try to think of my good and pure wife and they leave me at once. . . . You are truly my good Angel."[30] Women were called upon to be the guardians of morality—to make men virtuous.

This is the origin of the double standard, and on the surface, it may appear to empower women. After all, it accorded them the status of enforcers of virtue. But the underlying dynamic was actually very troubling: As Rotundo explains, in essence America was releasing men from the requirement to be virtuous. For the first time, moral and spiritual leadership were no longer viewed as masculine attributes. They became women's work. "Women took men's place as the custodians of communal virtue," Rotundo writes, but in doing so, they "were freeing men to pursue self-interest."[31] In other words, men were being let off the hook.

In the long run, this "de-moralizing" of the male character would not be in women's best interest, as we will see. Nor was it in men's best interest, either, for they were becoming content with a stunted definition of masculinity as tough, competitive, and pragmatic, which denied their moral and spiritual aspirations.

FEMINIZING THE CHURCH

Where was the Christian church in all this? Did it stand firmly against the "demoralization" of the male character? Sadly, no. Instead the American church largely acquiesced in the redefinition of masculinity. After centuries of teaching that husbands and fathers were divinely called to the office of household headship, the church began to pitch its appeal primarily to women. Churchmen began to speak of women as having a special gift for religion and morality. If you look carefully at illustrations of camp meetings, you often see women dominating the front rows, swooning and fainting (see fig. 12.1). In many evangelical churches, women began to outnumber men, often by two to one. When the British novelist Francis Trollope visited America in 1832, she commented that she had never seen a country "where religion had so strong a hold upon the women or a slighter hold upon the men."[32]

Fig. 12.1 **THE "FEMINIZATION" OF CHRISTIANITY:** The awakenings tended to attract more women than men. *(Library of Congress, Prints and Photographs Division [LC-USZC4-4554].)*

Even the tone of religion became feminized. In a classic book on the subject, *The Feminization of American Culture,* Ann Douglas writes that the ministry lost "a toughness, a sternness, an intellectual rigor which our society then and since has been accustomed to identify with 'masculinity,'" and instead took on "feminine" traits of care, nurturing, sentimentalism, and retreat from the harsh, competitive ethos of the public arena.[33] The trend was especially typical of liberal churches. "Religion in the old virile sense has disappeared, and been replaced by a feeble Unitarian sensibility," lamented Henry James, Sr., father of the famous novelist.[34] A Congregationalist minister complained that "the sword of the spirit" has been "muffled up and decked out with flowers and ribbons."[35]

The underlying dynamic is that the church was adopting a defensive strategy vis-a-vis the culture at large. Many churchmen simply retreated from making cognitive claims for religion that could be defended in the public sphere. Instead, they transferred faith to the private sphere of experience and feelings—which put it squarely into the domain of women. In 1820 the Unitarian minister Joseph Buckminster wrote,

> I believe that if Christianity should be compelled to flee from the mansions of the great, the academies of the philosophers, the halls of legislators, or the throng of busy men, we should find her last and purest retreat with women at the fireside; her last altar would be the female heart.[36]

The operative word here is "flee." There was a presumption that religion was on the run from the public realm of hard-headed men, retreating to the private realm of soft-hearted women.

In short, instead of challenging the growing secularism among men, the church largely acquiesced—by turning to women. Churchmen seemed relieved to find at least one sphere, the home, where religion still held sway. Whereas traditional church teaching had held that fathers were responsible for their children's education, in the early 1800s, says one historian, "New England ministers fervently reiterated their consensus that mothers were *more* important than fathers in forming 'the tastes, sentiments, and habits of children,' and more effective in instructing them."[37] As a result, "mothers increasingly took over the formerly paternal task of conducting family prayers."[38]

Once again, we detect a disturbing dynamic: The churches were releasing men from the responsibility of being religious leaders. They were turning religion and morality into the domain of women—something soft and comforting, not bracing and demanding. Charles Eliot Norton of Harvard spoke for many at the time when he complained of the intellectual flabbiness—he called it the "unmanliness"—of religion.[39]

MORALS AND MERCY

A similar transformation was taking place in the arena of social reform. If women were the moral guardians of the home, it seemed logical that they should be the guardians of society as well. After all, many women began to argue, it was impossible to hermetically seal off private life from public life.

Public vices like drunkenness and prostitution have private consequences. As the leader of the Women's Christian Temperance Union put it, women must seek to "make the whole world Homelike."[40]

Thus it was largely women who fueled the widespread reform movements of the progressive era in the nineteenth century. Working first through churches, women set out to reform the public sphere by dispensing Christian benevolence. They joined or started societies to feed and clothe the poor. They supported the Sunday school movement and missionary societies. They joined or founded organizations to abolish slavery, to outlaw prostitution and abortion, to stop public drunkenness and gambling. They supported orphan asylums and societies such as the YWCA to assist single women in the cities. They initiated movements to abolish child labor, establish juvenile courts, and strengthen food and drug laws.

This interlocking network of reform societies has been dubbed the Benevolent Empire, and one prominent reformer at the time credited its construction largely to women: "Scarcely without exception," he said, "it has been the members of the women's clubs . . . who have secured all the advanced legislation . . . for the protection of home and the child."[41]

The progressive era marked the birth of the secular feminist movement as well, which I will discuss later. But most of these early crusaders were definitely *not* feminists: They did not base their claim to work outside the home on the feminist argument that there are no important differences between men and women. Just the opposite: They accepted the doctrine that women are more loving, more sensitive, more pious—but then they argued that it was *precisely those qualities* that equipped them for benevolent work beyond the confines of the home. As one woman put it at the time, the affairs of government and industry have "been too long dominated by the crude, war-like, acquisitive, hardheaded, amoral qualities of men," and they "should no longer be deprived of the tempering influence of women's compassion, spirituality, and moral sensitivity."[42]

The locus of many of these reform activities was the church, and they were eagerly supported by the clergy, who declared that women's naturally pious influence was crucial for society. Again Joseph Buckminster gives an eloquent example:

> We look to you, ladies, to raise the standard of character of our own sex [i.e., men]; we look to you, to guard and fortify those barriers which still exist in society, against the encroachments of impudence and licentiousness. We look to you for the continuance of domestick purity, for the revival of domestick

religion, for the increase of our charities, and the support of what remains of religion in our private habits and publick institutions.[43]

But notice the same dangerous dynamic we noted before: When "ladies" are given responsibility for "raising the standard of character" among men, then men are freed to be less responsible. They are let off the hook. "The care of dependent populations" was "once the civic duty of town fathers and poor masters," writes one historian. But in the nineteenth century, it became "known as charity . . . and became the province of women."[44]

FEMALE STANDARDS, MALE RESENTMENT

Eventually the double standard created tensions in relationships between men and women. After all, who were the objects of all these reform movements? Who were the scoundrels so debauched that women must take them in hand? They were, well, . . . men. The temperance movement mobilized wives and mothers against hard-drinking husbands and fathers, to drive them out of the tavern and back to the hearth. The rhetoric of female abolitionists focused on male slave masters who took sexual advantage of slave women.[45] The movement to outlaw prostitution and abortion cast fallen women as victims and men as cruel seducers. Historian Mary Ryan sums up the gender dimension to the reform movements: "Almost all the female reform associations were implicit condemnations of males; there was little doubt as to the sex of slave masters, tavern-keepers, drunkards and seducers."[46]

The message sent by the doctrine of separate spheres was "that women must control men morally," explains historian Carl Degler. Women were urged to "work together to control the male tendency toward lasciviousness." For if the mother was "moral arbiter in the home," that role "vouchsafed to women the right—nay, obligation—to regulate men's sexual behavior."[47]

The ideology of separate spheres was nothing less than "a plan for female government of male passions," Rotundo agrees. But then he notes that it had a paradoxical effect: "It gave men the freedom to be aggressive, greedy, ambitious, competitive, and self-interested, then it left women with the duty of curbing this behavior."[48]

These themes were even reflected in the literature of the day. In the early nineteenth century, a full third of all novels published in the United States were written by women (inspiring Nathaniel Hawthorne's famous outburst that America had been taken over by a "mob of scribbling women").[49] One of the most common themes in these novels is the triumph of women against evil men. "The major repeated story," writes an English professor, "is that of the struggle of the good woman against the oppression and cruelties, covert and blatant, of men."[50] The message was that men are inherently coarse and immoral—and that virtue is a womanly trait, imposed upon men only through great travail. The very concept of virtue, which had once been primarily a masculine trait, defined as courage and disinterested civic duty, was transformed into a feminine trait, focused primarily on sexual purity.[51]

MANLY MEN

Ultimately, however, the attempt to make women the moral reformers of men was self-defeating. Why? Because when virtue is defined as a *feminine* quality instead of a *human* quality, then requiring men to be virtuous is seen as the imposition of a feminine standard—a standard that is alien to the masculine nature. Being virtuous took on overtones of being effeminate instead of manly. The Unitarian minister William Ellery Channing was once praised by a friend who described him as "almost feminine" and admired his "womanly temperament."[52]

By the late nineteenth and early twentieth century, a reaction set in and men began to rebel against female efforts to reform them. A new word entered the American language: *overcivilized*. Men began to worry that boys were now growing up far too exclusively under the tutelage of mothers and female teachers, with the result that they were becoming soft and effeminate.[53]

In reaction, a new emphasis was laid on the wild, untamed masculine nature. This is when legends of the lost frontier became popular—the lives of Davy Crocket and Daniel Boone. Theodore Roosevelt went west and began to celebrate the "strenuous life" of the outdoorsman. Ernest Thomas Seton dressed up in an Indian costume and founded the American Boy Scouts. A 1914 Scout manual expressed the new philosophy vividly:

> [The] Wilderness is gone, the Buckskin man is gone, the painted Indian has hit the trail over the Great Divide, the privations and hardships of pioneer life which did so much to produce sterling manhood are now but a legend, and we must depend on the Boy Scout movement to produce the MEN of the future.[54]

Literary works began to sound a tone of male rebellion against female standards of virtue. Around the turn of the century, says one historical account, there arose "new genres of cowboy and adventure fiction, written by such authors as Owen Wister [author of the first Western] and Jack London"—books that "celebrated the man who had escaped the confines of domesticity."[55] So-called "bad boy" books became a popular genre, the best-known being Mark Twain's *Tom Sawyer* and *Huckleberry Finn*. The latter ends with Huck taking off for lands unknown "because Aunt Sally she's going to adopt me and sivilize me, and I can't stand it." Note that "sivilizing" is something done by old maid aunts. Twain's books express a poignant ambivalence of "both reverence for and resentment of the home and female standards."[56]

Some writers began to celebrate the male as primitive and barbarian, praising his "animal instincts" and "animal energy." The Tarzan books, featuring a wild man raised by apes, became immensely popular. This new definition of masculine virtue reflected in part the influence of Darwin's theory of evolution. For if humans evolved from the animal world, the implication was that the animal nature is the core of our being. This was a startlingly new concept: From antiquity, virtue had been defined as the exercise of restraint of the "lower" passions by the "higher" faculties of the rational spirit and the moral will. But now, in a stunning reversal, the animal passions were held up as the true self. "It is a new sensation to come to see man as an animal—the master animal of the world," wrote John Burroughs (son of the author of *Tarzan*).[57] The rise of Social Darwinism exalted "the triumph of man over man in primitive struggle."[58]

Even churches sensed a problem and began recasting religion in a more masculine tone. Too long religion had been the domain of women, tinged with sentimental piety. In 1858 an *Atlantic Monthly* article scolded parents, saying that if a son was "pallid, puny, sedentary, lifeless, joyless," then he was directed to the ministry—while on the other hand the "ruddy, the brave, and the strong" were directed to secular careers.[59] The answer? "Muscular Christianity"—a concept that combined hardy physical manliness with ideals of Christian service.

The best-known advocate of muscular Christianity was the evangelist Billy Sunday, who proclaimed that Jesus was "no dough-faced, lick-spittle proposition" but "the greatest scrapper that ever lived." Sunday offered followers a "hard-muscled, pick-axed religion," not some "dainty, sissified, lily-livered piety."[60] Books appeared with titles like *The Manliness of Christ, The Manly Christ,* and *The Masculine Power of Christ.* A church-based movement appeared called the Men and Religion Forward movement, which lasted until the 1950s, stressing an image of Jesus as the Successful Businessman or Salesman. Organizers bought ads on the sports pages, alongside ads for cars and whisky, and proclaimed that women "have had charge of the Church work long enough." They promoted a manly religion that emphasized strength and social responsibility.[61]

ROMPER ROOM DADS

This welcome emphasis on male strength was tainted, however, by the continuing theme that genuine masculinity is attained only by resisting "feminine" standards. In 1926 an influential book called *The Mauve Decade* opened with a savage attack on what the author called "the Titanesse"—the American woman as arbiter of public taste and morals. The author worried about the masculinity of boys growing up in woman-dominated homes and schools.[62]

In the 1940s, Philip Wylie penned a best-selling book called *A Generation of Vipers,* in which he accused women of "Momism"—of smothering, controlling, and manipulating their sons.[63] I still remember as an adolescent seeing articles in women's magazines on the dangers of "Momism." In the 1950s, *Playboy* made its appearance, warning that women are economic parasites and that marriage is a trap that will "crush man's adventurous, freedom-loving spirit."[64] An early issue showed a full-page spread of a smiling bride and groom—but on the next page, the bride's nose and chin are elongated, her veil sticks out like spikes, and the poor man discovers he's married a harpy. The theme was that family life and values are imposed by women, but are oppressive to men.

For the first time it became socially acceptable for fathers not to be involved with their families. By the 1920s and 30s in urban areas, the father had become the secondary parent who covered the "extras": hobbies, sports, trips to the zoo. As one historian describes it, fathers were reduced to entertainers—Romper Room dads.[65]

There emerged the now-familiar image of fathers as incompetent bumblers in the home, who are patronized by long-suffering wives and clever children[66]—the image popularized today in the comic strip figure Dagwood Bumstead, Al Bundy on "Married with Children," and the beleaguered Father Bear in the popular Berenstain Bears picture-book series. When Mother Bear decides the family must stop eating junk food, it's Papa Bear who sneaks his favorite snacks. When Mother Bear decides the family must give up TV, it's Papa Bear who sneaks downstairs at night to watch the tube. The books present a stereotype where mothers impose rules, and childish fathers break them. Even the children scold Papa Bear for his infractions. It's all presented as humorous, of course. Ha-ha! Let's teach children to feel superior to their incompetent fathers.

When I was attending seminary, a professor opened class one day by telling a story of how he was left alone—*alone!*—with his two small sons one Saturday morning while his wife went shopping. Unable to restrain their lively behavior, he finally imposed order by settling one boy at one end of the couch, the other boy at the other end, while he stationed himself rigidly between them, forbidding them to move or talk until his wife returned and rescued him. The (male) students in the class all laughed. And I wondered: When did it become socially acceptable for a Christian man to admit that he is incompetent as a father?

As fatherhood lost status, not surprisingly, men showed a decreasing investment in being fathers. From 1960 to 1980 there was a striking 43 percent reduction in the amount of time men spend in a family environment where young children are present.[67] For many women today, on a personal level, the problem is not male dominance so much as male desertion.

FEMINIST FURY

As we noted earlier, the feminist movement began at roughly the same time women were swelling the ranks of the Benevolent Empire, so let's back up now to see where it fits into the cultural pattern. From the beginning, feminism was marked by considerable anger and envy—not toward individual men so much as toward the fact of the opportunities available to men in the public sphere. In 1912 one feminist wrote,

> Not since I started to do my own thinking have I been in any doubt as to which sphere most attracted me. The duties and pleasures of the average woman bore and irritate. The duties and pleasures of the average man interest and allure.[68]

As feminists saw it, the problem began when work was removed from the home. The solution, then, was obvious: Women should follow their work into the public arena. That's what men had done; why not women? Even science supported the idea of getting out of the house. The Social Darwinists of the day explained that the reason men were superior to women (a premise they did not question) was that, from their brute beginnings, males had fought for survival out in the world, where they were subject to competition and natural selection—a process that weeds out the weak and inferior. By contrast, women were at home nurturing the young, out of the reach of natural selection, with the result that they evolved more slowly.[69]

Ironically, even those who defended women against the Social Darwinist theories of biological inferiority did so by denigrating the home. Sociologist Lester Frank Ward argued that women were not *inherently* inferior; their faculties were merely underdeveloped because of their restriction to the home. Since nothing of significance happens in the home, those who spend time in it have only trivial matters upon which to exercise their minds, so it's no wonder they are stunted in their development.[70]

Feminists like Charlotte Perkins Gilman (a student of Ward's) concluded that women would never undergo evolutionary progress as long as they remained isolated in the pre-scientific environment of the home. Gilman urged that all the functions remaining in the home should be removed and put under the care of scientifically oriented professionals. Only when taken out of the amateurish hands of the housewife, she said, would any progress be made in cooking, cleaning, or childcare.[71] That may have sounded radical at the time but in our own day many women in essence follow Gilman's recommendations: Many rely on prepackaged foods or fast-food restaurants for much of their family's food; they hire crews to clean their houses; and hand their children over to be raised by day care workers.

What Hath Woman Lost?

How does this historical perspective give us a better understanding of contemporary "women's issues"? What principles can we draw out for crafting a more biblical view of marriage and family?

First, it is clear that we cannot understand the changes in women's roles and circumstances without relating them to parallel changes in men's roles. The two are intertwined in a dynamic interaction. The Industrial Revolution caused both men's and women's work to contract and become more specialized; the work of both sexes lost range and variety, and became more intensely focused. Men lost their traditional integration into the life of the household and family (no more of those cookbooks written for men!). They lost the close contact they once enjoyed with their children throughout the day, and as a result were unable to function as their children's primary parent and teacher.

For their part, women at home lost their former participation in economic production, along with the wide range of skills and activities that once involved. The loss of women's traditional productive role placed them in a new economic dependence: Whereas the preindustrial household was maintained by an interplay of mutual services, now women's unpaid service stood out as unique, feeding into a stereotype of women's character as selfless and giving—or more negatively, as dependent and helpless. Women also became more isolated: They lost their easy contact with the adult world, while at the same time, their responsibility for childrearing actually increased, since it was no longer shared by fathers and other adults in the household.

It might be asked why, since both sexes lost much of the integration of life and labor characteristic of the preindustrial household, only women protested.

Why has there been a women's movement but no men's movement (at least, not until recently)? The answer is that the contraction of women's sphere was more onerous because they were confined to the private sphere—which means they suffered from the *general devaluation* of the private sphere. The home was cut off from the "real" work of society, isolated from intellectual, economic, and political life, at the same time that the church was.[72] I suggest that just as it is not good for religion to be compartmentalized in the private realm, it is not good for women either.

REMORALIZING AMERICA

A second theme we can draw from history is that the goal of the reform movements of the Benevolent Empire was to "remoralize" the public sphere with the values of the private sphere—of religion and family. We could even say this was an early stage of today's "culture war": Politics, economics, and academia were beginning to declare autonomy from the old controls of religion and morality, and evangelical Christians were fighting back.

Yet there was a gender dimension to this conflict: Since men worked in the public sphere, they were the first to absorb the ethos of modernity—while social reform was largely fueled by the efforts of women (backed by the clergy). Thus, to be more precise, it was largely an attempt by *women* to remoralize the public sphere and draw men back to traditional values.

A third theme should be obvious: This strategy did not work and ought to be abandoned. Men perceived the attempt at remoralization as an attempt to impose "feminine" values, which they were bound to resist. The consequent male rebellion against religion and family led to a devaluation of both—a trend that continues even today.

Despite the adverse consequences, astonishingly, some social commentators persist in holding women responsible for "taming" men. In an article titled "Women Taming Men," columnist William Raspberry says crime and drugs among African-American men are the fault of . . . African-American women! "As long as women tolerate this behavior in men, it will continue," Raspberry writes. In support, he argues that it was women who "created marriage" and "domesticated" men, and who "are the civilizers of the society."[73]

Yet the historical record in America shows that this approach did not work. The truth is that men will be drawn back into family life only when they are convinced that being a good husband and father is a *manly* thing to do; that parental duty and sacrifice are masculine virtues; that marital love and fidelity are not female standards imposed upon men externally, but an integral part of the male character—something inherent and original, created by God.

NO DOUBLE STANDARD

Finally, the failure of the strategy of separate spheres illuminates why the feminist movement grew rapidly in the 1960s. It meant that many women were no longer willing to be the "moral guardians" of men or to "regulate men's sexual behavior." In short, they refused to maintain the double standard. Nor were they willing to remain isolated in a private sphere that had been devalued and emptied of much of its productive and personally fulfilling work. Feminists urged women to leave the empty husk of the home and to stake out a claim in the public arena, where "real" work was done and where they could regain some respect.

Of course, there was only one small problem—or actually several small problems: young children. Who would take care of the children? That's why it became so important to feminists to gain control of their reproductive lives through contraception and abortion; and when they did have children, to demand state-sponsored day care. These measures seemed crucial to gaining relatively equal access with men to the public realm.

Clearly, these "solutions" are morally objectionable to most evangelical Christians. Yet few have suggested realistic alternatives to the historical and economic trends that gave rise to them. In conservative circles, writes Dorothy Sayers, women are often simply "exhorted to be feminine and return to the home from which all intelligent occupation has been steadily removed."[74]

RECONSTITUTING THE HOME

A better course would be to challenge the trend toward emptying the home of its traditional functions. On the conceptual level, we need Christian economists willing to rethink the modern economy from the ground up, and creatively craft a biblically inspired philosophy of economics. What is the proper function of the family and of economic institutions, and how can they interrelate in ways that support rather than hinder each sphere's proper calling before the Lord?

Christians also need to challenge the "ideal-worker" standard in American corporate culture, which decrees that an employee should be available for full-time (even overtime) work without permitting his personal and family life to interfere—because he has turned all that over to a home-based spouse.[75] The ideal-worker standard did not function well even when wives and mothers were still home-based, filling in for absent fathers. Among the many causes of the rebellious youth culture of the 1960s was a great deal of "father hunger." The ideal-worker also helped create America's rootless, mobile society because it required workers to be willing to move anywhere at any time—tearing apart extended families and stable neighborhood communities. Family life became impoverished and more difficult to sustain without that traditional network of support systems.

Christian organizations ought to be the first to debunk the ideal-worker standard as harmful to families. They should be on the forefront in offering practical alternatives for reintegrating family responsibilities with income-producing work—through such things as home-based work, part-time work positions with prorated benefits, flexible hours, and telecommuting.

Heidi Brennan of Mothers At Home, a national group headquartered in Virginia, says the single most frequent question the organization receives from mothers around the country is, How can I earn an income and still be home with my family? Many women are finding that an effective way to combine work and family is to start a home-based business, and today women-owned small businesses are growing at a rapid pace. Home-based work has the added benefit of providing a means for children to participate, so that parents once again fulfill the role of training their children in basic work skills and values, just as in the preindustrial household.[76]

Nor are these suggestions just for women. One poll found that men (age 20 to 39) with young children said having time with their family was the most important issue in their jobs. A full 82 percent said a family-friendly schedule was "very important," while only 56 percent wanted more job security, 46 percent mentioned a high salary, and 27 percent mentioned status.[77]

What about single mothers, families living in poverty, and others who have no choice but to work? Even they would benefit from measures that allow them to integrate work with raising children, instead of putting them in day care. Some groups have discovered that strategies first developed among the poorest of the poor in places like Bangladesh work equally well in America's inner cities. For example, the Women's Self-Employment Project in Chicago works with poor women—mostly single mothers—using a rotating loan system developed in Third World countries in order to support the creation of "microenterprises" based in the home. Many work-training programs offered to low-income women channel them into hotel cleaning, data entry, and other positions that offer relatively little scope for creativity or responsibility. By contrast, self-employment gives women the opportunity to develop initiative and to take charge of their lives. It also gives them much more flexibility in working around their family responsibilities.[78]

At the same time, Christians must not fall into the trap of assuming that paid employment is the only thing that will give women a sense of dignity. That's a mistake secular feminists often make. Instead Christians need to challenge the prevailing ideology of success by insisting that individuals are most fulfilled when they enjoy a sense of calling or vocation—whether in paid *or* unpaid work. We all long for a sense that we are contributing to something larger than ourselves, to a greater good, to God's purposes in the world.

PRIVATE AND PERSONAL

To summarize the historical changes we have traced, in the nineteenth century the two-realm theory of truth came to be reflected in a deep social divide. Whereas in colonial times the social order was viewed as an organic whole, by the mid-nineteenth century it had splintered into a set of separate domains. Society was segmented, says Donald Scott, into "sacred and secular, domestic and economic, masculine and feminine, private and public."[79]

Yet these were all aspects of a single fundamental cleaveage. "The fissure in society divided the sexes," explains Newbigin: "the man dealt with public facts, the women with personal values." Read that sentence again and notice how succinctly it covers the split between public and private, facts and values, men and women.[80] We can better understand secular feminism by realizing that it was an attempt by women to cross this troubling chasm in order to join men in the public sphere. A better route, however, would be to find ways to *close* the gap itself, recovering some measure of integration of work and worship for both men and women.

Obviously, we could also raise exegetical questions about the way Scripture deals with the relations of husbands and wives, women's leadership in the church, and so on. But such questions go beyond the scope of this book. My goal has been to show how the social and intellectual context shapes the very way those questions are conceived. Though we no longer live in the nineteenth century, the tension between the public and private spheres continues to have profound personal consequences, especially for women. Most women today are trained, like men, for life and work in the public sphere. As a result, they may not even have much contact with the private sphere until they have children, which can then be a difficult and even traumatic transition.

My own interest in this subject grew out of the conflicts I experienced upon becoming pregnant with my first child. As a seminary student, I was profoundly ambivalent about this pregnancy. What would having a child mean for my future? How could I have children and still grow professionally? The only way I knew to pursue my deepest interests, to fulfill my calling before the Lord, was in the world of ideas, through academic study. But having a child seemed to pose a profound threat to the possibility of continuing my studies. I felt as though I were facing a black hole of uncertainty.

To jump ahead, I want to say that I greatly enjoyed becoming a mother, even homeschooling our son because I wanted to be intensely involved in his life. In addition, for most of my career, I have worked part-time and from a home office, which allows me to combine work and parenting responsibilities. Yet in my student days, unable to foresee all this, I went through an agonizing dilemma—and it was this experience that caused me to begin thinking about the pressures women face when they become mothers.

Let me highlight the issue by turning it around: My husband was about to become a father for the first time, but *he* did not have to wrestle with fears of giving up a central source of fulfillment, and the exercise of his gifts, for a significant portion of his life. When men have families, most are able to continue working in their chosen fields (though admittedly, they often do make difficult trade-offs between family and career advancement). At the time, I confess, it struck me as decidedly unfair that women should experience such intense pressure to choose between the two major tasks of adult life—between pursuing a calling and raising the next generation.

Rachel Cusk, in her book *A Life's Work,*[81] says many women describe becoming a mother as a "shock." Their lives are turned upside down by the constancy of a baby's demands. At the same time, they are astonished by the intensity of the love bond they form with their newborn. They feel like aliens entering a strange new world of home and childrearing.

Why does all this come as such a surprise? Because through young adulthood, most of us have been carefully primed for participation in the *public* world—while growing out of touch with the private world of babies and families. We probably haven't even baby-sat a neighbor's kids since we were teenagers. Our identity and sense of self-worth has been built primarily on our public persona and accomplishments, especially at work. By contrast, motherhood is still individual, personal, and private. As Cusk puts it, "In motherhood, a woman exchanges her *public* significance for a range of *private* meanings" for which she has not been prepared. Modern child-care manuals, she comments, "begin with a sort of apocalyptic scenario in which the world we know has vanished, replaced by another in whose principles we must be educated."[82]

Here the yawning gap between public and private spheres becomes a personal issue, as women find themselves catapulted into a new world that is not only unfamiliar but also undervalued. If they are feminists, as I was when I had my first child, they may even feel guilty about taking on "traditional" female roles and responsibilities in the home.[83] Women often face intense pressure from the outside world, including former colleagues urging them to return to the "real" world of professional work. Because of the unusually high percentage of professional women in the Washington, D.C., area where I live, there are no less than three support organizations that help mothers who want to leave the workplace, or at least cut back, while they have young children at home. The pressure is so relentless on professional women to stay in the workforce and put in long hours away from their families that women who want more time with their children need support from others who understand the strain.

BLUEPRINT FOR LIVING

Not only this topic but all the topics we have discussed up to this point have profound personal implications. These are not merely abstract intellectual matters fit for philosophers and historians to debate in the rarified atmosphere of academia. Ideas and cultural developments affect real people, shaping the way they think and live out their lives. That's why it is crucial for us to develop a Christian worldview—not just as a set of coherent ideas but also as a blueprint for living. Believers need a roadmap for a full and consistent Christian life. We also need to understand enough of modern thought to identify the ways it blocks us from living out the gospel the way God intends—both in terms of intellectual roadblocks and, as we have seen in this chapter, in terms of economic and structural changes that make it harder to live by scriptural principles. It is enormously difficult for fathers in a modern industrialized society to function as the primary parent, as Scripture calls them to—and as they *did* in earlier historical periods. It is likewise difficult for mothers to raise their children well, and still be faithful in honing their other gifts in a Christian calling. The distance between home and workplace, between public and private spheres, means most of us are required to specialize in either one or the other, at least for a substantial period of our lives.

The personal dimension to living out a Christian worldview typically gets short shrift in most books on the subject, yet it is by far the most important. What ultimate benefit do we gain from investing time and effort to develop a Christian worldview, if it is only a new way to think? A mental exercise? A slick set of arguments? New ideas have limited value unless they transform the way we actually live—the day-to-day decisions we make, the way we interact with other people, the way we run our organizations. The practical application of Christian worldview is so important that it is the subject of the next chapter. We cheat ourselves terribly unless we take the final step and restructure our entire lives by the life-giving truths in God's Word.

PART 4

WHAT NEXT?
LIVING IT OUT

13

TRUE SPIRITUALITY
AND CHRISTIAN WORLDVIEW

Moral character is assessed not by what a man knows
but by what he loves.
ST. AUGUSTINE[1]

A s Tony unfolded his life story,[2] I wondered how anyone who had suffered
so greatly had ever come to faith in God. Where had he encountered a witness that was authentic and powerful enough to cut through all the pain he had
endured?

Tony's parents claimed to be Christians, but they seemed content to do little more than go through the ritual of strict church attendance. In fact, the tone
of their home life could not have been better calculated to make atheists of all
their children. Which it pretty nearly did.

Tony's father was a workaholic, so driven to getting ahead professionally
that he was seldom home. And when he *was* home, he seldom stopped working there either. He organized the children in a constant round of chores and
home-building projects. A quiet, contemplative boy, Tony rarely seemed capable of pleasing his quick-tempered father—whose response was to beat him.
"I was awkward and uncoordinated, and when I was unable to meet his expectations, my reward was the fist."

Tony's own words tell the story with a grim repetitiveness that mirrors the
abuse he endured:

> I was often punished. I was punished for misunderstanding what my father
> wanted me to do. I was punished when I asked a question for clarification.
> I was punished when I didn't work fast enough. I was punished when my
> awkwardness caused me to knock things over or drop things. I was punished
> when I told the truth, and when I told a lie trying to avoid more punishment.
> I was punished! I was punished!

Tony's story, with its tragic refrain, echoed in my memory long after we had talked together. In time, he came to live in terror of his father. And it wasn't just the beatings. Along with the physical abuse came a constant torrent of verbal abuse. His father would tower over the trembling boy, his face contorted in rage, shouting what a stupid, incompetent idiot he was—as he punched him again and again.

By the time he reached high school, Tony had decided to commit suicide. "My parents told me that I was bad, and that a good Christian boy would obey them. But I just couldn't meet their expectations, and eventually I gave up trying. My life was misery. I could see no hope." The only thing that stopped him short was the thought that God might be real—and might send him to hell for killing himself. "The only way I could see out of my misery was suicide, but I was scared of the possibility of hell. That fear was the one thing that stayed my hand."

So Tony began to search out the question of God's existence—not with any hope of salvation but only to methodically clear the deck for taking his life. "I had to find out: Is there a God? Not that I'd seen any evidence of His existence, but suicide gives no second chances. So before I killed myself, I had to be sure."

One Sunday a gaunt, shabby man with a strong foreign accent appeared on the doorstep of the church where Tony, at the insistence of his parents, still attended. Tony showed him the way into the sanctuary, little knowing that this tall stranger held the key to the answers he was seeking. The man had good reason to look so haggard, for he had survived fourteen years in that hell on earth known as a communist prison camp in Romania. For what? For the crime of being a Lutheran pastor. On the minister's neck and head, Tony could see deep scars from the torture he had endured at the hands of his communist captors.

The man's name was Richard Wurmbrand, and he had only recently been released from communist Romania. The stories he related about communist persecution shocked Americans, who at that time knew little about conditions behind the Iron Curtain. (This was long before Alexander Solzhenitsyn smuggled out his massive *Gulag Archipelago,* documenting the Soviet Union's extensive prison camp system.) Later Wurmbrand would give a riveting testimony to a U.S. Senate subcommittee, which was picked up by the media and reported across the country.[3]

As Tony listened to Wurmbrand's account of his years behind bars, a faint glow of hope flickered within him. Here was a man who had been beaten just as he had been—in fact, far worse—and who understood what it meant to endure pain so searing that you don't want to live anymore. Yet he had come back from the edge of the abyss with a profound faith in a good God who loves us. "Humanly speaking, he should have been full of fury at his captors who had treated him so unjustly," Tony told me. "That I could understand. But instead he had responded in love."

Here was something entirely alien to Tony's experience: "This wasn't just a Sunday morning ritual. This was a life-giving power." He quickly recognized that it was the only power that could salvage his own damaged life. "I already knew a person's natural reaction to unjust suffering. But here was something new—something that opened up an alternative to what I had experienced." After that memorable Sunday, Tony began to read the Bible, and over time he too discovered a faith strong enough to bring him back from the edge of the abyss. "After this experience of seeing the reality of Christ in a person's life, I slowly started growing in the faith."

WURMBRAND'S FREEDOM

One reason I was so fascinated by Tony's story is that I, too, had seen Richard Wurmbrand shortly after his release from Romania—in fact, within only a few weeks. Wurmbrand was freed in 1965, when the Norwegian Lutheran Mission paid a $10,000 ransom to the Romanian government to purchase his liberty, and shortly afterward he traveled to Norway. My family was living in Oslo at the time, and on Wurmbrand's first Sunday there, since he could not speak Norwegian, he decided to visit the American Lutheran Church where we attended.

With hollow cheeks and sunken eyes, outfitted in secondhand clothing, Wurmbrand and his wife (who had also been imprisoned) stood out sharply from the well-heeled Western diplomats who made up most of the English-speaking congregation. Yet the couple radiated a strong personal magnetism that irresistibly drew attention. When they witnessed the sight of people worshiping freely and without fear of persecution, they broke down and wept uncontrollably.

That did it. The pastor of the church turned the service over to Reverend Wurmbrand to tell his strange tale of unspeakable persecution. The most vivid picture that remains in my mind is of the tears running down his face when he visited the Sunday school and saw children openly taught the Word of God. Openly! In Romania that was against the law. Many believers were in prison at that very moment because they had been caught secretly teaching young people about Christianity.

Though only thirteen at the time, I have never forgotten the terrible stories Wurmbrand told—of prisoners branded by red-hot irons, or hung upside down from a pole while their feet were beaten into a bloody mass, or locked into narrow closets with metal spikes in the walls. For religious prisoners, there were special tortures: Wurmbrand told of pastors forced to give the Lord's Supper in the form of urine and feces. He himself endured the worst trial of all: three years in solitary confinement in a cell thirty feet underground.

Casting my mind back to these memories, I could understand why Wurmbrand's testimony had worked so strongly upon Tony's heart. The Romanian pastor's message carried authenticity and conviction because he had suffered—and had come through it with a new spirit. His character was a testimony to the biblical principle that suffering is a crucible that tests the quality of a person's faith.

"We suffer with him in order that we may also be glorified with him," Paul writes (Rom. 8:17). Western Christians like to jump ahead to the second half of the verse, to the assurance that we will share in His glory. But spiritual growth doesn't work that way. Genuine sanctification begins with suffering and dying with Christ. "I have been crucified with Christ," Paul writes. "It is no longer I who live, but Christ who lives in me" (Gal. 2:20). Notice the order again: Only when we have faced trials so severe that we are crucified spiritually to this world can Christ truly give us His resurrection life.

Ultimately, this experience is the goal of developing a Christian worldview—not just studying and debating ideas, but dying and rising again in union with Christ. Without this inner spiritual reality, everything we have said about worldviews can become little more than a mental exercise—a way to solve intellectual puzzles, or, worse, a way to impress others by sounding smart and well-educated. Virtually anyone can learn to parrot high-sounding phrases, pronounce certain shibboleths, repeat a few punchy quotations, in order to craft an image of being cultured and sophisticated. Even worldview studies can become a seedbed for pride instead of a process of submitting our minds to the Lordship of Christ.

In fact, I would go even further and say that the first step in conforming our intellect to God's truth is to die to our vanity, pride, and craving for respect from colleagues and the public. We must let go of the worldly motivations that drive us, praying to be motivated solely by a genuine desire to submit our minds to God's Word—and then to use that knowledge in service to others.

We may do a great job of arguing that Christianity is total truth, but others will not find our message persuasive unless we give a visible demonstration of that truth in action. Outsiders must be able to see for themselves, in the day-to-day pattern of our lives, that we do not treat Christianity as just a private retreat, a comfort blanket, a castle of fairy-tale beliefs that merely make us feel better.

It is all but impossible for people to accept new ideas purely in the abstract, without seeing a concrete illustration of what they look like when lived out in practice. Sociologists call this a "plausibility structure"—the practical context in which ideas are fleshed out. The church is meant to be the "plausibility structure" for the gospel. When people see a supernatural dimension of love, power, and goodness in the way Christians live and treat one another, then our message of biblical truth becomes plausible.

But what if people see Christians practicing injustice and compromising with the world? Then who will believe our message? A verbal presentation of a Christian worldview message loses its power if it is not validated by the quality of our lives.

SCHAEFFER'S CRISIS

In doing research for this book, I reread several of the Christian classics that had shaped my thinking in the early years after my conversion some thirty years ago. Among them was Francis Schaeffer's *True Spirituality,* which he considered foundational to the rest of his writings. Why? Because it explains how to apply biblical principles to daily experience. He knew that without integrity at the personal level, a Christian worldview easily deteriorates into a lifeless set of ideas or a bare cognitive system. And while it is true that Christianity offers the best cognitive system for explaining the world, it is never *just* a system. *Knowing* the truth has meaning only as a first step to *living* the truth day by day.

And how do we drive our beliefs down into the reality of daily experience? By dying to ourselves, that we may live for God. From my earlier readings of *True Spirituality,* I did not remember that it opens with the theme of suffering. Spiritual giants like Richard Wurmbrand are not the only ones who grow spiritually through suffering. All of us discover at some point that the most profound spiritual growth typically comes through crises. Because we are fallen creatures living in a fallen world, the winnowing of our character is usually a painful process.[4]

Schaeffer himself underwent a crisis of faith after having been a pastor, then a mission worker, for more than ten years. At that point, he grew frustrated by the lack of spiritual reality in the lives of so many Christians he knew—including himself—and began to ask, How can we know experientially the Christian life described in the New Testament? How do we grasp hold of the love, the power, the abundant life that God promises?

"I walked in the mountains when it was clear," Schaeffer later recalled, "and when it was rainy I walked backward and forward in the hayloft we had in the old chalet in which we lived."[5] Pacing and praying, he retraced his think-

ing all the way back to the agnosticism he had held as a young man, reconsidering such basic questions as whether or not the Bible is true. After coming
to a new confidence that it *is* true, he then asked God to show him how its
redemptive message could become demonstrably real in his own life.

Over time he discovered that the key to inner transformation is the application of Christ's work on the cross for *this* life, not only for the life to come.
Theologically speaking, he had discovered that Christ's death and resurrection
are the basis not only for justification but also for sanctification—the growth
in holiness that is meant to take place in believers here and now.

IDOLS OF THE HEART

A pervasive theme throughout the New Testament is that Christ's death and
resurrection were not merely objective events that happened in history—
though certainly they were *that* first of all. We should never give up our conviction that the objective truths of Christ's death and resurrection are the basis
for our justification. But the next step is to take Christ as the ongoing model
for our lives. As the medieval spiritual writers put it, we are called to practice
"the imitation of Christ." Not in a moralistic sense of trying to mold our
behavior by certain ethical precepts, but rather in a mystical sense that our own
suffering becomes a participation in Christ's suffering. That's why Paul wrote,
"Our old self was crucified with him" (Rom. 6:6); and, "The world has been
crucified to me, and I to the world" (Gal. 6:14).

Only *after* sharing in Christ's death is there a promise of sharing in His
resurrection power. Again, the order is crucial. "Therefore we were buried with
him by baptism into death," Paul writes, "that, as Christ was raised from the
dead by the glory of the Father, so also we may walk in newness of life" (Rom.
6:4). It is impossible for us to receive a new life until we have truly given up
the old one. We do that at our conversion, of course, in a once-for-all transaction where God, as the Judge, declares us forgiven of our sins and adopts us
into His family. But being declared righteous in a judicial sense is only the
beginning. After that, we are called to begin a process in which we die spiritually, day by day, to deeply ingrained sinful patterns, so that we can be liberated
from sin and grow spiritually into a new person.

Moment by moment, we must learn to say no to sin and worldly motivations. In a world of moral relativism, where everything is reduced to personal
choice, simply saying no is in itself a very hard teaching. If it does not seem
hard, then we are probably accommodating to the world without realizing it.
If we are not saying no in ways that bring us to our knees to seek God's

enabling power, then it's likely that we are not standing against the sinful system of the world as we ought.

The principle of dying to worldly systems applies beyond obvious sins. In a culture that measures everything in terms of size, success, and influence, we have to say no to these worldly values as well. In a culture of material affluence, we have to say no to coveting a better house, a sleeker car, a more upscale neighborhood, a more impressive ministry. In a culture that judges people by reputation and achievements, we have to resist the lure of living for professional recognition and advancement. Not that these things are wrong in themselves. But when they fill our hearts and define our motivations, then they become barriers to our relationship with God—which means they become sin for us. As Paul says, *anything* not of faith is sin, because it blocks our single-minded devotion to God and hinders our growth in holiness.

God calls such barriers "idols of the heart" (see Ezek. 14:1-11)—and they can even include genuine needs that are completely right and proper in themselves. This is where the principle becomes really difficult. When our natural needs become a cause of anger and bitterness, or a reason to oppress or attack others, then we must say no to them as well. For example, it's perfectly proper to want intimacy and respect in our marriage. But people are sinners, and at times even Christian spouses may find themselves lonely and unloved. Then one of two things will happen: Either we will become angry and reject the other person—or we will learn how to die to even our valid personal needs, and trust God to work good even in an imperfect situation. Again, it is proper and right to want a job that fulfills our God-given talents, where we enjoy the respect of colleagues and supervisors. But in a fallen world, we may have to accept work that is less than fulfilling; we may not be successful; or we may work for bosses who are demeaning and exploitive. What then? Either we will find ourselves shaking our fist at God—or we will put our talents on the altar and die to them, trusting God to honor our sacrifice to Him.

Putting our valid needs on the altar does not mean shutting our mouths and closing our eyes to a sinful situation. If someone is truly in the wrong, then the loving response is not to give in but to confront the person. It is not an act of love to allow someone to sin against you with impunity. Sin is a cancer within the other person's soul, and genuine love must be strong and courageous in bringing that sin to the light, where it can be diagnosed and dealt with.

Yet it is all too easy to do the right thing in the wrong spirit. Only as we offer up to God our anger, fear, and drive for control do we develop the kind of spirit God can use in confronting others. "Christ also suffered for you, leaving you an example, so that you might follow in his steps," Peter writes—with the ultimate purpose "that He might bring us to God" (1 Pet. 2:21; 3:18). So, too, when we suffer, even unjustly, the ultimate purpose is to equip us to bring others to God. Moment by moment, as we suffer the effects of sin and brokenness in a fallen world, we need to ask Him to use those trials to unite us to Christ in His sacrifice and death—so that we can then be used to bring others to repentance and renewal.

THEOLOGY OF THE CROSS

Peter is telling us that the cross of Christ is a model for the deep structure of our own spiritual progress. Jesus makes this connection Himself in the Gospels: "The Son of Man must suffer many things and be rejected by the elders and chief priests and scribes, and be killed, and on the third day be raised." Immediately afterward He adds: "If anyone would come after me, let him deny himself, and take up his cross daily and follow me" (Luke 9:22, 23).

Notice the sequence: rejected and slain come first, before we can be raised.[6] In Jesus' case, the rejection came from the corrupt religious leaders of His day, whose hearts, hidden under their religious robes and their pious God-talk, were driven by worldly ambition and jealousy. They thus represented the world itself, in its rebellion against God and its rejection of His Son. In our own lives, too, rejection may come either from the world or from religious believers with worldly motivations in their hearts—parents who are neglectful or abusive, like Tony's; a spouse who is unloving or unfaithful; a child who rebels against his Christian upbringing; a church that is unwelcoming; a boss who is disrespectful and demeaning; a close friend who betrays you. Living in a world still under the dominion of sin, each of us will be rejected and wounded in some way.

As Martin Luther put it, Christians embrace a theology of the cross, not a theology of glory.[7] The mystery of our salvation was effectuated by Jesus' descent to earth not as a conquering hero but as a suffering servant—mocked, beaten, hung on a cross. True knowledge of Christ comes only as we are willing to give up our dreams of glory, praying to be identified with Him on the cross. While homeschooling my son Dieter, I taught him to play the recorder, and we used to play this moving hymn as a duet:

Jesus, I my cross have taken,
All to leave and follow Thee;
Destitute, despised, forsaken,
Thou from hence my all shall be.[8]

Try applying this outlook in the Washington, D.C., area, where I live, or any other place where the pressure is relentless to get ahead, make a good impression, pursue the right contacts, advance your cause. Destitute? Despised? Are we really willing to let God take us through times of defeat and despair, when we experience communion with Him in His crucifixion?

The wonder of God's goodness is that He can use these "crosses" for our sanctification, just as He used the death of Jesus to advance His redemptive plan. "You meant evil against me, but God meant it for good," Joseph told his brothers (Gen. 50:20). Christians sometimes think it a matter of piety to deny the evil done to them—to cover it up, say it wasn't so bad, wear a smile in public. But Joseph did not shrink from calling his brothers' actions *evil*, and neither should we. In this world, we too will be rejected by people with sinful motives, and for the sake of truth we should call it what it is. But we can also turn it to good by realizing that suffering gives us a chance to enter spiritually upon the journey that Jesus mapped out for us: rejected, slain (spiritually), and, finally, raised.

REJECTED, SLAIN, RAISED

In a fallen world, where nature itself has been thrown out of harmony, the greatest source of suffering for some people may be physical. The force that disrupts and threatens the normal course of life may be illness or injury. Over the past few years, a dear friend has suffered from cancer—at one point hovering between life and death for several months. Knowing that she is a spiritually sensitive person, I asked what she had learned from this harrowing experience. "I learned that I had to be willing to die," she replied, her eyes misting. "I was desperately holding on to life, to my family, and I had to let go and be willing to let God take everything from me."

That is exactly the point to which God has to bring each of us. Whether the suffering is physical or psychological, the way God brings us to see what we are *really* basing our life upon is to take it away. When we lose our health or family or work or reputation, and our lives come crashing down and we feel lost and empty—that's when we realize how much our sense of purpose and identity was actually bound up in those things. That's why we have to be willing to let Him take them away. We have to be "willing to die."

This principle may sound overly negative, and certainly there are strains of Christianity that teach a stern, tight-lipped asceticism—as though holiness consisted simply in saying no to fun and pleasure. But genuine spiritual death doesn't have a whiff of asceticism about it. It has nothing to do with monastic flight from the world. It is choosing to obey God's commands across the whole of life even when it is painful or costly. It is crying out to Him when our hearts are crucified by betrayal or oppression. It is letting go of the things we love or want the most, if hanging on to them is causing us to grow angry at God or to strike out against others. It is believing in God's goodness, sometimes by a sheer act of the will, in the face of overwhelming evil. And it is the whispered prayer that God would grant us to be united to Christ as we submit ourselves to the model He gave us—rejected, slain, raised.

We tend to have a limited concept of spiritual death as saying no only to things we want or covet—our guilty pleasures and selfish ambitions. But in reality it means dying inwardly to whatever has *control* over us. And the thing that really controls us may not be what we want; it may be what we fear. Fear can dominate our lives just as strongly as desire. It may be anger. Or pride. Or even futile wishes—a person disappointed in life may simply keep wishing that things had been different, and may find it all but impossible to let go of those dashed hopes and ruined dreams. Whatever it is that controls you, *that* is what you must place on the altar to be slain. Only then will we be released from our inner compulsions and be able to discover the freedom in which nothing but "the love of Christ controls us" (2 Cor. 5:14).

LIFE-PRODUCING MACHINES

Offering up the idols of our heart is only one step in the process, however. The next is to pray for spiritual deliverance. For whenever we give in to long-term, ingrained patterns of sin, we give Satan a foothold in our inner self—and become spiritually enslaved to him. As Paul writes, our bodies themselves can become "instruments for unrighteousness" (Rom. 6:13). This is a sobering thought: It means that it is possible for even a Christian to be controlled by Satan and do his work. There is no neutral ground in the spiritual battle between the forces of God and the forces of the devil. If some area of our lives is not fully submitted in obedience to God, then in practice we are under the control of Satan in that area—giving him the allegiance that belongs to God alone.

Paul seems to realize that this is a hard saying for Christians to accept, for he expounds further on the principle. "Do you not know that if you present yourselves to anyone as obedient slaves, you are slaves of the one whom you obey, either of sin, which leads to death, or of obedience, which leads to righteousness?" (Rom. 6:16). Paul is saying that even those saved by Christ can, in their day-to-day words and actions, produce either life or death. The terrible reality is that we may attend church regularly, read the Bible diligently, even work in a Christian ministry, yet still be what Schaeffer calls "death-producing machines"—"living contrary to our calling, yielding ourselves to the devil and therefore producing death in this poor world."[9]

How do we know whether we are producing life or death? By whether our lives exhibit the beauty of God's character. When people see the way you live, are they drawn closer to God or are they alienated from God? When they observe the way you treat others, do they find the gospel more credible or less credible? That is the standard by which we should measure our actions. Christians are called to be "life-producing machines," demonstrating by our actions and character that God exists. We may preach a God of love, we may even have opportunities to reach thousands through our ministries and church programs, but if nonbelievers do not observe *visible love* within those ministries and churches and Christian organizations, then we undermine the credibility of our message.

"The medium *is* the message," to use Marshall McLuhan's famous phrase. And for Christians, the medium is the way we treat one another. "By this all people will know that you are my disciples," Jesus said, "if you have love for one another" (John 13:35). God's strategy for reaching a lost world is for the church to function as a visible demonstration of His existence.

HIS WORK, HIS WAY

When Christians talk about the importance of developing a worldview message, they typically mean learning how to argue persuasively against the "isms" of the day. But having a Christian worldview is not just about answering intellectual questions. It also means following biblical principles in the personal and practical spheres of life. Christians can be infected by secular worldviews not only in their *beliefs* but also in their *practices*.

For example, a Christian church or ministry may be biblical in its *message* and yet fail to be biblical in its *methods*. Hudson Taylor, the great missionary to China, said that the Lord's work must be done in the Lord's way, if it is to have the Lord's blessing. We must express the truth not only in *what* we preach but also in *how* we preach it. A Christian organization may be doing the Lord's work—but if it is acting on human zeal and willpower, using secular methods of promotion and publicity, without visible love among staff and coworkers, then it is merely another form of human achievement, accomplishing little for the Kingdom of God.

Think back to the image of two chairs (discussed in chapter 6). For the nonbeliever sitting in the naturalist's chair, all that exists is a closed system of natural causes. The very definition of what counts as knowledge is limited by naturalism and utilitarianism. But for the believer sitting in the supernaturalist's chair, the natural world is only part of reality. A complete perspective includes both the seen and the unseen aspects of reality. Christians are called not merely to assent intellectually to the existence of both parts of reality but also to *function practically* on that basis. Day by day, they are to make choices that would make no sense unless the unseen world is just as real as the seen world.

Scripture gives a dramatic illustration of the two chairs in the account of Elisha when he was surrounded by Syrian troops (2 Kings 6:15-17). "Do not be afraid, for those who are with us are more than those who are with them," Elisha said to his anxious servant. But the servant could see no one. Then God opened the servant's eyes, and he saw that "the mountain was full of horses and chariots of fire all around Elisha." The same concept is echoed in the New Testament: "he who is in you is greater than he who is in the world" (1 John 4:4). We are called to make our decisions knowing that the unseen world has a powerful effect on the seen world, playing an active role in human history.

What does this mean in practice? It means we sometimes act in ways that seem irrational to those sitting in the naturalist's chair, who see only the physical world. It means we do what is right even at great cost, because we are convinced that what we gain in the unseen realm is far greater than what we lose from a worldly perspective.

Sadly, many Christians live much of their lives as though the naturalist were right. They give cognitive assent to the great truths of Scripture, but they make their practical, day-to-day decisions based only on what they can see, hear, measure, and calculate. When confessing their religious beliefs, they sit in the supernaturalist's chair. But in ordinary life, they walk over and sit in the naturalist's chair, living as though the supernatural were not real in any practical sense, relying on their own energy, talent, and strategic calculations. They may sincerely *want* to do the Lord's work, but they do it in the world's way—using worldly methods and motivated by worldly desires for success and acclaim.

The Bible calls this living in the "flesh" instead of in the Spirit, and Paul addresses the problem in the book of Galatians: "Having begun in the Spirit, are you now being perfected by the flesh?" (Gal. 3:3). Many believers act as though *becoming* a Christian were a matter of faith, but *being* a Christian afterward were a matter of their own drive and willpower. They are striving to be "perfected by the flesh."

Working in the flesh, they may well produce impressive results in the visible world. Churches and parachurch ministries may generate a great deal of publicity, hold glamorous conferences, attract huge crowds, bring in large donations, produce books and magazines, and wield political influence in Washington. But if that work is done in the flesh, then no matter how successful it appears, it does little to build God's kingdom. When the Lord's work is done in merely human wisdom, using human methods, then it is not the Lord's work any longer.[10]

The only way the church can establish genuine credibility with nonbelievers is by showing them something they cannot explain or duplicate through their own natural, pragmatic methods—something they can explain only by invoking the supernatural.

GOLD, SILVER, PRECIOUS STONES

If we find ourselves thinking can do the Lord's work in the world's way, as though worldly weapons were adequate, then we have drastically underestimated the nature of the battle. For the real battle is not in the seen world only, but chiefly in the unseen world. The battle is not "against flesh and blood," Paul says (Eph. 6:12), and if we try to fight it in the flesh, we will be merely shadowboxing. Sheer activism may bring about results that look impressive to those sitting in the naturalist's chair, whose only frame of reference is the visible world—but they will not be the results the Lord wants.

We can go so far as to say that if Christians win their battles by worldly methods, then *they have really lost*.[11] Visible results can be deceptive. In the seen world, we may appear to make a great advance—win professional recognition, attract people to our cause, raise money for our program, distribute tons of literature, win passage of an important bill. But if it was done by humanistic reliance on technical methods, without the leading of the Spirit, then we have accomplished little of value in the unseen world.

The opposite is likewise true: If Christians use the weapons God has ordained—if we lay our talents at His feet, dying to our own pride and ambition, obeying biblical moral principles, empowered by His Spirit, guided by a Christian worldview perspective—then even if by external standards we seem to have lost, *we have really won.* Outsiders looking on may conclude that we have failed. Even Christian friends and leaders may shake their heads disapprovingly and advise us that we've made a mistake. But if we have genuinely given our lives over to God's purposes and are being led by Him, then we have won a battle in the unseen world.

An old spiritual classic says the Christian life really begins when we understand by hard experience that "apart from me you can do nothing" (John 15:5). It's a verse many of us have memorized and can quote at the drop of a hat. But it rarely becomes real in practice until we encounter an overwhelming crisis that pushes us to the end of our own resources. For people with a lot of resources, that may not be until midlife or even later. But at some point, the realization crashes in on us that life is not what we had hoped for, and we ask,

Is this all there is? We realize that in a fallen world, even the good things cannot fully satisfy our deepest hungers, and everything we have loved and lived for turns to sawdust and slips through our fingers. If we are honest, we have to admit that our personal relationships are often driven by what *we* want and need from others, not by a genuinely unselfish love for them. Even our efforts at Christian ministry are often motivated more by personal zeal and ambition than by God's Spirit. And the greater our natural zeal, the greater the crisis God has to allow in order to bring us to the end of our rope. Only after dying to everything we have ever lived for do we genuinely come to believe, as a practical reality, that "apart from Me you can do nothing." And only then can God really pour His life and power into our work.

When life ends and we stand at the believers' judgment described in 1 Corinthians 3, some of our most successful and impressive projects may prove to be nothing but wood, hay, and stubble—devoured by the flames. But the activities that were truly led and empowered by God, in obedience to His truth, whether the results were visible or not, will sparkle as gold, silver, and precious stones. And God will set them as jewels in our heavenly crown.

RESULTS GUARANTEED

Looking back over the history of evangelicalism, we can understand better why there has been a strong temptation to split belief from practice—to do the Lord's work but in the world's way. As we saw in chapter 11, in the nineteenth century, evangelical scholars adopted methodological naturalism in dealing with subjects in the lower story, treating them as religiously neutral—as merely technical subjects where biblical truth did not apply in any integral way. As a result they tended to accept a largely functional and utilitarian approach to areas like science, engineering, politics, business, management, and marketing.

In the late nineteenth century, evangelicals even stopped sending their children to Christian liberal arts colleges, where the classics were still taught (they were suspicious of those pagan Greeks!). Instead they sent their children in droves to the newly founded state universities, to receive the technical training required to succeed in an increasingly technological society. Studies show a steady decline in church-related colleges, while the numbers in state institutions boomed. And the students attending those state colleges were predominantly evangelicals—Methodists, Baptists, Disciples of Christ, Presbyterians.[12] "Ironically," says historian Franklin Littell, "it was the misguided piety of revivalist Protestantism which . . . gave the first great impetus to the state colleges and universities."[13]

Littell calls it "misguided" precisely because it was shaped by the two-story division of knowledge. Christian students were avoiding fields like philosophy and literature and the classics, where they would have to deal with ideas, while avidly seeking technical and vocational training in fields that they thought were safely neutral. They were willing to accept an exclusively technological and utilitarian concept of knowledge in the technical fields (the lower story), as long as they were allowed to supplement their studies with campus religious activities designed to nurture the spiritual life (the upper story).

This explains why many Christian churches and ministries today continue to treat areas like business, marketing, and management as essentially neutral—technical fields where the latest techniques can simply be plugged into their own programs, without subjecting them to critique from a Christian worldview perspective. Start the business meeting with prayer, by all means, but then employ all the up-to-date strategies learned in secular graduate schools. Douglas Sloan calls this "the inner modernization of evangelicalism."[14] That is, we have resisted modernism in our *theology* but have largely accepted modernism in our *practices*. We want to employ the latest techniques and quantitative methods, where the results can be calculated and predicted.

For example, a Christian ministry once hired a young man who had just received his master's degree in marketing to head up its fundraising department. Immediately he set about implementing the standard techniques he had learned in his courses, including a sharp increase in the number of fundraising letters sent out. When other staff members questioned the new strategy, asking whether increased mailings were a good use of funds given sacrificially to the ministry, his response was, *but this works*. Brandishing graphs and studies, he said: "Statistics show that if you send out X number of letters, you will get Y rate of return—guaranteed."[15]

But if any secular organization can achieve the same results using the same "guaranteed" methods, where is the witness to God's existence? How does relying on statistically reliable patterns persuade a watching world that God is at work?

Doing the Lord's work in the Lord's way means forging a biblical perspective even on the practical aspects of running an organization, instead of relying on mechanical formulas derived from naturalistic assumptions. We may reject naturalism as a philosophy, but if our work is driven by the rationalized methods we have learned from the world, then we are naturalists *in practice*, no matter what we claim to believe.

"The *central* problem of our age is not liberalism or modernism," Schaeffer writes—or even hot-button social issues like evolution, abortion, radical feminism, or homosexual rights. The primary threat to the church is the "tendency to do the Lord's work in the power of the flesh rather than the Spirit." Many church leaders crave a "big name," he continues: They "stand on the backs of others" in order to achieve power, influence, and reputation—instead of exhibiting the humility of the Master who washed His disciples' feet. They "ape the world" in its publicity and marketing techniques, manipulating people's emotions to induce them to give more money.[16] No wonder outsiders see little in the church that cannot be explained by ordinary sociological forces and principles of business management. And no wonder they find our message unconvincing.

MARKETING THE MESSAGE

What are some examples of "aping the world"? In their marketing strategies, many Christian organizations borrow heavily from commercial enterprises, creating idealized images of their "product" to motivate people to "buy" it. For a familiar example, think of the ubiquitous fundraising letters that sound like they were all written by the same person—because they were ghostwritten by staffers all trained in the same techniques. Each letter creates a crisis mentality that is enhanced by melodramatic anecdotes, fake highlighting in the margins, and a signature produced by a machine. Often a little card is enclosed announcing a premium, a gimmick to induce us to reach for our checkbooks.

Where is the authenticity in all this? The name of a ministry leader appears at the bottom of the letter, but clearly it is not an authentic message from that person. It was produced by a committee of writers, marketers, and fund development professionals, carefully calculated to elicit a response. As often as not, the crisis is half-manufactured and the anecdotes half-fictionalized for greater emotional impact. A young man who traveled on staff with a respected Christian leader once told me that when their experiences were written up later as fundraising anecdotes, the stories were so heavily slanted, they were "practically unrecognizable to anyone who was actually there."

Should we shrug this off as benign deception? Or is it a serious moral failing that could spread corruption through an entire ministry? Can we compromise the truth without undermining our effectiveness for the Lord?

Several months ago, a fundraising letter arrived in my mailbox inviting me to "have your morning coffee with So-and So," a well-known Christian leader. The wording was obviously meant to stir up warm feelings associated with an intimate, personal chat around the kitchen table. But the reality? The ministry was offering a product that involved daily readings—something completely different from the image in the marketing pitch. What's more, the readings themselves were prepared by staff writers. The image of sipping coffee together with the author was a complete fabrication aimed at manipulating readers' emotions.

Where is our passion for truth and authenticity? Where is our respect for the reader as a person made in the image of God, not a mass of emotions to be manipulated? In short, where is a Christian worldview perspective on marketing and fundraising? *This is just as important as framing a worldview perspective on the "isms" of our day.*

Yet its importance is often overlooked in discussions of Christian worldview. Because evangelicals have historically accepted methodological naturalism in the lower-story, in their minds there *is* no distinctively Christian perspective in fields like marketing and management—and thus they have uncritically accepted whatever methods and techniques the secular world develops. In doing so, however, they have unwittingly limited their own thinking to the conceptual categories allowed within naturalism. They have absorbed what H. Richard Niebuhr calls a "depersonalized and disenchanted" perspective that lacks even the conceptual vocabulary to deal adequately with the human person. In this naturalistic framework, persons become merely "objects for objective manipulation in the market and the political arena."[17] Though Christians would never accept naturalism as a philosophy, many have absorbed a naturalistic approach to marketing, adopting techniques that treat a target audience essentially as passive "consumers" to be manipulated into buying a "product."

MORE MONEY, MORE MINISTRY

I once addressed a group of Christian graduate students earning advanced degrees from some of the nation's top universities in fields like philosophy, literature, and political theory. When I raised the need to develop a Christian worldview approach to practical fields as well, like business and marketing, they were startled. Having defined worldview study in terms of *ideas,* they had never even considered its relation to practical areas. Yet practical fields are not religiously neutral; they are shaped by fundamental assumptions about reality just as much as any other area of life.

By overlooking this fact, many ministry leaders have uncritically absorbed a nonbiblical view of business and success. "They are deeply infused with an American capitalist culture concerning the gospel," writes historian Joel Carpenter. They unconsciously assume "that God measures success by the numbers, that more money means more ministry, which means more success for God's kingdom. So they tend to measure their own success as disciples and servants of the Lord by the size of their ministry."[18]

Do we recognize a pattern here? We are witnessing history come home to roost. In earlier chapters on revivalism, we watched the seeds being sown. The appeal to the emotions. The pragmatic attitude of using whatever works. The habit of borrowing marketing techniques from the commercial world. The celebrity style of leadership. The focus on measurable results. "Religion is a work of man," Charles Finney said, meaning that conversions can be induced simply by manipulating the right conditions. All too often, today's ministries exhibit the same naturalistic attitude, the only difference being that they have access to vastly more sophisticated marketing and promotional techniques.

"The nonprofit economy has become more like the for-profit world," writes Thomas Berg. Religious fundraising has become "extremely fast-paced and sophisticated, relying more and more on high technology [and] carefully targeted direct-mail campaigns."[19] Many large religious organizations have entire departments of trained and credentialed marketers to create a constant flow of fundraising letters and promotionals. They conduct marketing surveys on how to position their "product" better. They organize focus groups to determine where to aim their efforts. They angle for articles and profiles in Christian magazines. They hire ghostwriters to write copy under the leader's name for columns, newsletters, daily devotionals, and websites. The overriding question is not, "Is this morally and spiritually right?" but rather, "Will it sell?"

Sometimes the marketing hype shades into subtle deception. Statistics are cited with no control group to make the numbers scientifically reliable. Successes are highlighted, while failures are swept under the carpet. Ken Blue tells the story of a ministry he started, which began including only the most striking success stories in its reports—until eventually he began to feel guilty about creating a "distorted image" of the ministry's impact. When he sought counsel from another pastor, however, the pastor only looked puzzled. "What's the problem?" he asked. "No one in ministry tells the unvarnished truth. We automatically take exaggeration into account."

But if that is true, Blue notes, "then the church regularly lies to itself and condones using people for its public relations needs."[20]

This is the ultimate danger of doing the Lord's work in the flesh: It may eventually lead to outright sin. We can be so driven by ministry goals that we are blinded to the use of unethical methods. Without really thinking, we begin to stretch the truth to enhance our image and attract donors. A former high-ranking executive at a parachurch organization told me he had resigned after discovering an internal "culture of lying"—a regular pattern of shading the truth and cutting ethical corners in order to look better and win influence—all for the good of the ministry, of course. It is a modern form of thinking we can "speak lies in the name of the Lord" (Zech. 13:3).

Imagine that you were to wake up tomorrow morning, Schaeffer says, and that by some magic, everything the Bible teaches about prayer and the empowering of the Holy Spirit was gone—it was erased from history and had never been said. Would that make any difference in practice in the way we run our churches and organizations? The tragic fact, Schaeffer says, is that in many Christian organizations, "there would be *no difference whatsoever.*" We function day by day sitting in the naturalist's chair, as though the supernatural were not real.[21]

OPERATING INSTRUCTIONS

The same contradictory pattern often emerges in the way Christian churches and organizations function—in their management of the workplace itself, treatment of employees, and leadership style. Many groups are Christian in what they *profess* but not in the way they *operate.*

Consider, for example, ministries that demand excessively long hours on the job. This common practice produces a line of destructive domino effects: It breaks up marriages, erodes family life, and eliminates outside sources of renewal, like involvement in a local church. Cut off from external emotional resources, a person often becomes overdependent on relationships at work and thus vulnerable to control and manipulation.

After working eight years in the U.S. Congress, a talented office manager switched to an executive position at a Christian parachurch ministry. "I wanted to get away from the typical congressional office, where everyone was so focused on the Big Name politician," she told me. "The staff was expected to sacrifice their personal lives, their families, their professional identities." And she added, "I hate to use the language of the recovery movement, but many staff really had codependent relationships with their member of Congress. They lived derivative lives, feeding off his fame and public identity."

When she started her new job, however, she was disappointed to discover exactly the same dynamics at the parachurch ministry. "Staff members were expected to live for the ministry—work long hours, have no outside life, make all their social relationships within the organization. It was the same codependent relationship with a Big Name." The emotionally unhealthy pattern was all too recognizable, and wisely she left the new position after only two months.

These patterns can be *physically* unhealthy as well, producing stress-related ailments that result in absenteeism and reduced productivity. An executive at a Washington think tank once worked at a Christian ministry where the atmosphere was so negative that he developed stress-related physical symptoms. When he sought medical treatment, the doctor said, "Why is it that everyone I see with this particular ailment *works at that same ministry?*"

Negative experiences are so common in churches and parachurch groups that a genre of self-help books has appeared on the market with titles like *The Subtle Power of Spiritual Abuse* and *Healing Spiritual Abuse*.[22] These books describe the signs of an unhealthy organizational system, marked by controlling, domineering leaders who drive people to perform in order to build a celebrity image. Believers who find themselves in such a system, whether in unpaid volunteer work or in a paid position, often find themselves subject to many of the classic forms of workplace abuse.

FROM GOOD TO GREAT

Happily, there are many positive counter-examples, and a study done in 2003 by the Best Christian Workplaces Institute[23] identified several of them. The study uncovered forty organizations that rank highest in worker satisfaction. It found that the most effective leaders are those who regard workers as part of their mission, not merely as a means to larger goals. Instead of asking, What can this person do for my ministry? they ask, What can I do to help this person develop spiritually and professionally?

In the top organizations, the study found, employees consistently described their leaders in terms like *humble, approachable, caring,* and *godly.* At Phoenix Seminary, President Darryl DelHousaye is known for asking his staff, "How can I help you? How can I bless you? How can I help you succeed?"[24] The best organizations regard the nurturing of their own employees as a spiritual mandate.

At Whitworth College, another top organization identified in the study, President Bill Robinson says, "I am trying to lead 'from amongst'." The reference is to John 1:14 ("the Word became flesh and dwelt among us, . . . full of grace and truth"). Robinson has a habit of wandering into the dining hall unannounced and sitting down with students to find out what they think of the college. "I hope it can be said of me that I dwelt among the people, bringing grace and speaking truth."[25]

Examples like these give concrete evidence that servant leadership is not an abstract ideal; it is completely practical and workable. Having a Christian worldview means being utterly convinced that biblical principles are not only true but also work better in the grit and grime of the real world.[26]

Even secular businesses are starting to recognize these principles. The bestseller *Good to Great,* popular in Christian management circles these days, is based on a study of business leaders who started with a *good* business but turned it into a *great* one, propelling it to the highest echelons of success. Contrary to the common stereotype, says author Jim Collins, these successful leaders "are not charismatic, nor are they celebrities." They are not "hard charging" leaders who feel they have to whip up employees to perform. Instead they are humble, modest, even self-effacing people, who share decision making with their staff.[27] One of the most damaging trends in recent history has been the tendency to select dazzling celebrity leaders, Collins concludes. It's a strategy that typically creates mediocre businesses, which eventually go into decline.

Clearly, biblical principles are not just Sunday school pieties. Because they are true to the real world, they actually work better in making people and companies more productive.

LOVING ENOUGH TO CONFRONT

Another common workplace abuse involves taking credit for another person's work or ideas. In the 1988 film *Working Girl,* starring Harrison Ford, Melanie Griffith, and Sigourney Weaver, a bright secretary named Tess comes up with a creative idea for a deal with a client. After winning her trust, however, her boss steals the idea, intending to pass it off as her own. At stake, of course, is not just a single project but also Tess's entire career, which could finally take off if clients had a chance to recognize her gifts.

Hard as it may be to believe, Christians sometimes exploit their workers in similar ways, denying them recognition for their God-given gifts. It can happen among coworkers—when someone discusses an idea with a colleague, who then presents it to the boss as his own. It can happen when a leader or supervisor takes credit for the success of a program without mentioning the creative work of team members. Or it can happen when a boss claims authorship of a work written by a staff writer. In every case, the offender is essentially co-opting someone else's spiritual gifts and calling by claiming them as his own.

In a journalism class I once taught, one of the students was agonizing over what to do. Fresh from earning a master's degree, she had landed a job doing policy analysis for a state-level Christian organization. On her first big project, she had worked for months analyzing the data and preparing an outstanding report. But when she was finished, to her shock, the boss announced that he was going to put his name on the final product.

"The message will get out better with my name on it," he said. "We'll get more attention, sell more copies, have greater impact." No matter that claiming to be the author was false and deceptive to the public. No matter that the woman who had done the real work was essentially reduced to a ghostwriter. Worse, the dishonesty was rationalized in religious language as the best way to "advance the ministry." Eventually the boss "graciously" agreed to include the writer's name on the cover as well, but the public was still misled into thinking that the ideas were his, while she was nothing but a staff writer.

It is scandalous that Christian ministries and publishing houses often turn a blind eye to this form of deception—especially when it involves top-selling names. Not long ago an editor at a major Christian publishing house told me that he had managed to get a Big Name to write a foreword to a forthcoming book—then added casually, "But of course he didn't really write it."

I recently met a conference speaker and author who once worked for a prominent ministry leader. To my amazement, she revealed that staff workers wrote everything that went out under his name—books, articles, radio programs. "The attitude among the staff is, let's not bother him with these projects. We'll just take care of them for him." Meanwhile the public is deceived into thinking they are getting this revered leader's own thoughts and insights.

Clearly, any practice that deceives the public ought to be off-limits—no matter how much money it brings in for the ministry. "Better is a little with righteousness than great revenues with injustice" (Prov. 16:8). There is nothing shameful in hiring someone to do things that you cannot do for yourself, says top-ranking journalist David Aikman. Hiring a professional writer to help you is like hiring an accountant to do your tax returns. But it *is* morally wrong to pretend to the public that you wrote something yourself when you did not.[28] When a Christian organization violates ethical principles in order to get results, it cannot expect God to use those results. We cannot "structure sin into our method of doing business" (to use a phrase my husband once coined), and then expect God to bless it.

No Little People

The operative principle is that each member in the Body of Christ has been given unique gifts—and the Body as a whole functions best when each is recognized, honored, and allowed to flourish. A Christian organization should aim to cultivate each worker's gifts, not stifle them or build up leaders at the expense of others. As Schaeffer put it, "with God there are no little people"— which means we cannot treat anyone as a mere means to other goals.[29]

A high-profile political commentator was approached by a Christian publisher to write a novel. "But I'm a columnist," he protested, "not a novelist."

"Don't worry," the publisher responded. "We'll get someone to write it for you."

To his credit, the columnist turned down the offer. But the incident reveals how willing many publishers are to use writers as mere means to putting a Big Name on a book cover. They seem to have forgotten that Christian leaders are called to nurture and build up the "little people," not to use them for personal gain.[30]

If you want to know what a Christian leader is really like, don't ask his peers or board members or adoring fans. Ask how he treats his support staff. That is a lesson Jerram Barrs presses upon seminary students at the Francis Schaeffer Institute at Covenant Seminary. "When I come to visit your church someday, I will not ask people about what a great preacher or leader you are," Barrs says. "Rather I will talk to the secretaries, the office staff, the janitors and cleaners and ask them what it is like to work with you. That will tell me far more about the kind of ministry taking place in the church, and whether you are the kind of leader Christ desires for His Church."[31]

To use biblical language, God charges shepherds (whether in the pulpit or in other forms of leadership) to feed the sheep, not to fleece them. He thunders against the leaders of ancient Israel: "You eat the fat, you clothe yourselves with the wool, and slaughter the fat ones, but you do not feed the sheep" (Ezek. 34:3). Bad shepherds are those who exploit other people's gifts and talents to meet their own needs and advance their own agendas, instead of asking what is good for the sheep themselves.

Paul was scrupulous in refusing to take credit for what others had accomplished: "We do not boast . . . in the labors of others" (2 Cor. 10:15). In the Body of Christ, the eye is not the ear (1 Cor. 12:14ff.), and it should not *pretend* to be, by claiming the ear's work as its own.

We can take a lesson from the political realm, where it is now standard for people to give public recognition to speechwriters. Everyone knows that President Bush's main speechwriter is Michael Gerson, because there have been several magazine and newspaper profiles about him. There is no attempt to hide the fact. A few years ago, I went to hear a lecture by Senator Rick Santorum at the Heritage Foundation. "Before I begin," he said, "I want to thank the two people on my staff, Mark Rodgers and Sydney Leach, who did the research for this lecture and wrote it." He then proceeded to deliver the lecture.[32] There are many ways to speak truthfully in order to build up those around us.

The other side of the coin is that it is quite proper for members of the Body to claim ownership of their own work. Psalm 95:5 is a key verse in a biblical defense of private property: "The sea is his, for he made it, and his hands formed the dry land." The implication is that the earth belongs to the Lord *because* He made it. The same principle applies to humans, who are made in God's image: What we create belongs to us. Taking responsibility for our own work—accepting both the credit and the blame, the benefits and the losses—is a crucial element in human dignity. Our work is one of the most important ways we express our inner self and character in external form—it is a principal "fruit" by which others can know who we really are. That is why it is profoundly dehumanizing to separate a person from the "fruit" of his work. Time and again in Scripture, a sign of God's blessing is that "you will eat the fruit of your own labor," whereas a sign of His chastisement is that "others will eat what you have planted" (for example, Deut. 28:30; Mic. 6:15; Mic. 4:4; Ps. 128:2). In the New Testament, Paul advises, "Let each one test his own work, and then his reason to boast will be in himself alone and not in his neighbor" (Gal. 6:4).

The overarching biblical principle is that we have a responsibility to practice stewardship of the gifts God has given us. Once when King David wanted to build an altar in a farmer's field, the farmer offered to simply give it to him, along with the bulls and the wood for the offering. But David refused to take any of it, and he presented this compelling reason: "I will not take for the LORD what is yours, nor offer burnt offerings that cost me nothing" (1 Chron. 21:24). The application to our own day is that we cannot "take for the Lord" work done by another person. Nor can we make an offering that "costs me nothing." Whoever does the actual work pays the cost in term of organizing the project, research, creative analysis, and so on—not to mention probably years of sacrificial study and preparation brought to the job in the first place. Each of us has a responsibility to develop our own gifts, and we cannot excuse exploitive practices by saying "but it's for the Lord."

The consequences of exploitive and deceptive practices ripple in ever-widening circles. There are many "little people" whom God has gifted with an important message or ministry that could benefit a wider segment of the church—if their work were properly recognized and better known. But who can compete with the head of an organization with the resources to hire half a dozen writers, editors, and PR professionals to put out material under a celebrity name? A larger-than-life standard is set up that attracts financial and other forms of support from donors and foundations that might otherwise have gone to worthier causes. The church as a whole then loses the benefit of their gifts. The purpose in assigning proper credit is to identify gifts within the Body of Christ, for the sake of more effective ministry.

REAL LEADERS SERVE

When Kurt Senske was only thirty-six years old, he took over leadership of a company that was losing money rapidly. Yet in only three years, he pulled together a team that turned the company around. The key to their success? "We followed sound Christian leadership strategies that included incorporating the principles of servant leadership from the bottom up, creating a healthy culture that valued its employees."

What is a servant leader? It is someone who, in Senske's words, refuses to use people as means to an end—who always asks, "Am I building people up, or am I building myself up and merely using those around me?" A servant leader creates an atmosphere of "transparency" in which all relevant information is shared openly, so that everyone has an opportunity to make responsible decisions. Finally, a servant leader lets go of command-and-control methods, and creates a culture that allows everyone to grow into leaders, stretching their own God-given talents.[33]

None of these biblical principles were merely fine phrases for Senske. He devoted months of sweat and prayer and sleepless nights to making them real. And his efforts paid off in terms of business success.

Every Christian needs to be equally convinced that biblical principles are true not only in some abstract sense but in the reality of our work, business, and personal lives. If we become aware that a ministry or business is violating biblical principles, we need to stop being enablers and start calling people to accountability—even if it means paying a price. An employee who takes a stand may not ultimately succeed in changing anything. In fact, he may run the risk of losing his job. The church's task is to make sure that he does not bear that risk alone. As Lesslie Newbigin writes, fellow Christians should stand ready to support those who speak the truth to power and pay a price for it, even providing financial assistance to those whose moral courage costs them their livelihood.[34]

We must never forget that going along with unbiblical practices is not only wrong, it is unloving. Acquiescing in an unjust situation typically stems not from love but from fear of possible negative repercussions. If we aspire to a godly, holy love for others, we must be willing to take the risk and practice loving confrontation.

There is too much at stake to be complacent. If you and I do not have the courage to confront worldly and sinful practices in our own ranks, what makes us think we will have the courage to stand against powerful secular leaders? If we cannot run with the footmen, we are fooling ourselves to imagine we will be able to run with the horses (see Jer. 12:5). Only by sitting in the supernaturalist's chair will we have the courage to do what's right even when it costs.

GETTING IT RIGHT BY DOING IT "WRONG"

It was just this kind of courage that Schaeffer demonstrated when he gave up everything to start L'Abri. In doing so, he developed an alternative model of ministry that remains instructive for us even now. Let's look beyond what he wrote and consider the practical model he constructed through his life and work.

In comparison with the strategies employed by many ministries today, we could say that *Schaeffer did everything wrong*. He shunned the celebrity circuit, and was willing to minister on the other side of the ocean in an obscure village that no one had ever heard of. While many Christian leaders are obsessed with getting publicity, visibility, and name recognition in order to raise money, Schaeffer was willing to start a small ministry completely invisible to the public, hidden away in the Swiss Alps. When he wrote about "dying" to our natural ambitions, he was not merely parroting a theological doctrine; his insights grew out of hard-won personal experience.

Nor did he use mass marketing techniques to get his name out and build a constituency. He did not have a fund-development department to churn out an endless flood of fundraising letters, advertising copy, and premium offers. Instead he started with a modest list of prayer supporters, while his wife, Edith, typed personal letters to send out.[35]

Even more remarkable, he was willing to get started by simply talking to his kids' friends. As his children grew older, they went down the mountain to Lausanne to attend university, and when their friends raised spiritual questions, they would say, "You ought to talk to my dad." Since their home was so inaccessible—a chalet perched on the side of the mountain—once students arrived, they would have to spend the night. Later they would tell *their* friends about the earnest little man with the goatee and a powerful message, hidden away in the Alps. And *they* would tell *their* friends, and after a while the Schaeffers had students sleeping everywhere—on couches, on floors, and in the hallways.

This is how L'Abri grew into a home-based ministry: It was a completely organic process, as the Schaeffers talked to real people about real questions. No five-year marketing plans, no lists of goals and objectives, no pumping donors for major gifts, no PR campaign to project an image. The ministry grew almost completely by word of mouth, as the Schaeffers prayed that God would bring to them the people of His choice.

Many of Schaeffer's former colleagues thought he was crazy to give up opportunities in the States to speak before large audiences and build a mega-organization. Some were angry and critical, accusing him of wasting his gifts. What kind of ministry is that, they asked, just *talking* to people? Later Schaeffer was to say in a sermon that if we can speak to thousands, we may have to die to that, and be willing to speak to one or two at a time. Clearly, his insights were not abstract, but were the fruit of his courage to follow God's leading in the face of sometimes vicious criticism.

This unique ministry was possible only because L'Abri was a team effort. Francis and Edith worked side by side, inviting people into their home and making themselves available as whole persons. Unfailingly gracious, Edith brought a touch of elegance and beauty to everything she did, always serving meals with candles and fresh-cut flowers on the table. She also labored alongside her husband in their evangelistic ministry, teaching and counseling and holding people's hands as they came down off drugs or agonized over the meaning of life. One of my closest friends at L'Abri was a fellow musician (we played duets together) who had once been a lesbian, using drugs and practicing the occult. It was Edith who had brought her to the Lord, through a stormy session of tears and prayers.

When a celebrity drops in to speak at a conference and then disappears, the audience has no way of knowing whether his personal character matches his message. But the Schaeffers lived alongside students day in and day out, providing a living demonstration that the Christian message is genuine under the tough pressures of real life. That's why their ministry eventually helped transform an entire generation of young people. When students left, many said the experience of genuine Christian community was at least as significant in their conversion as the intellectual answers given in lectures and discussions.

In many ministries, there is relentless pressure for constant growth: Every year, the numbers have to be bigger, the results more impressive, so that donors will be moved to write another check. By contrast, I once heard Schaeffer speak at a conference where he was asked what would happen if, someday, the money didn't come in. He responded simply, "I guess we'll be smaller." The conference hall errupted into applause at such a refreshing lack of pretentiousness. His mentality was that God had a time and a purpose for L'Abri, and when it had fulfilled that purpose, it might simply end.

How different from the driven, success-oriented attitude that pervades so many ministries today. Perhaps that's why Schaeffer had to leave, says philosopher John Vander Stelt—why he "had to 'flee' to the mountains of Switzerland, in order to be able to penetrate the citadels of our Western culture."[36] In both his message and his methods, Schaeffer left behind a compelling model that is even more relevant today than it was in his own lifetime.

TRUE SPIRITUALITY

A recent Zogby/Forbes ASAP poll asked respondents, What would you like most to be known for? For being intelligent? Good looking? Having a great sense of humor? A full half of respondents checked off an unexpected answer: They said they would like a reputation for "being authentic."[37] In a world of spin and hype, the postmodern generation is searching desperately for something real and authentic. They will not take Christians seriously unless our churches and parachurch organizations demonstrate an authentic way of life—unless they are communities that exhibit the character of God in their relationships and mode of living.

Advertising techniques that merely convey an image may bring in the money, but they are not the means to accomplishing a genuine spiritual work. The church's "manner of speaking the truth must not be aligned to the techniques of modern propaganda," writes Newbigin, "but must have the modesty, the sobriety, and the realism which are proper to a disciple of Jesus."[38] The church is called to be a witness to the gospel through an authentic demonstration of love and unity.

In the days of the early church, the thing that most impressed their neighbors in the Roman Empire was the community of love they witnessed among believers. "Behold how they love one another," it was said. In every age, the most persuasive evidence for the gospel is not words or arguments but a living demonstration of God's character through Christians' love for one another, expressed in both their words and their actions. The gospel is not meant to be "a disembodied message," Newbigin writes. It is meant to be fleshed out in "a congregation of men and women who believe it and live by it"—who exhibit in their relationships the beauty of God's character.[39]

In one sense, this chapter should have been the first, because its message is the pathway to everything else. The spiritual reality of *rejected, slain, raised* lies at the heart of everything in the Christian life, including the work of developing a Christian mind. Only as we cooperate with God in dying to sin and self are we open to receiving "the mind of Christ" (1 Cor. 2:16). May God give us the grace to be worldview missionaries, building lives and communities that give an authentic witness of His existence before a watching world.

APPENDICES

Appendix 1

HOW AMERICAN POLITICS
BECAME SECULARIZED

Social contract theory remains at the heart of political liberalism in America today. In chapter 4 we discussed Rousseau's version of the social contract, and in chapters 10 and 11 we talked about the enormous impact the theory had on America after the birth of our nation. We saw how a liberal view of society, with its atomistic individualism, was embraced by many evangelicals, and in chapter 12 how it altered the shape of the American family. Thus it is crucial that we understand this philosophical tradition more deeply.

And the most important point to grasp is why it was developed in the first place. The driving motivation behind the rise of social contract theory was the secularizing of political thought.

Throughout the Middle Ages, a constant tug-of-war was waged between church and state, between pope and emperor, with one gaining predominance for a period, then the other redressing the balance. An important turning point came after the Reformation. The split in the medieval church had fractured the religious unity of Christendom, yet both sides continued to hold a territorial view of the church. They simply assumed that everyone living within a certain nation or geographical region should belong to the same religion. As a result, for more than a hundred years, beginning in the late sixteenth century and continuing throughout most of the seventeenth century, Europe found itself embroiled in religious wars. Many people had to flee persecution in their homeland, becoming religious refugees.[1]

How did a century of religious warfare affect people's attitudes toward morality and politics? When people saw that Christians *were willing to shed blood over religious differences,* they began searching for an alternative basis for the social order. They sought a purely secular arena of discourse, autonomous from religion, that would function as "neutral" territory to bring peace to warring religious factions. As Jeffrey Stout explains, many came to think they could "contain the violent effects of religious disagreement only by creating *non*religious means for discussing and deciding matters of public importance."[2]

Up until this time, the state had been regarded as a moral and spiritual entity even though it was institutionally independent of the church. Ordained by God, its duty was to protect the "common good" of the body politic, conceived in moral terms like Justice, Mercy, and Righteousness (with the definition of these terms ultimately derived from divine revelation). Rulers regarded themselves as mediating, or participating in, God's own righteous rule over the nations—which included the duty of protecting "true religion" and upholding the church.

After the Reformation, however, people began to ask, *Which church?* Then, after a hundred years of warfare between conflicting churches, many began to answer that the state should not have the job of upholding *any* church. They even began to contest the moral function of the state: Since morality is derived from religion, any religious conception of the "common good" that was proposed might well be challenged by a competing religion. No, a purely secular basis would have to be found.[3]

The first to rise to the challenge was Thomas Hobbes. He proposed that the ultimate basis for the political order was the fear of violent death. The "state of nature," as Hobbes pictured it, was hostile and violent—a war of all against all. The threat of death hangs over everything and (in his famous phrase) life is "solitary, poor, nasty, brutish, and short." Each individual has a natural "right" to preserve his own life, taking whatever he needs, even if that means stealing or killing. The state arises when individuals decide that life would be more pleasant if they would give up certain rights, such as the right to defend themselves, and transfer those rights to a civil authority. This transferring of rights is called a contract, and for Hobbes it becomes the basis of all moral obligations.

The crucial point is that social duties no longer arise from a "common good" for civil society, constituted by transcendent principles such as Justice. Instead they are simply the product of individual choice—when people decide it is in their interests to contract away some of their own rights. This is a form of pre-Darwinian naturalism, where the foundation of civic society is not a higher good but merely the individual's biological urge for self-preservation.

John Locke presented a similar scenario, except that for him the ultimate source of the civil order is hunger. The most basic right is the right to eat, and the threat of death does not come from other people (as it did for Hobbes) but rather from hunger. By exerting his labor to find food, or to grow it himself, the individual creates private property—and to protect his property more effectively, he enters into a social contract with others. Now, Locke assigned a much more limited role to the state than either Hobbes or Rousseau did, which is why he became the favorite of political conservatives. Yet like the other social contract theorists, he did not base civil society on any higher good. Instead he portrayed it as the creation of individuals, motivated by enlightened self-interest. Locke's picture of society is atomistic, where all that exists ultimately are individuals and their needs or wants.

Rousseau, as we saw in chapter 4, derived civil society from the natural instinct of "self love" (*amour de soi*) or self-preservation. Thus for all the social contract theorists, the ultimate basis for the political order is purely secular. They based civil society not on moral ideals derived from religion but strictly on the natural, biological instinct of self-preservation. The sole source of political legitimacy is the consent of isolated, autonomous individuals.

Ironically, social contract theory presupposes a completely unrealistic conception of human nature. The atomistic creature that populates the state-of-nature scenarios appears to be an independent, fully developed, autonomous individual. "The theory starts with an image of, say, a 21-year-old adult male," comments Christian political theorist Paul Marshall.[4] Obviously, no one actually comes into the world that way. Each of us begins life as a dependent, helpless baby, born into a family and a complex social, religious, and civil order. Only through the love and sociality exercised toward us by others do we grow into mature, independent creatures. As Bertrand de Jouvenal once commented, social contract theories "are the views of childless men who must have forgotten their childhood."[5] Biology and history both teach that humans are intrinsically social beings.[6]

Yet, despite its unrealistic starting premise, social contract theory became the dominant political theory in America—while at the same time a powerful force for secularization. As we have seen, what united the various versions of social contract theories was their rejection of transcendent moral ideals, to be replaced by a lowest-common-denominator biological urge as the foundation of the political order. Religious perspectives were marginalized, while the state took over as the central institution in modern society.

Perhaps the greatest tragedy is that many evangelicals in the eighteenth and nineteenth century failed to recognize what was happening. Having embraced a two-story concept of truth, they assumed that political philosophy was a lower-story "science" that could be pursued apart from any distinctively Christian perspective. As a result, many evangelicals at the time simply adopted secular political philosophies—especially that of John Locke. Whatever Locke's personal religious faith was (which is endlessly debated), there can be no doubt that his political theory was at root secular, grounding civil society not in moral goods like Justice and Right but merely in individual self-interest.

How did evangelicals miss that? As George Marsden explains, "Locke's contract theory of government was, in practice, sufficiently like the Puritan concept of covenant that no one in the revolutionary era seems to have thought it significant to criticize its essentially secular theoretical base."[7] By treating the lower story as philosophically neutral, Christians failed to recognize *alien* philosophies—and sometimes even adopted them without being unaware of it.

In our own day, this same secularization process explains why politics leaves so many people disillusioned and spiritually dissatisfied. "The liberalism of Hobbes and Locke is founded upon the relatively 'low' human goals of self-preservation and the desire for wealth," writes Stanley Kurtz—which accounts for "the chronic disenchantment at the heart of modernity."[8] At the core, humans are moral beings, and we long to see our highest moral ideals expressed in our corporate life. Ultimately the secular version of civic life fails to satisfy the human longing to live together in moral communities, committed to Justice and Righteousness.

Appendix 2

MODERN ISLAM
AND THE
NEW AGE MOVEMENT

Christians sometimes find it easy to dismiss the New Age movement as the loony trappings left over from the counterculture of the 1960s. But that would be a dangerous underestimation. The core of the movement is a pantheistic religion (see chapter 4) deriving from an extraordinarily broad religious tendency that has appeared in virtually every age and culture—West, East, and Middle East (Islamic). In the aftermath of September 11, as the world focuses attention on Islamic cultures, Christians need to be equipped to identify this broader religious tendency in order to make sense of current cultural and political events.

Starting with the West, the quasi-pantheistic ideas we are talking about took root in the third century with the ancient Greeks. This was a period when Asian religions became fashionable in ancient Greek culture, much as they did in America in the 1960s. The result was a school of thought known as neo-Platonism, which merged Plato's philosophy with Indian pantheism. "Neo" means new, of course, so you might think of it as the ancient world's form of the New Age movement.

The main spokesman for this melding of East and West was Plotinus,[1] who taught that the world was an "emanation" or radiation of being from a nonpersonal Spirit or Absolute—somewhat as light is a radiation from the sun. The lowest level of this radiation was matter; and because it was farthest away from Infinite Goodness, that made it evil. In other words, having a physical, material body was itself regarded as a kind of sin, something negative from which we must be saved. How? By ascetic practices that suppress bodily desires. The goal was to liberate the spirit from the "prison house" of the body in order to be reabsorbed into the Infinite from which it came.

These ideas have obvious parallels with Eastern pantheism, and indeed some modern Hindus recognize Plotinus as a kindred spirit. Swami Krishnananda writes, "Plotinus, the celebrated mystic, comes nearest in his views to the Vedanta philosophy, and is practically in full agreement with the Eastern sages."² Other scholars agree: A book of essays titled *Neo-Platonism and Indian Philosophy* notes the "remarkable similarity between the philosophical system of Plotinus (205–270 A.D.) and those of various Hindu philosophers in various centuries."³ For both, God is not a personal being but a nonpersonal essence.

From the beginning, neo-Platonism was not just a philosophy but also a mystical religion. In fact, it was crafted in part in opposition to Christianity—as a weapon to be wielded by ancient paganism in its polemical battle against Christianity. In the fourth century, the emperor Julian the Apostate even tried to oust Christianity as the official religion of the Roman Empire by replacing it with neo-Platonism.

Surprisingly, many of the early Christians were nevertheless sympathetic to neo-Platonism and were greatly influenced by it—notably Clement of Alexandria, Origen, and Augustine. At the end of the fifth century this semi-Eastern philosophy was actually synthesized with Christianity by an unknown writer posing as a first-century convert of St. Paul's called Dionysius the Areopagite. Later known as pseudo-Dionysius, he presented a Christianized form of neo-Platonism that became enormously influential in the Middle Ages. His writings were translated into Latin by John Scotus Eriugena about the middle of the ninth century, and from then neo-Platonism became the major conduit of Greek thought to later ages. It greatly affected many mystical movements in the West, including those of Meister Eckhart and Jacob Boehme. It was popular among Renaissance humanists like Ficino and Pico della Mirandola. Even many of the early modern scientists held a neo-Platonist philosophy of nature, which inspired much of their scientific work.⁴

Later, neo-Platonism became an important influence on the Romantic movement of the nineteenth century with its philosophical idealism, in which ultimate reality was said to be Spirit, Mind, or the Absolute. In German historicism, the Absolute was given an evolutionary twist—it was said to evolve through a series of stages from lower levels of being to ever higher ones. In the early twentieth century, this notion was modernized in Process Thought, in which God Himself became embedded in the evolutionary process—an immanent, quasi-pantheistic deity that evolves along with the world (see chapter 8). Around the same time, a new blend of Eastern religion and Western occultism was launched under the name *perennial philosophy*—the same ideas I encountered in my teens when I read Aldous Huxley's book *The Perennial Philosophy* (see chapter 4).

The point of this rapid-fire historical survey is that long before the Beatles became disciples of the Maharishi, various forms of quasi-pantheistic thought were already prominent strands within the Western cultural tradition. The New Age movement was merely a more recent expression of a long-standing tendency to import Eastern pantheism into Western culture, which began with Plotinus and neo-Platonism.

What about the Middle East? Many of us do not realize that, historically, Islamic thinkers drew on ancient Greek sources just as heavily as Western thinkers did, so that neo-Platonism spread to Arabic cultures as well.[5] During the Golden Age of Islam in the seventh and eighth centuries, Muhammad's armies swept out from the Arabian peninsula, annexing territory from Spain to Persia. In the process, we might say, they also annexed the works of Plato, Aristotle, Plotinus, and other Greek thinkers. As a result, the Arab world had a rich tradition of commentary on the Greek philosophers long before Europe did. In college history courses, we often learn that the Renaissance was sparked by the recovery of ancient classical writings. But we rarely learn that it was *Muslim* philosophers who had preserved those texts and who reintroduced them to the West.

As a consequence, neo-Platonism became a strong influence on Islamic thought. Today several leading Muslim philosophers have embraced perennial philosophy, with its merging of Western and Eastern pantheism. In fact, the early proponents of this philosophy, who were Europeans, all ended up converting to Islam![6] To complete the circle, the man who launched perennial philosophy (a Frenchman named René Guenon) believed there was actually a common core uniting all three: neo-Platonism in the West, Hinduism in the East, and Islam in the Middle East.

Since September 11, we have heard it said again and again that Islam is just another Abrahamic faith—as though it were not really very different from Christianity. So it may come as a surprise to learn that the God of Islam is actually more akin to the nonpersonal Absolute of neo-Platonism and Hinduism than to the God of the Bible.

Yet it is true, and the central reason is that Islam rejects the Trinity. Without that concept, it cannot hold a fully personal conception of God. Why not? Because many attributes of personality can be expressed only within a relationship—things like love, communication, empathy, and self-giving.

Traditional Christian doctrine maintains a personal conception of God because it teaches that these interpersonal attributes were expressed from all eternity among the three Persons of the Trinity. A genuinely personal God requires distinct "Persons," because that alone makes it possible for love and communication to exist within the Godhead itself.

Islam denies the Trinity, however, which means there is no way for its conception of God to include these relational attributes. (At least, not until He created the world—but in that case He would be dependent on creation.) That's why it is correct to say, as some Islamic philosophers do, that Islam is actually akin to neo-Platonism and Hinduism.

This nonpersonal conception of God also explains why Muslims express their faith in near-mechanical rituals: Muslim believers recite the Koran over and over, in unison, word for word, in the original Arabic. They don't pray to God as a personal being, pouring their hearts out to Him as David did, or arguing with him as Job did. As one Muslim website puts it, "understanding [the Koran] is secondary" to recitation and ritual,[7] which makes sense only if God is not a personal being. As sociologist Rodney Stark explains, religions with nonpersonal gods tend to stress precision in the performance of rituals and sacred formulas; by contrast, religions with a highly personal God worry less about such things, because a personal Being will respond to a personal approach through impromptu supplication and spontaneous prayer.[8]

In our efforts to defend Christianity, we can easily be overwhelmed by the vast number of religions and philosophies being hawked in the marketplace of ideas today. The task becomes easier, however, when we realize they can all be grouped into two fundamental categories: The most crucial distinction falls between systems that begin with a personal God and those that begin with a nonpersonal force or essence. Typically we use the term *nonpersonal* to refer to secular "isms" like naturalism and materialism. But we should bear in mind that the same category includes religious beliefs as well—ones that begin with a nonpersonal spiritual essence. And although naturalism is fashionable among the highly educated, among ordinary people a vague generic spiritualism may actually be more widespread.

Instead, it was so widespread already half a century ago that C. S. Lewis said we often find ourselves opposed "not by the *ir*religion of our hearers but by their *real* religion"—by which he meant some diluted form of pantheism. People tend to like the idea that God is not a personal being but rather "a great spiritual force pervading all things, a common mind of which we are all parts, a pool of generalized spirituality to which we can all flow." So pervasive is this concept that Lewis considered it "the natural bent of the human mind"—"the attitude into which the human mind automatically falls when left to itself" apart from divine revelation.[9] If Lewis is right, then pantheism will always reemerge as a natural opponent of Christianity.

Over the long term, then, secularism is unlikely to last. Since humanity is naturally religious, ultimately Western culture will probably become spiritualized again. Having served its purpose in undercutting Christianity, secularism itself will die off, giving way to a pantheistic spirituality that is already at the core of so much thinking across the board in the West, the East, and the Middle East. It is crucial for Christians to learn how to analyze these nonpersonal, pantheistic worldviews—both to protect ourselves and to reach out in evangelism to the spiritually lost.

Appendix 3

THE LONG WAR BETWEEN
MATERIALISM AND CHRISTIANITY

Some of the most important figures in American history for Christians to
understand are the pragmatists, because they did so much to work out the
philosophical implications of Darwinism (see chapter 8). And one way to
gauge the impact of their ideas is to situate them within a larger historical context. Charles Sanders Peirce sometimes attributed his ideas about chance to the
philosopher Epicurus[1]—a comment that directs us all the way back to the
ancient Greek thinkers. Seen through a wider historical lens, pragmatism was
one stage in a long war between materialism and Christianity that began with
the ancient Greeks.

Virtually every conceivable philosophical position can be found in some
form at the dawn of Western culture among the Greek philosophers. In chapter 2, we traced the enormous impact that Plato and Aristotle had on Christian
thought. But there was also another stream of Greek thought, represented by
Epicurus and Democritus (and later the Roman poet Lucretius). They were the
materialists of ancient times, who taught that the universe consisted solely of
atoms in motion, combining and recombining to form living things by sheer
chance. As Lucretius declared in *On the Nature of the Universe,* living things
were brought about by "the purposeless congregation and coalescence of
atoms."[2]

This sounds strangely modern, very much like the materialism of our own
day. And except for lacking Darwin's mechanism of natural selection, ancient
materialism *did* have all the same basic elements: especially the core idea that
matter is capable of producing everything we see around us by chance colli-
sions of atoms, without plan or purpose.

In fact, already in ancient times, Epicurus had mapped out a complete
worldview based on materialism. First, if matter is all that exists, then we must
be empiricists: Knowledge is limited to what we know through the senses (atoms
impinging upon our sense organs). Second, morality must be based on the senses
too: Good and evil are defined by sensations of pleasure and pain. The sole principle of morality is that we ought to maximize pleasure and minimize pain—in

a word, hedonism. Students coming into Epicurus's garden, where he held his classes, were greeted by an inscription on the gate that read: "Stranger, here you will do well to tarry; here our highest good is pleasure." Yet Epicurus did not equate the term *hedonism* with unbridled indulgence, as we do today. He urged moderation and even asceticism, on the grounds that most pleasures bring pain in their wake (like drinking too much). Still, the main feature of his morality was that it was not based on any transcendent standard of the Good; instead it was based on our natural preference for certain sensations.

These ideas were as controversial in the ancient world as they are today. After the Hellenistic period (when Epicurus lived), philosophy once again fell under the sway of classical thought (Plato and Aristotle), whose followers vigorously opposed Epicurean materialism. They argued that if the world really did consist of chance configurations of atoms, then knowledge would be impossible. The constant stream of impressions coming into our minds through the senses would not be ordered in any rational patterns, but would be a meaningless scattershot of sights, sounds, tastes, and textures. The reason we can know anything at all, they said, is precisely that reality is *not* a random flow of atoms but is ordered into intelligible patterns—which they called Forms or Ideas. It is this rational order that our minds apprehend. Living things do not result from a chance collation of atoms; they consist of matter organized by intelligible Forms, which in Latin is *species*. (Recall the Form/Matter dualism discussed in chapter 2.)

What's more, classical philosophers argued, this rational order is teleological—directed by a goal or purpose (Greek *telos*). When an acorn becomes an oak, or an egg grows into a chicken, its development is a directed process that unfolds according to a built-in plan or purpose. The final goal or Form is the full-grown tree or the adult hen. (Aristotle had a pretty clear commonsense understanding of what we now call genetics.[3])

According to classical thought, the same teleological reasoning holds for morality. Morality is not based on the senses (pain and pleasure), as the Epicureans taught; it is based on transcendent Forms like Goodness and Justice. These are teleological in the sense that they express the purpose or ideal toward which humans ought to be developing: We should be striving to become ever more good and just.[4]

The intellectual world of ancient times was a battleground between these competing philosophies (along with several others), until Christianity appeared on the scene. When the early Christian thinkers surveyed the ongoing debate, they had no doubt which side was in the right: They aligned themselves firmly with Plato and Aristotle, while forcefully attacking Epicurean materialism. Indeed, Epicurus became a favorite whipping boy among the early Christian apologists.[5] Against his materialism, they affirmed the reality of the spiritual realm, along with the ability of the mind to know abstract ideals beyond the empirical world—Truth, Goodness, and Beauty. The concept of intelligible Forms was reinterpreted as "ideas in the mind of God"—the plans or designs He used in creating the world. The result was a kind of Christianized classicism that became the dominant philosophical position in Europe from late antiquity all through the Middle Ages and beyond, while Epicureanism was nearly forgotten.

Then, more than a millennium later, at the dawn of the scientific revolution, a seismic shift took place. Seeking to frame a new philosophy of nature, some of the early modern scientists began cautiously reconsidering Epicurean atomism. Many were Christians who broke with the negative judgment that early Christian apologists had pronounced on Epicureanism. Optimistically, these scientific thinkers hoped that atomism could be extracted from its materialistic philosophical context and baptized into a Christian worldview. The first to revive Epicurean atomism was the priest Pierre Gassendi, followed by the devout chemist Robert Boyle and the incomparable Isaac Newton.[6]

By resurrecting Epicurean atomism in *science*, however, they cracked open the door to Epicurean materialism in *philosophy*. In short order, materialism burst the door open and came charging through. Finally, with the evolutionary theory of Charles Darwin, materialism got the upper hand in Western thought. Darwin tossed out the concept of intelligible Forms (recall that the Latin word for Form is *species*), arguing that there are no real species in nature, but only a constantly shifting flux of individuals. The reason there *appear* to be species is only that evolutionary change is so slow—just as the earth appears to be flat only because its curve is so gradual. It is ironic that Darwin's book was titled *On the Origin of Species* because his purpose was actually to deny the real existence of species. He regarded taxonomic categories merely as useful mental constructs that *we* impose on the flux of nature. The organic world consists ultimately of individuals in constantly shifting chance interactions.[7] It is no exaggeration to say that Darwinism represents the triumph of Epicurean atomism in modern times.[8]

And if there are no species or Forms in nature, then there are none in morals or metaphysics either—no eternal ideals of Goodness, Truth, or Beauty. It was the pragmatists who took this next step: What Darwin did to species, they did to ideas. Tossing out the concept of Forms or Ideas, they concluded that all we know is the constantly shifting flux of experiences. In his famous essay "The Influence of Darwin on Philosophy," John Dewey said we must abandon the classical Greek approach of explaining things by reference to intelligible Forms, and replace it with knowledge that is "genetic and experimental."[9] Everything would now be explained as originating through historical processes ("genetic") that are knowable by empirical investigation ("experimental").

For example, instead of basing morality on human nature in its original and ideal form (the way God created us from the beginning), pragmatism explains morality as something that arises over time by a naturalistic process: As humans experiment with various behaviors, those that produce satisfactory results become imprinted in their brains. After all, according to evolution, there *is* no original and ideal human nature, normative for all times and places. Instead, moral practices come into being over the course of history as responses to environmental pressures, and are retained only if they pass the test of expedience and pragmatic results.

By the same token, as evolution proceeds and conditions change, then moral practices must change as well. The important thing is not to identify enduring normative principles but to learn strategies for managing change. For if species are not real, then the boundaries defining human nature become plastic and malleable—and who can assign humans any special moral status? Why not take control of the course of human evolution through social engineering? "Man, as he is, is obsolescent," announced Mary Calderone, former executive director of the Sexuality Information and Education Council of the United States (SIECUS), in 1968. The main question facing educators, she said, is "what kind [of man] do we want to produce in his place and how do we design the production line?" Calderone called on schools to begin producing "quality human beings by means of such consciously engineered processes as society's own best minds can blueprint."[10]

Such unvarnished calls for social engineering are chilling. Worse, we may soon have the scientific capacity to perform *genetic* engineering—which will put far greater power into the hands of technocrats eager to take charge of evolution. "Human nature disappears as a concept from neo-Darwinism," explains embryologist Brian Goodwin, "and so life becomes a set of parts, commodities that can be shifted around."[11] If there is no normative human nature, why *not* experiment? Why *not* shift genes around and manipulate life forms in any way that seems expedient?

By tracing the debate over Darwinism all the way back to Epicurus, we can place the theory within a much larger context. Darwinism was not entirely new, invented out of whole cloth. In many ways, it represented a revival of ancient Epicureanism. Having been decisively defeated by the early Christian apologists, Epicurean materialism lay dormant for a millennium and a half, only to rise once again to do battle with Christianity in modern times.[12] The pragmatists then applied Darwinism to the life of the mind. Thus pragmatism represents one stage in the long war between materialism and Christianity.

Appendix 4

ISMS ON THE RUN:
PRACTICAL APOLOGETICS
AT L'ABRI

When I first arrived at L'Abri, trudging through the early spring snow to the tiny alpine village nestled in the Alps, I had developed a motley set of "isms"—from determinism to subjectivism to moral relativism. But as I settled into a round of study and discussions, I was shocked to find those beliefs under constant and vigorous assault. Looking back, I realize that what finally persuaded me of the truth of Christianity was Schaeffer's apologetic method, which was a unique hybrid of Common Sense realism and Dutch neo-Calvinism (see chapter 11).

How did this method play out in actual apologetics with a skeptic—me, for example? In a nutshell, Schaeffer would argue that one way to test truth claims is to measure them against the standard of what we all know by direct experience—or as he put it, universal human experience (Common Sense realism). Then he would endeavor to show that Christianity alone gives an adequate *theoretical* account of what we know by *pre-theoretical* experience (Dutch neo-Calvinism). To borrow a phrase from a contemporary philosopher of science, the truths known by experience are "conclusions in search of a premise."[1] To make sense of them, we have to find a "premise" or systematic worldview that accounts for them.

SURVIVAL MACHINES?

To get a better grasp of this line of argument, walk with me through a few examples. How might we respond to the reductionism and determinism so widespread today, especially in the field of cognitive science? Just recently an article in *Nature* recited the current orthodoxy, insisting that the mind is "a survival machine with predetermined choices" and that free will is a subjective illusion.[2]

"The real causal story behind human behavior is deterministic," agrees another recent article. Free will is self-deception, for "we are experts at deluding ourselves that we are ideal agents. . . . We confabulate stories that keep the self in the driver's seat."³

Daniel Dennett, whom we met in earlier chapters, does not flinch at dismissing consciousness itself as an illusion. Since our brains are nothing but complicated computers, he reasons, we are merely robots—and like any robot, we can function perfectly well without subjective awareness (what we call mind, soul, or consciousness). Thus he concludes that humans are essentially zombies—not the movie monsters but "philosopher's zombies," creatures that exhibit all the behavior of a human being but without any consciousness.⁴

When I arrived at L'Abri, these were some of the ideas I had come to accept. What changed my mind? The counterargument is that determinism contradicts the data of experience. We all have an immediate awareness of being in situations where we must deliberate on alternative courses of action, and then select one of them. It is often exhilarating, and just as often agonizing, but in practice no one can really deny the direct awareness that we make choices.

"We find it impossible *not* to believe that we are radically free and responsible in our choices and actions," says philosopher Galen Strawson. In ordinary life, we find ourselves forced to believe that we have "ultimate, buck-stopping responsibility for what we do, of a kind that can make blame and punishment and praise and reward truly just and fair."⁵ Moreover, we find testimony to this belief in the literature of all ages and cultures throughout history. It is part of universal human experience.

To be consistent, the determinist is forced to deny the testimony of experience. But that is not a valid move in the worldview game: The point of offering a worldview is to *explain* the data of experience, not to *deny* it. Anything less is ducking the issue. Thus we can be confident that any philosophy that leads to determinism is simply false. It fails to account for the reality of human nature as we experience it.

Another way to frame the argument is to say that no one can live consistently on the basis of a deterministic worldview. In everyday life, we are forced to operate on the assumption that freedom and choice are real, no matter what we believe theoretically. This creates a point of tension for the nonbeliever. "The conviction of freedom is built into our experiences; we can't just give it up," said philosopher John Searle in an interview. "If we tried to, we couldn't live with it. We can say, OK, I believe in determinism; but then when we go into a restaurant we have to make up our mind what we're going to order, and that's a free choice."⁶ In his professional writings, Searle reduces all reality to particles moving by blind physical forces—yet when he leaves his laboratory and tries to function in the real world, he cannot live on that basis. His experience provides a practical contradiction of his philosophy.

By contrast, Christianity is completely consonant with human experience. It offers a rationally consistent explanation of human freedom as one aspect of the image of God. If ultimate reality is a personal God who wills and chooses, then the human person is no longer a misfit in a deterministic world. Christianity explains not only freedom but also the *other* dimensions of human personality that derive from freedom: creativity, originality, moral responsibility, and even love. The whole range of human personality is accounted for only by the Christian worldview, because it begins with a personal God. We don't need to make an irrational leap to the upper story in order to affirm the highest ideals of human nature; they are utterly logically consistent with the Christian worldview.

BUMPING UP AGAINST REALITY

What about subjectivism? During my second visit to L'Abri, I had the privilege of staying in the home of Udo and Debby Middelmann. One of Udo's frequent themes during dinner conversations was the objectivity of truth. It's a lesson we find ourselves learning, like it or not, from the time we are born, Udo would say. When a baby crawls to the edge of the crib and bumps his head against the wooden bars, he learns in a painful way that reality is objective. When a toddler tilts his high chair back until it falls to the floor, he learns that there is an objective structure to the universe. Reality does not bend itself to our subjective desires—a lesson that can be painful to learn even for adults. Thus we can confidently reject any philosophical position that leads to subjectivism. Why? Because it fails to account for what ordinary experience teaches us day by day. It is in tension with the data of experience.

Christianity, by contrast, treats truth as objective and explains why—because the world is the creation of God, not of my own mind. The doctrine of creation gives logical grounds for our belief that an objective, external world exists, with its own inherent structure and design.

What's more, the Creator is not silent. He has spoken, giving us divine revelation in Scripture. Since God sees and knows everything as it truly is, what He communicates in His Word is an objective, trustworthy basis for knowledge.

This is a revolutionary claim in today's postmodern world, with its pervasive subjectivism and relativism. We are not locked into the "prison house of language," as postmodernists put it. By *language* they mean belief systems, which are expressed in language, and which they regard as nothing more than products of history and cultural evolution. Over against this radical form of historicism, Christianity claims that we have access to *trans*historical truth, because God Himself has spoken.

It's Not Fair

If there is one prevailing characteristic of modern culture, it is moral relativism. Yet this is one of the "isms" that is easiest to shoot down. Why? Because, despite what a person says he believes, no one faced with genuine cruelty remains a moral relativist.

After World War II, when the atrocities of the Nazi concentration camps came to light, it created a crisis among many educated people. Steeped in the cynicism and relativism typical of their class, they perceived for the first time in a visceral way that evil is real. Yet their own secular philosophies gave them no basis for making objective, universal moral judgments—because those philosophies reduced moral judgments to merely personal preferences or cultural conventions. Thus they found themselves trapped in a practical contradiction, which created tremendous inner tension.

The dilemma is that humans irresistibly and unavoidably make moral judgments—and yet nonbiblical worldviews give no basis for them. When nonbelievers act according to their intrinsic moral nature by pronouncing something truly right or wrong, they are being inconsistent with their own philosophy—and thus condemn it by their own actions. "Whenever you find a man who says he does not believe in a real Right and Wrong, you will find the same man going back on this in a moment later," writes C. S. Lewis. "He may break his promise to you, but if you try breaking one to him he will be complaining 'It's not fair' before you can say Jack Robinson."

"It seems, then, we are forced to believe in a real Right and Wrong," Lewis concludes. "People may be sometimes mistaken about them, just as people sometimes get their sums wrong; but they are not a matter of mere taste and opinion any more than the multiplication table."[7] Yet what is the logical ground for this unavoidable belief in right and wrong? The only basis for an objective morality is the existence of a holy God, whose character provides the ultimate foundation for moral standards. Christianity explains why we are moral creatures, and establishes the validity of our moral sense.

These were some of the issues that I had to wrestle with personally in my studies at L'Abri before becoming a Christian. The form of apologetics I encountered there treated common human experience as the touchstone. The purpose of a *worldview* is to explain our experience of the *world*—and any philosophy can be judged by how well it succeeds in doing so. When Christianity is tested, we discover that it alone explains and makes sense of the most basic and universal human experiences. This is the confidence that should sustain us when we bring our faith perspective into the public arena, whether in personal evangelism or in our professional work.

NOTES

INTRODUCTION

1. *How Now Shall We Live?* was coauthored by Charles Colson and published by Tyndale (Wheaton, Ill., 1991) and is hereafter cited as *How Now?* I would also like to recognize the contribution of Harold Fickett, an outstanding writer and storyteller, who wrote the chapters in *How Now?* consisting of extended stories. In offering the current book in part as an advance on themes developed in *How Now?* I'd like to clarify that all citations of that earlier volume refer solely to chapters that I authored.

2. Bill Wichterman, in discussion with the author. Wichterman develops his thesis in greater detail in "The Culture: Upstream from Politics," in *Building a Healthy Culture: Strategies for an American Renaissance,* ed. Don Eberly (Grand Rapids, Mich.: Eerdmans, 2001), 76-101. "While cultural conservatives bemoan judicial activism that reinterprets the plain meaning of the written Constitution, they forget that the courts are only finishing on parchment a job already begun in the hearts of the American people. . . . Politics is largely an expression of culture."

3. Cited in Mary Passantino, "The Little Engine that Can," a review of Phillip Johnson's *The Right Questions* (foreword by Nancy Pearcey), in *Christian Research Journal,* April 2003.

4. Peter Berger, *Facing Up to Modernity: Excursions in Society, Politics, and Religion* (New York: Basic Books, 1977), 133.

5. Francis Schaeffer deals with the divided concept of truth in *Escape from Reason* and *The God Who Is There* (in *The Complete Works of Francis A. Schaeffer* [Wheaton, Ill.: Crossway, 1982]).

6. Phillip E. Johnson, *The Wedge of Truth: Splitting the Foundations of Naturalism* (Downers Grove, Ill.: InterVarsity Press, 2000), 148, emphasis added. See also my review of the book: "A New Foundation for Positive Cultural Change: Science and God in the Public Square," *Human Events* (September 15, 2000, at http://www.arn.org).

7. Lesslie Newbigin, *A Word in Season: Perspectives on Christian World Missions* (Grand Rapids, Mich.: Eerdmans, 1994), see especially the essay titled, "The Cultural Captivity of Western Christianity as a Challenge to a Missionary Church."

8. "Reeve: Keep Religious Groups Out of Public Policy," The Associated Press, April 3, 2003, emphasis added.

9. Michael Goheen, *"As the Father Has Sent Me, I Am Sending You": J. E. Lesslie Newbigin's Missionary Ecclesiology* (Zoetermeer: Uitgeverij Boekencentrum, 2000), 377.

10. Albert M. Wolters, *Creation Regained: Biblical Basics for a Reformational Worldview* (Grand Rapids, Mich.: Eerdmans, 1985), 4.

11. For a brief history of the term *worldview* from a Christian perspective, see Albert M. Wolters, "On the Idea of Worldview and Its Relation to Philosophy," in *Stained Glass,* ed. Paul Marshall, Sander Griffioen, and Richard J. Mouw (Lanham, Md.: University Press of America, 1989), 65-80. For a more detailed account, see David K. Naugle, *Worldview: The History of a Concept* (Grand Rapids, Mich.: Eerdmans, 2002). For a brief history from a non-Christian perspective, see the first two sections of Eugene F. Miller, "Positivism, Historicism, and Political Inquiry," *American Political Science Review* 66, no. 3 (September 1972): 796-817; at http://members. shaw.ca/compilerpress1/Anno%20Miller.htm. Miller writes: "All human expressions point beyond themselves to the characteristic worldview *(Weltanschauung)* of the epoch or culture to which they belong. This underlying impulse or spirit makes the culture a whole and determines the shape of all thought and evaluation within it. We grasp the documentary meaning of human objectifications by seeing them as unconscious expressions of a worldview. Even theoretical philosophy is but a channel through which the spirit of the age finds expression."

12. The first three parts of this book were delivered as three presentations at the Leadership Academy of the Association of Christian Schools International, June 22-26, 2001, under the titles "The Nuts and Bolts of a Christian Worldview" (part 1), "A Worldview Approach to Science" (part 2), and "Facing Our Past: Whatever Happened to the Christian Mind?" (part 3). They were later updated and presented at a L'Abri conference, February 6-7, 2004 in Rochester, Minnesota.

13. Nancy Pearcey, "Anti-Darwinism Comes to the University: An Interview with Phillip Johnson," *Bible-Science Newsletter,* June 1990. See also Nancy Pearcey, "Foreword," in

Phillip E. Johnson, *The Right Questions: Truth, Meaning, and Public Debate* (Downers Grove, Ill.: InterVarsity Press, 2002).

14. In *How Now?* material from the *Bible-Science Newsletter* contributed extensively to the chapters on science in part 2 and the chapters on redemption in part 4, among others. Readers interested in pursuing the original sources will find them referenced there (third printing) and more extensively throughout the present book.

CHAPTER 1: BREAKING OUT OF THE GRID

1. John D. Beckett, *Loving Monday: Succeeding in Business Without Selling Your Soul* (Downers Grove, Ill.: InterVarsity Press, 1998), 52.

2. "Sarah," in discussion with the author. The name has been changed to protect her privacy, but otherwise the story is completely true and accurate.

3. Francis Schaeffer explains this phenomenon in *A Christian Manifesto,* in *The Complete Works of Francis A. Schaeffer,* vol. 5 (Wheaton, Ill.: Crossway, 1982), 424-425: "Many Christians do not mean what I mean when I say Christianity is true, or Truth. They are Christians and they believe in, let us say, the truth of creation, the truth of the virgin birth, the truth of Christ's miracles, Christ's substitutionary death, and His coming again. But they stop there with these and other individual truths. When I say Christianity is true I mean it is true to total reality—the total of what is. . . . Christianity is not just a series of truths but *Truth*—Truth about all of reality."

4. Harry Blamires, *The Christian Mind* (New York: Seabury, 1963), 3, emphasis added.

5. Michael Weiskopf, "Energized by Pulpit or Passion, the Public Is Calling: 'Gospel Grapevine' Displays Strength in Controversy Over Military Gay Ban," *The Washington Post,* February 1, 1993, A1.

6. Blamires, *Christian Mind,* 3-4, emphasis in original.

7. Charlie Peacock, *At the Crossroads: An Insider's Look at the Past, Present, and Future of Contemporary Christian Music* (Nashville: Broadman & Holman, 1999).

8. Cited in Allen C. Guelzo, "The Return of the Will," in *Edwards in Our Time: Jonathan Edwards and the Shaping of American Religion,* ed. Sang Hyun Lee and Allen C. Guelzo (Grand Rapids, Mich.: Eerdmans, 1999), 133.

9. Martin Marty, *The Modern Schism: Three Paths to the Secular* (New York: Harper & Row, 1969), 40. See also 57, 92, 96.

10. Sidney Mead, *The Old Religion in the Brave New World: Reflections on the Relation Between Christendom and the Republic* (Los Angeles: University of California Press, 1977), 4.

11. Dorothy L. Sayers, *Creed or Chaos?* (Manchester, N.H.: Sophia, 1949), 77.

12. Bob Briner, *Roaring Lambs* (Grand Rapids, Mich.: Zondervan, 2000), 17-18.

13. Terry Mattingly, "Veggies Attack the Funny Gap," Scripps Howard News Service, October 2, 2002.

14. Fritjof Capra, *The Tao of Physics* (Boston: Shambhala, 2000).

15. Despite this discouraging conversation, I did end up writing that article on the new physics for the *Bible-Science Newsletter*—in fact, two articles: Nancy Pearcey, "The New Physics and the New Consciousness," parts 1 and 2, *Bible-Science Newsletter,* October 1986 and November 1986. I later expanded the material to form two chapters in a book on the history and philosophy of science, *The Soul of Science.* See chapter 8 on relativity theory, "Is Everything Relative? The Revolution in Physics," and chapter 9 on quantum mechanics, "Quantum Mysteries: Making Sense of the New Physics." I was joined in the project by Charles Thaxton, who provided scientific expertise and review (Nancy Pearcey and Charles Thaxton, *The Soul of Science: Christian Faith and Natural Philosophy* [Wheaton, Ill: Crossway, 1994], hereafter cited as *Soul of Science*).

16. See H. Evan Runner, *The Relation of the Bible to Learning* (Toronto: Wedge, 1970), 16.

17. "I will sprinkle clean water on you, and you shall be clean from all your uncleanness, and from all your idols" (Ezek. 36:25).

18. On these developments in the philosophy of science, see Nancy Pearcey, "The Science of Science," *Bible-Science Newsletter,* August 1983; Nancy Pearcey, "From Tyrant to Tool: A New View of Science," *Bible-Science Newsletter,* April 1986. For a later treatment, see *Soul of Science,* especially chapter 2.

19. Roy Clouser, *The Myth of Religious Neutrality: An Essay on the Hidden Role of Religious Belief in Theories* (Notre Dame, Ind.: University of Notre Dame Press, 1991), 87.

20. John Gray, "Exposing the Myth of Secularism," *Australian Financial Review,* January 3, 2003, at http://afr.com/review/2003/01/03/FFX9CQAJFAD.html.

21. R. G. Collingwood, *An Essay on Metaphysics* (Chicago: Regnery, 1972; orig., London: Oxford University Press, 1940), 253-257. "Matter in the Platonic sense, which must be 'prevailed upon' by reason, will not obey mathematical laws exactly: [On the other hand,] matter which God has created from nothing may well strictly follow the rules which its Creator has laid down for it. In this sense I called modern science a legacy, I might even have said a child, of Christianity" (Carl von Weizsacker, *The Relevance of Science* [New York: Harper & Row, 1964], 163).

22. For a historical account of the relationship between Christianity and mathematics, see Nancy Pearcy, "Mind Your Mathematics: A Two-Part Series on the Role of Mathematics in Science," *Bible-Science Newsletter,* March 1990; Nancy Pearcey, "The Rise and Fall of Mathematics," *Bible-Science Newsletter,* April 1990. I later expanded this material into two chapters in *Soul of Science* (chapters 6 and 7). A good treatment of the philosophy of mathematics can be found in Roy Clouser, *Myth of Religious Neutrality,* chapter 7.

23. *Getting to Know "Connected Mathematics Project,"* April 30, 1996, Teacher's Guide, 17; cited in Michael Chapman, "Worldview War in the Classroom," in *No Retreats, No Reserves, No Regrets,* ed. Brannon Howse (St. Paul, Minn.: Stewart, 2000), 149. Connected Mathematics Project is a complete grades 6–8 mathematics curriculum developed at Michigan State University with funds from the National Science Foundation.

24. *Minnesota State Statutes Governing the Licensing of Teachers,* 106, 111. Cited in ibid.

25. Reality is multilayered, and at levels where reality is simpler, agreement between Christians and non-Christians will be broader. The simplest level is sheer quantity—the level of mathematics. At a somewhat higher level is the application of mathematics to the physical world—physics—where theoretical constructs play a greater role. At a higher level yet is biology, where disagreements grow wider still. The most complex levels are the human sciences, and here the divergences are greatest—in subjects like psychology, morality, and finally religion. The higher you go up the scale, the greater the role played by philosophical and faith commitments, and hence the greater the differences in perspective. Herman Dooyeweerd calls this the "modal scale," and distinguishes fourteen levels: numerical, spatial, physical, biotic, psychical, logical, historical, linguistic, social, economic, aesthetic, juridical, moral, and pistic (faith). Each level is represented by an academic discipline. For a readable introduction, see L. Kalsbeek, *Contours of a Christian Philosophy: An Introduction to Herman Dooyeweerd's Thought,* ed. Bernard and Josina Zylstra (Toronto: Wedge, 1975). Dooyeweerd taught at the Free University of Amsterdam, which is housed in a building fourteen stories high, with each floor devoted to one of the levels in Dooyeweerd's "modal scale." The top floor houses the theology department; just under it is philosophy, then law, and so on. See David Caudill, "A Calvinist Perspective on the Place of Faith in Legal Scholarship," in Michael McConnell, ed., *Christian Perspectives on Legal Thought* (New Haven, Conn.: Yale University Press, 2001), 313.

26. Os Guinness, *The Gravedigger File: Papers on the Subversion of the Modern Church* (Downers Grove, Ill.: InterVarsity Press, 1984), 43, 44, emphasis added.

27. Clouser, *Myth of Religious Neutrality,* 80.

28. Other passages on this theme include Isaiah 6:9-10; 42:18-20; 43:8; Matthew 15:14; 23:16ff.; 2 Peter 1:9.

29. When I lecture on the Cultural Mandate, many people say that they have never encountered the concept before. Thus readers may benefit from my more detailed treatment of the Cultural Mandate in "Saved to What?" chapter 31 in *How Now?*

30. C. S. Lewis, *The Last Battle* (New York: HarperCollins, 1994), 211.

31. Francis Schaeffer makes this point in *True Spirituality,* in *Complete Works,* vol. 3, 200-201.

32. Gene Edward Veith, *God at Work: Your Christian Vocation in All of Life* (Wheaton, Ill.: Crossway, 2002). See also Veith's *The Spirituality of the Cross* (St. Louis: Concordia, 1999), 71ff.

33. Veith, *Spirituality of the Cross.* See also D. G. Hart, *Recovering Mother Kirk: The Case for Liturgy in the Reformed Tradition* (Grand Rapids, Mich.: Baker, 2003), chapter 12, "What Can Presbyterians Learn from Lutherans?"

34. "This small, intense man from the Swiss mountains delivered a message unlike any heard in evangelical circles in the mid-1960s. At Wheaton College, students were fighting to show films like Bambi, while Francis was talking about the films of Bergman and Fellini. Administrators

were censoring existential themes out of student publications, while Francis was discussing Camus, Sartre, and Heidegger. He quoted Dylan Thomas, knew the artwork of Salvador Dali, listened to the music of the Beatles and John Cage" (Michael Hamilton, "The Dissatisfaction of Francis Schaeffer" [*Christianity Today,* March 3, 1997], at http://www.antithesis.com/features/dissatisfaction.html).

35. Schaeffer has been criticized by some academic specialists for various aspects of his treatment of intellectual history. However, one need not agree with Schaeffer's analyses at every point in order to appreciate the way he conceptualized basic themes in philosophy, art, and culture so that questioning students and other seekers could understand and apply them. Many of those students went on to earn advanced degrees, specializing in various areas of scholarship. Thus Schaeffer played an important "bridging" role in leading young people into the intellectual and cultural world.

36. The apologetics arguments that I encountered at L'Abri, and that I eventually found persuasive, are woven throughout the rest of this book, especially in chapters 3, 7, and 11, and in appendix 4.

37. Augustine, *Confessions,* I.1.

38. This everyday artistry was a conscious attempt to express our relationship with a God of beauty. Edith Schaeffer explained her philosophy of finding beauty in ordinary life in *Hidden Art* (Wheaton, Ill.: Tyndale, 1972). For a shorter treatment, listen to her lecture titled "The Art of Life and the Courage to Be Creative," at http://www.soundword.com.

39. See, for example, Francis Schaeffer, *The New Super-Spirituality,* in *Complete Works,* vol. 3, 388; and *The God Who Is There,* in *Complete Works,* vol. 1, 27-31.

40. Schaeffer, *God Who Is There,* in *Complete Works,* vol. 1, 34.

41. The church is pastored by Erwin McManus, author of *An Unstoppable Force* (Loveland, Colo.: Group, 2001); and *Seizing Your Divine Moment* (Nashville: Nelson, 2002). See McManus's essay, "Fulfilling the Vision," at http://www.mosaic.org.

42. Quentin Smith, "The Metaphilosophy of Naturalism," in *Philo* 4, no. 2 (Fall/Winter 2001), at http://www.philoonline.org/library/smith_4_2.htm.

43. Smith debates William Lane Craig in *Theism, Atheism and Big Bang Cosmology* (New York: Oxford University Press, 1995).

44. Alvin Plantinga, *God and Other Minds: A Study of the Rational Justification of Belief in God* (Ithaca, N.Y., Cornell University Press, 1967, 1990).

45. Smith, "Metaphilosophy of Naturalism."

46. Sigmund Freud. *The Future of an Illusion,* trans. and ed. James Strachey (New York: Norton, 1961), 43.

47. Patrick Glynn, *God, The Evidence: The Reconciliation of Faith and Reason in a Postsecular World* (Rocklin, Calif.: Prima, 1997), 62.

48. Glynn, *God, The Evidence,* 20. I have described much more of the medical evidence supporting a positive relation between faith and health in, "Don't Worry, Be Religious," chapter 32 in *How Now?* See also Dale A. Matthews, Michael E. McCullough, David B. Larson, Harold G. Koenig, James P. Swyers, and Mary Greenwold Milano, "Religious Commitment and Health Status: A Review of the Research and Implications for Family Medicine," in *Archives of Family Medicine* 7, no. 2 (March/April 1998), at http://archfami.ama-assn.org/issues/v7n2/ffull/fsa6025.html.

49. Cited in a press release from the International Center for the Integration of Health and Spirituality, "Scientists, Doctors Gather to Define and Measure Spirituality," January 15, 1997, at http://www.nihr.org/programs/archivedreleases.cfm.

50. See, for example, the interview with Benson by John Koch in *The Boston Globe Magazine,* November 9, 1997, at http://www.boston.com/globe/magazine/11-16/interview/.

51. Guenter Lewy, *Why America Needs Religion* (Grand Rapids, Mich.: Eerdmans, 1996), x.

52. Ibid., 132-133.

53. For more on this topic, see chapter 12.

54. Cited in Marvin Olasky, *The Tragedy of American Compassion* (Washington, D.C.: Regnery; Wheaton, Ill.: Crossway, 1992), 48. See online at www.olasky.com/Archives/toac/03%20(word5).pdf. Chapter 3, page 8.

CHAPTER 2: REDISCOVERING JOY

1. Charles Malik, *The Two Tasks* (Westchester, Ill.: Cornerstone, 1980), 32.
2. Sealy Yates, in discussion with the author.
3. See Joseph G. Allegretti, *The Lawyer's Calling: Christian Faith and Legal Practice* (Mahwah, N.J.: Paulist, 1996). For an analysis of Christian approaches to law, see *Christian Perspectives on Legal Thought,* ed. Michael McConnell (New Haven, Conn.: Yale University Press, 2001).
4. Lesslie Newbigin, *Our Task Today.* An unpublished paper given to the fourth meeting of the diocesan council, Tirumangalam, India, December 18-20, 1951. Cited in Michael Goheen, "The Missional Calling of Believers in the World: Lesslie Newbigin's Contribution," at http://www.deepsight.org/articles/goheenb.htm.
5. Lesslie Newbigin, *Truth to Tell: The Gospel as Public Truth* (Grand Rapids, Mich.: Eerdmans, 1991), 49.
6. Andy Crouch, "Christian Esperanto: We Must Learn Other Cultural Tongues," in *Christianity Today,* April, 2003.
7. Wade Clark Roof, *Spiritual Marketplace: Baby Boomers and the Remaking of American Religion* (Princeton, N.J.: Princeton University Press, 1999), 7.
8. Peter Berger, *Facing Up to Modernity: Excursions in Society, Politics, and Religion* (New York: Basic Books, 1977), 18. Berger is referring specifically to the private sphere of the family, but it is an apt description of the private sphere generally.
9. Peter Berger, *The Sacred Canopy: Elements of a Sociological Theory of Religion* (New York: Doubleday, 1967), 134.
10. Walter Kasper, "Nature, Grace, and Culture: On the Meaning of Secularization," in *Catholicism and Secularization in America: Essays on Nature, Grace, and Culture,* ed. David L. Schindler (Huntington, Ind.: Our Sunday Visitor, Communio Books, 1990), 38.
11. Lesslie Newbigin, *Foolishness to the Greeks: The Gospel and Western Culture* (Grand Rapids, Mich.: Eerdmans, 1986), 31.
12. Lesslie Newbigin, *The Gospel in a Pluralist Society* (Grand Rapids, Mich.: Eerdmans, 1989), 172.
13. In 1995, Smith and his team conducted 130 two-hour interviews. In 1996, they conducted 2,591 telephone surveys (2,087 of which were with churchgoing Protestants). Later in 1996, they conducted 178 two-hour interviews with evangelical Protestants. They also did phone interviews with 8 people who had identified themselves in the phone interviews as "fundamentalists" and 6 who called themselves "liberal Protestants." See Christian Smith, with Michael Emerson, Sally Gallagher, Paul Kennedy, and David Sikkink, *American Evangelicalism: Embattled and Thriving* (Chicago: University of Chicago Press, 1998), 17.
14. The labels were based on self-definition: e.g., if someone identified himself as an evangelical Presbyterian, he was placed in the "evangelical" category, while if he identified himself as a liberal Presbyterian, he was slotted into the "liberal" category. As a result, the number of evangelicals is smaller (7 percent of the population) than in most other surveys, where subjects are identified according to standards selected by the survey-taker, such as denominational affiliation or specific doctrinal beliefs.
15. Surprisingly, evangelicals outrank even fundamentalists on all but one measure. The reason, Smith suggests, may be that fundamentalists tend to embrace a subculture mentality—remaining culturally isolated in their churches, schools, and parachurch organizations. Moreover, the doctrine of premillennial dispensationalism, which is more common among fundamentalists, is sometimes interpreted to imply that the world is on a downward slide, and thus that reform is useless. (Why polish the brass on a sinking ship?) This lack of engagement with the outside world may be the reason that fundamentalists demonstrated a slightly greater complacency about their faith as compared to evangelicals, who place more emphasis on reaching out to the surrounding culture. Regular confrontation with a hostile culture, Smith suggests, may actually make for a more alert and active faith commitment (Smith, *American Evangelicalism,* 145-147).
16. This is a result of an atomistic view of society, which conceives of social groups as merely aggregates of individuals. To understand the sources of this individualistic social philosophy among evangelicals, see part 3.
17. Smith, *American Evangelicalism,* 188, 190.
18. Ibid., 203.

402 TOTAL TRUTH

19. Ibid., 204, 205, 206.
20. Ibid., 194.
21. Ibid., 201, 198.
22. Plato, *Complete Works,* ed. John M. Cooper (Indianapolis: Hackett, 1997), Laws, book 10, 1542-1566.
23. Schaeffer critiques the two-story concept of truth in *Escape from Reason* and *The God Who Is There* (in *The Complete Works of Francis A. Schaeffer,* vol. 1 [Wheaton, Ill.: Crossway, 1982]), though he begins with Aquinas instead of the Greeks. Schaeffer's critique is similar to the more detailed analysis offered by Herman Dooyeweerd in *Roots of Western Culture: Pagan, Secular, and Christian Options* (Toronto: Wedge, 1979; orig., Zutphen, Netherlands: J. B. van den Brink, 1959); and *In the Twilight of Western Thought* (Nutley, N.J.: Craig, 1972; orig., Presbyterian & Reformed, 1960).
24. To be precise, we will be dealing with the religious interpretation of Plato, which began with the Jewish philosopher Philo and came to its fullest expression in the third century in the work of Plotinus. When I say "Plato," I will be referring to this religious interpretation of Plato, often referred to as neo-Platonism, which was the most powerful conduit of Greek thought to later centuries. (For greater detail, see appendix 2.) Historically, there was considerable merging and overlapping of Platonic with Aristotelian thought, though for simplicity's sake we will consider them separately here. For an accessible discussion of Plato and Aristotle and their impact on Christian thought, see Arthur Holmes, *Fact, Value, and God* (Grand Rapids, Mich.: Eerdmans, 1997).
25. See Charles Norris Cochrane, *Christianity and Classical Culture: A Study of Thought and Action from Augustus to Augustine* (New York: Oxford University Press, 1957), 342, 390, 417.
26. See J. P. Moreland and Scott B. Rae, *Body and Soul: Human Nature and the Crisis in Ethics* (Downers Grove, Ill.: InterVarsity Press, 2000).
27. Pastor and author John Piper says, "I've tried to define the flesh as Paul uses it. Most of the time . . . it does not simply refer to the physical part of you. (Paul does not regard the body as evil in itself.) The flesh is the ego which feels an emptiness and uses the resources in its own power to try to fill it. Flesh is the 'I' who tries to satisfy me with anything but God's mercy" (from a sermon titled "The War Within: Flesh Versus Spirit," at http://www.soundof grace.com/piper83/061983m.htm).
28. Robert Louis Wilken, *The Spirit of Early Christian Thought: Seeing the Face of God* (New Haven, Conn.: Yale University Press, 2003), chapter 1, passim.
29. For a readable account of the way many Christian thinkers were influenced by the dualistic thinking of Greek philosophy, see Brian Walsh and J. Richard Middleton, *The Transforming Vision* (Downers Grove, Ill.: InterVarsity Press, 1984), chapter 7.
30. Colin Gunton, *The One, the Three, and the Many: God, Creation, and the Culture of Modernity* (New York: Cambridge University Press, 1993), 2, 138.
31. Henry Chadwick, *Augustine: A Very Short Introduction* (Oxford: Oxford University Press, 2001), 64-65, 122.
32. G. K. Chesterton, *Saint Thomas Aquinas, "The Dumb Ox"* (1933; reprint, Garden City, N.Y.: Doubleday, 1956), 92.
33. Anglican philosopher Langmead Casserly says that Aquinas is best regarded as an apologist rather than as a philosopher per se: "The Aristotelian revival had put the Faith on the intellectual defensive in Europe for the first time since the collapse of the Western Empire." Thus Aquinas was not merely engaging in detached, objective philosophical inquiry; rather, "He is first and foremost an apologist, coping with a desperate intellectual situation. . . . He was the first apologist to perceive that the very essence of the strategy of apologetics is to concede as much as possible to one's opponent and to base one's argument on his assumptions. . . . This essential Thomistic strategy has been adopted by all wise Christian apologists since his time." In short, Aquinas's goal was to show the Aristotelians of his day that *even on their own premises* Christianity could account better for what they themselves believed to be true (J. V. Langmead Casserly, *The Christian in Philosophy* [New York: Scribner's, 1951], 77, 81-82).
34. Aquinas did not originate the juxtaposition of nature and grace; it was already part of the vocabulary of medieval theologians. An early example was a book by Augustine. Having read a work by Pelagius titled *Nature,* Augustine answered with his own *Nature and Grace.* See

Garry Wills, *Saint Augustine* (New York: Penguin, 1999), 125. What was innovative about Aquinas was that he gave "nature" an Aristotelian definition.

35. Roger French and Andrew Cunningham, *Before Science: The Invention of the Friars' Natural Philosophy* (Aldershot, Hampshire, UK: Ashgate, 1996), 202. The authors are describing the outlook of the Dominicans as a group, especially of Aquinas's teacher Albertus Magnus. For a summary, see Nancy Pearcey, "Recent Developments in the History of Science and Christianity," and "Reply," *Pro Rege* 30, no. 4 (June 2002): 1-11, 20-22.

36. French and Cunningham, *Before Science,* 183-202.

37. Thomas Aquinas, *Summa Theologica* I-II, q. 109, art. 2.

38. Michael Lapierre, S.J., "Grace in Thomas Aquinas," at http://www.catholic-church.org/grace/western/scholars/lap1.htm. Lapierre is endorsing this radical dualism.

39. Jacques Maritain, *Integral Humanism: Temporal and Spiritual Problems of a New Christendom,* trans. Joseph Evans (New York: Scribner's, 1968), 22.

40. Philip Melanchthon, *The Augsburg Confession* (1530), art. 26, "Of the Distinction of Meats," at http://www.iclnet.org/pub/resources/text/wittenberg/concord/web/augs-026.html.

41. Alister McGrath, "Calvin and the Christian Calling," *First Things* 94 (June/July 1999): 31-35.

42. John Kok, *Patterns of the Western Mind: A Reformed Christian Perspective* (Sioux Center, Ia.: Dordt College Press, 1998), 124, 125.

43. John D. Beckett, *Loving Monday: Succeeding in Business Without Selling Your Soul* (Downers Grove, Ill.: InterVarsity Press, 1998), 53.

44. Ibid., 58, 68, 69.

45. Gordon Clark, *Thales to Dewey: A History of Philosophy* (Boston: Houghton Mifflin, 1957), 192.

46. Albert M. Wolters, *Creation Regained: Biblical Basics for a Reformational Worldview* (Grand Rapids, Mich.: Eerdmans, 1985), 49ff.

47. Alexander Solzhenitsyn, *The Gulag Archipelago, 1918–1956: An Experiment in Literary Investigation,* III-IV (New York: Harper & Row, 1973), 615.

48. C. S. Lewis, *The Great Divorce* (New York: Macmillan, 1946), 28.

49. Beckett, *Loving Monday,* 72.

50. Paul Theroux, interview by Susan Olasky, "Agents of Virtue," *World,* March 15, 2003.

51. Robert Bellah, "At Home and Not at Home: Religious Pluralism and Religious Truth," *The Christian Century,* April 19, 1995, 423-428.

52. A brief description of the Holiness movement can be found in "American Holiness Movement," at http://mb-soft.com/believe/text/holiness.htm. The idea of perfection arose as a reaction against Roman Catholicism with its two-tiered spirituality, where ordinary believers were expected to fulfill only the minimum requirements of morality and religion, while the professionally religious (monks, nuns, priests) were to follow what were called the "counsels of perfection." (The phrase is based on Matthew 19:21, "If you would be perfect, go, sell what you possess and give to the poor.") Protestants rejected the Catholic two-tiered conception by insisting that *all* Christians are called to total commitment to God, and *all* are admonished to "Be perfect, as your heavenly Father is perfect" (Matt. 5:48). However, most Protestants do not think we are capable of fulfilling that calling this side of heaven.

53. Wolters, *Creation Regained,* 62-63.

54. The same argument is offered today by some Catholics to support priestly celibacy. "The triumph of celibacy is a holy anticipation of eternity 'where there is neither marrying nor giving in marriage, but all are like the angels of God,' those perfect heralds of his Word and doers of his Will" (Fr. Vincent Miceli, S.J., review of *Celibacy and the Crisis of Faith,* by Dietrich von Hildebrand, at http://www.ewtn.com/library/PRIESTS/HILDEBRA.HTM); "Celibacy, in the Church, thus draws attention to the new order of the gospel, whereas marriage has its roots in the old order. . . . [Celibacy] is a sign of the world to come" (Max Thurian, "The Theological Basis for Priestly Celibacy," at http://www.vatican.va/roman_curia/congregations/cclergy/documents/rc_con_cclergy_doc_01011993_theol_en.html). Of course, one may embrace singleness and celibacy for reasons that do *not* denigrate marriage, such as the freedom to give oneself wholly to ministry.

55. Paul denotes "perfect" with the term *teleios* (Col. 1:28; 4:12—ESV "mature"), which he contrasts to *nepios,* "childish" (1 Cor. 3:1), which denotes moral immaturity and deficiency.

The "perfect man," *teleion,* is the stable person who reflects "the measure of the stature of the fullness of Christ," in contrast to the children (*nepioi*) who are tossed about by every new wind of doctrine (Eph. 4:13-14).

56. One way this is reflected in Catholic theology is that original sin is conceived primarily as a *deprivation* of the super-added grace, leaving human nature weakened and vulnerable to disordered appetites but not morally corrupt, as Protestantism teaches. That is, according to Catholicism, sin is a subtraction from an original good, not the addition of a positive force of rebellion and evil. The *Catechism of the Catholic Church* says, "Adam and Eve transmitted to their descendants human nature wounded by their own first sin and hence deprived of original holiness and justice; this deprivation is called 'original sin'" (art. 417).

57. Hermann Dooyeweerd describes the nature/grace dualism (which he rejects) in these words: "Man lost this gift [of superadded grace] at the fall, and as a result he was reduced to mere 'human nature,' with all its weaknesses. But this human 'nature,' which is guided by the natural light of reason, was not corrupted by sin and thus also does not need to be restored by Christ" (*Roots of Western Culture,* 116-117; see also Dooyeweerd, *In the Twilight of Western Thought,* 191-194).

58. Louis Dupré, "Nature and Grace: Fateful Separation and Attempted Reunion," in *Catholicism and Secularization in America,* 59, 62, 61. Put another way, the nature/grace dualism implied "the assumed continuity of nature throughout the historical stages of innocence, fall, and redemption." (That is, the lower story is not affected by the fall and redemption.) The result was the idea of "an independent, quasi-autonomous natural order," a concept that "continued to hold sway over Catholic theology until the second half of the twentieth century" (61). In the mid-twentieth century there arose a school of thought within Catholicism (called *nouvelle theologie*) that rejected the nature/grace dualism. Excellent discussions by Catholic thinkers, echoing Schaeffer's imagery of "two stories," can be found in several of the essays in *Catholicism and Secularization in America.* For example, Walter Kasper describes the development of a "dualistic and separatist conception" of nature and grace, which he calls a "two-story system" ("Nature, Grace, and Culture," 41).

Similarly, in *Does God Exist?* (London: Collins, 1980), Hans Küng writes, "Cartesianism and Thomism clearly divide the two ways of knowing (natural reason and grace-inspired faith), two planes of knowledge (natural truth and grace-given revealed truth), two sciences (philosophy and theology). . . . Two spheres, even—as it were—like two floors of a building" (21). See also 23-24, 35-38, 67, 511, 518-522.

Catholic critics generally believe the problem lay not in Aquinas's formulation of nature and grace but in later scholasticism, as the two stories became increasingly independent and autonomous, e.g., in Cajetan, Molina, and Suarez. See Fr. Wojciech Giertych, OP, "Fundamental Moral Theology," at http://www.cfpeople.org/Books/Moral/cfptoc.htm; and International Catholic University, "Nature and Grace: Lesson One: The Natural Desire to See God—History," at http://icu.catholicity.com/c01601.htm. (Contrary to misreadings of his work, Francis Schaeffer was careful not to charge Aquinas with the dualism of later thinkers—see Ronald Nash's sensitive analysis in "The Life of the Mind and the Way of Life," in *Francis A. Schaeffer: Portraits of the Man and His Work,* ed. Lane Dennis [Westchester, Ill.: Crossway, 1986], 59-60.)

59. Cited in Richard Russell, "Biblical Foundations for Philosophy," at http://www.biblical creation.org.uk/theology_philosophy/bcs069.html.

CHAPTER 3: KEEPING RELIGION IN ITS PLACE

1. Freeman J. Dyson, "Is God in the Lab?" *The New York Review of Books,* May 28, 1998, emphasis added.

2. Alan Sears, in discussion with the author, December 30, 2002.

3. Christian Smith, "Introduction: Rethinking the Secularization of American Life," in *The Secular Revolution: Power, Interest, and Conflict in the Secularization of American Public Life,* ed. Christian Smith (Los Angeles: University of California Press, 2003), 2-3.

4. Kathleen Nielson, private correspondence, April 28, 2003.

5. See Roy Clouser, *The Myth of Religious Neutrality: An Essay on the Hidden Role of Religious Belief in Theories* (Notre Dame, Ind.: University of Notre Dame Press, 1991), 86-87.

6. Anselm of Canterbury, *Why God Became Man.* A similar defense had been made in the fourth

century by Athanasius. For readable introductions to both, see Tony Lane, *Exploring Christian Thought* (Nashville: Nelson, 1984).

7. Some contemporary Catholic thinkers concur with Protestant critics that the nature/grace dualism led to secularism. For example, Walter Kasper writes, "the two-story system . . . favored a humanism without God as well as a Christianity that had become alienated from the world. . . . In this way, the Baroque and neo-Scholastic understanding of the relation between nature and grace was one of the sources of modern secularization" ("Nature, Grace, and Culture: On the Meaning of Secularization," in *Catholicism and Secularization in America: Essays on Nature, Grace, and Culture,* ed. David L. Schindler [Huntington, Ind.: Our Sunday Visitor, Communio Books, 1990], 41).

8. Walker Percy, *Love in the Ruins* (New York: Avon, 1978), 181.

9. On the broad impact that Descartes' mechanistic philosophy had historically, see my discussion extended throughout several chapters in *Soul of Science* (chapters 1, 3, 4, and 6). The history of science gives a good handle on intellectual history generally, since every major system of thought includes a philosophy of nature, which is often foundational to everything else. (Regarding Newton, ironically, he himself did not hold what came to be called the Newtonian worldview. See *Soul of Science*, chapter 4.)

10. Hume pointed out that if we are strict empiricists, limiting our claims to what appears to the senses, then we cannot defend even concepts that are fundamental to science, such as causality. For we never perceive a cause as such; all we actually perceive are events following one another. We may say that fire "causes" heat, but all we actually perceive is the sight of fire followed by the sensation of heat. See *Soul of Science,* 138-139.

11. On Kant's nature/freedom dichotomy, see Francis Schaeffer, *Escape from Reason,* in *The Complete Works of Francis A. Schaeffer,* vol. 1 (Wheaton, Ill.: Crossway, 1982), 227-229; and Herman Dooyeweerd, *Roots of Western Culture: Pagan, Secular, and Christian Options* (Toronto: Wedge, 1979; orig., Zutphen, Netherlands: J. B. van den Brink, 1959), 171.

12. Immanuel Kant, *Groundwork of the Metaphysic of Morals* (New York: Harper & Row, 1964), 123.

13. Rousseau's thought is analyzed in greater detail in chapter 4.

14. Colin Gunton, *Enlightenment and Alienation: An Essay Towards a Trinitarian Theology* (Grand Rapids, Mich.: Eerdmans, 1985), 61.

15. Immanuel Kant, *Groundwork of the Metaphysic of Morals* (New York: Harper & Row, 1964), 116, 123.

16. Colin Brown, *Philosophy and the Christian Faith* (Downers Grove, Ill.: InterVarsity Press, 1968), 105. Arthur Holmes offers a more positive interpretation of Kant in *Fact, Value, and God* (Grand Rapids, Mich.: Eerdmans, 1997), chapter 10.

17. Richard Dawkins, *The Blind Watchmaker* (New York: Norton, 1986), 6.

18. See chapters 7 and 8 for a more detailed discussion of these themes.

19. Peter Kreeft, in an interview at http://www.christianbook.com/Christian/Books/cms_content/92165368?page=364779&insert=7843899&cvent=ESRC>100f743.jpg. Emphasis added.

20. For a briefer treatment, see Nancy Pearcey, "The Transforming Power of a Christian Worldview," delivered October 11, 2003, as part of a lecture series titled "Developing a Gospel Worldview," sponsored by Manna Christian Fellowship, Princeton University.

21. Steven Pinker, *How the Mind Works,* 55, emphasis added. See Phillip Johnson's discussion of Pinker in *The Wedge of Truth: Splitting the Foundations of Naturalism* (Downers Grove, Ill.: InterVarsity Press, 2000).

22. Pinker, *How the Mind Works,* 55-56, emphasis added.

23. Steven Pinker, *The Blank Slate: The Modern Denial of Human Nature* (New York: Viking, 2002), 240.

24. Marvin Minsky, *The Society of Mind* (New York: Simon & Schuster, 1985), 307, emphasis added.

25. Transcript of a television interview with John Searle from a program titled "Thinking Allowed: Conversations on the Leading Edge of Knowledge and Discovery," with Dr. Jeffrey Mishlove, at http://www.williamjames.com/transcripts/searle.htm, emphasis added.

26. Schaeffer, *Escape from Reason,* in *Complete Works,* vol. 1, 212. When Schaeffer was writing, the term *postmodernism* had not been coined yet, but clearly he was dealing with the same concept when he spoke about a "line of despair" (despair of finding rational grounds for

human morality and meaning), followed by a "leap of faith" to an irrational, upper-story experience. Millard Erickson notes Schaeffer's anticipation of postmodernism in *Postmodernizing the Faith: Evangelical Responses to the Challenge of Postmodernism* (Grand Rapids, Mich.: Baker, 1998), chapter 4.

27. Schaeffer, *True Spirituality,* in *Complete Works,* vol. 3, 172-173.

28. Schaeffer, *The God Who Is There,* in *Complete Works,* vol. 1, 122, emphasis added. This argument is developed in greater detail in chapter 11 of the present book.

29. John Searle, interview by Terry McDermott, "No Limits Hinder UC Thinker," *The Los Angeles Times,* December 28, 1999.

30. The forum is available at http://www.edge.org/3rd_culture/dawkins_pinker/debate_p1.html. Pinker makes similar claims in his latest book, *The Blank Slate: The Modern Denial of Human Nature* (New York: Viking, 2002).

31. See Paul M. Churchland and Patricia Churchland, *On the Contrary: Critical Essays, 1987–1997* (Cambridge, Mass.: Bradford/MIT Press, 1998). See also Phillip Johnson's analysis in *Wedge of Truth,* 118.

32. Daniel Wegner, *The Illusion of Conscious Will* (Cambridge, Mass.: MIT Press, 2002). For an excellent analysis of eliminative materialism from a Christian perspective, see Angus Menuge, *Agents Under Fire: Materialism and the Rationality of Science* (Lanham, Md.: Rowman & Littlefield, 2004).

33. This quotation is from a discussion of Dennett's views by Teed Rockwell, *Dictionary of Philosophy of Mind,* at http://www.artsci.wustl.edu/~philos/MindDict/eliminativism.html. See Daniel Dennett, *The Intentional Stance* (Cambridge, Mass.: Bradford, 1987).

34. The poll was taken for the National Association of Scholars and is discussed by John Leo in "Professors Who See No Evil," at http://www.usnews.com/usnews/issue/020722/opinion/22john.htm.

35. See Paul Gross and Norman Levitt, *Higher Superstition: The Academic Left and Its Quarrels with Science* (Baltimore: Johns Hopkins University Press, 1994).

36. Jacques Barzun, *The Use and Abuse of Art* (Princeton, N.J.: Princeton University Press, 1974), 53. Another good source on the subject is M. H. Abrams, *The Mirror and the Lamp: Romantic Theory and the Critical Tradition* (Oxford: Oxford University Press, 1953).

37. See Nancy Pearcey, "The Touch of Cold Philosophy: Darwinism and the Arts," paper presented at the Second Wedge conference at Biola University, December 12, 2003. I have touched on the same themes within a broader treatment of the relationship between Christianity and the arts in "Soli Deo Gloria," chapter 42 in *How Now?*

38. William Thompson, "The Imagination of Jerry Brown," *The New York Times,* February 24, 1978, op-ed page.

39. See Schaeffer, *God Who Is There,* in *Complete Works,* vol. 1, 51-55. I am using the term *liberalism* broadly to include both the earlier theological liberalism stemming from Friedrich Schleiermacher and the later neo-orthodoxy of figures like Karl Barth, Paul Tillich, Rudolf Bultmann, and the Niebuhr brothers (Richard and Reinhold). Though the neo-orthodox theologians sought to recover a richer grasp of biblical *content,* they never broke free from the two-realm *epistemology.* For a detailed discussion, see Douglas Sloan, *Faith and Knowledge: Mainline Protestantism and American Higher Education* (Louisville: Westminster John Knox, 1994). Sloan defines the two-realm theory of truth as "the view that on the one side there are the truths of knowledge as these are given predominantly by science and discursive, empirical reason. On the other side are the truths of the faith, religious experience, morality, meaning, and value." The problem is that "the latter are seen as grounded not in knowledge but variously in feeling, ethical action, communal convention, folk tradition, or unfathomable mystical experience" (ix). In short, for the neo-orthodox theologians, faith remained an upper-story, "existential leap into the unknown" (114).

40. For an example of the way history has been identified with philosophical naturalism, see Crane Brinton, *Ideas and Men: The Story of Western Thought,* 2nd ed. (Englewood Cliffs, N.J.: Prentice-Hall, 1963). As a historian, Brinton says he offers a "naturalistic-historical" study of Christianity (108-109), and a "naturalistic or positivistic explanation" of both Judaism and Christianity (78). "For the purposes of historical analysis," Brinton says he assumes that both religions are "products of human culture in historic time" (77). Brinton seems to assume that, when speaking as a professional historian, he must squeeze religion into naturalistic categories, reducing it to subjective belief, a product of the human mind.

41. William Reville, "God Knows, Richard Dawkins Is Wrong," *The Irish Times,* March 13, 2003.

42. See Schaeffer, *God Who Is There,* in *Complete Works,* vol. 1, 7-8.

43. Cited in Peter Berger, *Facing Up to Modernity: Excursions in Society, Politics, and Religion* (New York: Basic Books, 1977), 155.

44. Richard Cimino, "Choosing My Religion," *American Demographics,* April 1, 1999, at www.demographics.com/publications/ad/99_ad/9904_ad/ad990402.htm.

45. Wade Clark Roof, *A Generation of Seekers: The Spiritual Journeys of the Baby Boom Generation* (San Francisco: Harper, 1993), 30. See also Robert Fuller, "Spiritual, but Not Religious: More than One Fifth of Americans Describe Themselves With This Phrase. What Does It Mean?" at http://www.beliefnet.com (excerpted from Robert C. Fuller, *Spiritual, But Not Religious: Understanding Unchurched America* [New York: Oxford University Press, 2002]).

46. Terry Mattingly, "September 11's Impact on America's Faith Faded Fast," Scripps Howard News Service, September 13, 2002.

47. See Schaeffer, *God Who Is There,* in *Complete Works,* vol. 1, 11.

48. Bill Wichterman, "The Culture: Upstream from Politics," in *Building a Healthy Culture: Strategies for an American Renaissance,* ed. Don Eberly (Grand Rapids, Mich.: Eerdmans, 2001), 79.

49. Sidney Mead, *The Old Religion in the Brave New World: Reflections on the Relation Between Christendom and the Republic* (Los Angeles: University of California Press, 1977), 18-19.

50. Phillip E. Johnson, "Is God Unconstitutional? The Established Religious Philosophy of America," at http://www.arn.org/docs/johnson/unconst1.htm.

51. Nancy Pearcey, "Wedge Issue: An Intelligent Discussion with Intelligent Designer's Designer," *World,* July 29, 2000.

52. Sloan, *Faith and Knowledge,* 190.

53. C. S. Lewis, *Surprised by Joy* (New York: Harcourt Brace 1955), 170.

54. David Downing, *The Most Reluctant Convert* (Downers Grove, Ill.: InterVarsity Press, 2002), 148.

55. C. S. Lewis, *God in the Dock: Essays on Theology and Ethics,* ed. Walter Hooper (Grand Rapids, Mich.: Eerdmans, 1970), 66-67.

56. C. S. Lewis, *Surprised by Joy,* 235.

CHAPTER 4: SURVIVING THE SPIRITUAL WASTELAND

1. Albert M. Wolters, *Creation Regained: Biblical Basics for a Reformational Worldview* (Grand Rapids, Mich.: Eerdmans, 1985), 11.

2. Alan Watts, *Behold the Spirit* (New York: Pantheon, 1947); Aldous Huxley, *The Perennial Philosophy* (New York: Harper, 1945); Teilhard de Chardin, *The Phenomenon of Man* (New York: Perennial Library, 1959); and *Building the Earth* (Wilkes-Barre, Pa.: Dimension, 1965). The most prominent proponent of perennial philosophy today is Huston Smith, considered the premier scholar of world religions. For more on perennial philosophy, see appendix 2, "Modern Islam and the New Age Movement."

3. The ad was placed by Worldview Academy, based in New Braunfels, Texas.

4. Aldous Huxley, *The Doors of Perception* (New York: Harper & Row, 1963). When I first read Schaeffer's *The God Who Is There,* I was astonished to discover that, unlike most evangelical leaders at the time, he understood the philosophic motivation for using drugs: "This overwhelming desire for some nonrational [upper-story] experience was responsible for most of the serious use of the drugs LSD and STP in the 1960s. For the sensitive person, drugs were then not usually used for escape. On the contrary, he hoped that by taking them he would experience the reality of something which would give his life some meaning" (in *The Complete Works of Francis A. Schaeffer,* vol. 1 [Wheaton, Ill.: Crossway, 1982], 22). Similarly, in *The Church at the End of the Twentieth Century,* Schaeffer writes that every "serious" experimenter with drugs was following Aldous Huxley in looking for an "upper-story hope" (in *Complete Works,* vol. 4, 17).

5. For a charming account, see Thomas Cahill's *How the Irish Saved Civilization* (New York: Doubleday, 1995). You can also read my summary of Cahill's book in "Saved to What?" chapter 31 in *How Now?*

6. On behaviorism, see Nancy Pearcey, "Sensible Psychology: How Creation Makes the Difference," *Bible-Science Newsletter,* February 1986. Constructivist education is treated in greater detail in chapter 8 of the present book.

7. I have treated these themes in much greater detail in "Still at Risk," chapter 34 in *How Now?*

8. John Milton, "Of Learning" (1644), in *Tractate on Education* in *The Harvard Classics,* vol. 3, part 4 (New York: Collier, 1909–1914), at http://www.bartleby.com/3/4/1.html.

9. On New Age techniques in the classroom, see Nancy Pearcey, "East Meets West in Education," *Missourians for Educational Excellence,* April/May 1983; on bringing techniques from psychotherapy into the classroom, see Nancy Pearcey, "Classroom 'Therapy' and Family Alienation," *Missourians for Educational Excellence,* January/February 1983.

10. Bryce Christensen, *Utopia Against the Family: The Problems and Politics of the American Family* (San Francisco: Ignatius, 1990), 3, 11. Christensen writes from a Mormon perspective.

11. B. F. Skinner, *Walden Two* (New York: Macmillan, 1968), 297.

12. Ted Peters, *For the Love of Children: Genetic Technology and the Future of the Family* (Louisville: Westminster John Knox, 1997). For a review, see Nancy Pearcey, "I Take You . . ." in *First Things* 80 (February 1998): 48-53. On a similar note, British sociologist Anthony Giddens says that marriage and family should require separate contracts, such that each parent would sign an individual contract with each child. See Anthony Giddens, *The Third Way* (Cambridge: Polity, 2000).

13. Peters, *For the Love of Children,* 11, 31.

14. Process Theology is discussed in greater detail in chapter 8.

15. Francis Schaeffer, *True Spirituality,* in *Complete Works,* vol. 3, 344. See also Cornelius Van Til, *Christian Apologetics,* 2nd ed. (Phillipsburg, N.J.: Presbyterian & Reformed, 2003), 8; *The Defense of the Faith* (Philadelphia: Presbyterian & Reformed, 1955), 25; John D. Zizioulas, *Being As Communion: Studies in Personhood and the Church* (Crestwood, N.Y.: St. Vladimir's Seminary Press, 1985); Miroslav Volf, *After Our Likeness: The Church as the Image of the Trinity* (Grand Rapids, Mich.: Eerdmans, 1998), especially chapter 5, "Trinity and Church."

16. People who are not married can and should participate in other forms of relationship, preeminently in the church, in order to experience the spiritually maturing effects of being morally committed to others.

17. In epistemology (how we know things), the issue is phrased in terms of universals versus particulars. A universal is a common type or pattern used to interpret or make sense of the individual. For example, ideals such as Justice and Goodness function to organize and interpret a great number of particular experiences. When I encounter a particular event and ask, Is this just? my understanding of Justice provides the meaning or interpretation of the individual event. The ancient world regarded universals as "more real" than concrete particulars. In reaction, modern philosophy, starting with the nominalism of William of Ockham, insists that particulars alone are real; universals have been demoted to mere mental constructions.

18. Timothy Ware, *The Orthodox Church* (London: Penguin, 1997), 240; Kallistos [Timothy] Ware, *The Orthodox Way* (Crestwood, N.Y.: St. Vladimir's Seminary Press, 2002), 38-39.

19. For more detail, see Nancy Pearcey, "Religion of Revolution: Karl Marx's Social Evolution," *Bible-Science Newsletter,* June 1986; Nancy Pearcey, "Liberation, Yes . . . But How? A Study of Liberation Theology," *Bible-Science Newsletter,* July 1988. For a later treatment, see "Does It Liberate?" chapter 24 in *How Now?*

20. Historian John Hermann Randall explains that the Newtonian image of the universe as a finely tuned machine "practically forced men, as a necessary scientific hypothesis, to believe in an external Creator" (*The Making of the Modern Mind* [New York: Columbia University Press, 1976], 276).

21. Cited in Francis Nigel Lee, *Communism Versus Creation* (Nutley, N.J.: Craig, 1969), 28.

22. Robert G. Wesson, *Why Marxism? The Continuing Success of a Failed Theory* (New York: Basic Books, 1976), 30.

23. Ibid., 25.

24. Klaus Bockmuehl, *The Challenge of Marxism* (Leicester, UK: InterVarsity Press, 1980), 17.

25. John Gray, "Exposing the Myth of Secularism," *Australian Financial Review,* January 3, 2003, at http://afr.com/review/2003/01/03/FFX9CQAJFAD.html. On the religious character of neo-

Marxist feminist and multicultural movements, see Stanley Kurtz, "The Church of the Left: Finding Meaning in Liberalism," National Review Online, May 31, 2001; and "The Faith-Based Left: Getting Behind the Debate," National Review Online, February 5, 2001.

26. Leslie Stevenson and David L. Haberman, *Ten Theories of Human Nature* (New York: Oxford University Press, 1998), 147.

27. Cited in Robert Nisbet, *The Quest for Community: A Study in the Ethics of Order and Freedom* (1953; reprint, San Francisco: Institute for Contemporary Studies Press, 1990), 127, no source listed. Emphasis added. For greater detail on Rousseau and the other early modern political philosophers, see Nancy Pearcey, "The Creation Myth of Modern Political Philosophy," presented at the sixth annual Kuyper Lecture, the Center for Public Justice, 2000, at http://arn.org/pearcey/nphone.htm.

28. Nancey Murphy, *Anglo-American Postmodernity: Philosophical Perspectives on Science, Religion, and Ethics* (Boulder, Colo.: HarperCollins, 1997), 180. See also Nancey Murphy, *Beyond Liberalism and Fundamentalism: How Modern and Postmodern Philosophy Set the Theological Agenda* (Valley Forge, Pa.: Trinity Press International, 1996), 151.

29. Pierre Manent, *An Intellectual History of Liberalism* (Princeton, N.J.: Princeton University Press, 1994), 29.

30. Jean-Jacques Rousseau, *The Social Contract* (Chicago: Henry Gateway, 1954), 57. See also Manent, *Intellectual History,* 72.

31. For a discussion of the contrast between Christian and contractual views of marriage, see John Witte, Jr., *From Sacrament to Contract: Marriage, Religion, and Law in the Western Tradition* (Louisville: Westminster John Knox Press, 1997).

32. One source of Rousseau's philosophy of the state may well have been his personal decision to abandon all five of his children to a state orphanage. The state in essence liberated him from the moral demands of being a parent. I have recounted this sordid story in "Synanon and Sin," chapter 17 in *How Now?*

33. Glenn Tinder, *Political Thinking: The Perennial Questions* (New York: HarperCollins, 1995), 198-199. Henry May calls Rousseau a "prophet" who delivered the redemptive message that "the Fall was quite real but reversible" (Henry May, *The Enlightenment in America* [New York: Oxford University Press, 1976], 165). In France, in some quarters, May writes, Rousseau was "elevated into the status of . . . a new Christ, preaching a revolutionary redemption" (170).

34. Nancy Pearcey, "Century of Cruelty: Making Sense of Our Era," *Boundless,* December 1999.

35. "The masses grew out of the fragments of a highly atomized society. . . . The chief characteristic of the mass man is not brutality and backwardness, but his isolation and lack of normal social relationships" (*The Origins of Totalitarianism* [New York: Harcourt Brace, 1951], 310-311).

36. On neo-Calvinist political philosophy, see the writings of James Skillen, especially *The Scattered Voice: Christians At Odds in the Public Square* (Grand Rapids, Mich.: Zondervan, 1990); *Recharging the American Experiment: Principled Pluralism for Genuine Civic Community* (Grand Rapids, Mich.: Baker, 1994); and *Political Order and the Plural Structure of Society,* ed. James Skillen and Rockne McCarthy (Grand Rapids, Mich.: Eerdmans, 1991). See also Jonathan Chaplin, "Subsidiary and Sphere Sovereignty: Catholic and Reformed Conceptions of the Role of the State," in *Things Old and New: Catholic Social Teaching Revisited,* ed. Francis McHugh and Samuel Natale (Lanham, Md.: University Press of America, 1993).

37. Eric O. Springsted, *The Act of Faith: Christian Faith and the Moral Self* (Grand Rapids, Mich.: Eerdmans, 2002), x.

38. Michael J. Sandel, *Democracy's Discontent: America in Search of a Public Philosophy* (Cambridge, Mass.: Harvard University Press, 1996), 6, 12.

39. See ibid., especially chapter 4, "Privacy Rights and Family Law." On a similar note, Alasdair MacIntyre writes, "In many premodern, traditional societies it is through his or her membership in a variety of social groups that the individual identifies himself or herself and is identified by others. I am brother, cousin and grandson, member of this household, that village, this tribe. These are not characteristics that belong to human beings accidentally, to be stripped away in order to discover 'the real me.' They are part of my substance" (Alasdair MacIntyre, *After Virtue: A Study in Moral Theory,* 2nd ed. [Notre Dame, Ind.: University of Notre Dame Press, 1997], 33-34).

40. Mary Ann Glendon, *Rights Talk: The Impoverishment of Political Discourse* (New York: Free Press, 1993), 48.

41. Pierre Manent, *Modern Liberty and Its Discontents* (Lanham, Md.: Rowman & Littlefield, 1998), 158. See also Pierre Manent, "Modern Individualism," *Crisis* (October 1995): 35.

42. The study is summarized in Elana Ashanti Jefferson, "Sex 101: College Students Increasingly Casual About Bedfellows, Just as Casual About Condoms," *Denver Post,* October 24, 2002.

43. David Abel, "Porn Is Hot Course on Campus: Professors Seek Meaning Behind Flourishing Market," *Boston Globe,* August 20, 2001.

44. Margaret Sanger, *The Pivot of Civilization* (New York: Brentano's, 1922), 232. For greater detail on Sanger, Kinsey, and other architects of the sexual revolution, see Nancy Pearcey, "Creating the 'New Man': The Hidden Agenda in Sex Education," *Bible-Science Newsletter,* May 1990. For a later treatment, see "Salvation Through Sex?" chapter 25 in *How Now?* Sanger literally believed that sexual restraint caused a vast variety of physical and psychological dysfunctions—even mental retardation. If our sexuality were given full and free expression, she promised, we would literally become geniuses. "Modern science is teaching us that genius is not some mysterious gift of the gods. . . . Rather is it due to the removal of physiological and psychological inhibitions and constraints which makes possible the release and the channeling of the primordial inner energies of man into full and divine expression" (Sanger, *Pivot of Civilization,* 232-233).

45. Sanger, *Pivot of Civilization,* 271.

46. James Atlas, "The Loose Cannon: Why Higher Learning Has Embraced Pornography," *The New Yorker,* March 29, 1999, 60-65.

47. Margaret Sanger, *Pivot of Civilization,* 238.

48. Alfred Kinsey, Wardell Pomeroy, and Clyde Martin, *Sexual Behavior in the Human Male* (Philadelphia: W. B. Saunders, 1948), 7, 263, emphasis added.

49. Paul Robinson, *The Modernization of Sex,* 2nd ed. (Ithaca, N.Y.: Cornell University Press, 1988), 49-50, 85.

50. Atlas, "Loose Cannon."

51. Michael Medved, "Hollywood Chic," *The Washington Post,* October 4, 1992.

52. John Stuart Mill, *On Liberty* (Indianapolis: Hackett, 1978), 12.

53. Dominic Mohan, "In Bend with Madonna," *The Sun,* March 11, 2003.

54. On the "Westernizing" of Eastern pantheism, especially the way it has been merged with optimistic evolutionary views of progress, see Nancy Pearcey, "East Meets West in Science," *Bible-Science Newsletter,* February 1985; Nancy Pearcey, "Spiritual Evolution? Science and the New Age Movement," presentation at the National Creation Conference, Cleveland, Ohio, August 14-16, 1985. For a later treatment, see "The New Age Religion," chapter 28 in *How Now?*

55. Francis Hodgson Burnett, *The Secret Garden* (New York: Harper & Row, 1911), 250, 254.

56. Ibid., 236, 267, 251, 250. At one point in the story, several characters agree that whether you worship using the Christian doxology, or use the term *Magic* or some other name, "they are both the same thing" (285, 290).

57. Ibid., 250.

58. Ibid., 253-254, emphasis added.

59. Nancy Pearcey, "New Age for Kids," *Bible-Science Newsletter,* December 1988. This article gives additional documentation of the Eastern religious elements in the book.

60. Theosophy was the name given by Madame Blavatsky to Eastern religious teachings she learned in Tibet in the late 1800s. Burnett was highly influenced not only by Madame Blavatsky but also by Mind Healing and Christian Science. Her conception of the divine as a unified mind or spirit permeating all things was borrowed from these spiritualist philosophies. So were her ideas about the healing powers of the mind, which became a crucial motif in several of her books, including *The Secret Garden.*

Clearly not all stories that include magic incorporate a pantheistic worldview. For example, C. S. Lewis and J. R. R. Tolkein were Christian fantasy writers who used magic in the classic fairy tale manner—as a means of suggesting that there is more to reality than the mundane, ordinary, material world, while sparking a hunger for an unseen, transcendent spiritual realm. We cannot judge a piece of literature simply by whether it uses a particular term, like *magic,* but need to identify the underlying worldview.

61. See Francis Schaeffer, *Escape from Reason,* in *Complete Work,* vol. 1, 207-208.

62. Unfortunately, space does not permit the same kind of detailed analysis of the concepts of Fall and Redemption. However, readers might want to consult the relevant sections in *How Now?* Briefly, the section on the Fall (chapters 15, 17-21) describes what happens when the biblical doctrine of sin is denied, giving rise to various forms of utopianism, usually enforced by coercive means. The last of these chapters outlines the Bible's unique answer to the problem of evil and suffering. The Redemption section (chapters 23-29) shows that most modern ideologies are variations on the myth of progress—what philosopher Mary Midgely calls "the Escalator Myth"—including Marxism, sexual liberation, New Age thought, and so on. (On Midgely and the Escalator Myth, see Nancy Pearcey, "What Do You Mean, Evolution Is a Religion?" *Bible-Science Newsletter,* April 1988.)

CHAPTER 5: DARWIN MEETS THE BERENSTAIN BEARS

1. See "Huston Smith Replies to Barbour, Goodenough, and Peterson," *Zygon* 36, no. 2 (June 2001): 223-231.

2. Patrick Glynn, in discussion with the author. Glynn also talks about his personal experience in the first chapter of *God, The Evidence: The Reconciliation of Faith and Reason in a Postsecular World* (Rocklin, Calif.: Prima, 1997).

3. On the centrality of creation to the Christian worldview, see Nancy Pearcey, "Creation and the Unity of Scripture: Making the 'Simple Gospel' Simple," *Bible-Science Newsletter,* July 1984; Nancy Pearcey, "Did It Really Happen? Genesis and History," *Bible-Science Newsletter,* March 1987; Nancy Pearcey, "Everything You Wanted to Know About Evolution: But Don't Have Time to Read Up On," *Bible-Science Newsletter,* June 1988.

4. Edward A. Purcell, Jr., *The Crisis of Democratic Theory: Scientific Naturalism and the Problem of Value* (Lexington: University Press of Kentucky, 1973), 8, 21. See also Nancy Pearcey, "Darwinian Naturalism: Cultural and Philosophical Implications," Veritas Forum at UC Santa Barbara, October 25, 2003.

5. Elizabeth Flower and Murray G. Murphey, *A History of Philosophy in America,* vol. 2 (New York: Putnam, 1977), 553. On the unity of knowledge, I have written elsewhere: "Despite the differences among them all major civilizations have believed in a divine order that lays down the law for both natural and human realms. In the Far East it was called *Tao;* in ancient Egypt it was called *Ma'at;* in Greek philosophy it was called *Logos.* . . . John's Gospel borrows the Greek word for this universal plan of creation *(logos)* and, in a startling move, identifies it with a personal being—Jesus Christ himself. . . . In other words, Jesus himself is the source of the comprehensive plan or design of creation" (*How Now,* 297-298; see also C. S. Lewis, *The Abolition of Man*).

6. Nancy Pearcey, "The Birth of Modern Science," *Bible-Science Newsletter,* October 1982; Nancy Pearcey, "How Christianity Gave Rise to the Modern Scientific Outlook," *Bible-Science Newsletter,* January 1989. I later expanded this material into a major theme throughout *Soul of Science,* especially chapter 1, "An Invented Institution: Christianity and the Scientific Revolution."

7. Daniel Dennett, *Darwin's Dangerous Idea* (New York: Simon & Schuster, 1995), 63. See the review by Phillip Johnson in *The New Criterion,* October 1995.

8. Ibid., 519, 520. Nick Humphrey, professor of psychology at the New School for Social Research, uses even stronger language. In an Amnesty Lecture on human rights, he said, "Children have a right not to have their minds addled by nonsense. And we as a society have a duty to protect them from it. So we should no more allow parents to teach their children to believe in the literal truth of the Bible . . . than we should allow parents to knock their children's teeth out or lock them in a dungeon" ("What Shall We Tell the Children?" Amnesty Lecture, Oxford, February 21, 1997. Cited in Andrew Brown, *The Darwin Wars: The Scientific Battle for the Soul of Man* [New York: Simon & Schuster, 1999], 172).

9. PBS, "Evolution, Episode 1: Darwin's Dangerous Idea." See the critique of the series by the Discovery Institute: "Getting the Facts Straight: A Viewer's Guide to PBS's 'Evolution,'" at www.reviewevolution.com.

10. G. K. Chesterton, *Eugenics and Other Evils* (New York: Dodd, Mead, 1927), 98.

11. Stan and Jan Berenstain, *The Bears' Nature Guide* (New York: Random House, 1975). For a whimsical and well-written children's book giving the opposite position, see William Steig, *Yellow and Pink* (New York: Farrar, Straus, & Giroux, 1984). The story is about two wooden

marionettes who debate whether they were formed by natural processes or by Intelligent Design. See my review of the book in *Critique*, March/April 1985 (a publication of Ransom Fellowship), reprinted under the title "In the Language of Children," in the *Bible-Science Newsletter*, August 1985. A summary of the story is found in *How Now?* 94-95.

12. See Carl Sagan, *Cosmos* (New York: Random House, 1980), 4.

13. For a fuller discussion, see Nancy Pearcey, "Canonizing the Cosmos: Carl Sagan's Naturalistic Religion," *Bible-Science Newsletter*, October 1984. See also Norman Geisler, *Cosmos: Carl Sagan's Religion for the Scientific Mind* (Dallas: Quest, 1983). For a later discussion, see "Shattering the Grid," chapter 6 in *How Now?*

14. Jonathan Wells, *Icons of Evolution* (Washington, D.C.: Regnery, 2000).

15. See Nancy Pearcey, "The Galapagos Islands: A World All Its Own," *Bible-Science Newsletter*, February 1984; Nancy Pearcey, "The Origin of the Origin: Or, What Did Darwin Really Find?" *Bible-Science Newsletter*, December 1986.

16. Jonathan Weiner, "Kansas Anti-Evolution Vote Denies Students a Full Spiritual Journey," *Philadelphia Inquirer*, August 15, 1999.

17. See Phillip E. Johnson, *Reason in the Balance: The Case Against Naturalism in Science, Law, and Education* (Downers Grove, Ill.: InterVarsity Press, 1995). For a review of the book, see Nancy Pearcey, "Naturalism on Trial," *First Things* 60 (February 1996).

18. "If droughts occur about once every ten years on the islands, a new species of finch might arise in only about 200 years" (*Teaching About Evolution and the Nature of Science*, National Academy of Sciences, 1998, chapter 2, page 19, at http://www.nap.edu/readingroom/books/evolution98.).

19. Phillip E. Johnson, "The Church of Darwin," *Wall Street Journal*, August 16, 1999.

20. The reason is that the mutated form is less fit, so that the unmutated viruses quickly take over again. What happens is that a few unmutated viruses hide out in cells while the mutated, drug resistant varieties begin to dominate. When the coast is clear—that is, when drug treatment is stopped and the selective pressure is removed—these sequestered wild types quickly take over the population again because the drug resistant forms are much less fit. The PBS program does mention that drug resistance is completely reversible, but presents it misleadingly as evidence *for* evolution rather than as evidence *against* it.

21. See Nancy Pearcey, "What Species of Species? Or, Darwin and the Origin of *What?*" *Bible-Science Newsletter*, June 1989.

22. Technically, we are talking about neo-Darwinism here, rather than the classical version of the theory. Darwin did not know how variations in living things arise, and he was unfamiliar with the theory of genes that had already been developed by Gregor Mendel. Neo-Darwinian theory, which proposes genetic mutations as the source of new variations, arose in the 1930s and 40s and is sometimes called the "modern synthesis."

23. See the discussion of Goldschmidt in Norman Macbeth, *Darwin Retried* (New York: Dell, 1971), 33, 154.

24. Luther Burbank, quoted in ibid., 36. See Nancy Pearcy, "Progress and Limitations in Plant and Animal Breeding," *Bible-Science Newsletter*, November 1982; Nancy Pearcey, "Everybody Can Know: The Most Powerful Evidence Against Evolution," *Bible-Science Newsletter*, June 1987; and "Darwin in the Dock," chapter 9 in *How Now?*

25. Nancy Pearcey, "Natural Selection, the Point that Moved the World," *Bible-Science Newsletter*, November 1984. See also M. W. Ho and P. T. Saunders, "Beyond Neo-Darwinism—An Epigenetic Approach to Evolution," *Journal of Theoretical Biology* 78 (1979): 573-591.

26. In some cases, live moths were used, since they tend to be torpid during the day.

27. Peter D. Smith, "Darwinism in a Flutter," review of *Of Moths and Men: Intrigue, Tragedy, and the Peppered Moth*, by Judith Hooper, *The Guardian*, May 11, 2002.

28. Jerry Coyne, "Not Black and White," review of *Melanism: Evolution in Action*, by M. E. N. Majerus, *Nature* 396 (November 5, 1998): 35.

29. Bob Ritter, a Canadian textbook writer, was quoted in "Moth-eaten Darwinism: A Disproven Textbook Case of Natural Selection Refuses to Die," *Alberta Report Newsmagazine*, April 5, 1999. "High school students are still very concrete in the way they learn," Ritter said. "The advantage of this example of natural selection is that it is extremely visual." He went on: "we want to get across the idea of selective adaptation. Later on, they can look at the work critically." See Nancy Pearcey, "Creation Mythology: Defenders of Darwinism Resort to Suppressing Data and Teaching Outright Falsehoods," *World*, June 24, 2000.

30. From a letter to Asa Gray, September 10, 1860, in *The Life and Letters of Charles Darwin,* vol. 2, ed. Francis Darwin (New York: D. Appleton, 1896), 131.

31. Michael Richardson, quoted in Elizabeth Pennisi, "Haeckel's Embryos: Fraud Rediscovered," *Science* 277 (September 5, 1997): 1435.

32. Cited in Nancy Pearcey, "Michael Kinsley Out on a Limb: Stem-Cell Rationale Recalls Ideas of Debunked Scientist," *Human Events,* September 8, 2000.

33. In 2000, another piece of faked evidence emerged: an alleged feathered dinosaur. "National Geographic convened a press conference last October, heralding the fossil as a crucial missing link, the first solid evidence for a new theory that birds evolved from dinosaurs (contrary to an older theory that they evolved separately). But the prestigious journal soon had egg on its face. Chinese farmers have grown adept at gluing fossils together in ways that increase their black-market value, and in this case, the body turned out to be from an early toothed bird while the tail was from a dinosaur" (Nancy Pearcey, "The Missing Link that Wasn't: National Geographic's 'Bird Dinosaur' Flew Against the Facts," *Human Events,* March 10, 2000).

34. Melissa Ludwig, "New Force in the Fray on State's Textbooks: 'Intelligent Design' Adherents Use Science to Question Evolution," *Austin American-Statesman,* Wednesday, July 9, 2003.

35. Phillip E. Johnson, *Defeating Darwinism by Opening Minds* (Downers Grove, Ill.: InterVarsity Press, 1997), 37.

36. Jerry Alder and John Carey, "Is Man a Subtle Accident?" *Newsweek,* November 3, 1980, 95-96. See Nancy Pearcey, "Evolution After Darwin: What's Left?" *Bible-Science Newsletter,* August 1985.

37. Stephen Jay Gould, "Evolution's Erratic Pace," in *Natural History* 86 no. 5 (May 1977): 14.

38. The same year as the Macroevolution conference, Gould wrote that the neo-Darwinian synthesis "as a general proposition, is effectively dead, despite its persistence as textbook orthodoxy" ("Is a New and General Theory of Evolution Emerging?" *Paleobiology* 6, no. 1 [January 1980]: 120). Today, more than two decades later, the same "dead" proposition is still being flogged, largely because of the difficulty in finding anything with which to replace it: "A number of microbiologists, geneticists, theoretical biologists, mathematicians, and computer scientists are saying there is more to life than Darwinism. . . . I call them the 'postdarwinians.' . . . Their disagreement is with the very sweeping nature of the Darwinian argument, the fact that in the end it doesn't explain much, and the emerging evidence that Darwinism alone may not be sufficient to explain all we see. . . . [W]hat else is operating within or beyond evolution as we understand it?" (Kevin Kelly, *Out of Control: The New Biology of Machines, Social Systems, and the Economic World* [Cambridge, Mass: Perseus, 1994], 365-366).

39. See Michael Denton, *Evolution: A Theory In Crisis* (Bethesda, Md.: Adler & Adler, 1986).

40. Roger Lewin, "Evolutionary Theory Under Fire," in *Science* 210 (November 21, 1980): 883-887.

41. See Nancy Pearcey, "Fact vs. Theory: Does Gould Understand the Difference?" *Bible-Science Newsletter,* April 1987. "The required rapidity of the change implies either a few large steps or many and exceedingly rapid smaller ones. Large steps are tantamount to saltations and raise the problems of fitness barriers; small steps must be numerous and entail the problems discussed under microevolution. The periods of stasis raise the possibility that the lineage would enter the fossil record, and we reiterate that we can identify none of the postulated intermediate forms. Finally, the large numbers of species that must be generated so as to form a pool from which the successful lineage is selected are nowhere to be found. We conclude that the probability that species selection is a general solution to the origin of higher taxa is not great, and that neither of the contending theories of evolutionary change at the species level, phyletic gradualism or punctuated equilibrium, seem applicable to the origin of new body plans" (J. Valentine and D. Erwin, "Interpreting Great Developmental Experiments: The Fossil Record," in Rudolf A. Raff and Elizabeth C. Raff, eds., *Development as an Evolutionary Process* [New York: Alan R. Liss, 1987], 96).

42. Nancy Pearcey, "Foreword," in Phillip E. Johnson, *The Right Questions: Truth, Meaning, and Public Debate* (Downers Grove, Ill.: InterVarsity Press, 2002), 13.

43. Richard Dawkins, *The Blind Watchmaker* (New York: Norton, 1986), 287, emphasis in original.

44. S. C. Todd, "A View from Kansas on That Evolution Debate," *Nature* 401 (September 30, 1999): 423.

45. Mano Singham, a physicist at Case Western Reserve University, writing in *Physics Today,* June

2002, emphasis added. To buttress his argument, he quoted paleontologist George Gaylord Simpson, who wrote, "The progress of knowledge rigidly requires that no nonphysical postulate ever be admitted in connection with the study of physical phenomena. . . . the researcher who is seeking explanations must seek physical explanations only" (*Tempo and Mode in Evolution* [New York: Columbia University Press, 1944], 76).

46. John Rennie, "15 Answers to Creationist Nonsense," *Scientific American*, June 17, 2002.

47. See Del Ratzsch, *The Battle of Beginnings: Why Neither Side Is Winning the Creation-Evolution Debate* (Downers Grove, Ill.: InterVarsity Press, 1996), 167. For a more recent, and more academic, discussion of philosophical issues, see Del Ratzsch, *Nature, Design, and Science: The Status of Design in Natural Science* (New York: SUNY Press, 2001).

48. *BSCS Biology: A Molecular Approach,* 8th ed., Jon Greenberg, revision editor (Everyday Learning Corporation, 2001), 446.

49. Neil A. Campbell, Jane B. Reece, and Lawrence G. Mitchell, *Biology,* 5th ed. (Reading, Mass.: Addison Wesley, 1999), 426. A helpful analysis of textbooks can be found in Norris Anderson's "Education or Indoctrination 2001," at http://www.alabamaeagle.org/education_or_indoctrination_2001.htm.

50. Douglas Futuyma, *Evolutionary Biology,* 3rd ed. (Sunderland, Mass.: Sinauer, 1998), 15. See Jonathan Wells, "Opinions," *Topeka Capital-Journal,* November 23, 1999, at http://www.cjonline.com/stories/112199/opi_science.shtml.

51. Historian Neal Gillespie says Darwin's central innovation was a positivist definition of science that restricted it to natural causes. Once such a definition had been accepted, it "simply nullified special creation as a scientific idea." Put the other way around, "It was the prior success of positivism in science that assured the victory of evolution in biology." There was no need to directly attack religion, Gillespie explains, but only to adopt "positivism as the epistemological standard in science. And this eventually took God out of nature (if not out of reality) as effectively as atheism" (*Charles Darwin and the Problem of Creation* [Chicago: University of Chicago Press, 1979], 152, 146, 153. For more on this history, see Nancy Pearcey, "You Guys Lost," in *Mere Creation: Science, Faith, and Intelligent Design,* ed. William A. Dembski [Downers Grove, Ill.: InterVarsity Press, 1998], 73-92).

52. Tom Bethell, "Against Sociobiology," *First Things* 109 (January 2001): 18-24, emphasis added.

53. Charles Darwin, *The Descent of Man and Selection in Relation to Sex,* 2nd ed. (1871; reprint, London: John Murray, 1922), 92. The term "immutable" reveals that Darwin was reacting in part against an inadequate view of creation held by some in his day that all species came directly from the hand of God—that no new ones had ever appeared, nor had any died out (i.e., there was no extinction). In opposing this particular theory of creation, however, Darwin was also opposing the concept of creation or design per se.

54. Richard Lewontin, "Billions and Billions of Demons," *The New York Review of Books,* January 9, 1997, 28.

55. Cited in Roger Highfield, "Do Our Genes Reveal the Hand of God?" *Daily Telegraph* (London), March, 20, 2003, at http://www.telegraph.co.uk.

56. Cited in ibid.

57. Weinberg's comments were reported in "Free People from Superstition," *Freethought Today,* April 2000, at http://www.ffrf.org/fttoday/april2000/weinberg.html.

58. Cited in Michael Ruse, "Saving Darwinism from the Darwinians," *National Post,* May 13, 2000, B-3.

59. Ruse, ibid. Ruse makes the same argument in his most recent book, *Mystery of Mysteries: Is Evolution a Social Construction?* (Cambridge, Mass.: Harvard University Press, 1999).

60. See Tom Woodward, "Ruse Gives Away the Store, Admits Evolution Is a Philosophy," at http://www.leaderu.com/real/ri9404/ruse.html.

61. Cited in Ruse, "Saving Darwinism from the Darwinians." Elsewhere, Gould explicitly described Darwinism as a substitute for religion: "Evolution substituted a naturalistic explanation of cold comfort for our former conviction that a benevolent deity fashioned us directly in his own image" (Stephen Jay Gould, "Introduction," in Carl Zimmer, *Evolution: The Triumph of an Idea* [New York: HarperCollins, 2001], xi).

62. Ruse, "Saving Darwinism from the Darwinians."

63. Editorial, *Columbus Dispatch,* June 14, 2002.

64. Jacques Barzun, *Darwin, Marx, Wagner: Critique of a Heritage* (Chicago: University of Chicago Press, 1941), 37.
65. See Nancy Pearcey, "Scopes in Reverse," *Washington Times,* July 24, 2000.
66. Cited in Pearcey, "Foreword," in Johnson, *Right Questions,* 7-25.
67. For a general overview of the history of the Intelligent Design movement, see Nancy Pearcey, "The Evolution Backlash: Debunking Darwin," *World,* March 1, 1997, 12-15; Nancy Pearcey, "We're Not in Kansas Anymore: Why Secular Scientists and Media Can't Admit that Darwinism Might Be Wrong," *Christianity Today,* May 22, 2000.
68. Phillip E. Johnson, interview by James M. Kushiner, "Berkeley's Radical: An Interview with Phillip E. Johnson," *Touchstone,* June 2002, at http://www.touchstonemag.com/docs/issues/15.5docs/15-5pg40.html.
69. Phillip E. Johnson, *Darwin on Trial* (Downers Grove, Ill.: InterVarsity Press, 1993); *Reason in the Balance: The Case Against Naturalism in Science, Law, and Education* (Downers Grove, Ill.: InterVarsity Press, 1995).
70. I am often asked about the difference between creationism and Intelligent Design theory. The difference lies largely in the method of approach. Creationism starts with the Bible, and asks, What does the Bible say about science? That is a perfectly valid inquiry, just as we ask what the Bible implies for politics or the arts or any other field. But it is not the way to do apologetics. In speaking to a non-Christian culture, we must start with data that our audience finds credible. Thus Intelligent Design theory does not begin with the Bible—it begins with the scientific data and asks, Does the data itself give evidence of an intelligent cause? It makes the case that design be detected empirically.
71. L'Abri tapes are available at http://www.soundword.com/frontlabri.html.
72. "The Secular Web," at http://www.infidels.org/index.shtml.
73. Gillespie, *Charles Darwin and the Problem of Creation,* 16, emphasis added.
74. The position paper is posted at http://www.aristotle.net/~asta/science.htm. Interestingly, ASTA put out an earlier statement, in 1999, that still treated religion as a form of genuine knowledge: "People have many ways of knowing about their world including scientific knowledge, societal knowledge, religious knowledge and cultural knowledge. Science differs from these other ways of knowing in important ways" (posted on the same website). In only two years, religion was demoted from a type of knowledge to merely a social construction.
75. Ibid.
76. Huxley went on to say, "Darwin pointed out that no supernatural designer was needed; since natural selection could account for any new form of life, there is no room for a supernatural agency in its evolution" ("At Random: A Television Preview," in *Evolution After Darwin* [Chicago: University of Chicago Press, 1960], 41).
77. Douglas Sloan, *Faith and Knowledge: Mainline Protestantism and American Higher Education* (Louisville: Westminster John Knox, 1994), 190.
78. Allan Bloom, *The Closing of the American Mind* (Chicago: Chicago Review Press, 1989). This quotation is from *The Republic of Plato,* translated with notes and an interpretive essay by Allan Bloom (New York: Basic Books, 1968), x.
79. Cited in Victor Greto, "Delaware a Leader in Teaching Evolution," *The News Journal* (Wilmington, Del.), February 25, 2003, emphasis added.
80. Backgrounder for the PBS program "Evolution," titled "Emi and Nathan: Personal Testimonies," at www.pbs.org/wgbh/evolution/library/08/1/l_081_07.html.

CHAPTER 6: THE SCIENCE OF COMMON SENSE

1. Cited in Gerald Schroeder, "Can God Be Brought into the Equation?" review of *Science and Religion: Are They Compatible?* ed. Paul Kurtz and Barry Karr, in the *Jerusalem Post,* May 23, 2003, 13-B; at http://www.jpost.com/servlet/Satellite?pagename=JPost/A/JPArticle/ShowFull&cid=1\054002499080.
2. The survey was conducted by *Skeptic* editor Michael Shermer and MIT professor Frank Sulloway, and though it was sent out to a random sample of Americans, for unknown reasons respondents included a higher-than-average percentage of highly educated people. Results are reported in Michael Shermer, *How We Believe: The Search for God in an Age of Science* (New York: W. H. Freeman, 2000), 74-88. Ironically, when respondents were asked why *other* people believe in God, the number one reason cited was emotional comfort. In other words,

respondents claimed that they themselves had rational grounds for belief, but they regarded *everyone else* as being motivated by psychological need.

3. For a recent treatment of this theme, see Nancy Pearcey, "Shooting Down the Warfare Myth," Megaviews Forum, Los Alamos National Laboratory, September 24, 2003; Nancy Pearcey, "The War that Wasn't," Veritas Forum at USC, February 18, 2004; Nancy Pearcey, "How Science Became a Christian Vocation," in *Reading God's World: The Vocation of Scientist,* ed. Angus Menuge, forthcoming from the Cranach Institute, Concordia University in Milwaukee. For a brief introduction, see "The Basis for True Science," chapter 40 in *How Now?*

4. The difference between science and common sense is a matter of degree, not kind, says W. V. O. Quine, in *Ontological Relativity and Other Essays* (New York: Columbia University Press, 1997), 129.

5. This example is from my colleague Steve Meyer, director of the Center for Science and Culture at the Discovery Institute.

6. Eugenie Scott (executive director of the National Center for Science Education, Inc.), CNN Newsroom, May 3, 2001, at http://www.cnn.com/TRANSCRIPTS/0105/03/nr.00.html.

7. Michael Stroh, "The Office of Research Integrity—a.k.a., the Fraud Squad—Is on the Case," *Popular Science,* December 2003, at http://www.popsci.com/popsci/science/article/ 0,12543,519782,00.html. The article begins with an example:

> Cancer researcher Kenneth Pienta was flipping through a paper written by a promising young postdoc in his University of Michigan laboratory when he spotted something that made his stomach sink: two protein blots that looked remarkably similar.
> Too similar.
> Pienta knew there could be only one explanation for the identical images: The woman had doctored the data.

As this example shows, there are empirical markers of design—including unethical design!

8. David Postman, "Letourneau Lands on WASL as Answer, Raising Questions," *The Seattle Times,* April 27, 2001.

9. William A. Dembski and James M. Kushiner, eds., *Signs of Intelligence: Understanding Intelligent Design* (Grand Rapids, Mich.: Baker, 2001).

10. See Nancy Pearcey, "We're Not in Kansas Anymore," *Christianity Today,* May 22, 2000.

11. Neal C. Gillespie, *Charles Darwin and the Problem of Creation* (Chicago: University of Chicago Press, 1979), 83-85.

12. Richard Dawkins, *The Blind Watchmaker* (New York: Norton, 1986), 1, emphasis added.

13. George Gaylord Simpson, "Plan and Purpose in Nature," *Scientific Monthly* 64 (June 1947): 481-495; cited in Simpson *This View of Life: The World of an Evolutionist* (New York: Harcourt Brace, 1964), 190-191, 212, emphasis added. Simpson's best-known assertion is, "Man is the result of a purposeless and natural process that did not have him in mind. He was not planned" (Simpson, *The Meaning of Evolution: A Study of the History of Life and of Its Significance for Man* [1949; reprint, New Haven, Conn.: Yale University Press, 1960], 344).

14. William Paley, *Natural Theology,* is in the public domain and available online at http://www.hti.umich.edu/cgi/p/pd-modeng/pd-modeng-idx?type=HTML&rgn= TEI.2&byte=53049319.

15. Michael Behe, *Darwin's Black Box: The Biochemical Challenge to Evolution* (New York: Touchstone, 1996), 213. See also my review: Nancy Pearcey, "The Biochemical Challenge to Evolution," in *Books and Culture* (November/December 1996), at http://www.arn.org/docs/ pearcey/np_bc1296.htm; and "Darwin in the Dock," chapter 9 in *How Now?* Traditional arguments for design are discussed in Nancy Pearcey, "Design: The Oldest Argument for God," *Bible-Science Newsletter,* December 1982.

16. Nancy Pearcey, "Strangely Familiar: The New, but Not So New, World of the Cell," *Bible-Science Newsletter,* July 1987.

17. Francis Crick, *Life Itself: Its Origin and Nature* (New York: Simon & Schuster, 1981), 70-71. Similarly, Bruce Alberts writes, "The entire cell can be viewed as a factory that contains an elaborate network of interlocking assembly lines, each of which is composed of a set of large protein machines" (Bruce Alberts, "The Cell as a Collection of Protein Machines: Preparing the Next Generation of Molecular Biologists," *Cell* 92 [February 6, 1998]: 291-294).

18. See Ronald D. Vale, "The Molecular Motor Toolbox for Intracellular Transport," in *Cell* 112 (February 21, 2003): 467-480. "A cell, like a metropolitan city, must organize its bustling community of macromolecules. Setting meeting points and establishing the timing of transactions are of fundamental importance for cell behavior. The high degree of spatial/temporal organization of molecules and organelles within cells is made possible by protein machines that transport components to various destinations within the cytoplasm" (467).

19. David J. DeRosier, "The Turn of the Screw: The Bacterial Flagellar Motor," *Cell* 93 (April 3, 1998): 17

20. Behe, *Darwin's Black Box*, 39.

21. Charles Darwin, *On the Origin of Species,* facsimile of the first edition (Cambridge, Mass., and London: Harvard University Press, 1964), 189.

22. For a defense of Behe's argument, see William A. Dembski, "Evolution's Logic of Credulity: An Unfettered Response to Allen Orr," at http://www.designinference.com/documents/2002.12.Unfettered_Resp_to_Orr.htm.

23. Nancy Pearcey, "The Heavens Declare: The Origin of the Universe," *Bible-Science Newsletter,* September 1986; Nancy Pearcey, "A Universe Built for Us: The Anthropic Principle," in *Bible-Science Newsletter,* October 1990; and Nancy Pearcey, "The Anthropic Principle: The Closest Atheists Can Get to God," in *Bible-Science Newsletter,* November 1990. For a later treatment, see "Let's Start at the Very Beginning," chapter 7 in *How Now?*

24. George Greenstein, *The Symbiotic Universe: Life and Mind in the Cosmos* (New York: William Morrow, 1988), 85-90.

25. Paul Davies, "A Brief History of the Multiverse," *The New York Times,* April 12, 2003. Elsewhere Davies writes that "the seemingly miraculous concurrence of numerical values" for nature's fundamental contrasts is "the most compelling evidence for an element of cosmic design" (*God and the New Physics* [New York: Simon & Schuster, 1983], 189). For more on fine-tuning, see Dean Overman, *A Case Against Accident and Self-Organization* (Lanham, Md.: Rowman & Littlefield, 1997); Hugh Ross, *The Fingerprint of God* (New Kensington, Pa.: Whitaker, 2000); John Horgan, "Between Science and Spirituality," *Chronicle of Higher Education* 49, no. 14 (November 29, 2002), at http://chronicle.com/free/v49/i14/14b00701.htm; Guillermo Gonzalez and Jay Richards, *The Privileged Planet: How Our Place in the Cosmos Is Designed for Discovery* (Washington, D.C.: Regnery, 2004).

26. Dennis Overbye, "Zillions of Universes? Or Did Ours Get Lucky?" *New York Times,* October 28, 2003. See also John Barrow, *The Constants of Nature: From Alpha to Omega—The Numbers That Encode the Deepest Secrets of the Universe* (London: Jonathan Cape, 2002).

27. Heinz Oberhummer, "Stellar Production Rates of Carbon and Its Abundance in the Universe," *Science* 289 (July 7, 2000): 88-90, emphasis added. Cited in Nancy Pearcey, "Our 'Tailor-made Universe,'" *World,* September 2, 2000.

28. Arno Penzias, "Creation Is Supported by All the Data So Far," *Cosmos, Bios, Theos: Scientists Reflect on Science, God, and the Origins of the Universe, Life, and Homo sapiens,* ed. Henry Margenau and RoyAgraham Varghese (Chicago: Open Court, 1992), 83.

29. Arno Penzias, interview by Malcolm Browne, "Clues to the Universe's Origin Expected," *The New York Times,* March 12, 1978. See also Jerry Bergman, "Arno A. Penzias: Astrophysicist, Nobel Laureate," in *Perspectives on Science and Christian Faith* 46, no. 3 (September 1994): 183-187; also available online at http://www.asa3.org/ASA/topics/Astronomy-Cosmology/PSCF9-94Bergman.html#Penzias.

30. Fred Hoyle, "The Universe: Some Past and Present Reflections," *Annual Review of Astronomy and Astrophysics* 20 (1982): 16.

31. In a 1971 news conference, Hoyle said, "Human beings are simply pawns in the game of alien minds that control our every move. They are everywhere, in the sky, on the sea, and in the Earth. . . . It is not an alien intelligence from another planet. It is actually from another universe which entered ours at the very beginning and has been controlling all that has happened since." Cited in L. K. Waddill. "On Tip Toes Before Darwin," *Power of the Mind Magazine,* 1998, at http://www.btinternet.com/~meirionhughes/Pub/page14.htm.

32. Greenstein, *Symbiotic Universe*, 26-27, 223.

33. George Wald, quoted in Dietrick E. Thomsen, "A Knowing Universe Seeking to Be Known," *Science News* (February 19, 1983): 124.

34. Freeman Dyson, *Disturbing the Universe* (New York: Harper & Row, 1979), 250.

35. Gregg Easterbrook, "The New Convergence," *Wired,* December 2002, at www.wired.com/wired/archive/10.12.

36. Pagels concludes, with an ironic twist, that the anthropic principle "is the closest that some atheists can get to God" ("A Cozy Cosmology," *The Sciences* [March/April, 1985], 35-38).

37. Cited in Overbye, "Zillions of Universes?"

38. Nancy Pearcey, "Copying the Human Script: Genome Project Raises Hopes, Fears," *World,* July 8, 2000.

39. Richard Dawkins, "Genetics: Why Prince Charles Is So Wrong," Checkbiotech.org, January 28, 2003, at http://www.checkbiotech.org/root/index.cfm?fuseaction=news&doc_id=4575&start=1&control=173&page_start=1&page_nr=101&pg=1.

40. Scott McCabe and Alex Navarro, "Writer in Sky Sends Wrong Message," *Palm Beach Post,* January 2, 2002, 1A. See Nancy Pearcey, *"Which* God Is Great?" Salem radio editorial.

41. Jacques Monod, *Chance and Necessity: An Essay on the Natural Philosophy of Modern Biology,* trans. Austryn Wainhouse (New York: Knopf, 1971).

42. William A. Dembski, *The Design Inference* (Cambridge: Cambridge University Press, 1998). A more accessible form of his argument is given in his *Intelligent Design: The Bridge Between Science and Theology* (Downers Grove, Ill.: InterVarsity Press, 1999). Briefer treatments can be found in William A. Dembski, "Science and Design" in *First Things* 86 (October 1998): 21-27; at http://www.firstthings.com/ftissues/ft9810/articles/dembski.html; and William A. Dembski, "Redesigning Science," in *Mere Creation,* excerpted at http://www.arn.org/docs/dembski/wd_explfilter.htm.

43. David Adam, "Give Six Monkeys a Computer, and What Do You Get? Certainly Not the Bard," *The Guardian,* May 9, 2003.

44. The reason is that the production of simple compounds, like amino acids, are "downhill" processes, thermodynamically speaking, which means they involve chemical reactions that occur easily in nature, while the production of macromolecules, like protein and DNA, are "uphill" processes, which means they do not occur readily in nature. See Nancy Pearcey, "Running Down and Falling Apart: Thermodynamics and the Origin of Life," *Bible-Science Newsletter,* September 1987; Nancy Pearcey, "Code for Life: An Interview with Walter Bradley," *Bible-Science Newsletter,* February 1989.

45. A recent book arguing against the chance origin of life is David Swift, *Evolution Under the Microscope: A Scientific Critique of the Theory of Evolution* (Stirling University Innovation Park, UK: Leighton Academic, 2002). Swift writes that "biologically active proteins are such tiny and isolated islands of utility in a boundless ocean of possible but useless amino acid sequences, that it is not credible they could be happened upon by fortuitous drifting around" (183).

46. Norman Geisler, interview by Nancy Pearcey, in "Geisler's Rebuttal: An Appeal to Common Sense," *Bible-Science Newsletter,* March 1985.

47. See Charles Thaxton, Walter Bradley, and Roger Olsen, *The Mystery of Life's Origin* (Dallas: Lewis and Stanley, 1992; originally published by Philosophical Library, 1984). See also Nancy Pearcey, "The First Step—Chemical Evolution (an Interview with Charles Thaxton)," *Bible-Science Newsletter,* October 1985; and Nancy Pearcey, "A Science of Origins: An Interview with Charles Thaxton," *Bible-Science Newsletter,* January 1987.

48. Dean Kenyon and Gary Steinman, *Biochemical Predestination* (New York: McGraw-Hill, 1969). Kenyon also studied under a chemist named Melvin Calvin, though that probably *is* a coincidence.

49. Nancy Pearcey, "Up from Materialism: An Interview with Dean Kenyon," *Bible-Science Newsletter,* September 1989.

50. Like Behe, Kenyon is Catholic and had no religious motivation for questioning evolution; it was the scientific weaknesses of the theory that motivated his quest for an alternative. He is a low-voiced, irenic man who would never willingly attract controversy; yet his altered views cast him into a hostile tug-of-war with authorities at San Francisco State University, where he used to teach. When university officials heard that he had embraced Intelligent Design theory, they actually forced him out of his teaching responsibilities, despite his stature as a leader in his field. He was reinstated only after a long and acrimonious appeal process, during which both the university's Academic Freedom Committee and the American Association of University Professors agreed that Kenyon's academic freedom had been violated. These groups defended a professor's right to question orthodox opinion on the subjects he teaches. The story

is told in Phillip E. Johnson, *Reason in the Balance: The Case Against Naturalism in Science, Law, and Education* (Downers Grove, Ill.: InterVarsity Press, 1995), 29-30; and in John Myers, "A Scopes Trial in Reverse," at http://www.leaderu.com/real/ri9401/scopes.html. University officials held out until public opinion was stirred by a *Wall Street Journal* article that drew attention to the irony of the situation: "Unlike Scopes, the teacher was forbidden to teach his course not because he taught evolutionary theory (which he did) but because he offered a critical assessment of it" (Steve Meyer, "Danger: Indoctrination—A Scopes Trial for the '90s," *The Wall Street Journal,* December 6, 1993).

51. In fact, if the sequence in DNA *were* a regular, repeating pattern, describable by some law or formula, then mapping the human genome would have been a comparatively simple task: Merely find the formula and you've solved the puzzle. The reason the genome is so difficult to map is precisely that there *is* no general formula. Each individual chemical "letter" has to be specified, one by one.

52. Cited in Nancy Pearcey, "Phillip Johnson Was Right: The Unhappy Evolution of Darwinism," *World,* February 24, 2001.

53. The hope that complexity theory may provide an answer to the origin of life is still just that: a hope, not an accomplishment. Yet complexity theory is often cited as though it had already provided an answer. For example, the editor in chief of *Scientific American,* in opposing critics of evolution, writes, "Researchers into nonlinear systems and cellular automata at the Santa Fe Institute and elsewhere have demonstrated that simple, undirected processes can yield extraordinarily complex patterns. Some of the complexity seen in organisms may therefore emerge through natural phenomena that we as yet barely understand. But that is far different from saying that the complexity could not have arisen naturally" (John Rennie, "15 Answers to Creationist Nonsense," *Scientific American,* July 2002). Translation: We don't know what processes were involved, but we are absolutely sure they were natural. This is an example of the way evolutionists rely on philosophy to get over the gaps in empirical evidence.

54. Stuart Kauffman, *At Home in the Universe: The Search for the Laws of Self-Organization and Complexity* (Oxford: Oxford University Press), 1995. For a critique, see Nancy Pearcey, "The Molecule Is the Message," *First Things* (June/July 1996): 13-14.

55. Richard Dawkins, *River Out of Eden: A Darwinian View of Life* (New York: HarperCollins, 1995), 17.

56. See Nancy Pearcey, "Nature and Nature's God: What Information Theory Tells Us," *Bible-Science Newsletter,* July 1986; Nancy Pearcey, "Who Wrote the DNA Code? A Report on an Interdisciplinary Conference," *Bible-Science Newsletter,* March 1991. For a briefer treatment, see "Life in a Test Tube," chapter 8 in *How Now?*

57. George Williams, interview by John Brockman, "George C. Williams: 'A Package of Information,'" in John Brockman, *The Third Culture: Beyond the Scientific Revolution* (New York: Simon & Schuster, 1995), 43. The distinction between the medium and the message may have become clearer since the dawn of the computer age, Williams says: "The constant process of transferring information from one physical medium to another and then being able to recover the same information in the original medium brings home the separability of information and matter. In biology, when you're talking about things like genes and genotypes and gene pools, you're talking about information, not physical objective reality" (43).

58. Paul Davies, "How We Could Create Life: The Key to Existence Will Be Found Not in Primordial Sludge, but in the Nanotechnology of the Living Cell," *The Guardian,* December 11, 2002, emphasis added.

59. Both Dean Kenyon and Charles Thaxton were influenced by the works of Wilder-Smith. Thaxton in turn encouraged young scholars like Steve Meyer, Bill Dembski, and Paul Nelson. See A. E. Wilder-Smith, *The Creation of Life: A Cybernetic Approach to Evolution* (Costa Mesa, Calif.: The Word for Today, 1970); *Man's Origin, Man's Destiny: A Critical Survey of the Principles of Evolution and Christianity* (Minneapolis: Bethany, 1968); *The Natural Sciences Know Nothing of Evolution* (Costa Mesa, Calif.: The Word for Today, 1981); *The Scientific Alternative to Neo-Darwinian Evolutionary Theory: Information Sources and Structures* (Costa Mesa, Calif.: The Word For Today, 1987).

60. In *The Blind Watchmaker,* Richard Dawkins refers to complex systems that are independently specified—or "specified in advance" (7-8). In *The Fifth Miracle* (New York: Simon and Schuster, 1999), Paul Davies claims that life is not mysterious because of its complexity per se but because of its "tightly specified complexity" (112). For an accessible explanation of the

concept of specified complexity, see my treatment in *Soul of Science* (chapter 10, "A Chemical Code: Resolving Historical Controversies").

61. The term *specified complexity* appears to have been first used by Leslie Orgel in his 1973 book *The Origins of Life* (New York: John Wiley). The concept was developed in detail by Thaxton, Bradley, and Olsen in *Mystery of Life's Origin.* Thaxton also organized a historic conference in 1988 in Tacoma, Washington, named "Information Content of DNA." For more recent treatments, see Walter Bradley and Charles Thaxton, "Information and the Origin of Life," in *The Creation Hypothesis: Scientific Evidence for an Intelligent Designer,* ed. J. P. Moreland (Downers Grove, Ill.: InterVarsity: 1994); Stephen Meyer, "DNA and Other Designs," *First Things* 102 (April 2000): 30-38; at http://www.firstthings.com/ftissues/ft0004/articles/meyer.html; and Stephen Meyer, "DNA and the Origins of Life: Information, Specification, and Explanation," in *Darwinism, Design, and Public Education,* ed. John Angus Campbell and Stephen C. Meyer (Lansing: Michigan State University Press, 2003).

62. Pearcey, "Molecule Is the Message."

63. Daniel Dennett, *Darwin's Dangerous Idea* (New York: Simon & Schuster, 1995), 50.

64. In Darwin, ed., *Life and Letters of Charles Darwin,* vol. 2, 6-7, 28. For a more detailed discussion, see Nancy Pearcey, "You Guys Lost: Is Design a Closed Issue?" in *Mere Creation,* 73-92.

65. Douglas Futuyma, *Evolutionary Biology,* 3rd ed. (Sunderland, Mass.: Sinauer, 1998), 5.

66. David L. Hull, *Darwin and His Critics: The Reception of Darwin's Theory of Evolution by the Scientific Community* (Cambridge, Mass.: Harvard University Press, 1973), 54. For centuries, scholars have sought to draw a firm black line that would define what qualifies as genuine science. Various tests have been proposed for verifiability (and falsifiability). But every time a standard is set up, some scientific theory is found that knocks it down. This is called the "demarcation problem," and the consensus today is that there *is* no way to determine ahead of time what does or does not qualify for scientific status. The only recourse is to test each theory and see how well it explains the data. See Stephen Meyer, "The Methodological Equivalence of Design and Descent: Can There Be a Scientific 'Theory of Creation'?" in *The Creation Hypothesis;* Stephen Meyer, "The Demarcation of Science and Religion," in *The History of Science and Religion in the Western Tradition: An Encyclopedia* (New York: Garland, 2000).

67. Design theorists do not attribute *all* events to the direct activity of a Creator, as they are sometimes accused of doing. They recognize a role for chance and law acting through the history of the universe—what the early scientists called "secondary causes." Design theorists merely want to include an *additional* kind of cause, "primary causes," as an acceptable category within science. As Dembski writes, "All the tried and true tools of science will remain intact. But design adds a new tool to the scientist's explanatory tool chest" ("Science and Design," *First Things,* 86 [October 1998]: 21-27).

68. Phillip E. Johnson, *The Right Questions: Truth, Meaning, and Public Debate* (Downers Grove, Ill.: InterVarsity Press, 2002), 18.

69. His House was operated by Denis and Margie Haack, who became wonderful friends and graciously allowed me to stay with them for two summers when I was a young believer. Later the Haacks joined the staff of InterVarsity, and then founded Ransom Fellowship, a "Schaeffer-esque ministry" (their term) in Rochester, Minnesota. They also produce a monthly publication called *Critique,* designed "to help Christians develop skills in discernment."

70. Phillip E. Johnson, *The Wedge of Truth: Splitting the Foundations of Naturalism* (Downers Grove, Ill.: InterVarsity Press, 2000), 166.

71. Nancey Murphy, "Phillip Johnson on Trial: A Critique of His Critique of Darwin," *Perspectives on Science and Christian Faith* 45, no. 1 (1993): 33. See Johnson's response in *Reason in the Balance* (97-101). The tactic of separating *methodological* from *metaphysical* naturalism is ultimately incoherent: Methodological naturalism is thought to be sound precisely because it is deemed to reflect reality.

72. Ellen T. Charry, *By the Renewing of Your Minds: The Pastoral Function of Christian Doctrine* (New York: Oxford University Press, 1977), 6.

73. John Maddox, "Churchman Preaching to the Unconvertible," review of *God Outside the Box: Why Spiritual People Object to Christianity,* by Richard Harries, *The Times Higher Education Supplement,* February 7, 2003.

74. Francis Schaeffer, *Death in the City,* in *The Complete Works of Francis A. Schaeffer,* vol. 4 (Wheaton, Ill.: Crossway, 1982), see 288-299.

CHAPTER 7: TODAY BIOLOGY, TOMORROW THE WORLD

1. Robert Wright, *The Moral Animal: Why We Are the Way We Are* (New York: Vintage, 1994), 325.
2. John Calvert, in discussion with the author. Calvert has made similar statements in several contexts, many of which are available at http://www.intelligentdesignnetwork.org.
3. See Nancy Pearcey, "Design and the Discriminating Public: Gaining a Hearing from Ordinary People" (*Touchstone,* July/August, 1999); reprinted in *Signs of Intelligence: Understanding Intelligent Design,* ed. William A. Dembski and James M. Kushiner (Grand Rapids, Mich.: Baker, 2001). For a briefer treatment of many of the themes found in chapters 7 and 8, see Nancy Pearcey, "Darwin Meets the Berenstain Bears: How Evolution Changed American Thought," Veritas Forum at Ohio State University, November 6, 2002. The material is adapted and expanded in Nancy Pearcey, "Darwin Meets the Berenstain Bears: The Cultural Impact of Evolution," in *Uncommon Dissent: Intellectuals Who Find Darwinism Unconvincing,* ed. William A. Dembski (Wilmington, Del.: Intercollegiate Studies Institute, 2004).
4. Francis Schaeffer, *A Christian Manifesto,* in *The Complete Works of Francis A. Schaeffer,* vol. 5 (Wheaton, Ill.: Crossway, 1982), 423.
5. Richard Dawkins, *The Selfish Gene* (New York: Oxford University Press, 1976); Robert Wright, *The Moral Animal: Evolutionary Psychology in Everyday Life* (New York: Vintage, 1994); Leonard D. Katz, ed., *Evolutionary Origins of Morality* (New York: Norton, 1998).
6. E. O. Wilson and Michael Ruse, "The Evolution of Ethics," in *Religion and the Natural Sciences: The Range of Engagement,* ed. J. E. Hutchingson (Orlando: Harcourt & Brace, 1991), 310; E. O. Wilson and Michael Ruse, "Moral Philosophy as an Applied Science," *Philosophy* 61 (1986): 179.
7. Richard Wrangham and Dale Peterson, *Demonic Males: Apes and the Origins of Human Violence* (New York: Houghton Mifflin, 1996).
8. Scott Atran, *In Gods We Trust: The Evolutionary Landscape of Religion* (New York: Oxford University Press, 2002); and Pascal Boyer, *Religion Explained: The Evolutionary Origins of Religious Thought* (New York: Basic Books, 2001).
9. Paul H. Rubin, *Darwinian Politics: The Evolutionary Origin of Freedom* (New Brunswick, N.J.: Rutgers University Press, 2002); Arthur E. Gandolfi, Anna S. Gandolfi, and David P. Barash, *Economics as an Evolutionary Science: From Utility to Fitness* (New Brunswick, N.J.: Transaction, 2002); John H. Beckstrom, *Evolutionary Jurisprudence: Prospects and Limitations on the Use of Modern Darwinism Throughout the Legal Process* (Champaign, Ill.: University of Illinois Press, 1989); there is also the more recent book by Suri Ratnapala and Jason Soon, *Evolutionary Jurisprudence* (Aldershot, Hampshire, UK: Ashgate, 2003); Margaret Gruter and Paul Bohannan, eds., *Law, Biology, and Culture: The Evolution of Law* (Portola Valley, Calif.: Ross Erikson, 1983).
10. Dean Keith Simonton, *Origins of Genius: Darwinian Perspectives on Creativity* (New York: Oxford University Press, 1999); Joseph Carroll, *Evolution and Literary Theory* (Columbia: University of Missouri Press, 1994). See also Robert Storey, *Mimesis and the Human Animal: On the Biogenetic Foundations of Literary Representation* (Evanston, Ill.: Northwestern University Press, 1996).
11. Wenda Trevathan, James J. McKenna, and Euclid O. Smith, eds., *Evolutionary Medicine* (New York: Oxford University Press, 1999); Randolph M. Nesse and George C. Williams, *Why We Get Sick: The New Science of Darwinian Medicine* (New York: Vintage, 1996); Anthony Stevens and John Price, *Darwinian Psychiatry* (New York: Routledge, 2000); Paul Gilbert and Kent G. Bailey, eds., *Genes on the Couch: Explorations in Evolutionary Psychology* (London: Brunner-Routledge, 2000).
12. Kingsley Browne, *Divided Labours: An Evolutionary View of Women at Work* (New Haven, Conn.: Yale University Press, 1999); Martin Daly and Margo Wilson, *The Truth About Cinderella: A Darwinian View of Parental Love* (New Haven, Conn.: Yale University Press, 1999); Nigel Nicholson, *Executive Instinct: Managing the Human Animal in the Information Age* (New York: Crown, 2000).
13. David M. Buss, *Evolution of Desire: Strategies of Human Mating* (New York: Basic Books,

1995); Malcolm Potts and Roger Short, *Ever Since Adam and Eve: The Evolution of Human Sexuality* (New York: Cambridge University Press, 1999).

14. Geoffrey Miller, *The Mating Mind: How Sexual Choice Shaped the Evolution of Human Nature* (New York: Doubleday, 2000).

15. Natalie Angier, "Of Altruism, Heroism and Nature's Gifts in the Face of Terror," *New York Times,* September 18, 2001.

16. Cited in Hillary Rose and Steven Rose, ed., *Alas, Poor Darwin: Arguments Against Evolutionary Psychology* (London: Jonathan Cape, 2000), 249.

17. Nancy Pearcey, "Real Heroism," Salem radio editorial. See Jeffrey Schloss, "Evolutionary Accounts of Altruism and the Problem of Goodness by Design," *Mere Creation* (Downers Grove, Ill.: InterVarsity Press, 1998), 236-261. Many biologists "concede that the moral and sacrificial aspects of human behavior most needing explanation cannot be understood in terms of biological causation at all" (252).

18. Stephen Jay Gould seems to have coined the phrase. See Gould, "More Things in Heaven and Earth," in *Alas, Poor Darwin; Arguments Against Evolutionary Psychology,* ed. Hilary Rose and Steven Rose (London: Jonathan Cape, 2000), 94.

19. H. Allen Orr, "Dennett's Strange Idea: Natural Selection: Science of Everything, Universal Acid, Cure for the Common Cold . . . ," in the *Boston Review,* Summer 1996, at http://bostonreview.mit.edu/br21.3/Orr.html.

20. Randy Thornhill and Craig Palmer, "Why Men Rape," *The Sciences* (January/February 2000): 20-28; see also *The Natural History of Rape: Biological Bases of Sexual Coercion* (Cambridge, Mass.: MIT Press, 2000). The same theme is echoed in a recent book by Steven Pinker, *The Blank Slate: The Modern Denial of Human Nature* (New York: Viking, 2002), where he writes that rape is likely an adaptive strategy pursued by low-status males who are "alienated from a community" and "unable to win the consent of women" (364). Hence a gene that predisposes such males to rape will spread.

21. Nancy Pearcey, "Darwin's Dirty Secret," *World,* March 13, 2000.

22. Randy Thornhill, "Controversial New Theory of Rape in Terms of Evolution and Nature," National Public Radio, January 26, 2000, emphasis added.

23. Jerry Coyne and Andrew Berry, "Rape as an Adaptation," *Nature* 404 (March 9, 2000): 121-122.

24. Tom Bethell, "Against Sociobiology," *First Things* 109 (January 2001): 18-24.

25. Steven Pinker, "Why They Kill Their Newborns," *The New York Times,* November 2, 1997.

26. The *Newsweek* article appeared only a few months after a well-publicized infanticide case in Indiana ("Baby Doe"). See Nancy Pearcey, "Evolution and Murder," editorial, *Bible-Science Newsletter,* December 1982. For a longer treatment of the topic, see Nancy Pearcey, "Why People Kill Babies: Are Scientists Becoming Apologists for a New Ethic?" *Bible-Science Newsletter,* August 1986.

27. H. Allen Orr, "Darwinian Storytelling," *The New York Review of Books,* February 27, 2003. Orr describes Pinker's *New York Times* piece as "a nearly data-free account that comes perilously close to parody."

28. Cited in Ben Wiker, "Darwin and the Descent of Morality," *First Things* 117 (November 2001): 10-13; chapter 4 of Darwin's *Descent of Man,* where this quote occurs, may be viewed at http://www.literature.org/authors/darwin-charles/the-descent-of-man/chapter-04.html.

29. Provine's argument can be heard on the video, "Darwinism: Science or Naturalistic Philosophy?" a debate with Phillip Johnson at Stanford University, April 30, 1994. A transcript is available at http://www.arn.org/docs/orpages/or161/161main.htm.

30. Peter Singer, "Heavy Petting," review of *Dearest Pet: On Bestiality,* by Midas Dekkers, at http://www.nerve.com/Opinions/Singer/heavyPetting/main.asp.

31. The play is by Pulitzer Prize–winner Edward Albee, and it won four major awards for best new play (Tony, New York Drama Critics Circle, Drama Desk, and Outer Critics Circle).

32. Nancy Pearcey, "The Birds and the Bees: Pop Culture's Evolutionary Message," *World,* April 22, 2000.

33. For a discussion of Kinsey's thought, see Nancy Pearcey, "Creating the 'New Man': The Hidden Agenda in Sex Education," *Bible-Science Newsletter,* May 1990. For a later treatment, see "Salvation Through Sex?" chapter 25 in *How Now?*

34. For example, geneticist Theodosius Dobzhansky wrote that, in producing the genetic basis of

culture, "biological evolution has transcended itself," surrendering the primary role in human evolution to something that is non-biological (*Mankind Evolving: The Evolution of the Human Species* [New Haven, Conn.: Yale University Press, 1962], 20).

35. Cited in Nancy Pearcey, "Singer in the Rain," *First Things* 106 (October 2000): 57-63.

36. Peter Singer, *A Darwinian Left: Politics, Evolution, and Cooperation* (New Haven, Conn.: Yale University Press, 2000), 6.

37. Robin Dunbar, Chris Knight, and Camilla Power, eds., *The Evolution of Culture: An Interdisciplinary View* (New Brunswick, N.J.: Rutgers University Press, 1999); and Robert Aunger, ed., *Darwinizing Culture* (Oxford and New York: Oxford University Press, 2001).

38. Howard Kaye, *The Social Meaning of Modern Biology: From Darwinism to Sociobiology* (1986; reprint, New Brunswick, N.J.: Transaction, 1997). See also my review of Kaye's book in *First Things* 83 (May 1998): 59-62.

39. See Mary Midgely, "Why Memes?" in *Alas, Poor Darwin*, 72-73.

40. Robert Wright, *The Moral Animal: Why We Are the Way We Are* (New York: Vintage, 1994), 336, 351, 324-325, 350, 355, 325.

41. Ibid., 376, 336ff.

42. Dawkins, *Selfish Gene*, 215.

43. Steven Pinker, *How the Mind Works* (New York: Norton, 1997), 52.

44. Richard Dawkins, "The Evolution of Bill Clinton: Sex and Power," *The Observer* (London), Sunday, March 22, 1998.

45. See Francis Schaeffer, *The God Who Is There*, in *Complete Works*, vol. 1, 69, 133.

46. Singer, *Darwinian Left*, 62. See my review, "Singer in the Rain."

47. Singer, *Darwinian Left*, 63. In the last sentence, he is quoting Richard Dawkins.

48. Ibid.

49. C. S. Lewis, *God in the Dock: Essays on Theology and Ethics*, ed. Walter Hooper (Grand Rapids, Mich.: Eerdmans, 1970), part 1, chapter 12.

50. Ernst Mayr, "Evolution and God," *Nature* 248 (March 22, 1974): 285, emphasis added.

51. Richard Dawkins, *A Devil's Chaplain*, ed. Latha Menon (London: Weidenfeld & Nicolson, 2003). See also Richard Dawkins, "Viruses of the Mind," *Free Inquiry* 13 no. 3 (Summer 1993): 34-41.

52. Leo Strauss, *Natural Right and History* (Chicago: University of Chicago Press, 1950, 1953), 7-8. See also 166.

53. Dean E. Murphy, "Scout Not Prepared for Group's Ultimatum: Get Right with God," *The New York Times*, November 9, 2002.

54. Michael Shermer, *How We Believe: The Search for God in an Age of Science* (New York: W. H. Freeman, 2000), 2-3.

55. Michael Shermer, "How We Believe: The Search for God in an Age of Science," Michael Shermer's E-Skeptic of October 2, 1999, Skeptics Society, Altadena, Calif., at http://www.e-skeptic.de/021099.htm.

56. E. O. Wilson, "Toward a Humanistic Biology," *The Humanist* 42 (September/October 1982): 40.

57. E. O. Wilson, *Consilience: The Unity of Knowledge* (New York: Knopf, 1998), 4.

58. E. O. Wilson, *Naturalist* (Washington, D.C.: Island, 1994), 45. For additional detail on how Wilson turned evolution itself into a religion, see "The Drama of Despair," chapter 27 in *How Now?*

59. Abraham Kuyper, *Lectures on Calvinism* (Grand Rapids, Mich.: Eerdmans, 1931), 11.

60. Bill Overn (who later became executive director of the Bible-Science Association), in discussion with the author. One day when Bill was a student at the University of Minnesota, he found himself running late to class, and stuck out his thumb to hitchhike. When a car stopped, he was picked up by an engaging young man who introduced himself as Henry Morris, a graduate student in hydraulic engineering. Morris was later to become the founder of the Institute for Creation Research, and already he had written a book defending the scientific reliability of the Bible. By the time Bill got out of the car, he had become excited about the cause, and ever since he has been a tireless promoter of the scientific case for creation.

CHAPTER 8: DARWINS OF THE MIND

1. Robert Frost, "Accidentally on Purpose," in *Robert Frost; Collected Poems, Prose and Plays* (New York: Library of America, 1995), 438.

2. The story was originally told in E. Yaroslavsky, *Landmarks in the Life of Stalin* (Moscow: Foreign Languages Publishing House, 1940), 8-9.

3. Stow Persons, ed., *Evolutionary Thought in America* (New York: George Braziller, 1956).

4. John Dewey was heavily influenced by psychologist G. Stanley Hall, who was proud at having earned the nickname "Darwin of the mind," a moniker I've adapted for the title of this chapter. For a more general discussion on the impact of evolution on the social sciences, see Nancy Pearcey, "Where Is Evolution Taking Us? Sociology and the New World Order," *Bible-Science Newsletter,* February 1988.

5. Paul Conkin, *When All the Gods Trembled: Darwinism, Scopes, and American Intellectuals* (Lanham, Md.: Rowman & Littlefield, 1998), see especially 39-40, 143-144. Conkin gives greater detail in *Puritans and Pragmatists: Eight Eminent American Thinkers* (Bloomington: Indiana University Press, 1976).

6. See Albert W. Alschuler, *Law Without Values: The Life, Work, and Legacy of Justice Holmes* (Chicago: University of Chicago Press, 2000), 41.

7. Holmes recorded his thoughts a few years afterward in a notebook. Cited in Louis Menand, *The Metaphysical Club: A Story of Ideas in America* (New York: Farrar, Straus, & Giroux, 2001), 37.

8. Menand, *Metaphysical Club,* 4.

9. Oliver Wendell Holmes Jr., "Law in Science and Science in Law," *Harvard Law Review* 12:443 (1899), in *The Essential Holmes,* edited with an introduction by Richard A. Posner (Chicago: University of Chicago Press, 1996), 188-190. See also E. Donald Elliott, "The Evolutionary Tradition in Jurisprudence," *Columbia Law Review* 85, no. 38 (1985): 52-53. This article provides a good overview of legal theories that draw explicit metaphors to evolution.

10. Conkin, *When All the Gods Trembled,* 42.

11. John Dewey, "The Influence of Darwin on Philosophy," in *The Influence of Darwin on Philosophy and Other Essays in Contemporary Thought* (New York: Henry Holt, 1910), 9.

12. See Menand, *Metaphysical Club,* 361.

13. Ibid., 357-358, 369.

14. Ibid., 355, 358.

15. James Miller, "Holmes, Peirce, and Legal Pragmatism," *Yale Law Journal* 84 (1975): 1123, 1132.

16. As Christopher Kaiser explains, among the early modern scientists, the natural world was considered comprehensible because "the same Logos that is responsible for its ordering is also reflected in human reason" (*Creation and the History of Science* [Grand Rapids, Mich.: Eerdmans, 1991], 10). Likewise, historian Richard Cohen notes that the rise of science required a belief in a "rational creator of all things," with its corollary that "we lesser rational beings might, by virtue of that Godlike rationality, be able to decipher the laws of nature" ("Alternative Interpretations of the History of Science," in *The Validation of Scientific Theories,* ed. Philip Frank [Boston: Beacon, 1956], 227). On how the idea of the image of God persisted even among thinkers who were not Christian (where God was replaced by the Absolute, for example), see Edward Craig, *The Image of God and the Works of Man* (Oxford: Clarendon, 1987).

17. Cited in Menand, *Metaphysical Club,* 353.

18. Cited in ibid., 355-356. Elsewhere he wrote, "If theological ideas prove to have a value for concrete life, they will be true, for pragmatism, in the sense of being good for so much" ("What Pragmatism Means," in *Pragmatism: A New Name for Old Ways of Thinking* [New York: Longman, Green, 1907]). See also William James, *Varieties of Religious Experience* (New York: Touchstone, 1997).

19. Cited in Paul F. Boller, Jr., *American Thought in Transition: The Impact of Evolutionary Naturalism, 1865–1900* (Chicago: Rand McNally, 1969), 142, emphasis in original.

20. Bertrand Russell, *A History of Western Philosophy* (Forage Village, Mass.: Simon & Schuster, 1945), 818.

21. Jon Roberts and James Turner, *The Sacred and the Secular University* (Princeton, N.J.:

Princeton University Press, 2000). Part 1 of this book deals with the sciences, part 2 with the humanities.

22. As Conkin explains, the two-realm theory of truth seemed to divide the human person himself: The lower story exalted empirically verifiable facts, but it led to a determinism that denied "the validity of his ideals and his feelings of worth and purpose." Meanwhile the upper story affirmed the reality of moral and spiritual ideals, but "at the expense of logic [and] fact." It seemed one had to choose either a naturalism that cared about nothing but scientific facts, or else an airy idealism that offered sweeping visions of Purpose and Right (*Puritans and Pragmatists*, 275).

23. Morton White, *Science and Sentiment in America: Philosophical Thought from Jonathan Edwards to John Dewey* (New York: Oxford University Press, 1972). White even titles one chapter in his book "John Dewey: Rebel Against Dualism" (chapter 11).

24. James Kloppenberg, *Uncertain Victory: Social Democracy and Progressivism in European and American Thought, 1870–1920* (Oxford: Oxford University Press, 1986), 26. Dewey used the phrase "via media" specifically in describing the thought of William James, but Kloppenberg uses it as a rubric for all the pragmatists as well as others who sought to reconcile the rival traditions of empiricism and idealism.

25. Kloppenberg says James suffered the nineteenth century's "philosophical friction" between naturalism and idealism "as an acutely personal affliction" (*Uncertain Victory*, 37).

26. Conkin says James "saw science, as sponsored and popularized in America, as a new church, rich in prestige, imperialistic in its claims, and intolerable in its intellectual pretensions" (*Puritans and Pragmatists*, 276-277).

27. Henry Steele Commager says the two-realm division of truth seemed to confront people with a choice "between a 'brute,' tough-minded philosophy which banished idealism and mysticism in the name of science" (the lower story), and a "tender-minded philosophy which banished science in the name of mysticism and idealism" (the upper story) (*The American Mind: An Interpretation of American Thought and Character Since the 1880s* [New Haven, Conn.: Yale University Press, 1950], 93).

28. William James, "The Present Dilemma in Philosophy," in *Pragmatism* (New York: Longman, Green, 1907), at http://www.4literature.net/William_James/Pragmatism. Conkin says: "The noble goal of pragmatism, in James's own terms, was the bridging of fact and value, science and religion" (*Puritans and Pragmatists*, 324).

29. Bruce Kuklick, *Churchmen and Philosophers: From Jonathan Edwards to John Dewey* (New Haven, Conn.: Yale University Press, 1985), 223.

30. This was, in fact, *the* central concept that William James took from evolution. The "elusive but genuine character of individual spontaneity in both the external world and in man is in James's view of evolution epitomized by 'saltatory' mutations, original, spontaneous, irreducible phases of experience" (Philip P. Wiener, *Evolution and the Founders of Pragmatism* [Gloucester, Mass.: Peter Smith, 1969; orig., Cambridge, Mass.: Harvard University Press, 1949], 101). Peirce thought that even the laws of nature had evolved by chance—a view he said derived from Darwin: "My opinion is only Darwinism analyzed, generalized, and brought into the realm of Ontology" (cited in Menand, *Metaphysical Club*, 277).

31. James Ward Smith, "Religion and Science in American Philosophy," in *The Shaping of American Religion*, ed. James Ward Smith and A. Leland Jamison (Princeton, N.J.: Princeton University Press, 1961), 421 and passim. This is a tendency Smith himself supports, while deriding all other responses to evolution as "superficial." See also Stow Persons, "Religion and Modernity, 1865–1914," in the same volume.

32. See Wiener, *Evolution and the Founders of Pragmatism*, chapter 4. William James likewise taught a finite god, who is neither omnipotent nor omniscient. "His finiteness evaded all problems of evil and foreknowledge," says Conkin (*Puritans and Pragmatists*, 339). By the end of his life, James had come to see God as a cosmic consciousness, a pooling or weaving together of all individual consciousness.

33. "Hartshorne later claimed that Peirce and Whitehead were the two philosophers who influenced him most" (G. Douglas Browning, Robert Kane, Donald Viney, Stephen Phillips, "Hartshorne Tribute," *Proceedings and Addresses of the American Philosophical Association* [May 2001], at http://www.hyattcarter.com/hartshorne_tribute.htm. See also John B. Cobb, "Charles Hartshorne: The Einstein of Religious Thought, 1897–2000," Courtesy of the Center for Process Studies, Claremont, Calif., at http://www.ctr4process.org).

34. If you have read appendix 2, you will recognize this as a form of neo-Platonism—the world as an emanation of God's own essence.

35. See Boller, "William James and the Open Universe," in *American Thought in Transition,* especially 134-138. See also Allen C. Guelzo, "The Return of the Will," in *Edwards in Our Time: Jonathan Edwards and the Shaping of American Religion,* ed. Sang Hyun Lee and Allen C. Guelzo (Grand Rapids, Mich.: Eerdmans, 1999), 100-102. Some proponents of Open Theism acknowledge the influence of Peirce and Whitehead, while others insist that they are simply trying to explain how God can interact with a temporal and changing world (for example, responding to prayer) if He really is eternal, unchanging, immutable, and impassible. Philosopher John Passmore (who is not a professing Christian) shows that many conceptions of divine perfection were adopted from Greek philosophy and are incompatible with biblical theology (see *The Perfectibility of Man,* 3rd ed. [Indianapolis: Liberty Fund, 2000; orig., New York: Scribner's, 1970]).

36. The underlying problem for Christian thinkers is the rise of historical consciousness. In the Middle Ages, the church developed an essentially static or cyclical worldview. As a result, it had difficulty responding to the new sense of historical development that began in the Renaissance and came to full flower in the Romantic movement. See Nancy Pearcey, "Recent Developments in the History of Science and Christianity" and "Reply," *Pro Rege* 30, no. 4 (June 2002), 22.

   The two great challenges to the faith that arose at the end of the nineteenth century were German higher criticism and Darwinism, both representing the new historicist mindset—the first in theology, the second in science. Higher criticism insisted that Christianity itself had to be explained as a product of evolving religious ideas and customs. It did not regard Scripture as divine revelation but merely as the expression of evolving conceptions of God within human culture. Thus it imposed an evolutionary schema onto the Bible itself—a sequence from animism to totemism, to polytheism, and finally to monotheism. Where the biblical account did not fit that preconceived schema, the critics simply pronounced it unreliable and riddled with errors. See Nancy Pearcey, "Interpreting Genesis: A Reply to the Critics," *Bible-Science Newsletter,* August 1984; Nancy Pearcey, "Real People in a Real World: The Lessons of Archaeology," *Bible-Science Newsletter,* June 1985.

   The problem with historicism is that, like every "ism," it selects one aspect of the created world and elevates it into the single, unifying principle of interpretation for all reality. As Herman Dooyeweerd put it, historicism "absolutizes" the historical aspect of created reality. (Whenever God is rejected as the absolute reality, some part of creation will be elevated into an absolute, and everything else will be reduced to its categories.) Dooyeweerd also offered a Christian conceptualization of history as the "unfolding" of the inbuilt potentials of creation. For an accessible introduction to Dooyeweerd's philosophy, see L. Kalsbeek, *Contours of a Christian Philosophy,* ed. Bernard and Josina Zylstra (Toronto: Wedge, 1975), 111-113. See also C. T. McIntire, "Dooyeweerd's Philosophy of History," in *The Legacy of Herman Dooyeweerd* (Lanham, Md.: University Press of America, 1985).

37. The pragmatists adopted the Darwinian notion that law is merely "a human instrument for adjusting conflicting desires in the struggle for existence" (Wiener, *Evolution and the Founders of Pragmatism,* 153). For more on the impact of evolution on legal philosophy, see Nancy Pearcey, "Law and Democracy: Creation—A Complete Worldview," *Bible-Science Newsletter,* October 1983.

38. For more on the philosophical background of legal pragmatism, see Nancy R. Pearcey, "Darwin's New Bulldogs," *Regent University Law Review* 13, no. 2 (2000–2001): 483-511. An adapted version appeared as "Why Judges Make Law: The Roots and Remedies of Judicial Imperialism," *Human Events,* December 1, 2000, at http://arn.org/pearcey/nphome.htm.

39. Holmes, "Law in Science," 191.

40. Ibid., 92.

41. Holmes, "The Path of the Law," *Essential Holmes,* 170.

42. Holmes, "Law in Science," *Essential Holmes,* 198. The goal of studying law, Holmes said, is merely "the prediction of the incidence of the public force through the instrumentality of the courts." Phillip Johnson comments that for Holmes, law is "the science of state coercion"— the empirical study of how the state in fact uses its coercive power to enforce policies (*Reason in the Balance: The Case Against Naturalism in Science, Law, and Education* [Downers Grove,

Ill.: InterVarsity, 1995], 140). For a review see Nancy Pearcey, "Naturalism on Trial," *First Things* 60 (February 1996): 62-65.

43. As I was writing this chapter, I clipped an article from the *New York Times* announcing with great excitement that in the state's highest court, nineteen law professors had filed a brief arguing that judges should be free to make up their own minds about the acceptability of capital punishment, regardless of what the law says. The *Times* called this "a novel theory" but it was really just an application of Holmes's legal pragmatism. See "Law Professors Give State Court a Novel Theory on Executions," *New York Times,* May 6, 2002. See also the commentary by John Leo, "Stealth Strategy to Subvert Democracy," May 13, 2002, at http://www.townhall.com.columnists/johnleo/jl20020513.shtml.

44. Darwinism has influenced abortion even more directly by fostering the eugenics movement. See Richard Weikart, "Progress Through Racial Extermination: Social Darwinism, Eugenics, and Pacifism in Germany, 1860–1918," *German Studies Review* 26 (2003): 273-294; and "Darwinism and Death: Devaluing Human Life in Germany, 1860–1920," *Journal of the History of Ideas* 63 (2002): 323-344. See also Weikart's recent book, *From Darwin to Hitler: Evolutionary Ethics, Eugenics, and Devaluing Human Life in Germany* (New York: Palgrave Macmillan, 2004).

45. Kuklick, *Churchmen and Philosophers,* 230-231.

46. Cited in Menand, *Metaphysical Club,* 369. See Kuklick, *Churchmen and Philosophers,* 232-235, 219, 243.

47. Kuklick, *Churchmen and Philosophers,* 241. Conkin says, "Dewey remained a nominal Christian until his thirties" (*Puritans and Pragmatists,* 346).

48. Conkin, *Puritans and Pragmatists,* 354. Dewey's naturalistic faith permeated his highly influential educational philosophy—see Dewey's "Education as a Religion," *The New Republic,* August, 1922, 64ff.

49. See Nancy Pearcey, "The Evolving Child: John Dewey's Impact on Modern Education," parts 1 and 2, *Bible-Science Newsletter,* January and February 1991; and Nancy Pearcey, "What Is Evolution Doing to Education?" *Bible-Science Newsletter,* January 1986. For a later treatment, see "Still at Risk," chapter 34 in *How Now?*

50. Merrill Harmin, Howard Kirschenbaum, and Sidney Simon, *Clarifying Values Through Subject Matter: Applications for the Classroom* (Minneapolis: Hart, 1973), 31.

51. Thomas Lickona, *Educating for Character* (New York: Bantam, 1992), 237.

52. William Kilpatrick, *Why Johnny Can't Tell Right from Wrong: Moral Illiteracy and the Case for Character Education* (New York: Simon & Schuster, 1992), 93-94.

53. Catherine Fosnot, "Constructivism: A Psychological Theory of Learning," in *Constructivism: Theory, Perspectives, and Practice,* ed. Catherine Fosnot (New York: Teachers College Press, 1996), 8-33, emphasis added.

54. J. F. Osborne, "Beyond Constructivism," *Science Education* 80 (1996): 63.

55. Cited in Allen Quist, *FedEd: The Federal Curriculum and How It's Enforced* (St. Paul, Minn.: Maple River Education Coalition, 2002), 118.

56. "After looking at instructional methods textbooks, one could quickly conclude that constructivism is an instructional methodology," writes one educator. But "this conclusion would be incorrect. Constructivism is an epistemology, a philosophical explanation about the nature of knowledge. . . . In fact, according to constructivism, laws of nature do not exist; rather all knowledge is subjective and personal and is a product of our own cognitive acts" (Terry Simpson, "Dare I Oppose Constructivist Theory?" in *The Educational Forum* [Kappa Delta Pi] 66 [Summer 2002]: 347-354).

57. Ernst von Glasersfeld, "A Constructivist Approach to Teaching," in *Constructivism in Education,* ed. L. P. Steffe and J. Gale (Hillsdale, N.J.: Lawrence Erlbaum Associates, 1995), 3-15; also available online at http://platon.ee.duth.gr/~soeist7t/Lessons/lesson7.htm.

58. The school superintendent was from Brazil, which means this radical epistemology has already spread beyond the industrialized nations. Christian teachers often interpret constructivism in a strictly practical sense to mean that they should encourage students to actively figure out answers on their own, or that they should temporarily ignore students' mistakes for limited purposes (e.g., to encourage creative writing without the constant fear of being marked wrong). These are sound educational practices that good teachers have always adopted, especially in the early elementary grades. But Christian teachers need to be aware of the worldview implications of constructivism as well, understanding that in the secular world it is not merely

a pedagogical method but a relativistic epistemology based on the idea that truth is a social construction.

A balanced discussion of constructivism can be found in *Mathematics in a Postmodern Age: A Christian Perspective*, ed. Russell W. Howell and W. James Bradley (Grand Rapids, Mich.: Eerdmans, 2001). See especially chapter 12, "Teaching and Learning Mathematics: The Influence of Constructivism." For more on the impact of philosophical pragmatism on education, see Nancy Pearcey, "Darwin Meets the Berenstain Bears: The Cultural Impact of Evolution," in *Uncommon Dissent: Intellectuals Who Find Darwinism Unconvincing*, ed. William A. Dembski (Wilmington, Del.: Intercollegiate Studies Institute, 2004).

59. Though not all postmodernists are pragmatists, they hold many intellectual roots in common. See the first two sections of Eugene F. Miller, "Positivism, Historicism, and Political Inquiry," *American Political Science Review* 66, no. 3 (September 1972): 796-817; also available online at http://members.shaw.ca/compilerpress1/Anno%20Miller.htm.

60. Richard Rorty, *Contingency, Irony, and Solidarity* (Cambridge and New York: Cambridge University Press, 1989), chapter 1, passim. Interestingly, Rorty is echoed by educators who say that constructivism, too, hinges on the question, "Is knowledge made or discovered?" See D. C. Phillips, "The Good, the Bad, and the Ugly: The Many Faces of Constructivism," *Educational Researcher* 24, no. 7 (October 1995): 5-12.

61. Richard Rorty, "Untruth and Consequences," a review of *Killing Time* by Paul Feyerabend, in *The New Republic*, July 31, 1995, 32-36.

62. Rorty, *Contingency, Irony, and Solidarity*, 17.

63. Rorty, "Untruth and Consequences."

64. Rorty, *Contingency, Irony, and Solidarity*, 15.

65. In Francis Darwin, ed., *Life and Letters of Charles Darwin*, vol. 1 (New York: D. Appleton, 1898), 285. For several additional quotations from Darwin on this conundrum, see Nancy Pearcey, "The Influence of Evolution on Philosophy and Ethics," in *Science at the Crossroads: Observation or Speculation? Papers of the 1983 National Creation Conference* (Richfield, Minn.: Onesimus, 1985), 166-171.

66. Alvin Plantinga, *Warrant and Proper Function* (New York: Oxford University Press, 1993), 218.

67. Roger Trigg, *Philosophy Matters* (Oxford: Blackwell, 2002), 83.

68. If one begins with naturalistic evolution, explains historian George Marsden, then "the most consistent conclusion" is "postmodern skepticism" (*The Soul of the American University: From Protestant Establishment to Established Nonbelief* [New York: Oxford University Press, 1994], 440. See also 430-431).

69. Francis Schaeffer, *The God Who Is There*, in *The Complete Works of Francis A. Schaeffer*, vol. 1 (Wheaton, Ill.: Crossway, 1982), 140-142.

70. Phillip E. Johnson, "The Limits of Pragmatism," *First Things* 59 (June/July 1996): 52, 54.

71. "Lewis Mumford, Waldo Frank, and some years earlier Randolph Bourne, denounced what Mumford called 'the pragmatic acquiescence,' a phrase that caught their common conviction that pragmatism was a philosophy of means rather than ends, and that it took an unexamined conception of its ends, such as they were, from the surrounding culture" (Alan Ryan, in "Pragmatism, Social Identity, Patriotism, and Self-Criticism," a paper delivered at a conference titled "Conference on Identity: Personal, Cultural, and National," sponsored by the National Humanities Center, June 2–June 4, 1994; at http://www.nhc.rtp.nc.us:8080/publications/hongkong/ryan.htm).

72. Cited in Alschuler, *Law Without Values*, 59. This was a recurring theme in Holmes's writings. The law should be shaped "in accordance with the will of the de facto supreme power in the community," he wrote (cited in Alschuler, 58). And: "The ultimate question is what do the dominant forces of the community want and do they want it hard enough to disregard whatever inhibitions may stand in the way" (letter to John C. H. Wu, 1926, cited in Thomas C. Grey, "Holmes and Legal Pragmatism," *Stanford Law Review* 41 [1989]: 823). As Alschuler comments, Holmes's view means that "every government is good until it is ousted" (60).

73. Holmes, "Natural Law," in *Essential Holmes*, 180.

74. Bertrand Russell, "Pragmatism" (1909), in *Philosophical Essays* (London: Longmans, Green, 1910), 109.

75. Rorty, *Contingency, Irony, and Solidarity*, 5.

76. Jacob D. Bekenstein, "Information in the Holographic Universe," Scientific American.com,

July 14, 2003, at http://www.sciam.com/article.cfm?articleID=000AF072-4891-1F0A-97AE80A84189EEDF

77. Rorty, *Contingency, Irony, and Solidarity,* 21, emphasis added.

78. Schaeffer, *He Is There and He Is Not Silent,* in *Complete Works,* vol. 1.

79. Roberts and Turner, *The Sacred and the Secular University,* 90, emphasis added.

CHAPTER 9: WHAT'S SO GOOD ABOUT EVANGELICALISM?

1. James McGready, *Short Narrative of the Revival of Religion in Logan County, in the State of Kentucky, and the Adjacent Settlements in the State of Tennessee, from May 1797, Until September 1800,* cited in Iain Murray, *Revival and Revivalism: The Making and Marring of American Evangelicalism 1750–1858* (Edinburgh: Banner of Truth, 1994), 150.

2. "Denzel," in discussion with the author. The name has been changed to protect his privacy, but otherwise the story is completely true and accurate.

3. From John Wesley's journal for May 14, 1738, in *The Journal of the Rev. John Wesley,* ed. Nehemiah Curnock, 8 vols. (London: Epworth, 1938), 1:475-476.

4. Evangelicalism's "distinctive feature is not so much a theology as a devotional ethos" (Alister McGrath, *Evangelicalism and the Future of Christianity* [Downers Grove, Ill.: InterVarsity Press, 1995], 132; see also 57-59).

5. Ibid., chapter 6.

6. James Turner, *Without God, Without Creed: The Origins of Unbelief in America* (Baltimore: Johns Hopkins University Press, 1985), 75-76. Mark Noll calls the two wings "formalist" and "anti-formalist" (*America's God: From Jonathan Edwards to Abraham Lincoln* [Oxford: Oxford University Press, 2002], 175-176). Within contemporary American evangelicalism, James Davison Hunter identifies four major traditions: (1) Baptist, (2) Holiness-Pentecostal, (3) Anabaptist, (4) Reformational-Confessional (*American Evangelicalism: Conservative Religion and the Quandary of Modernity* [New Brunswick, N.J.: Rutgers University Press, 1983], 7-9). The first three of these would fall roughly within the populist wing, while the last would fall within the scholarly wing. For a helpful taxonomy by the Polis Center at Purdue University showing where individual denominations fit under broader categories, see http://www.polis.iupui.edu/RUC/Research/Glenmary_by_Polis_Types_as_table.htm.

7. The term itself has a longer history: "The term *evangelical* dates from the sixteenth century, and it was first used to refer to Catholic writers who wished to revert to more biblical beliefs and practices than those associated with the late medieval church." It was later applied to the Reformers (McGrath, *Evangelicalism and the Future of Christianity,* 19).

8. D. G. Hart, *That Old-Time Religion in Modern America: Evangelical Protestantism in the Twentieth Century* (Chicago: Ivan R. Dee, 2002), 9. For a list of the defining distinctives of evangelicalism, see David Bebbington, *Evangelicalism in Modern Britain: A History from the 1730s to the 1980s* (Grand Rapids, Mich.: Baker, 1992), 2-17.

9. For a discussion of the differences between confessional and evangelical churches, see the Introduction to D. G. Hart, *The Lost Soul of American Protestantism* (Lanham, Md.: Rowman & Littlefield, 2002). Presbyterians split during the first Awakening in 1741 (New Side versus Old Side), then reunited, then split again during the second Awakening in 1837 (New School versus Old School), only to reunite again in 1869. Thus the Presbyterians probably succeeded more than most groups in straddling both the populist and the scholarly strands of evangelicalism. Through the nineteenth century, they exercised strong intellectual leadership in the religious world and in American society generally, while also nurturing a warm and vibrant piety.

10. Mark Noll, *The Scandal of the Evangelical Mind* (Grand Rapids, Mich.: Eerdmans, 1994), 9.

11. Philip Jenkins, *The Next Christendom: The Coming of Global Christianity* (Oxford: Oxford University Press, 2002). An excellent introduction to Jenkins's book can be found in his article, "The Next Christianity," *The Atlantic Monthly,* October 2002, at http://www.theatlantic.com/issues/2002/10/jenkins.htm.

12. Roger Finke and Rodney Stark, *The Churching of America 1776–1990: Winners and Losers in Our Religious Economy* (New Brunswick, N.J.: Rutgers University Press, 1992).

13. This does not necessarily mean that people in early America were irreligious. The low rates are partly explained by the fact that the requirements for church membership were very rigorous, so that many attended church without becoming members. In addition, in frontier

areas there were often no churches to attend. Even taking these factors into account, however, the numbers are low compared to the common stereotype.

14. The percentages of religious adherents add up to less than 100 percent because the numbers do not include smaller groups, such as Lutheran, Dutch Reformed, Quaker, Mennonite, Huguenot, Moravian, Jewish, and so on.
15. Jon Butler, *Awash in a Sea of Faith: Christianizing the American People* (Cambridge, Mass.: Harvard University Press, 1990), see especially chapter 4. Butler offers a relatively positive view of the established churches, arguing that they served their constituents well. On suppression of dissenters, Nathan Hatch notes, "As late as the 1770s, Baptist preachers in Virginia were still being thrown in jail" (*The Democratization of American Christianity* [New Haven, Conn.: Yale University Press, 1989], 59).
16. Cited in Bebbington, *Evangelicalism in Modern Britain,* 11.
17. Cited in Finke and Stark, *Churching of America,* 19, emphasis added. For more detail, see chapter 2, "The Colonial Era Revisited."
18. The exceptions are places like Ireland and Quebec, where the Catholic church has also served as the primary vehicle for political resistance to external domination.
19. Finke and Stark, *Churching of America,* 238, 212.
20. "As the people moved westward after the Revolution, they were forever outrunning the institutions of settled society. . . . Organizations dissolved; restraints disappeared. Churches, social bonds, and cultural institutions often broke down, and they could not be reconstituted before the frontier families made yet another leap into the wilderness or the prairie" (Richard Hofstadter, *Anti-Intellectualism in American Life* [New York: Random House, 1966], 76).
21. Cited in Mark A. Noll, Nathan O. Hatch, and George M. Marsden, *The Search for Christian America* (Westchester, Ill.: Crossway, 1983), 111, emphasis added.
22. Finke and Stark, *Churching of America,* 33, emphasis added. This model applies even to the colonial period, when "the West" meant western Pennsylvania or Kentucky. Frontier conditions tend to be pretty much the same anywhere.
23. Hart, *That Old-Time Religion,* 7.
24. Hatch (*Democratization of American Christianity,* 87) cites a study finding that of the first 650 Methodist circuit riders, nearly half died before the age of thirty, almost 200 of them within their first five years of service. See also Finke and Stark, *Churching of America,* 153. The phrase God's "light artillery" is from Horace Bushnell, cited in Hatch, ibid., 67. The saying about "crows and Methodist preachers" is from Hofstadter, *Anti-Intellectualism in American Life,* 96.
25. Critics often accuse the revivalists of being anti-cultural and anti-intellectual, but to be fair many were simply responding to the condition of the frontier itself. Even Richard Hofstadter, generally critical of evangelical Christianity, wrote, "It must be said that they were not lowering the level of a high culture but trying to bring the ordinary restraints and institutions of a civilized society into an area which had hardly any culture at all" (*Anti-Intellectualism in American Life,* 79).
26. Cited in Hatch, *Democratization of American Christianity,* 127.
27. Hatch, *Democratization of American Christianity,* 102.
28. Cited in ibid., 104.
29. Among non-evangelical denominations, the ones that did best were those willing to adopt a similar approach. For example, Catholics began holding revival meetings using vernacular language and emotional appeals that were virtually identical to their Baptist and Methodist counterparts. In the early twentieth century, Catholics even built special vans and train cars outfitted with altars and religious symbols inside, which functioned as portable sanctuaries to take priests into unchurched areas. The vans, called "motor chapels," had wide doors on the side that opened outward, revealing an altar that could then be used to hold open-air masses in rural areas (see Finke and Stark, *Churching of America,* chapter 4).
30. Dean Kelley, *Why Conservative Churches Are Growing* (New York: Harper & Row, 1972). Of course the decline of the mainline churches has been slow and gradual, and their institutional power remained strong even as they lost numbers. For a good history, see Robert Handy, *A Christian America: Protestant Hopes and Historical Realities* (Oxford: Oxford University Press, 1984).
31. The achievement of the American evangelical movement stands out even more strongly when highlighted against the British experience. In England, John Wesley's Methodist movement was

eventually taken over by leaders more interested in maintaining rules and respectability than in reaching the poor and ragged masses—and they didn't care if that meant a loss in numbers. They banned camp meetings and expelled those who protested, until nearly one-third of their members had either left or been expelled. Eventually, the Methodist church in Britain lost contact with the working classes, with the result that today they are highly secularized. By contrast, in America the working classes remain *more* religious than the rest of the population. See Hatch, *Democratization of American Christianity*, 92-93. Here too, however, eventually the Methodist church followed the lure of respectability. Finke and Stark include a fascinating chapter on how the Methodist church became wealthy and went mainstream, and then began to decline almost as rapidly as it had once grown. See *Churching of America*, chapter 5.

32. Noll, *Scandal of the Evangelical Mind*, 63.

33. Stout, *The Divine Dramatist: George Whitefield and the Rise of Modern Evangelicalism* (Grand Rapids, Mich.: Eerdmans, 1991), xix. See also Harry Stout, "George Whitefield in Three Countries," in *Evangelicalism: Comparative Studies of Popular Protestantism in North America, the British Isles, and Beyond, 1700–1990*, ed. Mark Noll, David Bebbington, George Rawlyk (New York: Oxford University Press, 1994). Stephen Marini writes: "The Whitefieldian gospel . . . was Calvinist, but it neither dilated on theological problems nor spoke the language of doctrine and hermeneutic. It was more a matter of style and emphasis, drama and rhetoric designed to move emotions and change hearts" (*Radical Sects of Revolutionary New England* [Cambridge, Mass.: Harvard University Press, 1982], 12). For an inspiring account of Whitefield's life, see Arnold Dallimore, *George Whitefield: God's Anointed Servant in the Great Revival of the Eighteenth Century* (Wheaton, Ill.: Crossway, 1990).

34. Hart, *Lost Soul of American Protestantism*, 11. Whitefield relied so heavily on marketing techniques borrowed from the commercial world that one book calls him a "pedlar in divinity" (Frank Lambert, *"Pedlar in Divinity": George Whitefield and the Transatlantic Revivals, 1737–1770* [Princeton, N.J.: Princeton University Press, 2002]).

35. Stout, *Divine Dramatist*, xiii. Stout writes that Whitefield "was the first in a long line of public figures whose claim to influence would rest on celebrity and popularity rather than birth, breeding, or institutional fiat" (xiv).

36. Cited in Alan Heimert, *Religion and the American Mind: From the Great Awakening to the Revolution* (Cambridge, Mass.: Harvard University Press, 1966), 44.

37. Cited in ibid., 208.

38. Cited in ibid.

39. William H. Foote, *Sketches of North Carolina*, 396, cited in Murray, *Revival and Revivalism*, 149-150.

40. McGready, *Short Narrative*, cited in Murray, *Revival and Revivalism*, 150, emphasis added.

41. Heimert, *Religion and the American Mind*, 43. References to the joys of conversion are found throughout chapter 1, "The Nature and Necessity of the New Birth."

42. Heimert writes that defenders and opponents of the Awakening "each marked the independent fulfillment of one of the strains that in Puritanism had been held in precarious balance: 'piety' and 'reason'" (*Religion and the American Mind*, 3).

43. Patricia Bonomi, *Under the Cope of Heaven: Religion, Society, and Politics in Colonial America* (New York: Oxford University Press, 1986), 147.

44. Donald M. Scott, *From Office to Profession: The New England Ministry, 1750–1850* (Philadelphia: University of Pennsylvania Press, 1978). For a description of "Protestant communalism," see Barry Alan Shain, *The Myth of American Individualism: The Protestant Origins of American Political Thought* (Princeton, N.J.: Princeton University Press, 1994).

45. Harry Stout, *Divine Dramatist*, xx.

46. Cited in Bonomi, *Under the Cope of Heaven*, 158, 154, emphasis in original.

47. Bonomi, ibid., 158.

48. George Marsden, *The Soul of the American University: From Protestant Establishment to Established Nonbelief* (New York: Oxford University Press, 1994), 54.

49. Cited in Heimert, *Religion and the American Mind*, 119.

50. What the first Awakening did "was to plant seeds of individualism and immediatism that would eventually exert a profound effect on Christian thinking" (Noll, *Scandal of the Evangelical Mind*, 61). "The revivals led by Edwards and Whitefield planted seeds that would

challenge this older version of Protestantism and eventually yield the basic ingredients of evangelicalism" (Hart, *That Old-Time Religion,* 7).

CHAPTER 10: WHEN AMERICA MET CHRISTIANITY—GUESS WHO WON?

1. Thomas Paine, *Common Sense,* at www.pagebypagebooks.com/Thomas_Paine/Common_Sense/Appendix_p4.html.
2. Interestingly, camp meetings had roots in sacramental gatherings in Scotland. Since communion was observed infrequently, only two to four times a year, thousands of people would gather from miles around and camp out for several days to hear sermons and receive the Lord's Supper. See Leigh Eric Schmidt, *Holy Fairs: Scotland and the Making of American Revivalism,* 2nd ed. (Grand Rapids, Mich.: Eerdmans, 1989).
3. Gordon S. Wood, *The Radicalism of the American Revolution: How a Revolution Transformed a Monarchial Society into a Democratic One Unlike Any That Had Ever Existed* (New York: Knopf, 1992), 361-362, emphasis added.
4. Cited in Nathan Hatch, *The Democratization of American Christianity* (New Haven, Conn.: Yale University Press, 1991), 36-38, see also 186. Similar themes are found in Mark Noll, *The Scandal of the Evangelical Mind* (Grand Rapids, Mich.: Eerdmans, 1994), especially chapter 3. A more popular treatment of anti-intellectualism in American evangelicalism is found in Os Guinness, *Fit Bodies, Fat Minds: Why Evangelicals Don't Think and What to Do About It* (Grand Rapids, Mich.: Baker, 1994).
5. The identification of religion with politics began in the First Great Awakening and is treated in detail in Nathan O. Hatch, *The Sacred Cause of Liberty: Republican Thought and the Millennium in Revolutionary New England* (New Haven, Conn.: Yale University Press, 1977). Hatch opens the book with a telling anecdote contrasting Jonathan Edwards who prayed in 1747 for a revival, with a group of ministers who prayed in 1787 for "the spirit of true republican government" (1-2). Clearly there had been a shift in spiritual concern from holiness to liberty.
6. Alexis de Tocqueville, *Democracy in America,* vol. 1 (New York: Knopf, 1980), 306-307.
7. John Leland, "The Connecticut Dissenters' Strong Box: No. 1, New London, 1802," at http://www.uark.edu/depts/comminfo/cambridge/strongbox1.html.
8. Cited in Hatch, *Democratization of American Christianity,* 98.
9. D. G. Hart, *The Lost Soul of American Protestantism* (Lanham, Md.: Rowman & Littlefield, 2002), 18.
10. Cited in Hatch, *Democratization of American Christianity,* 69-70, emphasis in original.
11. Cited in ibid., 71.
12. Cited in Richard T. Hughes and C. Leonard Allen, *Illusions of Innocence: Protestant Primitivism in America, 1630–1875* (Chicago: University of Chicago Press, 1988), 105.
13. Evangelicals "appropriated the rhetoric of civil and religious liberty that the respectable clergy had made popular during the Revolution and marshaled it for an entirely new purpose: to topple its architects." The enemy was no longer the British but "elites of all kinds, particularly the clergy" (Hatch, *Democratization of American Christianity,* 76).
14. Cited in ibid.
15. Patricia Bonomi, *Under the Cope of Heaven: Religion, Society, and Politics in Colonial America* (New York: Oxford University Press, 1986), 158-159. Bonomi describes the new theology of conversion in connection with the First Great Awakening, but since its development was a gradual process, her description is, if anything, even more applicable to the Second Great Awakening.
16. The Puritans "elaborated a 'morphology of conversion,' successive states of consciousness through which the hopeful saint could evaluate the evidence of divine election. Every step in this lifelong process of growth in grace was carefully defined by appropriate attitudes and behavior. *In principle, the Puritans never knew they were saved;* they could only trust that their minds were enabled by grace to penetrate beyond the veil and dimly discern the hand of God leading them to glory" (Stephen Marini, *Radical Sects of Revolutionary New England* [Cambridge, Mass.: Harvard University Press, 1982], 12, emphasis added).
17. Hughes and Allen, *Illusions of Innocence,* 113, 115. John Walsh writes, "Evangelical preaching of an immediate, personal assurance came to some as a welcome surprise," especially to those "who had found it difficult to reach the experience of regeneration that their

Puritan culture expected of them" ("'Methodism' and the Origins of English-Speaking Evangelicalism," in *Evangelicalism: Comparative Studies of Popular Protestantism in North America, the British Isles, and Beyond, 1700–1990,* ed. Mark Noll, David Bebbington, George Rawlyk [New York: Oxford University Press, 1994], 29-31). David Bebbington writes, "Whereas the Puritans had held that assurance is rare, late, and the fruit of struggle in the experience of believers, the Evangelicals believed it to be general, normally given at conversion, and the result of simple acceptance of the gift of God" (*Evangelicalism in Modern Britain: A History from the 1730s to the 1980s* [Grand Rapids, Mich.: Baker, 1989], 43).

18. Gordon S. Wood, *The Creation of the American Republic, 1776–1787* (Chapel Hill: University of North Carolina Press, 1969), 599.

19. Cited in Henry May, *The Enlightenment in America* (New York: Oxford University Press, 1976), 163. Thomas Paine's book *Common Sense* is available online at www.pagebypage books.com/Thomas_Paine/Common_Sense/index.html, Appendix, 4.

20. Wood, *Creation of the American Republic,* 590, 601, 612, 607.

21. Richard Hofstadter, *Anti-Intellectualism in American Life* (New York: Random House, 1966), 82-83.

22. Sidney Mead, *The Lively Experiment: The Shaping of Christianity in America* (New York: Harper & Row, 1963), 108-111.

23. Charles Malik, *The Two Tasks* (Westchester, Ill.: Cornerstone, 1980), 33.

24. "So distinctive and so separated was the aristocracy from ordinary folk that many still thought the two groups represented two orders of being. Indeed, we will never appreciate the radicalism of the eighteenth-century revolutionary idea that all men were created equal unless we see it within this age-old tradition of difference. Gentlemen and commoners had different psyches, different emotional makeups, different natures. Ordinary people were made only 'to be born and eat and sleep and die, and be forgotten'" (Wood, *Radicalism of the American Revolution,* 27).

25. Wood, *Creation of the American Republic,* 418. See also Barry Alan Shain, *The Myth of American Individualism: The Protestant Origins of American Political Thought* (Princeton, N.J.: Princeton University Press, 1994); and Joyce Appleby, *Capitalism and a New Social Order: The Republican Vision of the 1790s* (New York: New York University Press, 1984), 8-9, 81. Appleby writes, "Classical republicanism taught that a carefully constructed constitution balancing the forces in society alone held out hope for checking the lust for power and selfish drives of human beings" (95). Noll describes the parallels between classical republicanism and Puritan theology in *Scandal of the Evangelical Mind,* 70-71.

26. Appleby, *Capitalism and a New Social Order,* 82, 36-37.

27. Since populist evangelicals privatized virtue by locating it in the individual heart and conscience, they tended to agree with liberals that the state was not the locus of any inherent virtue (Justice or Right). Thus they accepted the liberal view of a purely instrumental state— with a functional or procedural definition of the nature of government as a facilitator of economic progress. See Michael Gauvreau, "The Empire of Evangelicalism: Varieties of Common Sense in Scotland, Canada, and the United States," in *Evangelicalism,* ed. Noll, Bebbington, and Rawlyk, 225-233. By "privatized" I don't mean they retreated from the public square, for evangelicals initiated many social reforms. I mean they believed that the locus of virtue was not in external social structures but in the individual human heart, and that social reform itself had to start with personal transformation.

28. Cited in May, *Enlightenment in America,* 339, 304, see also 273, 274. The terminology can be confusing, because *republican* was sometimes used by liberals as well. (Recall the quotation from Elias Smith complaining that many are "but half republicans.") What's more, churchmen who were theologically *liberal* tended to be quite *conservative* politically and socially. Unitarians and other rationalists were mostly Federalists, striving to maintain the old elitism of classical republicanism (since they themselves were among the elites). See 350ff.; as well as Alan Heimert, *Religion and the American Mind: From the Great Awakening to the Revolution* (Cambridge, Mass.: Harvard University Press, 1966), viii, 15ff, 23, and passim.

29. Noll, *Scandal of the Evangelical Mind,* 75.

30. Appleby, *Capitalism and a New Social Order,* 27. In 1820 in America, the percentage of the labor force in agriculture still stood at nearly 80 percent (Wood, *Radicalism of the American Revolution,* 312).

31. Roger Finke and Rodney Stark, *The Churching of America 1776–1990: Winners and Losers in Our Religious Economy* (New Brunswick, N.J.: Rutgers University Press, 1992), 44.

32. Wood, *Radicalism of the American Revolution*, 359.

33. See Martin Marty, "The Revival of Evangelicalism and Southern Religion," in *Varieties of Southern Evangelicalism*, ed. David E. Jarrell, Jr. (Macon, Ga.: Mercer University Press, 1981), 14.

34. Gary Thomas, *Revivalism and Cultural Change: Christianity, Nation Building, and the Market in the Nineteenth-Century United States* (Chicago: University of Chicago Press, 1989), 8, 18, 83, 88-89. Carroll Smith-Rosenberg likewise draws parallels between the economic and the religious visions of society: During the Second Great Awakening, she writes, "The last vestiges of orthodox eighteenth-century Congregationalism—an insistence on an all-powerful Father-God, upon the passivity and powerlessness of man, upon an eternity patterned after agrarian patriarchy, and upon a spiritual economy of scarcity represented theologically by predestination—all were challenged and ultimately abandoned." Evangelicalism assumed a new freedom and self-assertion: "Renouncing a spiritual economy of scarcity, Finney preached a loving God who rewarded with limitless grace those who sought salvation. Anyone, rich or poor, who with her free will would assert her belief in God and her determination to do good could now achieve salvation" ("The Cross and the Pedestal: Women, Anti-Ritualism, and the Emergence of the American Bourgeoisie," in *Disorderly Conduct: Visions of Gender in Victorian America* [New York: Oxford University Press, 1985], 142, 153).

35. Wood, *Radicalism of the American Revolution*, 145.

36. Gauvreau, "Empire of Evangelicalism," 223. Gauvreau is speaking of Canadian evangelicalism, and his comment reminds us that evangelicalism was a phenomenon in Canada and Britain as well as in the United States. He writes, "Evangelical groups in both the United States and English Canada played a leading role in the democratization of politics and culture and reshaped social relationships according to the tenets of voluntarism" (220). In the same volume, another Canadian historian, George Rawlyck, writes: "Although British North America had rejected the American Revolution and all that American republicanism represented, . . . in Canada . . . evangelicalism was *more* radical, more anarchistic, more democratic and more popular than its American counterpart" ("'A Total Revolution in Religious and Civil Government': The Maritimes, New England, and the Evolving Evangelical Ethos, 1776–1812," in *Evangelicalism*, ed. Noll, Bebbington, and Rawlyk, 146). On Britain, see David Bebbington, *Evangelicalism in Modern Britain: A History from the 1730s to the 1980s* (Grand Rapids, Mich.: Baker, 1989).

37. In many ways, American evangelicals were echoing themes from the Radical Reformation. The Reformation consisted of three streams—Luther and his followers, Calvin and his followers, and a third group of separatists called Anabaptists and spiritualists, often termed the Radical Reformers. Luther and Calvin retained a territorial model of the church: Everyone living within a certain territory belonged to the same church as the ruler; they were baptized as infants; becoming a Christian was a matter of gradual growth and catechesis; the Christian life was defined primarily in terms of participating in the corporate, sacramental worship of the church. By contrast, the Radical Reformers promoted a "gathered church" or "believers' church" or "free church," which included only those who could claim a conscious conversion experience; thus subjective experience became more important than objective church membership. Only adults who had made a conscious choice were baptized (not infants). The sacraments were demoted from means of grace (something *God* does) to merely external symbols enacted out of obedience (something *we* do). The church was democratic and egalitarian, with the difference between clergy and laity being merely functional. As Ernst Troeltsch first noted in the late nineteenth century, the Anabaptists with their democratic conception of the church were actually quite "modern." See discussion in Steven Ozment, *The Age of Reform 1250–1550: An Intellectual and Religious History of Late Medieval and Reformation Europe* (New Haven, Conn.: Yale University Press, 1980), chapter 10.

    It's interesting that the evangelical movement in America came to reflect the views of the Radical Reformers more closely than those of the major Reformers. Roland Bainton says of the Radical Reformers that "they anticipated all other religious bodies in the proclamation and exemplification of three principles which, on the North American continent, are among those truths which we hold to be self-evident: the voluntary Church, the separation of Church and state, and religious liberty" (*Studies on the Reformation* [Boston: Beacon, 1963], 199).

38. Cited in Hofstadter, *Anti-Intellectualism in American Life*, 85.

39. Ibid., 86.

40. Donald M. Scott, *From Office to Profession: The New England Ministry, 1750–1850* (Philadelphia: University of Pennsylvania Press, 1978), 128, 153.

41. Cited in ibid., 143-147.

42. Hatch, *Democratization of American Christianity,* 134.

43. Hofstadter, *Anti-Intellectualism in American Life,* 86.

44. Hatch, *Democratization of American Christianity,* 133.

45. Hofstadter, *Anti-Intellectualism in American Life,* 86.

46. Jonathan Edwards, *A Faithful Narrative of the Surprising Work of God* (1790; reprint, Grand Rapids, Mich.: Baker, 1979).

47. Hofstadter, *Anti-Intellectualism in American Life,* 92.

48. Cited in Hatch, *Democratization of American Christianity,* 135.

49. Cited in Finke and Stark, *Churching of America,* 89-92; and Noll, *Scandal of the Evangelical Mind,* 96. See Charles Finney, "A Revival of Religion Is Not a Miracle," in *A Documentary History of Religion in America to the Civil War,* ed. Edwin Gaustad (Grand Rapids, Mich.: Eerdmans, 1982), 337.

50. Cited in Joel Carpenter, *Revive Us Again: The Reawakening of American Fundamentalism* (Oxford: Oxford University Press, 1997), 126.

51. Cited in Hatch, *Democratization of American Christianity,* 183.

52. Daniel Calhoun, *The Intelligence of a People* (Princeton, N.J.: Princeton University Press, 1973), 282; the Beecher citation is from 281.

53. Hatch, *Democratization of American Christianity,* 136.

54. Ronald Knox, *Enthusiasm: A Chapter in the History of Religion* (Notre Dame, Ind.: Notre Dame University Press, 1950).

55. Joel Carpenter, *Revive Us Again: The Reawakening of American Fundamentalism* (New York: Oxford University Press, 1997), 244.

56. A good one-chapter description of evangelicalism's transition from cultural dominance in the nineteenth century, through fundamentalism in the early twentieth century, to neo-evangelicalism in our own day can be found in Christian Smith, with Michael Emerson, Sally Gallagher, Paul Kennedy, and David Sikkink, *American Evangelicalism: Embattled and Thriving* (Chicago: University of Chicago Press, 1998), chapter 1, "Resurrecting Engaged Orthodoxy."

57. Richard Quebedeaux, *By What Authority? The Rise of Personality Cults in American Christianity* (New York: Harper & Row, 1982). See especially chapter 2, "Celebrity Leaders in the History of American Christianity: 1865–1960"; and chapter 3, "Celebrity Leaders in the History of American Christianity: 1960–present."

58. Carpenter, *Revive Us Again,* 237.

59. Alan Wolfe, *The Transformation of American Religion: How We Actually Live Our Faith* (New York: Free Press, 2003), 35, 3.

60. Another provocative book that makes a similar point is Harold Bloom's *The American Religion: The Emergence of the Post-Christian Nation* (New York: Simon & Schuster, 1992). Bloom argues that there is a distinctively American form of spirituality, which has taken over most Christian denominations. It is highly emotional, individualistic, and "gnostic," by which he means it focuses on the individual soul in immediate relationship to God, apart from our bodily existence as members of families and historically rooted churches. External expressions of religion, such as churches, creeds, and liturgy are regarded at best as unnecessary, and at worst as barriers to genuine worship.

61. Wade Clark Roof, *Spiritual Marketplace: Baby Boomers and the Remaking of American Religion* (Princeton, N.J.: Princeton University Press, 1999), 84-85, 130, emphasis added.

62. Wolfe, *Transformation of American Religion,* 80. See also Udo Middelmann, *The Market Driven Church: The Worldly Influence of Modern Culture on the Church in America* (Wheaton, Ill.: Crossway, 2004). Writing from a European perspective, Middelmann is well situated to discern both the positive and negative aspects of contemporary evangelicalism. While appreciating the way American Christians speak openly about their faith, he also warns that they often treat it as merely a matter of personal growth and private interpretation, having lost the sense that it is also public truth.

CHAPTER 11: EVANGELICALS' TWO-STORY TRUTH

1. Martin Marty, *The Modern Schism: Three Paths to the Secular* (New York: Harper & Row, 1969), 98.

2. See Donald Dayton, "'The Search for the Historical Evangelicalism': George Marsden's History of Fuller Seminary as a Case Study," in *Christian Scholar's Review,* September 1993, with responses by Marsden, Joel Carpenter, and others.

3. James Turner, *Without God, Without Creed: The Origins of Unbelief in America* (Baltimore: Johns Hopkins University Press, 1985), 75-76.

4. Theodore Dwight Bozeman, *Protestants in the Age of Science: The Baconian Ideal and Antebellum American Religious Thought* (Chapel Hill: University of North Carolina Press, 1977), 51, 132.

5. Herbert W. Schneider, cited in Daniel Walker Howe, *The Unitarian Conscience: Harvard Moral Philosophy, 1805–1861* (Cambridge, Mass.: Harvard University Press, 1970), 31.

6. Henry May, *The Enlightenment in America* (New York: Oxford University Press, 1976), 121.

7. Thomas Reid, the founder of Common Sense realism, "has almost disappeared from the canon used for teaching modern philosophy in the universities of the West. Yet from the last decade or two of the eighteenth century, on through most of the nineteenth, he was probably the most popular of all philosophers in Great Britain and North America and enjoyed considerable popularity on the continent of Europe as well" (Nicholas Wolterstorff, *Thomas Reid and the Story of Epistemology* [Cambridge: Cambridge University Press, 2001], ix).

8. Herbert Hovenkamp, *Science and Religion in America, 1800–1860* (Philadelphia: University of Pennsylvania Press, 1978), 5, 10, emphasis added.

9. Hume recognized that philosophy can never undermine what he calls "common life" (the equivalent of Reid's Common Sense). He wrote that "nature" will always assert its rights over any philosophical conclusions that contradict "common life" (David Hume, *An Inquiry Concerning Human Understanding,* ed. Charles W. Hendel [Indianapolis: Bobbs-Merrill, 1955 (1748)], 5.1, page 55). As he explains more fully: "The great subverter of *Pyrrhonism* or the excessive principles of scepticism is action, and employment, and the occupation of common life. These principles may flourish and triumph in the schools; where it is, indeed, difficult, if not impossible, to refute them. But as soon as they leave the shade, and by the presence of the real objects, which actuate our passions and sentiments, are put in opposition to the more powerful principles of our nature, they vanish like smoke, and leave the most determined sceptic in the same condition as other mortals" (12.2, page 167).

10. Thomas Reid, *Essays on the Intellectual Powers of Man,* 2.20.

11. British empiricists (starting with John Locke) tended to champion the inductive method of their fellow countryman Francis Bacon, over against Continental rationalists (starting with René Descartes), who championed the deductive method.

12. Thomas Reid, *Essays on the Intellectual Powers of Man,* 2.8.

13. "Reid's words [were] embalmed in the 'self-evident truths' of the Declaration of Independence" (Turner, *Without God, Without Creed,* 62). See also Garry Wills, *Inventing America: Jefferson's Declaration of Independence* (New York: Doubleday, 1978), chapter 12, "Self-Evident."

14. Cited in Charles Whitney, *Francis Bacon and Modernity* (New Haven, Conn.: Yale University Press, 1986), 11, 40. The momentous implications of the shift from a deductive model of knowledge (producing absolute certainty) to an inductive model of knowledge (producing only probability) is discussed in Jeffrey Stout, *The Flight from Authority: Religion, Morality, and the Quest for Autonomy* (Notre Dame, Ind.: University of Notre Dame Press, 1981).

15. Cited in Bozeman, *Protestants in the Age of Science,* 151.

16. Charles Hodge, *Introduction to Systematic Theology* (1872), excerpted in *The Princeton Theology 1812–1921: Scripture, Science, and Theological Method from Archibald Alexander to Benjamin Warfield,* ed. Mark Noll (Grand Rapids, Mich.: Baker, 2001), 119. See also George Marsden, "Everyone One's Own Interpreter? The Bible, Science, and Authority in Mid-Nineteenth-Century America," in *The Bible in America: Essays in Cultural History,* ed. Nathan Hatch and Mark Noll (New York: Oxford University Press, 1982), 84.

17. The Baconian method appealed to Protestants for other reasons as well—in particular, because its rejection of tradition and church authority was useful in their ongoing polemic against Roman Catholicism. By the same token, Catholics *rejected* the Baconian method because it supported the right of private interpretation apart from church authority. Catholics tended to

be more critical of Baconianism as a scientific method as well. They argued that its empiricism led to materialism (only what we know by the senses is real) and to hedonism (*good* and *evil* are just names we give to whatever causes sensations of pain and pleasure). (See George H. Daniels, *American Science in the Age of Jackson* [New York: Columbia University Press, 1968], 68, 79, 83, 84.) Catholics may have been more sensitized to the tendency of empiricism to lead to materialism because in France, that is precisely where it *did* lead. As Henry May explains, in Catholic France, Newtonian physics was interpreted to imply "a self-sufficient world machine of matter and motion"—thus supporting materialism. By contrast, in Protestant England, the Newtonian system led to an image of the universe as a cosmic machine requiring a Maker—thus supporting religion (May, *Enlightenment in America,* 108, 110).

18. Cited in Robert Richardson, *Memoirs of Alexander Campbell,* vol. 1 (1868), at http://www.mun.ca/rels/restmov/texts/rrichardson/mac/MAC103.HTM, emphasis in original.

19. Cited in Nathan Hatch, *The Democratization of American Christianity* (New Haven, Conn.: Yale University Press, 1991), 169, 176, 177.

20. Cited in Michael Casey, "The Origins of the Hermeneutics of the Churches of Christ. Part Two: The Philosophical Background," *Restoration Quarterly* 31, no. 4 (1989): 193-206.

21. Cited in Hatch, *Democratization of American Christianity,* 163.

22. Cited in Stephen E. Broyles, "James Sanford Lamar and the Substructure of Biblical Interpretation in the Restoration Movement," *Restoration Quarterly* 29, no. 3 (1987), 143-151, emphasis added; also available online at http://www.stephenbroyles.com/J.%20S.%20Lamar.htm.

23. In fact, Campbell added, he didn't trust his *own* judgments of a week ago, or even a day ago, but remained "on my guard" against *any* outside influence as he approached the Scripture completely fresh each day (cited in Hatch, *Democratization of American Christianity,* 179).

24. Walter H. Conser, Jr., *God and the Natural World: Religion and Science in Antebellum America* (Columbia: University of South Carolina Press, 1993), 72.

25. For historians of science, I want to clarify that I am not discussing Bacon himself but only the way his thought was interpreted and applied by eighteenth- and nineteenth-century American evangelicals.

26. When one reads the Bible as a random collection of data to be mined, "one does not so much read it consecutively for its own sake as ransack it for data bearing on a particular question" (Broyles, "James Sanford Lamar and the Substructure of Biblical Interpretation in the Restoration Movement").

27. C. S. Lewis, "On the Reading of Old Books," in *God in the Dock: Essays on Theology and Ethics,* ed. Walter Hooper (Grand Rapids, Mich.: Eerdmans, 1970).

28. Among nineteenth-century evangelicals, there were some who tried to stand against the anti-creedal implications of Baconianism—for example, the Old School Presbyterians. They abhorred the attempt by Campbell's "Christian" movement to do away with all systematic treatises, because they adamantly wished to retain their *own* existing confessions and statements of faith. But having adopted the Baconian model themselves, how could they avoid its implications?

    Some tried to have their cake and eat it too by drawing a parallel to science: Just as a scientist equips himself by studying precedents, they said, so the theologian should study preexisting systems and creeds simply as background information. Thus James Alexander wrote that a theological system is "a simple *hypothesis,* an approximation to the truth, and a directory for future inquiries" (cited in Bozeman, *Protestants in the Age of Science,* 152-153). Yet this strategy reduced existing theological statements to mere hypotheses for generating new discoveries. In this way, the logic of induction served to undercut doctrinal authority even among champions of orthodoxy.

29. "Not taking any chances, however, most sixteenth- and seventeenth-century Protestant groups doubly fortified their positions by drawing up creeds that effectively precluded private interpretations" (Marsden, "Everyone One's Own Interpreter?" 80).

30. Cited in Hatch, *Democratization of American Christianity,* 180.

31. Ibid., 81. For example, sentiment against creeds was so strong in 1845 that the Baptists who founded the Southern Baptist Convention refused to write a statement of beliefs, saying they would follow "no creed but the Bible."

32. Of course, the hypothetico-deductive method itself has been subject to critique and modifications, and there have been ongoing debates over how to define the scientific method:

Percy Bridgman's operationalism, Michael Polanyi's personal knowledge, Karl Popper's falsificationism, Imre Lakatos's research programs, Thomas Kuhn's paradigm shifts. These are reviewed in any basic text on the philosophy of science. A good one from a Christian perspective is Del Ratzsch, *Science and Its Limits: The Natural Sciences in Christian Perspective* (Downers Grove, Ill.: InterVarsity Press, 2000; originally published as *Philosophy of Science*).

33. Richard T. Hughes and C. Leonard Allen, *Illusions of Innocence: Protestant Primitivism in America, 1630–1875* (Chicago: University of Chicago Press, 1988), 130; see also 119.

34. Ibid., 168, 169. Similarly, E. Brooks Holifield discusses the embrace of Common Sense realism on the part of Southern theologians, and concludes, "Southern religious conservatives often claimed to be devotees purely and simply of Scripture, but their self-perception was inaccurate. . . . Religious conservatism in the Old South was always as much a matter of philosophical as of Biblical considerations" (*The Gentlemen Theologians: American Theology in Southern Culture 1795–1860* [Durham, N.C.: Duke University Press, 1978], 125).

35. Sidney Mead, *The Lively Experiment: The Shaping of Christianity in America* (New York: Harper & Row, 1963), 108.

36. Anthony Trollope, *Barchester Towers* (London: J. M. Dent, 1906), 96.

37. Mark Noll, *America's God: From Jonathan Edwards to Abraham Lincoln* (Oxford: Oxford University Press, 2002), 94.

38. Cited in Holifield, *Gentlemen Theologians,* 136-137.

39. Cited in Mark Noll, *The Scandal of the Evangelical Mind* (Grand Rapids, Mich.: Eerdmans, 1994), 89.

40. Cited in George Marsden, "The Collapse of American Evangelical Academia," in *Faith and Rationality,* ed. Alvin Plantinga and Nicholas Wolterstorff (Notre Dame, Ind.: University of Notre Dame Press, 1984), 231.

41. Allen Guelzo, "'The Science of Duty': Moral Philosophy and the Epistemology of Science in Nineteenth-Century America," in *Evangelicals and Science in Historical Perspective,* ed. David Livingstone, D. G. Hart, and Mark Noll (New York: Oxford University Press, 1999), 273.

42. John Witherspoon, "Lectures on Moral Philosophy," cited in Mark Noll, Nathan Hatch, and George Marsden, *The Search for Christian America,* expanded edition (Colorado Springs: Helmers & Howard, 1989), 90. See also Douglas Sloan, *The Scottish Enlightenment and the American College Ideal* (New York: Teachers College Press, Columbia University, 1971), 123.

43. Stow Persons, *American Minds: A History of Ideas* (New York: Henry Holt, 1958), 191. Another historian describes moral science as an "effort to offer moral theory independently of theological dogmatics" (D. H. Meyer, *The Instructed Conscience: The Shaping of the American National Ethic* [Philadelphia: University of Pennsylvania Press, 1972], 136). Holifield writes, "Morality was not dependent on Biblical revelation, which merely validated and enforced the conclusions of a sound moral philosophy" (*Gentlemen Theologians,* 127).

44. C. S. Lewis, *The Abolition of Man.*

45. Elizabeth Flower and Murray G. Murphey, *A History of Philosophy in America* (New York: Putnam, 1977), 1:234, emphasis added. Flower and Murphey are referring to Witherspoon's thought in particular, but their description applies to other forms of nineteenth-century moral science as well.

46. Turner, *Without God, Without Creed,* 59, 60.

47. George Marsden, *Understanding Fundamentalism and Evangelicalism* (Grand Rapids, Mich.: Eerdmans, 1991), 131.

48. Cited in Neal Gillespie, *Charles Darwin and the Problem of Creation* (Chicago: University of Chicago Press, 1979), 14.

49. George Marsden, *The Soul of the American University* (New York: Oxford University Press, 1994), 129, 199. For a discussion of evangelicals' embrace of Baconian ideals of "free inquiry," how they treated the disciplines as essentially autonomous, and how these same tactics were turned against them to introduce anti-Christian philosophies, see especially pages 85, 120, 154-155, and chapter 7.

50. "Darwin's rejection of special creation was part of the transformation of biology into a positive [positivistic] science, one committed to thoroughly naturalistic explanations based on material causes and the uniformity of nature" (Gillespie, *Charles Darwin and the Problem of Creation,* 19). Many historians treat the conflict as though it centered on the Baconian rejection of speculative hypotheses (e.g., Bozeman, *Protestants in the Age of Science,* 166-169), and that

was a genuine factor as well. Historian John Hedley Brooke explains, "These hypothetico-deductive structures were very effective, but they transgressed a popular perception of Baconian science. It meant that Darwin's theory would be attacked, and not just by clergymen, for its philosophical license. . . . In his *Origin of Species,* Darwin repeatedly wrote that natural selection 'could explain', 'might explain' phenomena previously inscrutable. This laid him open to the objection that he was launching a speculative programme rather than providing rigorous science. . . . Huxley himself once conceded that if there were a weak point in Darwin's armour it was that the transformation of one species into another could not be directly observed. . . . Darwin had introduced his assertions with statements like 'I do not doubt', 'it is not incredible', 'it is conceivable'. 'What new words are these', [Samuel] Wilberforce asked, 'for a loyal disciple of the true Baconian philosophy?'" (from a lecture delivered in the Queen's Lecture Theatre, Emmanuel College, Cambridge, on Monday, February 26, 2001 [no title given], at http://www.st-edmunds.cam.ac.uk/cis/brooke/lecture0.html).

51. Edward A. Purcell, Jr., *The Crisis of Democratic Theory: Scientific Naturalism and the Problem of Value* (Lexington: University of Kentucky Press, 1973), 8-9. For a good half century after Darwin, the majority of those who considered themselves Darwinians actually placed the theory within a philosophical context of purpose and progress. See Nancy Pearcey, "You Guys Lost: Is Design a Closed Issue?" in *Mere Creation,* ed. William A. Dembski (Downers Grove, Ill.: InterVarsity Press), 73-92.

52. Mark Noll and David Livingstone, eds., *B. B. Warfield—Evolution, Science, and Scripture: Selected Writings* (Grand Rapids, Mich.: Baker, 2000), 29.

53. McCosh regarded even natural evolutionary processes as merely the unfolding of a design that God had front-loaded into the creation. Marsden, *Soul of the American University,* 203-204.

54. This is Gillespie's interpretation of Gray. See *Charles Darwin and the Problem of Creation,* 111-114. A good discussion of Darwinism as a worldview can be found in John Greene, *Science, Ideology, and Worldview: Essays in the History of Evolutionary Ideas* (Los Angeles: University of California Press, 1981).

55. Charles Hodge, *What Is Darwinism? And Other Writings on Science and Religion,* ed. Mark Noll and David Livingstone (Grand Rapids, Mich.: Baker, 1994), 92, 155.

56. Phillip E. Johnson, *The Right Questions* (Downers Grove, Ill.: InterVarsity Press, 2002), 61-62. On a similar note, J. P. Moreland and William Lane Craig write that the debate "is not merely one about scientific fact. It never has been, because beginning with Darwin himself, the creation-evolution controversy has significantly been a debate about philosophy of science: Should theology directly interact and enter into the very fabric of science or should science adopt methodological naturalism?" Moreland and Craig then list various ways in which religious or theological concepts may function as control beliefs guiding the formation of testable hypotheses in science (J. P. Moreland and William Lane Craig, *Philosophical Foundations for a Christian Worldview* [Downers Grove, Ill.: InterVarsity Press, 2003], 354-356).

57. Gilman, *The Launching of a University* (1906), cited in Jon Roberts and James Turner, *The Sacred and the Secular University* (Princeton, N.J.: Princeton University Press, 2000), 105-106.

58. Friedrich Heinrich Jacobi, cited in Marty, *Modern Schism,* 41.

59. Douglas Sloan, *Faith and Knowledge: Mainline Protestantism and American Higher Education* (Louisville: Westminster John Knox, 1994), 23.

60. Marsden, *Understanding Fundamentalism and Evangelicalism,* 145, emphasis added.

61. The British theologian John Henry Newman enumerated some of those undeniable items of experience: "Of course we all believe, without any doubt, that we exist; that we have an individuality and identity all our own, that we think, feel, and act." We are also sure that "we have a present sense of good and evil, of a right and a wrong, of a true and a false." Finally, "We are sure beyond all hazard of a mistake that our own self is not the only being existing; that there is an external world." Newman concludes: "On all these truths we have an immediate and an unhesitating hold" (John Henry Newman, *An Essay in Aid of a Grammar of Assent* [1870; reprint Garden City, N.Y.: Doubleday, 1955], 148-150).

62. "Common Sense had a special appeal in America because it purported to be an anti-philosophy" (Marsden, "Everyone One's Own Interpreter?" 82).

63. Reid, *Inquiry,* 1.4.

64. Ibid., 7.4.

65. Cited in Bozeman, *Protestants in the Age of Science,* 58-59.

66. Noll, *Scandal of the Evangelical Mind,* 88, emphasis added.

67. Marsden, *Understanding Fundamentalism and Evangelicalism,* 151; see also chapter 5. Marsden designates the two groups the "Warfieldians" and the "Kuyperians."

68. Schaeffer studied at Westminster Theological Seminary under J. Gresham Machen, from whom he learned the Old Princeton tradition of Common Sense realism. He also studied under Cornelius Van Til, from whom he learned the Dutch neo-Calvinism of Kuyper and Dooyeweerd. In addition, after he moved to Europe, he was influenced by the Dutch art professor Hans Rookmaaker, who had come to faith in a Nazi prison camp, where he was tutored by a fellow prisoner, J. P. A. Mekkes, a student of Dooyeweerd. Schaeffer explains how he resolves these two approaches, not so much in theory as in practice, in "A Review of a Review," *The Bible Today,* May 1948, at http://www.pcanet.org/history/documents/schaefferreview.html. See also Francis Schaeffer, *The God Who Is There,* in *The Complete Works of Francis A. Schaeffer,* vol. 1 (Wheaton, Ill.: Crossway, 1982), 137-138. Analyses of Schaeffer's apologetic method can be found in Gordon Lewis, "Schaeffer's Apologetic Method," in *Reflections on Francis Schaeffer,* ed. Ronald Ruegsegger (Grand Rapids, Mich.: Zondervan, 1986); and Kenneth Boa and Robert Bowman, *Faith Has Its Reasons: An Apologetics Handbook* (Colorado Springs: NavPress, 2001).

69. Roy Clouser, *The Myth of Religious Neutrality: An Essay on the Hidden Role of Religious Belief in Theories* (Notre Dame, Ind.: University of Notre Dame Press, 1991), 69, emphasis added.

70. Herman Dooyeweerd, *In the Twilight of Western Thought: Studies in the Pretended Autonomy of Philosophical Thought* (Nutley, N.J.: Craig, 1972), 18.

71. Alvin Plantinga, *Warrant and Proper Function* (New York: Oxford University Press, 1993), especially chapter 5, "Perception." Thomas Reid wrote, "Our senses, our memory and our reason, are all limited and imperfect—this is the lot of humanity: but they are such as the Author of our being saw to be best fitted for us in our present state" (*Essays on the Intellectual Powers of Man,* 2.22).

72. Udo Middelmann, *Proexistence: The Place of Man in the Circle of Reality* (Downers Grove, Ill.: InterVarsity Press, 1974), 62.

73. Paul Davies, "Was Einstein Wrong?" *Prospect,* April 2003, at http://www.prospect-magazine.co.uk/ArticleView.asp?accessible=yes&P_Article=11889.

74. David Hume, *An Inquiry Concerning Human Understanding* (1748; reprint, LaSalle, Ill.: Open Court, 1956), 4.2, page 34.

75. Eugene Wigner, "The Unreasonable Effectiveness of Mathematics in the Natural Sciences," in *Mathematics: People, Problems, Results,* ed. Douglas M. Campbell and John C. Higgins, vol. 3 (Belmont, Calif.: Wadsworth, 1984), 117. See also Nancy Pearcey, "Mind Your Mathematics: A Two-Part Series on the Role of Mathematics in Science," *Bible-Science Newsletter,* March and April 1990; for a later treatment, see *Soul of Science,* chapters 6 and 7.

76. Morris Kline, *Mathematics: The Loss of Certainty* (New York: Oxford University Press, 1980), 35.

77. Plantinga, *Warrant and Proper Function,* 136.

78. Cited in Plantinga, *Warrant and Proper Function,* 50.

79. Hume, *A Treatise of Human Nature,* ed. L. A. Selby-Bigge (Oxford: Oxford University Press, 1978), 1.4.6, page 252.

80. See appendix 2 for more detail on Eastern and New Age thought.

81. Daniel Dennett, in *Freedom Evolves* (New York: Viking, 2003), concedes that genuine or pure altruism—doing good for another without any expectation of good for oneself—may be unattainable through natural selection. Evolution can give rise only to what he calls "pseudo-altruism"—a kind of far-sighted self-interest that recognizes the long-term benefits of cooperation and even of (temporary) self-sacrifice (196, 217).

82. Whether the nonbeliever is a brilliant professor or an uneducated dockworker, Schaeffer wrote, "you are facing a man in tension; and it is this tension which works on your behalf as you speak to him" (*The God Who Is There,* in *Complete Works,* vol. 1, 133). "If the man before you were logical to his non-Christian presuppositions, you would have no point of communication with him. . . . But in reality no one can live logically according to his own non-Christian presuppositions, and consequently, because he is faced with the real world and himself, in *practice* you will find a place where you can talk. . . . The nearer he is to the real world, the more illogical he is to his presuppositions" (ibid., 137, emphasis in original).

83. John Gray, review of *Freedom Evolves,* by Daniel Dennett, *The Independent* online, February 8, 2003, at http://enjoyment.independent.co.uk/books/reviews/story.jsp?story=376373.

84. John Gray, "Exposing the Myth of Secularism," *Australian Financial Review,* January 3, 2003, at http://afr.com/review/2003/01/03/FFX9CQAJFAD.html.

85. Plantinga's books include *Warrant: The Current Debate; Warrant and Proper Function;* and *Warranted Christian Belief* (New York: Oxford University Press, 1993, 1993, and 2002, respectively). The phrase cited is from *Warrant and Proper Function,* 13.

86. James Turner, "The Evangelical Mind Awakens," *Commonweal,* January 15, 1999.

87. The Yale historian was Jon Butler. See Darryl Hart, "What's So Special About the University, Anyway?" in *Religious Advocacy and American History,* ed. Bruce Kuklick and D. G. Hart (Grand Rapids, Mich.: Eerdmans, 1997), 137.

88. Marty, *Modern Schism,* 98, 135, 140.

89. Ibid., 98.

90. Cited in ibid., 129-130.

91. Richard Hofstadter, *Anti-Intellectualism in American Life* (New York: Random House, 1966), 87, emphasis added.

CHAPTER 12: HOW WOMEN STARTED THE CULTURE WAR

1. Peter Berger, *Facing Up to Modernity: Excursions in Society, Politics, and Religion* (New York: Basic Books, 1977), 133.

2. The article was by Sarah Grimké, cited in Carroll Smith-Rosenberg, "Beauty, the Beast, and the Militant Woman," in *Disorderly Conduct: Visions of Gender in Victorian America* (New York: Oxford University Press, 1985), 125.

3. Sarah Grimké, "Letters on the Equality of the Sexes, Addressed to Mary S. Parker, President of the Boston Female Anti-Slavery Society, 1837; Letter I: The Original Equality of Woman," at http://www.pinn.net/~sunshine/book-sum/grimke3.html.

4. Leon Podles, *The Church Impotent: The Feminization of Christianity* (Dallas: Spence, 1999), ix, emphasis added. On sex ratios in early America, see Roger Finke and Rodney Stark, *The Churching of America 1776–1990: Winners and Losers in Our Religious Economy* (New Brunswick, N.J.: Rutgers University Press, 1992), 33-35, 66-67. On sex ratios in contemporary America, see Christian Smith, with Michael Emerson, Sally Gallagher, Paul Kennedy, and David Sikkink, *American Evangelicalism: Embattled and Thriving* (Chicago: University of Chicago Press, 1998), 80, which contains the following findings from a 1996 survey on the percentage of men versus women in various branches of the American church:

	Male	Female
Evangelicals	43	57
Fundamentalists	35	65
Mainline Protestant	34	66
Liberal Protestant	33	67
Catholic	30	70

Exactly *when* women began to predominate in Christianity has been much debated. In *The Rise of Christianity* (Princeton, N.J.: Princeton University Press, 1996), Rodney Stark claims that Christianity attracted more women than men right from the first century. He writes that "Christianity was unusually appealing to pagan women" because in the Christian subculture women enjoyed far higher status than in the Greco-Roman world at large: Christianity recognized women as equal to men, children of God with the same supernatural destiny. Moreover, he says, the Christian moral code prohibiting polygamy, divorce, birth control, abortion, infanticide, etc., enhanced the dignity and well-being of women.

In contrast, Podles claims that "before the year 1200, men and women played an equal role in the life of the church. . . . Not until the High Middle Ages did something happen to the gender balance of the Church" (*Church Impotent,* 101). Finally, in America, Jon Butler sees a change in the years leading up to the First Great Awakening: "Between 1680 and 1740 a new spiritual couple emerged in New England, the member wife and the nonmember, or delayed-member, husband. Women made up the majority of members in most New England established churches in the 1680s. By the 1720s women dominated membership in virtually all known New England churches" (*Awash in a Sea of Faith: Christianizing the American People* [Cambridge, Mass.: Harvard University Press, 1990], 170).

5. Podles, *Church Impotent*, ix.

6. This chapter draws heavily on two journal articles: Nancy Pearcey, "Is Love Enough? Recreating the Economic Base of the Family," *The Family in America* 4, no. 1 (January 1990); and Nancy Pearcey, "Rediscovering Parenthood in the Information Age," *The Family in America* 8, no. 3 (March 1994). A combined and updated version of that material was delivered as a keynote address at "Gender and Faith: An Examination of Women's Roles in Society," a conference sponsored by the Francis Schaeffer Institute at Covenant Theological Seminary, February 2001.

7. Carl N. Degler, *At Odds: Women and the Family in America from the Revolution to the Present* (New York: Oxford University Press, 1980), 5.

8. Ferdinand Lundberg and Marynia F. Farnham, *Modern Woman, the Lost Sex* (New York: Grosset & Dunlap, 1947), 97.

9. Alice S. Rossi, "Social Roots of the Woman's Movement," in *The Feminist Papers,* ed. Alice S. Rossi (New York: Columbia University Press, 1973), 250. See also Lundberg and Farnham, *Modern Woman, the Lost Sex,* 130-131.

10. Degler, *At Odds,* 365. Degler notes that women were also "quite capable of taking over the business temporarily when their husbands traveled out of town." See also Ann Douglas, *The Feminization of American Culture* (New York: Knopf, 1977), 51. "Since a widow is by definition a woman suddenly deprived of male support, the opportunities her culture affords her, the attitude it adopts toward her, are especially revealing of its stance toward women more generally."

11. Dorothy Sayers, *Are Women Human?* (Grand Rapids, Mich.: Eerdmans, 1971), 43. Anthropologists sometimes dismiss the importance of women's work in traditional societies, classifying it as "household management." What they fail to understand is that when productive work is carried out in the home, household management *is* the management of the public economy. There is no dichotomy between public and private (Ruth Bleier, *Science and Gender: A Critique of Biology and Its Theories on Women* [New York: Pergamon Press, 1984], 148).

12. Gordon S. Wood, *The Creation of the American Republic, 1776–1787* (Chapel Hill: University of North Carolina Press, 1969). "The sacrifice of individual interests to the greater good of the whole formed the essence of republicanism" (53). "The representatives of the people would not act as spokesmen for private and partial interests, but all would be 'disinterested men, who could have no interest of their own to seek,' and 'would employ their whole time for the public good; then there would be but one interest, the good of the people at large'" (59, citing the Boston *Independent Chronicle,* July 10, 1777).

13. E. Anthony Rotundo, *American Manhood: Transformations in Masculinity from the Revolution to the Modern Era* (New York: Basic Books, 1993), 2, 12-14.

14. John Demos, *Past, Present, and Personal: The Family and the Life Course in American History* (New York: Oxford University Press, 1986), 44-47.

15. Maxine L. Margolis, *Mothers and Such: Views of American Women and Why They Changed* (Berkeley: University of California Press, 1984), 12-13, 18-22, 60.

16. John R. Gillis, *A World of Their Own Making: Myth, Ritual, and the Quest for Family Values* (New York: HarperCollins, 1996), 183.

17. Cited in ibid., 186.

18. See Robert Young, *Darwin's Metaphor: Nature's Place in Victorian Culture* (Cambridge: Cambridge University Press, 1981).

19. See Christopher Lasch, *Haven in a Heartless World: The Family Besieged* (New York: Basic Books, 1979). It should be noted that these changes happened gradually, and occurred in certain geographical areas and demographic groups earlier than in others. The Industrial Revolution took root first in the Northeast, which means that the social effects described in this chapter appeared there first. In the South, because of the plantation system with its separate slave culture, industrialization took place much later. Finally, through the end of the nineteenth century America always had a frontier moving steadily westward, so that a large segment of the nation remained in frontier conditions, with trappers, hunters, and small farmers. As we saw in chapter 9, in 1850 less than half the continent was even settled, while the eastern states already had a highly developed, two-hundred-year-old culture. In short, the dominant culture was focused in the Northeast and spread to other areas and groups only as they in turn became industrialized, entered the middle class, and absorbed its ethos. That

assimilation may not have been complete for some groups. For example, the loss of women's economic function was never as complete in fact as it was in rhetoric. But the dominant ethos and its rhetoric are still important, because they set the *ideals* to which people aspire.

20. Margolis, *Mothers and Such,* 6, 33.
21. Gillis, *World of Their Own Making,* 190.
22. For a history of the effects of the Industrial Revolution on families, see Allan Carlson, *From Cottage to Work Station: The Family's Search for Harmony in the Industrial Age* (San Francisco: Ignatius, 1993).
23. Douglas, *Feminization of American Culture,* 51.
24. Ibid.
25. See Wood, *Creation of the American Republic.*
26. Rotundo, *American Manhood,* 11-26, 227, 245-246. "Our current notion of a competitive person is a recent historical development. The word *competitive* did not even enter the English language until the early nineteenth century. When it did, it applied to situations ('competitive examination') or institutions ('competitive societies'), not to individuals. Nineteenth-century men and women did not have a language to describe in positive (or even neutral) terms a person who relished contest."
27. Lesslie Newbigin, *Foolishness to the Greeks: The Gospel and Western Culture* (Grand Rapids, Mich.: Eerdmans, 1986), 109.
28. Cited in Glenna Matthews, *"Just a Housewife": The Rise and Fall of Domesticity in America* (New York: Oxford University Press, 1987), 22. Peter Berger notes that both family and church were employed in a strategy for "'containing' the disruptive effects of modernization." These two institutions offered "shelter to the individual from the alienating forces of modernization." It is significant, Berger goes on, that in our own times, "it is precisely these two institutions that have been the major targets of the 'adversary culture' of the intellectuals" (*Facing Up to Modernity,* 65).
29. Kenneth Keniston and the Carnegie Council on Children, *All Our Children: The American Family Under Pressure* (New York: Harcourt Brace, 1977), 10.
30. Cited in Degler, *At Odds,* 31. See also Barbara Welter, "The Cult of True Womanhood: 1820–1860," in *The American Family in Social-Historical Perspective,* ed. Michael Gordon (New York: St. Martin's Press, 1973).
31. Rotundo, *American Manhood,* 18.
32. Cited in Michael Kimmel, *Manhood in America: A Cultural History* (New York: The Free Press, 1996), 176.
33. Douglas, *Feminization of American Culture,* 18. When churchmen wished to portray the Christian graces, they frequently used feminine examples, says Donald M. Scott: "Christian love was warm and caring, best exemplified by the selfless and sometimes suffering, but always receiving and forgiving, mother" (Donald M. Scott, *From Office to Profession: The New England Ministry, 1750–1850* [Philadelphia: University of Pennsylvania Press, 1978], 142).
34. Cited in Douglas, *Feminization of American Culture,* 17.
35. Joel Hawes, quoted in ibid., 113.
36. Cited in Nancy F. Cott, *The Bonds of Womanhood: "Woman's Sphere" in New England, 1780–1835* (New Haven, Conn.: Yale University Press, 1977), 129-130.
37. Ibid., 86, emphasis added.
38. Douglas, *Feminization of American Culture,* 75.
39. Cited in James Turner, *Without God, Without Creed: The Origins of Unbelief in America* (Baltimore: Johns Hopkins University Press, 1985), 203.
40. Frances Willard, cited in Matthews, *"Just a Housewife,"* 86.
41. Cited in Christopher Lasch, *Women and the Common Life: Love, Marriage, and Feminism,* ed. Elisabeth Lasch-Quinn (New York: Norton, 1997), 97.
42. Cited in Robert Smuts, *Women and Work in America* (New York: Columbia University Press, 1959), 129-130. Moreover, they argued, homemaking gives women skill in the management of practical affairs, and isn't the work of government merely homemaking on a larger scale? In the 1850s Theodore Parker defined the political economy as "national housekeeping" and asked, "Does any respectable woman keep house so badly as the United States?" (cited in Matthews, *"Just a Housewife,"* 88).
43. Cited in Cott, *Bonds of Womanhood,* 148.

44. Mary Ryan, *Womanhood in America: From Colonial Times to the Present,* 3rd ed. (New York: Franklin Watts, 1983), 150.

45. "The most vivid result of slavery (to which abolitionists turned again and again) was a system of lust, of unleashed, illicit sexuality. Slavery made the female slave the helpless victim of the master's insatiable sexual desires" (Scott, *From Office to Profession,* 90). For example, Sarah Grimké wrote with horror and indignation of a young slave woman, "remarkable for her beauty and intelligence," sold to an "ugly-looking bachelor" for a sum of $7,000 ("Letters on the Equality of the Sexes, Addressed to Mary S. Parker, President of the Boston Female Anti-Slavery Society, 1837; Letter VIII: On the Condition of Women in the United States," at http://www.pinn.net/~sunshine/book-sum/grimke3.html).

46. Ryan, *Womanhood in America,* 130.

47. Degler, *At Odds,* 287, 282, 283.

48. Rotundo, *American Manhood,* 25.

49. Cited in Degler, *At Odds,* 377.

50. Cited in ibid., 378-379.

51. The classic treatment of the change in the meaning of virtue is Ruth H. Bloch, "The Gendered Meanings of Virtue in Revolutionary America," *Signs* 13 (1987): 37-58.

52. Cited in Rotundo, *American Manhood,* 172.

53. Ibid., 25ff.

54. Cited in Kimmel, *Manhood in America,* 169.

55. Steven Mintz and Susan Kellogg, *Domestic Revolutions: A Social History of American Family Life* (New York: The Free Press, 1988), 117.

56. Matthews, *"Just a Housewife,"* 80-81. Twain himself married a woman who was determined to "sivilize" him: "Livy Clemens undertook to refine her rough-hewn husband as best she could, curbing his penchant for colorful profanity, his habit of eating, writing, and smoking in bed, his heavy drinking, and his spendthrift ways. Like the women in Huck Finn's life, Livy Langdon Clemens had set out to 'sivilize' him against his will. To keep domestic peace, Clemens endured his wife's insistence that he adapt to the niceties of middle-class morality; but he resented in himself the resulting hypocrisy he found blatant in the culture around him" (D. Bruce Lockerbie, *Dismissing God: Modern Writers' Struggle Against Religion* [Grand Rapids, Mich.: Baker, 1998], 114).

57. Cited in Rotundo, *American Manhood,* 229.

58. Rotundo, ibid., 229, 254.

59. Thomas Wentworth Higginson, "Saints and Their Bodies," cited in Kimmel, *Manhood in America,* 177.

60. Cited in ibid., 179.

61. The quotation is from Fred Smith, founder of the Men and Religion Forward Movement, cited in ibid., 180. See also Podles, *Church Impotent,* 158.

62. Cited in Lasch, *Women and the Common Life,* 100.

63. See Matthews, *"Just a Housewife,"* 207ff.

64. Cited in Barbara Ehrenreich, *The Hearts of Men: American Dreams and the Flight from Commitment* (New York: Doubleday, 1983), 47.

65. Robert Griswold, *Fatherhood in America: A History* (New York: Basic Books, 1993), 99.

66. Mintz and Kellogg, *Domestic Revolutions,* 117, 195-196. See also Demos, *Past, Present, and Personal,* 61.

67. David Eggebeen and Peter Uhlenberg, cited in Griswold, *Fatherhood in America,* 229.

68. Cited in Christopher Lasch, *The New Radicalism in America, 1889–1963: The Intellectual as a Social Type* (New York: Vintage, 1965), 58.

69. Nancy Pearcey, "War on the Family: How Social Darwinism Weakened the Home," *Bible-Science Newsletter,* January 1990. Notice the contempt that Social Darwinists expressed for both women's character and women's environment (i.e., the home). Home life was denounced as a drag on evolutionary development. As Matthews puts it, Herbert Spencer's theory of social Darwinism made the home "utterly irrelevant to human progress. Male struggle outside the home is the engine of change" (*"Just a Housewife,"* 121). Darwin's explanation of male superiority was slightly different. He proposed that from their savage beginnings males became strong by fighting over females (sexual selection instead of natural selection). While modern man did not literally fight for a mate, he did continue to struggle to maintain himself

and his family, which increases his mental powers. (It should be remembered that no one in the 1800s understood the mechanism of inheritance, and most assumed that males passed on more of their acquired traits to their sons, and females to their daughters.)

70. See Matthews, *"Just a Housewife,"* 131.

71. Charlotte Perkins Gilman, *The Home: Its Work and Influence,* introduction by William O'Neill (1903; reprint, Chicago: University of Illinois Press, 1972).

72. "Just as women were perceived as separated from 'real life,' so on an unarticulated level religion came to be felt as disjoined from the tangible realities of everyday life" (Turner, *Without God, Without Creed,* 81).

73. William Raspberry, "Women Taming Men," *The Washington Post,* November 24, 1993. Raspberry cites George Gilder (*Men and Marriage* [Gretna, La.: Pelican, 1986]), who defines the male nature as inherently brutish, barbarian, and war-like. By contrast, Gilder says, the female nature is shaped by the broader rhythms of her sexual functions: by the long-term commitments imposed on her through pregnancy, lactation, and infant care. The future of civilization, in Gilder's biological reductionism, depends on females accepting the task of taming men, persuading them to submit to the long-term horizons of female sexuality.

74. Dorothy Sayers, "The Human-Not-Quite-Human," in *Unpopular Opinions* (London: Victor Gollancz, 1946). For a response to abortion that takes into account historical forces affecting the family, see Nancy Pearcey, "A Plea for Changes in the Workplace," in *Pro-Life Feminism: Different Voices,* ed. Gail Grenier Sweet (Toronto: Life Cycle Books, 1985), 203-207.

75. For a discussion of the "ideal-worker" standard, see Joan Williams, *Unbending Gender: Why Family and Work Conflict and What to Do About It* (Oxford: Oxford University Press, 2002). The book includes a nice summary of the historical process described in this chapter (though the solutions offered are radical and not recommended).

76. See Nancy Pearcey, "The American Mother: Balancing Career and Family," *The World & I,* July 1990; Nancy Pearcey, "Rediscovering Motherhood," *The World & I,* May 1991; and Nancy Pearcey, "The Family that Works Together," *The World & I,* March 1989. Many Christians have also suggested measures to make the tax structure more family friendly—for example, increasing the child exemption or giving a tax credit, which would make it more financially feasible in many families for one parent to earn less and spend more time with children. Some have even proposed a "parental GI bill": Just as American men were given the GI bill to help make up for lost career time after serving in the armed forces during World War II, so parents who take time out to raise children would be given a bill to compensate for their contribution to society and to give them a boost in reentering the job market. See Don S. Browning, Bonnie J. Miller-McLemore, Pamela D. Couture, K. Brynolf Lyon, and Robert M. Franklin, *From Culture Wars to Common Ground: Religion and the American Family Debate* (Louisville: Westminster John Knox, 1997), 331.

77. Importance of Job Characteristics, By Age Group:

% Very Important	21-29	30-39	40-49	50-59
Schedule which allows family time	82	82	67	68
Relations with co-workers	72	75	74	82
Doing challenging work	76	78	80	76
Job security	56	59	64	53
Work which helps society or my community	40	50	35	40
A high salary	46	45	46	33
High prestige or status	27	26	24	22

Source: 2000 Life's Work Survey by Radcliffe Public Policy Center. See Mark Baumgartner, "On the Daddy Track: Fathers Opt for More Time with Families," ABCNews.com, June 15, 2001.

Several additional surveys are cited in James Levine and Todd Pittinsky, *Working Fathers: New Strategies for Balancing Work and Family* (New York: Harcourt Brace, 1997). Surveys show that fathers experience significantly higher work/family tensions than is generally acknowledged.

78. See Nancy Pearcey, "Unlikely Entrepreneurs," *The World & I,* December 1990.

79. Scott, *From Office to Profession,* 150-151.

80. Newbigin, *Foolishness to the Greeks,* 19, 31.

81. Rachel Cusk, *A Life's Work: On Becoming a Mother* (New York: Picador, 2001).

82. Cusk, *Life's Work,* 3.

83. The story of how my own attitudes changed profoundly through having my first child is told in Nancy Pearcey, "Why I Am Not a Feminist (Any More)," *The Human Life Review,* Summer 1987.

CHAPTER 13: TRUE SPIRITUALITY AND CHRISTIAN WORLDVIEW

1. Cited in Henry Chadwick, *Augustine: A Very Short Introduction* (Oxford: Oxford University Press, 2001), 54.
2. "Tony," in discussion with the author. The name has been changed to protect his privacy, but otherwise the story is completely true and accurate.
3. Wurmbrand later founded Voice of the Martyrs to minister to believers around the globe who are persecuted for their faith. See www.persecution.com. His best-known books are *Tortured for Christ* (Middlebury, Ind.: Living Sacrifice, 1969), and *In God's Underground* (London: W. H. Allen, 1968), which describe his years in captivity. His testimony before the Senate is at http://www.christianmonitor.org/Testimony/Wurmbrand.html.
4. I don't have the space here to treat the problem of evil, or what theologians call "theodicy" (how can a good God allow evil and suffering?), but readers may wish to see how I dealt with that question in "Does Suffering Make Sense?" chapter 21 in *How Now?* The related question of the origin of sin and evil is discussed in "A Snake in the Garden," chapter 20 in *How Now?*
5. Francis Schaeffer, *True Spirituality,* in *The Complete Works of Francis A. Schaeffer,* vol. 3 (Wheaton, Ill.: Crossway, 1982), 196.
6. "The order—*rejected, slain, raised*—is also the order of the Christian life of true spirituality: there is no other" (Schaeffer, ibid., 221).
7. See Gene Edward Veith, *The Spirituality of the Cross: The Way of the First Evangelicals* (St. Louis: Concordia, 1999).
8. Henry F. Lyte, "Jesus, I My Cross Have Taken," in *The Trinity Hymnal* (Atlanta: Great Commission Publications, 1998), 707.
9. Francis Schaeffer, *The Finished Work of Christ: The Truth of Romans 1–8* (Wheaton, Ill.: Crossway, 1998), 162, 161. "Sadly, it is all too possible for a Christian to give himself to the devil and become a weapon in the devil's battle against God" (171).
10. Schaeffer writes, "The Lord's work done in human energy is not the Lord's work any longer. It is something, but it is not the Lord's work" (*True Spirituality,* in *Complete Works,* vol. 3), 260.
11. Schaeffer, *No Little People,* in *Complete Works,* vol. 3, 47.
12. Douglas Sloan, *Faith and Knowledge: Mainline Protestantism and American Higher Education* (Louisville: Westminster John Knox, 1994), 23.
13. Franklin Hamline Littell, *From State Church to Pluralism: A Protestant Interpretation of Religion in American History* (Chicago: Aldine, 1962), 107-108.
14. Sloan, *Faith and Knowledge,* 241.
15. The stories told throughout this chapter were related to me by individuals from a variety of different ministries—local, statewide, national, and international.
16. Francis Schaeffer, *No Little People,* in *Complete Works,* vol. 3, 44ff.
17. H. Richard Niebuhr, *Radical Monotheism and Western Culture* (New York: Harper & Row, 1960), 140.
18. Joel Carpenter, "Contemporary Evangelicalism and Mammon: Some Thoughts," in *More Money, More Ministry: Money and Evangelicals in Recent North American History,* ed. Larry Eskridge and Mark Noll (Grand Rapids, Mich.: Eerdmans, 2000), 401.
19. Thomas Berg, "'Too Good to Be True': The New Era Foundation Scandal and Its Implications," in *More Money, More Ministry,* 383.
20. Ken Blue, *Healing Spiritual Abuse: How to Break Free from Bad Church Experiences* (Downers Grove, Ill.: InterVarsity, 1993), 70-71.
21. Schaeffer, *True Spirituality,* in *Complete Works,* vol. 3, 363.
22. David Johnson and Jeff VanVonderen, *The Subtle Power of Spiritual Abuse: Recognizing and Escaping Spiritual Manipulation and False Spiritual Authority Within the Church* (Minneapolis: Bethany, 1991); Blue, *Healing Spiritual Abuse.* Another title is George Bloomer, *Authority Abusers: Breaking Free from Spiritual Abuse* (New Kensington, Pa.: Whitaker, 1995).

Mistreatment of employees in the workplace has spawned a new genre of secular books on workplace abuse, including Gary Namie and Ruth Namie, *The Bully at Work: What You*

Can Do to Stop the Hurt and Reclaim Your Dignity On the Job (Naperville, Ill.: Sourcebooks, 2000); and Harvey Hornstein, *Brutal Bosses and their Prey* (New York: Riverhead, 1996). Despite the sensationalized titles, many of these books offer a sober assessment of the way supervisors can and do abuse the power they hold over a worker's career and livelihood.

23. The website for the Best Christian Workplaces Institute is http://www.bcwinstitute.com.

24. Quoted in Helen Lee, "The Forty Best Christian Places to Work," *Christianity Today,* April 2003.

25. Quoted in Lee, "Forty Best Christian Places to Work." See John D. Beckett's *Loving Monday* (Downers Grove, Ill.: InterVarsity Press, 2001) for additional ideas on how businesses can enact policies that express genuine respect for workers as made in the image of God.

26. Organizations like CBMC ("Connecting Business Men to Christ") and the Christian Labour Association of Canada bring a biblical worldview perspective to the world of business and industry, demonstrating that biblical principles actually work in guiding day-by-day decisions and procedures. Other groups include Marketplace Leaders (www.marketplaceleaders.org) and the International Coalition of Workplace Ministries (www.icwm.net). For additional groups and links, see http://www.elevate2004.com/main/marketplace_ministries_links.html.

27. Jim Collins, interview (on the website for the National Association of Convenience Stores), at www.nacsonline.com/NACS/Resource/ Corporate/cm_010901a_ir.htm - 36k. See also Jim Collins, *Good to Great* (New York: HarperCollins, 2001).

28. David Aikman, "A Christian Publishing Scandal," *Charisma,* July 2002.

29. Schaeffer, *No Little People,* in *Complete Works,* vol. 3, 5.

30. Of course, there can be morally acceptable forms of collaboration that are not deceptive. For example, if an expert genuinely contributes his own ideas, he might team up with a writer to give them literary form—as long as the writer has an equal byline, so that the public is not misled into thinking the expert has suddenly acquired the writer's talents. The moral principle at stake is telling the truth and avoiding deception.

31. Jerram Barrs, personal correspondence, March 18, 2003.

32. Rick Santorum, "The Necessity of Truth," Heritage Lecture #643. August 6, 1999, at http://www.heritage.org/Research/Religion/HL643.cfm.

33. Kurt Senske, *Executive Values: A Christian Approach to Organizational Leadership* (Minneapolis: Augsburg, 2003), 11, 22, 24-26. A website promoting the book says, "Senske is president and CEO of Lutheran Social Services of the South, Inc., a multi-faceted social service agency with an annual operating budget of more than $70 million. During his tenure at LSS, he has been responsible for more than doubling the size of the agency and steering the once-troubled agency back to financial stability."

34. Lesslie Newbigin writes: "We ought not to ask each Christian in solitude to bear the burden of the real front-line warfare. . . . the Church must find ways of expressing its solidarity with those who stand in these frontier situations, who have to make decisions that may cost not only their own livelihood but also that of their families" (Newbigin, "Basic Issues in Church Union," in *We Were Brought Together,* ed. David M. Taylor [Sydney: Australian Council for World Council of Churches], 155-169; address given at the National Conference of Australian Churches, Melbourne, February 1960). Newbigin is talking about the church's imperative to support Christians who suffer for confronting secular organizations, but the principle certainly applies equally well to those who confront unethical practices within Christian organizations.

35. Many of the letters were later gathered into a book (Edith Schaeffer, *Dear Family: The L'Abri Family Letters, 1961–1986* [San Francisco: HarperCollins, 1989]).

36. John Vander Stelt, professor emeritus of philosophy at Dordt College, personal communication, May 28, 2003.

37. "What Is 'True'? The ASAP Poll," *Forbes ASAP,* October 2, 2000. Margie Haack brought this article to my attention in her presentation, "Postmodern Credo: Authenticity Rules, Hypocrisy Rots," sponsored by the Francis Schaeffer Institute at Covenant Theological Seminary, January 24, 2002.

38. Lesslie Newbigin, *The Gospel in a Pluralist Society* (Grand Rapids, Mich.: Eerdmans, 1989), 229.

39. Ibid., 188, 227.

APPENDIX 1: HOW AMERICAN POLITICS BECAME SECULARIZED

1. See E. Harris Harbison, *The Age of Reformation* (Ithaca, N.Y.: Cornell University Press, 1955), chapter 3, "The Struggle for Power."

2. Jeffrey Stout, *The Flight from Authority: Religion, Morality, and the Quest for Autonomy* (Notre Dame, Ind.: University of Notre Dame Press, 1981), 175 (emphasis added). As Quentin Skinner explains, the Reformers, as much as the Catholics, believed that "one of the main aims of government must be to maintain 'true religion' and the Church of Christ." But "as soon as the protagonists of the rival creeds showed that they were willing to fight each other to the death, it began to seem obvious to a number of *politique* theorists that, if there were to be any prospect of achieving civic peace, the powers of the State would have to be divorced from the duty to uphold any particular faith" (*The Foundations of Modern Political Thought*, 2 vols. [Cambridge: Cambridge University Press, 1978], 2:352). Thus was born the idea that to be secular was to be religiously "neutral." Such an idea was plausible back in an age when religious institutions were powerful, while the secular arena was small. Today, when secularism itself is a powerful force, we more easily recognize that it is not "neutral" at all, but a definite philosophical stance in itself.

3. The following discussion relies heavily on Nancy Pearcey, "The Creation Myth of Modern Political Philosophy," presented at the sixth annual Kuyper Lecture, the Center for Public Justice, 2000. My interpretation in turn owes much to Pierre Manent, *An Intellectual History of Liberalism* (Princeton, N. J.: Princeton University Press, 1994).

4. Paul Marshall, in discussion with the author, December 2001. Marshall is author of *Thine Is the Kingdom: A Biblical Perspective on the Nature of Government and Politics Today* (Grand Rapids, Mich: Eerdmans, 1986), and *God and the Constitution: Christianity and American Politics* (Lanham, Md.: Rowman & Littlefield, 2002).

5. Cited in Joyce Appleby, *Capitalism and a New Social Order: The Republican Vision of the 1790s* (New York: New York University Press, 1984), 36; see also 20.

6. Christian social theory accounts much better for the social dimension of human nature, based on the doctrine of the interdependent unity of the three Persons in the Trinity. This starting premise provides the metaphysical grounds for a political order that supports both the dignity of the individual *and* the authority of the social institutions necessary for a humane existence. (Refer back to chapter 4 for a discussion of the social implications of the doctrine of the Trinity.)

7. George Marsden, *Understanding Fundamentalism and Evangelicalism* (Grand Rapids, Mich.: Eerdmans, 1991), 131-132.

8. Stanley Kurtz, "The Future of 'History'," *Policy Review* 113 (June/July 2002), at //www.policy review.org/JUN02/kurtz.html.

APPENDIX 2: MODERN ISLAM AND THE NEW AGE MOVEMENT

1. Neo-Platonism was founded by Ammonius Saccas, who explicitly acknowledged his debt to the religion of India. Plotinus was his student, and he was so enthralled with his teacher's ideas that he determined to travel to Persia and India to study Eastern philosophies firsthand, though historians are uncertain how far he actually got in his travels.

2. Swami Krishnananda, "Plotinus," in *Studies in Comparative Philosophy*, the Divine Life Society, at http://www.swami-krishnananda.org/com/com_plot.html.

3. Paulos Gregorios, ed., *Neo-Platonism and Indian Philosophy* (New York: SUNY Press, 2001). The quotation is from the back cover. The Bahá'í faith, which became trendy in the 1970s, likewise developed from neo-Platonism. Juan R. Cole points out that "the mystical theology of Plotinus (203–269/70 A.D.), the founder of Neoplatonism, particularly influenced the cultural context of the Bahá'í writings" (*The Concept of the Manifestation in the Bahá'í Writings*, originally published as *Bahá'í Studies* monograph 9 [1982]: 1-38, by the Association for Bahá'í Studies, Ottawa, Ontario; also available online at http://www-personal.umich.edu/~jrcole/bhmanif.htm).

4. I have discussed neo-Platonism's influence on the early modern scientists extensively in *Soul of Science*. A major theme in the book is that, since the scientific revolution, scientific theories have been shaped by three basic worldviews—Aristotelian, neo-Platonic, and mechanistic. Though the mechanistic worldview has become dominant, the other two remain as minority positions within science even today.

5. For recent treatments, see Parviz Morewedge, ed., *Neoplatonism and Islamic Thought*, Studies in Neoplatonism: Ancient and Modern, vol. 5 (New York: SUNY Press, 1992); Majid Fakhry,

Al-Farabi, Founder of Islamic Neoplatonism: His Life, Works and Influence (Rockport, Mass.: Oneworld, 2002); Ian Richard Netton, *Muslim Neoplatonists: An Introduction to the Thought of the Brethren of Purity (Ikhwan Al-Safa')* (New York: Routledge/Curzon, 2003). A helpful summary by Netton can be found under "Neoplatonism in Islamic Philosophy," at http://www.muslimphilosophy.com/ip/rep/H003.htm.

6. Prominent European proponents of perennial philosophy who converted to Islam include René Guenon, Fritjof Schuon, and Martin Lings. Today the best-known Muslim proponent of perennial philosophy is Sayyed Hossien Nasr.

7. Sachiko Murata and William C. Chittik, "The Koran," at http://www.quran.org.uk/ieb_quran_chittik.htm.

8. Rodney Stark, "Why Gods Should Matter in Social Science," *Chronicle of Higher Education* 49, no. 39 (June 6, 2003): B7; also available online at http://chronicle.com/free/v49/i39/39b00701.htm. The article was adapted from Stark's book *For the Glory of God: How Monotheism Led to Reformations, Science, Witch-Hunts, and the End of Slavery* (Princeton, N.J.: Princeton University Press, 2003).

9. C. S. Lewis, *Miracles: A Preliminary Study* (1947; reprint, New York: Macmillan, 1960), 81, 82, 83, emphasis added.

APPENDIX 3: THE LONG WAR BETWEEN MATERIALISM AND CHRISTIANITY

1. See the discussion of Peirce in Paul Conkin, *Puritans and Pragmatists: Eight Eminent American Thinkers* (New York: Dodd, Mead, 1968), 244ff. Epicurus accounted for an element of chance in the physical world by assuming that atoms sometimes "swerve" in unpredictable ways, which he presented as the physical basis for a belief in free will.

2. Lucretius, *On the Nature of the Universe,* book 2, line 98.

3. Elsewhere I have written, "In the 1970s Max Delbrück delivered an address titled 'How Aristotle Discovered DNA,' in which he half playfully suggested that, if Nobel Prizes were ever awarded posthumously, Aristotle ought to receive one. The Aristotelian concept of Form, Delbrück argued, is remarkably similar to the modern concept of a genetic program—a 'preimposed plan' according to which the embryo develops into an adult" (*Soul of Science,* 236).

4. On the importance of teleological concepts of morality in contemporary philosophy, see the brief discussion of Leo Strauss in chapter 4.

5. Attacks against Epicurus were included in Tatian's *Address to the Greeks,* Justin Martyr's *Hortatory Address to the Greeks* and *On the Resurrection,* Irenaeus's *Against the Heretics,* Tertullian's *The Prescription Against Heretics,* Hippolytus's *Refutation of All Heresies,* Origen's *Contra Celsum,* Lactantius's *The Divine Institutes,* Athanasius's *On the Incarnation,* Jerome's *Against Jovinian,* and many of Augustine's writings.

6. See Margaret Osler, *Divine Will and the Mechanical Philosophy: Gassendi and Descartes on Contingency and Necessity in the Created World* (Cambridge: Cambridge University Press, 1994).

7. See Nancy Pearcey, "What's in a Name? Taxonomy and the Genesis 'Kinds'," in *Bible-Science Newsletter,* September 1985.

8. Benjamin Wiker makes a strong case that Darwinism represents the revival of Epicurean metaphysics and ethics in *Moral Darwinism* (Downers Grove, Ill.: InterVarsity Press, 2002).

9. John Dewey, *The Influence of Darwin on Philosophy and Other Essays* (New York: Henry Holt, 1910), 9. See also John Dewey, *The Quest for Certainty* (1929; reprint, New York: Putnam, 1960).

10. Cited in Nancy Pearcey, "Creating the 'New Man': The Hidden Agenda in Sex Education," *Bible-Science Newsletter,* May 1990.

11. Cited in Nancy Pearcey, "Phillip Johnson Was Right: The Unhappy Evolution of Darwinism," *World* (February 24, 2001).

12. Scientists were not the only ones to resurrect ancient Epicurean philosophy. Think of the social contract theory of Hobbes, Locke, and Rousseau (appendix 2), which begins with the premise of atomistic individualism in a "state of nature." That was an application of Epicurean atomism to society. Likewise, moral philosophers (like the utilitarians Jeremy Bentham and John Stuart Mill) began to define morality in terms of pain and pleasure, just as Epicurus had done. Utilitarianism defined morality as the greatest happiness for the greatest number, and was essentially an attempt to formulate an ethical system compatible with an atomistic view of society, in which each person's interest carries the same weight,

and the good of all is arrived at by merely tabulating the pain/pleasure ratio of the sum of autonomous individuals.

APPENDIX 4: ISMS ON THE RUN: PRACTICAL APOLOGETICS AT L'ABRI

1. N. R. Hanson, *Patterns of Discovery* (London: Cambridge University Press, 1958), 90.
2. Melvin Konner, "The Buck Stops Here," *Nature* 423 (May 8, 2003): 17-18.
3. Thomas W. Clark, review of *The Illusion of Conscious Will*, by Daniel Wegner, in *Science and Consciousness Review* (May 2002), at http://psych.pomona.edu/scr/reviews/20020508.html.
4. This is the theme of Dennett's *Consciousness Explained* (Cambridge: MIT Press, 1992). For a critique from a Christian perspective, see Angus Menuge, *Agents Under Fire: Materialism and the Rationality of Science* (Lanham, Md.: Rowman & Littlefield, 2004).
5. Galen Strawson, "'Freedom Evolves': Evolution Explains It All for You," a review of "Freedom Evolves," by Daniel C. Dennett, *The New York Times,* March 2, 2003.
6. John Searle, interview by Jeffrey Mishlove, *Thinking Allowed: Conversations on the Leading Edge of Knowledge and Discovery,* PBS, at http://www.williamjames.com/transcripts/searle.htm.
7. C. S. Lewis, *Mere Christianity* (New York: Macmillan, 1952), 20.

RECOMMENDED READING

In the following list I have not sought to give a comprehensive listing of resources (for additional titles, see the footnotes). Instead I have focused on works that are particularly helpful in giving a worldview perspective on topics addressed throughout the book. Nor have I given a complete summary of each resource, instead highlighting only the themes that contribute to a better understanding of Christian worldview.

PART I: Crafting a Christian Worldview

Albert M. Wolters, *Creation Regained: Biblical Basics for a Reformational Worldview* (Grand Rapids, Mich.: Eerdmans, 1985).
> A great place to begin in understanding worldview concepts such as the structural elements of Creation, Fall, and Redemption.

C. S. Lewis, *Miracles, Mere Christianity,* and *The Abolition of Man* (all published most recently by HarperSanFrancisco, 2001); and *God in the Dock: Essays on Theology and Ethics,* ed. Walter Hooper (Grand Rapids, Mich.: Eerdmans, 1970).
> Lewis's books are indispensable for anyone who aspires to develop a Christian mind. His apologetics arguments are presented in such a lucid style that they can be understood by those with no philosophical background.

Paul Marshall with Lela Gilbert, *Heaven Is Not My Home: Living in the Now of God's Creation* (Nashville: Word, 1998).
> A delightful, colorful introduction to Christian worldview thinking. Marshall explains the framework of Creation-Fall-Redemption (he adds a fourth category: Consummation), and then explores what those categories mean for topics such as work, politics, the arts, and technology. The provocative title is meant to press home the theme that God's creation is good, even though fallen, and that our final destiny is not to live in a disembodied state but to inhabit a new earth.

James Sire, *The Universe Next Door: A Basic World View Catalog,* 3rd ed. (Downers Grove, Ill.: InterVarsity Press, 1997).
> Sire lines up various philosophies side by side, from theism to naturalism to New Age pantheism to postmodernism, comparing their answers to basic worldview questions such as: What is ultimate reality? What is human nature? Where is human history going? Working through Sire's comparisons provides a good lesson in how to do worldview analysis. He promotes similar themes in more recent titles such as *Habits of the Mind, Discipleship of the Mind,* and *Naming the Elephant.*

Arthur Holmes, *All Truth Is God's Truth* (Grand Rapids, Mich.: Eerdmans, 1977).
> A classic discussion of worldview that remains a useful introduction.

John Stott, *Your Mind Matters* (Downers Grove, Ill.: InterVarsity, 1973).
A small classic that I read myself as a recent convert to Christianity, and which has remained popular for three decades. Gives a forceful defense of the importance of the mind in Christian discipleship.

J. P. Moreland, *Love Your God with All Your Mind: The Role of Reason in the Life of the Soul* (Colorado Springs: NavPress, 1997).
Moreland makes a powerful case for the role of the mind in spiritual growth.

Gene Edward Veith, *Loving God with All Your Mind: Thinking as a Christian in the Postmodern World*, rev. ed. (Wheaton, Ill.: Crossway, 2003).
Veith urges Christians to affirm what is good about modernity, while exposing what is false and harmful. He has written several other books with a strong worldview perspective: a book on literature (*Reading Between the Lines*), one on the arts (*State of the Arts*), and another on postmodernism (*Postmodern Times*) (published by Crossway, 1990, 1991, and 1994, respectively). All are recommended as informative and accessible treatments of the impact of worldviews.

David Naugle, *Worldview: The History of a Concept* (Grand Rapids, Mich.: Eerdmans, 2002).
Naugle has done great service in tracing the source and development of the concept of "worldview" from the time the word was coined back in 1790 by Immanuel Kant ("Weltanschauung"). The term later was used by thinkers from Abraham Kuyper to Carl F. H. Henry to Francis Schaeffer to urge that Christianity must be understood as a comprehensive, holistic philosophy of life.

Abraham Kuyper, *Lectures on Calvinism* (Grand Rapids, Mich.: Eerdmans, 1931).
A good primer on Dutch neo-Calvinism. Kuyper argues that secularism is a comprehensive worldview, and that Christians will not be able to counter it unless they develop an equally comprehensive biblical worldview. He bases the call to worldview thinking on the Calvinist emphasis on God's sovereignty, which implies that the Lordship of Christ is meant to extend over all aspects of society—politics, science, the arts, and so on. This is not a theocratic vision, for the task is not to be accomplished by ecclesiastical control (that was the mistake of the Middle Ages) but rather by persuasion.

Roy Clouser, *The Myth of Religious Neutrality: An Essay on the Hidden Role of Religious Belief in Theories* (Notre Dame, Ind.: University of Notre Dame Press, 1991).
Clouser is a neo-Calvinist philosopher who shows that every theory (whether in physics, mathematics, or psychology) must make fundamental assumptions about what is ultimately real. Whatever a theory treats as ultimate, self-existent reality is essentially what plays the role of the divine. In this sense, every philosophy is religious: It takes some part of creation and absolutizes it into an ultimate principle that defines the parameters of what counts as genuine knowledge. This is the source of all forms of reductionism.

Etienne Gilson, *The Unity of Philosophical Experience: The Medieval Experiment, the Cartesian Experiment, the Modern Experiment* (San Francisco: Ignatius, 1937).
As a Thomist, Gilson writes from a very different perspective from Clouser, yet his theme is similar. The reason various philosophies fail, he shows, is that they fasten upon some aspect of creation and elevate it into an ultimate principle—and then reduce everything else to that single principle.

The Two-Realm Theory of Truth

H. Evan Runner, *The Relation of the Bible to Learning* (Toronto: Wedge, 1970).

Runner was a powerful teacher whose influence ran primarily through his students. He taught them to be Christians *in* their work but also to develop a Christian perspective *on* the work itself, in every field. Runner opposed any form of dualism that would compartmentalize Christianity or treat any area of learning as autonomous from God's truth.

Herman Dooyeweerd, *Roots of Western Culture: Pagan, Secular, and Christian Options* (Toronto: Wedge, 1979; originally published by J. B. van den Brink, 1959); and *In the Twilight of Western Thought* (Nutley, N.J.: Craig, 1972; originally published by Presbyterian & Reformed, 1960).

As a neo-Calvinist, Dooyeweerd offered what is arguably the most substantial systematic philosophy produced within Protestantism, and his work is worth getting to know for that reason alone. His treatment of intellectual history emphasized the two-story division of knowledge that Schaeffer later simplified and made accessible to a wider readership.

Francis Schaeffer, *Escape from Reason* (Downers Grove, Ill.: InterVarsity Press, 1977); and *The God Who Is There* (Downers Grove, Ill.: InterVarsity Press, 1998); both also available in *The Complete Works of Francis A. Schaeffer,* vol. 1 (Wheaton, Ill.: Crossway, 1982).

In these books, Schaeffer explains the history of the two-story division of knowledge, often referred to today as the fact/value split. He also describes his highly effective apologetics method, which combined elements of both evidentialism and presuppositionalism.

Lesslie Newbigin, *Truth to Tell: The Gospel as Public Truth* (Grand Rapids, Mich.: Eerdmans, 1991); and *Foolishness to the Greeks: The Gospel and Western Culture* (Grand Rapids, Mich.: Eerdmans, 1986).

When Newbigin returned to the West after forty years as a missionary in India, he was struck by the way the fact/value split locks Western Christianity into the private sphere of personal values. He writes persuasively on the need to present the gospel as "public truth."

Jon Roberts and James Turner, *The Sacred and the Secular University* (Princeton, N.J.: Princeton University Press, 2000).

An informative account of how the two-story division of knowledge was expressed in a division within the university curriculum between the sciences and the humanities. Part 1 deals with the sciences, and how they were taken over by philosophical naturalism. Part 2 with the humanities, and how they adopted relativism and historicism, giving birth in our own day to postmodernism.

Douglas Sloan, *Faith and Knowledge: Mainline Protestantism and American Higher Education* (Louisville: Westminster John Knox, 1994).

An outstanding treatment of the two-realm theory of truth. Sloan argues that believers will not be effective in introducing the *content* of a Christian worldview into the public arena (like the university) unless they first challenge the *epistemology* that defines knowledge in terms of philosophical naturalism.

Martin Marty, *The Modern Schism: Three Paths to the Secular* (New York: Harper & Row, 1969).

A good historical account of how Christian churches throughout the West gave in to a "division of labor," in which they were no longer permitted to speak to the public arena but only to private life.

Christian Smith, with Michael Emerson, Sally Gallagher, Paul Kennedy, and David Sikkink, *American Evangelicalism: Embattled and Thriving* (Chicago: University of Chicago Press, 1998).

This is a report of a massive, three-year survey of self-identified evangelicals. It found that though evangelicals are more likely than ever to be highly educated, they still largely compartmentalize their faith in the private realm of emotion and experience. The book also offers a theoretical explanation of why evangelicalism continues to thrive in modern culture, confounding sociologists who had predicted that it would die out.

David L. Schindler, ed., *Catholicism and Secularization in America: Essays on Nature, Grace, and Culture* (Huntington, Ind.: Our Sunday Visitor, Communio Books, 1990).

This collection of essays includes helpful critiques of the grace/nature division by several contemporary Catholic theologians.

Applications of Worldview

Gene Edward Veith, *God at Work: Your Christian Vocation in All of Life* (Wheaton, Ill.: Crossway, 2002).

Veith offers a good discussion of the Reformation theme of Christian vocation, which rejected the secular/sacred dualism while giving spiritual meaning to every kind of work.

Angus Menuge, ed., *Reading God's World: The Vocation of Scientist,* forthcoming from the Cranach Institute, Concordia University in Milwaukee.

A book of essays, produced by a Lutheran think tank, on the topic of why science is a valid calling for Christians.

Pierre Manent, *An Intellectual History of Liberalism* (Princeton, N.J.: Princeton University Press, 1994).

A former Marxist who converted to Christianity, Manent gives a penetrating analysis of the way early modern political philosophy was framed in terms that were specifically intended to eliminate religiously derived moral ideals as the foundation for civil society. Manent traces the development of the concept of the individual who has no goals outside the confines of the self, and of a state that has no purpose except to prevent individuals from dominating one another.

Alasdair MacIntyre, *After Virtue: A Study in Moral Theology* (Notre Dame, Ind.: University of Notre Dame Press, 1997).

An influential book that diagnoses the collapse of Enlightenment moral philosophy, while arguing for a traditional morality based on natural teleology. The only alternative today is a postmodern approach, derived from Nietzsche, that reduces morality to a mask for irrational power.

John D. Beckett, *Loving Monday: Succeeding in Business Without Selling Your Soul* (Downers Grove, Ill.: InterVarsity Press, 1998).

Influenced by Schaeffer, Beckett does a nice job of introducing worldview principles to men and women involved in business.

Udo Middelmann, *Pro-Existence: The Place of Man in the Circle of Reality* (Downers Grove, Ill.: InterVarsity Press, 1974).

> Middelmann gives a Christian worldview approach to topics such as work, creativity, and private property.

Glenn Stanton, *Why Marriage Matters: Reasons to Believe in Marriage in Postmodern Society* (Colorado Springs: Pinon, 1997); Patrick Glynn, *God, The Evidence: The Reconciliation of Faith and Reason in a Postsecular World* (Rocklin, Calif.: Prima, 1997); Guenther Lewy, *Why America Needs Religion: Secular Modernity and Its Discontents* (Grand Rapids, Mich.: Eerdmans, 1996); Linda Waite and Maggie Gallagher, *The Case for Marriage: Why Married People Are Happier, Healthier, and Better Off Financially* (New York: Doubleday, 2001).

> When Christian worldview principles are applied in the practical arena, they create a powerful witness to the truth of God's Word. Empirical research is accumulating to show that Christian principles work better in the real world—that they make people happier and healthier.

PART 2: DARWINISM AND INTELLIGENT DESIGN

Denyse O'Leary, *By Design or By Chance? The Growing Controversy over the Origin of Life in the Universe* (Oakville, Ontario, Canada: Castle Quay, 2004).

> Written in clear, punchy prose, this book takes an objective approach aimed at the undecided, so it is a good book to hand to friends who are not Christian. A former textbook writer, O'Leary maintains an informative tone and includes lots of little text boxes with interesting tidbits.

Jacques Barzun, *Darwin, Marx, Wagner: Critique of a Heritage* (Chicago: University of Chicago Press, 1941).

> Barzun's classic treatment of the philosophical issues at stake in Darwinism remains instructive. "By substituting Natural Selection for Providence, the new science . . . had to become a religion."

Jonathan Wells, *Icons of Evolution* (Washington, D.C.: Regnery, 2000).

> This is a great place to begin if you are new to the topic of Intelligent Design. Wells dissects what's wrong with the images employed most frequently to support Darwinism in textbooks and museums—the images that were no doubt implanted in your mind as a child, and that your own children will encounter as well.

Phillip E. Johnson, *Reason in the Balance: The Case Against Naturalism in Science, Law, and Education* (Downers Grove, Ill.: InterVarsity Press, 1995); and *The Wedge of Truth: Splitting the Foundations of Naturalism* (Downers Grove, Ill.: InterVarsity Press, 2000).

> As a lawyer, Johnson has led the way in framing the logic of the case for Intelligent Design. He is also adept at describing the broader cultural implications of Darwinian naturalism. In these two books, he highlights the way Darwinism cements the fact/value split, keeping Christianity marginalized in the private sphere.

Michael Behe, *Darwin's Black Box: The Biochemical Challenge to Evolution* (New York: Touchstone, 1996).

> Behe teaches science writing as well as biochemistry, which explains why his book is written in such a clear and readable style, sprinkled with illustrations and analo-

gies to bring it to life for the ordinary reader. Behe explicates the concept of "irreducible complexity," arguing that it cannot be accounted for by any gradualist, Darwinian process.

Neal Gillespie, *Charles Darwin and the Problem of Creation* (Chicago: University of Chicago Press, 1979).
  Gillespie focuses the debate over Darwinism on the question of what constitutes genuine knowledge. Darwin's goal, he shows, was to change the very definition of scientific knowledge to permit only unguided natural causes.

William A. Dembski, *The Design Inference* (Cambridge: Cambridge University Press, 1998); *Intelligent Design: The Bridge Between Science and Theology* (Downers Grove, Ill.: InterVarsity Press, 1999); *No Free Lunch: Why Specified Complexity Cannot Be Purchased Without Intelligence* (Lanham, Md.: Rowman & Littlefield, 2002).
  Dembski is a prolific theorist for the Intelligent Design movement. He has developed a three-stage Explanatory Filter to formalize the criteria we employ in determining whether an event is the product of chance, law, or design.

Mere Creation, ed. William A. Dembski (Downers Grove, Ill.: InterVarsity Press, 1998).
  A collection of substantial, sometimes technical essays given at the conference that officially started the Intelligent Design movement. The range of essays gives a sense of the breadth of issues involved in the debate.

Signs of Intelligence: Understanding Intelligent Design, ed. William A. Dembski and James M. Kushiner (Grand Rapids, Mich.: Baker, 2001).
  A less technical collection of essays on Intelligent Design theory, suitable for a general audience.

Darwinism, Design, and Public Education, ed. John Angus Campbell and Stephen C. Meyer (Lansing: Michigan State University Press, 2003).
  What makes this book significant is, first, that it was peer-reviewed and published by a mainstream university press. Second, it contains essays by both proponents and critics of Intelligent Design theory, engaging in genuine dialogue (though the pros outnumber the cons). Third, it contains some of the most recent, cutting-edge arguments.

Uncommon Dissent: Intellectuals Who Find Darwinism Unconvincing, ed. William A. Dembski (Wilmington, Del.: Intercollegiate Studies Institute, 2004).
  A fascinating collection of essays by public intellectuals from various theological perspectives who explain their reasons for questioning Darwinism.

Francis Beckwith, *Law, Darwinism, and Public Education: The Establishment Clause and the Challenge of Intelligent Design* (Lanham, Md.: Rowman & Littlefield, 2003).
  A brilliantly argued defense of the constitutionality of teaching Intelligent Design theory in the public schools. A thorough and comprehensive treatment of the legal issues.

Charles Thaxton, Walter Bradley, and Roger Olsen, *The Mystery of Life's Origin* (Dallas: Lewis and Stanley, 1992; originally published by Philosophical Library, 1984).
  Though somewhat dated, this book still gives an excellent critique of standard origin of life theories. It also gives a clear exposition of the concept of "specified complexity" as the defining characteristic of information.

A. E. Wilder-Smith, *The Creation of Life: A Cybernetic Approach to Evolution* (Costa Mesa, Calif.: The Word for Today, 1970); *Man's Origin, Man's Destiny: A Critical Survey of the Principles of Evolution and Christianity* (Minneapolis: Bethany, 1968); *The Natural Sciences Know Nothing of Evolution* (Costa Mesa, Calif.: The Word for Today, 1981).

With his creative and wide-ranging intellect, Wilder-Smith was the first to develop the argument for design based on information in DNA.

Guillermo Gonzalez and Jay Richards, *The Privileged Planet: How Our Place in the Cosmos Is Designed for Discovery* (Washington D.C.: Regnery, 2004).

The argument from design used to focus on examples from the world of living things, but today there is evidence for design in the physical universe itself.

Philosophical Implications of Darwin

Hillary Rose and Steven Rose, eds., *Alas, Poor Darwin: Arguments Against Evolutionary Psychology* (London: Jonathan Cape, 2000).

A collection of essays making the case against evolutionary psychology as nothing but pseudoscience.

Tom Bethell, "Against Sociobiology," *First Things* 109 (January 2001): 18-24.

In his trademark elegant style, Bethell identifies the weaknesses of sociobiology and of its offshoot, evolutionary psychology.

Philip P. Wiener, *Evolution and the Founders of Pragmatism* (Gloucester, Mass.: Peter Smith, 1969; originally published by Harvard University Press, 1949).

An older book giving a solid introduction to the way the founders of philosophical pragmatism sought to apply Darwinism to the human sciences.

Paul Conkin, *Puritans and Pragmatists: Eight Eminent American Thinkers* (New York: Dodd, Mead, 1968).

Conkin gives a clear, thorough history of the philosophical pragmatists. Also recommended is his book on the intellectual impact of the Scopes trial, *When All the Gods Trembled: Darwinism, Scopes, and American Intellectuals* (Lanham, Md.: Rowman & Littlefield, 1998).

Louis Menand, *The Metaphysical Club: A Story of Ideas in America* (New York: Farrar, Straus, & Giroux, 2001).

A readable and engaging account of the pragmatists' life and thought.

Nancy R. Pearcey, "Darwin's New Bulldogs," *Regent University Law Review* 13, no. 2 (2000–2001): 483-511.

A comprehensive philosophical treatment of legal pragmatism, from Oliver Wendell Holmes to Richard Posner, explaining the central role played by Darwinian concepts.

Albert W. Alschuler, *Law Without Values: The Life, Work, and Legacy of Justice Holmes* (Chicago: University of Chicago Press, 2000).

A critical evaluation of Oliver Wendell Holmes's legal philosophy, emphasizing his adoption of Social Darwinism.

Paul F. Boller, Jr., *American Thought in Transition: The Impact of Evolutionary Naturalism, 1865–1900* (Chicago: Rand McNally, 1969).

This book does exactly what the title says: It describes the rise and spread of the philosophy of evolutionary naturalism after Darwin, focusing on its broader cultural impact.

Edward A. Purcell, Jr., *The Crisis of Democratic Theory: Scientific Naturalism and the Problem of Value* (Lexington: University Press of Kentucky, 1973).

A legal historian, Purcell shows how Darwinism led to a new naturalistic view of knowledge, in which the concept of "value" was stripped of objective content. He then traces the difficulties this caused in providing a moral basis for American democracy.

Benjamin Wiker, *Moral Darwinism* (Downers Grove, Ill.: InterVarsity Press, 2002).

Wiker makes a strong case that Darwinism represents a revival of Epicurean metaphysics and ethics.

Richard Rorty, *Contingency, Irony, and Solidarity* (Cambridge: Cambridge University Press, 1989).

Rejecting the Enlightenment assumption that humans are capable of a "God's-eye" view, Rorty reduces all thought to historically contingent cultural conventions. He labels his own version of postmodernism "neo-pragmatism," claiming that it merely draws out the implications in Dewey's classic pragmatism—rooted ultimately in a Darwinian view of knowledge.

PART 3: EVANGELICALISM AND ITS HISTORY

Roger Finke and Rodney Stark, *The Churching of America 1776–1990: Winners and Losers in Our Religious Economy* (New Brunswick, N.J.: Rutgers University Press, 1992).

Written in readable, even sprightly prose, this book by two sociologists shows why evangelicalism has been such a powerful and vibrant force on the American religious scene. The authors explain why, historically, the evangelical denominations outstripped the established churches, and why evangelical groups continue to thrive and grow today.

Mark Noll, *The Scandal of the Evangelical Mind* (Grand Rapids, Mich.: Eerdmans, 1994).

A good place to start in seeking to understand why evangelicalism has historically had a weak intellectual tradition. "The scandal of the evangelical mind is that there is not much of an evangelical mind," Noll writes, adapting the most famous line from Harry Blamires's classic book *The Christian Mind*. Focusing on fundamentalism, Pentecostalism, and dispensationalism, Noll diagnoses the negative effect these movements have had on Christian intellectual life.

Os Guinness, *Fit Bodies, Fat Minds: Why Evangelicals Don't Think and What to Do About It* (Grand Rapids, Mich.: Baker, 1994).

A semi-popular treatment of anti-intellectualism in American evangelicalism. Guinness argues that "the real damage to evangelicals was self-inflicted," through internal trends such as pietism, primitivism, and populism.

The Bible in America: Essays in Cultural History, ed. Nathan O. Hatch and Mark A. Noll (New York: Oxford University Press, 1982); *Amazing Grace: Evangelicalism in Australia, Britain, Canada, and the United States,* ed. George A. Rawlyk and Mark A. Noll (Grand Rapids, Mich.: Baker, 1993); *Evangelicalism: Comparative Studies of Popular Protestantism in North America, the British Isles, and Beyond, 1700–1990,* ed.

Mark A. Noll, David Bebbington, and George Rawlyk (New York: Oxford University Press, 1994); *Reckoning with the Past: Historical Essays on American Evangelicalism from the Institute for the Study of American Evangelicals*, ed. D. G. Hart (Grand Rapids, Mich.: Baker, 1995); *Evangelicals and Science in Historical Perspective*, ed. David Livingstone, D. G. Hart, and Mark A. Noll (New York: Oxford University Press, 1999).

The scholarly study of evangelicalism has exploded in recent years, and much of the best and most current work is found in collections of essays like the titles above. In recent years, a cadre of evangelical historians (Marsden, Noll, Stout, Hart, Hatch, Wacker) has grown so prolific that some have warned of a "new evangelical thesis" taking over the study of American religious history.

Mark A. Noll, *America's God: From Jonathan Edwards to Abraham Lincoln* (Oxford: Oxford University Press, 2002).

Noll's latest and most comprehensive history of American religion. Its underlying thesis is that a specifically American evangelicalism, different from European forms of Christianity, was forged during and after the American Revolution through a unique synthesis of republicanism and Common Sense philosophy.

Iain Murray, *Revival and Revivalism: The Making and Marring of American Evangelicalism 1750–1858* (Edinburgh: Banner of Truth, 1994).

Murray cites frequently from original sources, conveying a good firsthand sense of the revivalists' warm piety and earnest efforts to bring people to salvation. He also explains why some supporters of the revival movement later broke away, objecting to new high-pressure techniques touted as the means to guarantee surefire, near-mechanical results.

Richard Hofstadter, *Anti-Intellectualism in American Life* (New York: Random House, 1966).

This older treatment still contains large elements of truth, especially in its critique of the anti-intellectual elements within evangelicalism.

David Bebbington, *Evangelicalism in Modern Britain: A History from the 1730s to the 1980s* (Grand Rapids, Mich.: Baker, 1989).

To put American evangelicalism within a wider context, it is good to understand evangelicalism in Britain as well.

The First Great Awakening

Allen C. Guelzo, "God's Designs: The Literature of the Colonial Revivals of Religion, 1735–1760," in *New Directions in American Religious History*, ed. Harry Stout and D. G. Hart (New York: Oxford University Press, 1997).

Guelzo surveys the literature on the First Great Awakening, explaining the interpretative slant taken by various historians. A good way to get oriented before digging into the literature itself.

Ronald Knox, *Enthusiasm: A Chapter in the History of Religion* (Notre Dame, Ind.: Notre Dame University Press, 1950).

As a Catholic, Knox started out as a critic of pietism and evangelicalism. But after spending a decade studying figures like Wesley and Whitefield, he ended up with a profound appreciation for the evangelicals' sincere and dedicated commitment to the gospel.

Alan Heimert, *Religion and the American Mind: From the Great Awakening to the Revolution* (Cambridge, Mass.: Harvard University Press, 1966).
> Heimert gives a good account of the emerging conflict between "head" and "heart" in the First Great Awakening, though his interpretation of the relationship between the awakening and the American Revolution remains controversial.

Patricia Bonomi, *Under the Cope of Heaven: Religion, Society, and Politics in Colonial America* (New York: Oxford University Press, 1986).
> Bonomi stresses how the revivalists "rehearsed" themes of autonomy and popular sovereignty that contributed to the revolutionary mentality in America's drive for independence from Britain.

Nathan O. Hatch, *The Sacred Cause of Liberty: Republican Thought and the Millennium in Revolutionary New England* (New Haven, Conn.: Yale University Press, 1977).
> Hatch emphasizes the identification of religion with revolutionary politics that was characteristic of the First Great Awakening. Whereas religion had traditionally concerned itself with *holiness,* religious leaders in pre-Revolutionary America became concerned with *liberty.* Whereas the enemy of religion had traditionally been identified as *heresy,* it was now identified as *tyranny.*

Harry Stout, *The Divine Dramatist: George Whitefield and the Rise of Modern Evangelicalism* (Grand Rapids, Mich.: Eerdmans, 1991); Stephen Marini, *Radical Sects of Revolutionary New England* (Cambridge, Mass.: Harvard University Press, 1982).
> Both books give a somewhat critical perspective on Whitefield as the initiator of many of the trends that have become problematic in evangelicalism today—the emotionalism, the focus on celebrities, the use of commercial marketing techniques, and so on. Balance this interpretation with the more positive account given by Arnold Dallimore in *George Whitefield: God's Anointed Servant in the Great Revival of the Eighteenth Century* (Wheaton, Ill.: Crossway, 1990).

Second Great Awakening

Nathan O. Hatch, *The Democratization of American Christianity* (New Haven, Conn.: Yale University Press, 1989).
> If you want to understand the history of American evangelicalism, this is the place to begin. It focuses on the Methodists, Baptists, Disciples, and other groups once dismissed as "upstarts" by the established churches, but whose form of spirituality has become in many ways the most widespread in America today.

Richard T. Hughes and C. Leonard Allen, *Illusions of Innocence: Protestant Primitivism in America, 1630–1875* (Chicago: University of Chicago Press, 1988).
> An excellent description of the tendency toward "primitivism" in American evangelicalism—the idea that it is possible and desirable to throw aside centuries of church history and recover the original New Testament church.

Donald M. Scott, *From Office to Profession: The New England Ministry, 1750–1850* (Philadelphia: University of Pennsylvania Press, 1978).
> A fascinating account of changes in the concept of the ministry from colonial times, when parishes were localized, communal, stable, hierarchical, and integrated into the whole of society—to the modern conception of the church as merely one

marginalized segment of a society, competing for power and influence, and offering a career track for aspiring religious professionals.

Gordon S. Wood, *The Creation of the American Republic, 1776–1787* (Chapel Hill: University of North Carolina Press, 1969); and *The Radicalism of the American Revolution: How a Revolution Transformed a Monarchial Society into a Democratic One Unlike Any that Had Ever Existed* (New York: Knopf, 1992).

> An outstanding historian, Wood explains how American concepts of social order changed from the classical republicanism of the colonial period, embracing hierarchy and deference, to a post-revolutionary embrace of democratic individualism. These social and political trends influenced the church, feeding into the "democratization" of Christianity described by Hatch. For a short introduction to Wood's thought, see his essay, "Religion and the American Revolution," in *New Directions in American Religious History*, ed. Harry Stout and D. G. Hart (New York: Oxford University Press, 1997).

Joyce Appleby, *Capitalism and a New Social Order: The Republican Vision of the 1790s* (New York: New York University Press, 1984).

> In this short, readable book, Appleby describes the same trend treated by Gordon Wood—the rise of democratic individualism—while focusing more narrowly on the economic sphere.

Michael Gauvreau, "The Empire of Evangelicalism: Varieties of Common Sense in Scotland, Canada, and the United States," in Mark Noll, David Bebbington, and George Rawlyk, eds., *Evangelicalism: Comparative Studies of Popular Protestantism in North America, the British Isles, and Beyond, 1700–1990* (New York: Oxford University Press, 1994).

> This Canadian historian is particularly attuned to how evangelicalism, despite its premodern message of sin and salvation, actually contributed to the ethos of modernity.

Gary Thomas, *Revivalism and Cultural Change: Christianity, Nation Building, and the Market in the Nineteenth-Century United States* (Chicago: University of Chicago Press, 1989).

> As a sociologist, Thomas is interested in the "plausibility structures"—the social and economic changes—that rendered the evangelical theology of the revivalists more attractive to Americans than the older Calvinist theology.

Joel Carpenter, *Revive Us Again: The Reawakening of American Fundamentalism* (Oxford: Oxford University Press, 1997).

> Carpenter gives an excellent history of what happened *after* the awakenings, during the fundamentalist era. He details both the humiliating defeat of fundamentalism during the Scopes trial, and its resilience and strength in building a vibrant subculture of churches, Bible schools, summer camps, and radio programs.

Richard Quebedeaux, *By What Authority? The Rise of Personality Cults in American Christianity* (New York: Harper & Row, 1982).

> Quebedeaux offers a good discussion of the rise of celebrityism in American evangelicalism.

Alan Wolfe, *The Transformation of American Religion: How We Actually Live Our Faith* (New York: Free Press, 2003).

> A sociologist examines religion in America and concludes that "we are all evan-

gelicals now"—by which he means that the evangelical style of worship has
become dominant even in non-evangelical denominations and religions. The characteristics of evangelicalism include an emphasis on emotional response, individual choice, and experiential engagement—along with a *de*-emphasis on doctrine
and theology.

D. G. Hart, *That Old-Time Religion in Modern America: Evangelical Protestantism in
the Twentieth Century* (Chicago: Ivan R. Dee, 2002); *The Lost Soul of American
Protestantism* (Lanham, Md.: Rowman & Littlefield, 2002); *Recovering Mother Kirk:
The Case for Liturgy in the Reformed Tradition* (Grand Rapids, Mich.: Baker, 2003).
　　Hart is a Presbyterian historian who gives a helpful description of the differences
　　between confessional and evangelical churches, while arguing for the ongoing
　　validity of the confessional church.

Evangelical Intellectual Traditions

Henry May, *The Enlightenment in America* (New York: Oxford University Press,
1976).
　　Because America started as a colony, it remained for a long time on the outskirts
　　of intellectual life, importing most of its ideas from Europe. May gives a helpful
　　analysis of *which* ideas successfully crossed the Atlantic and put down deep roots
　　in the soil of the New World. Those that proved most popular in America were
　　the ideas of the Scottish Enlightenment—which were in some ways actually *anti-*
　　Enlightenment because they were proposed in order to defend against radical skep-
　　ticism and atheism.

Norman Fiering, *Moral Philosophy at Seventeenth-Century Harvard: A Discipline in
Transition* (Chapel Hill: University of North Carolina Press, 1981); D. H. Meyer, *The
Instructed Conscience: The Shaping of the American National Ethic* (Philadelphia:
University of Pennsylvania Press, 1972); Allen Guelzo, "'The Science of Duty': Moral
Philosophy and the Epistemology of Science in Nineteenth-Century America," in
Evangelicals and Science in Historical Perspective, ed. David Livingstone, D. G. Hart,
and Mark A. Noll (New York: Oxford University Press, 1999).
　　When we hear the word *Enlightenment,* we typically think of the rise of modern
　　science and the mechanistic worldview. But equally significant historically was the
　　rise of a new moral philosophy (or "moral science"), which proposed a more nat-
　　uralistic approach to understanding human nature. Courses on moral philosophy
　　took the place once given to theology as the capstone of the university curriculum.

Jeffrey Stout, *The Flight from Authority: Religion, Morality, and the Quest for
Autonomy* (Notre Dame, Ind.: University of Notre Dame Press, 1981).
　　Stout shows how the concept of "the secular" arose as a reaction against a cen-
　　tury of religious warfare, which drove early modern thinkers to seek a "neutral"
　　arena between clashing religious factions. Thus Christians themselves, by being
　　willing to spill one another's blood, were partly the cause of the rise of secularism.

George Marsden, *Understanding Fundamentalism and Evangelicalism* (Grand Rapids,
Mich.: Eerdmans, 1991); *Fundamentalism and American Culture: The Shaping of
Twentieth-Century Evangelicalism, 1870–1925* (New York: Oxford University Press,
1980).
　　The doyen of evangelical historians, in these books Marsden offers an intellectual
　　history of evangelicalism.

George Marsden, *The Soul of the American University: From Protestant Establishment to Established Nonbelief* (New York: Oxford University Press, 1994).

> A comprehensive account of how American universities, most of which were founded as Christian institutions, eventually gave way to secularism. Marsden goes on to argue that today's secularized universities, which pride themselves on their diversity, have no reason to practice the deliberate exclusion of religiously based thinking.

The Secular Revolution: Power, Interest, and Conflict in the Secularization of American Public Life, ed. Christian Smith (Los Angeles: University of California Press, 2003).

> Essays by sociologists who reject the old adage that when societies modernize, secularization is inevitable. Instead, these essays identify specific historical forces that were responsible for the secularization process in fields such as education, law, and science—forces that were historically contingent, and therefore potentially reversible.

Men, Women, and the Family

Nancy Pearcey, "Is Love Enough? Recreating the Economic Base of the Family," *The Family in America* 4, no. 1 (January 1990); and "Rediscovering Parenthood in the Information Age," *The Family in America* 8, no. 3 (March 1994).

> The first journal article deals primarily with the effects of the Industrial Revolution on the status of women and their work in the home. The second describes the effects on men and the changing definitions of masculinity. (A taped lecture combining highlights of both articles can be obtained from the Francis Schaeffer Institute at Covenant Theological Seminary, delivered at a conference on "Gender and Faith," February 2001.)

Peter Berger, *Facing Up to Modernity: Excursions in Society, Politics, and Religion* (New York: Basic Books, 1977).

> Berger describes the rise of the dichotomy between public and private spheres in modern society, explaining how both the church and the family have been privatized and marginalized.

Barbara Welter, "The Cult of True Womanhood: 1820–1860," in *The American Family in Social-Historical Perspective,* ed. Michael Gordon (New York: St. Martin's Press, 1973).

> A seminal treatment of the emergence of the doctrine of "separate spheres" after the Industrial Revolution—a private sphere for women, home, and the gentler virtues, over against a public sphere of competitive individualism where men labored during the day.

Nancy F. Cott, *The Bonds of Womanhood: "Woman's Sphere" in New England, 1780–1835* (New Haven, Conn.: Yale University Press, 1977).

> An excellent historical account of the doctrine of "separate spheres," sometimes called "the cult of domesticity," and its impact on women—including the rise of a new concept of femininity and a drastic constriction of the scope of women's work.

Mary Ryan, *Womanhood in America: From Colonial Times to the Present,* 3rd ed. (New York: Franklin Watts, 1983).

> A good overall history of the changes in family structure brought about by the

Industrial Revolution—the reduction of women's role from producer to consumer, and at the same time the reduction of men's role from primary to secondary parent.

E. Anthony Rotundo, *American Manhood: Transformations in Masculinity from the Revolution to the Modern Era* (New York: HarperCollins, 1993); and Michael Kimmel, *Manhood in America: A Cultural History* (New York: Free Press, 1996).
    Read together, these two books paint a clear picture of changing concepts of masculinity throughout American history. The Puritan concept of "communal manhood," which placed men within an organic, hierarchical community, was supplanted by the modern concept of "individual manhood," autonomous selves who create their own place and status.

Robert Griswold, *Fatherhood in America: A History* (New York: Basic Books, 1993).
    As the Industrial Revolution took fathers out of the home, fatherhood was steadily devalued. Instead of passing on essential skills to prepare their children for adulthood, men were reduced to mere breadwinners, invisible throughout most of the day. With the rise of fields like child development and child psychology, a class of professionals began to take over the role of fathers in decreeing how children should be raised.

Christopher Lasch, *Haven in a Heartless World: The Family Besieged* (New York: Basic Books, 1979).
    In this classic book on the history of the family, Lasch explains how it has been marginalized, privatized, and devalued in modern society. The home has been stripped of its historic functions and reduced to a place of merely emotional succor.

Allan Carlson, *From Cottage to Work Station: The Family's Search for Harmony in the Industrial Age* (San Francisco: Ignatius, 1993).
    An economist, Carlson gives a good history of the effects of the Industrial Revolution on the family.

Glenna Matthews, *"Just a Housewife": The Rise and Fall of Domesticity in America* (New York: Oxford University Press, 1987).
    Matthews gives a sympathetic account of the history of women's household work, focusing on the way it was devalued after the Industrial Revolution, when much of the skilled work was removed to factories.

Carl N. Degler, *At Odds: Women and the Family in America from the Revolution to the Present* (New York: Oxford University Press, 1980).
    Degler gives a particularly clear account of the emergence of the double standard, whereby women were held responsible for controlling the unruly passions of men.

PART 4: APPLIED WORLDVIEW

Francis Schaeffer, *True Spirituality* (Wheaton, Ill.: Tyndale, 1979); also available in *The Complete Works of Francis A. Schaeffer*, vol. 3 (Wheaton, Ill.: Crossway, 1982).
    Schaeffer speaks to the crucial need to apply Christian worldview in the personal and practical domains, so that it does not become merely an abstract set of ideas. Those who aspire to develop a Christian mind must follow Christ to the cross—accepting suffering as a means of dying to old sinful patterns of behavior, in order to be resurrected with the mind of Christ.

Francis Schaeffer, *The Finished Work of Christ: The Truth of Romans 1–8* (Wheaton, Ill.: Crossway, 1998).

In these Bible studies, Schaeffer works out in detail the message of dying to personal zeal and ambition, in order to live in Christ's resurrection power, so that we may become "life-producing machines." "We produce either life or death as people around us either accept or reject God because of what we say to them and how we live before them."

Francis Schaeffer, *No Little People: Sixteen Sermons for the Twentieth Century* (Downers Grove, Ill.: InterVarsity Press, 1974); also available in *The Complete Works of Francis A. Schaeffer*, vol. 3 (Wheaton, Ill.: Crossway, 1982).

The sermon "The Lord's Work, the Lord's Way" is particularly relevant, warning that God will not honor those who try to do His work in their own strength. Christians must demonstrate something more than sheer activism, which the world can duplicate.

Gene Edward Veith, *The Spirituality of the Cross: The Way of the First Evangelicals* (St. Louis: Concordia, 1999).

Luther said Christian spirituality is focused not on glory (that comes later, with Christ's return) but rather on the cross—on identification and participation with the sufferings of Christ, finding renewal through an inversion of the world's values.

Ken Blue, *Healing Spiritual Abuse: How to Break Free from Bad Church Experiences* (Downers Grove, Ill.: InterVarsity Press, 1993); David Johnson and Jeff VanVonderen, *The Subtle Power of Spiritual Abuse: Recognizing and Escaping Spiritual Manipulation and False Spiritual Authority Within the Church* (Minneapolis: Bethany, 1991).

The suffering that Christians encounter in this life may come through relationships. Unhealthy relationships with a spiritual dimension—e.g., in a church or parachurch ministry—have dynamics that are unique enough that some have coined the phrase "spiritual abuse." These books describe situations where leaders use their spiritual authority to control and dominate others instead of serving them—using people to meet their own needs for importance, power, and image.

Henry Cloud and John Townsend, *Boundaries: When to Say Yes, When to Say No, to Take Control of Your Life* (Grand Rapids, Mich.: Zondervan, 1992).

This book and its many sequels and tapes offer helpful guidelines from Scripture and psychology on how to create healthy relationships, in the family as well as in churches and other Christian organizations.

INDEX

Against Our Wills (Brownmiller), 212

Aikman, David, 372

Alberts, Bruce, 416n. 17

Alexander, James, 299, 437n. 28

Allen, Richard, 265

Alliance Defense Fund (ADF), 97

Alston, William, 321

altruism, 210, 317-318, 440n. 81

American frontier, 262-263, 430n. 25; legends of, 338

American Manhood (Rotundo), 328

American Religion, The (H. Bloom), 435n. 60

Anderson, Norris, 414n. 49

Anglicans, 281

Anselm, 77, 100

Anti-Intellectualism in American Life (Hofstadter), 286

apologetics, 124-125, 134, 244

Apostle's Creed, 86, 281

Appleby, Joyce, 433n. 25

Aquinas, Thomas, 92, 100, 402n. 33; and Augustine, 78-79; overemphasis on creation, 92; reworking of the two stories, 79-80

Arendt, Hannah, 141

Aristotle, 74, 77, 389, 390

Arkansas Science Teacher's Association (ASTA), 176

artistic creativity, 57, 58

arts, the, 113-114

Athanasius, 405n. 6

atomism, 131, 133, 139, 233

Atran, Scott, 209

Augsburg Confession, 81-82

Augustine, 40, 42, 76-77, 351, 386, 402n. 34; and Aquinas, 78-79

Awakenings (the Great Awakenings), 260, 266, 269, 270; First, 263, 267-272, 274-275, 432n. 5; Second, 262, 263, 272, 273-274, 276, 326

Backus, Isaac, 283

Bacon, Francis, 298, 299, 303, 436n. 11. *See also* Baconian hermeneutics

Baconian hermeneutics, 299-300, 300-301; appeal to Protestants, 436n. 16; Old School Presbyterians' resistance to, 437n. 28; rejection of by Catholics, 436-437n. 17; seculariza-tion of moral philosophy, 305-307; secularization of the natural sciences, 307-310; sidelining of religion, 310-311; view of biblical interpretation, 303-305; weaknesses of, 301-302

Bahá'í, 448n. 3

Bainton, Roland, 434n. 37

Baptists, 256, 259, 260, 264-265, 269, 283; Southern Baptist Convention, 437n. 31

Barchester Towers (Trollope), 305

Barrs, Jerram, 373

Barzun, Jacques, 114, 173

Bear's Nature Guide, The (Berenstain and Berenstain), 157

Bebbington, David, 433n. 17

Beckett, John, 31, 83, 87

Beecher, Henry Ward, 287, 290

Behe, Michael, 185-186, 188

Behold the Spirit (Watts), 123

believers-church ecclesiology, 283

Bellah, Robert, 90

Benevolent Empire, 61, 336, 343

Benson, Herbert, 60

Bentham, Jeremy, 449n. 12

Berg, Thomas, 368

Berger, Peter, 20, 68, 325, 401n. 7, 443n. 28

Best Christian Workplaces Institute, 370

Bethell, Tom, 170, 212

Beyond Freedom and Dignity (Skinner), 320

Biochemical Predestination (Kenyon and Steinman), 194

Blackmun, Harry, 238

Blamires, Harry, 33-34; on the "Christian mind," 34

Blind Watchmaker, The (Dawkins), 183, 419n. 60

Bloom, Allan, 177

Bloom, Harold, 435n. 60

Blue, Ken, 368

Bockmuehl, Klaus, 137

Boehme, Jacob, 386

Boethius, 77

Bonaventure, 77

Bonomi, Patricia, 432n. 15

Boyer, Pascal, 209

Boyle, Robert, 391

Brabent, Siger de, 78

Bradley, Walter, 199, 420n. 61

Brennan, Heidi, 345

Bridgman, Percy, 438n. 32

Briner, Bob, 36

Brinton, Crane, 406n. 40

Brooke, John Hedley, 438-439n. 50

Brown, Colin, 106

Brownmiller, Susan, 212

Buckminster, Joseph, 335, 336-337

Buddhism, 146-147

Burbank, Luther, 161

Burnett, Frances Hodgson, 148; influences on, 410n. 60

Burroughs, John, 339

Bush, George W., 62

business and marketing, 365; Christian borrowing from commercial enterprises, 366-369

Butler, Jon, 430n. 15

Calderone, Mary, 392

Calvert, James, 421n. 2

Calvin, John, 82, 84, 303, 434n. 37

Calvinism, 284, 285. *See also* neo-Calvinism

Campbell, Alexander, 300-301, 437n. 23

Capra, Fritjof, 38

Carlson, Allan, 443n. 22

Carpenter, Joel, 291, 292, 367

catechisms, 303

Catholicism, 94, 257, 259, 261, 281, 291; and celibacy, 403n. 54; doctrine of original sin, 404n. 56; in Ireland and Quebec, 430n. 18; *nouvelle theologie* school, 404n. 58; and revival meetings, 430n. 29; two-tiered spirituality of, 403n. 52

causality, 315-316

Chalmers, Thomas, 260-261

Chance and Necessity (Monod), 192

Channing, William Ellery, 338

Chardin, Teilhard de, 124

Charry, Ellen, 203

Chesterton, G. K., 78, 157

Christian Mind, The (Blamires), 33

Christian workplace: and biblical principles, 370-371, 372-374; negative patterns in, 369-370; and violation of ethical principles, 371-372

Christian worldview, 17, 23, 24-25, 55-56, 73, 111, 121, 149-150, 157, 174, 193, 216, 219, 245, 316, 317-318, 348; and biblical principles, 361-363; and children, 19; and Christians as "life-producing machines," 360-361; constructing,

47-49, 127-128; and dying and rising with Christ, 354-355, 356-358, 359-360, 363-364; and the heart versus brain question, 20-22; and suffering, 51; and "thinking Christianly," 34-35; training, 25-26. *See also* public/private dichotomy; secular/sacred dichotomy

Christianity, 23, 25, 40, 52, 78, 91, 119, 172, 177-178, 222, 247, 255, 280, 284-285, 292; as irrational, 219; and liberalism, 116; and materialism, 389-392; and morality, 144; as objective truth, 176; and privatized values, 22; and the Roman empire, 265; and science, 155-156; and systems of thought, 41-42; as the "true myth," 119-121

Churches of Christ, 256, 260

Churching of America, The (Finke and Starke), 257-258

Clark, Gordon, 84

Clement of Alexandria, 77, 386

Clinton, Bill, 191, 218

Clinton, Hilary, 130

Closing of the American Mind, The (A. Bloom), 177

Clouser, Roy, 42, 45-46, 314

Cohen, Richard, 424n. 16

colleges/universities, 113-115, 310, 364-365; preparing young believers for, 125-127

Collingwood, R. G., 43, 399n. 21

Collins, Francis, 191

Collins, Jim, 370-371

Commager, Henry Steele, 425n. 27

Common Faith, A (Dewey), 239

Common Sense realism, 276-278, 311-312, 318; Southern theologians' embrace of, 438n. 34

complexity theory, 419n. 53

confessional churches, 257

Congregationalists, 256, 258, 260

Conkin, Paul, 425nn. 22, 26

conversion, 40; revivalism's focus on, 266, 269-70, 278

"Cosmos," 157

Craig, William Lane, 439n. 56

Creation, 42, 45, 47-48, 75, 83-84, 87-88, 88-89, 128-129, 130, 315; liberal view of, 116; and Redemption, 92

Creation/Fall/Redemption grid, 49, 87-88, 92-93, 95, 128, 134, 150; and Christian education, 128-130; and the family, 130-131; and Marxism, 134-137; and New Age thought, 147-148; and Rousseau, 138-140; and sexuality, 143-145

creationism, 415n. 70

creeds and confessions, 277, 302. *See also specific creeds*

Crick, Francis, 171, 185

Cross and the Switchblade, The (Wilkerson), 55

Crouch, Andy, 67

Cultural Mandate, the, 47, 48-49, 50, 72, 81, 129

Cusk, Rachel, 347

"Danger of an Unconverted Ministry, The" (Tennent), 271

Darwin, Charles, 155, 158, 163, 170, 183, 187, 200-201, 213, 230, 234, 243, 315, 391, 414n. 53, 438-439n. 50, 444n. 69; and Darwin's finches, 158-159

Darwin on Trial (Johnson), 174

"Darwinian fundamentalism," 210-211

Darwinian Left, A (Singer), 215, 219

Darwinism, 41, 106, 107, 153-156, 158, 160-161, 167-168, 174, 176, 178, 200, 207-208, 218, 242-243, 247, 291, 391-392, 426n. 36; as an alternative religion, 172-173; and Darwinian gradualism, 166-167; and the eugenics movement, 427n. 44; insertion of into a religious and providential framework, 308-309; and naturalism, 168-170; and rape, 210-212; universal, 208-209, 216; and values, 221-222. *See also* evolution; popular culture, "Darwinian fundamentalism"; neo-Darwinism; Social Darwinism

Darwinizing Culture (Aunger, ed.), 216

Darwin's Black Box (Behe), 185

Darwin's Dangerous Idea (Dennett), 156

David, 374

Davies, Paul, 189, 197-198, 417n. 25, 419n. 60

Dawkins, Richard, 106, 168, 183, 191, 197, 208, 218, 221, 419n. 60

Dayton, Donald, 295

Degler, Carl, 337, 442n. 10

Deists, 297

Delbrück, Max, 449n. 3

DelHousaye, Darryl, 370

della Mirandola, Pico, 386

Dembski, William A., 192, 417n. 22, 418n. 42, 420n. 67

Democracy's Discontent (Sandel), 141

Democritus, 389

Democratization of American Christianity, The (Hatch), 275

Demonic Males (Wrangham and Peterson), 209

Dennett, Daniel, 112, 156, 216, 317, 320, 394, 440n. 81

DeRosier, David, 187

Derrida, Jacques, 242

Descartes, René, 39, 41, 405n. 9, 436n. 11; and the mind/matter dichotomy, 102-103

Descent of Man, The (Darwin), 213

Design Inference, The (Dembski), 192

design theory. *See* Intelligent Design theory

determinism, 215, 393-394

Dewey, John, 228, 230, 233, 238-240, 391, 424n. 4, 425n. 24; and educational methodology, 238-240

Dionysius the Areopagite, 386

Disciples of Christ, 277, 283

Dobzhansky, Theodosius, 422n. 34

Doors of Perception, The (A. Huxley), 125

Dooyeweerd, Herman, 24, 93, 313, 314, 399n. 25, 402n. 23; 404n. 57, 426n. 36; on Kant's nature/freedom dichotomy, 405n. 11

Douglas, Ann, 334, 442n. 10

Dow, Lorenzo, 275-276

Duke of Argyll, 308

Dupré, Louis, 94

Dyson, Freeman, 97, 190

Easterbrook, Gregg, 190

Eastern thought, 146-149, 327. *See also* Buddhism; Hinduism; New Age movement

education, 238-242; Christian education, 37-38, 119, 128-129; constructivist approach, 241-242, 427n. 56; Dewey's influence on, 239; inquiry approach, 239-242

Edwards, Jonathan, 35, 269-270, 288

Eisenhower, Dwight D., 117

Elisha, 362

empiricism (British), 233, 234, 237

Engels, Friedrich, 137

Enlightenment, the, 38-41, 60, 101, 102, 104, 129, 233, 268, 269, 299, 308; and the arts and humanities, 113-114

Enthusiasm (Knox), 290-291

Epicurus, 389-391, 449n. 1; attacks on, 449n. 5

Episcopalians, 256, 258, 260, 265

Erickson, Millard, 405-406n. 26

Erigena, John Scotus, 77, 386

"Escalator Myth," 411n. 62

Escape from Reason (Schaeffer), 109, 125

"Evangelical Mind Awakens, The," 321

evangelicalism, 254-255, 278, 285-286, 295, 429n. 4; beginnings as a renewal movement, 253; in Canada and Britain, 434n. 36; and the "Christianizing" of American society, 257-260; as a force for modernization, 286; meaning of the term, 256-257; populist branch, 256, 257,

285, 286, 290, 292, 322, 433n. 27;
rationalist/scholarly branch, 256,
295-296; why it became anti-intellectual, 266-267, 268, 276, 291-292
evangelicals, 99, 173, 247, 267, 276,
281-282, 401n. 15; and politics, 18-
19, 22; separatist strategy of, 18;
views of, 70-71; the term *evangelical*,
429n. 7. *See also* neo-evangelicals
evangelism, 116-118; and moral and
metaphysical "lostness," 119
evolution, 170, 208-210, 214, 215; and
Darwin's finches, 158-160; and the
fossil record, 166; and fruit fly mutations, 160-161; macroevolution,
165-167; microevolution, 165; and
peppered moths, 161-162; as a product of Romantic historicism, 243-
244; punctuated equilibrium ("punk
eek"), 166, 167-168; and "selfish
genes," 208, 218; as self-refuting,
243-244; theistic, 203. *See also* evolutionary psychology
"Evolution" (PBS series), 160, 177-178,
209-210
Evolution of Culture, The (Dunbar,
Knight, and Power), 216
Evolutionary Origins of Morality (Katz,
ed.), 208
evolutionary psychology, 208, 210,
212-214, 215-216, 221. *See also*
pragmatism
Evolutionary Thought in America
(Persons, ed.), 227-228
Explanatory Filter, 200-201

fact/value dichotomy, 20, 22, 33, 95,
107-109, 111, 112, 113, 119, 154,
157, 177, 203, 221-222, 255
faith, 99; privatization of, 202-203; and
reason, 100-101
Fall, the, 45-46, 48, 84-85, 88-89, 90,
129, 130, 132-133; evangelicalism's
overemphasis on, 87; liberal view of,
116
family, the, 130-131

feminism, 113, 135, 341-342, 344, 346
Feminization of American Culture, The
(Douglas), 334
Ficino, 386
Fifth Miracle, The (Davies), 419n. 60
Finley, Samuel, 271
Finke, Roger, 257-258, 261-262, 263
Finney, Charles, 266, 275, 288-289,
368
Flight from Authority, The (Stout),
436n. 14
Flower, Elizabeth, 438n. 45
For the Love of Children (Peters), 131
Foucault, Michel, 242
free-church ecclesiology, 283
freedom. *See* human freedom
Freedom Evolves (Dennett), 320
Freud, Sigmund, 59
Frost, Robert, 227
fundamentalism, 18, 291

Gassendi, Pierre, 391
Gauvreau, Michael, 286, 434n. 36
Gaylord, George, 183-184
Geisler, Norman, 193
Generation of Vipers, A (Wylie), 340
Giddens, Anthony, 408n. 12
Gilder, George, 445n. 73
Gillespie, Neal, 414n. 51
Gillis, John, 329
Gilman, Charlotte Perkins, 342
Gilman, Daniel Coit, 310
Gish, Duane, 172
Gladden, Washington, 286
Glendon, Mary Ann, 142
Glynn, Patrick, 59-60, 153-154
God: The Evidence (Glynn), 59-60,
153, 154
God and Other Minds (Plantinga), 58
Goheen, Michael, 22
Goldschmidt, Richard, 160
Good to Great (Collins), 370-371
Goodwin, Brian, 392
Gould, Stephen Jay, 166, 172, 413n.
38, 414n. 61

grace, 79-80, 100; special, 42; common, 42-43. *See also* nature/grace dualism
Graham, Billy, 295
Gray, Asa, 309
Gray, John, 42, 137, 320
Great Divorce, The (Lewis), 86
Greene, John, 439n. 54
Greenstein, George, 188-190
Grimké, Sarah, 444n. 45
Gross, David, 190-191
Guenon, René, 387
Guinness, Os, 44
Gulag Archipelago (Solzhenitsyn), 352
Gunton, Colin, 77

Haack, Denis and Margie, 420n. 69
Haeckel, Ernst, 163-165
Haldane, J. B. S., 210
Hall, G. Stanley, 424n. 4
Harding, Sandra, 113
Hartshorne, Charles, 236, 425n. 33
Hatch, Nathan, 265, 275, 290, 321, 430nn. 15, 24, 432n. 5
Hawthorne, Nathaniel, 337
He Is There and He Is Not Silent (Schaeffer), 246
Healing from Spiritual Abuse, 370
"Heavy Petting" (Singer), 214
Hegel, Georg Wilhelm Friedrich, 234-235, 238
Heidegger, Martin, 242
Heimert, Alan, 431n. 42
higher criticism, 291, 426n. 36
Hinduism, 147, 148
historicism: Hegelian, 235; German, 386, 426n. 36; Romantic, 234
How the Mind Works (Pinker), 107
Hobbes, Thomas, 139, 140, 382, 384, 449n. 12
Hodge, Charles, 295, 299, 309
Hofstadter, Richard, 286, 287, 288, 323, 430n. 25
Holifield, E. Brooks, 438nn. 34, 43
Holmes, Arthur, 405n. 16
Holmes, Oliver Wendell, 228-229, 237-238, 245, 426n. 42, 428n. 72

home: before the industrial revolution, 326-329; and the ideal-worker standard, 344-345; impact of the industrial revolution on, 329-333, 342-343; reconstituting, 344-346
Hooper, Judith, 162
How Now Shall We Live? (Colson and Pearcey), 17, 397n. 1, 398n. 14
How the Mind Works (Pinker), 107
"How to Become a Christian" (Beecher), 287
Hoyle, Fred, 189, 417n. 31
human freedom, 105, 109, 395
human nature, 139, 144. *See also* Rousseau, Jean-Jacques
Hume, David, 104, 297, 298, 316, 317, 405n. 10, 436n. 9
Hunter, James Davison, 429n. 6
Huxley, Aldous, 124, 125, 386
Huxley, Julian, 176, 415n. 76

Icons of Evolution (Wells), 158
idealism (Romantic), 233, 234, 237
Illusion of Conscious Will, The (Wegner), 112
In Gods We Trust (Atran), 209
individualism, 270-272
industrial revolution, the, 161, 442n. 19. *See also* home, impact of the industrial revolution on
infanticide, 212-213
"Influence of Darwin on Philosophy, The" (Dewey), 230
Intelligent Design theory, 172-173, 174, 175, 178, 180-182, 199-201, 204-205, 223, 311, 415n. 70, 420n. 67; in biochemistry, 184-185; and the "blind watchmaker" metaphor, 182-184; in cosmology, 188-191; and the genetic code (DNA structure), 191-192, 195-196; and irreducible complexity, 187-188. *See also* origins of life, the
Islam, and the New Age movement, 385-388

James, Henry, Sr., 335

James, William, 228, 230, 231-232, 233-234, 424n. 18, 425nn. 30, 32; tolerance of religion, 231-232; view of God, 425n. 32

Jefferson, Thomas, 282-284, 288, 297

Jenkins, Philip, 257

Johnson, Phillip, 21, 22, 159, 165, 173-174, 202, 245, 310, 426n. 42; on privatizing Christian faith, 118-119

Jouvenal, Bertrand de, 383

Joyce, James, 88-89

Julian the Apostate, 386

justification, 49

Kaiser, Christian, 424n. 16

Kant, Immanuel, 103-106, 108; on human freedom (autonomy), 105; two-realm theory of truth, 104-106

Kasper, Walter, 69, 404n. 58, 405n. 7

Kauffman, Stuart, 196

Kaye, Howard, 216

Kelley, Dean, 266

Keniston, Kenneth, 333

Kenyon, Dean, 194-195, 418n. 50, 419n. 59

Kilpatrick, William, 240-241

Kinsey, Alfred, 144-145

Kinsley, Michael, 164

Kline, Morris, 316

Kloppenberg, James, 425nn. 24, 25

Knox, Ronald, 290-291

Kreeft, Peter, 107

Kuhn, Thomas, 438n. 32

Küng, Hans, 404n. 58

Kurtz, Stanley, 384; on the religious character of neo-Marxist feminist and multicultural movements, 408-409n. 25

Kuyper, Abraham, 24, 224, 313

L'Abri, 53, 376-377; practical apologetics at, 393-396

Lakatos, Imre, 438n. 32

Langmead Casserly, J. V., 402n. 33

Larson, David, 59, 60

"leap of faith" (secular), 108-110, 112, 219, 220

Leland, John, 276

Lenin, Vladimir Ilyich, 135

Lewin, Roger, 167

Lewis, C. S., 49, 86, 220, 302, 306, 388, 396, 410n. 60; and Christianity as the "true myth," 119-121

Lewontin, Richard, 170-171

Lewy, Guenter, 60

liberalism, 115-116, 141, 142, 261, 283, 320; 406n. 39

Lickona, Thomas, 240

Life's Work, A (Cusk), 347

Littell, Franklin, 364

Locke, John, 139, 140, 382-383, 384, 436n. 11, 449n. 12

Logos, 34-35, 201, 245, 246

London, Jack, 338

Loving Monday (Beckett), 83

Lucretius, 389

Luther, Martin, 50, 81, 174, 303, 329, 358, 434n. 37; and his "theology of the cross," 51

Lutherans, 118, 257

Machen, J. Gresham, 295, 440n. 68

Maddox, John, 204

Madonna, 146

Maguire, Bassett, 165

Malik, Charles, 63, 281-282

Manent, Pierre, 142

Manicheism, 77

"Many Worlds" hypothesis, 190

Marini, Stephen, 431n. 33, 432n. 16

Maritain, Jacques, 80

marriage, 132, 142; contemporary view of, 145; and the creation order, 92

Marsden, George, 296, 308, 311, 313, 321, 383-384, 428n. 68, 438n. 49

Marshall, Paul, 383

Marty, Martin, 35, 295, 322

Marx, Karl, 135, 137, 235

Marxism, 23, 134-137

mathematics, 43-44

Mating Mind, The (Miller), 210

Mattingly, Terry, 118
Mauve Decade, The, 340
May, Henry, 409n. 33
Mayr, Ernst, 221
McCosh, James, 309, 439n. 53
McGrath, Alister, 82, 255
McGready, James, 251, 269-270
Mead, Sidney, 35, 118, 281
Medved, Michael, 145
Meister Eckhart, 387
Mekkes, J. P. A., 440n. 68
men: loss of status as fathers, 340-341;
   and muscular Christianity, 338-339.
   See also home; women
Men and Religion Forward movement,
   339
Mencken, H. L., 204
Methodists, 256, 259, 260, 264, 265,
   283, 285, 430-431n. 31
Meyer, Steve, 196
Middelmann, Udo, 315, 395, 435n. 62
Middle Ages, the, 81, 99, 381, 426n. 36
Midgely, Mary, 411n. 62
Mill, John Stuart, 145, 449n. 12
Miller, Eugene F., 397n. 11
Miller, Geoffrey, 210
Miller, Samuel, 283
Milton, John, 129
Minsky, Marvin, 109
"modal scale," and Dooyeweerd, 399n.
   25
Modern Liberty and Its Discontents
   (Manent), 142
Modern Schism, 35, 322, 323
modernism, 18, 21
modernization, 20
monasticism, 81, 82, 91
Monod, Jacques, 192
Moody, Dwight L., 286, 291, 295
Moral Animal, The (Wright), 208, 217-
   218
Moral Darwinism (Wiker), 449n. 8
morality, 144, 208, 211, 213-214, 221,
   222; biblical, 214
Moreland, J. P., 439n. 56
Mothers At Home, 345

multiculturalism, 113, 135
Mumford, Lewis, 428n. 71
Murphey, Murray G., 438n. 45
Murphy, Nancey, 139, 203
Mystery of Life's Origin, The (Thaxton,
   Bradley, and Olsen), 199, 420b, 61
mysticism, 109, 110

National Academy of Science (NAS),
   159
National Institute for Healthcare
   Research (NIHR), 59
Natural History of Rape, The
   (Thornhill and Palmer), 211
natural selection, 183-184, 186, 208-
   209, 211
nature/grace dualism, 79-80, 93-94, 95,
   99, 100, 404nn. 57, 58
Nawrocki, Mike, 36-37
Nazarenes, 90
neo-Calvinism, 141, 313, 321
neo-Darwinism, 412n. 22
neo-evangelicals, 18
neo-Platonism, 385-387, 402n. 24,
   426n. 34, 448n. 1
Nevin, John, 289-290
New Age movement, 129, 147-149,
   317; and Islam, 385-388
Newbigin, Lesslie, 22, 67, 69, 332, 346,
   375, 378, 447n. 34
Newman, John Henry, 439n. 61
Newton, Isaac, 306, 307, 391; and the
   Newtonian worldview, 405n. 9
Newtonian physics, 103, 104, 105, 139,
   141
Next Christendom, The (Jenkins), 257
Nicene Creed, 281
Niebuhr, H. Richard, 367
Nielson, Kathleen, 99
Noll, Mark, 257, 266, 283, 306, 312,
   321, 429n. 6, 433n. 25
Norton, Charles Eliot, 335

Oberhummer, Heinz, 189
Olasky, Marvin, 61-62
Olsen, Roger, 192, 420n. 61

On the Nature of the Universe (Lucretius), 389
On the Origin of Species (Darwin), 391
ontological individualism, 131, 141-142
Open Theism, 236, 426n. 35
Orgel, Leslie, 420n. 61
Origen, 77, 386
Origin of Species (Darwin), 238
origin of life, the, 198-199; and chance theory, 193-194; and design, 197-198; and the laws of nature, 194-195
Origins of Totalitarianism, The (Arendt), 141
Orr, H. Allen, 211, 213
Overn, Bill, 224, 423n. 60
Overn, Oswald, 224

Pagels, Heinz, 190, 418n. 36
Paine, Thomas, 273, 276, 279
paleontology, 166
Paley, William, 183, 184-185, 308
Palmer, Craig, 211
panentheism, 236
pantheism, 133, 147, 148, 236, 410n. 54
Parker, Theodore, 443n. 42
Parkes, Frances, 333
Passmore, John, 426n. 35
Paul, on Mars Hill, 89-90
Peacock, Charlie, 34
Peirce, Charles Sanders, 228, 231, 235-236, 389, 425nn. 30, 33
Pender, William, 333
Penzias, Arno, 189
pentecostal-charismatic movement, 292
Percy, Walker, 103
Perennial Philosophy, The (Huxley), 386
perfection, 90, 403nn. 52, 55
personhood, 316-317
Peters, Ted, 131, 142
Philo, 402n. 24
philosophical naturalism, 239, 307
philosophy, 133; Christian, 58-59, 94; desecularization of, 58, 59; Greek,

74-76; legal, 141-142, 237; perennial, 123-124, 386, 449n. 6; political, 142, 284. *See also individually listed specific philosophies*
philosophy of science, 40-41
pietism, 269
Pinker, Steven, 107-109, 111-112, 212-213, 422n. 20; two-realm theory of, 108; on the unified self, 111-112
Pinnock, Clark, 236
Piper, John, 402n. 27
Plantinga, Alvin, 58-59, 244, 315, 321
Plato/Platonism, 74-76, 84, 130, 389, 390, 402n. 24; Platonic dualism, 75-76. *See also* neo-Platonism
Playboy, 340
Plotinus, 385-386, 402n. 24, 448n. 3
Podles, Leon, 441n. 4
Polanyi, Michael, 438n. 32
political correctness, 135
politics, secularization of, 381-384
Popper, Karl, 437-438n. 32
popular culture, 214; Darwinizing of, 215-216
"porn studies," 143, 145
Portrait of the Artist as a Young Man (Joyce), 88-89
positivism, 103
"Positivism, Historicism, and Political Inquiry" (Miller), 397n. 11
"Possible Answers to the Basic Philosophical Questions" (Schaeffer), 175
postmodernism, 21, 43-44, 110, 113, 114-115, 242-244; as defined by Tom Wolfe, 243
Power, Camilla, 216
pragmatism, 228-229, 232-233, 245, 392; as a Darwinian view of knowledge, 229-230, 234-235, 426n. 37
Presbyterians, 256, 257, 258-259, 265, 269, 295-296, 429n. 9
primitivism, 281, 304
Process Theology, 131, 236, 386
Protestant work ethic, 82
Provine, William, 214

public/private dichotomy, 20, 33-35, 65
Purcell, Edward, 309
Puritans, 82, 128, 332, 432n. 16, 432-433n. 17

quantum mechanics, 38
Quine, W. V. O., 416n. 4

Radical Reformation, 434n. 37
Randall, John Hermann, 408n. 20
Raspberry, William, 343
rationalism, 113, 114
Rawlyk, George, 434n. 36
reason, 100-101, 120, 129
Reason in the Balance (Johnson), 174
Redemption, 46, 49, 85-87, 89, 91-92, 129, 130, 133; liberal view of, 116
reductionism, 111
Reeve, Christopher, 22
Reformation, the, 80-82, 100, 128, 381. *See also sola Scriptura*
Reformed Epistemology, 321
Reformed tradition: German, 257; Dutch, 257, 313; Scottish, 313
Reid, Thomas, 297, 298, 311, 312, 316, 436n. 7, 440n. 71
religion, 41-42, 68-69, 100, 171, 173, 221, 261-262; Christians' views of, 201-202; compared to spirituality, 117-118; pre-Revolutionary, 260-261; positive impact on health, 59-61; and privatization, 68-69; as product of human subjectivity, 116-117; symbolic, 116-117
Religion Explained (Boyer), 209
Renaissance, the, 101, 426n. 36
Restoration movement, 256, 300-301. *See also* Churches of Christ; Disciples of Christ
Resurrection, the, 116, 117
revivalists/revivalism, 261, 265-266, 267-268, 269, 270-271, 286, 289-290
Rights of Man (Paine), 276
Rights Talk (Glendon), 142
Ritter, Bob, 412n. 29

Roaring Lambs (Briner), 36
Robinson, Bill, 370
Robinson, Paul, 145
Roe v. Wade (1973), 238
Roman Catholicism. *See* Catholicism
Romanticism, 101-102, 104, 129, 233, 234, 386, 426n. 36
Roof, Wade Clark, 117, 293
Rookmaaker, Hans, 440n. 68
Rorty, Richard, 242-244, 245-246
Rotundo, Anthony, 328, 333, 337, 443n. 26
Rousseau, Jean-Jacques, 104-105, 130, 137-142, 383, 409n. 32, 449n. 12; and the "state of nature" (self-love), 137-138. *See also* social contract theory
Ruse, Michael, 172, 208-209, 414n. 59
Russell, Bertrand, 53, 232, 245
Ryan, Mary, 337

Saccas, Ammonius, 448n. 1
Sagan, Carl, 157
sanctification, 24, 49; entire, 90
Sandel, Michael, 141
Sanger, Margaret, 143-146, 410n. 44
Sayers, Dorothy, 36, 328, 344
Schaeffer, Edith, 377, 400n. 38
Schaeffer, Francis, 53-54, 56, 110-111, 125, 208, 246, 313-314, 319-320, 363, 365-366, 369, 372, 399n. 34, 405n. 26, 440n. 82; on apologetics, 244; on Aquinas, 404n. 58; on "bridging" role he played, 400n. 35; on Christianity as total truth, 18, 398n. 3; crisis of faith, 355-356; critique of the two-story concept of truth, 397n. 5, 402n. 23; and cultural apologetics, 175; individuals he studied under, 440n. 68; on Kant's nature/freedom dichotomy, 405n. 11; on the "leap of faith," 108; on spirituality, 446nn. 6, 10; two-chairs image, 204, 361-362; two-story view of reality, 21, 74; on the use of drugs, 407n. 4. *See also* L'Abri

Schloss, Jeffrey, 422n. 17
scholasticism, 80, 82, 404n. 58
science: and the attack on the arts, 114; the demarcation problem, 420n. 66; as descriptive, 144; idealized image of, 168; imperialism of, 234; as model of unity, 301; and religion, 173 (see also Darwinism; evolution)
Science, Ideology, and Worldview (Greene), 439n. 54
scientific materialism, 101-102, 103, 111-112, 120, 157, 170-171, 317; and Christianity, 389-392; eliminative materialism, 112
scientific naturalism, 94, 110-111, 112, 115, 157-158, 168-170; Darwinian, 255; metaphysical, 203, 420n. 71; methodological, 203, 420n. 71
Scopes trial, 18
Scott, Donald, 287, 346, 443n. 33
Scottish realism. *See* Common Sense realism
search for extraterrestrial intelligence (SETI), 181
Searle, John, 109-110, 111, 394
Sears, Alan, 97-99
Secret Garden, The (Burnett), 148-149
secular/sacred dichotomy, 17, 36-37, 38-39, 69, 82-83, 95; danger of, 37
secularism, 42, 94, 101
secularization thesis, 71
Selfish Gene, The (Dawkins), 208, 218
Senske, Kurt, 375, 447b, 33
servant leadership, 375-376
Seton, Ernest Thomas, 338
Sex (Madonna), 146
Sexual Behavior in the Human Male (Kinsey), 144
sexual revolution, the, 142-146, 214-215
Shermer, Michael, 223, 415n. 2
Simpson, George Gaylord, 183-184, 414n. 45, 416n. 13
Simpson, Terry, 427n. 56
sin, Protestant doctrine of, 93
Singer, Peter, 214-216, 219-220

Skeptics' Society, 180
Skinner, B. F., 130
Skinner, Quentin, 448n. 2
Sloan, Douglas, 119, 311, 365, 406n. 39
Skillen, James, 409n. 36
Skinner, B. F., 130, 320
Smith, Adam, 284, 285, 332
Smith, Christian, 70, 73, 98, 401n. 13
Smith, Donald, 287
Smith, Elias, 277, 278
Smith, Huston, 153, 407n. 2
Smith, James Ward, 425n. 31
Smith, Quentin, 58-59
Smith-Rosenberg, Carroll, 434n. 34
Social Contract, The (Rousseau), 138
social contract theory, 140, 279-280, 282-283, 381, 383, 449n. 12
Social Darwinism, 215, 237, 339, 341, 444n. 69
social engineering, 392
Social Gospel, 238
Society of Mind, The (Minsky), 109
sociobiology, 215, 216
Socrates, 74
sola Scriptura, 302-303
Solzhenitsyn, Alexander, 85, 352
Soul of Science, The (Pearcey and Thaxton), 405n. 9, 411n. 6, 418n. 60, 448n. 4
Soul of the American University, The (Marsden), 438n. 49
"specified complexity," 198-199
Spencer, Herbert, 229, 237, 444n. 69
sphere sovereignty, 141
spirituality, 117-118
Spurgeon, Charles, 17
Stalin, Joseph, 227
Stark, Rodney, 257-258, 261-262, 263, 388, 441n. 4
statism, 131, 132
Steig, William, 411-412n. 11
Steinman, Gary, 194
Stevenson, Leslie, 137
Stone, Baron, 277
Stout, Harry, 268, 271

Stout, Jeffrey, 381, 436n. 14
Strauss, Leo, 222-223
Strawson, Galen, 394
subsidiarity, 141
Subtle Power of Spiritual Abuse, The, 370
Sulloway, Frank, 415n. 2
Sunday, Billy, 291, 339
Swami Krishnananda, 384-385
Swift, David, 418n. 45

Tao of Physics, The (Capra), 38
Taylor, Hudson, 361
Tennent, Gilbert, 271
Thaxton, Charles, 199, 419n. 59, 420n. 61
The Goat, or Who Is Sylvia? 214
theology of the cross, 358-359
theosophy, 149, 410n. 60
Theroux, Paul, 88
Thomas, Gary, 285
Thorndike, Edward, 230
Thornhill, Randy, 211, 212
Thornwell, James Henley, 312
Tocqueville, Alexis de, 263, 276, 323
Tolkein, J. R. R., 410n. 60
total depravity, 93
Tragedy of American Compassion, The (Olasky), 61-62
Trigg, Roger, 244
Trinity, doctrine of, 132-133, 138
Troeltsch, Ernst, 434n. 37
Trollope, Anthony, 305
Trollope, Francis, 334
True Spirituality (Schaeffer), 355
truth: divided concept of, 22-23; objectivity of, 395; private, 21; public, 21; two-realm theory of, 21
Twain, Mark, 338-339; marriage of, 444n. 56

Unbending Gender (J. Williams), 445n. 75
Unitarians, 261, 283, 296
universals versus particulars, 408n. 17
Universe Next Door, The, 23

"Unreasonable Effectiveness of Mathematics in the Natural Sciences, The" (Wigner), 316
U.S. Office of Research Integrity ("Fraud Squad"), 182
utilitarianism, 233
Utopia Against the Family (Christensen), 130
utopians, 130

Vale, Ronald D., 417n. 18
Valentine, J., 413n. 41
values, 177-178; reduction of to arbitrary, existential decisions, 20
Van Til, Cornelius, 440n. 68
Vander Stelt, John, 377
Veith, Gene Edward, 50
Vischer, Phil, 36-37

Wald, George, 190
Walden Two (B. F. Skinner), 131
Walsh, John, 432-433n. 17
Ward, Lester Frank, 341-342
Ware, Timothy, 134
Warfield, B. B., 295, 309
Watson, James, 171
Watts, Alan, 123-124
Wayland, Francis, 306
Wealth of Nations, The (A. Smith), 284, 332
Wegner, Daniel, 112
Weinberg, Steven, 114, 171, 202-203
welfare, Christian view of, 61-62
Wells, Jonathan, 158
Wesley, John, 253, 259, 265, 295
Wesleyans, 90
Wheeler, John, 179
Whitefield, George, 267-268, 431nn. 34, 35
Whitehead, Alfred North, 425n. 33
Why America Needs Religion (Lewy), 60
Why Conservative Churches Are Growing (Kelley), 266
Why Johnny Can't Tell Right from Wrong (Kilpatrick), 241

Wichterman, Bill, 18-19, 118, 397n. 2
Wigner, Eugene, 316
Wiker, Benjamin, 449n. 8
Wilder-Smith, A. E., 198, 419n. 59
Wilkerson, David, 55
William of Ockham, 100-101, 118, 408n. 17
Williams, George, 197, 419n. 57
Williams, Joan, 445n. 75
Wilson, E. O., 208-209, 224
Wister, Owen, 338
Witherspoon, , John, 297, 306
Witte, John, Jr., 409n. 31
Wolfe, Alan, 292-293
Wolfe, Tom, 243
Wolters, Albert M., 23, 123
Wolterstorff, Nicholas, 321
women: and the Awakenings, 326; domination of church membership, 441n. 4; and the feminization of the church, 334-335; and social reform, 335-338, 343. *See also* feminism; home; men

"Women Taming Men" (Raspberry), 343
Women's Christian Temperance Union, 336
Women's Self-Employment Project, 345
Wood, Gordon, 275, 279, 282, 284, 286, 433n. 24, 442n. 12
worldview, 17, 23-24, 134, 154, 220, 221, 397n. 11; history of the term, 397n. 11; purpose of, 317, 396; and sexual liberation, 143; starting point of, 175; testing of, 314. *See also* Christian worldview
Wrangham, Richard, 209
Wright, Robert, 207, 217-218
Wurmbrand, Richard, 352, 353-354, 446n. 3
Wylie, Philip, 340

Yates, Sealy, 63-66
Yellow and Pink (Steig), 411-412n. 11

ABOUT THE AUTHOR

NANCY RANDOLPH PEARCEY is the Francis A. Schaeffer Scholar at the World Journalism Institute, where *Total Truth* is the basis for a worldview curriculum. Pearcey studied violin in Heidelberg, Germany, in the early 1970s, then went to Switzerland to study Christian worldview under Schaeffer at L'Abri Fellowship. Later she graduated from Iowa State University with a Distributed Studies degree (philosophy, German, music). Pearcey earned a master's degree in Biblical Studies from Covenant Theological Seminary in St. Louis, followed by graduate work in the history of philosophy (with an emphasis on ancient philosophy and Dutch neo-Calvinism) at the Institute for Christian Studies in Toronto. Her current positions include visiting scholar at Biola University's Torrey Honors Institute and senior fellow at the Discovery Institute, where her focus is on the cultural and philosophical implications of the evolution controversy. She is also a frequent speaker at conferences and universities.

Pearcey began writing articles on science and Christian worldview in 1977 for the *Bible-Science Newsletter,* where she worked for thirteen years, analyzing many of the themes she would develop more fully in later writings. In 1991 she became the founding editor of "BreakPoint," a daily syndicated radio commentary program, and continued as the program's executive editor for nearly nine years, heading up a team of writers. Under her leadership, the program grew into an influential organ for teaching a Christian worldview perspective on current events, with an estimated weekly audience of five million. She was also policy director and senior fellow of the Wilberforce Forum, and coauthored a monthly column in *Christianity Today* for five years.

Pearcey has served as managing editor of the science journal *Origins & Design,* as an editorial board member for Salem Communications Network, and as a commentator on Public Square Radio. Her articles have appeared in several journals and magazines, including the *Washington Times, Human Events, First Things, Books and Culture, World, Pro Rege, Human Life Review, American Enterprise, The World & I, The Family in America, Christianity Today,* and the *Regent University Law Review.*

Pearcey has authored or contributed to several works, including *The Soul of Science,* on the history of science and Christianity since the scientific revolution; and the best-selling, award-winning *How Now Shall We Live?* She is featured in a video Sunday school curriculum based on the latter, produced by LifeWay Christian Resources.

She has contributed chapters to *Mere Creation, Of Pandas and People, Pro-Life Feminism, Genetic Ethics, Signs of Intelligence, Reading God's World,* and *Uncommon Dissent,* and most recently, a Phillip Johnson Festschrift titled *A Man for This Season.*

Pearcey resides in Northern Virginia with her husband and two sons. For speaking requests, please contact her agent, Susan Yates, at susanyates@yatesyates.com.